Time Out

London

www.timeout.com/london

Time Out Digital Ltd
4th Floor
125 Shaftesbury Avenue
London WC2H 8AD
United Kingdom
Tel: +44 (0)20 7813 3000
Fax: +44 (0)20 7813 6001
Email: guides@timeout.com
www.timeout.com

Published by Time Out Digital Ltd, a wholly owned subsidiary
of Time Out Group Ltd. Time Out and the Time Out logo are
trademarks of Time Out Group Ltd.

10 9 8 7 6 5 4 3 2 1

This edition first published in Great Britain in 2015 by Ebury Publishing.
20 Vauxhall Bridge Road, London SW1V 2SA

Ebury Publishing is part of the Penguin Random House group of companies
whose addresses can be found at global.penguinrandomhouse.com

Distributed in the US and Latin America by Publishers Group West
(1-510-809-3700)

For further distribution details, see www.timeout.com.

ISBN: 978-1-84670-352-2

A CIP catalogue record for this book is available from the British Library.

Printed and bound in China by Leo Paper Products Ltd.

Contents

124

200

277

99

360

Time Out London

Out

Editorial
Editor Simon Coppock
Copy Editor Edoardo Albert
Listings Editor Carol Baker
Proofreader John Shandy Watson

Editorial Director Sarah Guy
Group Finance Manager Margaret Wright

Design
Senior Designer Kei Ishimaru
Designers Darryl Bell, Christie Webster
Group Commercial Senior Designer Jason Tansley

Picture Desk
Picture Editor Jael Marschner
Deputy Picture Editor Ben Rowe
Picture Researcher Lizzy Owen

Advertising
Managing Director St John Betteridge
Advertising Sales Deborah Maclaren, Helen Debenham at The Media Sales House

Marketing
Senior Publishing Brand Manager Luthfa Begum
Head of Circulation Dan Collins

Production
Production Controller Katie Mulhern-Bhudia

Time Out Group
Founder Tony Elliott
Chief Executive Officer Tim Arthur
Managing Director Europe Noel Penzer
Publisher Alex Batho

Contributors

Written and researched by Simon Coppock, with features, boxes, reviews and additional research from Flo Wales Bonner, Katie Dailey, Richard Ehrlich, Euan Ferguson, Jonathan Lennie, Justin McDonnell, Sara O'Reilly, Pete Watts, Ben Williams and other contributors to *Time Out* magazine.

Maps JS Graphics Ltd (john@jsgraphics.co.uk).

Cover Photography Gonzalo Azumendi/Getty Images.

Back Cover Photography Clockwise from top left: villorejo/Shutterstock.com; Philip Bird/Shutterstock.com; Niall Clutton; American Bar at The Beaumont, London; © IWM.

Photography Pages 2/3, 15 (top), 62, 185 pcruciatti/Shutterstock.com; 4/5, 124 pablo/Shutterstock.com; 5 (top), 41, 136, 200 Michaelpuche/Shutterstock.com; 5 (middle right), 99 Ming Tang-Evans; 5 (bottom right), 360 (bottom) Mads Perch; 7 alice-photo/Shutterstock.com; 10, 91 © Victoria and Albert Museum, London; 10/11, 13 (bottom), 164/165, 302 (bottom), 334 (bottom) Philip Bird/Shutterstock.com; 11 Britta Jaschinski; 14 (top) Claudio Divizia/Shutterstock.com; 15 (bottom) Dafinka/Shutterstock.com; 16 (top) Patricia Niven; 16 (middle), 48, 55 © IWM; 16 (bottom) Luke Dyson Photography; 17 (top), 214/215, 233, 328/329 Kiev.Victor/Shutterstock.com; 17 (bottom), 173 Angelina Dimitrova/Shutterstock.com; 18/19, 131 (middle and bottom left) Scott Chasserot; 20 (bottom) Robby Whitfield; 21 Jonas Bengtsson/Wikimedia Commons; 23 Arup; 24 Anibal Trejo/Shutterstock.com; 24/25 (top) Sverlova Mariya/Shutterstock.com; 24/25 (bottom) Pete Spiro/Shutterstock.com; 25 (top) Perati Komson/Shutterstock.com; 25 (bottom) Seb Barros; 26 (top), 51 Giovanni G/Shutterstock.com; 26 (middle), 50, 337 (top) Neil Lang/Shutterstock.com; 27, 136/137 mikecphoto/Shutterstock.com; 29 Martin Mueller; 30/31, 174, 197, 206, 245 chrisdorney/Shutterstock.com; 34 Alison Henley/Shutterstock.com; 34/35 Jessica Gilbert; 35 JLOrtin/Shutterstock.com; 40, 243 Tadeusz Ibrom/Shutterstock.com; 42/43 (top), 181 Museum of London; 42/43 (middle), 84/85, 94, 138, 150, 183 IR Stone/Shutterstock.com; 42/43 (bottom), 82, 131 (top right, top left and bottom right), 236, 255 Rob Greig; 44, 307 (top) David Butler; 45 Will Pearson; 46/47 arturasker/Shutterstock.com; 48/49 John Holdship; 57 (left) Padmayogini/Shutterstock.com; 57 (right) Pawel Libera; 58 (top), 59 Pres Panayotov/Shutterstock.com; 58 (bottom), 298, 306 (bottom) Gordon Bell/Shutterstock.com; 60 Dazeley; 61, 225 Kris Piotrowski; 65 Celia Topping; 66 Courtesy Caruso St John and Tate; 66/67 Francesco R. Iacomino/Shutterstock.com; 68, 92, 241, 304, 337 (bottom) Ron Ellis/Shutterstock.com; 76 Dmitry Naumov/Shutterstock.com; 77 Institution of Civil Engineers (ICE); 79 r.nagy/Shutterstock.com; 81 villorejo/Shutterstock.com; 84 Daniel Gale/Shutterstock.com; 90 (left), 302 (top) Christian Mueller/Shutterstock.com; 90 (right) The Natural History Museum, London © Trustees of NHM, London; 97 (top) Charlie Hopkinson; 97 (bottom) Nick Bailey; 100 Anna Moskvina/Shutterstock.com; 100/101, 349 Tim Clinch; 107 Melvyn Vincent; 110 © By kind permission of the Trustees of the Wallace Collection; 112 David Loftus; 117 Nando Machado/Shutterstock.com; 121 © Fraser Marr; 122 Stephen Morris; 122/123 antb/Shutterstock.com; 135 Ben Rowe; 140 Paul Winch-Furness; 148 Lisa Buirski; 148/149 John Sturrock; 155 James Dillon; 159 chbaum/Shutterstock.com; 160 Gaztronome; 164 Cedric Weber/Shutterstock.com; 170 Toby Keane Photography; 176 KY CHO/Shutterstock.com; 177 Luciano Mortula/Shutterstock.com; 184 Jonathan Perugia; 186 david muscroft/Shutterstock.com; 190 Stuart Leech; 190/191 Will Rodrigues/Shutterstock.com; 196 Kim Lightbody; 198, 207 Jamie Lau; 205 pbombaert/Shutterstock.com; 208 Jael Marschner; 212 Courtesy of Typing Room; 214, 301 (bottom) PlusONE/Shutterstock.com; 220 Elena Rostunova/Shutterstock.com; 220/221 AC Manley/Shutterstock.com; 222 Baloncici/Shutterstock.com; 227 Alex Morris Visualisation; 228/229 Nagib/Shutterstock.com; 231, 331 Alastair Wallace/Shutterstock.com; 232 Alys Tomlinson; 235 Michael Franke; 246/247 Lee Arucci; 248 Ints Vikmanis/Shutterstock.com; 249 V&A Museum of Childhood; 251 Asenine/Wikimedia Commons; 257 SNAP/REX Features; 259 Al de Perez; 261 Mark Storey Photography; 264 Vladislav Gajic/Shutterstock.com; 266 Dave Swindells; 267 Tom Stapley; 274 Michelle Grant; 280 Pete Le May; 282, 286 Brinkhoff & Mögenburg; 283 Sebastian Hanel; 284 (top) Nick Guttridge; 284 (bottom left and bottom right) Benjamin Ealovega; 285 Joe Plommer; 287 Lucian Milasan/Shutterstock.com; 289, 333 (top) BasPhoto/Shutterstock.com; 291 (top left and bottom) Philip Vile; 291 (top right) Simon Annand; 292 Johan Persson; 293 Manuel Harlan; 296/297, 308 ian woolcock/Shutterstock.com; 300 Panglossian/Shutterstock.com; 301 (top left) St. Nick/Shutterstock.com; 301 (top right) Rachelle Burnside/Shutterstock.com; 305 SimonPRBenson/Shutterstock.com; 306 (top) EQRoy/Shutterstock.com; 307 (bottom left) Christopher Ison; 309 (top) Helen Hotson/Shutterstock.com; 309 (bottom) tlorna/Shutterstock.com; 310 CBCK/Shutterstock.com; 311 (left) S.m.u.d.g.e/Shutterstock.com; 311 (right) Mark Yuill/Shutterstock.com; 312/313 Julietphotography/Shutterstock.com; 314/315 Getty Images/Art Images; 316 David Sankey; 317, 320 Alamy; 318 Wellcome Images/Wikimedia Commons; 323 Getty Images; 330 Bikeworldtravel/Shutterstock.com; 332 Tupungato/Shutterstock.com; 333 (bottom) Paul J Martin/Shutterstock.com; 334 (top) Hal_P/Shutterstock.com; 335 Agnese Sanvito; 336 pio3/Shutterstock.com; 338/339, 341 (top left and top right) Niall Clutton; 341 (bottom) Ed Reeve; 344, 355 (bottom) Simon Brown; 348 CWMosier; 351 Tom Sullam Photography; 353 Richard Booth; 359 Nikolas Koenig; 360 (top) Andrew Meredith; 390/391 Bernhard Richter/Shutterstock.com

The following images were supplied by the featured establishments: 5 (bottom left), 13 (top), 14 (bottom), 20 (top), 26 (bottom), 64, 113, 115, 118, 132, 141, 142, 145, 154, 156, 163, 167, 178, 188, 189, 192, 195, 198/199, 211, 218, 228, 230, 239, 240, 252, 254, 262, 263, 265, 270, 271, 272, 277, 307 (bottom right), 340, 345, 346, 347, 354, 355 (top), 356, 362, 364, 365

About the Guide

GETTING AROUND

Each sightseeing chapter contains a street map of the area marked with the locations of sights and museums (❶), restaurants (❶), pubs and bars (❶), and shops (❶). There are also street maps of London at the back of the book, as well as an overview map of the city and a tube map. In addition, there is now a detachable fold-out street and tube map inside the back cover.

THE ESSENTIALS

For practical information, including visas, disabled access, emergency numbers, lost property, useful websites and local transport, see the Essential Information section. It begins on page 338.

THE LISTINGS

Addresses, phone numbers, websites, transport information, hours and prices are all included in our listings, as are selected other facilities. All were checked and correct at press time. However, business owners may alter their arrangements at any time, and fluctuating economic conditions can cause prices to change rapidly.

The very best venues in the city, the must-sees and must-dos in every category, have been marked with a red star (★). In the Explore chapters, we've also marked venues with free admission with a FREE symbol.

PHONE NUMBERS

The area code for London is 020, but within the city, dialling from a landline, you only need the eight-digit number as listed. From outside the UK, dial your country's international access code (011 from the US) or a plus symbol, followed by the UK country code (44), 20 for London (dropping the initial zero) and the eight-digit number as listed in the guide. So, to reach the British Museum, dial +44 20 7323 8000. For more on phones, including information on calling abroad from the UK and details of local mobile phone access, see pp374-375.

FEEDBACK

We welcome feedback on this guide, both on the venues we've included and on any other locations you'd like to see featured in future editions. Please email us at guides@timeout.com.

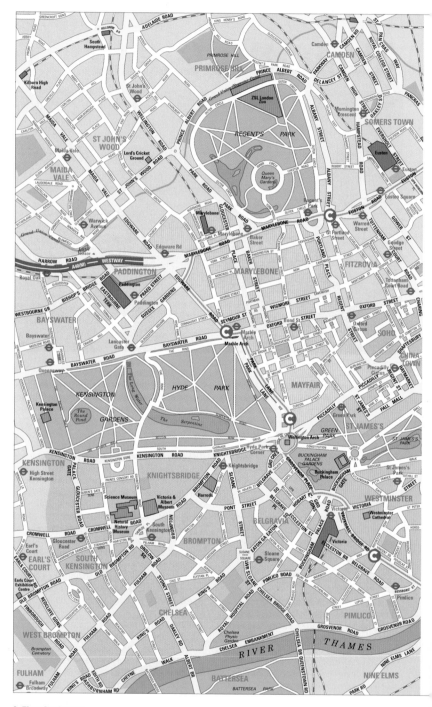

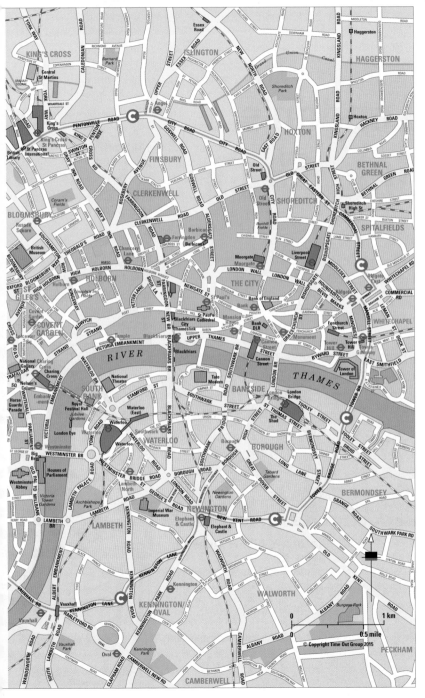

London's
Top 20

From swish cocktails to historic sights, we count down the capital's finest.

1 Victoria & Albert Museum
(page 90)

Stroll into the V&A's main entrance – that grand hall with the beautiful glass chandelier – and the scale of this museum of art and design, with its combination of stately historical context and cutting-edge modern design, is already apparent. It's gallery after grand and gorgeous gallery, with the reopened Weston Cast Court our absolute favourite.

2 Tate Britain
(page 77)

Since it opened in 2000, Tate Modern (*see p57*) has got all the plaudits. When its huge extension is done, it may do again. But the refurbishment of the original Tate nudged it ahead of its bombastic younger sibling in our affections: you get lovely premises and the entire chronological span of British art since 1545 to walk through.

3 Chiltern Firehouse
(page 110)

Sure, super-hotelier André Balazs is the name that appears on the many newspaper spreads, but we reckon the A-listers who come to his new hotel should pay at least as much attention to the culinary mastery of Nuno Mendes. We were huge fans of Mendes' skill and sense of adventure at his previous restaurant Viajante; now the chef is at the Firehouse, he seems to have reached a new peak of brilliance.

GENIUS

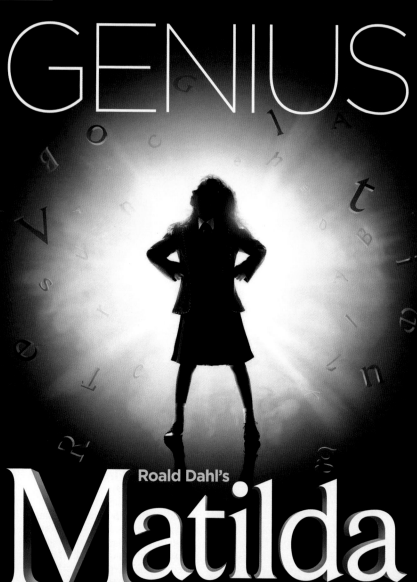

Roald Dahl's
Matilda

MatildaTheMusical.com

+44 (0)844 412 4652

CAMBRIDGE THEATRE, LONDON, WC2H 9HU

#MatildaPose

Supported using public funding by
ARTS COUNCIL
ENGLAND

4 Liberty
(page 116)

Liberty isn't quite our favourite shop – that accolade goes to Selfridges (*see p106*) – but it is certainly the most London, with its unique combination of up-to-the-minute fashion with those characteristic prints, of high Victorian, Tudor revival premises with modern shopping attitude.

5 British Museum
(page 150)

Under the departing Neil MacGregor, one of the world's great museums also became one of its most popular. No wonder: it's a compendium of key artefacts from most of the cultures of the world, from the Rosetta Stone and monumental Mesopotamian sculpture to Egyptian mummies and even an Easter Island head, with every visit uncovering further revelations.

6 The Walkie Talkie
(page 184)

Is it possible to have too much of a good thing? First there were soothing views from the Eye (*see p54*), then there were heart-stopping views from the Shard (*see p63*). But we reckon the vista from 20 Fenchurch Street tops them both. Even better – though you'll have to book a slot in advance – it won't cost a penny.

7 St James's Park
(page 89)

One of the city's joys is its chain of central parks, from Kensington Gardens and Hyde Park through Green Park to St James's. The last is our favourite. Why? It's the prettiest, has lovely lakes for waterfowl – not just ducks, but pelicans too – and lies between Buckingham Palace and Horse Guards Parade.

8 American Bar at the Beaumont
(page 118)

These aren't the most inventive cocktails in London – for those you call in on Tony Conigliaro (69 Colebrooke Row, *see p235*) or Ryan Chetiyawardana (White Lyan, *see p208*) – but there's something about a Mayfair hotel bar. The Beaumont's hits just the right note of suave glamour, respectful of cocktailing tradition without being too stuffed shirt.

9 Broadway Market
(page 213)

East London's dominance of all that's cool during the Hackney hipster era is drawing to a close, with its youthful energy increasingly dispersed by steepling rents. But there's life yet: a trip to Broadway Market – the perfect nexus of gourmet food stalls, quirky independent shops and people in whatever look is now – is still a must.

10 Shakespeare's Globe
(page 57)

London's West End is a powerhouse of international theatre, but the best bargain is undoubtedly seeing one of Shakespeare's plays authentically staged at the Globe. It costs only £5 if you're prepared to stand as a 'groundling' throughout the performance. More expensive, but a simply magical experience, are candlelit plays (and concerts) in the the Globe's Sam Wanamaker Playhouse.

12 Southbank Centre
(page 287)
Since Jude Kelly took over as artistic director – blessed with a refurbished Royal Festival Hall at the centre of the Southbank Centre's cluster of arts venues – she has given the place a new coherence, with events themed across all arts and venues, and buzzy events and markets all round the Centre.

13 Greenwich
(page 214)
The colonnades of Wren's Old Royal Naval College draw you into historic Greenwich Park, a fine introduction to London's most expansive UNESCO World Heritage Site, which combines the National Maritime Museum, an art gallery, an historic sailing ship and the Prime Meridian.

14 Changing the Guard
(page 33)
Almost everyone who comes to London wants to see some old-fashioned pomp and pageantry. We can't guarantee a sighting of the Queen, but we can provide the Changing the Guard. Either join the throng at Buckingham Palace, or do as we suggest and head to the less-crowded version of the ceremony at nearby Horse Guards Parade.

11 Tower of London
(page 187)
When William the Conqueror wanted to symbolise and emphasise his control of the city – and the country – in 1078, he built the White Tower, now the castle's central keep. It was witness to many of the key events in London's history and is now a fabulous showcase for the Crown Jewels, as well as giving a home to the traditionally dressed 'Beefeaters' (Yeoman Warders) and their ravens.

15 Royal Botanic Gardens (Kew Gardens)
(page 302)
Its origins reach back to 1759, when royal plant collector Queen Caroline began developing a garden, but Kew keeps up to date with temporary alfresco sculpture exhibitions and a focus on learning about

plant habitats and the environment. But relax: this isn't a visit to the classroom, it's time well spent strolling in a huge and gorgeous garden.

16 St John
(page 172)

This simple, relaxed restaurant – still one of the city's finest – can serve itself a healthy portion of responsibility for changing Britain's reputation for terrible food. Its owner, Fergus Henderson, pretty much invented 'modern British' cooking: striking combinations of well-sourced ingredients, traditional but out-of-favour cuts of meat and offal ('nose-to-tail' cooking) – it sounds so obvious now it seems extraordinary no one did it before.

17 Imperial War Museum
(page 55)

The World War I centenary in 2014, the 60th anniversary of World War II in 2015, a massive refurb… There's been no better time to visit the least regarded of London's major museums than now, when the complexities of our relationship to war feel so current – and the museum's combination of blockbuster, blood-thirsty artefacts and nuanced history drawn from small domestic and military objects feels completely right.

18 Westminster
(page 73)

The grand buildings of Parliament Square – collectively recognised as another UNESCO World Heritage Site – are mostly Victorian, but their core is

ancient: at the heart of the Houses of Parliament is Westminster Hall, a medieval Great Hall, and almost every British monarch has been crowned in Westminster Abbey. The palace sits on what was Thorney Island, one of the city's two original sites.

19 XOYO
(page 271)

A decade or so before the hen parties and post-office drinking mobs descended, the industrial buildings of Shoreditch made up the coolest slice of clubland in the country – perhaps the world. Now the bug-eyed are a bit further north in Dalston (*see pp236-241*), XOYO gives a good flavour of what was: industrial-not-terribly-chic decor, great music, and… what else do you need?

20 The Thames
(page 48)

The broad and muddy serpent of river that divides our city is the reason London is where it is and was, through seaborne trade, the source of its wealth. Ponder its importance from Waterloo Bridge or on board a boat tour (*see p29*) or Thames Clipper (*see p216*), or bone up on what the MP John Burns described as 'liquid history' at the Museum of London Docklands (*see p243*).

London
Today

*Peter Watts on a city
that is becoming bigger
than ever.*

London is a growing city. In February 2015, its population hit 8.6 million. Not only is that the largest it has ever been, it's bigger than Manchester, Birmingham, Glasgow, Leeds, Edinburgh and Liverpool put together. By 2050, it is estimated London will be home to 11 million people. To which Londoners have but one question: where on earth is everybody going to live? Londoners are used to the city's scale and often welcome the resulting bustle – for many, that's what brought them here in the first place – but they are increasingly realising that being a stat in London's historic boom does not come without its catches.

Cereal Killer Café.

BUILDING BIGGER

One of London's charms is the way it has always married its size with a humanising scale. The population has never taken to density, and terraces are still the most popular form of housing. But change is now being forced from above and without. London's growing population, rising land values and the constricting effect of the 'green belt' (a grassy noose around London that is protected from development), has seen developers build up and up in a completely new manner. The result is apparent all over London – particularly in patches at King's Cross, Earl's Court and Paddington – but most arrestingly at Nine Elms, a previously ignored sliver of land on the river between Battersea and Vauxhall, where a dozen shiny towers are being built. These developments, including several around the new US Embassy, due to open in 2017, are creating 16,000 new flats for 40,000 people – a completely new town, effectively.

Cass Gilbert, an American architect who built many New York skyscrapers, once described tall buildings as 'machines for making the land pay', and it's hard to disagree. While the Dubai-style skyscrapers are of mixed architectural merit, the real problem can be seen on the ground, where expensive retail units in draughty canyons are let to

Crossrail.

identikit chains, creating thoroughly unappealing living environments.

Moreover, these new streets are usually owned by developers rather than councils, so come with their own security personnel and restrictions, igniting a debate about private ownership of public space. Even the regeneration of the majestic 1930s industrial cathedral Battersea Power Station, for three decades a forlorn ruin on the western border of Nine Elms, is laced with regret as it will now be surrounded by glass developments, blocking long-loved views of Giles Gilbert Scott's majestic brick masterpiece.

Parakeets. *See p23.*

east-west train line that will provide a long-awaited fast service between Heathrow and Canary Wharf from 2018. Several new stations are being built, some of which are spellbinding. Tottenham Court Road will be one of the busiest interchanges, and the dramatic new station has already forced the demolition of the old Astoria music venue and the destruction of a few of the old station's prized mosaics by artist Eduardo Paolozzi.

As money pours into the area, ripples of redevelopment have spread further into Soho, leading to the closure of another popular club, Madame Jojo's. Londoners are used to change and do not fear it, but there is increasing anger that the current trend seems to be the replacement of anything fun in favour of private domiciles aimed squarely at the wealthy. It reached such a point that London's mayor, Boris Johnson, announced a 'task force' to look at ways of protecting London's live venues.

Cynicism is beginning to infect everything. Over in east London, where most exciting things spawn, there was an epic wave of surliness upon the opening of Cereal Killer Café, a Brick Lane café that serves 100 different types of cereal. What could have been amusingly silly was instead treated to the sort of sustained fury usually reserved for people who stand on the wrong side on escalators. That may have been something to do with the beards sported by the twin brothers who run the place, whose appearance jarred with a population that is beginning to treat 'hipsters' with the sort of folk-devil hatred previously applied to skinheads, muggers, Mods or bankers. Despite that, the cereal café appears to have kicked off a trend – there's another in Manchester – and was soon followed by a pop-up restaurant specialising in porridge. Whatever your breakfast choice, the savvy young go-getters of Hackney and Tower Hamlets continue to serve up some of London's most exciting and ridiculous offerings in just about any discipline, from food and fashion to art and technology.

MONEY VERSUS CULTURE

It's not even certain Londoners can afford to live in these new apartments. Londoners need homes, but few can pay £1 million for a centrally located one-bedroom studio flat overlooking the river. Many are therefore bought by foreign investors, who have taken advantage of stagnant interest rates to make themselves very rich at Londoners' expense, who are paying ever more for property. The result is a lack of empathy with London's past, present and future, as popular venues are sacrificed for housing designed to further enrich the super-rich.

One area of dispute has been St Giles, a previously untameable part of the West End that is home to the 'Tin Pan Alley' music shops of Denmark Street. A huge regeneration project is now under way, which features an enormous futuristic shopping mall boasting technology straight out of a Philip K Dick story. It has already led to the closure of the street's popular 12 Bar Club music venue and campaigners fear for survival of the remaining stores. Developers argue the regeneration is overdue and that when it is complete the street will retain its historic feel. Their intentions may be good, but the market has a way of deciding these things, and rarely in favour of heritage. Time will tell.

THE NEW UNDERGROUND

The transformation of St Giles has been made possible by the arrival of Crossrail, the

GARDENING LEAVE

Scorn also greeted Boris Johnson's final bid for immortality: the Garden Bridge. Johnson, who will stand down as mayor in 2016, first tried to create a lasting London landmark

MISS Saigon

+44 (0)207 812 7498 MISS-SAIGON.COM **PRINCE EDWARD THEATRE, LONDON**

TM © 1980 CML

Les Misérables

+44 (0)207 812 7498 lesmis.com QUEEN'S THEATRE, LONDON

TM © CMOL 1986

The PHANTOM of the OPERA

+44 (0)1158 960 138 thephantomoftheopera.com
HER MAJESTY'S THEATRE, LONDON

TM © RUG LTD 1986

Proposed Garden Bridge

'Londoners need homes, but few can pay £1m for a one-bedroom studio flat overlooking the river.'

when he blessed the city with its most pointless piece of infrastructure in decades: the cable car between North Greenwich and Royal Victoria (see p243). Having seen various other hare-brained schemes shot down, he finally hit paydirt with the Garden Bridge, a bridge-cum-park between Waterloo and Blackfriars that was proposed by actress Joanna Lumley and designed by Thomas Heatherwick, who created the 2012 Olympic Cauldron as well as Johnson's not-entirely-successful 'New Routemaster' bus fleet.

A lovely idea in principle, the Garden Bridge has clear flaws, not least the fact it's being built in an area already well served with cross-river transport. Most worrying is the fact that, while at least £60 million is coming from public funds (initially, it was understood it would be entirely privately funded, a miscomprehension common to most of Johnson's flagship projects), the bridge will still be closed to the public at night and several times a year for fund-raising. Lumley, Johnson and Heatherwick maintain that

Londoners will love the Garden Bridge when it opens in 2018 – and maybe they're right – but many feel they are being taken for a ride as Johnson desperately tries to mimic the popular grands projets of his predecessor Ken Livingstone's reign, with little success.

Those projects were largely cultural and paid for by National Lottery money, a well that has since run dry – or at least been diverted from such huge undertakings as the opening of the Tate Modern (see p57) or the new piazza of the British Museum (see p150). Big schemes haven't entirely disappeared: in December 2016, the Tate Modern extension is due to open, while the Design Museum (see p62) will move to a new home at the listed Commonwealth Institute in Kensington.

Impressive though these are, they haven't really captured the public imagination, which is where the Garden Bridge comes in. And the Garden Bridge does at least tap into one bubbling undercurrent of London life: a greater appreciation of nature. Writers, artists and poets are increasingly celebrating the diverse biospheres available in London, as seen in publications like Caught by the River, which riffs on an urban version of the landscape-obsessed musings of Robert MacFarlane. London's parks and numerous waterways are home to surprisingly exotic birds and plants – from growing numbers of noisy parakeets in the city's ancient trees to porpoises in the perenially muddy but ecologically clean Thames. It seems that it isn't just humans that are attracted by London's magnetic lights, as the city swells and seethes.

Itineraries

Let our step-by-step planner help you fall in love with London.

10AM

10.45AM

NOON

Day 1

10AM Start the day in **Trafalgar Square** (*p68*). The centre of London is an impressive sight, especially when it isn't too full of tourists snapping pictures of themselves with the lions: on the fourth pedestal, check out the skeletal horse on display in 2015, which will be followed by David Shrigley's giant thumbs-up in 2016. The masterpieces of the **National Gallery** (*p68*) – a veritable encyclopaedia of Western art – are on the pedestrianised northern side of the square.

10.45AM Head south down Whitehall, keeping an eye out for the cavalryman on sentry duty. You should arrive in time to see Horse Guards with shiny swords and helmets go through the daily **Changing the Guard** (*p41* **Stunning Ceremonials**; it's an hour earlier on Sunday). After the ceremonials, head through the parade ground into **St James's Park** (*p89*) to feed the ducks and admire

3PM

Clockwise from far left: **National Gallery**; **Changing the Guard**; **Millennium Bridge**; **Fabric**; **Parliament Square**.

Buckingham Palace (*p79*) at the end of the lake.

NOON Just out of the park's south-eastern corner is Parliament Square. Admire **Westminster Abbey**, **Parliament** and the **Queen Elizabeth Tower** ('Big Ben' to most visitors) – this is a UNESCO World Heritage Site. Next, cross Westminster Bridge for County Hall, the **London Eye** (*p54*) and a stroll east along the South Bank. This walk is modern London's biggest tourist cliché, but it's still great fun. The area around the **Southbank Centre** (*p50*) is busy with places to eat.

3PM Go with the flow past the ace repertory cinema **BFI Southbank** (*p256*) and the **National Theatre** (*p289*) to **Tate Modern** (*p57*) and **Shakespeare's Globe** (*p57*), and finish your afternoon by walking across the Millennium Bridge for the slow climb up to 17th-century architectural masterpiece,

St Paul's Cathedral (*p176*), right by St Paul's tube station.

8PM Enough history. Head north into Clerkenwell for brilliant food: modern British at **St John** (*p172*) or fusion at **Modern Pantry** (*p171*). If you're in town at the weekend and still have some energy, join the queue for enduringly cool superclub **Fabric** (*p267*).

8PM

This page
from the top:
**British
Museum**;
**Olympic
Park**;
Kanada-Ya.

10AM

Day 2

10AM Ready for one of the
world's finest museums? You
betcha – and you'll be early
enough to miss most of the
crowds. The **British Museum**
(*p150*) is so full of treasures,
you may not know where
to begin: try left out of the
middle of the covered
courtyard for monumental
antiquities, including the
Parthenon Marbles.

NOON Wander south to the
boutiques around Seven
Dials until lunch. **Great
Queen Street** (*p142*) is a
good option if you didn't try
St John; **Wahaca** (*p143*)
and **Kanada-Ya** (*p143*) are
cheaper for a quick snack.

3PM

Covent Garden Market
(*p138*) is here, but the
excellent **London Transport
Museum** (*p140*) or a coffee
on the lofty terrace of the
Royal Opera House (*p140*)
are better reasons to linger.

3PM If you're interested
in how London has been
changing, head to Bank
station and get the DLR: it
will take you to the **Olympic
Park** (*p237*) or the **Royal
Docks** (*p241*), with plenty
of walking opportunities
in the redeveloped former
industrial hinterland. Or
head to South Kensington's
trio of powerhouse museums:
the **V&A**, **Natural History
Museum** and **Science
Museum** (for all, *see pp87-
91*). If there's any walking
left in you, head to Hyde

Park for the grandiloquent
Albert Memorial (*p87*) and
Kensington Gardens for
the Zaha Hadid-redesigned
Serpentine Sackler gallery
(*p93*). You can eat in the
Sackler, but we recommend
a stroll north across the park
to **Le Café Anglais** (*p93*).

9PM Not yet ready for bed?
All you need do is get on the
Central (red) Underground
line and head to the **East End**
(*see pp198-213*): Liverpool
Street station is the gateway
to bleakly nondescript
Shoreditch and its plethora
of concept cocktail bars. Then
join the hipsters and take the
Overground from Shoreditch
High Street to Dalston
Junction for a taste of
Dalston's nightlife
(*see pp266-271*).

NOON

Shopping Around

COVENT GARDEN & SOHO

Shops around the former flower market have improved markedly over the last few years, but Neal Street and around Seven Dials rule for streetwear. In Soho, pedestrianised Carnaby Street is another key area.

OXFORD STREET

London's commercial backbone, Oxford Street heaves with department stores and big chains (especially to the west), which spill on to Regent Street. Marylebone has interesting small shops selling everything from jewellery to artisanal cheeses.

NOTTING HILL

Best known for Portobello Road market, Notting Hill also has posh boutiques, as well as rare vinyl and vintage-clothes shops.

MAYFAIR & ST JAMES'S

This patch is where to come for bespoke tailors, high-class jewellers, specialist hatters, cobblers and historic perfumers.

CHELSEA & KNIGHTSBRIDGE

King's Road is pretty bland, with a couple of notable exceptions, but boutiques line Sloane Street and mix with the deluxe department stores on Knightsbridge.

THE EAST END

Visit on Sunday for the Columbia Road Market and the best of Spitalfields, or on Saturday for Broadway Market at its busiest. Brick Lane and its offshoot Redchurch Street have great vintage clothes and home goods.

CAMDEN

The formerly grungy markets, still a natural habitat for under-25s, have grown up a bit – notably with food stalls at the Lock.

LONDON FOR FREE

Not everything in the city need cost the Mint.

MUSIC TO OUR EARS

There are a vast number of free gigs every week. They range from rock and pop at pub venues and in stores, notably at Rough Trade East, via lunchtime sessions at churches, including the atmospheric Union Chapel and, for classical, St Martin-in-the-Fields and St James's Piccadilly. The National Theatre, Barbican and Southbank Centre host regular foyer gigs, and Angel Comedy isn't just a free night – it's also a great one.

CULTURE GRATIS

All the key venues (the British Museum, both Tates and all three South Kensington museums are just the start) are free, as are many smaller ones (including the Soane's, Wallace, Grant and Horniman), and many prestigious private art galleries, including White Cube Bermondsey, the Saatchi and the South London Gallery.

FREE RIDERS

See the Changing the Guard at Buckingham Palace or Horse Guards Parade – early risers can catch the cavalry ride out through Hyde Park at 10.30am daily (9.30am Sundays). There are also mounted sentries on duty all day at Horse Guards and St James's Palace.

FOUNTAINS & SUMMER FUN

When the sun appears, roll up your trousers in the lovely fountain courtyards at Somerset House or Granary Square. Summer is also great for free alfresco theatre: try Greenwich & Docklands Festival or the Scoop near Tower Bridge.

PARK LIFE

London has a delightful array of green spaces, several surprisingly central; no visit to the city would be complete without a visit to one of Hyde, Regent's or St James's parks. Don't neglect the charming smaller spaces such as the City's Postman's Park, nor the wild acres of Hampstead Heath.

TAKE YOUR IMAGINATION INTO UNCHARTED TERRITORY!

CENTRAL LONDON'S
MUST SEE ATTRACTION

Ripley's
Believe *It or Not!* ®
LONDON

DISCOVER THE UK'S MOST EXTRAORDINARY ATTRACTION!

NO. 1 PICCADILLY CIRCUS • RIPLEYSLONDON.COM

Guided Tours

London Bicycle Tour Company.

ON FOOT

For free, self-guided walking tours, head to **www.walk london.org.uk** or the Greater London section of the Royal Geographical Society's **www. discoveringbritain.org**.

Good choices for paid group tours include **And Did Those Feet** (8806 4325, www.chr. org.uk), **Silver Cane Tours** (07720 715295, www. silvercanetours.com) and **Urban Gentry** (8149 6253, www.urbangentry.com). **Original London Walks** (7624 3978, www.walks.com) provides 140 different walks on a variety of themes.

For more idiosyncratic outings, follow **old London maps** (www.londontrails. wordpress.com); trace a route through the city's history via its **public conveniences** (http://lootours.com); or journey through the **art scene** (www.foxandsquirrel.com and streetartlondon.co.uk/tours). The politically minded might enjoy **East End Walks** (www. eastendwalks.com), David Rosenberg's tours through the history of radical London, or **Occupy London Tours** (http:// occupytours.org), the activist organisation's volunteer-led explorations of wealthy Canary Wharf, the City and Mayfair. **Unseen Tours** (07514 266774, www. sockmobevents.org.uk) are a terrific initiative: they are led by homeless guides, who bring their own perspective to well-known landmarks and the quirkier nooks of the city.

BY BICYCLE

The **London Bicycle Tour Company** (1 Gabriel's Wharf, 56 Upper Ground, South Bank, SE1 9PP, 7928 6838, www.londonbicycle.com) runs a range of tours in central London, while **Capital Sport** (01296 631671, www.the-carter-company.com) offers gentle cycling tours along the Thames. For self-starters, **Boris Bikes** can be an affordable option (p370).

BY BOAT

City Cruises: Red River Rover 7740 0400, www.citycruises. com. Rates from £13. Hop-on, hop-off river journeys.
Jason's Trip Canal Boats 7286 3428, www.jasons. co.uk. Rates £14 return; £13 reductions. Narrow-boat tours from Little Venice to Camden, running April to November.
London Kayak Tours 0845 453 2002, www.london kayaktours.co.uk. Rates from £29.99. Guided tours from Tower Bridge or Hampton Court Palace, or on the Regent's Canal, from March to October.
Thames RIB Experience 3613 2356, www.thames ribexperience.com. Rates £36-£52; £21.50-£24.50 reductions. One of several speedboat tour companies: zoom from the Embankment to Canary Wharf (50mins) or the Thames Barrier (75mins) and back. Bookings must be made by phone.

BY BUS

Both of these companies offer multiple hop-on, hop-off stops near the key central London sights. The tickets include a river cruise.
Big Bus Company 7808 6753, http://bigbustours. com. Rates from £32; £12 reductions; free under-5s.
Original London Sightseeing Tour 8877 1722, www. theoriginaltour.com. Rates £29; £14 reductions; £86 family; free under-5s.

BY AIR

Adventure Balloons 01252 844222, http:// adventureballoons.co.uk. Rates from £189. Flights run at dawn on weekdays from late April to mid August.
London Helicopter Tour 7887 2626, www.the londonhelicopter.com. Rates from £150. Half-hour flights from Battersea along the Thames and back.

BY CAR

Black Taxi Tours of London 7935 9363, www.black taxitours.co.uk. Rates £150. Tailored 2hr tours.
Small Car Big City 7839 6737, http://smallcarbigcity. com. Rates £54-£549. Themed tours in a classic Mini Cooper – for half an hour or the entire day.

Lord Mayor's Show.
See p39.

Diary

*Your guide to what's
happening when.*

Forget about British reserve. Festivals and events play ever more elaborate variations on the age-old themes of parading and dancing, nowadays with ever-larger sprinklings of arts and culture. Some are traditional, some innovative, from the outdoor spectacle of the Greenwich & Docklands International Festival to the splendid ritual of the Changing the Guard. Weather plays a part in the timing, with a concentration of things to do in the warmer – and sometimes drier – months of summer, but the city's calendar is busy for most of the year. Indeed, some of the most enjoyable events take place in winter – Bonfire Night, for example.

All year round

For **Changing the Guard**, *see p33* **Stunning Ceremonials**.

Ceremony of the Keys

Tower of London, Tower Hill, the City, EC3N 4AB (0844 482 7777, www.hrp.org.uk). Tower Hill tube or Tower Gateway DLR. **Date** 9.30pm daily (advance bookings only).

Join the Yeoman Warders after-hours at the Tower of London as they ritually lock the fortress's entrances in this 700-year-old ceremony. You enter the Tower at 9.30pm and it's all over just after 10pm, but places are hotly sought after – apply at least two months in advance; full details are available on the website.

Gun Salutes

Green Park, Mayfair & St James's, W1; Tower of London, the City, EC3. **Dates** 6 Feb (Accession Day); 21 Apr & 14 June (Queen's birthdays); 2 June (Coronation Day); 10 June (Duke of Edinburgh's birthday); 14 June (Trooping the Colour); State Opening of Parliament (*see p41*); Lord Mayor's Show (*see p39*); Remembrance Sunday (*see p39*); also for state visits.

There are gun salutes on many state occasions – see the list of dates given above for a complete breakdown of when the cannons roar out. A cavalry

PUBLIC HOLIDAYS

Good Friday
Fri 3 Apr 2015, Fri 25 Mar 2016

Easter Monday
Mon 6 Apr 2015, Mon 28 Mar 2016

May Day Holiday
Mon 4 May 2015, Mon 2 May 2016

Spring Bank Holiday
Mon 25 May 2015, Mon 30 May 2016

Summer Bank Holiday
Mon 31 Aug 2015, Mon 29 Aug 2016

Christmas Day
Fri 25 Dec 2015, Sun 25 Dec 2016
(bank holiday Tue 27 Dec 2016)

Boxing Day
Mon 28 Dec 2015, Mon 26 Dec 2016

New Year's Day
Fri 1 Jan 2016, Sun 1 Jan 2016
(bank holiday Mon 2 Jan 2016)

charge features in the 41-gun salutes mounted by the King's Troop Royal Horse Artillery in Hyde Park at noon (opposite the Dorchester Hotel; *see p350*), whereas, on the other side of town, the Honourable Artillery Company ditches the ponies and piles on the firepower with its 62-gun salutes (1pm at the Tower of London). If the dates happen to fall on a Sunday, the salute is held on the following Monday.

Summer

Spitalfields Music Summer Festival
7377 1362, www.spitalfieldsmusic.org.uk. **Date** June.
A series of mainly classical concerts in June, based at Christ Church Spitalfields, as well as local venues including Shoreditch Church and Spitalfields Market. The festival returns in December each year.

Field Day
Victoria Park, Victoria Park Road, Hackney, E3 5SN (www.fielddayfestivals.com). **Date** June.
One of the best music festivals in London, with a left-field booking policy. Acts range from weird pop and indie rock to underground dance producers and folk musicians. Held over a weekend.

★ London Festival of Architecture
www.londonfestivalofarchitecture.org. **Date** June.
An entertaining mix of talks, discussions, walks, screenings and other events, always gathered under a punchy theme.

LIFT (London International Festival of Theatre)
7968 6800, www.liftfest.org.uk. **Date** June.
Nearly 90 performances in a month under the inspirational directorship of Mark Ball.

Opera Holland Park
Holland Park (7361 3570, www.operaholland park.com). **Date** June-Aug.
A canopied outdoor theatre hosts a season of opera, including works aimed at children.

★ Epsom Derby
Epsom Racecourse, Epsom Downs, Surrey KT18 5LQ (01372 726311 information, 0844 579 3004 tickets, http://epsom.thejockeyclub.co.uk). Epsom Downs or Tattenham Corner rail. **Date** early June.
The world's most famous horse race on the flat, the Derby, is run over a distance of one and a half miles. Crowd-watching is a large part of the fun, with the race accompanied by all manner of hoopla.

★ Open Garden Squares Weekend
7839 3969, www.opensquares.org. **Date** mid June.
Secret – and merely exclusive – gardens are thrown open to the public for this horticultural shindig. You can visit roof gardens, children-only gardens and

STUNNING CEREMONIALS
London is a past master when it comes to military pomp.

On alternate days from 10.45am (www.royal.gov.uk/RoyalEventsandCeremonies/ChangingtheGuard/Overview.aspx has the details), one of the five Foot Guards regiments lines up in scarlet coats and tall bearskin hats in the forecourt of Wellington Barracks; at exactly 11.27am, the soldiers start to march to **Buckingham Palace**, joined by their regimental band, to relieve the sentries there in a 45-minute ceremony for **Changing the Guard**. The Guards regiments are the Grenadier, Coldstream, Scots, Irish and Welsh.

Not far away, at **Horse Guards Parade** in Whitehall, the Household Cavalry regiments – the Life Guards and Blues and Royals – mount the guard daily at 11am (10am on Sunday). Although this ceremony isn't as famous as the one at Buckingham Palace, it's more visitor-friendly: the crowds aren't as thick as they are at the palace, and spectators aren't held far back from the action by railings. After the old and new guard have stared each other out in the centre of the parade ground, you can nip through to the Whitehall side to catch the departing old guard perform their dismount choreography: a synchronised, firm slap of approbation to the neck of each horse before the gloved troopers all swing off.

As well as these near-daily ceremonies, London sees other, less frequent parades on a far grander scale. The most famous is **Trooping the Colour**, which is staged to mark the Queen's official birthday on 13 June (her real birthday is in April). At 10.45am, the Queen rides in a carriage from Buckingham Palace to Horse Guards Parade to watch the soldiers, before heading back to Buckingham Palace for a midday RAF flypast and the impressive gun salute from Green Park.

Also at Horse Guards, for two successive evenings in June, a pageant of military music and precision marching begins at 7pm when the Queen (or another royal) takes the salute of the 300-strong drummers, pipers and musicians of the Massed Bands of the Household Division. This is known as **Beating the Retreat** (0844 844 0444, tickets 7839 5323).

From left to right: **Wimbledon Tennis Championships**; **Wireless Festival**; **Notting Hill Carnival** (see p37).

prison gardens, as well as a changing selection of those tempting oases railed off in the middle of the city's finest squares. Some charge an entrance fee.

Tennis: Aegon Championships
Queens Club, Palliser Road, West Kensington, W14 9EQ (7386 3400, www.queensclub.co.uk). Barons Court tube. **Date** mid June.
The pros tend to treat this week-long grass-court tournament as a summer warm-up session for the world-famous Wimbledon Tennis Championships.

Royal Ascot
Ascot Racecourse, Ascot, Berkshire, SL5 7JX (0844 346 3000, www.ascot.co.uk). Ascot rail. **Date** mid June.
Major races include the Ascot Gold Cup on the Thursday, which is Ladies' Day. Expect sartorial extravagance and fancy hats.

★ Greenwich & Docklands International Festival
8305 5023, www.festival.org. **Date** late June.
This annual week of outdoor arts, theatre, dance and family entertainment is spectacular. Events take place at the Old Royal Naval College and other sites, including Canary Wharf and Mile End Park.

Pride London
0844 344 5428, www.prideinlondon.org. **Date** late June.

This historic celebration of the LGBT community (taking place since 1972, initially in support of the Stonewall rioters) now welcomes some 800,000 revellers to a week of events, culminating in a celebratory parade held on Saturday.

★ City of London Festival
0845 120 7502, www.colf.org. **Date** late June-mid July.
Last year, new CoLF director Paul Gudgin brought with him a new venue: a 30ft-tall inflatable bowler hat, in which he hosted comedy and children's theatre to enhance the traditional festival diet of classical music in a variety of genres, as well as some jazz and plenty of interesting talks. Many of the concerts are held in unusual venues (churches, courtrooms, ancient livery companies) and there's always a strong programme of free events.

★ Wimbledon Tennis Championships
All England Lawn Tennis Club, Church Road, Wimbledon, SW19 5AE (8944 1066, www. wimbledon.org). Southfields tube or Wimbledon tube/rail. **Dates** late June-mid July.
Getting into Wimbledon requires considerable forethought, as well as luck. Seats on the show courts are distributed by a ballot, which closes the previous year; enthusiasts who queue on the day may gain entry to the outer courts – and even get rare tickets for Centre Court. You can also turn up later in the day and pay reduced rates for seats vacated by spectators who've left the ground early.

Camden Lock Live

www.camdenlockmarket.com. Camden Town or Chalk Farm tube. **Date** mid July.
A free 'urban boutique' festival – in other words, small but perfectly formed out of gigs, food, fashion and other vaguely alternative entertainments.

★ BBC Proms

Royal Albert Hall, Kensington Gore, South Kensington, SW7 2AP (0845 401 5040, www.bbc.co.uk/proms). South Kensington tube. **Date** mid July-mid Sept.
The Proms overshadow all other classical-music festivals in the city, with around 70 concerts, covering everything from early-music recitals to orchestral world premières, and from boundary-pushing debut performances to reverent career retrospectives. BBC Radio 3 plays recordings of the concerts.

Camden Fringe

www.camdenfringe.org. **Date** Aug.
An eclectic bunch of new, experimental and short shows, staged by everyone from experienced performers to newcomers.

RideLondon

7902 0212, www.prudentialridelondon.com. **Date** early Aug.
This cycling festival encourages around 50,000 people to don branded fluorescent vests and ride an eight-mile traffic-free circuit from Buckingham Palace to the Tower. Competitive races also form part of the weekend's festivities.

Carnaval del Pueblo

Burgess Park, Southwark, SE5 7QH (www. carnavaldelpueblo.co.uk). Elephant & Castle tube/rail. **Date** early Aug.
This vibrant outdoor parade and festival is more than just a loud-and-proud day out for Latin American Londoners: with a procession from Elephant Road to Burgess Park, it attracts people from all walks of life (as many as 60,000, most years) looking to inject a little Latin spirit into the weekend.

Great British Beer Festival

Olympia London, Hammersmith Road, Kensington, W14 8UX (www.gbbf.org.uk). Kensington (Olympia) tube/Overground. **Date** mid Aug.

Wireless Festival

Finsbury Park, N4 2DW (www.wirelessfestival. co.uk). Manor House tube or Finsbury Park tube/ rail. **Date** early July.
Three nights of rock and dance acts, with the 2015 headliners including Drake, Kendrick Lamar, David Guetta and Nicki Minaj.

★ Lovebox Weekender

Victoria Park, Victoria Park Road, Hackney, E3 5SN (www.loveboxfestival.com). Mile End tube or Hackney Wick Overground. **Date** mid July.
Expect some of the best names that the London nightlife scene has to offer, over two days in myriad themed stages, tents and arenas.

Somerset House Summer Series

Somerset House, Strand, WC2R 1LA (7845 4600, www.somersethouse.org.uk/music). Temple tube. **Date** mid July.
Somerset House welcomes an array of big and generally pretty mainstream acts for roughly ten days of open-air shows.

IN THE KNOW DO MORE

You can buy tickets for the **BBC Proms** (see above) in advance, but many prefer to queue on the day for the £5 'promenade' tickets after which the festival is named. These allow entry to the standing-room stalls or gallery at the top of the auditorium.

A great chance to enjoy London's extraordinary beer renaissance in one place. Hiccup.

Meltdown
Southbank Centre, Belvedere Road, South Bank, SE1 8XX (www.southbankcentre.co.uk). **Date** mid Aug.
The Southbank Centre invites a guest artist – this year it's David Byrne – to curate a fortnight of gigs, films and whatever other events appeal to them.

London Mela
Gunnersbury Park, Ealing, W3 8LQ (8992 1612, www.londonmela.org). Acton Town, Gunnersbury or South Ealing tube. **Date** late Aug.
Thousands flock to this exuberant celebration of Asian culture, dubbed the Asian Glastonbury. You'll find urban, classical and experimental music, circus, dance, comedy, children's events and food.

★ Notting Hill Carnival
Notting Hill, W10 & W11 (www.thenottinghill carnival.com). Ladbroke Grove, Notting Hill Gate or Westbourne Park tube. **Date** late Aug.
Two million people stream into Notting Hill for Europe's largest street party. Massive mobile sound systems dominate the streets with whatever bass-heavy party music is currently hip, but there's plenty of tradition from the West Indies too: calypso music and a spectacular costumed parade. *Photo p34.*

South West Four
Clapham Common, SW4 (www.southwestfour. com). Clapham Common or Clapham South tube, or Clapham High Street Overground. **Date** late Aug.
London's key dance-music festival, held over the August bank holiday weekend.

Challenge Cup Final
Wembley Stadium, Stadium Way, Middlesex, HA9 0WS (www.thechallengecup.com). Wembley Park tube or Wembley Stadium rail. **Date** late Aug.
Rugby league is mainly played in the north of the country, but for the Challenge Cup Final the north heads south, bringing boisterous, convivial crowds to Wembley Stadium for some hard-tackling action.

Autumn

London African Music Festival
7328 9613, www.joyfulnoise.co.uk. **Date** Sept.
A wonderfully eclectic affair, held over a fortnight in September. Recent performers have included Osibisa (from Ghana), Modou Toure (Senegal) and Hanisha Solomon (Ethiopia).

Totally Thames Festival
Between Westminster Bridge & Tower Bridge (7928 8998, www.totallythames.org). Blackfriars or Waterloo tube/rail. **Date** Sept.

A giant party along the Thames, this month of events is London's largest free arts festival. It's a family-friendly mix of carnival, pyrotechnics, art installations, river events and live music alongside craft and food stalls. The highlight is the last-night lantern procession and firework finale.

Tour of Britain
www.thetour.co.uk. **Date** early Sept.
Join spectators on the streets of the capital for a stage of British cycling's biggest outdoor event.

★ Open-House London
3006 7008, www.open-city.org.uk. **Date** mid Sept.
An opportunity to snoop around other people's property, for one weekend only. Taking part are more than 500 palaces, private homes, corporate skyscrapers, pumping stations and bomb-proof bunkers, many of which are normally closed to the public.

Kings Place Festival
Kings Place, 90 York Way, King's Cross, N1 9AG (7520 1490, www.kingsplace.co.uk/festival). King's Cross St Pancras tube/rail. **Date** mid Sept.
Cramming in more than 100 events over three days – classical, jazz and experimental music, as well as spoken word and other events – this is a great little arts festival in a superb venue.

London Fashion Week
Somerset House, Strand, WC2R 1LA (www.londonfashionweek.co.uk). Temple tube. **Date** mid Sept.
Extraordinary biannual outbreak of fashionable happenings across London (it returns each February). Although mainly focused on Somerset House, events see gaggles of paparazzi and informal catwalks in the most unlikely places.

OnBlackheath
Blackheath, SE3 (www.onblackheath.com). **Date** mid Sept.
While the John Lewis sponsorship didn't imply wild times for the inaugural OnBlackheath weekend music and food festival in 2014, the line-up was less dad-rock than you might expect, with Massive Attack and Grace Jones among the headliners.

London Literature Festival
Southbank Centre, Belvedere Road, South Bank, SE1 8XX (7960 4200, www.southbankcentre. co.uk). **Date** mid-mid Oct.
The London Literature Festival combines superstar writers with stars from other fields: architects, comedians, sculptors and cultural theorists, examining anything from queer literature to migration.

Great River Race
River Thames, from Millwall Docks, Docklands, E14, to Ham House, Richmond, Surrey, TW10 (8398 8141, www.greatriverrace.co.uk). **Date** mid Sept.

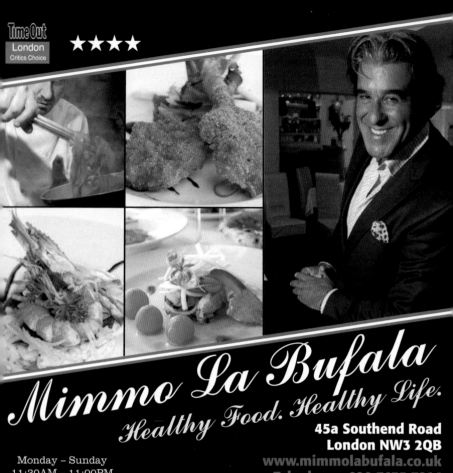

Much more interesting than the Boat Race (*see p41*), the Great River Race sees an exotic array of around 300 traditional rowing boats (including skiffs, canoes, dragon boats and Cornish gigs) from around the globe racing in the 'river marathon'. Hungerford Bridge, the Millennium Bridge and Tower Bridge are all good viewpoints.

American Football: NFL
Wembley Stadium, Stadium Way, Middlesex, HA9 0WS (www.nfluk.com). Wembley Park tube or Wembley Stadium rail. **Date** late Sept-early Nov.
The NFL took a regular-season match out of North America for the first time in 2007 – it was a huge success, and immediately became an annual fixture. Jacksonville Jaguars play a home game here in 2016.

The Big Draw
8351 1719, www.campaignfordrawing.org. **Date** Oct.
Engage with your inner artist at the month-long Big Draw, using anything from pencils to vapour trails.

Dance Umbrella
7407 1200, www.danceumbrella.co.uk. **Date** Oct.
A leading international dance festival, featuring a range of events (many free) in unusual spaces.

London Film Festival
www.bfi.org.uk/lff. **Date** mid Oct.
The most prestigious of the capital's film fests – in fact, the key film festival in the country. Over 200 new British and international features are screened each year, mainly at the BFI Southbank and Leicester Square's Vue West End, and there's always a smattering of red-carpet events for the celebrity-crazed.

★ London Frieze Art Fair
Regent's Park, NW1 (http://friezelondon.com). Regent's Park tube. **Date** mid Oct.
The biggest contemporary carnival in London's art calendar occupies a purpose-built venue at the south end of Regent's Park, where some 1,000 artists are displayed over the four-day festival. Highlights include the daily-changing Projects; debates and discussions as part of the Talks strand; and Live, showing performance-based installations.

Diwali
Trafalgar Square, WC2 (7983 4000, www.london. gov.uk). Charing Cross tube/rail. **Date** Oct/Nov.
A celebration of the annual Festival of Light by Hindu, Jain and Sikh communities.

Winter

London to Brighton Veteran Car Run
Departs Serpentine Road, Hyde Park, W2 2UH (01483 524433, www.veterancarrun.com). Hyde Park Corner tube. **Date** early Nov.

The London to Brighton Veteran Car Run is not so much a race as a sedate procession southwards by around 500 pre-1905 cars. The first pair trundles off at sunrise (around 7-8.30am), but you can catch them a little later crossing Westminster Bridge, or view them on a closed-off Regent's Street the day before the event (11am-3pm).

★ Bonfire Night
Date 5 Nov & around.
Britain's best-loved excuse for setting off fireworks: the celebration of Guy Fawkes's failure to blow up the Houses of Parliament in 1605. Check the dedicated page at www.timeout.com for a list of public displays right across town – several are put on for free, and many charge only a nominal entry fee.

★ Lord Mayor's Show
7606 3030, www.lordmayorsshow.org. **Date** early Nov.
This big show marks the traditional presentation of the new Lord Mayor for approval by the monarch's justices. The Lord Mayor leaves Mansion House in a fabulous gold coach at 11am, along with a colourful procession of floats and marchers. At 5pm, there's a fireworks display on the river. *Photo p30.*
▶ *The Lord Mayor is a City officer, elected each year by the livery companies and with no real power outside the City of London; don't confuse him with the Mayor of London, currently Boris Johnson (see pp18-23 London Today).*

Remembrance Sunday Ceremony
Cenotaph, Whitehall, Westminster, SW1. Charing Cross tube/rail. **Date** early Nov.
Held on the second Sunday in November, the Sunday nearest to 11 November – the day World War I ended – this solemn commemoration honours those who died fighting in the World Wars and later conflicts. The Queen, the prime minister and other dignitaries lay poppy wreaths at the Cenotaph. A two-minute silence at 11am is followed by a service of remembrance.

★ London Jazz Festival
7324 1880, www.londonjazzfestival.org.uk. **Date** mid Nov.
Covering most bases, from trad to free improv, this is the biggest London jazz festival of the year, lasting the best part of a fortnight.

Christmas Celebrations

Covent Garden (www.coventgardenlondonuk.com);
Bond Street (www.bondstreetassociation.com); St
Christopher's Place (www.stchristophersplace.com);
Marylebone High Street (www.marylebonevillage.
com); Trafalgar Square (www.london.gov.uk).
Date Nov-Dec.

Of the big stores, Fortnum & Mason (*see p82*) still
creates enchantingly old-fashioned Christmas
windows. Otherwise, though, skip the commercialised lights on Oxford and Regent streets and
head, instead, for smaller shopping areas such as St
Christopher's Place, Bond Street, Marylebone High
Street and Covent Garden. It's traditional to sing
carols beneath a giant Christmas tree in Trafalgar
Square – an annual gift from Norway in gratitude for
Britain's support during World War II – but you can
also join in a mammoth singalong at the Royal Albert
Hall, enjoy the starry choral Christmas Festival at St
John Smith Square or an evocative carol service at
one of London's historic churches. London's major
cathedrals all, naturally, celebrate Christmas with
splendid liturgies and music.

Chinese New Year Festival

Spitalfields Music Winter Festival

Date Dec.
See p33 **Spitalfields Music Summer Festival**.

New Year's Eve Celebrations

Date 31 Dec.
The focus of London's public celebrations has officially moved from overcrowded Trafalgar Square
to the full-on fireworks display launched from the
London Eye and rafts on the Thames. You have to get
there early for a good view. Those with stamina can
take in the New Year's Day Parade in central London
the next day (www.lnydp.com).

London International Mime Festival

www.mimelondon.com. **Date** Jan.
Theatrical magic in many forms, from haunting
visual theatre to puppetry for adults.

★ Chinese New Year Festival

Around Gerrard Street, Chinatown, W1, Leicester
Square, WC2 (7333 8118, www.chinatownlondon.
org). Leicester Square or Piccadilly Circus tube.
Date Feb.
Launch the Year of the Monkey (8 Feb 2016) in style
at celebrations that engulf Chinatown and Leicester
Square. Lion dancers gyrate alongside a host of acts
in the grand parade to Trafalgar Squarel.

London Fashion Week

Date mid/late Feb.
See p37 **London Fashion Week**.

Six Nations Tournament

Twickenham Stadium, Rugby Road, Middlesex,
TW1 1DZ (8892 2000, www.englandrugby.com).
Dates Feb-Mar.

This major rugby union tournament for the northern hemisphere teams sees England take on Wales,
Scotland, Ireland, France and Italy, with England's
home fixtures played at the code's headquarters at
Twickenham. Book a long way ahead.

Spring

League Cup Final

Wembley Stadium, Stadium Way, Middlesex, HA9
0WS (0800 169 2007, www.capitalonecup.co.uk).
Wembley Park tube. **Date** early Mar.
Less prestigious than the FA Cup, the League Cup
is a knockout football competition with a 50-year
history – but widely regarded as the annual trophy
that's 'better than nothing'. Still, the winners do get
to play in the UEFA Europa League.

Kew Spring Festival

Kew Gardens, Surrey, TW9 3AB (8332 5655,
www.kew.org). Kew Gardens tube/Overground,
Kew Bridge Overground/rail or riverboat to Kew
Pier. **Admission** £15; £14 reductions; £3.50
under-17s. **Date** early Mar-May.
Kew Gardens is at its most beautiful in spring, with
five million flowers carpeting the grounds.

National Science & Engineering Week

7019 4937, www.britishscienceweek.org.
Date mid Mar.
From the weird to the profound, this annual week
of events engages the public in celebrating science,
engineering and technology.

St Patrick's Day Parade & Festival

7983 4000, www.london.gov.uk. **Date** mid Mar.

London Marathon

Blackheath & Maze Hill rail (start), or Charing Cross tube/rail (end). **Date** mid Apr.
One of the world's elite long-distance races, the London Marathon is also one of the world's largest fundraising events – nearly 80% of participants run for charity, so zany costumes abound among the 36,000 starters. Held on a Sunday.

Breakin' Convention
Sadler's Wells, Rosebery Avenue, EC1R 4TN (0844 412 4300, www.breakinconvention.com). Angel tube. **Date** early May.
Hip hop and dance festival.

FA Cup Final
Wembley Stadium, Stadium Way, Middlesex, HA9 0WS (0800 169 2007 Wembley Stadium, www.thefa.com/thefacup). Wembley Park tube or Wembley Stadium rail. **Date** mid May.
The oldest domestic knockout tournament is an annual highlight for many international football fans. For all that the competition – which began in 1871 – has lost a little lustre for the top teams, who all fear being defeated by lowly opposition, it retains the capacity to surprise.

Covent Garden May Fayre & Puppet Festival
Garden of St Paul's Covent Garden, Bedford Street, WC2E 9ED (7375 0441, www.punchandjudy.com/coventgarden.htm). Covent Garden tube. **Date** 2nd Sun in May.
All-day puppet mayhem (10.30am-5.30pm) devoted to celebrating Mr Punch at the scene of his first recorded sighting in England in 1662. Mr P takes to the church's pulpit at 11.30am. Held on a Sunday.

Chelsea Flower Show
Royal Hospital, Royal Hospital Road, Chelsea, SW3 4SR (0844 338 7502, www.rhs.org.uk). Sloane Square tube. **Date** mid May.
Elbow through the huge crowds to admire perfect blooms, or get ideas for your own plot, with entire gardens laid out for the show, as well as tents with their walls packed with endless varietals. The first two days are reserved for Royal Horticultural Society members and tickets for the open days can be hard to come by.
▶ *The show closes at 5.30pm on the final day, but the display plants are sold off from around 4pm.*

State Opening of Parliament
Palace of Westminster, SW1A 0PW (7219 4272, www.parliament.uk). Westminster tube. **Date** May/June.
Pomp and ceremony attend the Queen's official reopening of Parliament after its recess, an event that marks the formal beginning of the parliamentary year. She arrives (at about 11.15am) and departs in the state coach, accompanied by troopers of the Household Cavalry.

Join the London Irish out in force for this annual parade through central London, which is followed by toe-tapping tunes in Trafalgar Square. Held on the Sunday closest to 17 March.

BFI Flare: London LGBT Film Festival
7928 3232, www.bfi.org.uk/flare. **Date** late Mar.
Highlighting the importance of the city's LGBT communities, the rebranded Lesbian & Gay Film Festival is the UK's third-largest film festival, cramming in a superb range of international films over the best part of a fortnight.

Oxford & Cambridge Boat Race
River Thames, from Putney to Mortlake (www.theboatrace.org). Putney Bridge tube, or Barnes Bridge, Mortlake or Putney rail. **Date** Apr.
Blue-clad Oxbridge students (dark blue for Oxford, light blue for Cambridge) race each other in a pair of rowing eights, as they have done since 1829, but now watched by tens of millions worldwide. Experience the excitement from the riverbank – along with 250,000 other fans. At the time of writing in 2015, the score is Cambridge 81, Oxford 79.

La Linea
www.comono.co.uk. **Date** early Apr.
A contemporary Latin-music festival, featuring everything from brass bands to flamenco guitar, held over a fortnight in April.

★ London Marathon
Greenwich Park to the Mall via the Isle of Dogs, Victoria Embankment & St James's Park (7902 0200, www.virginlondonmarathon.com).

London's
Best

*Check off the essentials
with our list of hand-
picked highlights.*

Sightseeing

BEST VIEWS
Hampstead Heath (p230)
From Parliament Hill the
cityscape is gorgeous.
London Eye (p54)
Let yourself be slowly rotated
through changing vistas.
Mondrian at Sea Containers
(p340)
The rooftop Rumpus Room
has ace river views.
The Monument (p186)
A stiff climb, a fine City vista.
The Shard (p63)
Revelatory views, not least
because you are so removed
from the city you're seeing.
Sky Garden (p189)
The Walkie Talkie's Sky
Garden opened in 2015
to instantly become our
favourite London viewpoint.

HISTORY LOCAL & GLOBAL
British Museum (p150)
Houses of Parliament tour
(p73)
Imperial War Museum (p56)
Museum of London (p180)
Tower of London (p187)

FINEST ART
Courtauld Gallery (p147)
An atmospheric, bijou setting
for modern masterpieces.
National Gallery (p68)
One of the world's greatest
collections of paintings.
Tate Britain (p77)
Do the blockbusters at Tate
Modern, but come here for a
chronology of British art.
Victoria & Albert Museum
(p90)
A staggering gathering of
decorative genius from
around the world.

top: **Museum of London**; middle: **Natural History Museum**; bottom: **Caravan King's Cross**.

Wallace Collection (p110)
Flamboyant interiors and an amazing Rembrandt self-portrait.

QUIRKY

Geffrye Museum (p206)
The history of interior design, winningly displayed.
Grant Museum (p154)
See a jar of moles and the rare skeleton of a quagga.
Horniman Museum (p238)
An amazing all-rounder: aquarium, global musical instruments, great gardens.
Leighton House (p226)
Experience serious tile envy.
Sir John Soane's Museum (p166)
You'll have to queue, but there's nowhere else like it.
Two Temple Place (p175)
Changing exhibitions as fascinating as the building that contains them.
Wellcome Collection (p155)
Takes your curiosity about medicine and science to places you didn't expect to go.

FRESH AIR

Chelsea Physic Garden (p96)
Granary Square (p158)
Queen Elizabeth Olympic Park (p241)
Regent's Park (p197)
Royal Botanic Gardens, Kew (p302)
St James's Park (p89)
WWT Wetland Centre (p239)

AMAZING ARCHITECTURE

30 St Mary Axe (p185)
Lloyd's of London (p184)
New London Architecture (p335)
Old Royal Naval College (p216)
St Paul's Cathedral (p176)

CHILDREN

Coram's Fields (p253)
No unaccompanied adults at these brilliant playgrounds.

Docklands Light Railway (p242)
Grab the front seat for a joyride on elevated tracks.
HMS Belfast (p63)
Zoom round a WWII warship.
London Transport Museum (p140)
Buses and trains to clamber around – and a brand new children's area. Ding ding!
Natural History Museum (p87)
Animatronic *T Rex*? You're going to have to queue – but you're going to have to go.
Science Museum (p87)
Full of play zones where learning really is fun.
Warner Bros Studio Tour (p303)
A must for Potter fans.
ZSL London Zoo (p197)
Costly, but an unbeatable day out with penguins, tigers, gorillas – even an armadillo.

Eating & drinking

ALL-DAY EATS

Caravan King's Cross (p159)
Excellent, relaxed venue for snacks, meals and drinks.
Delaunay (p147)
A grand brasserie in the Middle European tradition.
Dishoom (p141)
Unusual Indian snacks.
Duck & Waffle (p188)
Open all day and all night – with a side order of sensational views.
Kopapa (p143)
Superb fusion food.

MODERN BRITISH

Hereford Road (p224)
St John (p172)

LONDON CLASSICS

J Sheekey (p143)
The old-style fish restaurant that became a destination.

Moro (p172)
Spanish-North African food
that's still always special.
St John (p172)
The birthplace of modern
British cooking.

TREAT EATS
Chiltern Firehouse (p110)
Celeb-haunted, block-booked
and glorious.
Ledbury (p224)
An unshakeably high quality
west London favourite.
Pollen Street Social (p118)
The finest of Jason Atherton's
stable of over-achievers.

BUDGET EATS
Brick Lane Beigel Bake (p204)
Fuel for late-night ravers.
E Pellicci (p212)
Handsome and historic East
End greasy spoon.
M Manze (p63)
Cockney pie and mash.
Lanzhou Noodle Bar (p143)
West End location, late
opening hours, variable food.
Towpath (p237)
Watch the Hackney hipsters
as you tuck into breakfast.

GLOBAL
Gymkhana (p118)
Posh Indian in Mayfair.
Pachamama (p112)
Peruvian in Marylebone.
Sông Quê (p209)
Vietnamese in Shoreditch.
Trullo (p235)
Italian in Islington.

COCKTAILS
69 Colebrooke Row (p235)
Cocktail craftsman Tony
Conigliaro's tiny bar.
**American Bar at the
Beaumont** (p118)
Low-lit and glamorous.
White Lyan (p209)
Home to London's second
maestro of mixology:
Ryan Chetiyawardana.

Foyles.

**Worship Street Whistling
Shop** (p210)
Concoctions and confections
in a Victorian-themed bar.

PUBS
Black Friar (p174)
Not London's best pub,
but surely London's
best pub interior.
French House (p127)
Soho's best boozer.
Wenlock Arms (p209)
Incredible beer selection,
served the old-fashioned way.
Ye Olde Mitre (p170)
Wonderful historic pub.

WINE BARS
Gordon's Wine Bar (p147)
People come here for the
atmospheric basement
venue as much as the wine.
Terroirs (p144)
Uncover the secrets of
biodynamic wines.

Shopping

HISTORIC SHOPPING
Burlington Arcade (p121)
Early 19th-century shopping
mall – complete with beadles.

James Smith & Sons (p144)
Superb traditional brolly shop.

DEPARTMENT STORES
Liberty (p116)
Selfridge's (p107)

CONCEPT
Dover Street Market (p119)
High fashion sold from a
department store made to
look like a street market.
LN-CC (p241)
Hackney style goes sci-fi.
Shop at Bluebird (p99)
The Kings Road's best shop
is one London's best too.

GORGEOUS INTERIORS
House of Hackney (p210)
Liberty (p116)

VINTAGE
Blitz (p204)
Vintage Showroom (p146)

HIGH STREET FASHION
Topshop (p107)

FOOD & DRINK
Algerian Coffee Stores (p127)
Brixton Village (p245)
Maltby Street (p65)
Neal's Yard Dairy (p145)

Roundhouse.

Arts & culture

FESTIVALS
Chinese New Year Festival (p40)
Greenwich & Docklands International Festival (p34)
London Film Festival (p39)
London Jazz Festival (p39)
Lord Mayor's Show (p39)
Notting Hill Carnival (p37)
Open House London (p37)

SPORT
Epsom Derby (p33)
FA Cup Final (p41)
London Marathon (p41)
Wimbledon Tennis Championships (p34)

THEATRE
Donmar Warehouse (p293)
Intimate venue, stellar casts.
National Theatre (p291)
London's best theatre, mixing challenging drama with inventive musicals.
Open Air Theatre (p290)
Fun shows in Regent's Park.
Shakespeare's Globe (p290)
Authentic Shakespeare in the open-air Globe and candlelit atmospherics in the Sam Wanamaker Playhouse.
Wilton's Music Hall (p294)
Last of a dying breed.
Young Vic (p294)
Hottest off-West End stage.

OPERA & DANCE
English National Opera (p287)
The Place (p295)
Sadler's Wells (p295)
Royal Opera House (p288)

FILM
BFI Southbank (p256)
London's best repertory.
Phoenix (p258)
Perhaps the city's oldest cinema and certainly one of the best to spend time in.
Prince Charles Cinema (p255)
Great value West End flicks.

BOOKS & MUSIC
Cecil Court (p135)
A sweet alley of vintage and obscurantist booksellers.
Daunt Books (p113)
Beautiful Edwardian setting for browsing travel tomes and literary greats.
London Review Bookshop (p157)
Well curated stock, engaging events, charming little café.
Foyles (p126)
Superbly stocked, both with books and knowledgeable sales staff.
Rough Trade East (p204)
London's best record shop for the latest independent releases. Ace in-stores, too.

MARKETS
Broadway Market (p213)
Camden Market (p195)
Columbia Road Market (p213)
Portobello Road Market (p225)

Nightlife

CLUBBING
Bussey Building (p269)
The city's most varied programme, all of it good.
Dalston Superstore (p261)
The venue that created the Dalston scene.
Fabric (p267)
London's most credible superclub.
XOYO (p271)
Old-school Shoreditch warehouse club.

ROCK & POP MUSIC
Koko (p272)
02 Academy Brixton (p273)
02 Arena (p273)
Roundhouse (p273)

DIVES
100 Club (p274)
Nest (p270)
Shacklewell Arms (p276)

CLASSICAL MUSIC
Barbican (p283)
Kings Place (p284)
Royal Festival Hall at the Southbank Centre (p287)
Royal Opera House (p288)
Wigmore Hall (p287)

JAZZ, FOLK & COUNTRY
Cecil Sharp House (p277)
Ronnie Scott's (p279)
Union Chapel (p276)

EXPERIMENTAL MUSIC
Café Oto (p277)
Vortex (p279)

COMEDY
Angel Comedy (p281)
Terrific programmes – and put on for free.
Comedy Store (p281)
Where London's alternative comedy scene was born.

ALTERNATIVE NIGHTLIFE & CABARET
Bethnal Green Working Men's Club (p280)
The Glory (p263)
RVT (p261)

The South Bank & Bankside

An estimated 14 million people come this way each year, and it's easy to see why. Between the London Eye and Tower Bridge, the south bank of the Thames offers a two-mile procession of diverting arts and entertainment venues and events.

The area's modern-day life began in 1951 with the Festival of Britain, staged to boost morale in the wake of World War II. The Royal Festival Hall stands testament to the inclusive spirit of the project; it was later expanded into the Southbank Centre, alongside the BFI Southbank cinemas and the concrete ziggurat of the National Theatre.

But the riverside really took off in the new millennium, with the arrival of the London Eye, Tate Modern, the Millennium Bridge and the expansion of Borough Market.

EXPLORE

Imperial War Museum.

Don't Miss

1 London Eye The Shard is great, but we vote for the Eye's changing vistas (p54).

2 Tate Modern Power station turned artistic powerhouse (p57).

3 Dandelyan Exhilarating new cocktails, right by the Thames (p59).

4 Borough Market Gourmet goodies (p61).

5 Imperial War Museum Conflict histories in refreshed displays (p56).

EXPLORE

THE SOUTH BANK

Embankment or Westminster tube, or Waterloo tube/rail.

Thanks to the sharp turn the Thames makes around Waterloo, **Lambeth Bridge** lands you east of the river, not south, opposite the Tudor gatehouse of **Lambeth Palace**. Since the 12th century, it's been the official residence of the Archbishop of Canterbury. The palace is not normally open to the public, except on holidays. The church next door, St Mary at Lambeth, is now the **Garden Museum**.

The benches along the river here are great for viewing the Houses of Parliament opposite, before things get crowded after **Westminster Bridge**, where London's major riverside tourist zone begins. Next to the bridge is **County Hall**, once the seat of London government, now home to the **Sea Life London Aquarium** and the **London Dungeon**. In front of these attractions, in full view of the lovely **Jubilee Gardens**, the wheel of the **London Eye** rotates serenely.

When the **Southbank Centre** (*see p284*) was built in the 1950s, the big concrete boxes that together contain the Royal Festival Hall (RFH), the Queen Elizabeth Hall (QEH) and the Purcell Room were hailed as a daring statement of modern architecture. Along with the National Theatre and the Hayward, they comprise one of the largest and most popular arts centres in the world.

The centrepiece is Sir Leslie Martin's handsome **Royal Festival Hall** (1951), given a £91-million overhaul in 2007. The main auditorium has had its acoustics enhanced and seating refurbished; the upper floors include an improved Poetry Library, and event rooms in which readings are delivered against the backdrop of the Eye and, on the far side of the river, Big Ben. Behind the hall, **Southbank Centre Square** hosts a food market every weekend, and there are cafés and chain restaurants all around.

Next door to the Royal Festival Hall, just across from the building housing the QEH and the Purcell Room, the **Hayward Gallery** is a landmark of Brutalist architecture – all three venues are to close for a proposed multi-million pound refurbishment (*see p293* **Feeling Rattled**). Tucked under Waterloo Bridge is **BFI Southbank** (*see p254*); the UK's premier arthouse cinema, it's run by the British Film Institute. At the front is a second-hand book market – fun, but not brilliant for real finds. Due to its relative height and location just where the Thames bends from north–south to east–west, **Waterloo Bridge** provides some of the finest views of London, especially at dusk. It was designed by Sir Giles Gilbert Scott, the man behind Tate Modern, in 1942.

Southbank Centre.

East of the bridge is Denys Lasdun's terraced **National Theatre** (*see p287*), another Brutalist concrete structure, recently much improved (*see p294* **Grand National**). Shaded by trees dotted with blue LEDs, the river path leads past a rare sandy patch of riverbed, busy with sand sculptors in warm weather, to **Gabriel's Wharf**, a collection of eateries, and small independent shops that range from stylish to kitsch.

Next door, the deco tower of **Oxo Tower Wharf** was designed to circumvent advertising regulations for the stock-cube company that used to own the building. Saved by local action group Coin Street Community Builders, it now provides affordable housing, interesting designer shops and galleries, and restaurants (including a rooftop restaurant and bistro with more wonderful views). Next door, the new **Mondrian** hotel has brought a bit of buzz to this part of the South Bank – not least through the impressive ground-floor cocktail bar **Dandelyan**.

Sights & Museums

Florence Nightingale Museum

St Thomas's Hospital, 2 Lambeth Palace Road, SE1 7EW (7620 0374, www.florence-nightingale. co.uk). Westminster tube or Waterloo tube/rail. **Open** 10am-5pm daily. **Admission** £7; £4.80 reductions; £17 family; free under-5s. **Map** p52 A4 ❶

The nursing skills and campaigning zeal that made Nightingale a Victorian legend are honoured here. Reopened after refurbishment for the centenary of her death in 2010, the museum is now a chronological tour through a remarkable life via three key themes: family life, the Crimean War, health reformer. Among the period mementoes – clothing, furniture, books, letters and portraits – are Nightingale's lantern and stuffed pet owl, Athena.

Garden Museum

Lambeth Palace Road, SE1 7LB (7401 8865, www.gardenmuseum.org.uk). Lambeth North tube or Waterloo tube/rail. **Open** 10.30am-5pm Mon-Fri; 10.30am-4pm Sat. **Admission** £5; £3-£4 reductions; free under-16s. *During exhibitions* £7.50; £3-£6.50 reductions; free under-16s. **Map** p52 A5 ❷

The world's first horticulture museum fits neatly into the old church of St Mary's. A 'belvedere' gallery (built from eco-friendly Eurban wood sheeting) contains the permanent collection of artworks, antique gardening tools and horticultural memorabilia, while the ground floor is used for interesting temporary exhibitions. In the small back garden, the replica of a 17th-century knot garden was created in honour of John Tradescant, intrepid plant-hunter and gardener to Charles I; Tradescant is buried here. A stone sarcophagus contains the remains of William Bligh, the captain of the mutinous HMS *Bounty*.

Hayward Gallery

Southbank Centre, SE1 8XX, (0844 875 0073, www.southbankcentre.co.uk). Embankment tube or Waterloo tube/rail. **Open** noon-6pm Mon; 11am-7pm Tue, Wed, Sat, Sun; 11am-8pm Thur, Fri. **Admission** varies. **Map** p52 B2 ❸

This versatile gallery has no permanent collection, but runs a good programme of temporary exhibitions, with a particular taste for participatory installations: Antony Gormley's fog-filled chamber for 'Blind Light', a rooftop rowing boat for group show 'Psycho Buildings', even Carsten Höller's roller-coaster slides (from June to September 2015). Visitors can hang out in the industrial-look café downstairs (it's a bar at night), before visiting free contemporary exhibitions at the Hayward Project Space; take the stairs to the first floor from the glass foyer extension, an elliptical pavilion designed with light artist Dan Graham.

London Dungeon

County Hall, Westminster Bridge Road, SE1 7PB (0871 423 2240, www.thedungeons.com/london). Westminster tube or Waterloo tube/rail. **Open** *Term-time* 10am-5pm Mon-Wed, Fri; 11am-5pm Thur; 10am-6pm Sat, Sun. *School holidays* varies. **Admission** £25.95; £20.95 reductions; free under-4s. **Map** p52 A3 ❹

Visitors to this jokey celebration of torture, death and disease journey back in time to London's plague-ridden streets (rotting corpses, rats, vile boils, projectile vomiting) and meet some of the city's least savoury characters, from Guy Fawkes to Sweeney Todd. A cast of blood-splattered actors are joined by 'virtual' guests, such as Brian Blessed as Henry VIII, as well as 18 different shows and 'surprises' – which could see you on the run from Jack the Ripper or getting lost in London's Victorian sewers. There are two thrill rides too: a turbulent boat trip down the Thames for execution, and a dark drop ride that plunges three storeys in the pitch black.

▶ *The London Dungeon is not cheap, particularly for families, so to keep the prices to a minimum book in advance online.*

London Eye. *See p54.*

EXPLORE

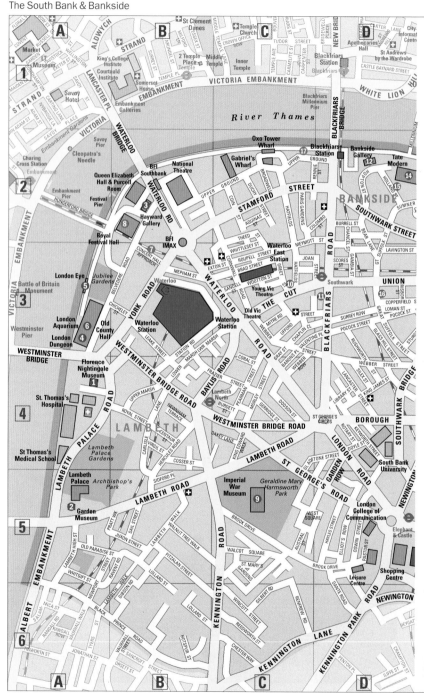

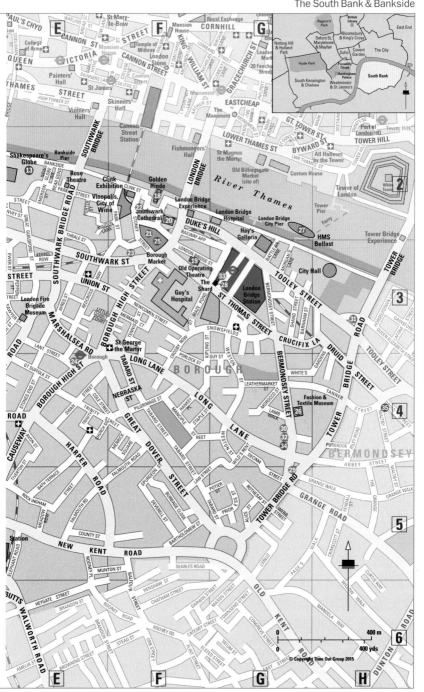

EXPLORE

★ London Eye

Jubilee Gardens, SE1 7PB (0870 500 0600, www. londoneye.com). Westminster tube or Waterloo tube/rail. **Open** varies. **Admission** £21.50; £15.50-£18.50 reductions; £74 family; free under-4s. **Map** p52 A3 ➎

Here only since 2000, the Eye is nonetheless up there with Tower Bridge and 'Big Ben' among the capital's most postcard-friendly tourist assets. Assuming you choose a clear day, a 30-minute circuit on the Eye affords predictably great views of the city. Take a few snaps from the comfort of your pod and, there, your sightseeing's just about done – and we'd suggest that the fact that the vista changes nudges it ahead of the Shard. The Eye was the vision of husband-and-wife architect team Julia Barfield and David Marks, who entered a 1992 competition to design a structure for the millennium. Their giant wheel idea came second, but the winning entry is conspicuous by its absence. The Eye was planned as a temporary structure but its removal now seems unthinkable. Owner Merlin Entertainments has completed a £12.5m renovation programme that reduced the Eye's carbon footprint and added a touchscreen sightseeing guide to each of the wheel's 32 pods. *Photo p51.*

Sea Life London Aquarium

County Hall, Westminster Bridge Road, SE1 7PB (0871 663 1678, tours 7967 8007, www. sealife.com). Westminster tube or Waterloo tube/ rail. **Open** *Term time* 10am-7pm daily. *School holidays* 10am-8pm daily. **Admission** £23.50; £16.95 reductions; £80 family; free under-3s. **Map** p52 A3 ➏

This is one of Europe's largest aquariums – and a huge hit with kids. The inhabitants are grouped by geographical origin, beginning with the Atlantic, where blacktail bream swim alongside the Thames Embankment. The 'Rainforests of the World' exhibit has introduced poison arrow frogs, crocodiles and piranhas. The Ray Lagoon is still popular, though touching the friendly flatfish is no longer allowed (it's bad for their health). Starfish, crabs and anemones can be handled in special open rock pools instead, and the clown fish still draw crowds. There's a mesmerising Seahorse Temple, a tank full of turtles and enchanting Gentoo peguins. The centrepieces, though, are the massive Pacific and Indian Ocean tanks, with menacing sharks quietly circling fallen Easter Island statues.

Restaurants

Around the Royal Festival Hall, you'll find plenty of chain restaurants (including Canteen, Feng Sushi, Giraffe, Pizza Express, Wahaca and Wagamama), while **Skylon** – a few floors up in the RFH building – has a grill and restaurant serving smart, seasonal British food. There are also crêpe and pizza restaurants at Gabriel's Wharf along the bank to the east.

Pubs & Bars

Bar Topolski

150-152 Hungerford Arches, Concert Hall Approach, SE1 8XU (7620 0627, www.bartopolski. co.uk). Waterloo tube/rail. **Open** 10am-11pm Mon-Wed; 10am-midnight Thur; 10am-1am Fri, Sat. **Map** p52 B3 ➐

The former Topolski Chronicles, an extensive mural by Polish-born artist Feliks Topolski depicting an extraordinary procession of 20th-century events and faces, has been turned into a bar-café. Occupying two capacious brick arches beneath Hungerford Bridge (some of Topolski's artworks are incorporated into the design), it serves cured meat, fish, cheese and other snacks, both savoury and sweet. There are assorted musical entertainments too.

Skylon

Royal Festival Hall, Belvedere Road, SE1 8XX (7654 7800, www.skylon-restaurant.co.uk). Waterloo tube/rail. **Open** noon-1am Mon-Sat; noon-10.30pm Sun. *Food served* noon-11pm Mon-Sat; noon-10.30pm Sun. **Map** p52 B2 ➑

There can't be many better river views in town – certainly for transport geeks. Sit at the cocktail bar (between the two restaurant areas), and gaze at trains trundling out of Charing Cross, cars and buses whizzing across Waterloo Bridge, and boats and cruisers pootling along the Thames. Drinks aren't cheap, but they're well made, and you're nicely insulated from the madness of the riverbank crowds.

WATERLOO & LAMBETH

Waterloo tube/rail or Lambeth North tube.

Surprisingly, perhaps, there's plenty of interest around the stone-meets-glass rail terminus of London Waterloo. The most obvious attraction is the massive **BFI IMAX** (*see p254*), located in the middle of a roundabout at the southern end of Waterloo Bridge. The £20-million cinema makes use of a desolate space that, in the 1990s, was notorious for its 'Cardboard City' of homeless residents.

South, on the corner of Waterloo Road and the Cut, is the restored Victorian façade of the **Old Vic** theatre (*see p288*), which will soon be getting used to life after outgoing artistic director Kevin Spacey. Further down the Cut is the **Young Vic** (*see p293*), a hotbed of theatrical talent with a stylish balcony bar. Both bring a touch of West End glamour across the river.

Further south, into Lambeth, is the impressive – and steadily revamped – **Imperial War Museum** (*see p55* **For the Fallen**). The imposing premises were built in 1814 as a lunatic asylum (the Bethlehem Royal Hospital, aka Bedlam). After the inmates were moved out in 1930, the central block became the war museum,

EXPLORE

FOR THE FALLEN

London's museums mark a series of key anniversaries.

London has been quietly immersed in a four-year-long commemoration of the First World War since the middle of 2014, when the **Imperial War Museum** (*see p56*) reopened after extensive refurbishment. One of the centrepieces was a new First World War gallery, which took a more considered, contemporary look at the conflict, examining the Home Front as much as the Western Front, and using the Imperial War Museum's heart-stopping collection of small, personal items alongside huge set-pieces like a walk-through trench. As we move towards the centenary of the war's end in 2018, the museum will continue to examine the war with temporary exhibitions and special events, with a focus on milestones, such as the Battle of the Somme, 100 years after the carnage began in 1916.

It's said that the guns on the opening day of the Somme were so loud, they could be heard in London. The battle, now a byword for pointless savagery on an industrial scale, will be the focus of a 2016 exhibition at the **Science Museum** (*see p87*) that will look at the medical impact of the First World War. Objects on display will include a giant magnet that was used to pull shrapnel from wounds.

Slightly less macabre is a new gallery at the **RAF Museum London** (Grahame Park Way, Hendon, NW9 5LL, 8205 2266, www.rafmuseum.org.uk), which opened in December 2014. Called 'The First World War in the Air', it looks at the birth of the RAF and includes personal artefacts such as medals, letters and uniforms, as well as early aircraft such as the magnificent Sopwith Camel biplane, which was used against the Zeppelin menace that threatened London directly.

Around 200 Londoners were killed in Zeppelin raids, and evidence remains on the infrastructure of the city. Head to 61 Farringdon Road and you'll find a plaque marking a building that was destroyed in a Zeppelin raid in 1917. There are several other such plaques in the area around Holborn, including New Square, Southampton Row and, happily, inside the **Dolphin Tavern** (44 Red Lion Street, WC1R 4PF, 7831 6298) beneath a clock with its hand stopped at 10.40pm, the time the bombs fell on 9 September 1915. It's as fine a place as any to stop and consider our considerable fortune to be born in different times. Check also http://bombsight.org which shows the location of every bomb that fell on the city.

EXPLORE

only to be damaged by air raids. Today, it provides a compelling, frequently hard-hitting history of armed conflict since World War I.

Sights & Museums

★ FREE Imperial War Museum

Lambeth Road, SE1 6HZ (7416 5000, www.iwm. org.uk). Lambeth North tube or Elephant & Castle tube/rail. **Open** 10am-6pm daily. **Admission** free. *Special exhibitions vary.* **Map** p52 C5 ❾

One of London's great museums – but probably the least famous of them – IWM London has had a major refit by Foster & Partners architects. When it reopened, in time for the 2014 centenary of the start of World War I, the Central Hall was the attention-grabbing repository of major artefacts: guns, tanks and aircraft hang from the ceiling (not least a Harrier GR9 that saw action in Afghanistan), while terraced galleries allow this section of the museum also to show a Snatch Land Rover from Iraq and an Argentine operating table from the Falklands. The already extensive World War I gallery has been expanded, then you head into the original displays for World War II.

The museum's tone darkens as you ascend. On the third floor, the Holocaust Exhibition (not recommended for under-14s) traces the history of European anti-Semitism and its nadir in the concentration camps. Upstairs, Crimes Against Humanity (unsuitable for under-16s) is a minimalist space in which a film exploring contemporary genocide and ethnic violence rolls relentlessly. At the top, a new gallery explores contemporary conflicts.

Restaurants

Anchor & Hope

36 The Cut, SE1 8LP (7928 9898, www. anchorandhopepub.co.uk). Southwark tube or Waterloo tube/rail. **Open** 5-11pm Mon; 11am-11pm Tue-Sat; 12.30-5pm Sun. *Food served* 6-10.30pm Mon; noon-2.30pm, 6-10.30pm Tue-Sat. **Main courses** £12-£22. **Map** p52 C3 ❿ **Gastropub**

Open for more than a decade, the Anchor & Hope is still a leading exponent of using 'head-to-tail' ingredients in simple but artful combinations, served in a relaxed setting. Bookings aren't taken, so most evenings you'll join the waiting list for a table (45mins midweek is typical) and hover at the crammed bar. The food is terrific: beautifully textured venison kofte, say, served on perkily dressed gem lettuce leaves; or rabbit served savagely red, with salty jus, fat chips and béarnaise sauce.

Baltic

74 Blackfriars Road, SE1 8HA (7928 1111, www. balticrestaurant.co.uk). Southwark tube. **Open** 5.30-11.15pm Mon; noon-3pm, 5.30-11.15pm Tue-Sat; noon-4.30pm, 5.30-10.30pm Sun. **Main courses** £5-£19. **Map** p52 D3 ⓫ **Eastern European**

A modern take on Polish/central European classics is served in surroundings of understated glamour, with pared-down monochrome decor punctuated by a supersized chandelier dripping shards of golden amber. You'll struggle to find elsewhere such enjoyable buckwheat blinis topped with smoked salmon or tender herring. Home-style pleasures abound, such as rabbit braised in a fragrant broth flavoured with sweet prune and smoky bacon, served with little knobbly spätzle dumplings. Start with a classy clear vodka such as Zytnia (rye), then move on to one of Baltic's own tasty ginger or spicy orange varieties.

BANKSIDE

Borough or Southwark tube, or Blackfriars or London Bridge tube/rail.

In Shakespeare's day, the area known as Bankside was the centre of bawdy Southwark, neatly located just beyond the jurisdiction of the City fathers. As well as playhouses such as the Globe and the Rose, there were the famous 'stewes' (brothels) presided over by the bishops of Winchester, who made a tidy income from the fines they levied on the area's 'Winchester Geese' (or, in common parlance, prostitutes). There's less drinking, carousing and mischief-making here these days, but the area's cultural heritage remains alive thanks to the reconstructed **Shakespeare's Globe** and, pretty much next door to it, **Tate Modern**, a former power station that's now a gallery.

Spanning the river in front of the Tate, the **Millennium Bridge** for pedestrians opened in 2000, when it became the first new Thames crossing in London since Tower Bridge (1894). Its early days were fraught with troubles: after just two days, the bridge was closed because of a pronounced wobble caused by the resonance of thousands of people crossing together, and didn't reopen until 2002. Its difficulties long behind it, the bridge is an elegant structure – a 'ribbon of steel' in the words of its conceptualists, architect Lord Foster and sculptor Anthony Caro. Cross it and you're at the foot of the stairs leading up to St Paul's Cathedral; to the west, the massively refurbished Blackfriars rail station not only has a brand-new entrance on the south bank of the river, but runs train platforms right across the river on the podiums of an earlier, incomplete version of **Blackfriars Bridge**.

Sights & Museums

FREE Bankside Gallery

48 Hopton Street, SE1 9JH (7928 7521, www. banksidegallery.com). Blackfriars tube/rail or Southwark tube. **Open** (during exhibitions) 11am-6pm daily. **Admission** free; donations appreciated. **Map** p52 D2 ⓬

EXPLORE

Shakespeare's Globe.

EXPLORE

In the shadow of Tate Modern, this tiny gallery is the home of the Royal Watercolour Society and the Royal Society of Painter-Printmakers. The gallery runs a changing programme of exhibitions, with many of the displayed works for sale.

★ Shakespeare's Globe

21 New Globe Walk, SE1 9DT (7902 1400, www. shakespearesglobe.com). Blackfriars tube/rail or Southwark tube. **Open** *Exhibition* Feb-Oct 9am -5.30pm daily. Nov-Jan 10am-5.30pm daily. *Globe Theatre tours* daily; *Rose Theatre tours* Mar-Oct, times vary. **Admission** £13.50; £8-£12 reductions; £36 family; free under-5s. **Map** p53 E2 **⑬**

The original Globe Theatre, where many of William Shakespeare's plays were first staged and which he co-owned, burned to the ground in 1613 during a performance of *Henry VIII*. Nearly 400 years later, it was rebuilt not far from its original site, using construction methods and materials as close to the originals as possible, and it is now open to the public for tours throughout the year (allow 90 minutes for the visit). During matinées, the tours go to the site of the Rose (21 New Globe Walk, SE1 9DT, 7261 9565, www.rosetheatre.org.uk), built by Philip Henslowe in 1587 as the first theatre on Bankside; red lights show the position of the original theatre. Funds are being sought to continue excavations and to preserve the latter site.

Under the adventurous artistic directorship of Dominic Dromgoole (who steps down in April 2016), the Globe is also a fully operational theatre (*see p289*). From 23 April, conventionally regarded as the bard's birthday, into early October, Shakespeare's plays and the odd new drama are performed in the open air. Year-round performances can be seen in the adjoining 350-seat indoor theatre, the Sam Wanamaker Playhouse, which opened in 2014.

★ FREE Tate Modern

Bankside, SE1 9TG (7887 8888, www.tate.org.uk). Blackfriars tube/rail or Southwark tube. **Open** 10am-6pm Mon-Thur, Sun; 10am-10pm Fri, Sat. *Tours* 11am, noon, 2pm, 3pm daily. **Admission** free. *Temporary exhibitions* vary. **Map** p52 D2 **㉔**

Thanks to its industrial architecture, this powerhouse of modern art is awe-inspiring even before you enter. Built after World War II as Bankside Power Station, it was designed by Sir Giles Gilbert Scott, architect of Battersea Power Station. The power station shut in 1981; nearly 20 years later, it opened as an art museum, and has enjoyed spectacular popularity ever since. The gallery attracts five million visitors a year to a building intended for half that number, hence the vast tower that is emerging behind the original red-brick building. The first fruits of the immensely ambitious (and now rather delayed) extension opened in 2012: the Tanks, so-called because they occupy vast, subterranean former oil tanks, stage performance and film art. As for the rest, a huge new origami-like structure, designed by Herzog & de Meuron (who were behind the original conversion), will unfold above the Tanks until 2016, when six new levels (four for new galleries, which will focus on international art) and a south-facing entrance will open.

Tate Modern. *See p57.*

The continuing work won't interrupt normal service in the main galleries. It's service as usual in the cavernous turbine hall, which continues to be used to jaw-dropping effect with the ongoing series of massive installations. Beyond, the permanent collection draws from the Tate's many post-1900 international works, featuring heavy-hitters such as Matisse, Rothko and Beuys – a collection that begins to feel slightly thin in comparison to the riches of the rehung Tate Britain (*see p77*). The art tends to be grouped according to movement or theme (Surrealism, Minimalism, Post-war Abstraction) rather than artist, which can mute its impact, leading many to visit for the very busy blockbuster shows rather than spending much time on the permanent collection.

▶ *The polka-dotted Tate-to-Tate boat zooms to Tate Britain every 40 minutes, with a stop-off at the London Eye. Tickets are available at both Tates, on board, online or by phone (7887 8888; £6.50, £2.15-£5.85 reductions).*

Restaurants

There are some handy chain restaurants (Pizza Express, The Real Greek, Tas Pide) on the river near the Globe Theatre, plus more (Tsuru, Leon) behind Tate Modern on Canvey Street. **Tate Modern Café: Level 2** (*see p250*) is good for those with children.

Albion Neo Bankside
Pavilion B, Holland Street, SE1 9FU (3764 5550, www.albioncafes.com). Southwark tube. **Open** 8am-11pm Mon-Fri; 9am-11pm Sat, Sun. **Main courses** £6-£14. **Map** p52 D2 ⑮ **British**
This glass-walled eaterie just behind Tate Modern is the second of Terence Conran's poshed-up British cafés. A secluded outdoor terrace overlooks a beautifully landscaped garden of mature silver birches – perfect for summer dining. Breakfast runs from toast and Marmite to a full English or kidneys on sourdough. Later on, the menu expands to include fish and chips, pies, bread and butter pudding and classic afternoon teas.

Union Street Café
47-51 Great Suffolk Street, SE1 0BS (7592 7977, www.gordonramsay.com). Southwark tube. **Open** *Restaurant* noon-3pm, 6-11pm Mon-Fri; noon-4pm, 6-10.30pm Sat; noon-5pm Sun. *Bar* 5pm-2am Thur-Sun. **Main courses** £12-£25. **Map** p52 D3 ⑯ Italian
A mish-mash of styles – with exposed ducts and wiring, but also parquet flooring and leather seats, – greets diners at this addition to the Gordon Ramsay empire. The intentionally casual, smiling service and Italian style of the daily-changing menu can be undermined by meagre portions: a 'secondi' octopus dish of two meaty tentacles perched on braised borlotti beans, or a soup bowl-sized seafood stew.

EXPLORE

Golden Hinde.

Highlights might include a chocolate and peanut-butter cake topped with vanilla ice-cream, with espresso poured over over it.

Pubs & Bars

★ Dandelyan
Mondrian London, 20 Upper Ground, SE1 9PD (3747 1000, www.morganshotelgroup.com/mondrian). Blackfriars or Southwark tube. **Open** 4pm-1am Mon-Wed; noon-1.30am Thur-Sat; noon-12.30am Sun. **Map** p52 C2 ⑰
The second bar opened by Ryan Chetiyawardana (aka bartender Mr Lyan) couldn't be more different from his first (*see p208* **He's Not Lyan**). Rather than occupying a converted Hoxton pub, Dandelyan has a prime spot off the lobby of the multimillion-pound Mondrian (*see p340*). The bar might be glamorous, luxurious and a bit formal, but the drinks show Chetiyawardana's invention and attention to detail are intact: the botanically themed drinks list includes ingredients such as 'chalk bitters', 'crystal peach nectar' and the archaic-sounding 'dandelion capillaire'. Everything is surprising without being show-off, and, importantly, it's all drinkable.

BOROUGH

Borough or Southwark tube, or London Bridge tube/rail.

On the east side of Blackfriars Bridge, you'll find the **Anchor Bankside** pub (34 Park Street, SE1

9EF, 7407 1577, www.taylor-walker.co.uk). Built in 1775 on the site of an even older inn, the Anchor has, at various points, been a brothel, a chapel and a ship's chandlers. The outside terrace, across the pathway, offers fine river views – a fact lost on no one each summer, when it's invariably crammed with people.

All that's left of the Palace of Winchester, home of successive bishops, is the ruined rose window of the Great Hall on Clink Street. It stands next to the site of the bishops' former Clink prison, where thieves, prostitutes and debtors all served their sentences; it's now the **Clink Prison Museum** (1 Clink Street, SE1 9DG, 7403 0900, www.clink.co.uk). At the other end of Clink Street, St Mary Overie's dock contains a terrific full-scale replica of Sir Francis Drake's ship, the **Golden Hinde**.

The main landmark here is the Anglican **Southwark Cathedral**, formerly St Saviour's and before that the monastic church of St Mary Overie. Shakespeare's brother Edmund was buried in the graveyard; there's a monument to the playwright inside. Just south of the cathedral is **Borough Market**, a busy covered food market dating from the 13th century, although with its new glass-fronted premises you'd hardly think so. There's still plenty of Victorian ironwork to enjoy. The market is wholesale only for most of the week, but hosts London's foodiest public food market on Wednesdays, Thursdays, Fridays and Saturdays (when it gets very crowded). It's surrounded by good places to eat and drink. Not far away, the **George** (77 Borough High Street, 7407 2056) is London's last surviving galleried coaching inn. Owned by the National Trust, it hosted Charles Dickens among many others.

Fans of gore should head to the interesting and thoroughly grisly **Old Operating Theatre, Museum & Herb Garret**, with its body parts and surgical implements.

Sights & Museums

Golden Hinde
Pickfords Wharf, Clink Street, SE1 9DG (7403 0123, www.goldenhinde.com). London Bridge tube/rail. **Open** 10am-5.30pm daily. **Admission** £7; £5 reductions; £20 family; free under-3s. **Map** p53 F2 ⑱
This meticulous replica of Sir Francis Drake's 16th-century flagship is thoroughly seaworthy: the ship has even reprised the privateer's circumnavigatory voyage. You can visit by means of a self-guided tour, but if you've got kids it's much more fun to join in on a 'living history' experience (some overnight): participants dress in period clothes, eat Tudor fare and learn the skills of the Elizabethan seafarer; book well in advance. At weekends, the ship swarms with children dressed up as pirates for birthday dos.

EXPLORE

Old Operating Theatre, Museum & Herb Garret.

Old Operating Theatre, Museum & Herb Garret

9A St Thomas's Street, SE1 9RY (7188 2679, www.thegarret.org.uk). London Bridge tube/rail. **Open** 10.30am-5pm daily. **Admission** £6.50; £3.50-£5 reductions; £13.90 family; free under-6s. **No credit cards. Map** p53 F3 ⑲

The tower that houses this reminder of the surgical practices of the past used to be part of the chapel of St Thomas's Hospital. Before moving there, operations took place in the wards. Visitors enter via a vertiginous spiral staircase to inspect a pre-anaesthetic operating theatre dating from 1822, with tiered viewing seats for students. The operating tools look more like torture implements.

FREE Southwark Cathedral

London Bridge, SE1 9DA (7367 6700, www. cathedral.southwark.anglican.org). London Bridge tube/rail. **Open** 10am-5pm daily (closing times vary on religious holidays). *Services* 8am, 8.15am, 12.30pm, 12.45pm, 5.30pm Mon-Fri; 9am, 9.15am, 4pm Sat; 8.45am, 9am, 11am, 3pm, 6.30pm Sun. **Admission** free; suggested donation £4. **Map** p53 F2 ⑳

The oldest bits of this building date back more than 800 years. The retro-choir was the setting for several Protestant martyr trials during the reign of Mary Tudor. Inside, there are memorials to Shakespeare, John Harvard (benefactor of the American university) and Sam Wanamaker (the motivation and driving force behind the reconstruction of the Globe); Chaucer features in the stained glass. There are displays throughout the cathedral explaining its history. The courtyard is one of the area's prettiest places for a rest; there's also a café.

Restaurants

Borough Market, full of stalls selling all kinds of wonderful food, is a superb foraging place for street-food enthusiasts.

Arabica Bar & Kitchen

3 Rochester Walk, Borough Market, SE1 9AF (3011 5151, www.arabicabarandkitchen.com). London Bridge tube/rail. **Open** 11am-11pm Mon-Wed; 8.30am-11pm Thur; 8.30am-11.30pm Fri, Sat. **Main courses** £6-£14. **Map** p53 F2 ㉑ Middle Eastern

With its fashionable buzz, there's no other Levantine restaurant in London quite like Arabica – it manages to steer a safe course between 'Arabian Nights' theme park and brightly lit marble palace, in a room with lots of bare brick and steel, but low lighting for atmosphere. Meze dishes are the highlight of Lebanese cooking, and here the fried snacks such as lamb or aubergine kibbeh – which look a bit like scotch eggs – are excellent. There's also clay-oven cooking and a charcoal grill. The vegetarian dishes are inventive and, if you sit at the polished concrete bar, you can watch the kitchen at work.

Elliot's

12 Stoney Street, SE1 9AD (7403 7436, www.elliotscafe.com). London Bridge tube/rail. **Open** noon-3pm, 6-10pm Mon-Fri; noon-4pm, 6-10pm Sat. **Main courses** £7-£16. **Map** p53 F2 ㉒ Brasserie

Light and airy, with stripped brick walls and a contemporary feel, Elliot's is a busy spot. The choices are to sit out front while watching the world going by, to perch at the bar or to take a seat in the bright back area. The seasonal menu is short but innovative, and the ingredients are carefully sourced. Smaller plates such as pickled mackerel with apple and rye cracker are listed alongside larger plates such as lox cheek, polenta horse radish and pickled walnut. Drinks include a selection of natural wines (orange wines are listed alongside the expected white, red and rosé).

Gelateria 3bis

4 Park Street, SE1 9AB (7378 1977, www. gelateria3bis.it). London Bridge tube/rail. **Open**

Summer 8am-10pm Mon-Sat; 10am-6pm Sun. *Winter* 8am-8pm Mon-Sat; 11am-6pm Sun. **Map** p53 F3 ㉙ **Ice-cream**

The menu at one of our favourite gelaterias encompasses frozen yoghurt, ice-cream cakes, brioches and crêpes, plus speciality coffees – but the real star is the gelato. It's made on the premises and the repertoire includes Italian classics as well as creative English innovations (eton mess, anyone?). Behind a green frontage, the bright, spacious dining room has full-length windows opening on to the pavement in summer.

Pubs & Bars

If top-quality beer is your priority, you're in luck: there's a superb range at the tiny **Rake** (14A Winchester Walk, SE1 9AG, 7407 0557).

Gladstone Arms
64 Lant Street, SE1 1QN (7407 3962, www. thegladpub.com). Borough tube. **Open** noon-11pm Mon-Thur; noon-midnight Fri; 1pm-midnight Sat; 1-10.30pm Sun. *Food served* noon-10pm Mon-Fri; noon-9pm Sat, Sun. **Map** p53 E4 ㉘

While the Victorian prime minister glares from the massive mural on the outer wall, inside is funky, freaky and candlelit. Gigs (blues, folk, acoustic, five nights a week) take place at one end of a cosy space; opposite is the bar. Pies provide sustenance. Retro touches include an old-fashioned 'On Air' studio sign and a Communist-style railway clock.

Shops & Services

★ Borough Market
Southwark Street, SE1 (7407 1002, www. boroughmarket.org.uk). London Bridge tube/rail. **Open** 10am-5pm Wed, Thur; 10am-6pm Fri; 8am-5pm Sat. **No credit cards. Map** p53 F3 ㉕ **Market**

The food hound's favourite market is also London's oldest, dating back to the 13th century. It's the busiest, too, occupying a sprawling site near London Bridge. Gourmet goodies run the gamut, from fresh loaves and rare-breed meats, via fish, game, fruit and veg, to cakes and all manner of preserves, oils and teas; head out hungry to take advantage of the numerous free samples. A rail viaduct, vigorously campaigned against, is now in place, which means

restored historic features have been returned and works disruption should now be at an end. As if to celebrate, a new Market Hall, facing on to Borough High Street, has been opened: it acts as a kind of greenhouse for growing plants (including hops), as well as hosting workshops, tastings and foodie demonstrations. You can also nip in with your snack if the weather's poor.

▶ *Although the market's open on Monday and Tuesday, those days are mainly for tradespeople, and there are fewer stalls open to the general public. Given that weekends are almost always mobbed, Wednesday and Thursday are normally the best days on which to visit.*

LONDON BRIDGE TO TOWER BRIDGE

Bermondsey tube or London Bridge tube/rail.

Nothing can compete with the colossal, 1,016-foot **Shard** development at London Bridge station – it towers over the immediate area, and the London skyline from pretty much everywhere – but there's are more modest discoveries to be made further to the east. Next to the Thames is **Hay's Galleria**. Once an enclosed dock, it's now dominated by a peculiar kinetic sculpture called *The Navigators*. Exiting on the riverside, you can walk east past the great grey hulk of **HMS Belfast** to Tower Bridge. Beyond the battleship you'll pass the pristine environs of the **More London** complex – sold off to Kuwaiti investors in a £1.7-billion property deal – part of which is **City Hall**, home of London's current government. There's a pleasant outside area called the Scoop, used for outdoor events, and a handful of chain cafés.

South of here, many of the historic houses on Bermondsey Street now host hip design studios or funky shops. This is also where you'll find the **Fashion & Textile Museum**, as well as the largest and newest of Jay Jopling's **White Cube** art galleries (nos.144-152, 7930 5373, www.whitecube.com, closed Mon). At the street's furthest end, the redevelopment of Bermondsey Square created an arthouse cinema and the Bermondsey Square Hotel (*see p341*), alongside a charming cemetery park, but old-timers linger on: the classic eel and pie shop **M Manze** and a Friday **antiques market** – great for browsing, but get there early.

If the Borough Market crowds are getting too much for you on a Saturday, there is a winning cluster of food stalls around **Maltby Street**, **Druid Street** and nearby **Spa Terminus**, and on the redeveloped **Ropewalk**.

Back on the riverfront, a board announces when Tower Bridge is next due to be raised. The bridge is one of the lowest to span the Thames, hence its twin lifting sections (or bascules). The original steam-driven machinery can be seen at the **Tower Bridge Exhibition** (*see p187*). Further east, the former warehouses of **Butler's Wharf** are now mainly given over to expensive riverside dining; one of them currently houses the **Design Museum**.

Sights & Museums

The **Design Museum** (Shad Thames, SE1 2YD, www.designmuseum.org, £14, free-£10.50 reductions) will move to grand premises in Kensington in 2016 (*see p227* **The Future of Design**). Until then, the programme of fine temporary exhibitions continues here.

Fashion & Textile Museum

83 Bermondsey Street, SE1 3XF (7407 8664, www.ftmlondon.org). London Bridge tube/rail. **Open** 11am-6pm Tue, Wed, Fri, Sat; 11am-8pm Thur; 11am-5pm Sun. **Admission** £8.80; £4.40-£6.60 reductions; free under-12s. **Map** p53 G4 ㉓ As flamboyant as its founder, fashion designer Zandra Rhodes, this pink and orange museum holds 3,000 of Rhodes's garments and her archive of paper designs, sketchbooks, silk screens and show videos.

Shard.

EXPLORE

The varied and always interesting temporary exhibits explore the work of trend-setters or themes such as the development of underwear. A quirky shop sells ware by new designers.

HMS Belfast

The Queen's Walk, SE1 2JH (7940 6300, www. iwm.org.uk). London Bridge tube/rail. **Open** *Mar-Oct* 10am-6pm daily. *Nov-Feb* 10am-5pm daily. **Admission** £14; £11.60 reductions; free under-16s (must be accompanied by an adult). **Map** p53 G2 ❷
This 11,500-ton 'Edinburgh' class large light cruiser is the last surviving big-gun World War II warship in Europe. It's also a floating branch of the Imperial War Museum, and is a popular if unlikely playground for children, who tear around its complex of gun turrets, bridge, decks and engine room. The *Belfast* was built in 1936, ran convoys to Russia, supported the Normandy Landings and helped UN forces in Korea before being decommissioned in 1963.

★ Shard

32 London Bridge Street, SE1 9SG (0844 499 7111, www.theviewfromtheshard.com). London Bridge tube/rail. **Open** 10am-8.30pm daily. **Admission** *In advance* £24.95; £18.95-£19.95 reductions; free under-4s. *On the day* £29.95; £24.95-£23.95 reductions; free under-4s. **Map** p53 G3 ❷
You can't miss the Shard – which is, after all, the point of the structure. It shoots into the sky 'like a shard of glass' – to use the words of its architect, Renzo Piano, looking oddly similar to Saruman's tower in *The Lord of the Rings*. In 2011, it became the tallest building in the EU, but didn't reach its full height until 2012, when it topped out at 1,016ft. As is the fate of skyscrapers, the Shard's claims to be the tallest are relative: it's beaten in Moscow, the Arab Emirates and across South-east Asia. But this slim, slightly irregular pyramid is the centrepiece of views from right across London – except, ironically, from in those Victorian alleys at its foot, where the monstrous building plays peek-a-boo with visitors as they scurry around looking for a good snapshot. High-speed lifts whisk passengers up to stunning 360°, 40-mile views, but the real joy of a visit is looking down: even seasoned London-watchers find peering down on the likes of the Tower of London from this extreme height oddly revelatory.
▶ *Note there are no toilets or refreshments on the viewing platforms – if you plan to take your time up there, then go prepared.*

Restaurants

As well as the **Shangri-La** hotel (*see p341*), the Shard contains numerous eating options: a ground-floor deli (Láng), four restaurants (Aqua Shard, Level 31; Oblix, Level 32; Hutong, Level 33; Tīng, Level 35) and, our current favourite, London's highest bar **Gŏng**.

IN THE KNOW KAPOW!

Wondering where those big forward guns on **HMS Belfast** (*see left*) are pointing? Exploiting an effective range of a bit less than 12 miles, they'd put a shell through the plate-glass windows of a service station on the M1 motorway.

M Manze

87 Tower Bridge Road, SE1 4TW (7407 2985, www.manze.co.uk). Bus 1, 42, 188. **Open** 11am-2pm Mon; 10.30am-2pm Tue-Thur; 10am-2.30pm Fri; 10am-2.45pm Sat. **Main courses** £2.75-£5.20. **Map** p53 G5 ❷
Pie & mash
One of the few remaining purveyors of the dirt-cheap traditional foodstuff of London's working classes. It's the oldest pie shop in town, established in 1902, with tiles, marble-topped tables and wooden benches – and is almost as beautiful as L Manze's on Walthamstow High Street, now Grade II-listed. Orders are simple: minced beef pies or, for braver souls, stewed eels with mashed potato and liquor (a thin parsley sauce).

Pizarro

194 Bermondsey Street, SE1 3TQ (7378 9455, www.pizarrorestaurant.com). Borough tube or London Bridge tube/rail. **Open** noon-11pm Mon-Sat; 10am-10pm Sun. **Main courses** £12-£24. **Map** p53 G4 ❸ Spanish
José Pizarro's restaurant continues in the style set in his tapas bar, José, up the street (no.104, SE1 3UB, 7403 4902, http://joserestaurant.co.uk). Menus are more extensive than at the tapas-only José; the selection of mostly traditional dishes prepared with care and skill, and fine ingredients, includes an expertly slow-braised beef stew. The space artfully combines old-Spanish touches – tiles, warm wood, exposed brick – with a stripped-down 'New Bermondsey' look.

Restaurant Story

199 Tooley Street, SE1 2JX (7183 2117, www. restaurantstory.co.uk). London Bridge tube/rail. **Open** noon-5pm, 6.30-9.30pm Tue-Thur; noon-5pm, 6-9.30pm Fri, Sat. **Set meal** £35 6 courses; £85 10 courses. **Map** p53 H3 ❹ British
Story, from starry young chef Tom Sellers, continues this area's rise to foodie heaven, securing a Michelin star within months of opening. It's set in a sparse room – all the better to emphasise the view of the Shard through floor-to-ceiling windows, and, of course, the food: an enjoyable procession of modernist dishes layered with culinary puns (bread and dripping, for instance, features a lit candle made from dripping) and tastebud challenges (mackerel versus green strawberries).

EXPLORE

▶ *As with many of London's coolest restaurants, you'll need to book far ahead: a month's notice at time of writing.*

Zucca
184 Bermondsey Street, SE1 3TQ (7378 6809, www.zuccalondon.com). Bermondsey tube or London Bridge tube/rail. **Open** noon-3pm, 6-10pm Tue-Fri; noon-3.30pm, 6-10pm Sat; noon-4pm Sun. **Main courses** £14-£18. **Map** p53 G4 ㉒ Italian
The sleek interior and light streaming in through the floor-to-ceiling windows lend a sophisticated Sydney vibe to Zucca. Own-made breads might be followed by burrata with broad beans in a garlicky dressing, or spider crab served prettily in its shell. The own-made pasta is superb, served with sauces such as a sweetly earthy combination of lentils, walnuts and basil.

Pubs & Bars

This is one of the best bits of London in which to explore the recent extraordinary proliferation of craft breweries (*see below* **Meet Your Makers**).

MEET YOUR MAKERS
Say 'hi' to the Bermondsey 'Beer Mile'.

London has always been awash with beer – literally in 1814, when an exploding brewery on Tottenham Court Road created the London Beer Flood – but the current ubiquity of craft ale is remarkable. For a taster, explore Bermondsey's 'Beer Mile': half a dozen microbreweries occupying railway arches south of London Bridge. All six open their tap rooms – the small bar attached to the brewery – every Saturday, allowing curious drinkers to savour some of London's tastiest brews in an intoxicating crawl. Start at South Bermondsey station and take a map (or make sure your smartphone's got juice) as the walk isn't straightforward, especially after a few pints.

The grandaddy of the scene is **Kernel** (Arch 11, Dockley Industrial Estate, SE16 3SF), who set up in the first wave of the London beer renaissance in 2007. Their tap is now so popular they almost have to turn people away. They were followed by **Partizan** (8 Almond Street, SE16 3LR), who used some of Kernel's old equipment, then **Brew By Numbers** (79 Enid Street, SE16 3RA), **Fourpure** (22 Trading Estate, Rotherhithe New Road, SE16 3LL) and, sharing premises, **Bullfinch** and **Anspach & Hobsday** (118 Druid Street, SE1 2HH) – Anspach & Hobsday also opens on Friday and Sunday, which are generally less busy than Saturday.

Collectively, they offer tasty evidence of the way London has embraced craft beer. When Kernel began, there were less than half-a-dozen breweries in London; now there are more than 70. As drinking habits have been transformed, pubs that once served gassy lagers and tasteless bitters now compete to serve the widest range of new beers. As one Hackney landlord commented, 'You might not get more customers if you serve good beers, but you will definitely lose them if you don't.'

Partizan

For once London was behind the curve. The microbrewery trend started in the United States in the 1980s, and parts of Scotland have had thriving scenes for years. But when it hit London, it hit big. That moment came with the 2008 recession, which lowered costs for new businesses. Craft ale tapped into a wider foodie trend that celebrated local produce and embraced more complex tastes, as found in hoppy IPAs ('India Pale Ale' – a light, hoppy, refreshing beer).

But London was also able to tap into a strong, lost tradition of brewing: IPAs, porters and several other varieties were created in London centuries ago, allowing canny current brewers to provide an experience that felt new and exciting, but was also deep in taste and rich in history. Where better to enjoy that heady brew, six times over, than under a railway arch in south-east London?

EXPLORE

Gŏng

*Level 52, The Shard, 31 St Thomas Street, SE1
9SY (7234 8208, www.gong-shangri-la.com).
London Bridge tube/rail.* **Open** 5pm-2am Mon-
Sat; 5pm-midnight Sun. **Map** p53 G3 ㉝

Take the express lift up the Shard to the 52nd floor
to find London's highest bar. At this altitude, it's
actually not so easy to pick out landmarks, but the
views of the City are simply spectacular, especially
if you book a two-hour slot across sunset. Be
warned: you'll pay a premium for drinking in such
an elevated location. Our Bermondsey Bubbles –
made with Jensen's gin, rose liqueur and champagne
– was perfectly pleasant, but it didn't leave much
change from a £20 note.

▶ *There's a minimum £30 spend per person, but on
Sunday, Monday or Tuesday (except bank holidays)
you can enjoy the view for the price of a bottle of
beer or a glass of wine.*

Shops & Services

The **Design Museum** has a superb shop, full
of inspirational design and funky gifts.

Bermondsey Square
Antiques Market

*Corner of Bermondsey Street & Long Lane,
SE1 3UN (www.bermondseysquare.co.uk).
Borough tube or London Bridge tube/rail.*
Open 4am-1pm Fri. **No credit cards**.
Map p53 G4 ㉞ **Market**

Following the redevelopment of Bermondsey
Square, the antiques market – which started in 1855
in north London – continues in an expanded space
that now accommodates 200 stalls. Traditionally
good for china and silverware, as well as furniture
and glassware, there are now also food, fashion and
crafts stalls. It's famous for being the spot where,
back in the day, thieves could sell their goods with
impunity: it's half car boot sale, half chic Parisian
fleamarket. Get there early – lunchtime arrivals will
be disappointed to find grouchy antiques sellers
(well, they did start work at 4am) packing up.

Maltby Street

*Maltby Street, Druid Street, Spa Terminus,
Ropewalk, SE1 (www.maltby.st). Bermondsey or
Southwark tube.* **Open** 9am-4pm Sat; 11am-4pm
Sun. **Map** p53 H4 ㉟ **Food & drink**

Borough Market's trade has been challenged by
former stallholders who have set up camp under
the railway arches around Maltby Street and
further south. Head here for delicious raclette
from Kappacasein (Arch 1), craft beer from Kernel
Brewery (Arch 12) and the city's finest custard
doughnuts, courtesy of St John Bakery (Arch 72).
Most producers are open on Saturday mornings,
some on Sundays too – the website www.spa-
terminus.co.uk has a useful map showing locations
and opening hours.

Maltby Street.

Westminster & St James's

The whole of the United Kingdom is ruled from Westminster. The monarchy has been in residence here since the 11th century, when Edward the Confessor moved west from the City; the government of the day also calls it home. It's a key destination for visitors as well, with the most significant area designated a UNESCO World Heritage Site back in 1987.

As well as being home to some of London's most impressive buildings, it's also packed with culture: Tate Britain, the National Gallery and the National Portrait Gallery are all here. For such an important part of London, it's surprisingly spacious. St James's Park is one of London's finest green spaces, Trafalgar Square is a tourist hotspot, and the Mall offers a properly regal approach route to Buckingham Palace.

Tate Britain.

Don't Miss

1 St James's Park Central London's prettiest park, with great birdlife (p79).

2 National Gallery One masterpiece after another (p68).

3 Westminster Abbey Magnificent, sacred and packed to its reredos with history (p75).

4 Tate Britain The original Tate, now revamped and rehung (p77).

5 Fortnum & Mason The ultimate for traditional foodie souvenirs (p82).

TRAFALGAR SQUARE

Leicester Square tube or Charing Cross tube/rail.

Laid out in the 1820s by John Nash, Trafalgar Square is the heart of modern London. Tourists come in their thousands to pose for photographs in front of **Nelson's Column**. It was erected in 1840 to honour Vice Admiral Horatio Nelson, who died at the point of victory at the Battle of Trafalgar in 1805. The statue atop the 150-foot Corinthian column is foreshortened to appear in perfect proportion from the ground. The granite fountains were added in 1845; Sir Edwin Landseer's bronze lions joined them in 1867 – the metal has in places been worn very thin by tourists clambering over them. Stay off!

Once surrounded on all sides by busy roads, the square was improved markedly in 2003 by the pedestrianisation of the North Terrace, right in front of the **National Gallery**. A ban on feeding pigeons was another positive step. The square feels more like public space now, and is a focus for performance and celebration.

Around the perimeter are three plinths bearing statues of George IV and two Victorian military heroes, Henry Havelock and Sir Charles James Napier. The long-empty fourth plinth, which never received its planned martial statue, has been used since 1998 to display temporary, contemporary art. An equine skeleton with a London Stock Exchange ticker attached to its raised foreleg – *Gift Horse* by Hans Haacke – currently stands there, to be followed in 2016 by David Shrigley's huge thumbs-up, *Really Good*. Other points of interest around the square include an equestrian statue of Charles I dating from the 1630s, with a plaque behind it that marks the original site of Edward I's Eleanor Cross, the official centre of London. (A Victorian replica of the cross is outside Charing Cross Station.) At the square's north-east corner is **St Martin-in-the-Fields**.

Sights & Museums

★ FREE **National Gallery**

Trafalgar Square, WC2N 5DN (7747 2885, www. nationalgallery.org.uk). Charing Cross tube/rail. **Open** 10am-6pm Mon-Thur, Sat, Sun; 10am-9pm Fri. *Tours* 11.30am, 2.30pm Mon-Thur; 11.30am, 2.30pm, 7pm Fri; 11.30am, 2.30pm, 4pm Sat, Sun. **Admission** free. *Special exhibitions* vary. **Map** p71 B5 ❶

Founded in 1824 to display 36 paintings, the National Gallery is now one of the world's great repositories for art. There are masterpieces from virtually every European school of art, from austere 13th-century religious paintings to the sensual delights of Caravaggio and Van Gogh. One of the most important, Titian's *Diana and Actaeon*, was

Trafalgar Square.

secured for the gallery by outgoing director Nicholas Penny, who leaves in August 2015 having led the gallery to record attendance figures in 2013. His replacement, Gabriele Finaldi, comes from the Prado in Madrid; he will take over a gallery that continues to host sell-out blockbuster shows – not least recent exhibitions of Rembrandt and the Impressionists – but faces industrial turmoil over its new policy of outsourcing its gallery assistants.

The gallery itself is huge. Furthest to the left of the main entrance, the modern Sainsbury Wing extension contains the gallery's earliest works: Italian paintings by masters such as Giotto and Piero della Francesca, as well as the *Wilton Diptych*, the finest medieval English picture in the collection, showing Richard II with the Virgin and Child.

In the West Wing (left of the main entrance) are Italian Renaissance masterpieces by Correggio, Titian and Raphael. Straight ahead on entry, in the North Wing, are 17th-century Dutch, Flemish, Italian and Spanish Old Masters, including works such as Rembrandt's *A Woman Bathing in a Stream* and Caravaggio's *Supper at Emmaus*. Velázquez's *Rokeby Venus* is one of the artist's most famous paintings. Also in this wing are works by the great landscape artists Claude and Poussin. Turner insisted that his *Dido Building Carthage* and *Sun Rising through Vapour* should hang alongside two Claudes here that particularly inspired him.

In the East Wing are some of the gallery's most popular paintings: you'll find works by the French Impressionists and Post-Impressionists, including Monet's *Water-Lilies*, one of Van Gogh's *Sunflowers* and Seurat's *Bathers at Asnières*. Don't miss Renoir's astonishingly lovely *Les Parapluies*.

You shouldn't plan to see everything in one visit, but free guided tours, audio guides and the superb

Art Start computer (which allows you to tailor and map your own itinerary of must-sees) help you make the best of your time.

▶ *Downstairs from the main entrance, the scruffily endearing 'secret gallery' Room A has been rehung. A two-year refurb left it better lit and curated, showing a lovely mix of barely known artists and lost works, some dating back to 1250. It opens on Wednesdays and the first Sunday of the month.*

★ FREE National Portrait Gallery

St Martin's Place, WC2H 0HE (7306 0055, www. npg.org.uk). Leicester Square tube or Charing Cross tube/rail. **Open** 10am-6pm Mon-Wed, Sat, Sun; 10am-9pm Thur, Fri. **Admission** free. *Special exhibitions* vary. **Map** p71 A5 ❷

Since 2002, director Sandy Nairne has proved that portraits don't have to be stuffy, not least with his stellar Lucian Freud retrospective in 2012; his successor, Nicholas Cullinan, who arrived from New York's Metropolitan Museum of Art in spring 2015, has much to follow. But the NPG is in fine health, with displays showing everything from oil paintings of stiff-backed royals to photographs of soccer stars and gloriously unflattering political caricatures. The portraits of musicians, scientists, artists, philanthropists and celebrities are arranged in chronological order from top to bottom.

On the second floor, are the earliest works, portraits of Tudor and Stuart royals and notables, including Holbein's 'cartoon' of Henry VIII and the 'Ditchley Portrait' of his daughter, Elizabeth I, her pearly slippers placed firmly on a colourful map of England. On the same floor, the 18th-century collection features Georgian writers and artists, with one room devoted to the influential Kit-Cat Club of bewigged Whig (leftish) intellectuals, the playwright Congreve and the poet Dryden among them. More famous names include Wren and Swift. The second floor also shows Regency greats, military men such as Wellington and Nelson, plus Byron, Wordsworth and other Romantics. The first floor is devoted to the Victorians (Dickens, Brunel, Darwin) and to 20th-century luminaries, such as TS Eliot and Ian McKellen.

FREE St Martin-in-the-Fields

Trafalgar Square, WC2N 4JJ (7766 1100, www. smitf.org). Leicester Square tube or Charing Cross tube/rail. **Open** 8.30am-1pm, 2-6pm Mon, Tue, Thur, Fri; 8.30am-1.15pm, 2-5pm Wed; 9.30am-6pm Sat; 3.30-5pm Sun. *Brass Rubbing Centre* 10am-6pm Mon-Wed; 10am-8pm Thur-Sat; 11.30am-5pm Sun. **Admission** free. *Brass rubbing* £4.50. **Map** p71 B6 ❸

There's been a church 'in the fields' between Westminster and the City since the 13th century, but the current one was built in 1726 by James Gibbs, using a fusion of neoclassical and Baroque styles. The parish church for Buckingham Palace (note the royal box to the left of the gallery), St Martin's bright interior was fully restored a few years back, with Victorian furbelows removed and the addition of a brilliant altar window that shows the Cross, stylised as if rippling on water. Downstairs in the crypt are a fine café and the London Brass Rubbing Centre. The lunchtime and evening concerts in the church (which rarely wander far from the embrace of Mozart and Bach) are often delightful, especially when candlelit.

Restaurants

Aside from chains that are all shine and no soul or tourist traps, there are few dining options. If you don't fancy the National, head 10 minutes north to explore the multifarious dining opportunities in nearby **Soho** (*see pp122-135*).

National Dining Rooms

Sainsbury Wing, National Gallery, Trafalgar Square, WC2N 5DN (7747 2525, www. peytonandbyrne.co.uk). Charing Cross tube/rail. **Open** *Bakery* 10am-5pm Mon-Thur, Sat, Sun; 10am-8pm Fri. *Restaurant* 10am-5.30pm Mon-Thur, Sat, Sun; 10am-8.30pm Fri. **Main courses** *Bakery* £6.50-£17.50. *Restaurant* £16.50-£32.50. **Map** p71 B5 ❹ **British**

Ascend the stairs to Oliver Peyton's first-floor dining room – in the quieter Sainsbury Wing of the National Gallery – and enter a professionally run and peaceful place, where the views (over the Square in one direction, of a vast Paula Rego mural in the other) are matched by the superb food. Dishes are light, artfully presented and with clever additions.

IN THE KNOW
GOING, GOING... GONE?

Trundling these streets since the 1950s, the hugely popular **Routemaster** bus, London's original hop-on, hop-off double-decker, was retired in 2005 – to howls of protest that, in part, fuelled the rise to power of the incumbent mayor. The irony is lost on no one that, under Boris Johnson, the 'heritage routes' are now under threat: one has already closed. He argues his expensively designed New Bus for London – by coincidence, officially renamed the New Routemaster – will run right across London, so keeping on any of the old buses at all is an unnecessary luxury. For the time being, refurbished buses from the 1960-64 Routemaster fleet run on route 15 (between Trafalgar Square and Tower Hill); head to stop F, on the Strand to the east of the square. Buses run every 15 minutes from around 9.30am; fares match ordinary buses, but you must have a ticket or valid card before boarding (see p368).

EXPLORE

EXPLORE

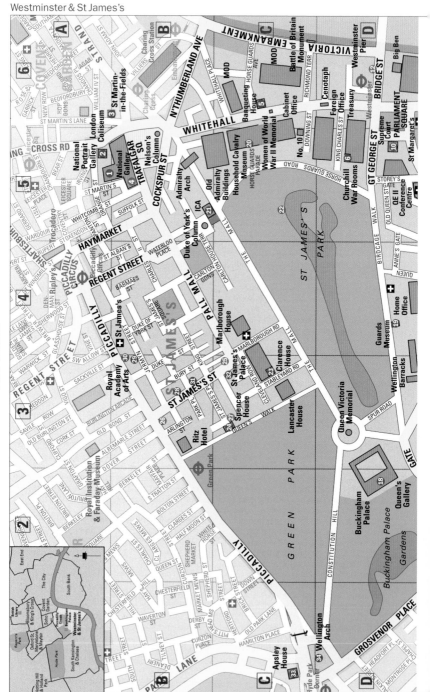

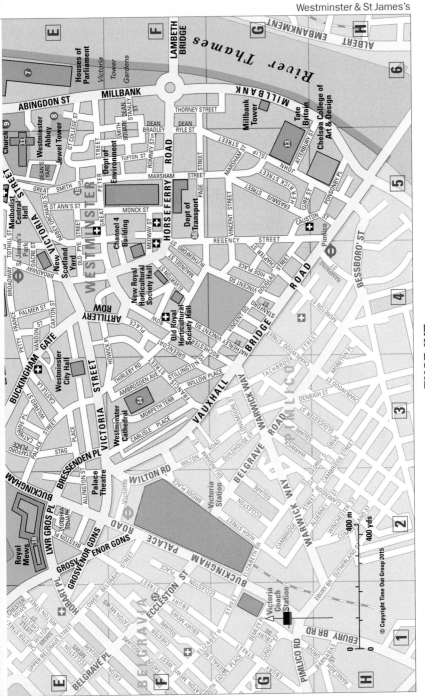

EXPLORE

Walk through 2,000 years of

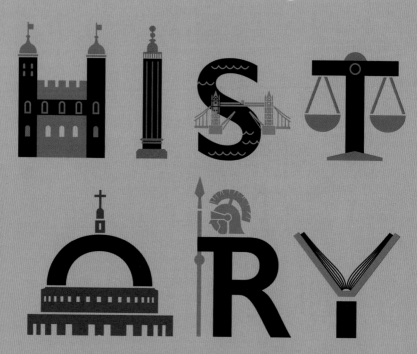

in just 90 mins

Walk the City Visitor Trail in just 90 minutes and discover
a vibrant culture and fascinating history.
Pick up our free map from the City Information Centre
or download our App.

CITY OF LONDON

Discover more at
www.cityoflondon.gov.uk/cvt

DIOCESE OF
LONDON

VISITLONDON.COM
OFFICIAL VISITOR GUIDE

Available on the
App Store

ANDROID APP ON
Google play

WHITEHALL TO PARLIAMENT SQUARE

Westminster tube or Charing Cross tube/rail.

The offices of the British government are lined along **Whitehall**, itself named after Henry VIII's magnificent palace, which burned to the ground in 1698. Walking south from Trafalgar Square, you pass the old **Admiralty Offices** and **War Office**, the **Ministry of Defence**, the **Foreign Office** and the **Treasury**, as well as the **Banqueting House**, one of the few buildings to survive the blaze. Also here is **Horse Guards**, headquarters of the Household Cavalry, the elite army unit that protects the Queen.

Either side of **Downing Street** – home to the prime minister (no.10) and chancellor (no.11), but closed to the public after IRA attacks in the 1980s – are significant war memorials. The millions who died in the service of the nation in World Wars I and II are commemorated by Sir Edwin Lutyens' dignified **Cenotaph**, focal point of Remembrance Day (*see p39*), while a separate memorial to the women of World War II, by sculptor John Mills, recalls the seven million women who contributed to the war effort. Just past the Cenotaph and hidden beneath government offices at the St James's Park end of King Charles Street, the claustrophobic **Churchill War Rooms** are where Britain's wartime PM planned the struggle.

The broad sweep of Whitehall is an apt introduction to the monuments of **Parliament Square**. Laid out in 1868, this green space is flanked by the **Houses of Parliament**, the neo-Gothic Middlesex Guildhall (now the **Supreme Court**) and the twin spires of **Westminster Abbey**. Parliament Square can seem little more than a glorified traffic island, despite all the statues of British politicians (Disraeli, Churchill) and foreign dignitaries (Lincoln, Mandela and, since spring 2015, Gandhi), but its symbolic value has been brought back into focus through court battles over its suitability as a site for political protest: initially against the occupation of Iraq, more recently over austerity and corruption.

Parliament itself simply dazzles. An outrageous neo-Gothic fantasy, the seat of the British government is still formally known as the Palace of Westminster, though the only remaining parts of the medieval palace are **Westminster Hall** and the **Jewel Tower**. At the north end of the palace is the clocktower housing the huge **'Big Ben'** bell that gives the clocktower its popular name; more than seven feet tall, the bell (itself formally known as the 'Great Bell') weighs over 13 tons. The tower was, in fact, renamed in 2012: rather than bowing to common usage, it became the Elizabeth Tower – in honour of the Queen's Diamond Jubilee.

Sights & Museums

Banqueting House

Whitehall, SW1A 2ER (0844 482 7777, www.hrp. org.uk). Westminster tube. **Open** 10am-5pm Mon-Sat; phone to check. **Admission** £6.60; £5.50 reductions; free under-16s. **Map** p71 C6 ➎

This handsome Italianate mansion, which was designed by Inigo Jones and constructed in 1620, was the first true Renaissance building in London. The sole surviving part of the Tudor and Stuart kings' Whitehall Palace, the Banqueting House features a lavish painted ceiling by Rubens, glorifying James I, 'the wisest fool in Christendom'. Regrettably, James's successor, Charles I, did not rule so wisely. After losing the English Civil War to Cromwell's Roundheads, he was executed in front of Banqueting House in 1649 – the subject of a set of displays here.

▶ *Charles I's execution is marked by a dogged bunch of royalists every 31 January at his equestrian statue just south of Trafalgar Square.*

Churchill War Rooms

Clive Steps, King Charles Street, SW1A 2AQ (7930 6961, www.iwm.org.uk). St James's Park or Westminster tube. **Open** 9.30am-6pm daily. **Admission** £16.35; £8.15 reductions; free under-16s. **Map** p71 D5 ➏

Out of harm's way beneath Whitehall, this cramped and spartan bunker was where Winston Churchill planned the Allied victory in World War II, and the rooms powerfully bring to life the reality of a nation at war. The cabinet rooms were sealed on 16 August 1945, keeping the complex in a state of suspended animation: every pin stuck into the vast charts was placed there in the final days of the conflict. The humble quarters occupied by Churchill and his deputies give a tangible sense of wartime hardship, an effect reinforced by the wailing sirens and wartime speeches on the audio guide (free with admission).

★ Houses of Parliament

Parliament Square, SW1A 0AA (Commons information 7219 4272, Lords information 7219 3107, www.parliament.uk). Westminster tube. **Open** (when in session) *House of Commons Visitors' Gallery* 2.30-10.30pm Mon; 11.30am-7.30pm Tue, Wed; 9.30am-5.30pm Thur; 9.30am-3pm Fri. *House of Lords Visitors' Gallery* 2.30-10pm Mon, Tue; 3-10pm Wed; 11am-7.30pm Thur; from 10am Fri. *Tours* 9.15am-4.30pm Sat & summer recess; check website for details. **Admission** *Visitors' galleries* free. *Tours* £25; £10-£20 reductions; free under-15s with adult. **Map** p70 E6 ➐

The British parliament has an extremely long history, with the first parliamentary session held in St Stephen's Chapel in 1275. The Palace of Westminster, however, only became the permanent seat of Parliament in 1532, when Henry VIII moved

EXPLORE

to a new des-res in Whitehall. The current Palace is a wonderful mish-mash of styles, dominated by Gothic buttresses, towers and arches. It looks much older than it is: the Parliament buildings were designed in 1860 by Charles Barry (ably assisted by Augustus Pugin) to replace the original building, which had been destroyed by fire in 1834. Now, the compound contains 1,000 rooms, 11 courtyards, eight bars and six restaurants, plus a small cafeteria for visitors. Of the original palace, only the Jewel Tower and Westminster Hall remain.

Visitors are welcome (subject to stringent security checks at St Stephen's Gate, the only public access point into Parliament) to observe the political debates in the House of Lords and House of Commons, but tickets must be arranged in advance through your embassy or MP, who can also arrange tours – even free trips up the 334 spiral steps of the Elizabeth Tower to hear 'Big Ben'. The experience of listening in on the Houses of Parliament in session is often soporific, but Prime Minister's Question Time at noon on Wednesday is often sparky: the PM has alternately to rebuff a barrage of hostile questions from the opposition (and occasionally their own rebellious backbenchers) and massage value out of soft questions from loyal backbenchers eager to present the government in a good light.

▶ *The best way to see these historic buildings is to book on one of the revealing 90min guided tours (7219 4114, www.parliament.uk/visiting/) on Saturday or during summer recess. Tours take in both Houses, Westminster Hall, the Queen's Robing Room and the Royal Gallery.*

Jewel Tower

Abingdon Street, SW1P 3JY (7222 2219, www. english-heritage.org.uk). Westminster tube. **Open** *Apr-Oct* 10am-5pm daily. *Nov-Mar* 10am-4pm Sat, Sun. **Admission** £4; £2.40-£3.60 reductions; free under-5s. **Map** p70 E6 ❽

This easy-to-overlook little stone tower opposite Parliament was built in 1365 to house Edward III's treasure. It is, with Westminster Hall, all that remains of the medieval Palace of Westminster. It contains a small exhibition on Parliament's history.

▶ *Nowadays, the Crown Jewels are on display in the Tower of London; see p187.*

FREE St Margaret's Church

Parliament Square, SW1P 3PA (7654 4840, www.westminster-abbey.org). St James's Park or Westminster tube. **Open** 9.30am-3.30pm Mon-Fri; 9.30am-1.30pm Sat; 2-4.30pm Sun (times vary due to services). *Services* times vary; check website for details. **Admission** free. **Map** p70 E6 ❾

Tucked in next to the grandeur of Westminster Abbey, this little church was founded in the 12th century; since 1614, it's served as the official church of the House of Commons. The interior features some of the most impressive pre-Reformation stained glass in London. The east window (1509)

commemorates the marriage of Henry VIII and Catherine of Aragon; others celebrate Britain's first printer, William Caxton (buried here in 1491), explorer Sir Walter Raleigh (executed in Old Palace Yard in 1618) and writer John Milton (1608-74), who married his second wife here in 1656.

FREE Supreme Court

Parliament Square, SW1P 3BD (7960 1900, www. supremecourt.uk). St James's Park or Westminster tube. **Open** 9.30am-4.30pm Mon-Fri. *Tours* 11am, 2pm, 3pm Fri. **Admission** free. *Tours* £5; £3.50 reductions. **Map** p71 D5 ❿

In 2005, Parliament made a momentous decision – not that anyone noticed. The right to adjudicate final appeals was taken from the House of Lords and given to a new, independent Supreme Court, which was duly opened by the Queen in 2009, directly opposite Parliament. Part of the notion was to open up higher processes of law to the public – in plain English, you can visit any time you like (through airport-style security gates) to see lawyers debate 'points of law of general public importance' in front of the country's most senior judges. Recent cases have included whether an MP can be tried in a magistrate's court for alleged criminal misconduct within Parliament, and how binding a prenuptial agreement should be. You can also look around the lovely Grade II*-listed, neo-Gothic premises, built for Middlesex County Council in 1913. There's even a café and souvenirs on sale.

▶ *The Supreme Court doesn't sit on Friday.*

★ Westminster Abbey

20 Dean's Yard, SW1P 3PA (7222 5152 information, 7654 4834 tours, www.westminster-abbey.org). St James's Park or Westminster tube. **Open** *May-Aug* 9.30am-3.30pm Mon, Tue, Thur-Sat; 9.30am-6pm Wed. *Sept-Apr* 9.30am-3.30pm Mon, Thur, Fri; 2-3.30pm Tue; 9.30am-6pm Wed; 9.30am-1.30pm Sat. *Abbey Museum, Chapter House & College Gardens* times var; phone for details. *Tours* May-Aug 10am, 10.30am, 11am, 2pm, 2.30pm Mon-Fri; 10am, 10.30am, 11am Sat. Sept-Apr 10.30am, 11am, 2pm, 2.30pm Mon-Fri; 10.30am, 11pm Sat. **Admission** £20; £9-£17 reductions; £45 family; free under-10s with adult. *Tours* £5. **Map** p70 E5 ⓫

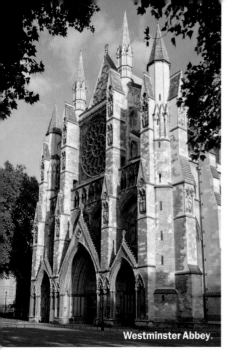

Westminster Abbey.

In the vaulted area under the former monks' dormitory, one of the abbey's oldest parts, the Abbey Museum celebrated its centenary in 2008. You'll find effigies and waxworks of British monarchs, among them Edward II and Henry VII, wearing the robes they donned in life. The 900-year-old College Garden is one of the oldest cultivated spaces in Britain and a useful place to escape the crowds. For snacks, there's a refectory-style restaurant – the Cellarium Café & Terrace (7222 0516, www.cellariumcafe.com).

Pubs & Bars

While the **Red Lion** (48 Parliament Street, SW1A 2NH, 7930 5826, http://redlionwestminster.co.uk) is, by tradition, the politicians' favourite pub and the **Westminster Arms** (9-10 Storey Gate, SW1P 3AT, 7222 8520, www.shepherdneame.co.uk) has its own 'division bell' to summon drinkers back into the House to vote, most MPs nowadays prefer to drink in the privacy of Parliament's own taxpayer-subsidised bars.

St Stephen's Tavern

10 Bridge Street, SW1A 2JR (7925 2286, www. hall-woodhouse.co.uk). Westminster tube. **Open** 10am-11.30pm Mon-Sat; 10.30am-10pm Sun. *Food served* 10am-10pm daily. **Map** p71 D6 ⑫

Done out with dark woods, etched mirrors and Arts and Crafts-style wallpaper, this is a handsome pub. The food is reasonably priced and the ales are decent, but drinks can be expensive. Opposite Big Ben, its location is terrific, yet it's neither too touristy nor too busy. If the downstairs bars are full, head upstairs and look for a seat on the mezzanine.

MILLBANK

Pimlico or Westminster tube.

Running south from Parliament along the river, Millbank leads eventually to **Tate Britain**, built on the site of a pentagonal prison that held criminals destined for transportation to Botany Bay. If you're walking south from the Palace of Westminster, look out on the left for **Victoria Tower Gardens** (*see right* **Unsung Hero**).

On the other side of the road, Dean Stanley Street leads to Smith Square, home to the architecturally striking **St John's Smith Square** (*see p285*), built as a church in grand Baroque style and now a venue for classical music. **Lord North Street**, the Georgian terrace running north from here, has long been a favourite address of politicians; note, too, the directions on the wall for wartime bomb shelters.

Across the river from Millbank is **Vauxhall Cross**, the oddly conspicuous HQ of the Secret Intelligence Service (SIS), commonly referred to by its old name, MI6. In case any enemies of the state were unaware of its location, the cream and

The cultural, historic and religious significance of Westminster Abbey is impossible to overstate, but also hard to remember as you're shepherded around, forced to elbow fellow tourists out of the way to read a plaque or see a tomb – even more so after the 2012 Royal Wedding 'twixt Prince William and Kate Middleton, which resulted in an impressive 36% boost in the number of visitors (the number has subsided somewhat since then). The best plan is to get here as early in the day as you can. Edward the Confessor commissioned a church to St Peter on the site of a 7th-century version, but it was only consecrated on 28 December 1065, eight days before he died. William the Conqueror subsequently had himself crowned here on Christmas Day 1066 and, with just two exceptions, every English coronation since has taken place in the abbey.

Many royal, military and cultural notables are interred here. The most haunting memorial is the Grave of the Unknown Warrior, in the nave. Elaborate resting places in side chapels are taken up by the tombs of Elizabeth I and Mary Queen of Scots. In Innocents Corner lie the remains of two lads believed to be Edward V and his brother Richard (their bodies were found at the Tower of London), as well as two of James I's children. Poets' Corner is the final resting place of Chaucer, who was the first writer to be buried here. Few of the other writers who have stones here are buried in the abbey, but the remains of Dryden, Johnson, Browning and Tennyson are all present. Henry James, TS Eliot and Dylan Thomas have dedications – on the floor, fittingly for Thomas.

green block appeared as itself in the 1999 James Bond film *The World is Not Enough* – reprising the role (and suffering serious bomb damage along the way) in 2012's *Skyfall*.

Sights & Museums

★ FREE Tate Britain

Millbank, SW1P 4RG (7887 8888, www.tate.org. uk). Pimlico tube. **Open** 10am-6pm daily. *Tours* 11am, noon, 2pm, 3pm daily. **Admission** free. *Special exhibitions* vary. **Map** p70 G5 ⑲

Tate Modern (*see p58*) gets the attention, but the original Tate Gallery, founded by sugar magnate Sir Henry Tate, has a broader brief – broad enough, in fact, that some argue it lacks focus. Opened in a stately riverside building in 1897 with a display of 245 British paintings, Tate Britain is second only to the National Gallery (*see p68*) when it comes to British art. It's also looking to steal back a bit of the limelight from its starrier sibling with a 20-year redevelopment plan called the Millbank Project: conserving the building's original features, upgrading the galleries, opening new spaces to the public and adding a new café.

The first move – a comprehensive rehang of the collections, unveiled in 2013 – may seem modest, but we found it revelatory. Covering British art from Holbein in the 1540s up to the present, the gallery's major holdings are now largely shown in chronological order on the building's main floor – allowing you to trace the development of British art through

UNSUNG HERO

A modest new plaque to the man who quietly saved thousands.

Central London is so endearingly littered with small green spaces that it is easy for some such as **Victoria Tower Gardens**, beside the Thames and in the shadow of Parliament, to get overlooked. This wonderful spot is sometimes occupied only by its commemorative furniture: a distinguished statue of suffragette Emmeline Pankhurst, a fine cast of Rodin's *The Burghers of Calais* and a magnificent neo-Gothic folly/water fountain that celebrates the abolition of slavery. A more recent, less eye-catching but hugely significant addition to these arrived in 2014, in the form of a small green plaque on the river wall.

London loves a plaque, but so many different bodies now distribute them that Londoners can be forgiven for becoming a little blasé. But this one is worth noting. It is for Sir Thomas Peirson Frank, chief engineer of the London County Council from 1931 to 1946. Frank worked on several important London infrastructure projects during his tenure – including the extension of County Hall and rebuilding of Waterloo Bridge – but this commemoration is for his less well-known role during the Second World War. Frank directed the Thames Flood Prevention Emergency Repairs service, which had the vital job of repairing damage to the Thames wall during the Blitz as swiftly as possible. The wall was hit more than 120 times by the Luftwaffe – indeed, the plaque has been placed on part of the wall that still displays scarring from bomb damage – but it was never breached. Frank has subsequently been dubbed 'the man who saved London from drowning'.

This is not hyperbole. Frank's work repairing roads and flood defences was crucial – if the Thames wall was breached, London's low-level tube stations could have flooded, drowning the thousands of Londoners who used them as bomb shelters at the height of the Blitz. So important was Frank's role that it was kept a state secret, and the full extent of his achievements was only rediscovered in recent years, when researchers found examples of the extensive repair work covertly undertaken to protect the capital. It is now known that Frank began his work before war was even declared, identifying particularly vulnerable locations, introducing secondary defences and drilling rapid-response teams. This small plaque is testament to his huge success.

EXPLORE

history – and with a minimum of hectoring curatorial captions. A few key artists are given more substantial treatment: the Turners remain together in the Clore Gallery, and works by Henry Moore and William Blake are grouped.

Caruso St John architects improved the fabric of the oldest part of the building as part of this initial £45m tranche of improvements. Sturdier floors mean that more sculpture can be displayed, and the amount of natural light has been increased. At the Millbank entrance, there's now a stained-glass window and a striking spiral staircase; downstairs in the restaurant, a new ceiling mural has been designed by Alan Johnston to complement the restored 1926-27 Rex Whistler wall mural *Pursuit of Rare Meats*. There is also a new space for temporary exhibitions,.

Given the high regard we have for the rehang, we are sad to see the controversial director, Penelope Curtis, moving on: a combination of critical opprobrium heaped on some of her temporary exhibitions and some bad visitor numbers seem to have done for her. Her successor will need a steady hand.

VICTORIA

Pimlico tube or Victoria tube/rail.

Victoria is chaotic. The rail station is a major hub for trains to southern seaside resorts and ferry terminals, while the nearby coach station is served by buses from all over Europe, and theatres dotted around the area add up to a kind of western outpost of the West End's Theatreland, but there's no real focus here, just one stand-out attraction: **Westminster Cathedral**. Not to be confused with Westminster Abbey (*see p75*), it is the headquarters of the Roman Catholic Church in England. South and east of Victoria Station are the Georgian terraces of **Pimlico** and **Belgravia**. Antiques stores and restaurants line Pimlico Road, and Tachbrook Street has some intriguing independent shops.

North of Victoria Street, towards Parliament Square, is **Christchurch Gardens**, burial site of Thomas ('Colonel') Blood, who stole the Crown Jewels in 1671. He was apprehended making his

getaway but, amazingly, managed to talk his way into a full pardon. Also in the area is **New Scotland Yard**, with its famous revolving sign, all sold in late 2014 to the Abu Dhabi Financial Group for £370 million – the rumours are that the site will become residential property, offices and a hotel. The fabulous art deco headquarters of **London Underground** at 55 Broadway are also to become private property, with Transport for London due to move out in 2015. Public outrage about Jacob Epstein's graphic nudes on the façade almost led to the resignation of the managing director in 1929; there was no such outrage at this more recent management decision.

Sights & Museums

FREE **Westminster Cathedral**
42 Francis Street, SW1P 1QW (7798 9055, www. westminstercathedral.org.uk). Victoria tube/rail.
Open 7am-7pm Mon-Fri; 8am-8pm Sat, Sun.
Admission free; donations appreciated.
Map p70 F3 ㉔

With its domes, arches and soaring tower, the most important Catholic church in England looks surprisingly Byzantine. There's a reason: architect John Francis Bentley, who built it between 1895 and 1903, was heavily influenced by Hagia Sophia in Istanbul. Compared to the candy-cane exterior, the interior is surprisingly restrained (in fact, it's unfinished), but there are still some impressive marble columns and mosaics. Eric Gill's sculptures of the Stations of the Cross (1914-18) were dismissed as 'Babylonian' when they were first installed, but worshippers have come to love them. An upper gallery holds the 'Treasures of the Cathedral' exhibition, where you can see an impressive Arts and Crafts coronet, a Tudor chalice, holy relics and Bentley's amazing architectural model of his cathedral, complete with tiny hawks.

Restaurants

Cinnamon Club
Old Westminster Library, 30-32 Great Smith Street, SW1P 3BU (7222 2555, www.cinnamonclub.com). St James's Park or Westminster tube. **Open** 7.30-9.30am, noon-2.45pm, 6-10.30pm Mon-Fri; noon-2.45pm, 6-10.30pm Sat. **Main courses** £16-£34.
Map p70 E5 ㊲ Indian

There's a gentlemen's club feel to this grand, Grade II-listed Victorian building (once a library). It's an established haunt of sharp-suited power brokers and Westminster politicians who enjoy a fine-dining menu of updated rustic and regal pan-Indian dishes, such as sliced veal escalope with its toasted coriander seasoning. The kitchen particularly excels in seafood preparations.
Other locations Cinnamon Kitchen, 9 Devonshire Square, the City, EC2M 4YL; Cinnamon Soho, 5 Kingly Street, Soho, W1B 5PF (7437 1664).

EXPLORE

Buckingham Palace

Regency Café
17-19 Regency Street, SW1P 4BY (7821 6596).
St James's Park tube or Victoria tube/rail. **Meals
served** 7am-2.30pm, 4-7.15pm Mon-Fri; 7am-noon
Sat. **Main courses** £2.70-£6.55. **Map** p70 F5 ⑯
Behind its black-tiled art deco exterior, this classic
caff has been here since 1946. Customers sit on
brown plastic chairs at Formica-topped tables,
watched over by muscular boxers and Spurs stars of
yore, whose photos hang on the tiled walls. Lasagne,
omelettes, salads, every conceivable cooked
breakfast and mugs of tannin-rich tea are meat and
drink to the Regency. Still hungry? The improbably
gigantic cinnamon-flavoured bread and butter pud
will see you right for the rest of the week.

Pubs & Bars

Boisdale of Belgravia
*13-15 Ecclestone Street, SW1W 9LX (7730 6922,
www.boisdale.co.uk). Victoria tube/rail.* **Open/
food served** noon-1am Mon-Fri; 6pm-1am Sat.
Admission free before 10pm, then £12.
Map p70 F1 ⑰
There's nowhere quite like this posh, Scottish-themed
enterprise, and that includes its sister branches in
the City and Canary Wharf. If you're here to drink,
you'll be drinking single malts from a terrific range.
That said, the outstanding wine list is surprisingly
affordable, with house selections starting at under
£20. Additional appeal comes from live jazz (six
nights a week) and a heated cigar terrace.
Other locations Swedeland Court, 202
Bishopsgate, the City, EC2M 4NR (7283 1763);
Cabot Place, Canary Wharf, E14 4QT (7715 5818).

AROUND ST JAMES'S PARK
St James's Park tube.

Handsome **St James's Park** was founded as a
deer park for the royal occupants of St James's
Palace, and remodelled by John Nash on the
orders of George IV. The central lake is home
to various species of wildfowl; pelicans have
been kept here since the 17th century, when the
Russian ambassador donated several of the bag-
jawed birds to Charles II. The pelicans are fed
between 2.30pm and 3pm daily. Lots of humans
picnic here, too, notably around the bandstand
during the summer weekend concerts. The bridge
over the lake offers good views of Buckingham
Palace. Head that way and you'll see Green Park,
the beginning of a relaxing stroll that will take
you under trees as far as Hyde Park Corner.
  Along the north side of the park, the Mall
connects Buckingham Palace with Trafalgar
Square. It looks like a classic processional route,
but the Mall was actually laid out as a pitch for
Charles II to play 'pallemaille' (an early version of
croquet imported from France) after the pitch at
Pall Mall became too crowded. On the south side
of the park, Wellington Barracks contains the
Guards Museum; to the east, Horse Guards
contains the **Household Cavalry Museum**.
  Carlton House Terrace, on the north
flank of the Mall, was the last project completed
by John Nash before his death in 1835. Part of the
terrace now houses the **ICA** (*see p80*). Just behind
is the **Duke of York column**, commemorating
Prince Frederick, Duke of York, who led the
British Army against the French. He's the
nursery rhyme's 'Grand old Duke of York',
who marched his 10,000 men neither up nor
down Cassel hill in Flanders.

Sights & Museums

Buckingham Palace & Royal Mews
*The Mall, SW1A 1AA (Palace 7766 7300, Royal
Mews 7766 7302, Queen's Gallery 7766 7301,
www.royalcollection.org.uk). Green Park tube or
Victoria tube/rail.* **Open & admission** times &
prices vary. **Map** p70 E2 ⑱
Although the nearby St James's Palace (*see p81*)
remains as the official seat of the British court,

EXPLORE

EXPLORE

every monarch since Victoria has used Buckingham Palace as their primary home. Originally known as Buckingham House, the present home of the British royals was constructed as a private house for the Duke of Buckingham in 1703, but George III liked it so much he purchased it for his German bride Charlotte in 1761. George IV decided to occupy the mansion himself after taking the throne in 1820 and John Nash was hired to convert it into a palace befitting a king. Construction was beset with problems, and Nash – whose expensive plans had always been disliked by Parliament – was dismissed in 1830. When Victoria came to the throne in 1837, the building was barely habitable. The job of finishing the palace fell to the reliable but unimaginative Edward Blore ('Blore the Bore'). The neoclassical frontage now in place was the work of Aston Webb in 1913.

As the home of the Queen, the palace is usually closed to visitors, but you can view the interior for a brief period each year while the Windsors are away on their holidays; you'll be able to see the State Rooms, still used to entertain dignitaries and guests of state, and part of the garden. There's even a café – paper cups, sadly, but coloured a pretty blue-green and clearly marked with the palace crest for souvenir-hunters. At any time of year, you can visit the Queen's Gallery to see her personal collection of treasures, including paintings by Rubens and Rembrandt, Sèvres porcelain and the Diamond Diadem crown. Further along Buckingham Palace Road, the Royal Mews is a grand garage for the royal fleet of Rolls-Royces and home to the splendid royal carriages and the horses, individually named by the Queen, that pull them.

Guards Museum

Wellington Barracks, Birdcage Walk, SW1E 6HQ (7414 3428, www.theguardsmuseum.com). St James's Park tube. **Open** 10am-4pm daily. **Admission** £6; £2-£3 reductions; free under-16s. **Map** p71 D4 ⑲

Just down the road from Horse Guards, this small museum tells the 350-year story of the Foot Guards, using flamboyant uniforms, period paintings, medals and intriguing memorabilia, such as the stuffed body of Jacob the Goose, the Guard's Victorian mascot, who was regrettably run over by a van in barracks. Appropriately, the shop is well stocked with toy soldiers of the British regiments.

▶ *The Guards assemble on the parade ground here before marching on to the palace for the Changing the Guard; see p33* **Stunning Ceremonials**.

Household Cavalry Museum

Horse Guards, Whitehall, SW1A 2AX (7930 3070, www.householdcavalrymuseum.co.uk). Westminster tube or Charing Cross tube/rail. **Open** *Apr-Oct* 10am-6pm daily. *Nov-Mar* 10am-5pm daily. **Admission** £7; £5 reductions; £18 family; free under-5s. **Map** p71 C5 ⑳

Household Cavalry is a fairly workaday name for the military peacocks who make up the Queen's official guard. They tell their stories through video diaries at this small but entertaining museum, which also offers the chance to see medals, uniforms and shiny cuirasses (breastplates) up close. You also get a peek – and sniff – of the magnificent horses that parade just outside every day: the stables are separated from the main museum by no more than a screen of glass.

▶ *The entrance to the museum is from the parade ground where the cavalry assemble for Changing the Guard; see p33* **Stunning Ceremonials**.

FREE ICA (Institute of Contemporary Arts)

The Mall, SW1Y 5AH (7930 0493 information, 7930 3647 tickets, www.ica.org.uk). Piccadilly Circus tube or Charing Cross tube/rail. **Open** 11am-11pm Tue-Sun. *Galleries* (during exhibitions) 11am-6pm Tue, Wed, Fri-Sun; 11am-9pm Thur. **Admission** free. **Map** p71 B5 ㉑

Founded in 1947 by a collective of poets, artists and critics, the ICA has recently found itself somewhat adrift. The institute moved to the Mall in 1968 and set itself up as a venue for arthouse cinema, performance art, philosophical debates, exhibitions, art-themed club nights and anything else that might challenge convention – but 'convention' is much harder to challenge now that everyone's doing it. Director Gregor Muir has quietly developed some interesting ideas, including off-site exhibitions and lunchtime talks from top contemporary artists.

Restaurants

Inn the Park

St James's Park, SW1A 2BJ (7451 9999, www. peytonandbyrne.co.uk). St James's Park tube. **Open** *Summer* 8am-11pm Mon-Fri, 9am-10pm Sat, Sun. *Winter* 8am-5pm Mon-Fri; 9am-5pm Sat, Sun. **Main courses** £13-£18.50. **Map** p71 C5 ㉒ **British**

It's all about the location at this beautifully appointed and designed café-restaurant. The seasonal British cooking isn't always up to expectations, especially given the prices, but there is plenty on the plus side: staff are lovely, and the setting (overlooking the duck lake, with trees all around and the London Eye in the distance) is really wonderful.

ST JAMES'S

Green Park or Piccadilly Circus tube.

One of London's most refined residential areas, St James's was laid out in the 1660s for royal and aristocratic families, some of whom still live here. It's a rewarding district, a sedate bustle of intriguing mews and grand squares. Bordered by Piccadilly, Haymarket, the Mall and Green Park, the district is centred on **St James's Square**.

Just south of the square, **Pall Mall** is lined with members-only gentlemen's clubs (in the old-fashioned sense of the word). Polished nameplates reveal such prestigious establishments as the **Reform Club** (nos.104-105), site of Phileas Fogg's famous bet in *Around the World in Eighty Days*, and the former home of the **Institute of Directors** (no.123), which in 2015 briefly became (to quote the *Evening Standard*) 'London's poshest squat'; the IoD is now at no.116. Around the corner on St James's Street, the **Carlton Club** (no.69) is the official club of the Conservative Party, founded in 1832; until the club's rules were finally changed in 2008, Lady Thatcher was the only woman to have been granted full membership. The world's oldest fin-art auctioneers, **Christie's** (7839 9060, www. christies.com), is on King Street.

At the south end of St James's Street, **St James's Palace** was built for Henry VIII in the 1530s. Extensively remodelled over the centuries, the red-brick palace is still the official address of the Royal Court, even though every monarch since 1837 has lived at Buckingham Palace. Here, Mary Tudor surrendered Calais, Elizabeth I led the campaign against the Spanish Armada, and Charles I was confined before his 1649 execution. The palace is home to the Princess Royal (the title given to the monarch's eldest daughter, currently Princess Anne); it's closed to the public, but you can attend Sunday services at its historic **Chapel Royal** (1st Sun of mth, Oct-Good Friday; 8.30am, 11.15am).

Adjacent to St James's Palace is **Clarence House**, former residence of the Queen Mother; a few streets north, delightful **Spencer House** is the ancestral home of the family of the late Princess Diana. Across Marlborough Road lies the pocket-sized **Queen's Chapel**, designed by Inigo Jones in the 1620s for Charles I's Catholic queen Henrietta Maria, at a time when Catholic places of worship were officially banned. The Queen's Chapel can only be visited for Sunday services (Easter-July; 8.30am, 11.15am).

Sights & Museums

Clarence House

St James's Palace, The Mall, SW1 1BA (7766 7303, www.royalcollection.org.uk). Green Park tube. **Open** *Aug* 10am-4.30pm Mon-Fri; 10am-5.30pm Sat, Sun. Closed Sept-July. **Tours** £9.50; £5.50 reductions; free under-5s. **Map** p71 C3 ㉓

Currently the official residence of Prince Charles and the Duchess of Cornwall, this austere royal mansion was built between 1825 and 1827 for Prince William Henry, Duke of Clarence, who stayed on in the house after his coronation as King William IV. Designed by John Nash, the house has been much altered. Five receiving rooms and the late Queen Mother's British art collection are open to the public in August.

Spencer House

27 St James's Place, SW1A 1NR (7499 8620, www. spencerhouse.co.uk). Green Park tube. **Open** *Feb-July, Sept-Dec* 10.30am-5.45pm Sun. Last tour 4.45pm. Closed Jan, Aug. **Admission** £12; £10 reductions. Under-10s not allowed. **Map** p71 C3 ㉔

One of the last surviving private residences in St James's, this handsome mansion was designed for John Spencer by John Vardy, but was completed in 1766 by Hellenophile architect James Stuart, hence the mock Greek flourishes. Lady Georgiana, the 18th-century socialite and beauty – played by Keira Knightley in *The Duchess* (2008) – lived here, but the Spencers left generations before their most famous scion, Diana, married into the Windsor family. The palatial building has painstakingly restored interiors, and a wonderful garden, which is sometimes open to the general public).

EXPLORE

St James's Park. See p79.

Restaurants

Boulestin
*5 St James's Street, SW1A 1EF (7930 2030,
www.boulestin.com). Green Park tube.* **Open**
7am-3pm, 5-10.30pm Mon-Fri; 11am-3pm,
5-10.30pm Sat. **Main courses** £14.50-£32.50.
Set dinner (5-7pm) £19.50 2 courses; £24.50
3 courses. **Map** p71 C3 ❷ French
Named after Marcel Boulestin – a pioneer of pre-war
London cooking – this new Boulestin is no relation,
though it does pay homage to the era of the great
chef. The menu lists oeufs en gelée – a dish which,
much like old-school St James's, is preserved in aspic.
Classic French cooking at its best shines in dishes
such as daube of beef or boudin noir. A few dishes
seem almost daringly modern with their rocket and
preserved lemons; but for the most part, this menu
is as classic, French and retro as the grand setting.
▶ *The all-day Café Marcel at the same address is
cheaper and less formal, and serves good-value
pre- and post-theatre menus.*

★ Wolseley
*160 Piccadilly, W1J 9EB (7499 6996, www.
thewolseley.com). Green Park tube.* **Open**
7am-midnight Mon-Fri; 8am-midnight Sat;
8am-11pm Sun. **Main courses** £11.25-£44.75.
Cover £2. **Map** p71 B3 ❷ Brasserie
A self-proclaimed 'café-restaurant in the grand
European tradition', the Wolseley combines London
heritage and Viennese grandeur. The kitchen is
much celebrated for its breakfasts, and the scope
of the main menu is admirable. From oysters, steak
tartare or soufflé suisse, via wiener schnitzel or
grilled halibut with wilted spinach and béarnaise,
to Portuguese custard tart or apple strudel, there's
something for everyone. On Sunday afternoons,
three-tiered afternoon tea stands are in abundance.
▶ *Owners Chris Corbin and Jeremy King now run a
number of London's favourite venues, including the
Delaunay (see p147) and Bar Américain (see p114),
and have just opened their first hotel, the Beaumont
(see p348).*

Pubs & Bars

★ Dukes Bar
*Dukes Hotel, 35 St James's Place, SW1A 1NY
(7491 4840, www.dukeshotel.com). Green Park
tube.* **Open** 2-11pm Mon-Sat; 4-10.30pm Sun.
Map p71 C3 ❷
If you want to go out for a single cocktail, strong
and expensive and very well made, go to Dukes. It's
in a luxury hotel, but everyone gets the warmest of
welcomes. There are three small rooms, all decorated
in discreetly opulent style; you feel cocooned. The
bar is famous for the theatre of its Martini-making
– at the table, from a trolley, using vermouth made
exclusively for them at the Sacred distillery in
Highgate – but other drinks are just as good.

Dukes Bar.

Shops & Services

DR Harris
*29 St James's Street, SW1A 1HB (7930 3915,
www.drharris.co.uk). Green Park or Piccadilly
Circus tube.* **Open** 8.30am-6pm Mon-Fri;
9.30am-5pm Sat. **Map** p71 B3 ❷ Health
& beauty
Founded in 1790, this venerable chemist has a royal
warrant – and is on the verge of reopening after a
major refurb and expansion, probably in September
2015. You can still expect wood-and-glass cabinets
full of bottles, jars and old-fashioned shaving
brushes. Until the grand day, the shop can be found
round the corner at 35 Bury Street.

Floris
*89 Jermyn Street, SW1Y 6JH (7930 2885,
www.florislondon.com). Green Park tube.*
Open 9.30am-6pm Mon-Sat. **Map** p71 B3 ❷
Health & beauty
Enterprising young Spaniard Juan Floris set up his
fragrance shop in 1730 and it has been run by the
same family ever since. One imagines not too much
has changed. Everything is behind glass cabinets
and oak panelled counters in the manner of an
old-fashioned apothecary, and smartly dressed men
and women guide you through the selection process;
much more civilised than a department store.

★ Fortnum & Mason
*181 Piccadilly, W1A 1ER (7734 8040, www.
fortnumandmason.co.uk). Green Park or Piccadilly
Circus tube.* **Open** 10am-8pm Mon-Sat; noon-6pm
Sun. **Map** p71 B3 ❸ Department store
In business for over 300 years, Fortnum & Mason
is as historic as it is inspiring. A sweeping spiral
staircase soars through the four-storey building,
while light floods down from a central glass dome.
The iconic eau de nil blue and gold colour scheme
with flashes of rose pink abounds on both the
store design and the packaging of the fabulous

EXPLORE

ground-floor treats, such as chocolates, biscuits, teas and preserves. A food hall in the basement has a good range of fresh produce; Fortnum's Bees honey comes from beehives on top of the building. There are various eateries, including an ice-cream parlour. The famous hampers start from £50 – though they rise to a whopping £2,000 for the most luxurious.

James J Fox

19 St James's Street, SW1A 1ES (7930 3787, www. jjfox.co.uk). Green Park tube. **Open** 9.30am-5.45pm Mon-Wed, Fri; 9.30am-9.30pm Thur; 9.30am-5pm Sat. **Map** p71 B3 ③ **Cigars**
There are other cigar shops in London, but Fox is the grandest and most storied. Oscar Wilde died owing them money and the iconic image of Winston Churchill, with a cigar clenched between his teeth, is down to the fact he used to buy his Montecristos here. It's worth a visit just to see the clientele: a curious mixture of ageing Euro playboys, old Etonians and Mayfair gents. There's also a small museum.

Lock & Co Hatters

6 St James's Street, SW1A 1EF (7930 8874, www.lockhatters.co.uk). Green Park tube. **Open** 9am-5.30pm Mon-Fri; 9.30am-5pm Sat. **Map** p71 C3 ③ **Milliners**
Lock & Co is perhaps the most famous hat shop in the world. It is certainly one of the oldest, dating from 1759, and has been frequented by such names as Charlie Chaplin and Admiral Lord Nelson. But, history aside, it is simply very good. It has one of the most comprehensive selections of classic hats to be found anywhere in London: bowlers, top hats, homburgs, berets, panamas – all exquisitely made.

GREEN PARK & HYDE PARK CORNER

Green Park or Hyde Park Corner tube.

The flat green expanse just beyond the Ritz on Piccadilly is **Green Park**; it's rather dull in itself (except in spring, when the daffodils jolly things up), but does make a very pleasant middle section of a walk through three Royal Parks, connecting St James's Park (*see p79*) to Hyde Park (*see p92*).

Work your way along Piccadilly, following the northern edge of Green Park past the queue outside the **Hard Rock Café** (where the Vault's displays of memorabilia are free to visit and open every day; www.hardrock.com) to the Duke of Wellington's old home, **Apsley House**, opposite **Wellington Arch**. This is hectic **Hyde Park Corner**; Buckingham Palace (*see p79*) is just a short walk south-east, while Hyde Park and the upper-crust enclave of Belgravia are to the west, but it also has a collection of memorials that are worth lingering over. The newest is the **Bomber Command Memorial**. Unveiled in 2012, it recognises the sacrifice of the 55,573 men of

Bomber Command, killed between 1939 and 1945 as they pulverised Nazi-held Europe into submission. But we find Charles Sargeant Jagger's thoughtful tribute to the 49,076 men of the Royal Regiment of Artillery, slain between 1914 and 1919, to be more deeply moving. It's both vast – a huge Portland stone slab with giant gunners on three sides – and strangely muted, with a dead soldier lying peacefully in giant hobnail boots on the monument's north side.

Sights & Museums

Apsley House

149 Piccadilly, W1J 7NT (7499 5676, www.english-heritage.org.uk). Hyde Park Corner tube. **Open** *Nov-Mar* 10am-4pm Sat, Sun. *Apr-Oct* 11am-5pm Wed-Sun. *Tours* by arrangement. **Admission** £6.90; £4.10-£6.20 reductions; £23.10 family; free under-5s. *Joint ticket with Wellington Arch* £8.90; £5.30-£8 reductions; £23.10 family. **Map** p71 C1 ③
Called No.1 London because it was the first London building encountered on the road to the city from the village of Kensington, Apsley House was built by Robert Adam in the 1770s. The Duke of Wellington kept it as his London home for 35 years. Although his descendants still live here, several rooms are open to the public, providing a superb feel for the man and his era. Admire the extravagant porcelain dinnerware and plates or ask for a demonstration of the crafty mirrors in the scarlet and gilt picture gallery, where a fine Velázquez and a Correggio hang near Goya's portrait of the Iron Duke after he defeated the French in 1812. This was a last-minute edit: X-rays have revealed that Wellington's head was painted over that of Joseph Bonaparte, Napoleon's brother.
▶ *Atmospheric twilight tours are held here in winter.*

Wellington Arch

Hyde Park Corner, W1J 7JZ (7930 2726, www.english-heritage.org.uk). Hyde Park Corner tube. **Open** *Apr-Oct* 10am-5pm daily. *Nov-Mar* 10am-4pm daily. **Admission** £4.20; £2.50-£3.80 reductions; £23.10 family; free under-5s. *Joint ticket with Apsley House* £8.90; £5.30-£8 reductions; £23.10 family. **Map** p71 D1 ③
Built in the late 1820s to mark Britain's triumph over Napoleonic France, Decimus Burton's Wellington Arch was initially topped with an out-of-proportion equestrian statue of Wellington. However, Captain Adrian Jones's 38-ton bronze *Peace Descending on the Quadriga of War* has finished it with a flourish since 1912. The Arch has three floors, with an English Heritage bookshop and various displays, covering the history of the arch and the Blue Plaques scheme, and in the Quadriga Gallery providing space for excellent temporary exhibitions. There are great views from the balcony in winter (leafy trees obscure the sightlines in spring and summer).

EXPLORE

South Kensington & Chelsea

There can be few cities in the world with a square mile so crammed with cultural highlights as you'll find in South Kensington: three of the world's greatest museums, some extraordinary colleges, a grand concert hall and an expansive park.

Neighbouring Knightsbridge, on the other hand, has no cultural pretensions: a certain type of Londoner comes here to spend, spend, spend – or, at least, to hang around with the non-doms and hyperwealthy incomers who are spend, spend, spending in the designer shops and world-famous department stores. Chelsea, running between them and the river, has long since left its raffish youth behind – but there are still pleasures to be found amid its red-brick gentility.

EXPLORE

Science Museum.

Don't Miss

1 Science Museum How the world works (p87).

2 Harrods Legendary department store (p95).

3 Victoria & Albert Museum Applied arts from around the world (p90).

4 Chelsea Physic Garden Botanical marvel (p96).

5 Natural History Museum Life on earth from prehistory to today (p87).

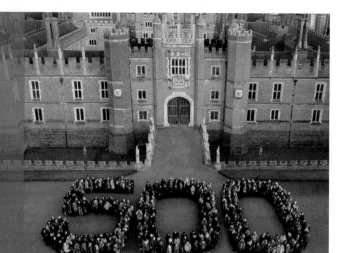

SOUTH KENSINGTON

Gloucester Road or South Kensington tube.

As far as cultural and academic institutions are concerned, this is the land of plenty. It was Prince Albert who oversaw the inception of its world-class museums, colleges and concert hall, using the profits of the 1851 Great Exhibition; the area was nicknamed 'Albertopolis' in his honour. You'll find the **Natural History Museum**, the **Science Museum** and the **Victoria & Albert Museum**, **Imperial College**, the **Royal College of Art** and the **Royal College of Music** (Prince Consort Road, 7591 4300; call for details of the musical-instrument museum). The last forms a unity with the **Royal Albert Hall** (*see p283*), open since 1871 and variously used for boxing, motor shows, marathons, table-tennis tournaments, fascist rallies and rock concerts. Directly opposite is the wonderfully pompous **Albert Memorial**.

Sights & Museums

FREE Albert Memorial
Kensington Gardens (0300 061 2000, www. tourguides.co.uk). South Kensington tube. **Tours** *Mar-Dec* 2pm, 3pm 1st Sun of mth. **Tickets** £7; £6 reductions. **Map** p88 B2 ❶
'I would rather not be made the prominent feature of such a monument,' was Prince Albert's reported response when the subject of his commemoration arose. Hard, then, to imagine what he would have made of this extraordinary thing, unveiled 15 years after his death. Created by Sir George Gilbert Scott, it centres on a gilded Albert holding a catalogue of the 1851 Great Exhibition, guarded on four corners by the continents of Africa, America, Asia and Europe. The pillars are crowned with bronze statues of the sciences, and the frieze at the base depicts major artists, architects and musicians. It's one of London's most dramatic monuments.

★ FREE Natural History Museum
Cromwell Road, SW7 5BD (7942 5000, www.nhm. ac.uk). South Kensington tube. **Open** 10am-5.50pm daily. **Admission** free. Special exhibitions vary. *Tours* free. **Map** p88 C4 ❷
Both a research institution and a fabulous museum, the NHM opened in Alfred Waterhouse's purpose-built, Romanesque palazzo on the Cromwell Road in 1881. Now joined by the splendid Darwin Centre extension, the original building still looks quite magnificent. The pale blue and terracotta façade just about prepares you for the natural wonders within.

Taking up the full length of the vast entrance hall is the cast of a *Diplodocus* skeleton. A left turn leads into the west wing, or Blue Zone, where long queues form to see animatronic dinosaurs – especially the endlessly popular *T rex*. Here too, in

the Mammals Hall, is the actual skeleton of a blue whale, staggering in its scale; it is planned that the whale will replace the *Diplodocus* replica in the entrance hall in 2017. A display on biology features an illuminated, man-sized model of a foetus in the womb along with graphic diagrams of how it might have got there.

A right turn from the central hall leads past the 'Creepy Crawlies' exhibition to the Green Zone. Stars include a cross-section through a Giant Sequoia tree and an amazing array of stuffed birds, including the chance to compare the egg of a hummingbird, – smaller than a little finger nail – with that of an elephant bird (now extinct), almost football-sized.

Beyond is the Red Zone. 'Earth's Treasury' is a mine of information on a variety of precious metals, gems and crystals; 'From the Beginning' is a brave attempt to give the expanse of geological time a human perspective.

Many of the museum's 22 million insect and plant specimens are housed in the new Darwin Centre, where they take up nearly 17 miles of shelving. With its eight-storey Cocoon, this is also home to the museum's research scientists, who can be watched at work. But a great deal of this amazing institution is hidden from public view, given over to labs and specialised storage.

Outside, the delightful Wildlife Garden (Apr-Oct only) showcases a range of British lowland habitats, including a 'Bee Tree', a hollow tree trunk that opens to reveal a busy hive. *Photo p90.*
▶ *Especially in school holidays, there are often huge queues at the main entrance from Cromwell Road. Try the side entrance from Exhibition Road, instead: it is usually less busy, it provides a pretty impressive introduction to the collections, past a newly installed* Stegosaurus *skeleton and up an escalator into the Earth Galleries.*

★ FREE Science Museum
Exhibition Road, SW7 2DD (switchboard 7942 4000, information 0870 870 4868, www. sciencemuseum.org.uk). South Kensington tube. **Open** 10am-6pm daily. **Admission** free. Special exhibitions vary. **Map** p88 C3 ❸
The Science Museum is a celebration of the wonders of technology in the service of our daily lives. On the ground floor, the shop – selling brilliant toys, not least because you can pretend they're educational – is part of the 'Energy Hall', which introduces the museum's collections with impressive 18th-century steam engines. In 'Exploring Space', rocket science and the lunar landings are illustrated by dramatically lit mock-ups and full-size models, before the museum gears up for its core collection in 'Making the Modern World'. Introduced by Puffing Billy, the world's oldest steam locomotive (built in 1815), the gallery also contains Stephenson's Rocket. Also here are the Apollo 10 command module, classic cars and an absorbing collection of everyday technological marvels from 1750 up to the present.

EXPLORE

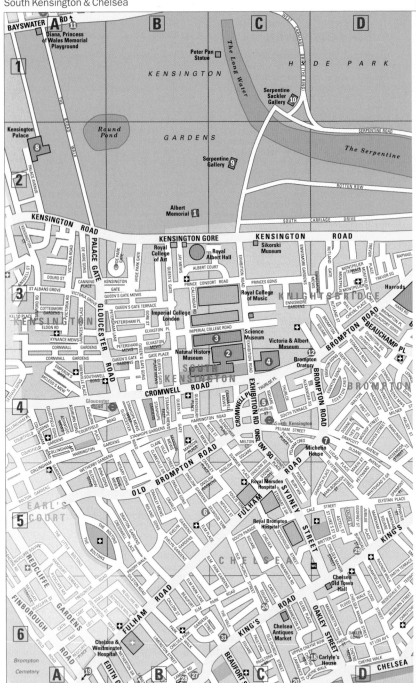

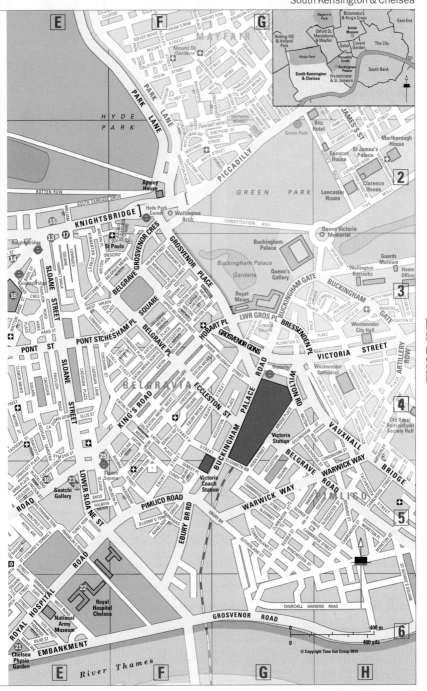

EXPLORE

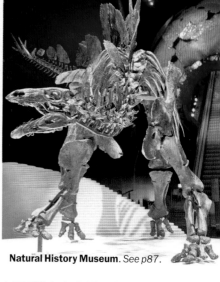

Natural History Museum. *See p87.*

In the main body of the museum, the second floor holds displays on computing, marine engineering and mathematics; the third floor is dedicated to flight, among other things, including the hands-on Launchpad gallery, which has levers, pulleys, explosions and all manner of experiments for children (and their associated grown-ups). On the fifth floor, you'll find an old-fashioned but intriguing display on the science and art of medicine.

Beyond 'Making the Modern World', bathed in an eerie blue light, the three floors of the Wellcome Wing are where the museum makes sure it stays on the cutting edge of science. On the ground floor, 'Antenna' is a web-savvy look at breaking science stories, displaying video interviews and Q&As with real research scientists alongside the weird new objects they've been working on. Upstairs is the enjoyable and troubling 'Who Am I?' gallery. A dozen silver pods surround brightly lit cases of objects with engaging interactive displays – from a cartoon of ethical dilemmas that introduces you to your dorsolateral prefrontal cortex to a chance to find out what gender your brain is. Compelling objects include a jellyfish that's 'technically immortal', the statistically average British man (he's called Jose),a pound of human fat, displayed alongside a gastric band, and half of Charles Babbage's brain (the other half is in the Hunterian Museum).

The second floor has a couple of the museum's newer additions. There's the Media Space, for excellent temporary exhibitions drawn from the museum's impressive photographic archive, and – since October 2014 – 'Information Age', the UK's first permanent gallery dedicated to the history of communications technology. It follows developments from the 19th-century establishment of an international telegraph network through broadcasting all the way up to the worldwide web.

★ FREE Victoria & Albert Museum

Cromwell Road, SW7 2RL (7942 2000, www.vam.ac.uk). South Kensington tube. **Open** 10am-5.45pm Mon-Thur, Sat, Sun; 10am-10pm Fri. *Tours* 10.30am, 12.30am, 1.30pm, 3.30pm daily. **Admission** free. Special exhibitions vary. **Map** p88 C4 ❹

The V&A is one of the world's – let alone London's – most magnificent museums, its foundation stone laid on this site by Queen Victoria in her last official public engagement in 1899. It is a superb showcase for applied arts from around the world, appreciably calmer than its tearaway cousins on the other side of Exhibition Road. Some 150 grand galleries on seven floors contain countless pieces of furniture, ceramics, sculpture, paintings, posters, jewellery, metalwork, glass, textiles and dress, spanning several centuries. Items are grouped by theme, origin or age: for advice, tap the patient staff, who field a formidable combination of leaflets, floor plans, general knowledge and polite concern.

Highlights include the seven Raphael Cartoons painted in 1515 as tapestry designs for the Sistine Chapel; the finest collection of Italian Renaissance sculpture outside Italy; the Ardabil carpet, the world's oldest and arguably most splendid floor covering, in the Jameel Gallery of Islamic Art; and the Luck of Edenhall, a 13th-century glass beaker from Syria. The fashion galleries run from 18th-century court dress right up to contemporary chiffon numbers; the architecture gallery has videos, models, plans and descriptions of various styles; and the photography collection holds over 500,000 images.

Over more than a decade, the V&A's ongoing FuturePlan transformation has been a revelation. The completely refurbished Medieval & Renaissance Galleries are stunning, but there are many other eye-catching new or redisplayed exhibits: they were preceded by the restored mosaic floors and beautiful stained glass of the 14th- to 17th-century sculpture rooms, just off the central John Madejski Garden, and followed by the Furniture Galleries – another immediate hit on opening. On a smaller scale, the Gilbert Collection of silver, gold and bejewelled ornaments arrived from Somerset House (*see p147*); the Ceramics Galleries have been renovated and supplemented with an eye-catching bridge; and the Theatre & Performance Galleries took over where Covent Garden's defunct Theatre Museum left off.

Its the range of galleries that fascinates us most. On one hand, the V&A has turned Gallery 74 into a 'Rapid Response Collection', an adaptable space that aims to keep abreast of contemporary design and architecture, particularly work relating to important events and current affairs; on the other, the grand openings continue with the septet of ambitious 'Europe 1600-1800' galleries, a £12.5m development built around a stunning 12ft-long table fountain – carefully reconstructed from 18th-century fragments – and taking a chronological and thematic approach to European clothes, furniture and other artefacts. And then there are the magnificent Cast Courts – one of which, the Weston (Gallery 46b), has finally opened again for the public to ogle an 18ft-high plaster-cast of *David* and other monumental sculptures in a painstakingly restored double-height gallery that dates to 1873.

▶ *The V&A also runs the Museum of Childhood in Bethnal Green (see p211).*

Restaurants

Daquise
20 Thurloe Street, SW7 2LT (7589 6117, www.daquise.co.uk). South Kensington tube. **Open** noon-11pm daily. **Main courses** £15-£22. **Set lunch** (noon-4pm Mon-Fri) £9 2 courses. **Map** p88 C4 ❺ **Polish**
In 2013, regulars were distressed at news that this much-loved grande dame of London Polish restaurants (established 1947) was to close – but staff and the restaurant's previous owners rallied round to save it. In the shabby-chic, light and airy interior, enlivened with fresh flowers, robust, flavourful, no-nonsense traditional dishes are served with great charm. Classic cold starters of meltingly tender herring with cream, apple, onion and flax oil, or beetroot with subtly warming horseradish, are ladled directly from capacious earthenware bowls, while mains are assembled directly at the table from well-worn saucepans, borne by the chefs who lovingly prepared the dishes.

Pubs & Bars

Anglesea Arms
15 Selwood Terrace, SW7 3QG (7373 7960, www.metropolitanpubcompany.com). South Kensington tube. **Open** 11am-11pm Mon-Sat; noon-10.30pm Sun. *Food served* noon-3pm, 6-10pm Mon-Fri; noon-5pm, 6-10pm Sat; noon-5pm, 6-9.30pm Sun. **Map** p88 B5 ❻
The local of both Charles Dickens and DH Lawrence, this old boozer is packed on summer evenings, the front terrace and main bar filled with professional blokes chugging back ale, and their female equivalents putting bottles of Sancerre on expenses. But the Anglesea has always had more aura than the average South Kensington hostelry; perhaps it's because of the link with the Great Train Robbery, which was reputedly planned here.

Shops & Services

The **V&A** has a superb gift shop, stuffed with stylish exhibition-related buys, the **Science Museum** has a lively range of geek-free science presents for kids and the **Natural History Museum** has cute cuddly dinosaurs.

Conran Shop
Michelin House, 81 Fulham Road, SW3 6RD (7589 7401, www.conranshop.co.uk). South Kensington tube. **Open** 10am-6pm Mon, Tue, Fri; 10am-7pm Wed, Thur; 10am-6.30pm Sat; noon-6pm Sun. **Map** p88 D4 ❼ **Homewares**
Sir Terence Conran's flagship store in the Fulham Road's beautiful 1909 Michelin Building showcases furniture and design for every room in the house as well as the garden. In addition to design classics, such as the Eames DAR chair, there are plenty of

EXPLORE

Victoria & Albert Museum.

portable accessories, gadgets, books, stationery and toiletries that make great gifts or souvenirs. **Other location** 55 Marylebone High Street, W1U 5HS (7723 2223).

HYDE PARK & KENSINGTON GARDENS

Hyde Park Corner, Knightsbridge, Lancaster Gate or Queensway tube.

At one and a half miles long and about a mile wide, **Hyde Park** (0300 061 2000, www. royalparks.org.uk) is one of the largest of London's Royal Parks. The land was appropriated in 1536 from the monks of Westminster Abbey by Henry VIII for hunting deer. Although opened to the public in the early 1600s, the parks were favoured only by the upper echelons of society.

At the end of the 17th century, William III, averse to the dank air of Whitehall Palace, relocated to **Kensington Palace**. A corner of Hyde Park was sectioned off to make grounds for the palace and closed to the public, until King George II opened it on Sundays to those wearing formal dress. Nowadays, **Kensington Gardens** is delineated from Hyde Park only by the line of the Serpentine and the Long Water. Beside the Long Water is a bronze statue of **Peter Pan**, erected in 1912: it was in Kensington Gardens beside the Round Pond eight years earlier that playwright JM Barrie met Jack Llewelyn Davies, the boy who was the inspiration for Peter. The **Diana, Princess of Wales Memorial Playground** (*see p253*) is a kids' favourite, as is Kathryn Gustafson's ring-shaped **Princess Diana Memorial Fountain**. Near the fountain, Simon Gudgeon's giant bird *Isis* was in 2009 the first sculpture added to the park for half a century. There are changing exhibitions of contemporary art at the **Serpentine Gallery**, which also has a Zaha Hadid-designed counterpart just across the bridge.

The **Serpentine** itself is London's oldest boating lake, home to ducks, coots, swans, tufty-headed grebes and, every summer, gently perspiring blokes rowing their children or lovers about. The lake is at the bottom of Hyde Park, which isn't a beautiful park, but is of historic interest. The legalisation of public assembly in the park led to the establishment of **Speakers' Corner** in 1872 (close to Marble Arch tube), where political and religious ranters – sane and otherwise – still have the floor every Sunday afternoon. Marx, Lenin, Orwell and the Pankhursts all spoke here. It has made the park a traditional destination for protest marches: notably the million opponents of the Iraq War in 2003; more recently, trades union protests against government austerity measures in 2012. There is also a moving memorial in the south-east corner of the park. On 7 July 2005, 52 people were killed by Islamist suicide bombers as they made their way to work. Their commemoration, set between the Lovers' Walk and busy Park Lane, consists of 52 ten-foot-tall, square steel columns, one for each fatality; each is marked with the date, time and location of that person's death.

The park perimeter is popular with skaters, as well as with bike- and horse-riders. If you're exploring on foot and the vast expanses defeat you, look out for the **Liberty Drives** (May-Oct). Driven by volunteers, these electric buggies, each with space for a wheelchair, pick up groups of sightseers and ferry them around; there's no fare, but offer a donation if you can.

Serpentine Sackler Gallery.

Sights & Museums

Kensington Palace

Kensington Gardens, W8 4PX (information 0844 482 7777, reservations 0844 482 7799, www.hrp.org.uk). High Street Kensington or Queensway tube. **Open** *Mar-Oct* 10am-6pm daily. *Nov-Feb* 10am-5pm daily. **Admission** £17.50; £14.90 reductions; free under-16s. **Map** p88 A2 ❸

Sir Christopher Wren extended this Jacobean mansion to palatial proportions on the instructions of William III, initiating the palace's long love affair with royalty – which culminated with the floral memorials for one particular resident, Princess Diana, that were placed at the palace's gate after her fatal accident in 1997. Wren's work too was adapted, under George I, with the addition of intricate trompe l'oeil ceilings and staircases. Visitors can now follow a whimsical trail that focuses on four 'stories' of former residents – Diana, of course; William and Mary, and Mary's sister Queen Anne; Georges I and II; Queen Victoria – unearthing the facts through handily placed 'newspapers'. Artefacts include paintings by the likes of Tintoretto, contemporary art and fashion installations, and even Victoria's (tiny) wedding dress.

★ FREE Serpentine & Serpentine Sackler Galleries

Kensington Gardens, near Albert Memorial, W2 3XA (7402 6075, www.serpentinegalleries.org). Lancaster Gate or South Kensington tube. **Open** 10am-6pm Tue-Sun. **Admission** free; donations appreciated. **Map** p88 C2 ❾ & C1 ❿

The Serpentine Gallery – much-loved for its sometimes challenging exhibitions of contemporary art – originally had just the one secluded location in a small 1930s tea-house building south-west of the Long Water and Serpentine, into which were squeezed exhibition spaces and a bijou bookshop. Here, the rolling two-monthly programme of exhibitions features a mix of up-to-the-minute artists and edgy career retrospectives, but – perhaps symbolic of the gallery's limitations of space – every spring it also commissions a renowned architect, who's never before built in the UK, to build a temporary pavilion outside. The pavilion then hosts a packed programme of cultural events (June to September).

A permanent solution to the issue of space was found in 2013, when the gallery opened a second location, the Serpentine Sackler, just across the bridge from the original. Devoted to emerging art in all forms, the Sackler is a Grade II-listed, Palladian former gunpowder store, with a clean-lined restaurant over which architect Zaha Hadid has cast a billowing white cape of a roof.

▶ *Hadid designed the first Serpentine Pavilion back in 2000, but her singular architectural vision is now represented in London by both the Sackler and the Aquatics Centre in the Olympic Park (see p241).*

Restaurants

★ Le Café Anglais

8 Porchester Gardens, W2 4DB (7221 1415, www.lecafeanglais.co.uk). Bayswater tube. **Open** noon-3.30pm, 6.30-10.30pm Mon-Thur; noon-3.30pm, 6.30-11pm Fri; 11am-3.30pm, 6.30-11pm Sat; noon-3.30pm, 6.30-10pm Sun. **Main courses** £9.50-£27.50. **Map** p88 A1 ⓫ Modern European

The far side of the park from Knightsbridge and South Ken, this celebrated brasserie looks as good as when it opened in 2008, with its art deco lines, tall leaded windows and graceful grey-green banquettes. At one end, beneath a stunning chandelier, is the café/oyster bar; at the other, the open kitchen. The appealing menu is nicely varied, from raw, cured and smoked seafood and meat (oysters, pickled herrings, rabbit rillettes) via assorted appetisers (the famous parmesan custard with anchovy toast) to straightforward bistro fare (omelette, burger, fish pie) and dishes such as roast chicken leg with oregano and skordalia.

KNIGHTSBRIDGE

Knightsbridge tube.

Knightsbridge in the 11th century was a village celebrated for its taverns, highwaymen and the legend that two knights once fought to the death on the bridge spanning the Westbourne River (later dammed to form Hyde Park's Serpentine lake). In modern Knightsbridge, urban princesses would be too busy unsheathing the credit card to notice such a farrago. Voguish **Harvey Nichols** holds court at the top of **Sloane Street**, which leads down to Sloane Square. Expensive brands – Gucci, Prada, Chanel – dominate. East of Sloane Street is **Belgravia**, characterised by a cluster of embassies around **Belgrave Square**. Hidden behind the stucco-clad parades fronting the square are numerous mews, worth exploring for the pubs they conceal, notably the **Nag's Head** (53 Kinnerton Street, SW1X 8ED, 7235 1135).

For many tourists, Knightsbridge means one thing: **Harrods**. From its olive-green awning to its green-coated doormen, it's an instantly recognisable retail legend. Further along is the imposing **Brompton Oratory**.

Sights & Museums

FREE Brompton Oratory

Thurloe Place, Brompton Road, SW7 2RP (7808 0900, www.bromptonoratory.com). South Kensington tube. **Open** 6.30am-8pm daily. **Admission** free; donations appreciated. **Map** p88 D4 ⓬

The second-biggest Catholic church in the country (after Westminster Cathedral; *see p78*) is formally the Church of the Immaculate Heart of Mary, but

Harrods.

almost universally known as the Brompton Oratory. Completed in 1884, it feels older, partly because of the Baroque Italianate style but also because much of the decoration pre-dates the structure: Mazzuoli's 17th-century apostle statues, for example, are from Siena cathedral. The church is popular with young, traditionally minded Catholics. The 11am Solemn Mass sung in Latin on Sundays is enchanting, as are Vespers, at 3.30pm; the website has details.

▶ *During the Cold War, KGB agents used the church as a dead-letter box.*

Restaurants

There's a branch of the popular – and self-explanatory – mini-chain **Burger & Lobster** (*see p127*) in **Harvey Nichols**.

★ Bar Boulud
Mandarin Oriental Hyde Park, 66 Knightsbridge, SW1X 7LA (7201 3899, www.barboulud.com). Knightsbridge tube. **Open** noon-11pm Mon-Sat; noon-10pm Sun. **Main courses** £13-£32. **Map** p89 E3 ⑬ French
Overseen by renowned chef Daniel Boulud, the restaurant has an eye-catching view of the open-plan kitchen, where chefs work in zen-like calm. Charcuterie from Gilles Verot is a big draw, as are the elegant French brasserie options and finger-licking American staples. We've had burgers here and loved every bite – try a beef patty topped with pulled pork and green chilli mayonnaise. On our latest visit, we enjoyed such culinary gems as a robust french onion soup, resplendent with caramelised onions and topped with molten gruyère.

★ Zuma
5 Raphael Street, SW7 1DL (7584 1010, www.zumarestaurant.com). Knightsbridge tube. **Open** *Restaurant* noon-2.45pm, 6-10.45pm Mon-Fri; 12.30-3.15pm, 6-10.45pm Sat, Sun. *Bar* noon-11pm Mon-Fri; 12.30-11pm Sat, Sun. **Main courses** £14.80-£70. **Map** p89 E3 ⑭ Japanese
Out of simplicity can come excellence, and the food at Zuma is a case in point. The venue may be swish but when it comes to the food, much of the wow factor is down to high-class ingredients that haven't been messed around with too much. Own-made silken tofu, presented in a cedar saké cup, is rich, creamy and light. More indulgent dishes such as spicy miso with lobster have a clarity of flavour. Give the saké list a proper look too: there are more than 40 to choose from.

Pubs & Bars

Mandarin Bar
Mandarin Oriental Hyde Park, 66 Knightsbridge, SW1X 7LA (7201 3724, www.mandarinoriental. com/london). Knightsbridge tube. **Open** 10.30am -1.30am Mon-Sat; 10.30am-12.30am Sun. **Map** p89 E2 ⑮
The Mandarin Oriental is in part famous as the location of Heston Blumenthal's Dinner, so some customers at the bar are praying for a walk-in space to become available in the restaurant. If you're going to choose a waiting room, you really couldn't do much better than this. The room is dazzling, with a central bar and an array of glass, wood and marble. The drinks are done expertly. House cocktails are devised with good sense, and the classics are well

handled – and with serving sizes that match the high prices. They're combined with polished, attentive service and excellent bar snacks.

Shops & Services

Harrods

87-135 Brompton Road, SW1X 7XL (7730 1234, www.harrods.com). Knightsbridge tube. **Open** 10am-8pm Mon-Sat; noon-6pm Sun (browsing from 11.30am). **Map** p89 E3 ⑲ **Department store**
It might be unashamedly ostentatious, stuffed with tourists and in possession of the world's most vulgar statue (Dodi and Diana in bronze by the Egyptian escalators), but Harrods – London's most-famous department store – is still spectacular. Serious shoppers browse the elegantly tiled and fragrant food halls on the ground floor or the wealth of exclusives in the beauty halls. But indulge the excesses too: Harrods has an art gallery, a stunning new interiors department and a kitchenware floor that hosts live cooking lessons from household names. Got kids? Head straight to Toy Kingdom on the third floor, with its enchanted forest, intergalactic science lab and bespoke sweets-maker. Elsewhere, Harrods excels at shoes – with a gargantuan footwear department stocking labels such as Ferragamo, Charlotte Olympia and Giuseppe Zanotti – and the Fashion Lab, on the fourth floor, is dedicated to young designer labels such as Zadig & Voltaire, Wildfox and the Kooples.

Harvey Nichols

109-125 Knightsbridge, SW1X 7RJ (7235 5000, www.harveynichols.com). Knightsbridge tube. **Open** 10am-8pm Mon-Sat; noon-6pm Sun. **Map** p89 E3 ⑰ **Department store**
Once the watchword for luxury Knightsbridge shopping, Harvey Nicks lost ground to Liberty (*see p115*), Selfridges (*see p106*) and even Harrods, which were engaging better with their customers and seemed to get the idea of hosting dynamic shopping events. But it's beginning to fight back: there's the beauty hall that will provide bespoke nail polish and scents, and 2015's Sneaker Concept for high-fashion sports shoes. The rails are full of top labels such as Alexander Wang, Balenciaga and Givenchy, and there's an excellent array of accessories and beauty buys from luxurious brands such as Tom Ford and COR (whose soap contains real silver). Finish off proceedings with lunch on the fifth floor, where the buzzy food department is located and a branch of Burger & Lobster (*see p127*).

CHELSEA

Sloane Square tube then various buses.

Chelsea is where London's wealthy classes play in cultural and geographical isolation. Originally a fishing hamlet, the area was a 'village of palaces'

by the 16th century, home to the likes of Henry VIII's ill-fated advisor Sir Thomas More. Artists and poets (Whistler, Carlyle, Wilde) followed from the 1880s, before the fashionistas arrived with the opening of Mary Quant's Bazaar in 1955. Soon after, Chelsea had acquired a raffish reputation and was at the forefront of successive youth-culture revolutions. Synonymous with the Swinging Sixties and immortalised by punk, the dissipated phase of the **King's Road** is now a matter for historians as the street teems with pricey fashion houses and air-conditioned poodle parlours. Yet on a sunny day, it does make a vivid stroll. For one thing, you don't have to take yourself as seriously as the locals. And for another, the area is figuratively rich in historical associations, and literally so with the expensive red-brick houses that slumber down leafy mews and charming, cobbled side streets.

At the top (east end) of the King's Road is **Sloane Square**. It's named after Sir Hans Sloane, whose collections formed the basis of the British Museum (*see p150*). The shaded benches in the middle of the square provide a lovely counterpoint to the looming façades of Tiffany & Co and the enormous Peter Jones department store, in a 1930s building with excellent views from its top-floor café. A certain edginess is lent to proceedings by the **Royal Court Theatre** (*see p288*), which shocked the nation with its 1956 première of John Osborne's *Look Back in Anger*.

To escape the bustle and fumes, head to **Duke of York Square**, a pedestrianised enclave of boutiques and restaurants presided over by a statue of Sir Hans. In the summer, the cooling fountains attract hordes of children, their parents sitting to watch from the outdoor café tables or taking advantage of the Saturday food market. The square is also home to the mercilessly modern art of the **Saatchi Gallery**, housed in former military barracks.

The once-adventurous shops on the King's Road are now a mix of trendier-than-thou fashion houses and high-street chains. Wander Cale Street for some pleasing boutiques, or head for the **Chelsea Farmers' Market** on adjoining Sydney Street to find a clutter of artfully distressed rustic sheds housing restaurants and shops selling everything from cigars to garden products. Sydney Street leads to **St Luke's Church**, where Charles Dickens married Catherine Hogarth in 1836.

Towards the western end of the King's Road is **Bluebird**, a dramatic art deco former motor garage housing a café, a restaurant and the hip **Shop at Bluebird**, one of Chelsea's most notable remaining boutiques. A little further up the road, the **World's End** store (no.430) occupies what was once Vivienne Westwood's notorious leather- and fetishwear boutique Sex; a green-haired Johnny Rotten auditioned for the Sex

EXPLORE

Pistols here in 1975 by singing along to an Alice Cooper record on the shop's jukebox.

Running parallel to the King's Road, Chelsea's riverside has long been noted for its nurseries and gardens, lending a village air that befits a place of retirement for the former British soldiers living in the **Royal Hospital Chelsea**. In summer, the Chelsea Pensioners, as they're known, regularly don red coats and tricorn hats when venturing beyond the gates. The Royal Hospital's lovely gardens host the **Chelsea Flower Show** (*see p41*) each spring. Next door, the **National Army Museum** is closed until late 2016 for major refurbishment.

West from the river end of Royal Hospital Road is **Cheyne Walk**. Its river-view benches remain good spots for a sit-down, but the tranquillity of the **Chelsea Physic Garden** (*see p97* **Take Your Physic**) – established on land bought by Sir Hans Sloane – is the real treat.

Further west on Cheyne Walk, the park benches of **Chelsea Embankment Gardens** face Albert Bridge, where signs still order troops to 'Break step when marching over this bridge'. In the small gardens, you'll find a statue of the great historian Thomas Carlyle – the 'sage of Chelsea', whose home is preserved (**Carlyle's House**). Nearby, a gold-faced statue of Sir Thomas More looks out over the river from the garden of **Chelsea Old Church**, where he once sang in the choir and may well be (partially) buried. Follow Old Church Street north and you'll find the **Chelsea Arts Club** (no.143), founded in 1871 by Whistler and now host to occasional public events, including classical recitals.

North of the western extremity of Cheyne Walk are **Brompton Cemetery** (suffragette Emmeline Pankhurst is buried here) and the home ground of London's first Champions League winners: Chelsea FC. Tickets for league games are hard to come by, but **Stamford Bridge** (Fulham Road, SW6 1HS, 0871 984 1905, www.chelseafc.com) does have the excellent **Chelsea Centenary Museum**.

Sights & Museums

The **National Army Museum** is closed for major rebuilding until late 2016.

Carlyle's House

24 Cheyne Row, SW3 5HL (7352 7087, www.nationaltrust.org.uk). Sloane Square tube or bus 11, 19, 22, 49, 170, 211, 319. **Open** *Mar-Oct* 11am-4.30pm Wed-Sun. Closed Nov-Feb. **Admission** £5.10; £2.60 children; £12.80 family. **No credit cards. Map** p88 D6 ⑱
Thomas Carlyle and his wife Jane moved to this four-storey, Queen Anne house in 1834. The house was inaugurated as a museum in 1896, 15 years after Carlyle's death, offering an intriguing snapshot of

Victorian life. The writer's quest for quiet (details of his valiant attempts to soundproof the attic) strikes a chord today: he was plagued by the sound of revelry from Cremorne Pleasure Gardens.

Chelsea Centenary Museum

Stamford Bridge, Fulham Road, SW6 1HS (0871 984 1955, www.chelseafc.com/the-club/Museum-stadium-tours.html). Fulham Broadway tube. **Open** 10.30am-4.30pm daily. **Admission** £11; £9-£10 reductions; free under-5s. **Map** p88 A6 ⑲
Opened in 1877 as an athletics track (it was thought track and field had a more promising financial future than mere Association Football), Stamford Bridge was soon a football ground in search of a team. It became the home of the Blues in 1905; for its 100th anniversary the club celebrated with the opening of this fine museum. It provides a terrific social history of the game, helped along by the narrative of Chelsea's journey from music-hall joke to oil-money-funded Premier League titans. There are interactives, trophies – Chelsea are the only London club to have won the prestigious Champions League (in 2012) and the only British club to have won all three major European trophies – and some ace memorabilia, including a photo of Raquel Welch in Chelsea strip making a valiant attempt to side-foot the ball.

FREE Chelsea Old Church

Old Church Street, SW3 5DQ (7795 1019, www.chelseaoldchurch.org.uk). Sloane Square tube or bus 11, 19, 22, 49, 319. **Open** 2-4pm Tue-Thur; 1.30-5pm Sun. *Services* 8am, 10am, 11am, 12.15pm Sun. *Evensong* 6pm Sun. **Admission** free; donations appreciated. **Map** p88 C6 ⑳
Legend has it that the Thomas More Chapel, which remains on the south side, contains More's headless body buried somewhere under the walls (his head, after being spiked on London Bridge, was 'rescued' and buried in a family vault in St Dunstan's church, Canterbury). There's a striking statue of More outside the church. Guides are on hand on Sundays.

★ Chelsea Physic Garden

66 Royal Hospital Road, SW3 4HS (7352 5646, www.chelseaphysicgarden.co.uk). Sloane Square tube or bus 11, 19, 22. **Open** *Apr-June, Sept, Oct* 11am-6pm Tue-Fri, Sun. *July, Aug* 11am-6pm Mon, Tue, Thur, Fri, Sun; 11am-10pm Wed. *Nov-Mar* 9.30am-4pm Mon-Fri. *Tours* times vary; phone to check. **Admission** £9.90; £6.60 reductions; free under-5s. *Tours* free. **Map** p89 E6 ㉑
See p97 **Take Your Physic.**

FREE Royal Hospital Chelsea

Royal Hospital Road, SW3 4HT (7881 5200, www.chelsea-pensioners.org.uk). Sloane Square tube or bus 11, 19, 22, 137, 170. **Open** 10am-4pm Mon-Fri. *Tours* 10am, 1.30pm Mon-Fri. **Admission** free. Tours £10; £7 reductions; under-6s free. **Map** p89 E6 ㉒

TAKE YOUR PHYSIC

Chelsea is home to one of London's most restorative spaces.

When we first nosed into one of the Victorian greenhouses at the **Chelsea Physic Garden** (for listings, *see p96*), a gardener was giving the ferns a mist from his backpack sprayer. He told us about the delicate filmy ferns, their scarcity and the strange beauty of their leaves – just a single cell thick, hence their characteristic translucence. He explained how a garden curator here kicked off the Victorian 'Fern Craze' – which led to collectors hunting these particular ferns almost to extinction.

When you pass through the modest red-brick walls here, you enter a secret garden, by the Thames but separated from it into its own microclimate, a place where rare plants from Britain and across the globe have been collected – and now thrive.

Consider for a moment: by allowing plants to survive carriage over long distances a humble, sealed, hand-carried greenhouse called a Wardian Case (a model of which you can see) changed world agriculture, creating the tea industry of India and the rubber plantations of south-east Asia. Or look at the rockery, created in 1773 from black Icelandic basalt imported by Joseph Banks, the most-famous plant hunter of all, and decorated with masonry from the Tower of London; western Europe's oldest rockery, this structure is Grade II-listed, yet it provides perfect growing conditions for exotic plants such as the carnivorous pitcher plant. Or hunt out the fascinating section of plants labelled with a skull-and-crossbone motif – not everything is healthy fun.

Set up by apothecaries in 1673, the garden was saved by Sir Hans Sloane – whose discoveries of quinine and drinking chocolate made him wealthy. Sloane remembered training in the garden fondly, so – having bought up most of Chelsea – he bequeathed these four acres to apothecaries in perpetuity: the peppercorn rent of £5 is still paid to his descendants, and his statue (*pictured*) presides over the garden.

If you don't stumble across a gardener with time to chat, pick up the beautifully illustrated new guide, with its maps and plant histories. Like the garden itself, it only costs a fiver.

EXPLORE

Around 350 Chelsea Pensioners (retired soldiers) live at the Royal Hospital, founded in 1682 by Charles II for those 'broken by age or war' and designed by Sir Christopher Wren (with adjustments by Robert Adam and Sir John Soane). Retired soldiers are still eligible to apply for a final posting here if they're over 65 and in receipt of an Army or War Disability Pension for Army Service. The pensioners have their own club room, bowling green and gardens, and get tickets to Chelsea FC home games. The museum (same times) has more about their lives. The annual Chelsea Flower show is held in the grounds.

FREE Saatchi Gallery
Duke of York's HQ, King's Road, SW3 4RY (7811 3070, www.saatchigallery.com). Sloane Square tube. **Open** 10am-6pm daily. **Admission** free. **Map** p89 E5 ㉓
Charles Saatchi's gallery offers 50,000sq ft of space for temporary exhibitions. Given his fame as a promoter in the 1990s of what became known as the Young British Artists – Damien Hirst, Tracey Emin, Gavin Turk, Sarah Lucas et al – it will surprise many that the focus of exhibitions here has been internationalist in outlook, with China, Africa and India all featuring. Still, Richard Wilson's superb oil-sump installation *20:50* has survived from the Saatchi Gallery's previous incarnations and remains here as the only permanently displayed artwork.

Restaurants

Cadogan Arms
298 King's Road, SW3 5UG (7352 6500, www. thecadoganarmschelsea.com). Sloane Square tube then bus 19, 22, 319. **Open** 11am-11pm Mon-Sat; 11am-10.30pm Sun. *Food served* noon-3.30pm, 6-10.30pm Mon-Fri; noon-10.30pm Sat; noon-9pm Sun. **Main courses** £13-£24. **Map** p88 C6 ㉔
Gastropub
In 2009, this 19th-century Chelsea pub was given a major rebuild by its new owners, the Martin brothers. It now has a countrified look, complete with stuffed animals and fly-fishing displays, and remains a proper boozer, with top-quality real ales, notwithstanding the snug and smoothly run dining area, where great food is on offer.
▶ *On Sloane Square, the Martin brothers' Botanist (no. 7, 7730 0077) provides a similar mix of fine booze and hearty food.*

Colbert
51 Sloane Square, SW1W 8AX (7730 2804, www. colbertchelsea.com). Sloane Square tube. **Open** 8am-11pm Mon-Thur; 8am-11.30pm Fri, Sat; 8am-10.30pm Sun. **Main courses** £6.95-£30. **Map** p89 E4 ㉕ **Brasserie**
Paying homage to Continental grand cafés with marble, linen napkins and mirrors aplenty, Colbert feels more casual and local than its siblings – the Wolseley (*see p82*), the Delaunay (*see p147*) and

Brasserie Zédel (*see p114*) – and the posters in the booth-lined bar area advertising performances by Olivier and Vivien Leigh next door at the Royal Court Theatre (*see p288*) lend a sense of history. It also trumps the others with pavement tables from which to admire the beautiful people. More importantly, it serves the best lunch in the area: perhaps a deliciously decadent smoked haddock florentine served on spinach, under a perfectly poached egg, in a buttery cream sauce; or a croque madame – perfectly fried brioche filled with melted comté cheese, jambon blanc and béchamel sauce, topped with a fried egg.

Gallery Mess
Saatchi Gallery, Duke of York's HQ, King's Road, SW3 4RY (7730 8135, www.saatchi gallery.com/gallerymess). Sloane Square tube. **Open** *Bar* 10am-11pm Mon-Sat; 10am-7pm Sun. *Restaurant* noon-9.30pm Mon-Sat; noon-6.30pm Sun. **Main courses** £14.25-£25. **Map** p89 E5 ㉖
Brasserie
As befits its Chelsea location, this welcoming brasserie at the Saatchi art gallery is smarter than most, with white linen tablecloths, exposed brickwork and impressive bar all somewhat in thrall to the vaulted ceiling and expansive curtain of floor-to-ceiling arched windows. There's also a large outdoor terrace. Service is disarmingly friendly and mains offer comforting flavours and proportions. So you'll find cod and chips, steak sandwich, charcuterie and smoked fish platters, caesar salad and afternoon tea.

Medlar
438 King's Road, SW10 0LJ (7349 1900, www. medlarrestaurant.co.uk). Fulham Broadway tube or bus 11, 22. **Open** noon-3pm, 6.30-10.30pm daily. **Set lunch** (Mon-Fri) £28 3 courses; (Sat) £30 3 courses; (Sun) £35 3 courses. **Set dinner** (Mon-Sat) £46 3 courses; (Sun) £35 3 courses. **Map** p88 B6 ㉗ **Modern European**
The decor here is understated: a soothing grey-green colour scheme and unobtrusive artwork. The real artistry arrives on the plates, dishes of astounding excellence. Assemblies are complex and have lengthy names: crisp calf's brain with smoked duck breast, aïoli, pink fir potatoes and tardivo (radichio), for example. But every ingredient justifies its place in entirely natural-seeming juxtapositions of flavour, texture and colour. And the execution is nearly flawless. Save room for wonderful (and relatively simple) puddings, such as cardamom custard with saffron oranges, pomegranate and langues de chat.

Mona Lisa
417 King's Road, SW10 0LR (7376 5447). Fulham Broadway tube or bus 11, 22. **Open** 7am-11pm Mon-Sat; 8.30am-5.30pm Sun. **Main courses** £6-£18.95. **Map** p88 B6 ㉘ **Italian/café**

Rabbit.

Not much to look at, either inside or out, the Mona Lisa is hidden away at the 'wrong' end of the King's Road, just beyond World's End. But the bonhomie is infectious, and if you order the right thing, such as the meltingly tender calf's liver alla salvia (with butter and sage), served with old-school potatoes and veg, you won't give a fig about the homely decor. The menu ranges across breakfasts, sandwiches, burgers, omelettes, jacket potatoes and pastas to three-course blow-outs (at lunch, the latter comes in at the astonishingly cheap price of £8.95).

★ **Rabbit**
172 King's Road, SW3 4UP (3750 0172, www.rabbit-restaurant.com). Sloane Square tube. **Open** 6-11pm Tue-Sat; noon 4pm Sun.
Main courses £6-£14. **Map** p88 D5 ㉙ **British**
More than a restaurant, Rabbit feels a bit like a theme bar that does food, right down to a 'stable door' entrance, outside which smokers linger. But to see it as a party venue does the cooking a disservice: the Gladwins dish up inventive mouthfuls of joy that warm you up for heavy, slow-cooked mains (perhaps pigs' cheeks with malt, stout, garlic and pennywort) and lighter, faster-cooked dishes (such as tempura duck liver). However, the 'British with a twist' ethos is best summed up by the desserts: try a Viennetta parfait made of Magnum ice-cream lollies or an intriguing cep and white-chocolate bourbon.

Shops & Services

John Sandoe
10 Blacklands Terrace, SW3 2SR (7581 2084, www.johnsandoe.com). Sloane Square tube. **Open** 9.30am-6.30pm Mon-Sat; 11am-5pm Sun. **Map** p89 E5 ㉚ **Books & music**
Tucked away on a side street, this 50-year-old independent has always looked just as a bookshop should, with stock literally packed to the rafters. The enthusiasm and knowledge of the staff can be taken as, forgive us, read – several have worked here for decades, their passion for books undimmed.

★ Shop at Bluebird
350 King's Road, SW3 5UU (7351 3873, www. theshopatbluebird.com). Sloane Square tube. **Open** 10am-7pm Mon-Sat; noon-6pm Sun. **Map** p88 C6 ㉛ **Fashion/homewares**
Browsing at the Shop at Bluebird is an unusually tranquil experience. The 10,000sq ft space, which began life as a garage back in the 1930s, has a white tiled floor and lots of natural light, tempting shoppers to roam calmly through its delightfully curated mix of fashion, beauty, homewares, books and music. The Shop was opened by John and Belle Robinson in 2005; it now has a reputation for tempting luxury brands and for discovering up-and-coming designers. There's an in-store spa, too.

Oxford Street, Marylebone & Mayfair

Oxford Street is working hard to stay top of London's shopping destinations, with a revamped roundabout at Marble Arch, wider pavements, the innovative pedestrian crossings at Oxford Circus, and an all-new 'eastern gateway' development near the shiny new Tottenham Court Road superstation, already partially open in anticipation of Crossrail's arrival in 2018.

North are the luxury cafés and boutiques of Marylebone, bounded there by Regent's Park and to the west by the Arab shisha cafés and juice bars of the Edgware Road. South of Oxford Street, Mayfair oozes wealth, while to the south-east, neon-lit Piccadilly Circus is a bit of town every Londoner does their best to avoid.

EXPLORE

Selfridges.

Don't Miss

1 **Royal Academy of Arts** Impressive home to blockbuster shows (p120).

2 **Liberty** A sweet combination of tradition and fashion (p116).

3 **American Bar at the Beaumont** A place for civilised cocktailing (p118).

4 **La Fromagerie** Where to visit to enter cheese nirvana (p112).

5 **Selfridges** London's leading department store (p106).

OXFORD STREET

Bond Street, Marble Arch, Oxford Circus or
Tottenham Court Road tube.

Official estimates put the annual footfall at
somewhere near 200 million people per year,
but few Londoners love **Oxford Street**. A
shopping district since the 19th century, it's
unmanageably busy on weekends and in the
run-up to Christmas. Even outside these times,
it's rarely pretty, lined as it is with over-familiar
chain stores and choked with bus traffic. The
New West End Company (www.newwestend.
com) has been charged with changing all that,
and Oxford Circus, Marble Arch and Regent
Street are beginning to feel the benefits.

The street gets smarter as you walk from east
to west. The eastern end around Tottenham Court
Road station is under major redevelopment for
Crossrail, but its lack of destination shops was
solved a couple of years ago by the opening of
teen-magnet fashion flagship **Primark** (nos.14-
28, 7580 5510); more will follow in what is, as we
go to press, mostly a building site. Still, the first
sight of the future Crossrail and tube superstation
at Tottenham Court Road in 2015 was rather
appealing. The string of classy department
stores – **John Lewis** (nos.278-306, 7629 7711),
Debenhams and **Selfridges** – begins west of
Oxford Circus, always chaotic with shoppers.
Next stop along, Bond Street station, is also in the
throes of Crossrail disruption. Apart from the art
deco splendour of Selfridges, architectural
interest along Oxford Street is largely limited to
Oxford Circus's four identical convex corners,
constructed between 1913 and 1928. The crowds
and rush of traffic hamper investigations, a
problem the council addressed by widening
pavements, removing street clutter and creating
Tokyo Shibuya-style diagonal crossings, which
actually work rather well.

Oxford Street gained notoriety as the route
by which condemned men were conveyed from
Newgate Prison to the old Tyburn gallows,
stopping only for a last pint at the **Angel** (61-62
St Giles High Street, 7240 2876), in the shadow of
Centre Point. For over six centuries, crowds would
gather to watch executions at the west end of the
street, at Tyburn; held in 1783, the final execution
to be carried out here is marked by an X on a
traffic island at the junction of the Edgware
and Bayswater roads.

Close by, also at the western end of Oxford
Street, stands **Marble Arch**, with its Carrara
marble cladding and sculptures celebrating
Nelson and Wellington. It was designed by
John Nash in 1827 as the entrance to a rebuilt
Buckingham Palace, but the arch was moved
here in 1851, after – it is said – a fuming Queen
Victoria found it to be too narrow for her coach.

Now given a £2-million revamp, it's been joined
by renovated water fountains and gardens that
contain an ongoing series of large-scale public
sculpture commissions.

North of Oxford Circus

Great Portland Street, Oxford Circus or
Regent's Park tube.

North of Oxford Circus runs **Langham Place**,
notable for the Bath stone façade of John Nash's
All Souls Church (Langham Place, 2 All Souls
Place, 7580 3522, www.allsouls.org). Its bold
combination of a Gothic spire and classical
rotunda wasn't popular: in 1824, a year after it
opened, the church was condemned in Parliament
as 'deplorable and horrible'; a statue of Nash now
stands outside, looking forlornly away.

Tucked to one side of the church you'll find
the BBC's **Broadcasting House**, an oddly
asymmetrical art deco building, much extended
by recent redevelopment. Over the road is the
Langham Hotel, which opened in 1865 as
Britain's first grand hotel and has been home at
various points to Mark Twain, Napoleon III and
Oscar Wilde; it has a swanky bar, **Artesian**.

North, Langham Place turns into **Portland
Place**, designed by Robert and James Adam as
the glory of 18th-century London. Its Georgian
terraced houses are now mostly occupied by
embassies and swanky offices. At no.66 is the
Royal Institute of British Architects (RIBA;
see p335). Parallel to Portland Place are **Harley
Street**, famous for its high-cost dentists and
doctors, and **Wimpole Street**, erstwhile home
to the poet Elizabeth Barrett Browning (no.50),
Sir Paul McCartney (no.57) and Sir Arthur Conan
Doyle (2 Upper Wimpole Street).

Sights & Museums

BBC Broadcasting House

*Portland Place, Upper Regent Street, W1A 1AA
(0370 901 1227, www.bbc.co.uk/showsandtours/
tours). Oxford Circus tube.* **Tours** *(pre-booked only)*

EXPLORE

EXPLORE

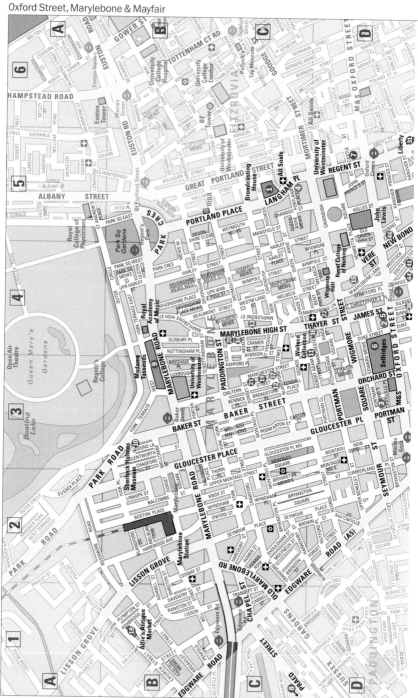

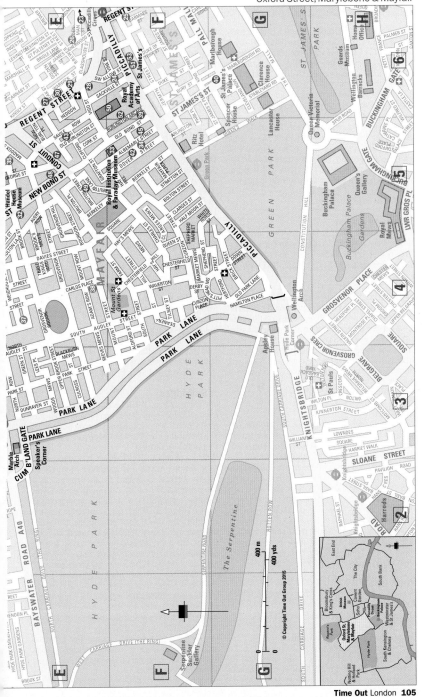

EXPLORE

© Copyright Time Out Group 2015

from 10am daily. **Tickets** £15; £10-£13 reductions; £43.50 family. No under-9s. **Map** p104 C5 ❶
Completed in 1932, this was Britain's first purpose-built broadcast centre; in 2013, it acquired a neighbour, New Broadcasting House. There are daily tours of the BBC, but you'll need to book ahead on the website – and under-9s are not admitted. Tours take in the studios, including those for television and radio news, and you'll be able to read the news and weather on an interactive set. The guides also explain the history of the BBC and the original building. The Radio Theatre in the original BBC building is especially gorgeous; there you can join the audience for radio and TV shows, with ticketing information at www.bbc.co.uk/showsandtours.

Restaurants

★ Busaba Eathai
8-13 Bird Street, W1U 1BU (7518 8080, www.busaba.com). Bond Street tube. **Open** noon-11pm Mon-Thur; noon-11.30pm Fri, Sat; noon-10pm Sun. **Main courses** £7.90-£14.50. **Map** p104 D4 ❷
Thai
Busaba is a ten-strong chain – but it's not your average Thai joint. The dark, handsome interior combines dark wood, incense and dimly lit lanterns. With spacious shared tables, no reservations and brisk service, it remains a great spot for a casual meal with friends. Among the Thai classics, you'll find a few dishes that aren't often seen in London, such as sen chan pad thai (a pimped pad thai with crab originating from the Chanthaburi province of eastern Thailand).
Other locations throughout the city.

Roti Chai
3-4 Portman Mews South, W1H 6HS (7408 0101, www.rotichai.com). Marble Arch tube. **Open** noon-10.30pm Mon-Sat; 12.30-9pm Sun. **Main courses** £4.20-£8.50. **Map** p104 D3 ❸ Pan-Indian
The ground-floor 'street kitchen', with its utilitarian furniture and canteen vibe, is ideal for a swift midday feed – and the alert young staff keep things pacy. The menu is modelled on those of urban India's snack shacks, so you'll find food such as bhel pooris, chilli paneer and puri puri. Larger dishes include 'railway lamb curry' (tender meat and potato in a rich gravy spiced with star anise and cinnamon bark). In the basement, the evening-only 'dining room' is a darker, sexier (and pricier) space.

Pubs & Bars

Artesian
Langham Hotel, 1C Portland Place, W1B 1JA (7636 1000, www.artesian-bar.co.uk). Oxford Circus tube. **Open** 11am-2am Mon-Sat; 11am-midnight Sun. **Map** p104 C5 ❹
The Artesian is very nearly a very great bar. Its elegant space on the ground floor of the Langham

Hotel is lovely. Tables are well spaced. Service is friendly and ultra-efficient even when – as so often happens – it's packed out. A free plate of tasty canapés may arrive unbidden. Their own cocktails are well conceived, and the classics are flawlessly rendered and generously poured. Two downers: piping in incredibly loud Euro-pop, which is completely at odds with the room, and the pricing of the drinks, among London's most expensive.

Shops & Services

Debenhams
334-348 Oxford Street, W1C 1JG (0344 561 6161 www.debenhams.com). Oxford Circus tube. **Open** 9.30am-9pm Mon-Sat; noon-6pm Sun. **Map** p104 D4 ❺ Department store
Until its £25m refurbishment, the Debenhams flagship was one of Oxford Street's drabbest and most downmarket department stores. But things have changed dramatically for the 200-year-old brand. The seven-floor store has been completely redesigned, with a new interior, an impressive shimmering kinetic metal façade (which resembles a wave) and a chichi new shoes department. There's also a chic bistro in the basement. The store now features 21 designer collaborations, including Henry Holland, Matthew Williamson and Jenny Packham, but our favourites are the Todd Lynn and Jonathan Saunders Edition ranges. Up on the fifth floor, you'll find children's clothing and toys plus an airy new family-friendly restaurant. Finally, it's a light-filled, easy-to-navigate store you'll want to linger in.

★ Selfridges
400 Oxford Street, W1A 1AB (0800 123400, www.selfridges.com). Bond Street or Marble Arch tube. **Open** 9.30am-9pm Mon-Sat; noon-6.15pm Sun (browsing from 11.30am). **Map** p104 D4 ❻ Department store
With its plethora of concession boutiques, store-wide themed events and collections from all the hottest brands, Selfridges is as dynamic as a department store could be. Although the store layout changes regularly (and, with the announcement in June 2014 of a £300m, five-year facelift, this will continue), the useful floor plans make navigating the place easy-peasy. While the basement is chock-full of hip home accessories and stylish kitchen equipment, it's Selfridges' fashion floors that really get hearts racing. With a winning combination of new talent, hip and edgy labels, high-street brands and luxury high-end designers, the store stays ahead of the pack. Highlights include the huge denim section, and the extensive Shoe Galleries, the world's biggest women's footwear department. Level 4 hosts the predictably excellent Toy Shop. There are always new draws in the food hall, ranging from great deli and bakery produce to classy packaged goods. Regularly changing pop-ups and special events keep customers on their toes.

Topshop.

Topshop
36-38 Great Castle Street, W1W 8LG (0844 848 7487, www.topshop.com). Oxford Circus tube. **Open** 9am-9pm Mon-Sat; 9am-7pm Sun. **Map** p104 D5 ❼ **Fashion**
Topshop has been the queen of the British high street for the past decade, and walking into the busy Oxford Street flagship, it's easy to see why. Spanning three huge floors, the place lays claim to being the world's largest fashion shop, and is always buzzing with fashion-forward teens and twentysomethings keen to get their hands on the next big trends. The store covers a huge range of styles and sizes, and includes free personal shoppers, boutique label concessions, capsule collections, a Metalmorphosis tattoo parlour, a Daniel Hersheson Blow Dry Bar, a café and sweet shop. Topman is as on-the-ball and innovative as its big sister, stocking niche menswear labels such as Garbstore, and housing a trainer boutique, a suit section, and a new personal shopping suite, featuring consultation rooms, Xbox 360s and an exhibition space. Both shops are even more of a hive of activity than normal during London Fashion Week, when a series of special events are held at them.
Other locations throughout the city.

MARYLEBONE & BAKER STREET

Baker Street, Bond Street, Marble Arch, Oxford Circus or Regent's Park tube.

North of Oxford Street, the fashionable district known to its boosters as 'Marylebone Village' has become a magnet for moneyed Londoners, especially since the opening of André Balazs's **Chiltern Firehouse** effected the area's transformation from merely rich to actively fashionable (*see p111* **Walk**). However,

most visitors to the area head directly for the unfashionable but deathlessly popular waxworks of **Madame Tussauds**; there's also a small and oft-overlooked museum at the neighbouring **Royal Academy of Music** (7873 7373, www. ram.ac.uk), while the northern end of **Baker Street** is unsurprisingly heavy on nods of respect to the world's favourite freelance detective: there's the **Sherlock Holmes Museum**, but studious fans may find more of interest among the books and photos of the **Sherlock Holmes Collection** at Marylebone Library (7641 6200, by appointment only). The Beatles painted 94 Baker Street with a psychedelic mural before opening it in December 1967 as the Apple Boutique, a clothing store run on such whimsical hippie principles that it had to close within six months due to financial losses. Fab Four pilgrims head to the **London Beatles Store** (no.231, 7935 4464, www. beatlesstorelondon.co.uk), where the ground-floor shop offers a predictable array of Beatles-branded accessories alongside some genuinely collectible items.

For Londoners, the area's beating heart is **Marylebone High Street**, teeming with interesting shops. The name of the neighbourhood is a contraction of the church's earlier name, St Mary by the Bourne; the 'bourne' in question, Tyburn stream, still filters into the Thames near Pimlico, but its entire length is now covered. **St Marylebone Church** stands in its fourth incarnation at the northern end of the street. The church's garden hosts designer clothing and artisan food stalls at the **Cabbages & Frocks** market on Saturdays (www.cabbagesandfrocks.co.uk).

Lovely boutiques can be found on winding **Marylebone Lane**, along with the **Golden Eagle** (no.59, 7935 3228), which hosts regular

EXPLORE

singalongs around its piano. There's fine food here, too, with smart, often upmarket eateries snuggling alongside delicatessens such as **La Fromagerie** and century-old lunchroom **Paul Rothe & Son** (35 Marylebone Lane, 7935 6783). **Marylebone Farmers' Market** takes place in the Cramer Street car park every Sunday.

Further south, the soaring neo-Gothic interior of the 19th-century **St James's Roman Catholic Church** (Spanish Place, 22 George Street, 7935 0943, www.sjrcc.org.uk) is lit dramatically by stained-glass windows; Vivien Leigh (née Hartley) married barrister Herbert Leigh Hunt here in 1932. Other cultural diversions include the **Wallace Collection** and the **Wigmore Hall** (*see p287*).

Part of the Romans' Watling Street from Dover to Wales, **Edgware Road** rules a definite north–south line marking the western edge of the West End. It's now the heart of the city's Middle East end: if you want to pick up your copy of *Al Hayat*, cash a cheque at the Bank of Kuwait or catch Egyptian football, head here.

The fact that the name Paddington has been immortalised by a certain small, ursine Peruvian émigré is appropriate, given that the area has long been home to refugees and immigrants. It was a country village until an arm of the Grand Union Canal arrived in 1801, linking London to the Midlands, followed in the 1830s by the railway. **Paddington Station**, with its fine triple roof of iron and glass, was built in 1851 to the specifications of the great engineer Isambard Kingdom Brunel. Paddington's proximity to central London eventually drew in developers. To the east of the station, gleaming **Paddington Central** now provides a million square feet of office space, canalside apartments and restaurants. In St Mary's Hospital, the old-fashioned **Alexander Fleming Laboratory Museum** gives a sense of what the district used to be like.

Sights & Museums

Alexander Fleming Laboratory Museum

St Mary's Hospital, Praed Street, W2 1NY (3312 6528, www.medicalmuseums.org). Paddington tube/rail. **Open** 10am-1pm Mon-Thur. *By appt* 2-5pm Mon-Thur; 10am-5pm Fri. **Admission** £4; £2 reductions; free under-5s. **No credit cards**. **Map** p104 C1 ❺

Buzz in at the entrance on your left as you enter the hospital and head up the stairs to find this tiny, dusty, instrument-cluttered lab. Enthusiastic guides conjure up Professor Alexander Fleming who, in 1928, noticed that mould contamination had destroyed some staphylococcus bacteria on a set-aside culture plate: he had discovered penicillin. The keen entrepreneurs across the street immediately began to advertise their pub's healthful properties,

claiming the miracle fungus had blown into the lab from them. The video room has a documentary on Fleming's life and discovery.

Madame Tussauds

Marylebone Road, NW1 5LR (0871 894 3000, www.madametussauds.com/london). Baker Street tube. **Open** varies. **Admission** £30; £25.80 reductions; £111.60 family; free under-4s. **Map** p104 B3 ❾

Streams of humanity jostle excitedly here for the chance to take pictures of one another planting a smacker on a waxen visage of fame and fortune. Madame Tussaud brought her show to London in 1802, 32 years after it was founded in Paris, and it's been expanding ever since, on these very premises since 1884. There are now some 300 figures in the collection: current movie A-listers who require no more than a first name (Angelina, Brad), as well as their illustrious forebears for whom the surname seems more fitting (Chaplin); a bevy of Royals (not least Wills and Kate), and sundry sports stars – not just Nadal and Bobby Moore, but an Athletes' Village of 2012 Olympians, among them Jessica Ennis-Hill, Mo Farah and Usain Bolt. Rihanna and One Direction can be found hanging out among the Music Megastars, while Dickens, Einstein and Madame Tussauds herself kick back in the Culture section. If you're not already overheating, your palms will be sweating by the time you descend to the Chamber of Horrors in 'Scream', where only teens claim to enjoy the floor drops and scary special effects. Much more pleasant is the kitsch 'Spirit of London' ride, whisking you through 400 years of London life in a taxi pod.

Tussauds also hosts Marvel Super Heroes 4D. Here, interactives and waxworks of Iron Man, Spider-man and an 18ft Hulk provide further photo ops, but the highlight is the nine-minute film in '4D' (as well as 3D projections, there are 'real' effects such as a shaking floor and smoke in the auditorium).

A major new attraction opened in spring 2015. Expertly finished Star Wars sets are spread over two new floors, so visitors can explore Yoda's swamp and the lava fields of Mustafar, where Anakin turns to the dark side. Life-like waxworks show Luke Skywalker fighting Darth Vader, Obi-Wan Kenobi and (teenage boys and their dads take note) a captive Princess Leia in Jabba's Throne Room.

▶ *The new Star Wars isn't going to make the queues at Madame Tussauds any shorter. The owners now issue only timed tickets, so book online in advance if you can (it's cheaper); if you can't, you'll probably have to queue for a time slot later that day – fill the time at the Sherlock Holmes Museum (see below).*

Sherlock Holmes Museum

221B Baker Street, NW1 6XE (7224 3688, www. sherlock-holmes.co.uk). Baker Street tube. **Open** 9.30am-6pm daily. **Admission** £10 £8 reductions. **Map** p104 B3 ❿

EXPLORE

Wallace Collection.

Founded in 1989 at what used to be no.239, the museum fought long and hard for the right to claim the address 221B Baker Street as its own. When you visit, you are likely to be greeted by an august person wearing a bowler hat and whiskers; this, you will deduce, is Dr Watson. And every lovingly recreated detail – murder weapons, Victoriana, waxwork tableaux of key scenes from Conan Doyle's stories – conspires to persuade visitors to suspend their disbelief and feel themselves travelling back in time to a preserved fragment of historical reality. Perhaps most interesting is a folder of letters upstairs in Mrs Hudson's room: they were all actually sent to Holmes by fans from all over the world, asking for help or offering their assistance as wannabe sleuths.

★ FREE Wallace Collection

Hertford House, Manchester Square, W1U 3BN (7563 9500, www.wallacecollection.org). Bond Street tube. **Open** 10am-5pm daily. **Admission** free. **Map** p104 D4 ⓬

Built in 1776 and tucked away on a quiet square, this handsome house contains an exceptional collection of 18th-century French furniture, painting and objets d'art, as well as an amazing array of medieval armour and weaponry taking up much of the ground floor. It all belonged to Sir Richard Wallace, who, as the illegitimate offspring of the fourth Marquess of Hertford, inherited in 1870 the treasures his father had amassed in the last 30 years of his life. Room after grand room contains Louis XIV and XV furnishings and Sèvres porcelain; the galleries are hung with paintings by Titian, Gainsborough and Reynolds, as well as Fragonard's *The Swing*.

Thoroughly refurbished, the Wallace is looking wonderful these days, especially upstairs, where the West Galleries display 19th-century and Venetian paintings (including a room of Canalettos) and the East Galleries are dedicated to Dutch paintings,

among them a wonderful Rembrandt self-portrait hung directly opposite his less characterful painting of Titus, his son. At the back, the Great Gallery – following painstaking improvements to lighting and decor – is now the loveliest gallery room in London, with Franz Hals's *Laughing Cavalier*, Poussin's *A Dance to the Music of Time*, Velázquez's *The Lady with a Fan* and Rubens' *The Rainbow Landscape* shown to their very best advantage.

Restaurants

★ Chiltern Firehouse

1 Chiltern Street, W1U 7PA (7073 7676, www. chilternfirehouse.com). Baker Street tube. **Open** 8am-10.30am, noon-2.30pm, 5-10.30pm Mon-Fri; 11am-3pm, 6-10.30pm Sat, Sun. **Main courses** £21-£75. **Map** p104 C3 ⓬ **Modern European**
This lovely 1889 Grade II-listed Victorian Gothic fire brigade building has been rebuilt from the inside out to create London's buzziest hotel (*see p349*), but the discreetly gated garden is also the entrance to one of London's finest restaurants. The kitchen can do fiddly and pretty, exemplified by appetisers such as the tiny, slider-like 'doughnuts' filled with crab meat, but pretty is only part of the story. The restaurant's success is built on its reputation as a celeb-magnet but when that fades, the flavour combinations and exemplary modern cooking techniques, as 'curated' by Portuguese superchef Nuno Mendes, will remain. The best seats are at the kitchen counter, from which you can watch the chefs work their magic.

Fischer's

50 Marylebone High Street, W1U 5HN (7466 5501, www.fischers.co.uk). Baker Street or Regent's Park tube. **Open** 8am-10.30pm Mon-Sat; 8am-10pm Sun. **Main courses** £11.50-£31.50. **Map** p104 C4 ⓭ **Austrian**

WALK MEET MARYLEBONE

Discover the inner London village that's becoming cool again.

West of Marble Arch tube is a traffic island where Edgware Road joins Oxford Street. Set into the ground is the most euphemistic **circular plaque** in London: around a humble cross, it says just 'The site of the Tyburn Tree'. This was the gallows that was London's main place of execution from 1388 to 1783, silent witness to the death of highwayman Jack Sheppard (who drew crowds of 200,000) and the hanging of Cromwell's exhumed corpse.

What has this to do with Marylebone? Marylebone is a euphemism too. The Tyburn was a village stream (now buried) that lent its name not only to the gallows, but also to the medieval estate it flowed through. By the 1600s residents were referring to their village by the name of its church: St Mary by the Bourne (meaning Tyburn). By degrees, St Marylebone and eventually plain old Marylebone were born.

Walk east along **Oxford Street** through the inevitably hellish crowds. Though you'll pass such highlights as Selfridges (see p106), it's a relief to turn left into pedestrianised **St Christopher's Place** (www.stchristophers place.com), with its boutiques and cafés, plus a little square with a fountain sculpture.

Turn right on to Wigmore Street – passing the funky Comptoir Libanais restaurant (no.65, 7935 1110, www.comptoirlibanais. com) – and then left on to **Marylebone Lane**. The slanted curve of this street mirrors the course of the Tyburn beneath. It also gathers a sweet collection of shops, from fashionable boutiques such as KJ's Laundry (see p113) to eccentrics such as Paul Rothe (see p109) and the self-explanatory Button Queen (no.76, 7935 1505, www.thebuttonqueen.co.uk).

The whole lane is a short and pleasant browse, but turn off at Hinde Street, crossing Thayer Street and continuing into the rather grand **Manchester Square**, home to the Wallace Collection (see p110), a flamboyantly decorated house full of armour and paintings. It's a favourite with the fashion crowd – a glance at the wallpaper will explain why.

Head north via Manchester Street, then right along George Street. You're now on **Marylebone High Street**. Here, the innovative fusion restaurant Providores (no.109, 7935 6175, www.theprovidores.co.uk) remains a draw (although we prefer its cheaper offshoot Kopapa, see p143), while the boutiques include a hot drink and Gaultier collaboration

at Kusmi Tea (no.15), Sicilian perfumier Ortigia (no.23), American import J Crew (no.19; for the Regent Street branch, see p115) and the unapologetically British and thoroughly lovely Daunt Books (see p113).

Turn left on to Paddington Street, past the delightful Paddington Street Gardens, proud winner of 'Loo of the Year' and home to some interesting mausoleums, until you reach **Chiltern Street**. This is arguably the most fashionable street in London, mostly due Chiltern Firehouse. Eat at the restaurant (see p110) if can get a reservation, but on your way south down the street, also note John Simons (see p113), Cadenhead's (see p113) the sitar shop and – since you don't really have a reservation – the cool little Monocle café (no.18, 7135 2040, http://cafe.monocle. com/), the coffee shop of Tyler Brûlé's magazine. Want to drown your sorrows that you're not with the in-crowd across the road? Just round the corner is the excellent basement bar Purl (see p112).

EXPLORE

Fischer's. See p110.

Meat Liquor
74 Welbeck Street, W1G 0BA (7224 4239, www. meatliquor.com). Bond Street tube. **Meals served** noon-2.30pm, 5-10.30pm Mon-Fri; 1-10.30pm Sat; 2-9.30pm Sun. **Main courses** £4.50-£11.50. **Map** p104 D4 ⑮ **North American**
Inside, this cult destination is dark and loud: more hell-raising nightclub than restaurant. Signs point out the rules ('No suits', 'No ballet pumps'). The graffiti murals are occult-themed, and the staff heavily tattooed. The Deep South cooking is gutsy stuff, with the likes of crunchy-coated 'bingo wings' served not only with a terrific Louisiana-style hot sauce but also a feisty blue-cheese dip. There are cheese steaks and dogs, though the real show-stoppers are the burgers. Staff make a mean cocktail.

★ Pachamama
18 Thayer Street, W1U 3JY (7935 9393, http:// pachamamalondon.com). Bond Street tube. **Open** noon-3pm, 6pm-midnight Mon-Fri; noon-midnight Sat; noon-10.30pm Sun. **Dishes** £6. **Map** p104 D4 ⑯ **Peruvian**
In Peru, the goddess Pachamama is the earth mother; in London, her avatar appeared as an unheralded Peruvian restaurant. And what a surprise she was. Looks: gorgeous, a thoughtful mix of rough and smooth, like a beautiful old hacienda in the process of being done up, with similarly attractive diners. Food: tasty and modish Peruvian plates – listed under sections named land, sea and soil – that combine finesse and flavour, and never confuse innovation with wackiness.

Pubs & Bars

Purl
50-54 Blandford Street, W1U 7HX (7935 0835, www.purl-london.com). Bond Street tube. **Open** 5-11.30pm Mon-Thur; 5pm-midnight Fri, Sat. **Map** p104 C3 ⑰
Purl, one of London's first speakeasy-type bars, is popular, which means that booking is advisable – though walk-ins will be seated if there's space. The layout of the bar, over a number of smallish spaces in a vaulted basement, gives the opportunity for genuine seclusion, if that's what you're looking for. And if you're interested in cutting-edge cocktail making, you're also in luck. Novel methods and unusual ingredients are used in many of the unique drinks, but the classics are always sound too. And the music is chosen by someone who has very good taste in jazz.

Shops & Services

Alfie's Antique Market
13-25 Church Street, NW8 8DT (7723 6066, www.alfiesantiques.com). Edgware Road tube or Marylebone tube/rail. **Open** 10am-6pm Tue-Sat. **No credit cards**. **Map** p104 B1 ⑲ **Antiques**

Chris Corbin and Jeremy King have made a habit of producing destination restaurants that don't feel stand-offish. This revival of the Mittel-European grand café is no exception. It's another celebrity hotspot – they love both Fischer's ageless elegance and its two-track booking system (fast-track for slebs; sidings for the hoi polloi) – but the prices here, in a setting where the monthly bill for wood polish might cause a Habsburg lip to tremble, are not as inflated as you'd expect. The main menu would be familiar to someone touring the Austro-Hungarian Empire in their charabanc, but there is fabulous sachertorte and strudel for those who can't manage a full meal.

La Fromagerie
2-6 Moxon Street, W1U 4EW (7935 0341, www. lafromagerie.co.uk). Baker Street or Bond Street tube. **Open** 8am-7.30pm Mon-Fri; 9am-7pm Sat; 10am-6pm Sun. **Main courses** £6.95-£18.50. **Map** p104 C4 ⑭ **Café**
There are cheeseboards and there are La Fromagerie cheeseboards. We'd like to live in a world in which we were only ever served the latter – carefully sourced, themed by nation (with suggested wines to match) and prettily arranged on a wooden slab at the back of an enticing deli and cheese shop. The café doesn't take bookings, so time your visit with care.

For almost four decades, Alfie's three floors and basement have hosted a hundred dealers in vintage furniture and fashion, art, books, maps and the like behind the rather bold art deco façade. There's a pleasant rooftop café to revive flagging browsers.

▶ *Alfie's has been an encouragement – and, in some cases, a stepping stone – for other dealers to set up businesses at the east end of Church Street. There's now a cluster of shops, many of which are focused on 20th-century collectibles.*

Cadenhead's Whisky Shop & Tasting Room

26 Chiltern Street, W1U 7QF (7935 6999, www.whiskytastingroom.com). Baker Street tube. **Open** 10.30am-6.30pm Mon-Sat. **Map** p104 C3 ⑲ **Food & drink**

Cadenhead's is a survivor of a rare breed: the independent whisky bottler. And its shop is one of a kind, at least in London. Cadenhead's selects barrels from distilleries all over Scotland and bottles them without filtration or any other intervention.

★ Daunt Books

83-84 Marylebone High Street, W1U 4QW (7224 2295, www.dauntbooks.co.uk). Baker Street tube. **Open** 9am-7.30pm Mon-Sat; 11am-6pm Sun. **Map** p104 C4 ⑳ **Books & music**

This beautiful Edwardian shop's elegant three-level back room – complete with oak balconies, viridian-green walls and stained-glass window – houses a much-praised travel section featuring guidebooks, maps, language reference, travelogues and related fiction. Travel aside, Daunt is also a first-rate stop for literary fiction, biography, gardening and more. **Other locations** throughout the city.

John Simons

46 Chiltern Street, W1U 7QR (3490 2729, www.johnsimons.co.uk). Baker Street tube. **Open** 11am-6pm Tue-Sat. **Map** p104 C3 ㉑ **Menswear**

The foundation of the Ivy League wardrobe is here: Harrington jackets, button-down shirts, knit ties, chinos and penny loafers – the kind of clothes you see on the cover of Blue Note albums. Lots of shops now sell this look but John Simons is the correct, authentic version; probably, it's the one Miles Davis would have approved of.

KJ's Laundry

74 Marylebone Lane, W1U 2PW (7486 7855, www.kjslaundry.com). Bond Street tube. **Open** 10am-7pm Mon-Sat; 11am-5pm Sun. **Map** p104 D4 ㉒ **Fashion**

Since opening in 2006, proprietors Kate Allden and Jane Ellis have curated a delightful mix of both established and lesser-known designers from around the globe, with the emphasis on timeless elegance rather than cutting-edge style. Luxury knits, skinny jeans, floaty tops, cowboy boots and charm jewellery are all hardy perennials here.

PICCADILLY CIRCUS & REGENT STREET

Oxford Circus or Piccadilly Circus tube.

Busy **Piccadilly Circus** is an uneasy mix of the tawdry and the grand, a mix that has little to do with the vision of its architect. John Nash's 1820s design for the intersection of Regent Street and Piccadilly, two of the West End's most elegant

Pachamama.

streets, was a harmonious circle of curved frontages. But 60 years later, Shaftesbury Avenue muscled in. A revamp of the traffic junction (by the same design consultants who successfully remodelled Oxford Circus) is now complete, with a mile of railings ripped out.

Alfred Gilbert's memorial fountain in honour of child-labour abolitionist Earl Shaftesbury was erected in 1893. It's properly known as the **Shaftesbury Memorial**, with the statue on top intended to show the Angel of Christian Charity, but critics and public alike recognised the likeness of **Eros** and their judgement has stuck.

The illuminated advertising panels around the intersection (www.piccadillylights.co.uk) appeared late in the 19th century and have been present ever since: a Coca-Cola ad has been here since 1955, making it the world's longest-running advertisement, but TDK quit the site in March 2015 after 25 years. Running *Sky News* broadcasts indicate the likely media-saturated future for these illuminations.

Opposite the memorial, the **Trocadero Centre** (www.londontrocadero.com) has seen several ventures come and go, in a prime but tired location; many a London teenager ended a night begun in hope and promise with a deflated session on the video games that once bleeped and buzzed within. However, **Ripley's Believe It or Not!** is now well established – and will surely benefit if the massive budget hotel that has been mooted for the site over many years finally happens, as now seems likely.

Connecting Piccadilly Circus to Oxford Circus to the north and Pall Mall to the south, the broad curve of **Regent Street** was designed by Nash in the early 1800s with the aims of improving access to Regent's Park and bumping up property values in Haymarket and Pall Mall. Much of Nash's architecture was destroyed in the early 20th century, but the grandeur of the street remains impressive.

Sights & Museums

Ripley's Believe It or Not!

The London Pavilion, 1 Piccadilly Circus, W1J 0DA (3238 0022, www.ripleyslondon.com). Piccadilly Circus tube. **Open** 10am-midnight daily (last entry 10.30pm). **Admission** £26.95; £19.95-£24.95 reductions; £79.95 family; free under-4s. **Map** p105 E6 ㉓
This 'odditorium' follows a formula more or less unchanged since Robert Ripley opened his first display at the Chicago World Fair in 1933: an assortment of 800 curiosities is displayed, ranging from the world's smallest road-safe car to da Vinci's *Last Supper* painted on a grain of rice – via the company's signature shrunken heads. There are occasional temporary displays too: you might just catch the end of the Spice Girls exhibition that began in 2015.

Restaurants

Set in a grand art deco basement just off Piccadilly Circus, **Brasserie Zédel** is a huge, all-day French eaterie run by the team behind the Wolseley (*see p82*); good on its own terms, it's also home to **Bar Américain**.

Bentley's Oyster Bar & Grill

11-15 Swallow Street, W1B 4DG (7734 4756, www.bentleys.org). Piccadilly Circus tube. **Open** *Oyster Bar* 11.30am-midnight Mon-Sat; 11.30am-10pm Sun. *Restaurant* noon-3pm, 5.30-11pm Mon-Fri; 5.30-11pm Sat. **Main courses** *Oyster Bar* £8.50-£75. *Restaurant* £19-£48. **Map** p105 F6 ㉔ **Fish & seafood**
Richard Corrigan first overhauled this grande dame of the capital's restaurant scene (established 1916) in 2005. The interior remains as polished as ever, with art deco windows, the original marble oyster bar and wood panelling. Week nights in the more formal first-floor Grill restaurant have a restrained business-dinner vibe, but the downstairs oyster bar is pleasingly laid-back. Theatrics at the gleaming marble counter (part staff speedily shucking, part competitive knocking 'em back) provide entertaining distraction as you decide between menu classics and imaginative daily specials.
▶ *Corrigan also runs the estimable Corrigan's Mayfair (28 Upper Grosvenor Street, W1K 7EH, 7499 9943), which serves high-class British food.*

Shoryu Ramen

9 Regent Street, SW1Y 4LR (no phone, www.shoryuramen.com). Piccadilly Circus tube. **Open** 11.15am-midnight Mon-Sat; 11.15am-10.30pm Sun. **Main courses** £9-£14.90. **Map** p105 F6 ㉕ **Japanese**
Shoryu pips its West End tonkotsu rivals when it comes to the texture and stock of its broth. As well as Hakata-style ramen (noodles in a rich, boiled-down, pork-bone broth), the other notable feature is speed. Both help to ease the hassle of no-bookings dining. Dracula tonkotsu – with caramelised garlic oil, balsamic vinegar and garlic chips – packs a flavoursome punch. Extra toppings such as bamboo shoots and boiled egg are to be expected, but kaedama (plain refill noodles) are a godsend for anyone sharing soup stock between small children. There's a varied choice of sides, sakés and sweets. **Other locations** 3 Denman Street, Soho, W1D 7HA; G3-5 Kingly Court, Soho, W1B 5PJ.

Pubs & Bars

Bar Américain

Brasserie Zédel, 20 Sherwood Street, W1F 7ED (7734 4888, www.brasseriezedel.com). Piccadilly Circus tube. **Open** 4.30pm-midnight Mon-Wed; 4.30pm-1am Thur, Fri; 2.30pm-1am Sat; 4.30-11pm Sun. **Map** p105 E6 ㉖

Liberty. *See p116.*

We love the simplicity of the cocktail list here: around 20 drinks, most of them tried and tested classics. Martinis, manhattans and daiquiris are all expertly rendered, and you can get the true Vesper, James Bond's own-recipe martini made with gin, vodka and Lillet Blanc. For a quiet drink in the West End, in a beautiful art deco interior with widely spaced tables, and without paying ultra-high prices, you can't do much better than the Américain.

▶ *Also here is Brasserie Zédel, another example of Chris Corbin and Jeremy King's characteristic flair for combining glamour and approachability.*

Shops & Services

Burberry
121 Regent Street, W1B 4TB (7806 8904, www.burberry.com). Piccadilly Circus tube. **Open** 10am-9pm Mon-Sat; 11am-6pm Sun. **Map** p105 E6 ㉗ **Fashion**
The flagship store of the Burberry brand melds together the building's near-200 years of history with the attributes of hyper-modern retailing, but the gracious surroundings and an emphasis on natural light create a welcoming atmosphere. There's a beauty room here, as well as fashion and accessories. **Other locations** throughout the city.

Hamleys
188-196 Regent Street, W1B 5BT (03871 704 1977, www.hamleys.com). Oxford Circus tube. **Open** 10am-9pm Mon-Fri; 9.30am-9pm Sat; noon-6pm Sun. **Map** p105 E6 ㉘ **Children**
Visiting Hamleys is certainly an experience – whether a good one or not will depend on your tolerance for noisy, over-excited children, especially during school holidays and the run-up to Christmas, when the store runs special kids' events. As you doubtless know, Hamleys is a ginormous toy shop, perhaps *the* ginormous toy shop, with attractive displays of all this season's must-have toys across five crazed floors, and perky demonstrators ramping up the temptation levels.

J Crew
165 Regent Street, W1B 4AD (7292 1580, www.jcrew.com). Oxford Circus tube. **Open** 10am-8pm Mon-Sat; noon-6pm Sun. **Map** p105 E6 ㉙ **Fashion**
America's hottest fashion export – a firm favourite with Michelle Obama – landed in London in 2013 and has since spread across London. This outpost is handsomely designed and easy to navigate. Women's clothing is on the ground floor, upstairs is menswear and the Crewcuts kids' range. **Other locations** throughout the city.

Karl Lagerfeld
145-147 Regent Street, W1B 4JB (7439 8454, www.karl.com). Piccadilly Circus tube. **Open** 10am-8pm Mon-Sat; noon-6pm Sun. **Map** p105 E6 ㉚ **Fashion**

EXPLORE

Lagerfeld's first dedicated UK store is a temple to the man himself. Having cultivated an instantly recognisable appearance (slimline black tailoring, smoothly quiffed silver ponytail, black shades and superfluous fingerless gloves), the designer is set on flogging the hell out of it. In fact, the first thing that you see when you enter the store is a run of Karl robots and dolls. Behind them are neatly stacked Union Jack T-shirts emblazoned with Karl cameos, and trainers with a dogtooth-print that on closer inspection is a micro Karl motif.

★ Liberty

Regent Street, W1B 5AH (7734 1234, www. liberty.co.uk). Oxford Circus tube. **Open** 10am-8pm Mon-Sat; noon-6pm Sun. **Map** p104 D5 ③

Department store

Charmingly idiosyncratic, Liberty is housed in a 1920s mock Tudor structure. The store was given a major revamp in early 2009, and a further boost as the subject of a TV documentary series in 2013.

The expanded beauty hall on the ground floor goes from strength to strength, with a perfumerie selling scents from cult brands such as Le Labo and Byredo, and skincare from the much-celebrated Egyptian Magic; the basement holds a Margaret Dabbs Sole Spa, for pedicures, polishing and shaping. At the main entrance to the store is Wild at Heart's exuberant floral concession, and just off from here you'll find yourself in a room devoted to the store's own label. Fashion brands focus on high-end British designers, such as Vivienne Westwood and Christopher Kane. But despite being up with the latest fashions, Liberty still respects its dressmaking heritage with a range of cottons in the third-floor haberdashery department. Stationery also pays homage to the traditional, with beautiful Liberty of London notebooks, address books and diaries embossed with the art nouveau 'Ianthe' print, while the interiors departments showcase new furniture designs alongside a dazzling collection of 20th-century classics. Artful and arresting window displays, exciting new collections and luxe labels make it an experience to savour.

MAYFAIR

Bond Street or Green Park tube.

The gaiety suggested by the name of Mayfair, derived from a long-gone spring celebration, isn't matched by its atmosphere today. Even on Mayfair's busy shopping streets, you may feel out of place without the reassuring heft of a platinum card in your pocket. Nonetheless, there are many pleasures to enjoy if you fancy a stroll, not least the rapidly changing roster of blue-chip commercial art galleries.

The Grosvenor and Berkeley families bought the rolling green fields that would become Mayfair in the middle of the 17th century. In the 1700s,

they developed the pastures into a posh new neighbourhood, focused on a series of landmark squares. The most famous of these, **Grosvenor Square** (1725-31), is dominated by the supremely inelegant US Embassy, due to close in 2017 for its move to Vauxhall. The embassy's only decorative touches are a fierce eagle and a mass of post-9/11 protective barricades. Out front, pride of place is taken by a statue of President Dwight Eisenhower, who stayed in nearby **Claridge's** (*see p349*) when in London; Roosevelt presides over the square itself, and its rather eloquent 9/11 memorial: 'Grief is the price we pay for love.' About the Ronald Reagan statue – complete with some of his oratorical greatest hits – the less said the better.

Brook Street has impressive musical credentials: GF Handel lived and died at no.25, and Jimi Hendrix roomed briefly next door at no.23, adjacent buildings that have been combined into the **Handel House Museum**. For most visitors, however, this part of town is all about shopping. Connecting Brook Street with Oxford Street to the north, **South Molton Street** is home to the fabulous boutique-emporium **Browns** and the excellent **Grays Antique Market**, while **New Bond Street** is an A-Z of top-end, mainstream fashion houses.

Beyond New Bond Street, **Hanover Square** is another of the area's big squares, now a busy traffic chicane. Just to the south is **St George's Church**, built in the 1720s and once everyone's favourite place in which to be seen and to get married. Handel, who married nobody, attended services here. South of St George's, salubrious **Conduit Street** is where fashion shocker Vivienne Westwood (no.44) faces staid **Rigby & Peller**, corsetière to the Queen.

Running south off Conduit Street is the most famous Mayfair shopping street of all, **Savile Row**. Gieves & Hawkes (no.1) is a must-visit for anyone interested in the history of British menswear; at no.15, the estimable Henry Poole & Co has cut suits for clients including Napoleon III, Charles Dickens and 'Buffalo' Bill Cody. No.3 was the home of the Beatles' Apple Records and their rooftop farewell concert, while the rock 'n' roll fashion designer **Alexander McQueen** has his menswear shop at no.9.

Two streets west, **Cork Street** was long the heart of the West End art scene – but Fitzrovia's Eastcastle Street these days mounts a pretty serious challenge. Still, **Flowers Central** (21 Cork Street, 7439 7766, www.flowersgalleries. com) is one of Mayfair's notable small galleries, facing off against heavy competition from major US art dealers: notably, the 10,000sq ft **David Zwirner** gallery (24 Grafton Street, 3538 3165, www.davidzwirner.com). **Pace** (no.6, 3206 7600, www.pacegallery.com), which shares premises at 6 Burlington Gardens with the **Royal Academy** (*see p120*), also stages arresting shows. A couple of streets over is Albemarle Street, where you'll find the **Royal Institution**.

Just west of Albemarle Street, **44 Berkeley Square** is one of the original houses in this grand square. Built in the 1740s, it was described by architectural historian Nikolaus Pevsner as 'the finest terrace house of London'. Curzon Street, which runs off the south-west corner of Berkeley Square, was home to MI5, Britain's secret service, from 1945 until the '90s. It's also the northern boundary of **Shepherd Market**, named after a food market set up here by architect Edward Shepherd in the early 18th century and now a curious little enclave. From 1686, this was where the raucous May Fair was held, until it was shut down in the late 18th century due to 'drunkenness, fornication, gaming and lewdness'. You'll still manage the drunkenness easily enough at a couple of good pubs, but the flavour of the place is now captured by the presence of a tobacconist and a couple of leather-bag makers.

Sights & Museums

Handel House Museum

25 Brook Street, W1K 4HB (7495 1685, www.handelhouse.org). Bond Street tube. **Open** 10am-6pm Tue, Wed, Fri, Sat; 10am-8pm Thur; noon-6pm Sun. **Admission** £6.50; £2-£5.50 reductions; free under-5s. **Map** p105 E5 😊

George Frideric Handel moved to Britain from his native Germany aged 25 and settled in this house 12 years later, remaining here until his death in 1759. The house has been beautifully restored with original and recreated furnishings, paintings and a welter of the composer's scores. The programme of events includes Thursday recitals on the museum's period instruments.

As recorded by a blue plaque outside, Jimi Hendrix lived with his girlfriend in an upstairs flat next door at no.23 in 1968 – so impressed was he by his illustrious former neighbour that he bought the *Messiah* and *Water Music* on vinyl. The flat is now museum offices, but plans are afoot to refurbish the room as it was in Hendrix's day; depending on funding, it could reopen permanently to the public in autumn 2015.

▶ *The price of admission is waived for under-17s at the weekend.*

FREE Royal Institution & Faraday Museum

21 Albemarle Street, W1S 4BS (7409 2992, www. rigb.org). Green Park tube. **Open** 9am-6pm Mon-Fri. Closes for events; phone ahead. **Admission** free. *Tours* £3. **Map** p105 F5 😊

The Royal Institution was founded in 1799 for 'diffusing the knowledge… and application of science to the common purposes of life'; from behind its neoclassical façade, it's been at the forefront of London's scientific achievements ever since. In 2008, Sir Terry Farrell completed a £22m rebuild, hoping to improve accessibility and lure people in with more open frontage, a licensed café and spruced-up events. Instead, the RI found itself in a recession and saddled with major debt – after reports in early 2013 that the premises would have to be sold, illustrious benefactors stepped in to help.

The Michael Faraday Laboratory, a replica of the great scientist's former workspace, is in the basement, alongside a working laboratory in which Royal Institution scientists can be observed researching their current projects. Some 1,000 of the RI's 7,000-odd scientific objects are on display, including the world's first electric transformer, a prototype Davy lamp and, from 1858, a print of the first transatlantic telegraph signal.

EXPLORE

New Bond Street.

American Bar at the Beaumont.

▶ *The RI holds a terrific rolling programme of talks and demonstrations in its lecture theatre.*

Restaurants

★ Gymkhana
42 Albemarle Street, W1S 4JH (3011 5900, www. gymkhanalondon.com). Green Park tube. **Open** noon-2.30pm, 5.30-10.30pm Mon-Sat. **Main courses** £7.50-£40. **Map** p105 F5 ㉔ Indian

Justly lauded, Gymkhana looks and feels like an Indian colonial club, with its retro ceiling fans, marble-topped tables and yesteryear photos of polo and cricket team triumphs. It serves a splendid spread of modern Indian dishes based on regional masalas and marinades: a starter of South Indian fried chicken wings, steeped in chilli batter, perhaps, followed by Goan pork vindaloo – slow-cooked chunks of suckling pig cheek, with a vinegary red chilli and garlic masala, spiced with sweet cinnamon and pounded coriander.

★ Pollen Street Social
8-10 Pollen Street, W1S 1NQ (7290 7600, www. pollenstreetsocial.com). Oxford Circus tube. **Open** *Bar* noon-midnight Mon-Sat. *Restaurant* noon-2.30pm, 6-10.30pm Mon-Sat. **Main courses** £14.50-£35.50. **Map** p105 E5 ㉕ Modern European

Pollen Street Social's philosophy is 'deformalised fine dining', and to this end the decor is smart but approachable – white-walled, linen-draped and wood-panelled. Dishes are grounded in French and English tradition and embellished with occasionally esoteric side notes of texture and taste. The delicious subtlety and artistry of Cornish sea bass and red mullet with bouillabaisse sauce, fennel, cuttlefish and saffron potato (self-served from the pan) revealed real zest in the kitchen, as did a masterly strawberry and basil eton mess.

Smack Deli
26-28 Binney Street, W1K 5BN (no phone, www.smackdeli.com). Bond Street tube. **Open** 11am-10.30pm Mon-Sat; noon-10pm Sun. **Main courses** £7.50-£12. **Map** p104 D4 ㊱ Seafood

An idea so simple, you could smack yourself for not thinking of it: lobster rolls, sold from a takeaway counter. There's a choice of four fillings, all served in a rich, toasted brioche bun for £7.50 takeaway or £9 eat-in. There's also a fantastic lobster chowder that was halfway to being a bisque: rich, warming and only £4.80 (eat-in) for a substantial pot; if you're feeling particularly indulgent, tuck into a whole lobster. If you do sit in, head downstairs: the basement is spacious and attractively decorated, as well as playing good tunes and serving craft beer and wines by the glass.

Pubs & Bars

★ American Bar at the Beaumont
Brown Hart Gardens, W1K 6TF (7499 1001, www.thebeaumont.com/dining/american-bar). Bond Street tube. **Open** 11.30am-midnight Mon-Sat; 11.30am-11pm Sun. **Map** p105 E4 ㊲

About as far from the British pub as a drinking experience could get, the American Bar at the Beaumont (*see p348*) purred into action in 2014 – but, like a classic Cadillac, it's already hard to imagine a time it didn't exist. Service is Stateside slick. Cocktails are strong and liberating. The free snacks are diligently refilled. The wood-panelled room is dark and discreet, with portraits of 20th-century American greats looking down approvingly from the walls. Stop here for an americano, a bronx, or just a martini, made just as they would have been 100 years ago.

▶ *Several London bars channel the art deco, Prohibition-era vibe. Our other favourites are the American Bar at the Savoy (see p355), a fine rebirth of the bar that pioneered cocktailing in the city in the 1890s, and Bar Américain (see p114).*

Coburg Bar
The Connaught, Carlos Place, W1K 2AL (7499 7070, www.the-connaught.co.uk). Bond Street or Green Park tube. **Open** 8am-11pm Mon, Sun; 8am-1am Tue-Sat. **Map** p105 E4 ㊳

EXPLORE

The Connaught has always had the most country-house-like feeling of London's great hotels, and the effect reaches perfection in the Coburg. It seems effortlessly beautiful, from the deep patterned carpet to the moulded ceiling; the wing chairs, a long-time fixture, can induce torpor even if you're drinking a double espresso. Great champagnes and cognacs feature prominently on the drinks menu, and the cocktail list focuses on classics. Execution is flawless. Bowls of crisps and olives, both outstanding in quality, are replaced when empty.

▶ *If the Coburg isn't 'scene' enough for you, try the hotel's other, noisier and busier bar, the Connaught.*

Shops & Services

This is a focal area for British designer showcases, with **Stella McCartney** and **Alexander McQueen** our top picks.

★ Alexander McQueen

4-5 Old Bond Street, W1S 4PD (7355 0088, www. alexandermcqueen.com). Green Park tube. **Open** 10am-6pm Mon-Wed, Fri, Sat; 10am-7pm Thur; noon-6pm Sun. **Map** p105 F6 ❸ **Fashion**
McQueen had quite the year in 2015: the 'Savage Beauty' exhibition at the V&A (*see p90*) was a massive sell-out success, but it was only one of several shows dedicated to the artistry of the late designer. Here, you can see – and buy – the best of his designer womenswear. This is a very posh shop, full of baroque wood panels, marble and gilt mirrors, but – as with all things McQueen – in among the splendour something sinister must lurk. Look at the feet of chairs and tables and you'll see claws and hoofs. Gargoyles and skulls grimace and twist furtively from the flora and fauna of the moulded plaster panels. A real shopping experience.

▶ *Alexander McQueen Menswear (9 Savile Row, W1S 3PF, 7494 8840) has similarly macabre touches – as well as a bespoke tailoring workshop in the basement – and there's also a diffusion line, McQ (14 Dover Street, W1S 4LW, 7318 2220).*

Berry Bros & Rudd

3 St James's Street, SW1A 1EG (7022 8973, www.bbr.com). Green Park tube. **Open** 10am-6pm Mon-Fri; 10am-5pm Sat. **Map** p105 G6 ❹ **Food & drink**
Britain's oldest wine merchant has been trading in the same premises since 1698, and its heritage is reflected in its panelled sales and tasting rooms. Burgundy-and claret-lovers will drool at the hundreds of wines, but there are also decent selections from elsewhere in Europe and the New World.

Browns

24-27 South Molton Street, W1K 5RD (7514 0016, www.brownsfashion.com). Bond Street tube. **Open** 10am-6.30pm Mon-Wed, Fri, Sat; 10am-7pm Thur. **Map** p104 D4 ❹ **Fashion**

Browns has been on the fashion cutting-edge for more than four decades. Among the 100-odd designers jostling for attention in Joan Burstein's five interconnecting shops (menswear is at no.23) are Chloé, Christopher Kane and Balenciaga, with plenty of fashion exclusives. No.24 now also houses Shop 24, selling 'staple items you can't live without'. Browns Focus is younger and more casual; Labels for Less is loaded with last season's leftovers. **Other location** 160 Sloane Street, Chelsea, SW1X 9BT (7514 0040).

★ Dover Street Market

17-18 Dover Street, W1S 4LT (7518 0680, www. doverstreetmarket.com). Green Park tube. **Open** 11am-7pm Mon-Sat; noon-5pm Sun. **Map** p105 F5 ❷ **Fashion**
Comme des Garçons designer Rei Kawakubo's groundbreaking six-storey space combines the edgy energy of London's indoor markets – concrete floors, tills inside corrugated iron shacks, Portaloo dressing rooms – with a fine range of rarefied labels. All 14 of the Comme des Garçons collections are here, alongside exclusive lines from such designers as Lanvin and Azzedine Alaïa.

▶ *News broke in late 2014 that, after a decade here, DSM would be moving to premises on Haymarket, the site of the original Burberry flagship. No timescale had been announced as we went to press.*

Drake's

3 Clifford Street, W1S 2LF (7734 2367, www. drakes-london.com). Green Park tube. **Open** 10am-6pm Mon-Fri; 11am-6pm Sat. **Map** p105 E5 ❸ **Menswear**
The subtle interplay between exuberance and understatement is what makes Drake's unique. Its parquet floors and soft white walls provide a neutral backdrop to showcase the Drake's look: classic British style, as it might be imagined by Italians. The place to release your inner gent.

Grays Antique Market & Grays in the Mews

58 Davies Street, W1K 5LP & 1-7 Davies Mews, W1K 5AB (7629 7034, www.graysantiques.com). Bond Street tube. **Open** 10am-6pm Mon-Fri; 11am-5pm Sat. **Map** p104 D4 ❷ **Antiques**
Sibling of Alfie's (*see p112*), Grays gathers more than 200 dealers in a smart covered market building. They sell everything from antique furniture and rare books to vintage fashion and jewellery.

Paul Smith

9 Albemarle Street, W1S 4BL (7493 4565, www.paulsmith.co.uk). Green Park tube. **Open** 10am-6pm Mon-Wed; 10am-7pm Thur-Sat; noon-6pm Sun. **Map** p105 F5 ❺ **Fashion**
The Paul Smith flagship is as big, glossy and imposing as an oligarch's art gallery, with the whimsical flourishes that made Smith Britain's most popular

EXPLORE

designer replaced by something on a much grander scale. There's that huge wrought-iron façade, which jars brilliantly with the Georgian elegance of the surrounding buildings, and white pillars within that spring from the parquet floor to showcase nostalgic record players and vintage radios. The full men's and women's collections are here, displayed on more wrought-iron and on chunks of reclaimed wood.
▶ *Samples and previous season's stock are sold at discounts of up to 50% at the Paul Smith Sale Shop (23 Avery Row, W1X 9HB, 7493 1287).*

Postcard Teas
9 Dering Street, W1S 1AG (7629 3654, www. postcardteas.com). Bond Street or Oxford Circus tube. **Open** 10.30am-6.30pm Mon-Sat. **Map** p104 D5 ⓺ **Food & drink**
The range in this exquisite little shop is not huge, but it is selected with great care, and all teas are sourced from small co-operatives. There's a central table for those who want to try a pot; or book in for one of the tasting sessions held on Saturdays between 10am and 11am. Tea-ware and accessories are also sold.

Rigby & Peller
22A Conduit Street, W1S 2XT (7491 2200, www.rigbyandpeller.com). Oxford Circus tube. **Open** 9.30am-6pm Mon-Wed, Fri, Sat; 9am-7pm Thur. **Map** p105 E5 ⓻ **Fashion**
Rigby & Peller make Elizabeth II's smalls – if it's good enough for Her Majesty, it's good enough for us. Established in 1939, the brand's royal warrant was granted in 1960. Book an appointment for the bespoke bra-making service or to be expertly fitted for ready-to-wear lingerie and swimwear. Premium brands such as Aubade, Lejaby, Huit and Simone Perele are also stocked, along with sports, bridal, mastectomy and maternity bras.
Other locations throughout the city.

Smythson
40 New Bond Street, W1S 2DE (7629 8558, www.smythson.com). Bond Street tube. **Open** 9.30am-7pm Mon-Wed, Fri; 10am-8pm Thur; 10am-7pm Sat; noon-6pm Sun. **Map** p105 E5 ⓽ **Stationery**
London's poshest and best-loved stationers is a vertiable paradise for paper-lovers. Established in 1887, Smythson made its name from selling extraordinarily desirable pigskin diaries, notebooks and personalised stationery – and they have designed invitations and notelets for everyone from Stella McCartney to the Queen herself.

Stella McCartney
30 Bruton Street, W1J 6QR (7518 3100, www. stellamccartney.com). Bond Street or Green Park tube. **Open** 10am-6pm Mon-Wed, Fri, Sat; 10am-7pm Thur. **Map** p105 E5 ⓽ **Fashion**
It's hard not to adore Stella's flagship, all super-sleek in shiny black with the brand emblazoned on it in

fuchsia. Her current collection presides over a main space decked out in lots of white marble with pops of pink: if you can't afford £1,000 for a chic tailored blazer or this year's 'It' bag, look to signature shades or some delicate jewellery. There's children's wear in a well-lit atrium towards the back, just before you get to the footwear shrine in a cosy back chamber. And there's a simply gigantic fitting room, where you have all the space you need to play dress up.

PICCADILLY
Green Park, Hyde Park Corner or Piccadilly Circus tube.

Piccadilly's name is derived from the 'picadil', a type of suit collar that was in vogue during the 18th century. The first of the area's main buildings was built by tailor Robert Baker and, indicating the source of his wealth, nicknamed 'Piccadilly Hall'. A stroll through the handful of Regency shopping arcades confirms that the rag trade is still flourishing mere minutes away from Savile Row and Jermyn Street. At the renovated **Burlington Arcade**, the oldest and most famous of these arcades, top-hatted security staff known as 'beadles' ensure there's no singing, whistling or hurrying in the arcade: such uncouth behaviour is prohibited by archaic by-laws. Formerly Burlington House (1665), the **Royal Academy of Arts** is next door to the arcade's entrance. It hosts several lavish, crowd-pleasing exhibitions each year.
To the west along Piccadilly, smartly uniformed doormen mark former car showroom turned restaurant, the **Wolseley** (*see p82*), and the expensive, exclusive **Ritz** (*see p343*).

Sights & Museums

FREE Royal Academy of Arts
Burlington House, W1J 0BD (7300 8000, www. royalacademy.org.uk). Green Park or Piccadilly Circus tube. **Open** 10am-6pm Mon-Thur, Sat, Sun; 10am-10pm Fri. **Admission** free. *Exhibitions* vary. **Map** p105 F6 ⓾
Britain's first art school was founded in 1768 and moved to the extravagantly Palladian Burlington House a century later, but it's now best known not for education but for exhibitions. Ticketed blockbusters

Royal Academy of Arts.

are generally held in the Sackler Wing or the main galleries; shows in the John Madejski Fine Rooms are drawn from the RA's holdings, which range from Constable to Hockney, and are free. The biggest event here is the annual Summer Exhibition, which for more than two centuries has drawn from works entered by the public. The RA's restaurant, the Keeper's House, has a little courtyard 'garden'.

The RA has also expanded into a nearby 19th-century building: 6 Burlington Gardens. Conveniently located directly behind the main location, it has been exhibiting unabashedly contemporary art, from Tracey Emin and David Hockney to lightworks by Mariko Mori. There's a Peyton & Byrne café here, and the Studio Shop.

FREE St James's Piccadilly

197 Piccadilly, W1J 9LL (7734 4511, www.sjp.org).
Piccadilly Circus tube. **Open** 8am-6.30pm daily.
Evening events times vary. **Admission** free.
Map p105 F6 ③

Consecrated in 1684, St James's is the only church Sir Christopher Wren built on an entirely new site. A calming building with few architectural airs or graces, it was almost destroyed in World War II, but painstakingly reconstructed. Grinling Gibbons, the woodcarver, created the delicate limewood garlanding around the sanctuary which thankfully survived the bombing and is one of the few real frills. Beneath a new tiled roof, the church stages regular classical concerts, provides a home for the William Blake Society (Blake was baptised here) and hosts markets in the churchyard: food on Monday, antiques on Tuesday, and arts and crafts from Wednesday to Saturday. There's also a handy café in the basement with plenty of tables.

Restaurants

Just across Piccadilly in St James's is one of the grandest brasseries to be found in London: the **Wolseley** (*see p82*).

Shops & Services

The Royal Arcades are a throwback to shopping of the past – the **Burlington Arcade** is both the largest and grandest, but the **Piccadilly Arcade**, opposite it, and the **Royal Arcade**, at 28 Old Bond Street, are also worth a visit.

★ Burlington Arcade

51 Piccadilly, W1J 0QJ (7493 1764, www.
burlington-arcade.co.uk). Green Park tube.
Open 9am-7.30pm Mon-Sat; 11am-6pm Sun.
Map p105 F6 ㉜ **Mall**

In 1819, Lord Cavendish commissioned Britain's very first shopping arcade. Nearly two centuries later, the Burlington is still one of London's most prestigious shopping 'streets', patrolled by 'beadles' decked out in top hats and tailcoats. Highlights include collections of classic watches at David Duggan, established British fragrance house Penhaligon's, and Sermoneta, selling Italian leather gloves in a range of bright colours. High-end food shops come in the form of Luponde Tea and Ladurée; head to the latter for exquisite Parisian macaroons. Burlington also houses a proper shoe-shine boy working with waxes and creams for just £4. This may not offer the best shopping in London, but it's certainly one of the best shopping experiences.

Waterstones Piccadilly

203-206 Piccadilly, W1J 9HD (7851 2400,
www.waterstones.co.uk). Piccadilly Circus tube.
Open 9am-10pm Mon-Sat; noon-6.30pm Sun.
Map p105 F6 ㉝ **Books**

The flagship store of the chain is located in a handsome art deco former department store, where six floors are now stuffed with some 200,000 books, as well as two Café Ws (one on the lower ground-floor, one on the mezzanine) and, on the top floor, the 5th View Bar & Restaurant. The programme of readings, reading groups and workshops is lively and varied. London's only rival to Foyles (*see p126*).

EXPLORE

Soho & Leicester Square

For more than two centuries, poseurs, spivs, tarts, toffs, drunks and divas have gathered in Soho. But the district's time as the focus of all that's benevolently naughty – and a proportion of the truly wicked too – has gone. Prostitution has largely been cleared out; many of the area's music, film and advertising businesses have moved on, and even the once-thriving gay scene faces frequent venue closures. Instead, the sizeable residential community that remains is faced with an almost inconceivable number of bars, restaurants and shops. There are more chains among them than there used to be, but independents still dominate.

Just to the south of Soho, beyond London's bustling Chinatown, Leicester Square – known for cinemas and, for many years, drunk out-of-towners – is inching towards a classier reputation.

Foyles.

Don't Miss

1 Algerian Coffee Stores An aromatic piece of Soho history (p127).

2 Arbutus Affordable fine dining (p124).

3 Bar Termini Coffee, aperitivi – what more could you want (p127)?

4 Foyles London's best bookshop (p126).

5 Carnaby Street Back in fashion (p132).

EXPLORE

Soho Square.

SOHO SQUARE & AROUND

Tottenham Court Road tube.

Forming the area's northern gateway, **Soho Square** was laid out in 1681. It was initially called King's Square; a weather-beaten statue of Charles II stands in it. One of the square's benches is dedicated to singer Kirsty MacColl, in honour of her song named after the square.

Two classic Soho streets run south from the square. **Greek Street**, its name a nod to a church that once stood here, is lined with restaurants and bars, among them 50-year-old Hungarian eaterie the **Gay Hussar** (no.2, 7437 0973, http://gayhussar.co.uk) and the nearby **Pillars of Hercules** pub (no.7, 7437 1179), where the literati once enjoyed long, liquid lunches. Just by the Pillars, an arch leads to Manette Street and Charing Cross Road, where you'll find the reborn **Foyles**. Back on Greek Street, no.49 was once Les Cousins, a folk venue (note the mosaic featuring a musical note); Casanova lived briefly at no.46.

Parallel to Greek Street is **Frith Street**, once home to Mozart (1764-65, no.20) and painter John Constable (1810-11, no.49). Humanist essayist William Hazlitt died in 1830 at no.6, now a discreet hotel named in his memory (*see p352* **Hazlitt's**). Further down the street are **Ronnie Scott's** (*see p279*), Britain's best-known jazz club, and, across from Ronnie's, the similarly mythologised 24-hour coffee haunt **Bar Italia** (no.22, 7437 4520).

Restaurants

★ 10 Greek Street
10 Greek Street, W1D 4DH (7734 4677, www.10greekstreet.com). Tottenham Court Road tube. **Open** noon-2.30pm, 5.30-10.45pm Mon-Sat. **Main courses** £18-£19. **Map** p125 D3 ❶ Modern European

This small, unshowy restaurant has made a name for itself with a short but perfectly formed menu and an easygoing conviviality. Dishes are seasonal and the kitchen produces lots of interesting but ungimmicky combinations – such as a special of halibut fillet with yellow beans, chilli and garlic, on a vivid romesco sauce. It's good value too. Tables are closely packed, and in the evening it can get noisy; bookings are taken for lunch but not dinner.

★ Arbutus
63-64 Frith Street, W1D 3JW (7734 4545, www.arbutusrestaurant.co.uk). Tottenham Court Road tube. **Open** noon-2.30pm, 5-11pm Mon-Thur; noon-2.30pm, 5-11.30pm Fri, Sat; noon-3pm, 5.30-10.30pm Sun. **Main courses** from £19. **Map** p125 C3 ❷ Modern European

This smart modern eaterie is successfully creative with unusual and less-used ingredients: saddle of rabbit, prettily presented with small root vegetables and stuffed with liver, accompanied by shepherd's pie, for example. We like the good-value set lunch and pre-theatre menus, the posh but proper puds and the fact that every wine is available by 250ml carafe.
▶ *Also try sister restaurant Wild Honey (12 St George Street, Mayfair, W1S 2FB, 7758 9160, www.wildhoneyrestaurant.co.uk).*

Ceviche
17 Frith Street, W1D 4RG (7292 2040, www.cevicheuk.com). Leicester Square tube. **Open** noon-11.30pm Mon-Sat; noon-10.15pm Sun. **Tapas** £4.50-£13. **Map** p125 C3 ❸ Peruvian

Ceviche showcases citrus-cured fish. It is available in half a dozen different forms, though the menu also includes everything from terrific chargrilled meat and fish skewers (anticuchos) to a simple but perfectly executed corn cake. Factor in the seating options (trendy at the steel counter-bar, more comfortable in the rear dining area), the charismatic, attentive staff and the party atmosphere, and it's no wonder this place has been such a huge hit.

Koya
49 Frith Street, W1D 4SG (7434 4463, www.koya.co.uk). Tottenham Court Road tube. **Open** noon-3pm; 5.30-10.30pm Mon-Sat; 5.30-10pm Sun. **Main courses** £6.90-£14.90. **Map** p125 C3 ❹ Japanese

With blond-wood sharing tables, white walls and a generally fresh-faced crowd of diners, this venue feels more like a friendly caff than a slick West End eaterie. The handmade udon noodles produced here are top-notch, which explains why expectant diners often queue out of the door (no bookings are taken).

Pizza Pilgrims
11 Dean Street, W1D 3RP (7287 8964, http://pizzapilgrims.co.uk). Tottenham Court Road tube. **Meals served** noon-10.30pm Mon-Sat; noon-9.30pm Sun. **Main courses** £7-£11. **Map** p125 C3 ❺ Pizza

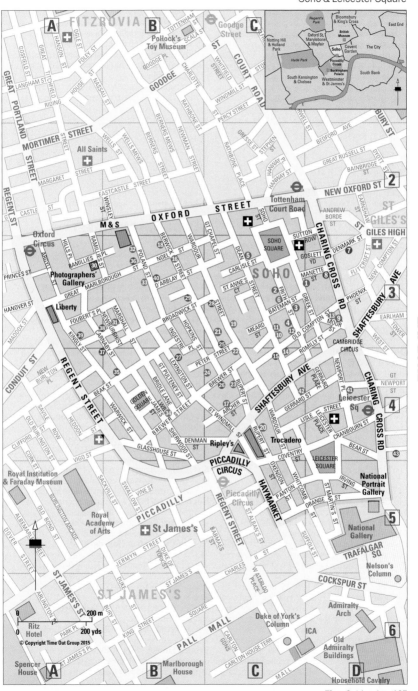

The main basement dining area is intimate, with wipe-clean green checked tablecloths and 1960s Italian film posters creating the feel of a retro Soho trattoria. The friendly, slightly trendy mood is helped by an alcove for table football. Pizzas are chewy and soft in the Neapolitan style, the appealing, thick bases layered with on-trend toppings: 'nduja, a spicy Calabrian sausage, is paired well with a simple marinara sauce, for example. No bookings.

Pubs & Bars

Dog & Duck

18 Bateman Street, W1D 3AJ (7494 0697, www. nicholsonspubs.co.uk). Tottenham Court Road tube. **Open** 10am-11pm daily. **Map** p125 C3 ❻
This venerable boozer is owned by the Nicholson's chain, hence the branded menus; ignore them and look around you at the lovely tiled walls, big mirrors, original light fixtures and well-seasoned wood instead. The pub is incredibly popular, though weekday afternoons are relatively leisurely for a quiet pint chosen from a small, changing list of real ales. At night, you'll be lucky to get a seat and even luckier to get one at the prized copper-topped tables at the back. In any weather more clement than a typhoon, the crowd spills out on to the pavement.

Shops & Services

Denmark Street

Map p125 D3 ❼ **Musical instruments**
Just off the Charing Cross Road, Denmark Street is in the 1960s the site of the legendary recording studio Regent Sounds; it is now a hub for music shops, principally selling guitars, amps and FX pedals, but you'll also find such esoterica as an early-music specialist (no.11) that can supply all your recorder and Baroque cello needs. There's an upmarket Fernandez & Wells café at the far end of the short street, plus a swanky burger joint halfway along, while to the north there's much evidence of Crossrail.

★ Foyles

107 Charing Cross Road, WC2H 0EB (7437 5660, www.foyles.co.uk). Tottenham Court Road tube. **Open** 9.30am-9pm Mon-Sat; noon-6pm Sun.
Map p125 D3 ❽ **Books & music**
News that Foyles was moving and that its beloved café would close was greeted with dismay by *Time Out* readers, but when the vast new premises opened in 2014 just a couple of doors down the same street, it was easy to understand the decision. CEO Sam Husain, entering retirement now the move is complete, described the new store as 'a bookshop for the 21st century': it gathers 37,000sq ft of floorspace, laid out immaculately by architects Lifschutz Davidson Sandilands, around an impressive central atrium. The shop's eight levels (four actual floors) are packed with more than 200,000 books, as well as CDs and a variety of

more-or-less literary gifts. Wherever you stand, you can see every part of the building, and the place is bathed in a gentle, contemplation-inducing glow. It's light years away from the dusty nooks and crannies of the old building.

The shop's focus is on the social aspect of reading. A whole floor is dedicated to events, from readings by Michael Palin and Jarvis Cocker, to themed reading groups or literary tours, and there's a space dedicated to contemporary art. The swish new café is run by Leafi, the people behind the gallery cafés at the Whitechapel (*see p205*) and Courtauld (*see p147*). Foyles veterans may have found the new premises a smidge anodyne, but such reservations were soon forgotten by most – this great bookshop finally has premises that really work.
Other locations throughout the city.

OLD COMPTON STREET & AROUND

Leicester Square or Tottenham Court Road tube.

Linking Charing Cross Road to Wardour Street and crossed by Greek, Frith and Dean streets, **Old Compton Street** is London's gay catwalk. Tight T-shirts congregate around **Balans** (*see p260*), **Compton's** (nos.51-53) and the **Admiral Duncan** (no.54). However, the street has an interesting history that dates back long before rainbow flags were hung above its doors: no.59 was formerly the 2i's Coffee Bar, the skiffle venue where stars and svengalis mingled in the late 1950s and early '60s.

Visit Old Compton Street in the morning for a sense of the mostly vanished immigrant Soho of old. Cheeses and cooked meats from **Camisa** (no.61, 7437 7610, www.icamisa.co.uk) and roasting beans from the **Algerian Coffee Stores** scent the air, as **Pâtisserie Valerie** (no.44, 7437 3466, www.patisserie-valerie.co.uk), first of a now significant national chain, does a brisk trade in croissants and cakes.

Valerie's traditional rival is the older **Maison Bertaux** (7437 6007, www.maisonbertaux.com), an atmospheric holdover from the 19th century that sits near the southern end of Greek Street. At the corner of Greek and Romilly streets is **Norman's Coach & Horses** (29 Greek Street, 7437 5920, www.coachandhorsessoho.co.uk), where irascible Soho flâneur Jeffrey Bernard held court for decades; it is now London's only vegetarian pub. It's almost opposite the members' club **Soho House** (40 Greek Street, 7734 5188; for the club's hotels, *see p352* **Dean Street** and *p363* **Shoreditch Rooms**), where media types and wannabes hope to channel the same vibe. Two streets along, Dean Street holds the **French House**; formerly the York Minster pub, it was de Gaulle's London base for French resistance in World War II and in later years became a favourite of painters Francis Bacon and Lucian Freud.

North of Old Compton Street on Dean Street sits the **Groucho Club** (no.45, 7439 4685), a members-only media hangout that was founded in the mid 1980s and named in honour of the Groucho Marx quote about not wanting to join any club that would have him as a member. A few doors along, at no.28, the other famous Marx lived in a garret from 1850 to 1856; he would probably not have approved of the high-class, high-cost dinners served there now – at **Quo Vadis** (nos.26-29). To the north is the **Soho Theatre** (*see p294*), which programmes comedy, cabaret and new plays.

Restaurants

La Bodega Negra
9 Old Compton Street, WE1D 5JF (7758 4100, www.labodeganegra.com). Leicester Square tube.
Open *Café* noon-midnight Mon-Wed; noon-1am Thur-Sat; noon-11pm Sun. *Restaurant* 6pm-1am Mon-Sat; 6-11.30pm Sun. **Main courses** £12-£29. **Map** p125 D3 ❾ Mexican
It's so dark and loud in this nightclub-like basement restaurant that you'll need a moment to adjust. The cooking is perhaps the least thrilling aspect of the place, though effort is put into presentation. Soft flour tacos with a tender beef filling are beautifully arranged on a wooden board. Factor-in the small portions and two-hour table limits and you might wonder what the fuss is all about. But that would be missing the point. You come here to see and be seen.

Burger & Lobster
36 Dean Street, W1D 4PS (7432 4800, www. burgerandlobster.com). Leicester Square tube.
Open noon-10.30pm Mon-Wed; noon-11pm Thur-Sat; noon-10pm Sun. **Main courses** £20. **Map** p125 C3 ❿ American
With its no-nonsense choice of, you've guessed it, burger or lobster, this place has been a runaway hit. Food costs £20, an all-in price that includes a huge carton of thin-cut fries and a side salad: you won't go hungry here. The burger is good, but for ultimate value, choose the lobster (boiled, grilled or in a brioche roll with mayonnaise).
Other locations throughout the city.

Cây Tre
42-43 Dean Street, W1D 4PZ (7317 9118, www. caytresoho.co.uk). Leicester Square tube. **Open** 11am-11pm Mon-Thur; 11am-11.30pm Fri, Sat; 11am-10pm Sun. **Main courses** £8-£13. **Map** p125 C3 ⓫ Vietnamese
Cây Tre is chic, with minimal decor, impeccably smart and efficient black-clad staff, and beautifully served food. The chain prides itself on using fresh ingredients with impeccable provenance – witness the barbecued Somerset ribs with lemongrass, Sriracha chilli sauce and galangal. Counters with

stools have been provided by the entrance, facing the street, for those in a hurry or singletons.
Other location 301 Old Street, Shoreditch, EC1V 9LA (7729 8662).

★ Herman Ze German
33 Old Compton Street, W1D 5JU (7734 0431, www.herman-ze-german.co.uk). Leicester Square tube. **Open** 11am-11.30pm Mon-Thur, Sun; 11am-midnight Fri, Sat. **Main courses** £4.45-£9.95. **Map** p125 C3 ⓬ German
Herman Ze German is a purveyor of German sausages. The sausages are from the Schwarzwald (the Black Forest), and are *sehr gut*: high-quality pork. *See p131* **London's Best Dishes**.
Other locations 19 Villiers Street, Charing Cross, WC2N 6ND (7839 5264); 43 Charlotte Street, W1T 1RS (7323 9207).

Pubs & Bars

★ Bar Termini
7 Old Compton Street, W1D 5JE (07860 945 018, www.bar-termini.com). Leicester Square or Tottenham Court Road tube. **Open** 7.30am-midnight daily. **Map** p125 C3 ⓭
The newest of cocktail-maestro Tony Conigliaro's outposts (his drinks lab is at 69 Colebrooke Row; *see p235*), Bar Termini does two things: coffee and cocktails, in a room for 25, with seated service only, though you may stand if you order a single 'espresso al bar' (£1) – then drink and run in the Italian style. The coffee list has just six brews, all of them classics but with a twist. The alcohol list has three negronis, four 'aperitivi', three wines, one bottled beer. There are also baked goods by day, and charcuterie and cheese in the evening.
▶ *You'll need to book for visits later than 5pm, when there's also a 90-minute time limit.*

★ French House
49 Dean Street, W1D 5BG (7437 2799, www. frenchhousesoho.com). Leicester Square tube. **Open** noon-11pm Mon-Sat; noon-10.30pm Sun. *Food served* noon-4pm daily. **Map** p125 C4 ⓮
Through the door of this venerable establishment have passed many titanic drinkers of the pre- and post-war eras. The venue's French heritage enticed de Gaulle to run a Resistance operation from upstairs – it's now a tiny restaurant. De Gaulle's image survives behind the bar, where beer is served in half-pints, and litre bottles of Breton cider are still plonked on the famed back alcove table.

Shops & Services

★ Algerian Coffee Stores
52 Old Compton Street, W1D 4PB (7437 2480, www.algcoffee.co.uk). Leicester Square tube. **Open** 9am-7pm Mon-Wed; 9am-9pm Thur, Fri; 9am-8pm Sat. **Map** p125 C4 ⓯ Food & drink

EXPLORE

For over 125 years, this unassuming little shop has been trading over the same wooden counter. The range of coffees is broad, with house blends sold alongside single-origin beans; some serious teas and brewing hardware are also available.

▶ *Passing by? Take away a single or double espresso for £1, or a cappuccino or a latte for £1.20.*

WARDOUR STREET & AROUND

Leicester Square or Tottenham Court Road tube.

Parallel to Dean Street, **Wardour Street** provides offices for film and TV production companies, but is also known for its rock history. No.100 was, for nearly three decades, the Marquee, where Led Zeppelin played their first London gig and Hendrix appeared four times. The latter's favourite Soho haunt was the nearby **Ship** pub (no.116), still with a sprinkling of music-themed knick-knacks. There's more music history at Trident Studios on nearby **St Anne's Court**: Lou Reed recorded *Transformer* here, and David Bowie cut both *Hunky Dory* and *The Rise and Fall of Ziggy Stardust* on the site.

When he was still known as David Jones, Bowie played a gig at the Jack of Clubs on Brewer Street, most recently the now also lamented Madame JoJo's. But this corner of Soho is most famous not for music but for its position at the heart of Soho's almost vanished but still notorious sex trade. The Raymond Revuebar opened on the neon alleyway of Walker's Court in 1958, swiftly becoming London's most famous strip club. It closed in 2004, became a series of short-lived gay clubs, then reopened as edgy, celebrity-infested, exclusive alt-cabaret club the **Box** (11-12 Walker's Court, W1F 0SD, www.theboxsoho.com), the London branch of a New York original.

North of here, **Berwick Street** clings on to its mix of old-school London raffishness and new-Soho style. The former comes courtesy of the fruit and veg market, and the egalitarian, old-fashioned and unceasingly popular **Blue Posts** pub (no.22, 7437 5008), where builders, post-production editors, restaurateurs and market traders gabble and glug as one beneath a portrait of Berwick Street-born star of stage and radio Jessie Matthews (1907-81). The likes of coffee bar **Flat White** (no.17, 7734 0370) and **Ember Yard** herald the likely future.

Restaurants

Berwick Street Market
Berwick Street, W1F 0PT (no phone, www. berwickstreetlondon.co.uk/market). Piccadilly Circus tube. **Open** 9am-6pm Mon-Sat. **Map** p125 B3 ⓭ **Street food**
Berwick Street sits smack-dab in the middle of Soho, one of the most restaurant-rich patches of Britain.

The street has been home to a fruit and vegetable market since 1778. There's less fresh produce nowadays, but stalls selling takeaway food – anything from a virtuous but vivid salad of couscous with charred vegetables to a juicy, dripping cheeseburger – have filled in the gaps nicely. The roster changes, but among the Monday-to-Friday regulars you can expect to find meat specialists Tongue 'n' Cheek, Freebird Burritos and the Bread Man.

Bocca di Lupo
12 Archer Street, W1D 7BB (7734 2223, www. boccadilupo.com). Piccadilly Circus tube. **Open** 12.15-2.45pm, 5.15-11pm Mon-Sat; 12.15-3pm, 5.15-9.30pm Sun. **Dishes** £6-£26.50. **Map** p125 C4 ⓱ Italian
The buzz is as important as the food at this popular restaurant. The menu is a slightly confusing mix of small and large plates to share: buttery brown shrimp on soft, silky white polenta, say, or a deep-fried mix of calamari, soft-shell crab and lemon. The radish, celeriac, pomegranate and pecorino salad with truffle dressing is a much-imitated Bocca di Lupo signature.

▶ *The same team runs Gelupo, the gelateria at no.7 (7287 5555, www.gelupo.com). Their blood-orange granita – dark, intense and made with only fruit and cane sugar – is one of our favourite desserts.*

Ember Yard
60 Berwick Street, W1F 8SU (7439 8057, http:// emberyard.co.uk). Oxford Circus or Tottenham Court Road tube. **Open** noon-midnight Mon-Sat; noon-10.30pm Sun. **Tapas** £4.50-£9. **Map** p125 B3 ⓲ Tapas
The fourth in a growing chain of new-style tapas bars, Ember Yard builds on the strengths of its forebears, following their template of combining Italian and Spanish influences, but places an even greater emphasis on the grill. The result is reminiscent of the fabulous charcoal-grill restaurants of the Basque country, especially if you're sitting near the glowing coals. Every flavour combination here is a winner, with the bar snacks among the best in Soho.

★ Hummus Bros
88 Wardour Street, W1F 0TH (7734 1311, www. hbros.co.uk). Oxford Circus or Tottenham Court Road tube. **Open** 7.30am-10pm Mon-Fri; noon-10pm Sat; noon-9pm Sun. **Dishes** £3.95-£8.85. **Map** p125 C3 ⓳ Café
The humble chickpea paste is elevated to something altogether more delicious in the hands of Hummus Bros. Though the wraps aren't bad, go for the bowls of silky-smooth houmous sprinkled with paprika and olive oil. Mashed, cumin-scented fava beans is a good choice of topping, but our favourite is the chunky slow-cooked beef. Side dishes are heartily recommended, with deliciously smoky barbecued aubergine and zingy tabouleh particular highlights. Service is quick and casual.

EXPLORE

Other locations 62 Exmouth Market, Clerkenwell, EC1R 4QE (7812 1177); 37-63 Southampton Row, Bloomsbury, WC1B 4DA (7404 7079); 128 Cheapside, the City, EC2V 6BT (7726 8011).

Palomar

34 Rupert Street, W1D 6DN (7439 8777, http:// thepalomar.co.uk). Leicester Square or Piccadilly Circus tube. **Open** noon-2.30pm, 5.30-11pm Mon-Wed; noon-2.30pm, 5.30-11.30pm Thur-Sat; noon-3.30pm Sun. **Main courses** £9.50-£19. **Map** p125 C4 ⑳ Israeli

Pulse-quickening dance music, free-flowing drink and vibrantly flavoured dishes are common in Israel's fashionable eateries, but rare in London's often po-faced Jewish restaurants. Palomar is set to buck the trend: run by Israeli-born nightclub entrepreneurs, it has become the West End's most unlikely hit. Many of its dishes are recognisably Sephardic. So you might start with Yemeni-style bread, kubaneh – a yeast bread served with rich tahini and tomato dips – and continue with Moroccan-style chermoula-stuffed sardines. Jew or Gentile doesn't matter: bring an appetite for fun as well as for food.

★ Polpetto

11 Berwick Street, W1F 0PL (7439 8627, www. polpo.co.uk). Oxford Circus tube. **Open** noon-11pm Mon-Sat; noon-4pm Sun. **Dishes** £5-£10. **Map** p125 C3 ㉑ Italian

The new incarnation of Polpetto (previously, it was in a room above the French House; *see p127*) is a winner. This long, low-lit dining room bubbles with attentive staff serving Italian-inspired small plates to an appreciative crowd who don't seem to mind being seated at tightly packed tables. In the basement dining room, there's the bonus of a view of chef Florence Knight and her skilled team at work in the glass-fronted kitchen.

Other locations (Polpo) 6 Maiden Lane, Soho, WC2E 7NA (7836 8448); 41 Beak Street, Covent Garden, W1F 9SB (7734 4479); 3 Cowcross Street, Clerkenwell, EC1M 6DR (7250 0034); 126-128 Notting Hill Gate, W11 3QG (7229 3283).

Princi

135 Wardour Street, W1F 0UF (7478 8888, www.princi.co.uk). Leicester Square or Tottenham Court Road tube. **Open** 8am-midnight Mon-Sat; 8.30am-10pm Sun. **Main courses** £7.50-£12.50. **Map** p125 C4 ㉒ Bakery/café

This smart outpost of a Milanese bakery chain remains a popular all-day option. It's an airy, good-looking room, and the food is varied: as well as cakes, pastries and breads, there's a choice of filled focaccia (parma ham, say, or mortadella), hot dishes (lasagne, aubergine parmigiana), slices of pizza and lots of salads. It's all quality, seasonal stuff. Finding a seat at the communal counters can be something of a trial. Opt out by dining in the pizzeria, which offers table service and a calmer atmosphere.

Spuntino

61 Rupert Street, W1D 7PW (no phone, www. spuntino.co.uk). Piccadilly Circus tube. **Open** noon-midnight Mon-Wed; noon-1am Thur-Sat; noon-11pm Sun. **Main courses** £5-£10. **Map** p125 C4 ㉓ North American

A challenge to find (look for 'number 61'), this venue is laid out as a bar – and a tiny one at that, with a smattering of fixed, backless seats allowing diners to perch along the counter. This is no wholesome 1950s-style diner, but a dark, grungy space where dim lights dangle in cages, the walls are cracked and battered, and the staff sport daring tattoos under flimsy vests (and that's just the girls). The menu is Italian-American with plenty of 'additude', featuring big bold flavours packed into tiny portions. No bookings are accepted.

▶ *Owner Russell Norman also runs the excellent Polpo mini-chain (www.polpo.co.uk), of which Polpetto (see left) is our current favourite.*

Yalla Yalla

1 Green's Court, W1F 0HA (7287 7663, www. yalla-yalla.co.uk). Piccadilly Circus tube. **Open** 10am-11pm daily. **Main courses** £9.75-£14.50. **Map** p125 C4 ㉔ Lebanese

The 'Beirut street food' resonates well with the upbeat informality of these dinky Soho premises. Diners cram on to faux-rustic tables, while others nip in for takeaway wraps – filled with everything from falafel to spicy sujuk sausage – from the prepared selection behind the counter. A concise list of classic meze dishes includes a chunky, smoky baba ganoush and a flavour-packed fattoush salad. There's also a selection of grills. Cocktails are served in the evening.

Other location 12 Winsley Street, Marylebone, W1W 8HQ (7637 4748).

Shops & Services

Berwick Street is really the heart of Soho, with its breezy street market (9am-6pm Mon-Sat), one of London's oldest, in an area better known for its lurid, neon-lit trades. Dating back to 1778, it's seeing a bit of a revival with popular street-food stalls. The indie record shops that used to cluster here took a pasting in the noughties, but **Reckless Records** (no.30, 7437 4271, http:// reckless.co.uk) and **Sister Ray** (nos.34-35, 7734 3297, www.sisterray.co.uk) are now beneficiaries of the vinyl revival – along with nearby **Sounds of the Universe**.

Gosh!

1 Berwick Street, W1F 0DR (7636 1011, www. goshlondon.com). Oxford Circus tube. **Open** 10.30am-7pm daily. **Map** p125 C3 ㉕ Books & music

There's nowhere better to bolster your comics collection. There's a huge selection of manga, but

EXPLORE

LONDON'S BEST DISHES

Our food experts did the research – now you enjoy the grub.

BOCKWURST, £4.45

Imported from a German butcher called Fritz, the sausages at **Herman ze German** (see p127) are fat, juicy and made with the highest quality ingredients. Our favourite – the bockwurst, made of smoked pork – has a delicate flavour, a springy middle and plenty of 'knack' when you bite into it. Just add ketchup and mustard.

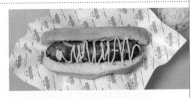

TOASTED FERMENTED CORN BRIOCHE WITH BURNT LEEKS AND SLOW-POACHED DUCK EGG, £7

The **Grain Store** (see p159) isn't a vegetarian restaurant per se, but it does put veg first in all its dishes. And this terrific, just-toasted fermented corn brioche topped with braised 'burnt' leeks, a wobbly, slow-poached duck egg and a drizzle of lovage oil is so good, even card-carrying carnivores fight over them.

BBQ-SPICED CRISPY PIGS' EARS, £5

Duck & Waffle (see p188) serves these beauties in a little brown paper bag, complete with a red wax seal. Inside is a tumble of long, deep-fried piggy strips, with a warmly spiced barbecue flavour and plenty of crunch. The fact that you can munch on them at any time of day or night, while gazing out at the breathtaking skyline, is a big bonus.

TOASTED CHEESE SANDWICH, £6

The folks at **Kappacasein** are cheese over-achievers. Owner Bill Oglethorpe developed Ogleshield, a sweet, nutty little alpine number with brilliant powers of melting that was soon incorporated in toasties across town. But join the queue at his stall at Borough Market (see p61) to taste the best: eight parts Montgomery cheddar, one part Ogleshield and one part Comté, on a base of Poilâne sourdough, with sliced leeks, minced onions and crushed garlic for extra oomph.

QUAIL BRUNCH WITH 'CEREAL', 'EGG', 'TEA' AND 'TOAST', £15.50

Jason Atherton is known for his witty reconstructions of familiar dishes. At **Pollen Street Social** (see p118), his 'quail brunch' comes as a bowl of 'cereal' (a savoury risotto with wild mushrooms), a slice of 'toast' (brioche, topped with a rich quail terrine) and a cup of 'tea' (quail stock and lapsang souchong, poured from a teapot at the table). And that's before they open the wooden box that's sitting next to you, which – hey, presto! – reveals two pieces of pine-smoked quail (breast and confit leg), which are gently placed on the risotto. Culinary theatre of the best – and most delicious – kind.

EXPLORE

Social Eating House.

graphic novels take centre stage, from early classics such as *Krazy Kat* to Alan Moore's erotic Peter Pan adaptation *Lost Girls*. Classic children's books, of the *This is London* vein, are another strong point.

Machine-A

13 Brewer Street, W1F 0RH (7734 4334, www.machine-a.com). Oxford Circus tube. **Open** 11am-7pm Mon-Wed; 11am-8pm Thur-Sat; noon-6pm Sun. **Map** p125 C4 ㉖ **Fashion**

Hats off (make it an Alex Mattsson baseball cap) to Machine-A for championing London's most exciting emerging designers at its Soho concept store. Pieces practically sizzle with energy inside this small space. Outside, its neon signage is a cheeky nod to its massage-parlour neighbours on Brewer Street. A natural habitat for the young, bold and brave.

Pokit

34 Lexington Street, W1F 0LH (01843 448 517, www.pokit.co.uk). Piccadilly Circus tube. **Open** by appt. **Map** p125 B4 ㉗ **Menswear**

Pokit has swept away all the pointless ritual of tradi-tional bespoke tailoring to create something faster, better value and, ultimately, a lot more relevant to how people dress today. But they do it without los-ing any of the quality. Their cloth is sourced from the best British mills, and the fit and make compare favourably with anything on Savile Row.

Sounds of the Universe

7 Broadwick Street, W1F 0DA (7734 3430, www.soundsoftheuniverse.com). Tottenham Court Road tube. **Open** 11am-7.30pm Mon-Sat; 11.30am-5.30pm Sun. **Map** p125 C3 ㉘ **Books & music**

SOTU's remit is broad. This is especially true on the ground floor (new vinyl and CDs), where grime and dubstep 12-inches jostle for space alongside new wave cosmic disco, electro-indie re-rubs and Nigerian compilations. The second-hand vinyl basement is big on soul, jazz, Brazilian and alt-rock.

Universal Works

40 Berwick Street, W1F 8RX (3 581 1501, www.universalworks.co.uk). Tottenham Court Road tube. **Open** 11am-7pm Mon-Sat; 11am-5pm Sun. **Map** p125 B3 ㉙ **Menswear**

One of a number of newish men's brands that draw on Brit heritage in terms of design and craftsman-ship, UW has a street-orientated outlook on style. There's an aversion to flashiness, which lends indi-vidual pieces and the store a quiet, understated feel. **Other location** 37 Lamb's Conduit Street, Bloomsbury, WC1N 3NG (3632 2115).

WEST SOHO

Piccadilly Circus tube.

The area west of Berwick Street was rebranded 'West Soho' in a misplaced bid to give it some kind of upmarket identity. **Brewer Street** does have some interesting places; among them is the **Vintage Magazine Store** (nos.39-43, 7439 8525), offering everything from retro robots to pre-war issues of *Vogue*. Star restaurant **Hix** with its hip downstairs bar (**Mark's Bar**) is also here. On Great Windmill Street is the **Windmill Theatre** (nos.17-19), which gained fame in the 1930s and '40s for its 'revuedeville' shows with erotic 'tableaux' – naked women who remained stationary in order to stay within the law. The place is now a lap-dancing joint. North of Brewer Street is **Golden Square**. Developed in the 1670s, it became the political and ambassadorial district of the late 17th and early 18th centuries, and remains home to some of the area's grandest buildings (many now bases for media firms) and a purveyor of cinnamon buns: the **Nordic Bakery** (no.14A, 3230 1077, www.nordicbakery.com).

Just north of Golden Square is **Carnaby Street**, which became a fashion mecca shortly after John Stephen opened His Clothes here in 1956; Stephen, who went on to own more than a dozen fashion shops on the street, is now commemorated with a plaque at the corner with Beak Street. After thriving during the Swinging Sixties, Carnaby Street became a rather seamy commercialised backwater. However, along with nearby **Newburgh Street** and **Kingly Court**, it's revived, with the tourist traps and chain stores joined by a wealth of independent stores.

A little further north, just short of Oxford Street, is the **Photographers' Gallery**.

Sights & Museums

FREE Photographers' Gallery

16-18 Ramillies Street, W1F 7LW (7087 9300, www.thephotographersgallery.org.uk). Oxford Circus tube. **Open** 10am-6pm Mon-Wed, Fri, Sat; 10am-8pm Thur; 11.30am-6pm Sun. **Admission** free. *Temporary exhibitions* vary. **Map** p125 A3 ⑩

Given a handsome refit by Irish architects O'Donnell+ Tuomey, this old, brick corner building reopened in 2012 as the new home for London's only gallery dedicated solely to the photographic arts. The upper floors have two airy new exhibition spaces, while a bookshop, print sales room and café (open from 9.30am Mon-Fri) are tucked into the ground floor and basement. The exhibitions are varied, and enhanced by quirky details such as the camera obscura in the third-floor Eranda Studio and a projection wall in the café.

Restaurants

Pitt Cue Co

1 Newburgh Street, W1F 7RB (no phone, www.pittcue.co.uk). Oxford Circus tube. **Food served** noon-3pm, 6-10.30pm Mon-Sat; noon-4pm Sun. **Main courses** £9.50-£16. **Map** p125 B3 ㉛

North American

Come to this trailblazing 30-seat rib joint on a Friday or Saturday night and there's one certainty: a painfully long queue. For rib-lovers, it'll be worth it. The Pitt Cue-ers' cooking rarely misses a beat. The gargantuan signature ribs arrive with blistered, blackened skin, revealing ruby fall-off-the-bone meat that is both smoky and dangerously rich. A fine 'slaw, with two kinds of cabbage, coriander seeds and a zingy vinaigrette, cuts through the cholesterol.

★ Social Eating House

58 Poland Street, W1F 7NR (7993 3251, www.socialeatinghouse.com). Oxford Circus tube. **Open** noon-2.30pm, 6-10.30pm Mon-Sat. **Main courses** £17-£33.50. **Set lunch** (noon-2.30pm Mon-Sat) £19 2 courses; £23 3 courses. **Map** p125 B3 ㉜ British

This is arguably star restaurateur Jason Atherton's best venue. It comprises a ground-floor dining room, where the mirrored ceiling creates the sensation of space in a low room, and a smart upstairs cocktail bar, called the Blind Pig, which has a separate entrance. Most of the action is in the dining room, with a kitchen brigade who are clearly at the top of

their game. Smoked duck 'ham', egg and chips is a dish typical of chef Paul Hood's playfulness: 'ham' is cured and smoked from duck breast on the premises, served with a breadcrumbed duck egg that's molten in the middle, but with an aroma of truffle oil. Service is sweet and eager, and the dishes arrive fast.

Pubs & Bars

Lucky Voice

52 Poland Street, W1F 7NQ (7439 3660, www.luckyvoice.com). Oxford Circus tube. **Open** 5.30pm-1am Mon-Wed; 5.30pm-3am Thur, Fri; 3pm-3am Sat; 3-10.30pm Sun. **Map** p125 B3 ㉝

There are nine rooms at this karaoke venue, each with space for between four and 12 singers; some come with props such as hats, wigs and inflatable electric guitars. A drinks menu includes cocktails (£7.95), saké and spirits, brought to your room when you press the 'thirsty' button; food is pizza and snacks. The place to discover your inner Beyoncé. **Other location** 173-174 Upper Street, Islington, N1 1RG (7354 6280).

Mark's Bar

Hix, 66-70 Brewer Street, W1F 9UP (7292 3518, www.marksbar.co.uk). Piccadilly Circus tube. **Open** noon-1am Mon-Sat; noon-midnight Sun. **Map** p125 B4 ㉞

The basement cocktail bar at Mark Hix's restaurant is a first-rate establishment. The historical drinks manage to be both interesting and good, especially those in the Cocktail Explorer's Club list. Rum drinkers should go for the Royal Bermuda Yacht Club: Mount Gay Barbados rum with orange curaçao, Mark's own falernum and lime juice. The selection of scotch would take several months to drink through. The bar 'snax' are terrific, and the place looks great, with its big, smoked mirrors.

Shops & Services

As famous as the King's Road back when the Sixties swung, **Carnaby Street** was, until a decade ago, more likely to sell you a postcard of the Queen snogging a punk rocker than a fishtail parka. But the noughties were kind and Carnaby is cool again, with **Kingly Court** a pioneer that brought in several hip boutiques.

Albam

23 Beak Street, W1F 9RS (3157 7000, www.albamclothing.com). Oxford Circus tube. **Open** 11am-7pm Mon-Sat; noon-5.30pm Sun. **Map** p125 B4 ㉟ Menswear

With contemporary, pared-down British menswear having a bit of a renaissance, it's easy to forget who did it first and best. These days, big ticket items such as Shetland wool jumpers, floral printed cagoules and quilts abound, but Albam can still pull off a tapered chino, crisp shirt and a brilliant basic tee.

EXPLORE

Harold Moores Records

*2 Great Marlborough Street, W1F 7HQ (7437
1576, www.hmrecords.co.uk). Oxford Circus tube.*
Open 10am-6.30pm Mon-Sat. **Map** p125 B3 ⓰
Books & music

Harold Moores is not your stereotypical classical-
music store: young, open-minded staff and an
expansive stock of new and second-hand music
bolster its credentials. This collection sees some
great stuff from old masters complemented by a
range of eclectic contemporary music. There's a
basement dedicated to second-hand classical vinyl,
including an excellent selection of jazz music.

Kingly Court

*Carnaby Street, opposite Broadwick Street, W1B
5PJ (7333 8118, www.carnaby.co.uk). Oxford
Circus tube.* **Open** 11am-7pm Mon-Sat; noon-6pm
Sun. **Map** p125 B4 ⓱ Mall

If you want to shop modern Carnaby Street, Kingly
Court is the place to start – in fact, it's also the place
that started the area's revival as a cool shopping
destination. It's a three-tiered complex that contains
a funky mix of established chains, independents,
vintage and vintage-style boutiques, with courtyard
cafés in the centre.

★ Monki

*37 Carnaby Street, W1V 1PD (7287 0620, www.
carnaby.co.uk/store). Oxford Circus tube.* **Open**
10am-8pm Mon-Sat; noon-6pm Sun. **Map** p125 A3
⓳ Fashion

Hailing from Sweden, Monki's aesthetic is a bold
urban one featuring cute animal prints, oddly
shaped sweater dresses and eccentric accessories
– current hits include the animal-print backpacks,
chunky leather ankle boots and cute woolly mittens
emblazoned with big logos for less than a fiver.

OTHER/shop

*21 Kingly Street, W1B 5QA (7734 6846, www.
other-shop.com). Oxford Circus tube.* **Open**
10.30am-6.30pm Mon-Sat; noon-5pm Sun.
Map p125 A3 ⓳ Fashion

Founders Matthew Murphy and Kirk Beattie have
more than a decade's experience of running an indie
boutique. Other occupies the same site as its (now
defunct) predecessor – b Store – and sells similar
stock (even a continuation of the excellent b Clothing
brand – now called Other). A sunlit basement stocks
Other's edit of brands such as Peter Jensen, Our
Legacy and Sophie Hulme. The store often houses
installations and exhibitions by artists, and also
stocks a range of magazines and coffee-table books.

YMC

*11 Poland Street, W1F 8QA (7494 1619, www.
youmustcreate.com). Oxford Circus tube.* **Open**
11am-7pm Mon-Sat. **Map** p125 B3 ⓴ Fashion
Impeccably designed staples are the forte of this
London label, which opened its first store in 2010. It's

the place to head to for simple vest tops and T-shirts,
stylish macs, tasteful knits and chino-style trousers,
for both men and women.
Other location 23 Hanbury Street, Spitalfields, E1
6QR (3432 3010).

CHINATOWN
& LEICESTER SQUARE

Leicester Square tube.

Shaftesbury Avenue is the very heart of
Theatreland. The Victorians built seven grand
theatres here, six of which still stand. The most
impressive is the gorgeous **Palace Theatre**
on Cambridge Circus, which opened in 1891
as the Royal English Opera House; when grand
opera flopped, the theatre reopened as a music
hall two years later. Appropriately, it's most
famous for the musicals it has staged: *The
Sound of Music* (1961) and *Jesus Christ
Superstar* (1972) had their London premières
here, and *Les Misérables* racked up 7,602
performances between 1985 and 2004. (The
Les Mis juggernaut continues to rumble a few
blocks west on Shaftesbury Avenue: there, the
Queen's Theatre proudly proclaims it the
world's longest-running musical.)

Marks & Co, the shop that was made famous
by Helene Hanff's book *84 Charing Cross Road*,
used to stand just opposite the Palace Theatre,
on a road that was once a byword for bookselling.
Barely any second-hand bookshops remain on
Charing Cross Road, though some appealing
new shops are opening in their stead; bibliophiles
should keep on south towards Leicester Square,
where **Cecil Court** continues to fight the good
fight for readers. West of Charing Cross Road and
south of Shaftesbury Avenue, officially just
outside Soho, is London's **Chinatown**.

The Chinese are relative latecomers to this
part of town. The city's original Chinatown
was set around Limehouse in east London,
but hysteria about Chinese opium dens and
criminality led to 'slum clearances' in 1934
(interestingly, the surrounding slums were
deemed to be in less urgent need of clearance).
It wasn't until the 1950s that the Chinese put
down roots here, attracted by the cheap rents
along Gerrard and Lisle streets.

The ersatz oriental gates, stone lions and
pagoda-topped phone boxes around Gerrard
Street suggest a Chinese theme park, but this
remains a close-knit residential and working
enclave, a genuine focal point for London's
Chinese community. The area is crammed
with restaurants, Asian grocery stores, great
bakeries and a host of small shops selling iced-
grass jelly, speciality teas and cheap air tickets
to Beijing, but even here rising rents are pricing
out some long-established family businesses.

South of Chinatown, **Leicester Square** was one of London's most exclusive addresses in the 17th century; in the 18th, it became home to the royal court of Prince George (later George II). Satirical painter William Hogarth had a studio here (1733-64), as did 18th-century artist Sir Joshua Reynolds – busts of both once resided in the small gardens at the heart of the square, along with a now vanished statue of Charlie Chaplin. They've been swept away in the fine refurbishment of the square, which has left just a statue of a wistful Shakespeare presiding over modish white 'ribbon' seating and the cut-price theatre-tickets booth, **tkts** (see p288).

For many years, locals left the square to the unimaginative tourists and drunk suburban kids that were its only denizens. But the arrival in 2011 of a couple of high-class hotels (for the **W**, see p351) and the reopening in 2012 of the Frank Matcham-designed, castle-like, red-brick Hippodrome on the corner of Cranbourn Street and Charing Cross Road as a high-rolling casino gave the area a bit of pull. Not all memories of the square's cheerfully tacky phase have gone, however: the Swiss glockenspiel has returned, with its 27 bells and mechanical mountain farmers chiming out the time on behalf of Switzerland Tourism.

Film premières are still regularly held in the monolithic **Odeon Leicester Square** (see p255), which once boasted the UK's largest screen and probably still has the UK's highest ticket prices; this is where the **London Film Festival** (see p258) kicks off every year. Its 1930s counterpart, the **Odeon West End**, is currently under threat of redevelopment into 10 storeys of

chain hotel-cum-cinema – a move excoriated by many heritage groups. Get a price-conscious cinema fix just north of the square on Leicester Place, at the excellent **Prince Charles** rep cinema (see p255).

Restaurants

Chinatown stalwarts such as **Mr Kong** (21 Lisle Street, 7437 7341), **Wong Kei** (41-43 Wardour Street, 7437 8408) and **Imperial China** (White Bear Yard, 25A Lisle Street, WC2H 7BA, 7734 3388, www.imperialchina-london.com) still ply their reliable Anglo-Cantonese trade, but for a cheap feed we prefer **Jen Café**.

Jen Café
4-8 Newport Place, WC2H 7JP (7287 9708). Leicester Square tube. **Open** 10.30am-6.30pm Mon-Wed; 10.30am-9.30pm Thur-Sun. **Main courses** £5-£16. **Map** p125 D4 ㊶ **Chinese**
This plain, green-painted café has a prominent corner site, where you can often see the cooks sat in front of the windows hand-wrapping dumplings. There are plenty of other dishes served, from buttered toast through barbecued pork to Hong Kong-style tea and Taiwanese-style bubble teas, but it's those fresh dumplings that keep us coming back – try the 'Beijing dumplings': eight white sachets like overfilled ravioli, with pork or vegetarian, for just a fiver.

Pubs & Bars

★ Experimental Cocktail Club
13A Gerrard Street, W1D 5PS (7434 3559, www.chinatownecc.com). Leicester Square tube. **Open** 6pm-3am Mon-Sat; 6pm-midnight Sun. **Admission** £5 after 11pm. **Map** p125 C4 ㊷
ECC is all elegant opulence, arranged over three floors of an old townhouse. Booking isn't essential (half of the capacity is kept for walk-ins) but is recommended (email only, between noon and 5pm). The cocktails are among London's best: sophisticated, complex and strong – try the Havana (cigar-infused bourbon, marsala wine, Bruichladdich Octomore single malt 'wash').

Shops & Services

★ Cecil Court
Between Charing Cross Road & St Martin's Lane, WC2N (www.cecilcourt.co.uk). Leicester Square tube. **Map** p125 D4 ㊸ **Books & music**
Quaint Cecil Court is known for its antiquarian book, map and print dealers, housed in premises that haven't changed in a hundred years. Notable residents include children's specialist Marchpane (no.16, 7836 8661); 40-year veteran David Drummond of Pleasures of Past Times (no.11, 7836 1142), with his playbills and Victoriana; and the mystical, spiritual and occult specialist Watkins (nos.19-21, 7836 2182).

Jen Café.

EXPLORE

Covent Garden & the Strand

Covent Garden has always been an index of the extremes of London life: on one hand, it had a previous existence as the capital's wholesale fruit and veg market; on the other, it has been home since the 1700s to the Royal Opera House, purveyor of the most refined of all the arts.

The masses now descend daily on the restored 19th-century market and its cobbled 'piazza' to peruse the increasingly high-end shops and gawp at the street entertainment, with even the most crowd-averse Londoner finding some aspects appealing: grudgingly the buskers, eagerly the London Transport Museum. Down towards the river on the grubbily historic Strand, the Courtauld Gallery and vast courtyard of Somerset House are further attractions.

EXPLORE

Somerset House.

Don't Miss

1 London Transport Museum Fun for all the family, especially train and bus geeks (p140).

2 Covent Garden Piazza A pedestrian-friendly gem (p138).

3 J Sheekey The fish restaurant that always a star (p143).

4 Vintage Showroom An experience as much as a shop (p146).

5 Somerset House The Thameside palace reinvented with exhibitions and fountains (p147).

COVENT GARDEN

Covent Garden (until late 2015: exit only; only eastbound Piccadilly line trains stop at weekends) or Leicester Square tube.

Covent Garden was once the property of the medieval Abbey ('convent') of Westminster. When Henry VIII dissolved the monasteries, it passed to John Russell, first Earl of Bedford, in 1552; his family still owns land hereabouts. During the 16th and 17th centuries, they developed the area: the fourth Earl employed Inigo Jones to create the Italianate open square that remains the area's centrepiece.

A market was first documented here in 1640 and grew into London's pre-eminent fruit and vegetable wholesaler, employing over 1,000 porters; its success led to the opening of coffee-houses, theatres, gambling dens and brothels. A flower market was added (where the London Transport Museum now stands).

In the second half of the 20th century, it became obvious that the congested streets of central London were unsuitable for such market traffic and the decision was taken to move the traders out. In 1974, with the market gone, the threat of property development loomed for the empty stalls and offices. It was only through demonstrations that the area was saved. It's now a pleasant place for a stroll, especially if you catch it early before the crowds descend.

Covent Garden Piazza

Centred on Covent Garden Piazza, the area now offers a combination of gentrified shops, restaurants and cafés, supplemented by street artists and busking musicians in the lower courtyard. The majority of the entertainment takes place under the portico of **St Paul's Covent Garden**. Tourists favour the 180-year-old **covered market**, which combines upmarket chain stores with a collection of small, sometimes quirky but often rather twee independent shops. Its handsome architecture is best viewed from the Amphitheatre Café Bar's terrace loggia at the **Royal Opera House**.

Since 2006, property investor Capco has consumed great chunks of prime real estate in Covent Garden, scooping up property on the Piazza, King Street, James Street, Long Acre and beyond – £780 million of it, to be exact. As a result, a slew of ho-hum shops have been replaced by high-street heavyweights and luxury brands. Fred Perry, Whistles, L'Artisan Parfumier, Kurt Geiger, Ralph Lauren's Rugby brand and Burberry Brit have all appeared. The world's largest **Apple Store** has also set up shop. Perhaps most tellingly, the West Cornwall Pasty Co became a Ladurée café, with waistcoated staff

Apple Market

dispensing dainty orange-blossom macaroons where once they trowelled out pastries. Classy restaurateurs have also been lured in: **Terroirs** and **Delaunay** are near, while celeb-magnet the Ivy (due to reopen after refurbishment in summer 2015) has opened a new restaurant, **Ivy Market Grill**, right on the Piazza.

Change is barely evident elsewhere in Covent Garden. The **Apple Market**, in the North Hall, still has arts and crafts stalls from Tuesday to Sunday, and antiques on Monday. Across the road, the tackier **Jubilee Market** deals mostly in novelty T-shirts and other tat. And the always excellent **London Transport Museum** remains the stand-out attraction.

Elsewhere in Covent Garden

Outside Covent Garden Piazza, the area offers a mixed bag of entertainment, eateries and shops. Nearest the markets, most of the more unusual shops have been superseded by a homogeneous mass of cafés, while big fashion chains – and the **St Martin's Courtyard** mall (www.stmartinscourtyard.co.uk) – have all but domesticated Long Acre. There are more interesting stores north of here on Neal Street and Monmouth Street; Earlham Street is also home to the **Donmar Warehouse** (*see p293*), a former banana-ripening depot that's now an intimate and groundbreaking theatre. On tiny Shorts Gardens next door is the **Neal's Yard Dairy**, purveyor of exceptional UK cheeses; down a passageway one door along is **Neal's Yard** itself, a pleasant courtyard with communal seating. Always a welcome remnant of a less corporate Covent Garden, even Neal's Yard is changing: in 2015, old-school vegetarian café Food for Thought, here since 1971, announced it could no longer meet rising rents and would close.

South of Long Acre and east of the Piazza, historical depravity was called to account at the former **Bow Street Magistrates Court**. Once

EXPLORE

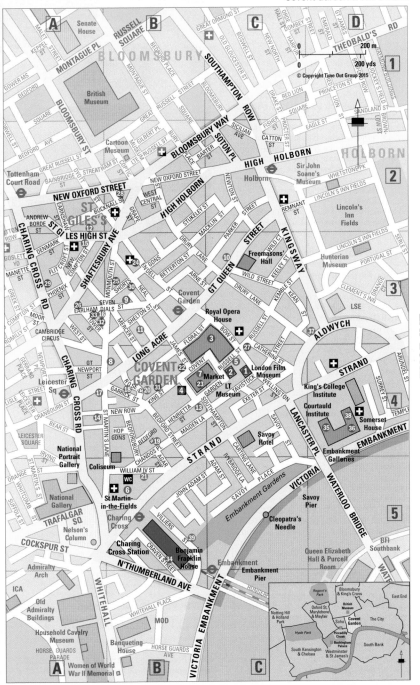

EXPLORE

home to the Bow Street Runners, the precursors of the Metropolitan Police, this was also where Oscar Wilde entered his plea when arrested for 'indecent acts' in 1895. Plans to convert it into a hotel have been long in gestation: Jason Atherton is the latest name on the planning notices; given his recent run of stellar successes (he's the man behind hit restaurants such as Pollen Street Social; *see p118*), we reckon he'll soon have the place up and running. To the south, Wellington and Catherine streets mix restaurants and theatres, including the grand **Theatre Royal** (0844 412 4660, www.reallyusefultheatres.co.uk). Other diversions in and around Covent Garden include the museum at **Freemasons' Hall** (7395 9257, www.freemasonry.london.museum; call for details of tours), the eye-catchingly bombastic white stone building where Long Acre becomes Great Queen Street; and the **Coliseum** (*see p287*), home of the English National Opera.

Sights & Museums

London Film Museum
45 Wellington Street, WC2E 7BN (7836 4913, www.londonfilmmuseum.com). Covent Garden tube. **Open** 10am-6pm Mon-Fri, Sun; 10am-7pm Sat. **Admission** £14.50; £9.50 reductions; £38 family; free under-5s. **Map** p139 C4 ❶
Having left its former home on the South Bank, the film museum relaunched its collection of Brit film memorabilia in 2014 with 'Bond in Motion' – a display of 50 of 007's most covetable high-end motors. New exhibits include vehicles from the latest Sam Mendes-directed Bond film, *SPECTRE*.

★ London Transport Museum
Covent Garden Piazza, WC2E 7BB (7379 6344, www.ltmuseum.co.uk). Covent Garden tube. **Open** 10am-6pm Mon-Thur, Sat, Sun; 11am-6pm Fri. **Admission** £15; £11.50 reductions; free under-17s. **Map** p139 C4 ❷
The London Transport Museum traces the city's transport history from the horse age to the present day. It does so in an engaging and inspiring fashion, with a focus on social history and design, illustrated by a superb array of preserved buses, trams and trains, and backed up by some brilliant temporary exhibitions. The collections are in broadly chronological order, beginning with the Victorian gallery, where a replica of Shillibeer's first horse-drawn bus service in 1829 takes pride of place. Another gallery is dedicated to the museum's truly impressive collection of poster art. Under the leadership of Frank Pick, in the early 20th century London Transport developed one of the most coherent brand identities in the world. The museum also raises some interesting and important questions about the future of public transport in the city, even offering a fanciful imagining of London's travel network in the years ahead.

Barrafina.

▶ *Already thoroughly child-friendly, the Transport Museum opened a small but terrific children's play area in 2015.*

FREE Royal Opera House
Bow Street, WC2E 9DD (7304 4000, www.roh.org. uk). Covent Garden tube. **Open** 10am-3.30pm Mon-Sat. **Admission** free. **Tours** £12; £8.50-£11 reductions. **Map** p139 C3 ❸
The ROH was founded in 1732 by John Rich on the profits of his production of John Gay's *Beggar's Opera*; the current building, constructed roughly 150 years ago but extensively remodelled since, is the third on the site. Visitors can explore the massive eight-floor building as part of an organised tour, including the main auditorium, the costume workshops and sometimes even a rehearsal. Certain parts of the building are also open to the general public, including the glass-roofed Paul Hamlyn Hall, the Crush Bar (so named because in Victorian times the only thing served during intermission was orange and lemon crush) and the Amphitheatre Restaurant & Terrace, which has great views over the covered market. Major improvements are planned, in part to 'open up' the Opera House even further to the public: work should begin in early 2016, for completion before the end of 2017.
▶ *For music at the Royal Opera House, see p288.*

FREE St Paul's Covent Garden
Bedford Street, WC2E 9ED (7836 5221, www. actorschurch.org). Covent Garden tube. **Open** 8.30am-5pm Mon-Fri; 9am-1pm Sun. Times vary Sat; phone for details. *Services* 1.10pm Tue, Wed; 11am Sun. *Choral Evensong* 4pm 2nd Sun of mth. **Admission** free; donations appreciated. **Map** p139 B4 ❹

EXPLORE

Known as the Actors' Church for its long association with Covent Garden's theatres, this pleasingly spare building was designed by Inigo Jones in 1631. A lovely limewood wreath by the 17th-century master carver Grinling Gibbons hangs inside the front door as a reminder that he and his wife are interred in the crypt. But most visitors come to see the memorial plaques: many thespians are commemorated here, among them Vivien Leigh, Charlie Chaplin and Hattie Jacques of *Carry On* fame.

Restaurants

Balthazar

4-6 Russell Street, WC2B 5HZ (3301 1155, www.balthazarlondon.com). Covent Garden tube. **Open** 7.30am-midnight Mon-Fri; 9am-midnight Sat; 9am-11pm Sun. **Main courses** £12-£35. **Map** p139 C4 ❺ Brasserie
NYC import Balthazar presents a Manhattan interpretation of a French brasserie, with signature dishes such as the onion soup (grilled gruyère lid on thick country bread, immersed in a rich and sweet chicken stock); duck shepherd's pie is another powerfully flavoured treat. The premises mimic the New York original perfectly, with red awnings, red leather banquettes, giant antique mirrors on the walls and mosaic floors. Balthazar's bread, from master baker Jon Rolfe, is a must-try – and is sold to take away at the Boulangerie next door.

Barrafina

10 Adelaide Street, WC2N 4HZ (7440 1456, http://barrafina.co.uk). Charing Cross or Leicester Square tube. **Open** noon-3pm, 5-11pm Mon-Sat; 1-3.30pm, 5.30-10pm Sun. **Tapas** £3.80-£10. **Map** p139 B5 ❻ Tapas
Like its predecessor in Soho, Barrafina Covent Garden takes no reservations, so arrive early if you don't want to queue at this perennially popular tapas restaurant. The menu is studded with tempting Mallorcan and Catalan dishes but watch out if you're properly hungry, as the bill adds up fast. Despite the fancy prices, remember that Barrafina isn't a 'proper' restaurant: it's a modern Spanish tapas bar, which means that the list of sherries, cavas and other wines by the glass are as much a part of the draw as the food, and perfect for experimenting with as you nibble.

Battersea Pie

Lower-ground floor, 28 The Market, WC2E 8RA (7240 9566, www.batterseapiestation.co.uk). Covent Garden tube. **Open** 11am-7pm Mon-Thur, Sun; 11am-8pm Fri, Sat. **Main courses** £7.50-£8.50. **Map** p139 B4 ❼ British
Serving proper British food at bargain prices, this pie-and-mash house is something of an anomaly in Covent Garden Market. Housed in one of the refurbished subterranean arches, it retains the traditional exterior and flagstone floor, but the fixtures and fittings are stylish and modern: bright white tiles, polished marble tables and a shiny counter. Besides traditional fillings such as steak and mushroom with stout are less expected versions, such as butternut squash and goat's cheese. Even for a counter-service place, this is a terrific little caff.

Dishoom

12 Upper St Martin's Lane, WC2H 9FB (7420 9320, www.dishoom.com). Covent Garden or Leicester Square tube. **Open** 8am-11pm Mon-Thur; 8am-midnight Fri; 9am-midnight Sat; 9am-11pm Sun. **Main courses** £5.90-£16.50. **Map** p139 B4 ❽ Pan-Indian
A swish, self-styled 'Bombay café', Dishoom is filled with retro features: whirring ceiling fans, low-level lighting and vintage Bollywood posters. The place is crowded all day, from breakfast (for sausage naan rolls with chilli jam) to dinner (for the usual curries and tandoori grills). Quality can vary: vada pau (potato croquettes with sharp chutney in a fluffy Portuguese-style bun) and bhel (crunchy puffed rice with tangy tamarind chutney) are tasty; kebabs and curries are fairly standard renditions.
Other locations 5 Stable Street, King's Cross, N1C 4AB (7420 9321); 7 Boundary Street, Shoreditch, E2 7JE (7420 9324).

Battersea Pie.

EXPLORE

Flesh & Buns

41 Earlham Street, WC2H 9LX (7632 9500, www.bonedaddies.com/flesh-and-buns). Covent Garden tube. **Open** noon-3pm, 5-10.30pm Mon, Tue; noon-3pm, 5-11.30pm Wed-Fri; noon-11.30pm Sat; noon-9.30pm Sun. **Main courses** £17-£32. **Tasting menu** £35 per person (minimum 2). **Map** p139 B3 ❾ Taiwanese

Flesh & Buns is hidden in a capacious basement, with industrial-chic decor and young, pierced and tattooed staff setting the tone. It serves hirata buns – a US take on Taiwanese street food – with a side order of rock music. Sweet, fluffy dough is folded, then steamed and brought to table. Diners then stuff these pockets with their choice of 'flesh'. Mustard miso and a few slices of subtly pickled apple make a foil for tender pulled pork; crisp-skinned grilled sea bass is served with fresh tomato salsa.

Great Queen Street

32 Great Queen Street, WC2B 5AA (7242 0622, www.greatqueenstreetrestaurant.co.uk). Covent Garden or Holborn tube. **Open** *Bar* 5pm-midnight Tue-Sat. *Restaurant* noon-2.30pm, 6-10.30pm Mon-Sat; 1-4pm Sun. **Main courses** £14-£25. **Map** p139 C3 ❿ British

The excellent location ensures Great Queen Street's perennial popularity. The outdoor tables are almost never vacant, but walk-ins may find space at the bar, where the full menu is served. The menu changes daily, is produce-led and is predominantly British. There's minimal fussing with ingredients: a plump piece of bone-in smoked mackerel might be served with a dollop each of cooked gooseberries and horseradish; slow-cooked pork could arrive in a stew with a generous quantity of cockles.

Hawksmoor Seven Dials

11 Langley Street, WC2H 9JG (7420 9390, www.thehawksmoor.co.uk). Covent Garden tube. **Open** noon-3pm, 5-10.30pm Mon-Thur; noon-3pm, 5-11pm Fri, Sat; noon-9.30pm Sun. **Main courses** £13-£50. **Map** p139 B3 ⓫ Steakhouse

The short main menu centres on steak (ribeye, T-bone, porterhouse, fillet, sirloin and more), at serious prices, plus the likes of grilled chicken, lobster with garlic butter, monkfish grilled over charcoal, and a meat-free choice for the odd misplaced vegetarian. A good kick-off is one of Hawksmoor's renowned cocktails.

Other locations 157A Commercial Street, Shoreditch, E1 6BJ (7426 4850); 10 Basinghall Street, City, EC2V 5BQ (7397 8120); 5A Air Street, Piccadilly Circus, W1J 0AD (7406 3980).

Ippudo

3 Central St Giles Piazza, St Giles High Street, WC2H 8AG (7240 4469, www.ippudo.co.uk). Tottenham Court Road tube. **Open** noon-3pm, 5-10.30pm Mon-Fri; noon-10.30pm Sat, Sun. **Main courses** £7-£16. **Map** p139 A2 ⓬ Japanese

Ippudo, a super-slick international ramen chain, has around 120 restaurants but this was the Japanese company's first foray into Europe (a second branch is due to open in Canary Wharf). The interior is dark, polished and brooding, with lots of glass and metal, and the staff make liberal use of a handful of Japanese phrases. The speciality is tonkotsu with pork loin slices, crunchy kikurage (cloud ear mushroom) and thin, own-made noodles. Vegetarians are not left out: there's a seaweed and mushroom broth-based version that's topped with fried tofu.

Ivy Market Grill

1A Henrietta Street, WC2E 8PS (3301 0200, www.theivymarketgrill.com). Covent Garden tube. **Open** 7am-midnight Mon-Fri; 8am-midnight Sat; 8am-11pm Sun. **Main courses** £9.75-£29.50. **Map** p139 B4 ⓭ Modern European

This is no mere cash-in on the celeb-courted Ivy: the interior's lovely, in a classy, bourgeois brasserie, my-family-own-Dorset way. The menu's a good read, with a pleasingly retro Continental feel to the dishes, but using mainly British ingredients. However, if you're after a culinary superstar, go elsewhere. You

Kanada-Ya.

can forget about spotting stars too: rather than being located in a discreet side street, this Ivy's bang on the Piazza – where no ordinary Londoner, never mind an A-list celeb, sets foot. Yet we liked the place: it's good-looking, with good service, and opens late, serving breakfast, tea and all-day snacks.
Other locations 1 West Street, Covent Garden, WC2H 9NQ (7836 4751, www.the-ivy.co.uk); 197 King's Road, Chelsea, SW3 5ED (3301 0300, http://theivychelseagarden.com).

★ J Sheekey
28-35 St Martin's Court, WC2N 4AL (7240 2565, www.j-sheekey.co.uk). Leicester Square tube. **Open** noon-3pm, 5pm-midnight Mon-Fri; noon-3.30pm, 5.30pm-midnight Sat; noon-3.30pm, 5.30-11pm Sun. **Main courses** £15.75-£51.50. **Map** p139 A4 ⓮
Fish & seafood
After well over a century of service, Sheekey's status as a West End institution is assured. With its monochrome photos of stars of stage and screen, wooden panelling and cream crackle walls, and array of silver dishes atop thick white tablecloths, it oozes old-fashioned glamour. The menu runs from super-fresh oysters and shellfish via old-fashioned snacks (herring roe on toast) to upmarket classics (dover sole, lobster thermidor). The fish pie – a rich, comforting treat – is acclaimed, but we feel the shrimp and scallop burger merits similar status.
▶ *The adjoining J Sheekey Oyster Bar (nos.33-35) serves a similar menu to customers sitting at the counter, and with an expanded choice of oysters.*

★ Kanada-Ya
64 St Giles High Street, WC2H 8LE (7240 0232, www.kanada-ya.com). Tottenham Court Road tube. **Open** noon-3pm, 5-10pm Mon-Sat. **Main courses** £10-£12. **Map** p139 A3 ⓯ Japanese
Small, brightly lit and minimal, this is not the place for a leisurely meal: there are always lengthy meal-time queues outside its doors. But there's a reason for Kanada-Ya's already-large fan base: exceptional ramen. If you don't eat pork, forget it; but those pork bones are simmered for 18 hours to create the smooth, rich, seriously savoury tonkotsu broth – one of the best in London.
▶ *If you can't queue, the wait at Ippudo (see p142), just opposite, is always more bearable.*

Kopapa
32-34 Monmouth Street, WC2H 9HA (7240 6076, www.kopapa.co.uk). Covent Garden or Leicester Square tube. **Open** 8.30-11.30am, noon-11pm Mon-Fri; 9.30am-4pm, 4.30-11pm Sat; 9.30am-4pm, 4.30-9.45pm Sun. **Main courses** £12.50-£23. **Map** p139 A3 ⓰ Fusion
The exciting, well-executed menu at this handily located all-dayer includes Turkish eggs (poached eggs with yoghurt, hot chilli butter and flatbread) for breakfast and brunch. Lunch features weighty sandwiches (steak on focaccia with caramelised onion,

mustard cream cheese, roast tomatoes and pickles) and burgers (soft-shell crab burger with Asian salad, spicy peanut mayonnaise and avocado), alongside salads and a selection of more inventive dishes, many of which also appear on the evening menu. Quality produce, imaginatively paired, served by smiling, clued-up staff.

Lanzhou Noodle Bar
33 Cranbourn Street, WC2H 7AD (7836 4399). Leicester Square tube. **Open** 10am-2am Mon-Thur; 10am-5am Fri, Sat; 10am-11pm Sun. **Main courses** £5-£7.50. **Map** p139 A4 ⓱ Chinese
This Chinese noodle bar is cheap, fast and open into the early hours. It's also a humble place, and many of the dishes – those slathered with brightly coloured sauces in the window, for instance – are not worthy of your attention. But the hand-pulled noodles? They're another matter. Made to order, they're served in three variations – in soup, dry or fried – and a hundred-plus permutations.

★ Lima Floral
14 Garrick Street, WC2E 9BJ (7240 5778, www.limalondon.com). Leicester Square tube. **Open** noon-2.30pm, 5.30-10.30pm Mon-Fri; 10.30am-2.30pm, 5.30-10.30pm Sat; 10.30am-2.45pm Sun. **Main courses** £19-£28. **Set meals** (noon-2.30pm, 5.30-6pm Mon-Sat) £17.50 2 courses; £19.50 3 courses. **Map** p139 B4 ⓲ Peruvian
Lima Floral is Virgilio Martinez's showcase of classic Peruvian dishes. There's a little less fuss, a reasonable price tag, and a bar in the basement that serves pisco cocktails. Lima Floral is perfect for diners looking for a new kick, with Martinez's dishes combining playfulness and sheer imagination. *See also p162* Lima London.

Wahaca
66 Chandos Place, WC2N 4HG (7240 1883, www.wahaca.co.uk). Covent Garden or Embankment tube. **Open** noon-11pm Mon-Sat; noon-10.30pm Sun. **Main courses** £3.80-£10.50. **Map** p139 B4 ⓳ Mexican
Thomasina Miers' Mexican 'market food' concept is a successful mini-chain, with a dozen branches across London. The restaurants share a cheery vibe, with young, efficient staff buzzing round bright interiors. Tortillas loom large – in soft, crisp, toasted and chip variations – and in flour and corn versions – though there are also a few grills (fish, steak or chicken served with green rice). Particular favourites include the steak burrito.
Other locations throughout the city.

Pubs & Bars

Lamb & Flag
33 Rose Street, WC2E 9EB (7497 9504, www.lambandflagcoventgarden.co.uk). Covent Garden tube. **Open** 11am-11pm Mon-Thur; 11am-11.30pm

EXPLORE

Fri, Sat; noon-10.30pm Sun. *Food served* noon-8pm Mon-Thur; noon-5pm Fri, Sat; noon-9pm Sun. **Main courses** £5.75-£15.95. **Map** p139 B4 ⓴

Rose Street used to be a pit of prostitution and bare-knuckle bashes, the latter of which were hosted at this historic, low-ceilinged Covent Garden tavern back when it was called the Bucket of Blood; poet John Dryden was beaten up here in 1679. The place is popular and space is always at a premium. Two centuries of mounted cuttings and caricatures amplify the sense of character.

★ Terroirs
5 William IV Street, WC2N 4DW (7036 0660, www.terroirswinebar.com). Charing Cross tube/rail. **Open** noon-11pm Mon-Sat. *Food served* noon-3pm, 5.30-11pm Mon-Sat. **Map** p139 B5 ㉑

Terroirs – a wine bar with excellent food – is really two places under one roof. The always-crowded ground floor has a casual wine-bar feel and a menu to match, focused on small plates for sharing. You can sample some of the same dishes in the atmospheric and surprisingly roomy basement, although the menu here, with a focus on rustic French dishes, seems designed to guide diners more towards a starter-main-dessert tradition. The wine list is an encyclopaedia of organic and biodynamic bottles.

Shops & Services

Apple Store
1-7 The Piazza, WC2E 8HA (7447 1400, www.apple.com/uk/retail). Covent Garden tube. **Open** 10am-9pm Mon-Sat; noon-6pm Sun. **Map** p139 B4 ㉒ **Electronics & photography**

A temple to geekery, this is the world's biggest Apple Store, with separate rooms – set out over three storeys – devoted to each product line. The exposed brickwork, big old oak tables and stone floors make it an inviting place, and it's also the world's first Apple Store with a Start Up Room, where staff will help to set up your new iPad, iPhone, iPod or Mac, or transfer files from your old computer to your new one – all for free.

Benjamin Pollock's Toy Shop
44 The Market, WC2E 8RF (7379 7866, www.pollocks-coventgarden.co.uk). Covent Garden tube. **Open** 10.30am-6pm Mon-Wed; 10.30am-6.30pm Thur-Sat; 11am-6pm Sun. **Map** p139 B4 ㉓ **Children**

Best known for its toy theatres, Pollock's is also superb for traditional toys such as knitted animals, china tea sets, masks, glove puppets, cards, spinning tops and fortune-telling fish.

Blackout II
52 Endell Street, WC2H 9AJ (7240 5006, www.blackout2.com). Covent Garden tube. **Open** 11am-7pm Mon-Fri; 11.30am-6.30pm Sat. **Map** p139 B3 ㉔ **Vintage clothing**

There are dozens of good vintage stores in London, but this remains a firm favourite. Blackout II has been providing bright and beautiful frocks, hand-bags, shoes and all the trimmings for the past two-and-a-half decades. Here, you will find a wonderful array of dress-up clothes, from 1930s cocktail frocks to full-skirted '50s dresses and some slinky numbers that might have graced the sets of *Dynasty*.

★ Coco de Mer
23 Monmouth Street, WC2H 9DD (7836 8882, www.coco-de-mer.com). Covent Garden tube. **Open** 11am-7pm Mon-Sat; noon-6pm Sun. **Map** p139 B3 ㉕ **Accessories**

London's most glamorous erotic emporium sells a variety of tasteful books, toys and lingerie, from glass dildos that double as objets d'art to a Marie Antoinette costume of crotchless culottes and corset. Trying on items can be fun as well: the peepshow-style velvet changing rooms allow your lover to peer through and watch you undress from a 'confession box' next door.

★ Fopp
1 Earlham Street, WC2H 9LL (7845 9770, www.fopp.com). Leicester Square tube. **Open** 10am-10pm Mon-Wed; 10am-11pm Thur-Sat; noon-6.30pm Sun. **Map** p139 A3 ㉖ **Books & music**

Three floors of new music releases and back-catalogue surprises, plus good selections of books and DVDs, all at competitive prices, make this a great place for bargains. Look out for world cinema, arthouse masterpieces and anime – plus '80s teen classic DVDs on the ground floor and basement, with Fopp's full music selection upstairs.

Hope & Greenwood
1 Russell Street, WC2B 5JD (7240 3314, www.hopeandgreenwood.co.uk). Covent Garden tube. **Open** 11am-7.30pm Mon-Fri; 10.30am-7.30pm Sat; noon-6pm Sun. **Map** p139 C4 ㉗ **Food & drink**

Everything from chocolate gooseberries to sweetheart candies is prettily displayed in plastic beakers, cellophane bags, glass jars, illustrated boxes, porcelain bowls and cake tins. Indulge in a bag of sherbet Flying Saucers or gobstoppers. Gift possibilities include retro gumball machines.

James Smith & Sons
53 New Oxford Street, WC1A 1BL (7836 4731, www.james-smith.co.uk). Holborn or Tottenham Court Road tube. **Open** 10am-5.45pm Mon-Fri; 10am-5.15pm Sat. **Map** p139 B2 ㉘ **Accessories**

More than 175 years after it was established, this charming shop, with Victorian fittings still intact, is holding its own in the niche market of umbrellas and walking sticks. The stock here isn't the throwaway type of brolly that breaks at the first sign of a bit of wind. Lovingly crafted 'brellas, such as a classic City umbrella with a malacca cane handle at £165, are built to last. A repair service is also offered.

Made Showroom

100 Charing Cross Road, WC2H 0JG (no phone, www.made.com). Tottenham Court Road tube. **Open** 10am-8pm Mon-Sat; noon-6pm Sun. **Map** p139 A3 ㉙ **Homewares** *See below* **Made for Browsing**.

★ Neal's Yard Dairy

17 Shorts Gardens, WC2H 9AT (7240 5700, www.nealsyarddairy.co.uk). Covent Garden tube. **Open** 10am-7pm Mon-Sat. **Map** p139 B3 ㉚ **Food & drink**

Neal's Yard buys from small farms and creameries and matures the cheeses in its own cellars until they're ready to sell in peak condition. Names such as Stinking Bishop and Lincolnshire Poacher are as evocative as the aromas in the shop. It's best to walk in and ask what's good today: you'll be given tasters by the well-trained staff. **Other location** 6 Park Street, Borough, SE1 9AB, (7367 0799).

Opening Ceremony

35 King Street, WC2E 8JG (7836 4978, www.openingceremony.us). Covent Garden tube. **Open** 11am-8pm Mon-Sat; noon-6pm Sun. **Map** p139 B4 ㉛ **Fashion**

Humberto Leon and Carol Lim have the Midas touch when it comes to fashion. Opening Ceremony is their joint brand, with a winning formula that combines their own zeitgeist-tapping designs with hot-off-the-press new labels and revivals of long-forgotten brands, as well as exclusives from the likes of Chloë Sevigny, who produces a winning collection for them every season.

Poste Mistress

61-63 Monmouth Street, WC2H 9EP (7379 4040, www.office.co.uk). Covent Garden tube. **Open** 10am-7pm Mon-Wed, Fri, Sat; 10am-8pm Thur; 11.30am-6.30pm Sun. **Map** p139 A3 ㉜ **Footwear**

This Covent Garden boutique opened in 2001 disguised as a decadent boudoir. Floral wallpaper,

MADE FOR BROWSING

The high-flying online retailer takes its first steps back on earth.

In spring 2015, the 'future of online shopping' surprised us by opening an honest-to-goodness stand-alone shop. E-tailer **Made**, the super-successful furniture store established on the principle that it could make its customers savings by selling wares directly from the supplier without the cost of bricks-and-mortar premises, has unveiled a new high-tech flagship (for listings, *see above*) on the less fashionable fringe of Covent Garden, almost opposite Foyles (*see p126*).

It's by no means the first. Hipster online operation **Cubitts** (37 Marshall Street, W1F 7EZ, 7287 0564, www.cubitts.co.uk), which designs very cool horn and thick-rimmed spectacles, hand-finished in London, sold with lenses for from £125, opened a shop above their workshop not far from Made in west Soho. Stylishly fitted out with antique fixtures, the place has a real sense of permanence. And even **Google**, perhaps mindful of the roaring success of London's Apple Stores (for the Covent Garden branch, *see p144*), opened a shop – tucked into the Curry's PC World to the north on Tottenham Court Road (nos.145-149, W1T 7NE, 0344 561 0000, www.currys.co.uk).

It seems the shopper is a complex beast: intent on bargains of a severity that only the internet can provide, while still craving the social rituals of shopping in person – hence the popularity of in-store events, exemplified

in London by the ever-imaginative Selfridges (*see p106*) and here-today-gone-next-week pop-ups, as well as the annual ritual of the Boxing Day sales.

What can you expect from Made off-line? With prices the same as on the web, this is really more a shop window than a shop – allowing customers to try (or at least see) the furniture before they buy. The shop features virtual full-size projections of products, till-free iPad ordering, a flashy window installation and, in a charmingly old-tech touch, a wall of takeaway postcards with pictures and details of the 600 products on them. Importantly, you can also view a selection of pieces on the shopfloor, fondle fabric samples to your heart's content, and get information and advice from, you know, human staff.

EXPLORE

velvet drapes and gilt-framed mirrors create enticing surroundings in which women can treat themselves to designer shoes. Its eponymous line sits alongside niche and quirky brands such as Opening Ceremony, Melissa, Dries Van Noten and Chie Mihara, but tempting shoppers into real sin are bigger brands including Miu Miu, Jil Sander and Vivienne Westwood.

★ Vintage Showroom

14 Earlham Street, WC2H 9LN (7836 3964, www.thevintageshowroom.com). Covent Garden tube. **Open** varies. **Map** p139 A3 ⑨ **Vintage menswear**

In the old FW Collins & Sons ironmongery, Roy Luckett and Doug Gunn show a tiny selection of their famous west London menswear archive, which they routinely loan out to big-name designers, denim brands and vintage obsessives. With stock sourced from around the world (Roy and Doug have some hair-raising stories of dealings with collectors and hoarders in obscure locations), it follows that the pair occasionally find it hard to part with an item, and they've been known to try to dissuade shoppers from buying the rarer pieces on display. But the shop has London's best men's vintage collection, with an emphasis on Americana (denim, sweats, a few choice tees) and classic military and British pieces.

STRAND, EMBANKMENT & ALDWYCH

Embankment or Temple tube, or Charing Cross tube/rail.

Until as recently as the 1860s, Strand ran beside the Thames; indeed, it was originally the river's bridlepath. In the 14th century, it was lined with grand residences with gardens that ran down to the water. It wasn't until the 1870s that the Thames was pushed back with the creation of the Embankment and its adjacent gardens. By the time George Newnes's famed *Strand* magazine was introducing its readership to Sherlock Holmes (1891), the street boasted the Cecil Hotel (long since demolished), **Simpson's** (likely soon to be taken over by a more fashionable chef), **King's College** and **Somerset House**. Prime Minister Benjamin Disraeli described it as 'perhaps the finest street in Europe'. Nobody would make such a claim today, but there's still plenty to interest visitors.

In 1292, the body of Eleanor of Castile, consort to King Edward I, completed its funerary procession from Lincoln to the small hamlet of Charing, at the western end of what is now Strand. The occasion was marked by the erection of the last of 12 elaborate crosses. A replica of the Eleanor Cross (originally set just south of nearby Trafalgar Square; *see p68*) was placed in 1865 on the forecourt of **Charing Cross Station**; it

remains there today, looking like the spire of a sunken cathedral. Across the road, behind **St Martin-in-the-Fields** (*see p69*), is Maggi Hambling's weird memorial to a more recent queen, *A Conversation with Oscar Wilde*.

The Embankment itself can be reached down Villiers Street. Pass through the tube station to the point at which boat tours with on-board entertainment depart. Just to the east stands **Cleopatra's Needle**, an obelisk presented to the British nation by the viceroy of Egypt, Mohammed Ali, in 1820 but not set in place by the river for a further 59 years. The obelisk was originally erected around 1500 BC by the pharaoh Tuthmosis III at a site near modern-day Cairo, before being moved to Alexandria, Cleopatra's capital, in 10 BC. By this time, however, the great queen was 20 years dead.

Back on Strand, the majestic **Savoy** hotel (*see p355*) was first opened in 1889, financed by profits from Richard D'Oyly Carte's productions of Gilbert and Sullivan's light operas at the neighbouring **Savoy Theatre**. The theatre, which pre-dates the hotel by eight years, was the first to use electric lights. Two grand hotels guard Aldwych, at the eastern end of the Strand: **One Aldwych** (*see p354*) and, directly opposite, **ME by Meliá London** (*see p352*). This grand crescent dates only from 1905, but the name 'ald wic' (old settlement or market) has its origins in the 10th century. To the south is **Somerset House**. Almost in front of it is **St Mary-le-Strand** (7836 3126, www.st marylestrand.org, closed Mon, Fri, Sat), James Gibbs's first public building, completed in 1717. On Strand Lane, reached via Surrey Street, is the so-called **'Roman' bath** where Dickens took the waters – you have to peer through a dusty window.

On a traffic island just east of Aldwych is **St Clement Danes** (7242 8282, www.raf.mod.uk/stclementdanes). It's believed that a church was first built here by the Danish in the ninth century and dedicated to one of the many patron saints of mariners, but the current building is mainly Wren's handiwork. It's the principal church of the RAF. Just beyond the church are the Royal Courts of Justice (*see p175*) and the original site of Temple Bar (*see p175*).

EXPLORE

Sights & Museums

Benjamin Franklin House
36 Craven Street, WC2N 5NF (7925 1405, www. benjaminfranklinhouse.org). Charing Cross tube/ rail. **Open** noon-5pm Mon, Wed-Sun. *Tours* noon, 1pm, 2pm, 3.15pm, 4.15pm Mon, Wed-Sun. **Admission** £7; £5 reductions; free under-16s. **Map** p139 B5 ❸❹

This is the house where Franklin – scientist, diplomat, philosopher, inventor and Founding Father of the US – lived between 1757 and 1775. It isn't a museum in the conventional sense: there are few artefacts on display. Rather, it is explored through 45-minute 'experiences' (Wed-Sun, booking advised). These are led by an actress playing Franklin's landlady's daughter, Polly Hewson, using sound and visual projections on the plain walls of the house to conjure up the world in which Franklin lived. From noon on Mondays, there are more straightforward architectural tours (20 mins, £3.50).

★ Courtauld Gallery
Strand, WC2R 0RN (7848 2526, www.courtauld. ac.uk/gallery). Temple tube. **Open** 10am-6pm daily. *Tours* phone for details. **Admission** £7; £6 reductions; £3 Mon; students, unwaged & under-18s free. **Map** p139 D4 ❸❺

Located for the last two decades in the north wing of Somerset House (*see below*), the Courtauld has one of Britain's greatest collections of paintings, and contains several works of world importance. Although there are some outstanding early works (Cranach's *Adam & Eve*, for one), the collection's strongest suit is in Impressionism and Post-Impressionism. Popular masterpieces here include Manet's *A Bar at the Folies-Bergère*, but there are also superb works by Monet and Cézanne, important Gauguins, and some Van Goghs and Seurats. On the top floor, there's a selection of gorgeous Fauvist pieces and a lovely room of Kandinskys. Hidden downstairs, the little gallery café is delightful.

FREE Somerset House & the Embankment Galleries
Strand, WC2R 1LA (7845 4600, www. somersethouse.org.uk). Temple tube. **Open** 10am-6pm daily (last entry to galleries 5pm). *Tours* phone for details. **Admission** *Courtyard & terrace* free. *Embankment Galleries* prices vary; check website for details. *Tours* phone for details. **Map** p139 D4 ❸❻

The original Somerset House was a Tudor palace commissioned by the Duke of Somerset. In 1775, it was demolished to make way for the first purpose-built office block in the world. Architect Sir William Chambers spent the last 20 years of his life working on this neoclassical edifice overlooking the Thames, built to accommodate learned societies such as the Royal Academy and government departments. The taxmen are still here, but the rest of the building is open to the public. Attractions include the Courtauld, the handsome fountain court and several eating options: from a terrace café and Fernandez & Wells to Skye Gyngell's Spring, a pricey Italian restaurant; several rooms around the courtyard are used to host lively art exhibitions. Downstairs on the Thames side of the building, the Embankment Galleries house exhibitions on a grander scale, and a Christmas market. In summer, children never tire of running through the choreographed fountains while parents watch from café tables; in winter, an ice rink takes over the courtyard.

Restaurants

★ Delaunay
55 Aldwych, WC2B 4BB (7499 8558, www. thedelaunay.com). Covent Garden or Temple tube. **Open** 7am-11.30pm Mon-Fri; 8am-midnight Sat; 9am-11pm Sun. **Main courses** £6.50-£33. **Cover** £2. **Map** p139 D3 ❸❼ **Brasserie**

European grand cafés are the inspiration here, resulting in a striking interior of green leather banquette seating, dark wood, antique mirrors and a black and white marble floor. The menu runs from breakfast to dinner, taking in afternoon tea (try the Austrian-biased cakes, all made in-house). There's a dish of the day, soups, sandwiches, salads and egg dishes, plus savouries and crustacea.

▶ *If the restaurant is full, try the no-bookings Counter café next door for cakes and light meals.*

Fernandez & Wells
East Wing, Somerset House, the Strand, WC2R 1LA (7420 9408, www.fernandezandwells.com). Temple tube. **Open** 8am-7.30pm Mon-Wed; 8am-9pm Thur, Fri; 10am-6.30pm Sat, Sun. **Tapas** £4.50-£15. **Map** p139 D4 ❸❽ **Café**

Four impressive rooms in the east wing of Somerset House (*see left*) are set up for all-day grazing. Meat is central: the 'ham room' has carving slices of lomito ibérico, jamón de lampiño, or wild fennel Tuscan salami, while morcilla and the like arrive from an open grill. Breakfasts are simple but good. **Other locations** throughout the city.

Pubs & Bars

★ Gordon's Wine Bar
47 Villiers Street, WC2N 6NE (7930 1408, www.gordonswinebar.com). Embankment tube or Charing Cross tube/rail. **Open** 11am-11pm Mon-Sat; noon-10pm Sun. **Map** p139 B5 ❸❾

Gordon's was established in its present form as long ago as 1890, but the exposed brickwork and flickering candlelight make this basement feel older still. Although this is the definitive old-school wine bar, it gets packed with a young and lively crowd. The wine list is surprisingly modern; still, in such surroundings, it seems a shame not to drink the fortified wines, drawn from casks behind the bar.

EXPLORE

Bloomsbury, King's Cross & Fitzrovia

L ondon's neighbourhoods north of Oxford Street are bookish and bohemian. Bloomsbury is best known as the home of the British Museum. The unofficial heart of the area is the Brunswick Centre and the buzzing network of surrounding streets.

To the west, Fitzrovia is a favourite source of stories for London nostalgists, but the days of post-war spivs and drunken poets have given way to an era of new-media offices. At least they keep the pubs lively and the quality of the restaurants high.

To the north of Bloomsbury, the legendarily seedy King's Cross has gone the way of formerly raffish Fitzrovia, with the arrival of the British Library, the rebirth of St Pancras Station as an international rail hub and the emergence of King's Cross Central as an entirely new district.

EXPLORE

British Museum.

Don't Miss

1 **British Museum**
A treasure trove (p150).

2 **Wellcome Collection**
Science made
scintillating (p155).

3 **Lima London** Get into
Peruvian eats (p162).

4 **Novelty Automation**
Coin-op giggles (p154).

5 **London Review
Bookshop** Find yourself
some inspiration (p157).

BLOOMSBURY

Euston Square, Holborn, Russell Square or Tottenham Court Road tube.

Bloomsbury's florid name is, prosaically, taken from 'Blemondisberi' – the manor ('bury') of William Blemond, who acquired the area in the 13th century. It remained rural until the 1660s, when the fourth Earl of Southampton built Bloomsbury Square around his house. The Southamptons intermarried with the Russells, the Dukes of Bedford; together, they developed the area as one of London's first planned suburbs.

Over the next two centuries, the group built a series of grand squares. **Bedford Square** (1775-80) is London's only complete Georgian square (regrettably, its central garden is usually closed to the public); huge **Russell Square** has been restored as a public park with a popular café. To the east, the cantilevered postwar **Brunswick Centre** is full of shops, flats, restaurants and a cinema. The nearby streets, particularly **Marchmont Street**, are some of the more characterful in the West End.

Bloomsbury's charm is the sum of its parts, best experienced on a meander through its bookshops (many on **Great Russell Street**), pubs and squares. The blue plaques are a *Who's Who* of literary modernists – TS Eliot, Virginia Woolf, WB Yeats – with a few interlopers from more distant history: Edgar Allan Poe (83 Southampton Row), Anthony Trollope (6 Store Street) and, of course, Dickens (48 Doughty Street; now the **Charles Dickens Museum**).

On Bloomsbury's western border, Malet, Gordon and Gower streets are dominated by the **University of London**. The most notable building is Gower Street's University College,

founded in 1826. Inside is the 'autoicon' of utilitarian philosopher and founder of the university, Jeremy Bentham: his preserved cadaver, fully clothed, sits in a glass-fronted cabinet. The university's main library is housed in towering **Senate House** on Malet Street, one of the city's most imposing examples of monumental art deco. It was the model for Orwell's Ministry of Truth in *1984* – but don't be scared to step inside: the lower floors and little café are open to the public.

South of the university sprawls the **British Museum**, the must-see of all London must-sees. Running off Great Russell Street, where you'll find the museum's main entrance, are three attractive parallel streets (Coptic, Museum and Bury) and, nearby, the **Cartoon Museum**; also close by, Bloomsbury Way is home to Hawksmoor's restored **St George's Bloomsbury**. Across from here, **Sicilian Avenue** is an Italianate, pedestrian precinct of colonnaded shops – take it in over a fine ale at the **Holborn Whippet** (3137 9937, www.holbornwhippet.com).

North-east of the British Museum, **Lamb's Conduit Street** is a convivial thoroughfare lined with interesting shops. At the north end of the street is **Coram's Fields**, a delightful children's park on the grounds of the former Thomas Coram's Foundling Hospital. Coram's legacy is commemorated in the **Foundling Museum**.

Sights & Museums

★ FREE British Museum

Great Russell Street, WC1B 3DG (7323 8299, www. britishmuseum.org). Russell Square or Tottenham Court Road tube. Open *Galleries* 10am-5.30pm Mon-Thur, Sat, Sun; 10am-8.30pm Fri. *Great Court*

British Museum.

9am-6pm Mon-Thur, Sat, Sun; 9am-8.30pm Fri. *Multimedia guides* 10am-4.30pm Thur, Sat, Sun; 10am-7.30pm Fri. *Eye Opener tours* (40mins) phone for details. **Admission** free; donations appreciated. *Temporary exhibitions* vary. *Multimedia guides* £5; £3.50-£4.50 reductions. *Eye Opener tours* free. **Map** p153 G4 ❶

Officially the country's most popular tourist attraction, the British Museum opened to the public in 1759 in Montagu House, which then occupied this site. The current building is a neoclassical marvel built in 1847 by Robert Smirke, one of the pioneers of the Greek Revival style. In 2000, Lord Foster added a glass roof to the Great Court, now claimed to be 'the largest covered public square in Europe' and a popular public space ever since. This £100m landmark surrounds the domed Reading Room (used by the British Library until its move to King's Cross), where Marx, Lenin, Dickens, Darwin, Hardy and Yeats once worked. In 2014, the museum added a new building to its western corner, containing the Sainsbury Exhibitions Gallery. This will be hosting the fabulous, sell-out blockbuster shows (China's Terracotta Army, Pompeii, Ice Age art, Greek sculpture) that have characterised Neil MacGregor's tenure as the museum's director; he steps down in 2015 after over a decade in charge.

In the museum proper, star exhibits include ancient Egyptian artefacts – the Rosetta Stone on the ground floor (with a barely noticed, perfect replica in the King's Library), mummies upstairs – and Greek antiquities, including the marble friezes from the Parthenon known as the Elgin Marbles. Room 41 displays Anglo-Saxon artefacts, including the famous Sutton Hoo treasure. Also upstairs, the Celts gallery has Lindow Man, killed in 300 BC and so well preserved in peat you can see his beard, while the ground-floor Wellcome Gallery of Ethnography holds an Easter Island statue and regalia collected during Captain Cook's travels. The King's Library provides a calming home to a permanent exhibition entitled 'Enlightenment: Discovering the World in the 18th Century', a 5,000-piece collection devoted to the extraordinary formative period of the museum. The remit covers archaeology, science and the natural world; the objects displayed range from Indonesian puppets to a beautiful orrery.

You won't be able to see everything in one day, so buy a souvenir guide and pick out the show-stoppers, concentrate on a particular area or plan on making several visits. Highlights tours focus on specific aspects of the huge collection; Eye Opener tours offer specific introductions to world cultures.

▶ *Seeking refreshment? Check out the fine cask beers at the historic Museum Tavern (49 Great Russell Street, 7242 8987), opposite the front gate.*

Cartoon Museum

35 Little Russell Street, WC1A 2HH (7580 8155, www.cartoonmuseum.org). Tottenham Court Road tube. **Open** 10.30am-5.30pm Mon-Sat;

noon-5.30pm Sun. **Admission** £7; £5 reductions; free under-18s. **Map** p153 G4 ❷

The best of British cartoon art is displayed on the ground floor of this former dairy. The displays start in the early 18th century, when high-society types back from the Grand Tour introduced the Italian practice of *caricatura* to polite company. From Hogarth, it moves through Britain's cartooning 'golden age' (1770-1830) to examples of wartime cartoons, ending up with modern satirists such as Gerald Scarfe and the wonderfully loopy Ralph Steadman. Upstairs is a celebration of UK comic art, with original 1921 *Rupert the Bear* artwork by Mary Tourtel, Frank Hampson's Dan Dare, Leo Baxendale's Bash Street Kids and a painted *Asterix* cover by that well-known Briton, Albert Uderzo.

Charles Dickens Museum

48 Doughty Street, WC1N 2LX (7405 2127, www.dickensmuseum.com). Chancery Lane or Russell Square tube. **Open** 10am-5pm daily. *Tours* by arrangement. **Admission** £8; £4-£6 reductions; free under-6s. **Map** p153 F6 ❸

London is scattered with plaques marking addresses where Dickens lived, but this is the only one to have been preserved as a museum. He lived here from 1837 to 1840, writing *Nicholas Nickleby* and *Oliver Twist* while in residence. Ring the doorbell to gain access to four floors of Dickensiana, collected over the years from various former residences. Some rooms are arranged as they might have been when he lived here (especially atmospheric during the occasional candlelit openings); others deal with different aspects of his life, from struggling hack to famous performer. Refurbishment has created a pleasant downstairs café and courtyard garden.

▶ *The museum displays the chair and desk at which Dickens wrote* Great Expectations: *they were bought for the nation by the National Heritage Memorial Fund in 2015. You'll find them in the Study.*

Foundling Museum

40 Brunswick Square, WC1N 1AZ (7841 3600, www.foundlingmuseum.org.uk). Russell Square tube. **Open** 10am-5pm Tue-Sat; 11am-5pm Sun. **Admission** £7.50; £5 reductions; free under-16s. **Map** p153 E5 ❹

This museum recalls the social history of the Foundling Hospital, set up in 1739 by shipwright and sailor Thomas Coram. Returning to England from America in 1720, Coram was appalled by the number of abandoned children he saw. Securing royal patronage, he persuaded Hogarth and Handel to become governors; it was Hogarth who made the building Britain's first public art gallery; works by artists as notable as Gainsborough and Reynolds are on display. The most heart-rending display is a tiny case of mementoes that were all mothers could leave the children they abandoned here. Recover your composure over a cuppa in the café, run by local social enterprise the People's Supermarket.

EXPLORE

EXPLORE

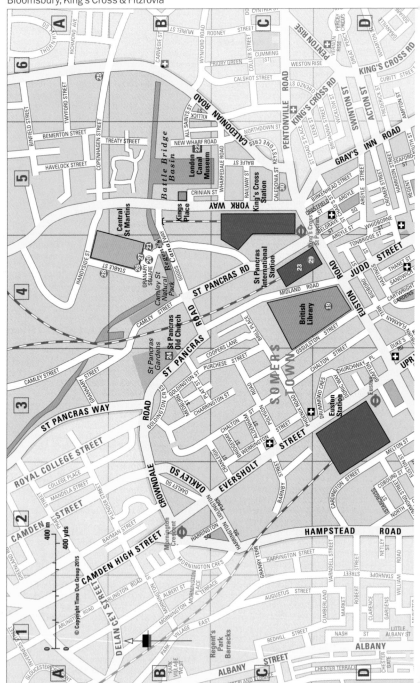

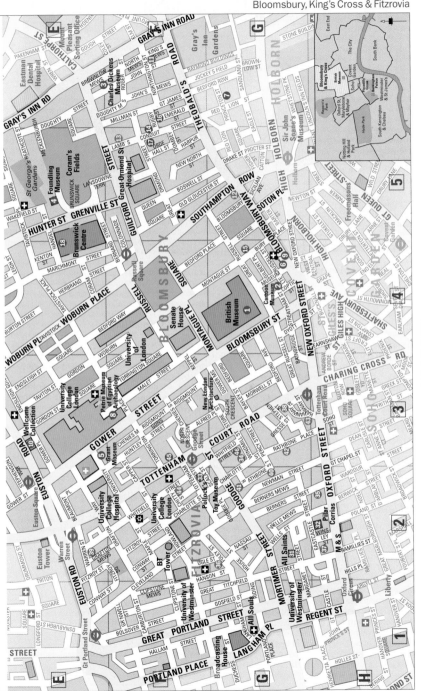

EXPLORE

Reading Room, Wellcome Collection.

★ FREE **Grant Museum**
Rockefeller Building, 21 University Street, WC1E
6JJ (3108 2052, www.ucl.ac.uk/museums/zoology).
Goodge Street tube. **Open** *1-5pm Mon-Sat.*
Admission free. **Map** p153 E3 ❺
Now rehoused in a former Edwardian library in
the University College complex, the Grant Museum
retains the air of an avid Victorian collector's house.
Its 67,000 specimens include the remains of many
rare and extinct creatures, including skeletons of
the dodo and the zebra-like quagga (which lived in
South Africa and was hunted out of existence in
the 1880s). Visitors are engaged in dialogue about
the distant evolutionary past via the most modern
means available, including iPads and smartphones.
Don't miss the Micrarium – a kind of booth walled
with illuminated microscope slides.

Museum of Comedy
Undercroft, St George's Church, Bloomsbury
Way, WC1A 2SR (7534 1744, www.museumof
comedy.com). Holborn tube. **Open** *noon-6pm*
Tue-Sun. **Admission** £5; £4 reductions. **Map**
p153 G4 ❻
The crypt below St George's Church in Bloomsbury
is the unlikely location of the country's first museum
dedicated to comedic artefacts. It's the brainchild of
Martin Witts, owner of the Leicester Square Theatre
(*see p281*). Over decades working alongside the
heroes of British comedy, Witts has collected thousands of remarkable curiosities, including Tommy
Cooper's magic props (all made by Cooper himself)
and the Two Ronnies' glasses. His artefacts are now
on permanent display – along with temporary photographic exhibitions. Attached to the museum, the
Cooper Room is a 100-seat stand-up/theatre venue.
And you can sup on a lager (the comic's drink of
choice) at the Comedians' Arms bar – itself an arte-
fact, recycled from Wilton's Music Hall (*see p294*).

▶ *Taking a charmingly old-school approach to*
interactivity, the museum has a portable TV on
which you can watch, yes, videos of old comedy
shows, as well as a record player for the many LPs.

★ **Novelty Automation**
1A Princeton Street, WC1R 4AX (http://novelty-
automation.com). Chancery Lane or Holborn tube.
Open *11am-6pm Wed, Fri, Sat; noon-8pm Thur.*
Admission free; tokens £1 each. **Map** p153 G6 ❼
See p155 **Silliness as an Art Form**.

FREE **Petrie Museum of**
Egyptian Archaeology
University College London, Malet Place, WC1E
6BT (7679 2884, www.petrie.ucl.ac.uk). Warren
Street tube. **Open** *1-5pm Tue-Sat.* **Admission** free;
donations appreciated. **Map** p153 F3 ❽
Set up in 1892 by eccentric traveller and diarist
Amelia Edwards, the refurbished museum is named
after Flinders Petrie, tireless excavator of ancient
Egypt. Where the British Museum's Egyptology
collection is strong on the big stuff, the Petrie is dim
case after dim case of minutiae: pottery sherds,
ancient linen, beads, pieces of papyrus. Highlights
include artefacts from heretic pharaoh Akhenaten's
capital Tell el Amarna. Computers offer 3D views of
select objects from the 80,000-strong collection.

FREE **St George's Bloomsbury**
Bloomsbury Way, WC1A 2HS (7242 1979,
www.stgeorgesbloomsbury.org.uk). Holborn or
Tottenham Court Road tube. **Open** *vary. Services*
9am Tue, Thur; 9am, 1.10pm Wed, Fri; 10.30am
Sun. **Admission** free. **Map** p153 G4 ❾
Consecrated in 1730, St George's is a grand and
disturbing Nicholas Hawksmoor church, with an
offset, stepped spire that was inspired by Pliny the
Elder's account of the Mausoleum at Halicarnassus.

EXPLORE

Highlights of its renovation include the mahogany reredos and the sculptures of lions and unicorns clawing at the base of the steeple. The opening hours are erratic, but on Sundays, the church always remains open for visitors after the regular service. Check online for details of concerts.

▶ *The Undercroft contains a compelling (and free) little exhibition on the building of the church above – and also the Museum of Comedy (see p154).*

★ FREE Wellcome Collection

183 Euston Road, NW1 2BE (7611 2222, www. wellcomecollection.org). Euston Square tube or Euston tube/Overground. **Open** 10am-6pm Tue, Wed, Fri, Sat; 10am-10pm Thur; 11am-6pm Sun. *Library* 10am-6pm Mon-Wed, Fri; 10am-8pm Thur; 10am-4pm Sat. **Admission** free. **Map** p153 E3 ⑩ Less than a decade after this gathering of international and historic oddities (Napoleon's toothbrush, Victorian amulets, Polynesian medical aids) opened, its brilliant temporary exhibitions ('High Society' dealt with drugs, 'The Institute of Sexology' was all about bumping uglies) were already attracting 500,000 visitors a year – far more than the premises could cope with. So the ground-floor exhibition gallery, shop and café-restaurant,

SILLINESS AS AN ART FORM

Put a coin in the slot and enter Tim Hunkin's world of crazy.

Want a divorce? Fancy a cheap holiday? Need to launder money or lose weight? All these things and many others can be achieved for the modest outlay of a pound (sometimes two) at the nutty slot machines of **Novelty Automation** (see p154).

These lovingly crafted moving sculptures are almost all the work of Tim Hunkin, a cartoonist who fell in love with coin-in-the-slot machines. There are one or two by other exponents of this most idiosyncratic of arts: for instance, Paul Spooner's *The Dream*, which sees a couple's sleep disturbed by something nasty in the woodshed, is both funny and alarming.

Visitors to London with long memories and a long-established taste for quirky attractions may remember Cabaret Mechanical Theatre, which resided on the lower level of Covent Garden's Apple Market from 1984 to 2000. Some of its exhibits then found a home in the arcade on Southwold Pier in Suffolk, while others travelled the world, and a selection of these lovely handmade jokes operated by cogs and levers has returned to London.

Now, in a small shabby space behind a Bloomsbury shopfront, people of all ages are shown a good time. When some brave soul has a go at *Test Your Nerve* – a slot machine that invites you to place your hand beneath the jowls of a huge, red-eyed dog and keep it there while the horrible hound growls and drools – the entire place erupts.

The antidote to that experience is *Microbreak*: strap yourself into a battered easy chair on a wobbly platform and 'enjoy all the benefits of a holiday with none of the downsides' – you even get a hot blast of sun, courtesy of the lamp on top of the telly in front of you. Nerves steadied, you might be ready to juggle nuclear waste with the 'remote manipulator arm' in *My-Nuke*, or to offer yourself for to the *Autofrisk* machine, which invites visitors to have themselves patted down by a pair of disembodied hands in heavy-duty rubber gloves. Where else can you get fun of that calibre for a quid?

EXPLORE

and well-displayed permanent collection and medicine-themed contemporary art upstairs have been enhanced by a typically ingenious adaptation. Connected to the lower floors with a showpiece spiral staircase, space has been found upstairs for a new restaurant and the handsome Reading Room. Still part of the library, the latter has a slightly studious air and a mezzanine stuffed with medical and scientific books, but it's now a public space too, manned by explainers and librarians who can introduce you to historic artwork (some of it in boxes that must be opened with protective white gloves) and extraordinary artefacts (a dentist's workstation, a 'Smoky Sue Smokes for Two' doll). Fascinating interactives include the 'Virtual Autopsy' table – effectively a giant tablet where you can swipe cuts through 3D cadavers – and a replica of Freud's couch, complete with Rorschach tests.

Restaurants

Lady Ottoline
11A Northington Street, WC1N 2JF (7831 0008, www.theladyottoline.com). Chancery Lane or Russell Square tube. **Open** noon-11pm Mon-Sat; noon-5pm Sun. *Food served* noon-10.30pm Mon-Fri; noon-4pm, 6-10pm Sat; noon-4pm Sun. **Main courses** £10.95-£19.50. **Map** p153 F6 ⓫
Gastropub
One of a group of upmarket gastropubs, all of which have a commitment to drink as well as food, with space for drinkers and a selection that runs from cocktails and real ales to a thoughtful wine list. Food is served in the ground-floor bar at the Lady Ottoline, but for a more sedate meal, it's best to dine in the pleasant first-floor room. The menu is a bit more adventurous than at most gastropubs – witness creamy rabbit pie with pomegranate salad. **Other locations** Princess of Shoreditch, 76-78 Paul Street, Shoreditch, EC2A 4NE (7729 9270); Pig & Butcher, 80 Liverpool Road, Islington, N1 0QD (7226 8304).

Pubs & Bars

All Star Lanes
Victoria House, Bloomsbury Place, WC1B 4DA (7025 2676, www.allstarlanes.co.uk). Holborn tube. **Open** 4-11.30pm Mon-Wed; 4pm-midnight Thur; noon-2am Fri; 11am-2am Sat; 11am-11pm Sun. *Food served* 5-10pm Mon-Thur; noon-10pm Fri-Sun. **Rates** £6.95-£8.95/person per game; £5.95 under-13s. **Map** p153 G5 ⓬
Of Bloomsbury's two subterranean bowling dens (*see also p157* **In the Know**), this is the one with aspirations. Walk past the lanes and smart, diner-style seating, and you'll find yourself in a comfortable, subdued side bar with chilled glasses, classy red furnishings, an unusual mix of bottled lagers and some impressive cocktails. There's an American menu and, at weekends, DJs.

Other locations Whiteleys, 6 Porchester Gardens, Bayswater, W2 4DB (7313 8363); Old Truman Brewery, 95 Brick Lane, Spitalfields, E1 6QL (7426 9200); Westfield Stratford City, Stratford, E20 1ET (3167 2434).

Lamb
94 Lamb's Conduit Street, WC1N 3LZ (7405 0713, www.youngs.co.uk). Holborn or Russell Square tube. **Open** noon-11pm Mon-Wed; noon-midnight Thur-Sat; noon-10.30pm Sun. *Food served* noon-9pm daily. **Map** p153 F5 ⓭
The standard range of Young's beers is dispensed from a central horseshoe bar in this 280-year-old pub, around which are ringed original etched-glass snob screens, used to prevent Victorian gentlemen from being seen when liaising with 'women of dubious distinction'. A sunken back area gives access to a convenient square of summer patio.

Shops & Services

Darkroom
52 Lamb's Conduit Street, WC1N 3LL (7831 7244, www.darkroomlondon.com). Holborn tube. **Open** 11am-7pm Mon-Fri; 11am-6pm Sat; noon-5pm Sun. **Map** p153 F5 ⓮ **Fashion**
This shop is quite literally dark (with black walls and lampshades), creating a striking backdrop for the carefully chosen selection of unisex fashion, accessories and interiors items for sale. The space doubles up as an art gallery.

Darkroom.

EXPLORE

▶ *For more clothes, check out Folk (www.folkclothing. com). The menswear at no.49 (7404 6458) focuses on the stylish own-label, with additional pieces from Scandi brands Our Legacy and Han Kjøbenhavn, while no.53 (8616 4191) is a godsend for women, with labels such as Sweden's Acne, Humanoid from the Netherlands and Sessùn from France.*

London Review Bookshop

14 Bury Place, WC1A 2JL (7269 9030, www.lrb shop.co.uk). Holborn or Tottenham Court Road tube. **Open** 10am-6.30pm Mon-Sat; noon-6pm Sun. **Map** p153 G4 ⑮ **Books & music**
From the inviting presentation to the sheer quality of the books selected, this is an inspiring bookshop – no wonder it was able to celebrate its tenth anniversary in 2014. Politics, current affairs and history are well represented on the ground floor; downstairs, audio books lead on to exciting poetry and philosophy sections – everything you'd expect from a shop owned by the *London Review of Books*. Browse through your purchases in the sweet little adjoining café, and check the website for stimulating events.

Pentreath & Hall

17 Rugby Street, WC1N 3QT (7430 2526, www.pentreath-hall.com). Holborn tube. **Open** 11am-6pm Mon-Sat. **Map** p153 F6 ⑯ **Homewares**
This petite store looks like the drawing room of a smart country house scaled to the size of a Shoreditch studio flat, scattered with beautifully made decorative artefacts and accessories such as watercolours above the mantelpiece, vintage maps and fine chinaware mugs. Alongside design and architecture books (Ben Pentreath is an architect), there's a notable range of découpage plates and trays from Bridie Hall (the designer is a joint owner of the shop) with designs from archival natural-history and geographical sources.

Persephone Books

59 Lamb's Conduit Street, WC1N 3NB (7242 9292, www.persephonebooks.co.uk). Russell Square tube. **Open** 10am-6pm Mon-Fri; noon-5pm Sat. **Map** p153 F5 ⑰ **Books**
Persephone Books independently publishes the works of 20th-century women writers (and a few men) in beautifully rendered publications, lined with prints of female artists of the period. Pick from a range that includes Diana Athill's *Midsummer Night in the Warehouse*, which includes a classic memoir about a failed love affair, or Virginia Woolf's *A Writer's Diary*. The shop itself spills over into the Persephone office at the back (or is it the other way around?), giving the store a slightly ramshackle, writer's room feel where herbal tea and upscale literary chit-chat always seem to be on the table.

Skoob

Unit 66, The Brunswick Centre, WC1N 1AE (7278 8760, www.skoob.com). Russell Square tube. **Open** 10.30am-8pm Mon-Sat; 10.30am-6pm Sun. **Map** p153 E5 ⑲ **Books & music**
A back-to-basics basement beloved of students from the nearby University of London, Skoob showcases some 50,000 titles covering virtually every subject, from philosophy and biography to politics and the occult. Prices are very reasonable.

KING'S CROSS & ST PANCRAS

King's Cross St Pancras tube/rail.

North-east of Bloomsbury, King's Cross is becoming a major European transport hub, thanks to a £500m makeover of the area. The renovated and restored **St Pancras International** was the key arrival, but neighbouring King's Cross station has since benefited with a handsomely restored 1851 façade overlooking a public square, nicely balancing the splendidly restored **Great Northern Hotel** (*see p356*), plus an expanded station concourse with snazzy cascading roof, much-improved restaurants and cafés, and – yes – a sawn-in-half luggage trolley that symbolises Harry Potter's **Platform 9¾**. If joining the queue for a photo-op doesn't satisfy your cravings, there are plenty of souvenirs in the **Harry Potter Shop** (7803 0500, www.harrypotterplatform934.com).

It's the area to the north that holds our attention, however. **King's Cross Central** is impressive in stats alone: 67 acres, 20 'historic structures' being refurbed, 'up to 2,000 homes and serviced apartments', 'up to 500,000sq ft of retail space', 20 new streets, three new bridges, ten new parks and squares, and 400 trees planted. The concept behind the numbers is interesting too. The developers have tried to create from scratch a 'mixed-use' development – one with the virtues of multiplicity and resilience normally found in communities that have grown up over time. To this end, they are paying careful attention to the area's industrial heritage, to attracting the right mix of residents, and to the kind of events that might draw in visitors. So, heading north-east from the station, King's Boulevard leads directly to the fine **Granary Square**, where the University of the Arts London is the most important new resident. (There's also a rather sci-fi illuminated tunnel

EXPLORE

connecting the new offices beside King's Boulevard to King's Cross station itself.) The whole area seems more cohesive and populous than it did, with the **Kings Place** arts complex (*see p284*), **London Canal Museum** and **St Pancras Old Church** no longer feeling as though they are isolated in a wasteland.

Sights & Museums

★ FREE British Library
96 Euston Road, NW1 2DB (01937 546060, www.bl.uk). Euston or King's Cross St Pancras tube/rail. **Open** 9.30am-8pm Mon-Thur; 9.30am-6pm Fri; 9.30am-5pm Sat; 11am-5pm Sun. **Admission** free; donations appreciated. **Map** p152 D4 ⑲

'One of the ugliest buildings in the world,' opined a Parliamentary committee on the opening of the new British Library in 1997. But don't judge a book by its cover: the interior is a model of cool, spacious functionality, the collection is unmatched (150 million items and counting), and the reading rooms (open only to cardholders) are so popular that regular users complain that they can't find a seat. The focal point of the building is the King's Library, a six-storey glass-walled tower housing George III's collection, but the library's main treasures are on permanent display in the John Ritblat Gallery: the Lindisfarne Gospels, a Diamond Sutra from AD 868, original Beatles lyrics. There is also a great programme of temporary exhibitions and associated events: the Folio Society Gallery is free and hosts focused little shows based around key artefacts, while the engaging blockbuster shows are ticketed but cover meaty themes such as sci-fi, Gothic literature, the 800th anniversary of Magna Carta and the English language itself.

Granary Square
Map p152 B4 ⑳
Filled with choreographed fountains (1,080 water spouts, operating 8am-8pm daily, and lit in many colours at night), the square's terracing down to the canal is already populated most sunny days. No wonder: there's a ready supply of students from Central Saint Martins college of art, which in 2011 moved into the building behind – a sensitively and impressively converted, Grade II-listed 1850s

---

IN THE KNOW HEY, SQUIRT!

You'll have seen choreographed fountains in squares elsewhere, but have you ever controlled them? Download the Granary Squirt app and then – if you're in **Granary Square** (*see above*) between 5pm and 8pm and using the Cloud Wi-Fi – you can play games (currently retro arcade classic Snake) with the water jets.

---

industrial building. Fronting on to the square are two restaurants and a café, with the House of Illustration tucked around the corner, and the Coal Drops Yard and Lewis Cubitt Square beginning to open up the industrial land beyond it.

▶ *For information on the ongoing development, visit the King's Cross Visitor Centre (Western Transit Shed, 11 Stable Street, N1C 4AB, 3479 1795, www.kingscross.co.uk, closed Sun).*

House of Illustration
2 Granary Square, N1C 4BH (3696 2020, www.houseofillustration.org.uk). King's Cross St Pancras tube/rail. **Open** 10am-6pm Tue-Sun. **Admission** £7; £4-£5 reductions; free under-5s. **Map** p152 B4 ㉑

The world's first gallery dedicated to the art of illustration has demonstrations, talks, debates and hands-on workshops covering all aspects of illustration, from children's books and scabrous cartoons to advertising and animation, as well as a regular programme of exhibitions.

London Canal Museum
12-13 New Wharf Road, off Wharfdale Road, N1 9RT (7713 0836, www.canalmuseum.org.uk). King's Cross St Pancras tube/rail. **Open** 10am-4.30pm Tue-Sun (until 7.30pm 1st Thur of mth). **Admission** £4; £2-£3 reductions; free under-5s. **Map** p152 B5 ㉒

Housed on two floors of a former 19th-century ice warehouse, the London Canal Museum has a barge cabin to sit in and models of boats, but the displays (photos and videos about ice-importer Carlo Gatti) on the history of the ice trade are perhaps the most interesting. The canalside walk (download a free MP3 audio tour from the museum website) from Camden Town to the museum is lovely.

▶ *In summer, don't miss tours organised by the museum that explore dank Islington Tunnel, an otherwise inaccessible Victorian canal feature.*

FREE St Pancras International
Pancras Road, N1C 4QP (7843 7688, www. stpancras.com). King's Cross St Pancras tube/rail. **Open** 24hrs daily. **Admission** free. **Map** p152 C4 ㉓

The redeveloped St Pancras station has become a destination in more ways than the obvious, now containing large sculptures, the self-proclaimed 'longest champagne bar in Europe', high-end boutiques – even a gastropub and farmers' market. But the new additions are mere window-dressing for the stunning original structures: famously, George Gilbert Scott's grandiloquent red-brick exterior (much of which is now the St Pancras Renaissance hotel; *see p357*), but even more impressively, William Barlow's Victorian glass-and-iron roof to the train shed, a single span that is airy and light, as though he wished to create some kind of cathedral to 19th-century industry and transport.

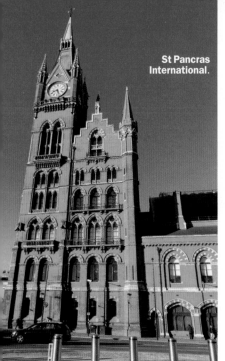

St Pancras
International.

noon-6pm Mon-Fri. Closed Oct-Mar. **Hot dogs**
£3-£6. **Map** p152 A6 ㉕ American

Big Apple Hot Dogs uses specially commissioned
sausages made from free-range pork, and buns
baked by a local bakery. There are various sizes and
meat combinations (pork, beef, pork and beef) and a
full range of condiments. The taste is a revelation –
coarsely meaty, flavoursome and evocative of baseball games, world's fairs and competitive eating.

★ Caravan King's Cross

*Granary Building, 1 Granary Square, N1C 4AA
(7101 7661, www.caravankingscross.co.uk). King's
Cross St Pancras tube/rail.* **Open** 8am-10.30pm
Mon-Fri; 10am-10.30pm Sat; 10am-4pm Sun. **Main
courses** £7-£15.50. **Map** p152 B4 ㉖ Global

This offshoot of Caravan is an altogether bigger,
more urbane operation than the original in Exmouth
Market. The ethos is the same in both branches:
welcoming staff and a menu of what they call
'well-travelled food'. Most are small plates – deep-
fried duck egg with baba ganoush, chorizo oil and
crispy shallots, say, or grits, collard greens and
brown shrimp butter – plus a few large plates and
(at King's Cross only) a handful of first-class pizzas.
Recent favourites include a naughty-but-nice crispy
fried chicken with jerk mayo and pawpaw salsa.
The setting, overlooking the fountains of Granary
Square, is another plus.

Other location 11-13 Exmouth Market,
Clerkenwell, EC1R 4QD (7833 8115).

Grain Store

*Granary Square, 1-3 Stable Street, N1C 4AB
(7324 4466, www.grainstore.com). King's Cross St
Pancras tube/rail.* **Open** noon-2.30pm, 6-10.30pm
Mon-Fri; 11am-3pm, 6-10.30pm Sat; 11am-4pm Sun.
Main courses £9.50-£16. **Set dinner** £35 5
courses. **Map** p152 B4 ㉗ Modern European

Grain Store occupies just one part of a vast former
Victorian warehouse, next to Caravan. Most of
the rest of the building has been imaginatively
transformed into Central Saint Martins arts college.
The restaurant is run by Bruno Loubet, whose
cooking is grounded in the classical traditions of
south-west France, but not bound by them. The
menu is a pick 'n' mix of ingredients and cuisines: a
dish such as sticky pork belly with a corn and quinoa
tamale is typical.

Other location Grain Store Unleashed, St John's
Square, 86-88 Clerkenwell Road, Clerkenwell, EC1M
5RJ (7324 4455, www.grainstoreunleashed.com).

Kerb

*Lewis Cubitt Square, N1 (7324 4466, www.kerb
food.com/kings-cross). King's Cross St Pancras
tube/rail.* **Open** noon-2pm Mon-Fri. **Main courses**
£3-£7. **Map** p152 A4 ㉘ Street food

Kerb runs a series of street-food sites across
London, but had made first King's Boulevard, then
Granary Square their main focus of activities. Now,

FREE St Pancras Old Church & St Pancras Gardens

*St Pancras Road, NW1 1UL (7419 6679, www.
camden.gov.uk). Mornington Crescent tube or
King's Cross St Pancras tube/rail.* **Open** *Church
& gardens* 9am-dusk. *Services* times vary; check
website (www.posp.co.uk/old-st-pancras) for
details. **Admission** free. **Map** p152 B3 ㉔

St Pancras Old Church has been ruined and rebuilt
many times. The current structure is handsome,
but it's the churchyard that delights. Among those
buried here are writer William Godwin and his
wife, Mary Wollstonecraft; over their grave, their
daughter Mary Godwin (author of *Frankenstein*)
declared her love for poet Percy Bysshe Shelley. Also
here is the last resting place of Sir John Soane, one
of only two Grade I-listed tombs (the other is that
of Karl Marx, in Highgate Cemetery; *see p232*).
Designed for his wife, the tomb's dome influenced
Gilbert Scott's design for the red British phone box.

Restaurants

The new area behind King's Cross station is
shaping up to be something of a gastronomic
destination, with an excellent set of restaurants
and a healthy street-food scene.

Big Apple Hot Dogs

*170 Caledonian Road, N1 0SQ (3592 5526, www.
bigapplehotdogs.com). Angel tube.* **Open** *Apr-Sept*

EXPLORE

EAT ON THE STREET

Hot from the stall, cheap at the price.

Kerb.

It's a measure of how comprehensive streetfood's takeover of bargain nosh in the city has been that three of our top ten cheap eats – as voted for by readers of our magazine and website – were not restaurants or caffs with permanent premises but changing combinations of stalls at south London markets: **Borough** (see p61), **Brixton Village** (see p245) and Brockley. Developers haven't been slow to notice Londoners' obsession with food stalls: getting the **Kerb** collective (see p159) to set up their food stalls along King's Cross Boulevard seems such an obvious idea in retrospect that its success in bringing people and atmosphere to the vast King's Cross Central development is easily overlooked. That Kerb have now been moved on to the next new square in the development tells its own story.

In this edition of the London guide, we've made a point of including a selection of our favourite street-food areas. In addition to the places highlighted above, you'll find **Berwick Street Market** (see p130) in Soho and **Exmouth Market** (see p171) in Clerkenwell, but there's also fine foraging at **Broadway Market** (see p213) and **Camden Market** (see p195). The line-up of stalls is unpredictable, of course, but the places we've picked out always have something good to get your teeth into – as well as a diversity of dishes and buzz that make snacking on the street such an enjoyable way to get yourself fed.

they've moved two minutes' walk further north and expanded, with up to ten different traders a day, serving anything from Sri Lankan kothu roti or barbecue ribs to houmous salads and black pudding rolls – the website has details of who's selling what on any particular day.

Pubs & Bars

Booking Office

St Pancras Renaissance London Hotel, Euston Road, NW1 2AR (7841 3566, www.booking officerestaurant.com). King's Cross St Pancras tube/rail. **Open** 6.30am-1am Mon-Wed, Sun; 6.30am-3am Thur-Sat. **Map** p152 C4 ㉙

Sit indoors at this smart cocktail bar and you'll gaze at Sir George Gilbert Scott's lofty interior, a stirring example of the Victorian architect's interpretation of Gothic revival. Outside, under spacious canopies, you'll have a nearly ceiling-level view of St Pancras International station. The cocktail list gives a prominent place to traditional punches, served in mugs, but the list is a long one. Martinis are well made, and the gin fix (a variant on gin fizz using fresh berries) is a wonderful and refreshing potion. Warning: the free bar snacks – coated peanuts – are dangerously addictive.

VOC

2 Varnishers Yard, Regent Quarter, N1 9AW (7713 8229, www.voc-london.co.uk). King's Cross St Pancras tube/rail. **Open** 5pm-midnight Mon-Thur, Sun; 5pm-2am Fri, Sat. **Map** p152 C5 ㉚

VOC bar occupies a smallish, cosy space. The name derives from the Dutch East India Company, and there's a nautical and historical theme to the drinks list. Punches based on old recipes figure large, though modern technology brings them right up to date. Playing it safe with the classics is by no means the inferior option, however, as textbook martinis and caipirinhas prove. On our visit, more people were on beer or wine than cocktails. More fool them.

FITZROVIA

Goodge Street or Tottenham Court Road tube.

Squeezed in between Tottenham Court Road, Oxford Street, Great Portland Street and Euston Road, Fitzrovia isn't as famous as Bloomsbury, but its history is just as rich. The origins of the name are hazy: some believe it comes from **Fitzroy Square**, named after Henry Fitzroy (son of Charles II); others insist it's due to the famous **Fitzroy Tavern** (16A Charlotte Street, 7580 3714), focal venue for London bohemia of the 1930s and '40s and a favourite with the likes of Dylan Thomas and George Orwell. Fitzrovia also had its share of artists: James McNeill Whistler lived at 8 Fitzroy Square, later taken over by British Impressionist Walter Sickert, while Roger

EXPLORE

Fry's Omega Workshops, blurring the distinction between fine and decorative arts, had its studio at no.33. Fitzrovia's raffish image is largely a thing of the past (media offices are in the ascendance these days) but the steady arrival of new galleries – notably the likes of **Pilar Corrias** along Eastcastle Street – has given the district back some of its artiness, even if local rents mean it will never again be home to the dissolute.

The district's icon is the **BT Tower**, completed in 1964 as the Post Office Tower. Its revolving restaurant and observation deck featured in any film that wanted to prove how much London was swinging (*Bedazzled* is just one example). The restaurant is now reserved for corporate functions, but **Charlotte Street** and neighbouring byways have plenty of good options for food and drink.

Sights & Museums

FREE All Saints

7 Margaret Street, W1W 8JG (7636 1788, www. allsaintsmargaretstreet.org.uk). Oxford Circus tube. **Open** 7am-7pm daily. *Services* 7.30am, 8am, 1.10pm, 6pm, 6.30pm Mon-Fri; 7.30am, 8am, 6pm, 6.30pm Sat; 8am, 10am, 11am, 5.15pm, 6pm Sun. **Admission** free. **Map** p153 G2 ③①

Providing respite from the tumult of Oxford Street, this 1850s church was designed by William Butterfield, one of the great exponents of the Victorian Gothic revival. The church looks as if it has been lowered on to its tiny site, so tight is the fit; its lofty spire is the second-highest in London. Behind the polychromatic brick façade, the lavish interior is one of the capital's finest ecclesiastical triumphs, with luxurious marble, flamboyant tile work and glittering stones built into its pillars.

FREE Pilar Corrias

54 Eastcastle Street, W1W 8EF (7323 7000, www.pilarcorrias.com). Oxford Circus tube. **Open** 10am-6pm Mon-Fri; 11am-6pm Sat. **Admission** free. **Map** p153 H2 ③②

Formerly a director at the pioneering Lisson and Haunch of Venison galleries, Corrias opened this 3,800sq ft, Rem Koolhaas-designed gallery in 2008 with a giant aluminium Christmas tree by Philippe Parreno. It was one of the first of an influx of private galleries to the area – several coming here from the art-saturated East End.

Pollock's Toy Museum

1 Scala Street, W1T 2HL (7636 3452, www. pollocksmuseum.com). Goodge Street tube. **Open** 10am-5pm Mon-Sat. **Admission** £6; £3-£5 reductions; free under-3s. **Map** p153 F2 ③③

Named after Victorian toy theatre printer Benjamin Pollock, this place is in turns beguiling and creepy, a nostalgia-fest of old board games, tin trains, porcelain dolls and gollies – fascinating for

adults but less so for children; describing a pile of painted woodblocks in a cardboard box as a 'Build a skyscraper' kit may make them feel lucky to be going home to Minecraft.

▶ *The attached shop is good for wind-up toys and other funny little gifts for children.*

Restaurants

★ Barnyard

18 Charlotte Street, W1T 2LY (7580 3842, www. barnyard-london.com). Goodge Street tube. **Open** noon-10.30pm Mon-Wed; noon-11pm Thur, Fri; 11am-11pm Sat; 11am-9pm Sun. **Main courses** £8-£15. **Map** p153 G3 ③④ American

Barnyard's walls are corrugated iron, the tables stripped planks; plates are enamelled, some seats are oil drums. But wait a minute, isn't this the latest venture from cutting-edge chef Ollie Dabbous? It is, and it proves Dabbous can also do family-friendly and affordable. Barnyard's menu can read like a motorway service station caff until you delve a bit deeper. Despite the affordable pricing and no-bookings policy, there is haute cuisine precision in many of the dishes. Service is charming, the low bill even more agreeable; be prepared to queue: the place is tiny.

▶ *The original Dabbous restaurant is just round the corner (7323 1544, www.dabbous.co.uk), with Oskar's Bar (see p163) above it.*

Berners Tavern

10 Berners Street, W1T 3NP (7908 7979, www. bernerstavern.com). Oxford Circus or Tottenham Court Road tube. **Open** *Bar* 11am-midnight daily. *Restaurant* 7-10.30am, noon-3pm, 3-5.15pm, 6-10.30pm, 10.30pm-midnight daily. **Main courses** £15-£30. **Map** p153 H2 ③⑤ Modern European

The huge lobby bar of the London Edition hotel (*see p357*) looks fabulous, but the vast dining room, with its ornate plasterwork ceiling and lively bar area, looks even better. Food is playful and appealing: tender pork belly with capers, golden raisins and apple coleslaw, and cod with fennel and cider sauce, are sublime. Any caveats? Sometimes dizzy service; frequent upselling of extras; and lighting so low it's hard to read the menu. But Berners Tavern is glamtastic. Wear your best threads, and book ahead for a preliminary cocktail in the adjoining Punch Room bar to steel yourself for the bill.

Bonnie Gull

21A Foley Street, W1W 6DS (7436 0921, www. bonniegull.com). Goodge Street tube. **Open** noon-2.45pm, 6-9.45pm Mon-Fri; noon-3.45pm, 6-9.45pm Sat; noon-3.45pm, 6.30-8.45pm Sun. **Main courses** £15-£26. **Map** p153 G2 ③⑥ Fish

After starting as a pop-up in Hackney in 2011, Bonnie Gull landed in Fitzrovia in 2012. The premises do a good job of evoking a seaside shack. The menu changes daily, but super-fresh crab, with

EXPLORE

the brown meat mixed with mayo in the shell and the white meat ready to be cracked out, is often featured. More complex dishes, such as hake with courgette purée, are beautifully presented and equally good.
▶ *They also run a seafood bar on Exmouth Market (nos.55-57, EC1R 4QL, 3122 0047).*

★ Ethos

48 Eastcastle Street, W1W 8DX (3581 1538, http://ethosfoods.com). Oxford Circus or Tottenham Court Road tube. **Open** 8am-10pm Mon-Fri; 10am-10pm Sat; noon-5pm Sun. **Dishes** Breakfast £5.95. Lunch £2.50/100. *Dinner* £2.75/100g. **Map** p153 H2 ❼ Vegetarian
Ethos is a vegetarian, self-serve buffet, where you pay for your food by its weight. It opens early in the day with a short breakfast menu (avocado on toast, fruit salad, granola, porridge), then rolls on through to lunch and dinner with dishes with a pretty broad global range. Although it's most popular as a midday spot, the drinks list (three beers and a dozen wines) and the rarity of affordable vegetarian eateries in the West End mean it's also a good dinner destination.

Hakkasan

8 Hanway Place, W1T 1HD (7927 7000, www.hakkasan.com). Tottenham Court Road tube. **Open** noon-3.15pm, 5-11.15pm Mon-Wed; noon-3.15pm, 5.30-12.15am Thur, Fri; noon-4.15pm, 5.30-12.15am Sat; noon-4.45pm, 5.30-11.15pm Sun. **Main courses** £17-£61. **Set lunch** £35 2 courses; £58 dim sum (Sun). **Map** p153 G3 ❻ Chinese
More than a decade after it started wowing London's big spenders with its classy Cantonese cooking, this Michelin-starred trendsetter remains a benchmark against which high-end Chinese restaurants should be judged. The basement's stylish interior (all dark wood lattice screens and moody lighting) still attracts beautiful people, who come for signature dishes such as silver cod roasted in champagne, and jasmine tea-smoked organic pork ribs. Drinks run from cocktails via high-priced wines to specialist teas.
Other location 17 Bruton Street, Mayfair, W1J 6QB (7907 1888).

Honey & Co

25A Warren Street, W1T 5LZ (7388 6175, www.honeyandco.co.uk). Warren Street tube. **Open** 8am-10.30pm Mon-Fri; 9.30am-10.30pm Sat. **Main courses** £8.50-£12.50. **Set dinner** (Mon-Sat) £26.50 2 courses; £29.50 3 courses. **Map** p153 E2 ❻ Middle Eastern
A bijou delight, with small tables and chairs packed closely together. The kitchen is run by an accomplished Israeli husband-and-wife team. This pedigree shines in a daily-changing menu that draws influences from across the Middle East. The meze selection includes fabulously spongy, oily bread, sumac-spiked tahini, smoky taramasalata, crisp courgette croquettes with labneh, pan-fried feta and a bright salad with lemon and radishes. A

main might be a whole baby chicken with lemon and a chilli and walnut muhamara paste. It's imaginative home-style cooking, and service is charming.

Koba

11 Rathbone Street, W1T 1NA (7580 8825). Goodge Street or Tottenham Court Road tube. **Open** noon-2.30pm, 6-11pm Mon-Sat; 6-11pm Sun. **Main courses** £8.50-£12. **Set lunch** £6.50-£11.50. **Set meal** £25-£35. **Map** p153 G2 ❿ Korean
Koba is one of the strongest players on the West End Korean scene. Barbecue meats such as beef kalbi or bulgogi are well marinated, and grilled at the table by efficient staff. Barbecued squid is fresh as a daisy, with just the right amount of tongue-tingling heat in the vibrant red sauce. Stews make a sound choice too, with umami-rich stocks and accompanying bowls of pearly rice. Service is polished but not too formal, and the dark, modern, east Asian meets industrial, interior is slick. Drinks include Korean beers, soju and a short wine list.

Lantana

13 Charlotte Place, W1T 1SN (7637 3347, www.lantanacafe.co.uk). Goodge Street tube. **Open** 8-11.30am, noon-3pm Mon-Fri; 9am-3pm Sat, Sun. **Main courses** £6-£12. **Map** p153 G2 ⓫ Café
Lantana is a lively spot. Its look – wooden tables, mismatched chairs, small pieces of art on white walls – is now commonplace, but the staff pride themselves on their coffee-making and baking skills, and rightly so. The flat whites are super-smooth and go well with a moist raspberry friand or an Aussie 'cherry ripe' cake slice. The breakfast and brunch menu includes the likes of maple french toast with streaky bacon, grilled banana and candied pecans. Savoury dishes can be ordered with a glass of wine. The kiosk next door sells some dishes as takeaways.
Other location 1 Oliver's Yard, 55 City Road, Shoreditch, EC1Y 1HQ (7253 5273).

★ Lima London

31 Rathbone Place, W1T 1JH (3002 2640, www.limafitzrovia.com). Tottenham Court Road tube. **Open** noon-2.30pm, 5.30-10.30pm Mon-Sat; noon-3.30pm Sun. **Main courses** £16-£29. **Set meal** (noon-2.30pm, 5.30-6pm Mon-Fri) £20 2 courses; £23 3 courses. **Map** p153 G3 ⓬ Peruvian
Part of the 'Peruvian wave' of restaurants to hit the capital in 2012, Lima London pitched itself squarely at the high end. The modish rear dining room mixes the hum of low-level beats with polite chatter. Well-drilled staff bring out a medley of carefully crafted small plates, the likes of sea bream ceviche flecked with hot aji limo chilli and pieces of roasted corn, and thick wedges of suckling pig – part dense meat, part salty, crispy crackling – matched by a rough corn mash spiked with two kinds of peppers. *See also p143* Lima Floral.

Barnyard. See p161.

Pubs & Bars

Bradley's Spanish Bar
42-44 Hanway Street, W1T 1UT (7636 0359, www.bradleysspanishbar.co.uk). Tottenham Court Road tube. **Open** noon-11.30pm Mon-Thur; noon-midnight Fri, Sat; 3-10.30pm Sun. **Map** p153 G3 ⓭
There's something of the Barcelona dive bar about this place, and San Miguel or Cruzcampo on draught, but Bradley's isn't really very Spanish. A hotchpotch of local workers, shoppers and foreign exchange students fill the cramped two-floor space, unperturbed by routinely unpleasant toilets and the madness of Crossrail-led construction 20 yards away on Oxford Street. After all, there's a good jukebox (playing vinyl, retro fans) and a good atmosphere – what more could anyone want?

Oskar's Bar
Dabbous, 39 Whitfield Street, W1T 2SF (7323 1544, www.dabbous.co.uk). Goodge Street tube. **Open** 5.30-11.30pm Tue-Sat. **Map** p153 F2 ⓮
Downstairs from Ollie Dabbous' first restaurant, this cocktail bar has plenty of unorthodox ingredients: the Giddy Up contains tequila, bramley and gage slider (traditional sloe-infused cider from Devon), elderflower cordial, lemon juice and camomile-infused acacia honey topped with Sierra Nevada IPA. More conservative drinkers are also catered for, with plenty of other drinks that stay close to the classics, and service is sweet and solicitous.

Shops & Services

The electronics shops that congregated at the south end of **Tottenham Court Road** have pretty much vanished, but the arrival of the first Google Shop (*see p145* **Made For Browsing**), a 'shop in a shop' at Currys PC World (nos.145-149), caused a bit of a cyberstir in 2015.

Heal's
196 Tottenham Court Road, W1T 7LQ (7636 1666, www.heals.co.uk). Goodge Street tube. **Open** 10am-7pm Mon-Wed, Fri, Sat; 10am-8pm Thur; noon-6pm Sun. **Map** p153 F3 ⓯ **Homewares**
The store's 2013 redesign emphasises dramatic lighting, its showroom filled with show-stopping designs from Tom Dixon, Bocci (who designed the glass pendant chandelier over the spiral staircase) and Squint. Heal's also rules for kitchen goods such as copper saucepans. Despite the luxe labels, you can find real value for money: wool Tuareg rugs cost under £200 and a solid oak chest of drawers might go for less than £600 in the sale. A wide range of toiletries completes the picture.

Lewis Leathers
Mottram House, 3-5 Whitfield Street, W1T 2SA (7636 4314, www.lewisleathers.com). Tottenham Court Road tube. **Open** 11am-6pm Mon-Sat. **Map** p153 G3 ⓰ **Fashion**
It's the heritage leather biker brand that boasts Cara Delevingne and Kate Moss as customers. Established in 1892, the history of Lewis Leathers is plastered on the wall in nostalgic posters from TT racer days of the 1920s through to the '60s and '70s. Here, you can pick and choose from a wide range of leather goods, whether it's a classic racer jacket, trousers, a studded belt or some seriously sleek heeled boots. The shop also stocks a variety of denim, T-shirts, sneakers, goggles and even books, including its current issue of *Men's File Archive*. Of course, quality leather like this costs (jackets retail at upwards of £600).

The City

The City's current fame merely as the financial heart of London does no justice to its 2,000-year history. Here – on top of a much more ancient ritual landscape – the Romans founded the city they called Londinium, building a bridge to the west of today's London Bridge. Here were a forum-basilica, an amphitheatre, public baths and the defensive wall that still defines what we now call the Square Mile (an area, in fact, of 1.21 square miles).

Although the City has just over 9,000 residents, 330,000 people arrive each weekday to work as bankers, lawyers and traders, taking over 85 million square feet of office space. Tourists come, too, to see St Paul's Cathedral, the Tower of London and, in increasing numbers, the Museum of London, but there's much else besides. No area of London offers quite so much in so small a space. Roman ruins? Medieval churches? Iconic 21st-century towers? You're in the right place.

EXPLORE

St Paul's Cathedral.

Don't Miss

1 St Paul's Cathedral Sir Christopher Wren's masterpiece (p176).

2 Sir John Soane's Museum Former home packed with art, furniture and ornamentation (p166).

3 Tower of London Crown Jewels, Beefeaters, armour: a historic attraction par excellence (p187).

4 Sky Garden London's best view? Head up 20 Fenchurch Street (p187).

5 Museum of London Life in the city from prehistory to the present (p180).

To understand the City properly, visit on a weekday when the great economic machine is running at full tilt and the commuter is king. Despite efforts by the City authorities to improve the district's prospects as a weekend leisure destination, many of the streets still fall eerily quiet on Saturday and Sunday. If you do visit at the weekend, try the Cheapside shops and the street's anchor mall, the rather antiseptic **One New Change**; drop in on the always wonderful **Museum of London**; or just do as a discerning minority of locals do – potter about the place's odd nooks and crannies, from unexpected parks to disregarded churches, in relative tranquillity.

We begin this chapter with a couple of rather more lived-in adjuncts to the City proper: **Holborn**, where London-connoisseurs can wander some of the city's finest small museums, and **Clerkenwell**, where you'll find some of the best places to eat anywhere in London. They are underscored by historic **Fleet Street**, famous for its now-absent newspaper industry, to the south of which you can ponder powdered wigs and legal quiddities in the calm surrounds of **Temple** and the **Inns of Court**.

Newcomers to the City are advised to head straight to St Paul's, not just for the beauty of the architecture, but because the spiky-roofed **City of London Information Centre** (7332 1456, www.cityoflondon.gov.uk) is there, on the river side of the cathedral. Open 9.30am-5.30pm daily (10am-4pm Sun), it has information on sights, events, walks and talks, as well as offering tours with specialist guides, and has free Wi-Fi.

HOLBORN

Holborn tube.

A sharp left turn out of Holborn tube on to Kingsway and then another left leads to the unexpectedly lovely **Lincoln's Inn Fields**. Surely London's largest square (indeed, it's more of a park), it's blessed with gnarled oaks casting dappled shade over a tired bandstand. On the south side of the square, the neoclassical façade of the Royal College of Surgeons hides the **Hunterian Museum**; facing it from the north is the magical **Sir John Soane's Museum**.

East of the square lies **Lincoln's Inn** (7405 1393, www.lincolnsinn.org.uk), one of the city's four Inns of Court. Its grounds are open to the public, ogling an odd mix of Gothic, Tudor and Palladian buildings. On nearby Portsmouth Street lies the **Old Curiosity Shop** (nos.13-14, WC2A 2ES, 7405 9891), its timbers apparently known to Dickens, but now selling decidedly modern shoes. Nearby, Gray's Inn Road runs north alongside the sculpted gardens at **Gray's Inn** (7458 7800, www.graysinn.org.uk), dating to 1606; they are open noon-2.30pm weekdays.

Opened in 1876 on Chancery Lane as a series of strongrooms in which the upper classes could secure their valuables, the **London Silver Vaults** (7242 3844, www.thesilvervaults.com) are now a hive of dealers buying, selling and repairing silverware. There are also glittering displays on **Hatton Garden**, the city's jewellery and diamond centre – which suffered a dramatic heist in 2015. It's no distance to walk but a million miles in nature from the Cockney fruit stalls and sock merchants of the market on **Leather Lane** (10am-2pm Mon-Fri).

Further on is **Ely Place**, its postcode absent from the street sign as a result of it technically falling under the jurisdiction of Cambridgeshire. The church garden of ancient **St Etheldreda** produced strawberries so delicious that they made the pages of Shakespeare's *Richard III*; a celebratory Strawberrie Fayre is still held on the street each June. The 16th-century **Ye Olde Mitre** is one of the city's most atmospheric pubs, hidden down a barely marked alley.

Sights & Museums

FREE **Hunterian Museum**

Royal College of Surgeons, 35-43 Lincoln's Inn Fields, WC2A 3PE (7869 6560, www.rcseng.ac.uk/ museums). Holborn tube. **Open** 10am-5pm Tue-Sat. **Admission** free. **Map** p168 A4 ❶

The collection of medical specimens once held by John Hunter (1728-93), physician to King George III, can be seen in this museum. The main room's sparkling glass cabinets offset the goriness of the exhibits, which include Charles Babbage's brain and Churchill's dentures, as well as shelf after shelf of diligently classified, pickled body parts. The upper floor holds a brutal account of surgical techniques. Interesting kids' activities have included demonstrations by a 'barber surgeon', and there are monthly lunchtime lectures (held on a Tuesday, £4).

FREE **St Etheldreda**

14 Ely Place, EC1N 6RY (7405 1061, www. stetheldreda.com). Chancery Lane tube. **Open** 8am-5pm Mon-Sat; 8am-12.30pm Sun. **Admission** free; donations appreciated. **Map** p168 C3 ❷

Dedicated to the saintly seventh-century Queen of Northumbria, this is Britain's oldest Catholic church and London's only surviving example of 13th-century Gothic architecture; it was saved from the Great Fire by a change in the wind. The crypt is darkly atmospheric, untouched by traffic noise, and the stained glass (actually from the 1960s) is stunning. It's a peaceful place.

★ FREE **Sir John Soane's Museum**

13 Lincoln's Inn Fields, WC2A 3BP (7405 2107, www.soane.org). Holborn tube. **Open** 10am-5pm Tue-Sat; 10am-5pm, 6-9pm 1st Tue of mth. *Tours* 11.30am Tue, Fri; 3.30pm Wed, Thur. **Admission** free; donations appreciated. *Tours* £10; free for reductions. **Map** p168 A4 ❸

When he wasn't designing notable buildings (among them the original Bank of England), Sir John Soane (1753-1837) obsessively collected art, furniture and architectural ornamentation. In the 19th century, he turned his house into a museum to which, he said, 'amateurs and students' should have access. The result is this perfectly amazing place. The modest rooms were modified by Soane with ingenious devices to channel and direct daylight, and to expand space, including walls that fold out to display paintings by Canaletto, Turner and Hogarth. The Tivoli Recess – the city's first gallery of contemporary sculpture, with a stained-glass window and plaster sunbursts – has been restored, and further stained glass illuminates a bust of Shakespeare. The Breakfast Room has a beautiful domed ceiling, inset with convex mirrors, while the Monument Court contains a sarcophagus of alabaster, so fine that it's almost translucent, that was carved for the pharaoh Seti I (1291-78 BC) and discovered in the Valley of the Kings. There are also numerous examples of Soane's eccentricity, not least the cell for his imaginary monk. Formerly a treasured secret, the museum now welcomes 93,000 people a year: expect to queue to get in. The old entrance was far too cramped, so a cloakroom was established next door in no.12. You now exit that way, past a shop full of one-off gifts and commissions. There's also an Exhibition Room where, since his arrival from the V&A (*see p90*), director Abraham Thomas has hosted terrific shows on Piranesi's drawings, 3D printing and archaeological illustrations.

In 2016, the entire second floor will open to the public – including private rooms not seen since Soane's death. You'll even be able to visit the Model Room for the first time since 1850: it holds Britain's largest collection of historical architectural models.

▶ *The museum provides a discount voucher for coffee and a cake at Fields Bar & Kitchen (Lincoln's Inn Fields, WC2A 3LJ, 7242 5351, www.fieldsbar andkitchen.com), in the lovely little park opposite.*

Restaurants

Leather Lane has daytime street food and good coffee bars: **Department of Coffee & Social Affairs** (nos.14-16, EC1N 7SU, www.department ofcoffee.co.uk) and **Prufrock Coffee** (nos.23-25 EC1N 7TE, 7242 0467, www.prufrockcoffee.com).

Daddy Donkey
50B Leather Lane, EC1N 7TP (7404 4173, www.daddydonkey.co.uk). Chancery Lane tube or Farringdon tube/rail. **Open** 11am-4pm Mon-Fri. **Main courses** £5.25-£5.95. **Map** p168 B3 ❹
Mexican

Started by Joel Henderson in 2005, the Daddy Donkey street-food stall grew massively and in 2014 moved to a permanent site. Whether you're having the 'naked burrito' (sans tortilla, replaced with salad) or the Daddy D burrito, choose from five fillings (a step above other burrito stalls), including shredded beef (cooked with green tomatillos and lime salsa), or carnitas (pork shoulder cooked with garlic, cola, spices and chilli). The combinations are endless, but there is one constant – be prepared to queue.

EXPLORE

Daddy Donkey.

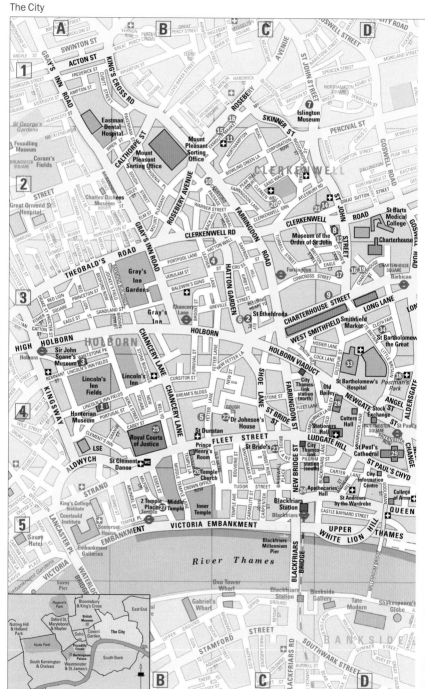

EXPLORE

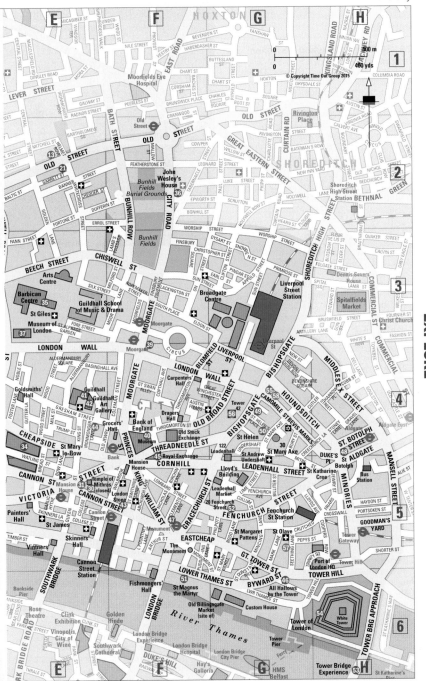

Pubs & Bars

28°-50° Wine Workshop & Kitchen

140 Fetter Lane, EC4A 1BT (7242 8877, www.2850.co.uk). Farringdon tube/rail. **Open** noon-11pm Mon-Fri. *Food served* noon-2.30pm, 6-9.30pm Mon-Fri. **Map** p168 B4 ⑤

The Fetter Lane branch of 28°-50°, in a basement with a French country-kitchen vibe, has a French-inspired menu and a bright, on-the-ball attitude. The wine list is a thing of joy, offering upwards of 30 varied and delicious wines, many of them from small producers, plus a changing themed selection. It's well worth exploring: order 75ml glasses and follow the young staff's enthusiastic advice.

Other locations 17-19 Maddox Street, Mayfair, W1S 2QH (7495 1505); 15-17 Marylebone Lane, Marylebone, W1U 2NE (7486 7922).

Ye Olde Mitre

1 Ely Court, EC1N 6SJ (7405 4751, www.yeolde mitreholborn.co.uk). Farringdon tube/rail. **Open** 11am-11pm Mon-Fri. **Map** p168 C3 ⑥

Largely due to its location – down a barely marked alley between Hatton Garden's jewellers and Ely Place – this little traditional pub, the foundation of which dates to 1546, is a favourite of 'secret London' lists. There's always a good range of ales on offer at the tiny central bar, but people come for the atmosphere: lots of cosy dark wood and some overlooked curiosities, such as the tree in the front bar. It's a cherry tree that Good Queen Bess is said to have danced around, but now supports a corner of the bar.

CLERKENWELL

Farringdon tube/rail.

Few places encapsulate London's capacity for reinvention quite like Clerkenwell, an erstwhile religious centre that takes its name from the parish clerks who once performed Biblical mystery plays on its streets. The most lasting holy legacy is that of the 11th-century knights of the **Order of St John**; the remains of their priory can still be seen at St John's Gate, a crenellated gatehouse that dates from 1504 and is home to the **Museum of the Order of St John**. For a little peace and quiet, stroll by the **Charterhouse** in Charterhouse Square. This Carthusian monastery, founded in 1370, is now Anglican almshouses which retain the original 14th-century chapel and a 17th-century library. It's opening to the public for the first time in 2016 – curated by the Museum of London, which has hatched serious plans itself to move nearby to Smithfield Market. Until then, there are occasional guided tours (£10; check the museum's website for details). The Charterhouse is right beside the **Malmaison** hotel (*see p358*).

Foxlow.

By the 17th century, Clerkenwell was a fashionable locale, but the Industrial Revolution soon buried it under warehouses and factories. Printing houses were established, and the district gained a reputation as a safe haven for radicals, from 15th-century Lollards to 19th-century Chartists. In 1903, Lenin is believed to have met Stalin for a drink in what is now the **Crown Tavern** (43 Clerkenwell Green, 7253 4973, www. thecrowntavernec1.co.uk), one year after moving the publication of the newspaper *Iskra* to no.37A (now the **Marx Memorial Library**; 7253 1485, www.marx-memorial-library.org).

Industrial dereliction and decay were the theme until property development in the 1980s and '90s turned Clerkenwell into a desirable area to live in and visit. The process was aided by a slew of artfully distressed gastropubs (following the lead of the **Eagle**), and the food stalls, fashion boutiques, restaurants and bars along the colourful strip of **Exmouth Market**. Now, the area is one of London's dining powerhouses, with **St John** the acknowledged pioneer of the new British cuisine – reviving the taste for unfavoured cuts of meat and offal under the catchy motto of 'nose-to-tail eating'.

Sights & Museums

FREE Islington Museum

245 St John Street, beneath Finsbury Library, EC1V 4NB (7527 2837, www.islington.gov.uk). Angel tube. **Open** 10am-5pm Mon, Tue, Thur-Sat. **Admission** free. **Map** p168 C1 ⑦

The museum covers local history and the political and ethical credentials of the borough, exemplified by local residents such as reformist preacher John Wesley, playwright Joe Orton and eminent feminist Mary Wollstonecraft.

FREE Museum of the Order of St John

St John's Gate, St John's Lane, EC1M 4DA (7324 4005, www.museumstjohn.org.uk). Farringdon tube/rail. **Open** 10am-5pm Mon-Sat. *Tours* 11am, 2.30pm Tue, Fri, Sat. **Admission** free. Suggested donation £5; £4 reductions. *Tours* free. **Map** p168 D2 ❽

Now best known for its ambulance service, the Order of St John's roots lie in Christian medical practices from the Crusades of the 11th to 13th centuries. Artefacts related to the Order of Hospitaller Knights, from Jerusalem, Malta and the Ottoman Empire, are displayed (among them Caravaggio's *The Cardsharps*); there's a separate collection relating to the ambulance service. A major refurbishment has reorganised the galleries in the Tudor gatehouse and, across St John's Square, opened the Priory Church (11am-5pm Mon-Sat), its secluded garden, and the pleasingly gloomy 12th-century crypt to the public.

Restaurants

Comptoir Gascon

61-63 Charterhouse Street, EC1M 6HJ (7608 0851, www.comptoirgascon.com). Farringdon tube/rail. **Open** noon-2.30pm, 6-10pm Tue-Sat. **Main courses** £9-£14.50. **Map** p168 D3 ❾
French

This bistro/deli specialises in the cuisine of Gascony: richer than Depardieu and earthier than Gainsbourg. Pork and duck appear in various dishes – grilled duck hearts, crackling with duck egg, duck confit – while starters include the must-order 'piggy treats', a charcuterie board with saucisson, pâté, rillettes and slivers of cured tongue. Rustic, yes, but sophisticated too, and every dish comes with a bold whack of flavour. The oddly shaped space is stripped back to brick in that typical Farringdon way, but manages to be cosy and welcoming.
▶ *The smarter, similarly excellent Club Gascon (57 West Smithfield, EC1A 9DS, 7600 6144, www.clubgascon.com) is across the meat market.*

Eagle

159 Farringdon Road, EC1R 3AL (7837 1353, www.theeaglefarringdon.co.uk). Farringdon tube/rail. **Open** noon-11pm Mon-Sat; noon-5pm Sun. *Food served* noon-3pm, 6.30-10.30pm Mon-Fri; 12.30-3.30pm, 6.30-10.30pm Sat; 12.30-4pm Sun. **Main courses** £11-£18. **Map** p168 B2 ❿
Gastropub

Widely credited with launching the food-in-pubs revolution when it opened in its current form in 1991, the Eagle has long since passed into both legend and middle age. But this high-ceilinged corner room remains a cut above the competition. Globetrotting mains are chalked twice daily above the bar/open kitchen. You can just drink but few do, aware they're missing the big-flavoured likes of moreish tomato and bread soup; daisy-fresh scallops, pan-fried and

served on toast with chorizo; and succulent leg of lamb with jansson's temptation (a potato gratin-style Swedish dish).

Exmouth Market

Exmouth Market, EC1R 4QE (www.exmouth-market.com). Farringdon tube/rail. **Open** noon-3pm Mon-Fri. **Map** p168 C2 ⓫ Street food
Stalls serving a great variety of takeaway food to satisfy omnivorous and vegetarian appetites. Regulars might include Spinach & Agushi (Ghanaian stews), Pasean pastas, Mac & Cheese, Meat Head BBQ, La Cochinita Spanish dishes, and Freebird burritos, among others.

★ Foxlow

69-73 St John Street, EC1M 4AN (7014 8070, www.foxlow.co.uk). Farringdon tube/rail. **Open** 11am-3.30pm, 5.30-10.30pm Mon-Sat; 11am-3.30pm Sun. **Main courses** £10-£21.50. **Map** p168 D2 ⓬
International

Will Beckett and Huw Gott, the duo behind the very popular Hawksmoor steakhouses, have scored again. It has a cosily masculine vibe (warm woods, low lighting and comfy retro-themed furniture) and a compact menu of meaty dishes to comfort and soothe, plus impeccably sourced steaks. 'Smokehouse rillettes' sees a smoky mound of beef, turkey, pork and lardo knocked into shape by a tart jumble of cucumber, pickles and capers. The youthful staff are an absolute marvel, with bags of personality, beaming smiles and a nothing's-too-much-trouble attitude.
Other location 71-73 Church Street, Stoke Newington, N16 0AS (7481 6377).

Look Mum No Hands

49 Old Street, EC1V 9HX (7253 1025, www.lookmumnohands.com). Barbican tube or Old Street tube/rail. **Open** 7.30am-10pm Mon-Fri; 9am-10pm Sat; 9.30am-10pm Sun. **Main courses** £5-£10. **Map** p169 E2 ⓭ Café
Look Mum is a cycle-friendly café-bar with cycle parking in a courtyard, a small workshop and plenty of space to hang out, snack, use the Wi-Fi and – in the evenings – drink bottled beer or well-priced wine. Live afternoon screenings of cycle races take place in the big main room. The food is simple: expect cured meat platters, baked tarts, pastries and cakes.
Other location 125-127 Mare Street, Hackney, E8 3RH (07985 200 472).

Modern Pantry

47-48 St John's Square, EC1V 4JJ (7553 9210, www.themodernpantry.co.uk). Farringdon tube/rail. **Open** *Café* 8am-11am, noon-10pm Mon; 8am-11am, noon-10.30pm Tue-Fri; 9am-4pm, 6-10.30pm Sat; 10am-4pm, 6-10pm Sun. *Restaurant* noon-3pm, 6-10.30pm Tue-Fri; 11am-4pm, 6-10.30pm Sat; 11am-4pm Sun. **Main courses** £7.20-£20.50. **Map** p168 D2 ⓮ International

EXPLORE

Chef Anna Hansen creates enticing fusion dishes that make the most of unusual ingredients sourced from around the globe. Antipodean and Asian flavours (yuzu, tamarind) pop up frequently, alongside plenty of seasonal British fare (wild garlic, purple sprouting broccoli); the combinations can seem bewildering on the page, but rarely falter in execution, and the signature dish of sugar-cured prawn omelette with chilli, coriander and spring onion is still a winner. The stylish ground-floor café is quite feminine in feel, with soothing white and grey paintwork, white furniture and burnished copper light fittings; there's a more formal restaurant upstairs.

★ Moro

34-36 Exmouth Market, EC1R 4QE (7833 8336, www.moro.co.uk). Farringdon tube/rail or bus 19, 38, 341. **Open** *Bar* noon-10.30pm Mon-Sat; 12.30-2.45pm Sun. *Restaurant* noon-2.30pm, 6-10.30pm Mon-Sat; 12.30-2.45pm Sun. **Main courses** £19.50-£22. **Tapas** £3.50-£14.50. **Map** p168 C2 ⓯ North African/Spanish

Sam(antha) and Sam Clark's Exmouth Market restaurant and cookbooks set the benchmark for a distinctly British style of 'Iberian with a North African twist' Mediterranean cooking, and they're still in the front rank some 17 years later. Moro provides a spectacular showcase for modern Spanish and Portuguese wines, and vibrantly fresh food that throws out surprising and pleasurable flavours at every turn.

▶ *Next door, Morito (no.32, EC1R 4QE, 7278 7007) is a fine no-booking tapas bar offshoot.*

★ St John

26 St John Street, EC1M 4AY (7251 0848, www. stjohngroup.uk.com). Barbican tube or Farringdon tube/rail. **Open** noon-3pm, 6-11pm Mon-Fri; 6-10.45pm Sat; 1-3pm Sun. **Main courses** £13.50-£23.80. **Map** p168 D3 ⓰ British

Fergus Henderson and Trevor Gulliver's restaurant has been praised to the skies for reacquainting the British with the full possibilities of native produce, and especially anything gutsy and offal-ish. Perhaps as influential, however, has been its almost defiantly casual style. The mezzanine dining room in the former Smithfield smokehouse has bare white walls, battered floorboards and tables lined up canteen-style. St John's cooking is famously full-on, but also sophisticated, concocting flavours that are delicate as well as rich, as in black cuttlefish and onions, with a deep-flavoured ink-based sauce with a hint of mint. The airy bar here is a great place for a drink and a no-fuss snack.

Other location St John Bread & Wine, 94-96 Commercial Street, Spitalfields, E1 6LZ (7251 0848).

Vinoteca

7 St John Street, EC1M 4AA (7253 8786, www. vinoteca.co.uk). Barbican tube or Farringdon tube/ rail. **Open** noon-11pm Mon-Sat. *Food served* noon-2.45pm, 5.45-10pm Mon-Fri; noon-4pm, 5.45-10pm Sat. **Main courses** £11.50-£16.50. **Map** p168 D3 ⓱ Wine bar

Charmingly but sparingly decorated, and with delightfully friendly staff, this bijou spot is the original branch in the small chain. Serious about its commitment to the grape, Vinoteca offers 25 wines by the glass, 300 by the bottle, all available to take away. But even without the fabulous wines, it would still be a great restaurant. Dishes such as mussels, clams and john dory with chorizo, or barnsley chop with greens, are excellent combinations of light, bright flavours – and go perfectly with the recommended wines.

Other locations 55 Beak Street, Soho, W1F 9SH (3544 7411); 18 Devonshire Road, Chiswick, W4 2HD (3701 8822); 15 Seymour Place, Marylebone, W1H 5BD (7724 7288).

Pubs & Bars

Clerkenwell has a compelling claim to being the birthplace of the now ubiquitous gastropub: the **Eagle** kicked things off. **St John** and **Vinoteca** are both good options for a relaxed glass of wine.

Café Kick

43 Exmouth Market, EC1R 4QL (7837 8077, www. cafekick.co.uk). Angel tube or Farringdon tube/rail. **Open** 11am-11pm Mon-Thur; 11am-midnight Fri, Sat; noon-10.30pm Sun. *Food served* noon-3pm Mon-Fri; noon-10pm Sat, Sun. **Map** p168 C1 ⓲

Clerkenwell's most likeable bar is this table football-themed gem. The soccer paraphernalia is authentic, retro-cool and mainly Latin (you'll find a Zenit St Petersburg scarf amid the St Etienne and Lusitanian gear); bar staff, beers and bites give the impression you could be in Lisbon. A modest open kitchen ('we don't microwave or deep-fry') dishes out tapas, sandwiches and charcuterie platters.

Other location Bar Kick, 127 Shoreditch High Street, Shoreditch, E1 6JE (7739 8700).

Fox & Anchor

115 Charterhouse Street, EC1M 6AA (7250 1300, www.foxandanchor.com). Barbican tube or Farringdon tube/rail. **Open** 7am-9.45pm Mon-Fri; 8.30am-9.45pm Sat; 8.30am-8.45pm Sun. *Food served* 7am-noon, 1-9.30pm Mon-Fri; 8am-noon, 1-9.30pm Sat; 8.30am-noon, 1-8.30pm Sun. **Map** p168 D3 ⓳

Pristine mosaic tiling, etched glass and a dark wood front bar lined with pewter tankards help make this refurbished old pub a local treasure. To the back is the Fox's Den, a series of intimate rooms used for both drinking and dining. Local sourcing is a priority and a pleasure: in addition to the own-label ale, cask beers might include Red Poll and Old Growler from Suffolk's fine Nethergate brewery. There are plenty more delights among the bottles.

Three Kings of Clerkenwell

7 Clerkenwell Close, EC1R 0DY (7253 0483).
Farringdon tube/rail. **Open** noon-11pm Mon-Fri;
5.30-11pm Sat. *Food served* noon-3pm, 6-10pm
Mon-Fri. **Map** p168 C2 ⑳
Rhinoceros heads, Egyptian felines and photos of
Dennis Bergkamp provide the decorative backdrop
at this great little boozer. Glug Scrumpy Jack, Beck's
Vier, Old Speckled Hen or London Pride, and tap
the well-worn tables to the Cramps and other gems
from an outstanding jukebox that is crammed with
fabulous old platters.

★ Zetter Townhouse

49-50 St John's Square, EC1V 4JJ (7324 4545,
www.thezettertownhouse.com). Farringdon tube/
rail. **Open** 7am-midnight Mon-Wed, Sun; 7am-1am
Thur-Sat. **Map** p168 D2 ㉑
The decor at Townhouse embodies a 'more is more'
philosophy: every square inch of surface area is
occupied by something lovely. The result: one of
the most beautiful bars in London. The cocktail list
is high quality, devised by Tony Conigliaro. Even
though Conigliaro is known as a techno-wizard, the
original drinks here are fairly simple and restrained.
And wonderful. Among the house cocktails, check
out the Köln Martini, Les Fleurs du Mal, and the Silk
Road gimlet. Service is friendly and helpful.

FLEET STREET

Temple tube or Blackfriars tube/rail.

Without Fleet Street, the daily newspaper
might never have been invented. Named after
the vanished River Fleet, Fleet Street was a major
artery for the delivery of goods into the City,
including the first printing press, which was
installed behind **St Bride's Church** in 1500 by
William Caxton's assistant, Wynkyn de Worde,
who also set up a bookstall in the churchyard of
St Paul's. London's first daily newspaper, the
Daily Courant, rolled off the presses in 1702; in
1712, Fleet Street saw the first of innumerable
libel cases when the *Courant* leaked the details
of a private parliamentary debate.

By the end of World War II, half a dozen
offices were churning out scoops and scandals
between Strand and Farringdon Road. Most of
the newspapers moved away after Rupert
Murdoch won his war with the print unions in
the 1980s; the last of the news agencies, Reuters,
finally followed suit in 2005. Until recently, the
only periodical published on Fleet Street was a
comic, the much-loved *Beano*, but in 2009 left-
wing weekly the *New Statesman* moved into
offices around the corner from Fleet Street on
Carmelite Street. Relics from the media days
remain: the Portland-stone **Reuters building**
(no.85), the Egyptian-influenced **Daily
Telegraph building** (no.135) and the sleek,

black **Daily Express building** (no.120),
designed by Owen Williams in the 1930s and
arguably the finest art deco building in London.
Tucked away on an alley behind St Bride's Church
is the **St Bride Foundation**, (7353 3331, www.
sbf.org; closed Sat, Sun), dedicated to printing
and typography. There are events, a library
and temporary exhibitions showing off its
collections, which include rare works by Eric
Gill and maquettes for Kinnear and Calvert's
distinctive road signs.

At the top of Fleet Street itself is the church
of **St Dunstan-in-the-West** (7405 1929, www.
stdunstaninthewest.org), where the poet John
Donne was rector in the 17th century. The church
was rebuilt in the 1830s, but the eye-catching
clock dates from 1671. The clock's chimes are
beaten by clockwork giants who are said to
represent Gog and Magog, tutelary spirits of
the City. Next door, no.186 is the house where
Sweeney Todd, the 'demon barber of Fleet Street',
reputedly murdered his customers before selling
their bodies to a local pie shop. The legend, sadly,
is a porky pie: Todd was invented by the editors
of a Victorian penny dreadful in 1846 and
propelled to fame rather later by a stage play.

Fleet Street was always known for its pubs;
half the newspaper editorials in London were
composed over liquid lunches, but there were

Fleet Street.

also more literary imbibers. If you walk down Fleet Street, you'll see **Ye Olde Cheshire Cheese** (no.145, 7353 6170), a favourite of Dickens and Yeats. In its heyday, it hosted the bibulous literary salons of Dr Samuel Johnson, who lived nearby at 17 Gough Square (**Dr Johnson's House**). It also had a famous drinking parrot, the death of which prompted hundreds of newspaper obituaries. At no.66, the **Tipperary** (7583 6470) is the oldest Irish pub outside Ireland: it sold the first pint of Guinness on the British mainland in the 1700s. Just south of Fleet Street, near Blackfriars station, is the **Black Friar**, a lovely, art nouveau meets Arts and Crafts pub. The bridge itself – designed by Thomas Cubitt and dating from 1869 – is handsome, with its red-and-white painted ironwork. It also gives a great view of London's first cross-river railway station: needing extended platforms to accommodate longer trains, the designer simply ran them across the Thames. Now commuters can peer out along the river from inside the station.

Sights & Museums

Dr Johnson's House

17 Gough Square, off Fleet Street, EC4A 3DE (7353 3745, www.drjohnsonshouse.org). Chancery Lane tube or Blackfriars tube/rail. **Open** *May-Sept* 11am-5.30pm Mon-Sat. *Oct-Apr* 11am-5pm Mon-Sat. *Tours* by arrangement; groups of 10 or more only. **Admission** £4.50; £1.50-£3.50 reductions; £10 family; free under-5s. *Tours* £3.50. **No credit cards**. **Map** p168 C4 ②

Famed as the author of one of the first – as well as the most significant and unquestionably the wittiest – dictionaries of the English language, Dr Samuel Johnson (1709-84) also wrote poems, essays, literary criticism, a novel and an early travelogue, an acerbic account of a tour of the Western Isles with his biographer James Boswell. You can tour the stately Georgian townhouse where he came up with

St Bride's Church.

his inspired definitions – 'to make dictionaries is dull work' was his definition of the word 'dull' while 'oats' is a 'grain, which in England is generally given to horses, but in Scotland supports the people'.

▶ *A neat statue of Johnson's cat Hodge sits contentedly in the square outside.*

🆓 St Bride's Church

Fleet Street, EC4Y 8AU (7427 0133, www.stbrides. com). Temple tube. **Open** 9am-5pm Mon-Fri; 10am-6.30pm Sun. Times vary Sat; phone to check. **Admission** free. **Map** p168 C4 ㉓

Hidden down an alley south of Fleet Street, St Bride's is known as the journalists' church: in the north aisle, a shrine is dedicated to hacks killed in action. Down in the crypt, a surprisingly interesting little museum displays fragments of the churches that have existed on this site since the sixth century, as well as some portions of Roman tessellated floor (*see p324* **Walk**).

Pubs & Bars

Black Friar

174 Queen Victoria Street, EC4V 4EG (7236 5474, www.nicholsonpubs.co.uk). Blackfriars tube/rail. **Open** 10am-11pm Mon-Sat; noon-10.30pm Sun. **Map** p168 C5 ㉔

Built in 1875 on the site of a medieval Dominican friary, the Black Friar had its interior completely remodelled in the Arts and Crafts style. It is now a Nicholson's (they run most of the trad pubs in the City, serving moderate food but decent real ales), but

---

IN THE KNOW
BIRTH OF A TRADITION

An 18th-century Fleet Street pâtissier, William Rich, was famous for tiered wedding cakes, which he modelled on the lovely Wren-designed spire of **St Bride's** (*see right*) – the template for bride cakes ever since, as the tour guides never tire of explaining. Intriguingly, the church's marital connections might run much deeper than that. It's likely that the holy well that gave the original church its location had been a site of pagan worship – including the blessing of relationships.

---

the bright panes, intricate friezes and carved slogans ('Industry is Ale', 'Haste is Slow') of the main saloon make it a stunning work of art. Admittedly, there's a far more prosaic bar adjoining it but this remains one of London's most interesting pub interiors.

TEMPLE & THE INNS OF COURT

Temple tube.

At its eastern end, the arterial Strand becomes Fleet Street at **Temple Bar**, the City's ancient western boundary and once the site of Wren's great gateway (which was removed to Hertfordshire but is now in Paternoster Square beside St Paul's). A newer, narrower, but still impressive wyvern-topped monument marks the original spot. The area has long been linked to the law, and here stands the splendid neo-Gothic **Royal Courts of Justice**. On the other side of the road, stretching almost to the Thames, are the several courtyards that make up **Middle Temple** (7427 4800, www.middletemple. org.uk) and **Inner Temple** (7797 8250, www.innertemple.org.uk), two of the Inns of Court that provided training and lodging for London's medieval lawyers. Anybody may visit the grounds, but access to the grand, collegiate buildings is for lawyers and barristers only.

The site was formerly the headquarters of the Knights Templar, a religious order of warrior monks founded in the 12th century to protect pilgrims to the Holy Land. The Templars built the original **Temple Church** in 1185, but fell foul of Philip IV of France, who pressured the pope into suppressing their order.

Almost due south of Temple Bar, alongside Middle Temple, is the virtually unknown and fabulous **Two Temple Place**.

Sights & Museums

FREE Royal Courts of Justice
Strand, WC2A 2LL (7947 6000, www.justice.gov. uk). Temple tube. **Open** 9am-4.30pm Mon-Fri. **Admission** free. *Tours* £12; £5-£10 reductions. **Map** p168 B4 ㉕
Two of the highest civil courts in the land sit in these imposing buildings: the High Court and the Appeals Court. Visitors are welcome to observe the process of law in any of the 88 courtrooms, but very little happens in August and September. There are also two-hour tours (11am or 2pm; pre-book on 07789 751 248 or rcjtours@talktalk.net). Cameras and children under 14 are not allowed on the premises.

Temple Church
Off Fleet Street, EC4Y 7BB (7353 3470, www. templechurch.com). Chancery Lane or Temple tube. **Open** varies. **Admission** £5; free-£3 reductions. **Map** p168 B5 ㉖

Inspired by Jerusalem's Church of the Holy Sepulchre, the Temple Church was the chapel of the Knights Templar. The rounded apse contains the worn gravestones of several Crusader knights, but the church was refurbished by Wren and the Victorians, and was damaged in the Blitz. Not that that puts off the wild speculations of fans of Dan Brown's *The Da Vinci Code*. There are organ recitals most Wednesdays at 1.15pm.

★ FREE Two Temple Place
2 Temple Place, WC2R 3BD (7836 3715, www. twotempleplace.org). Temple tube. **Open** *Late Jan-mid Apr* 10am-4.30pm Mon, Thur-Sat; 10am-9pm Wed; 11am-4.30pm Sun. Closed mid Apr-late Jan. **Admission** free. *Tours* free. **Map** p168 B5 ㉗
The pale Portland-stone exterior and oriel windows here are handsome – but the interior is extraordinary. You get a hint about what's to come before you open the door: look right and there's a cherub holding an old-fashioned telephone to his ear. Built as an estate office in 1895 to the close specifications of William Waldorf Astor, Two Temple Place now opens to the public for three months a year with exhibitions of 'publicly-owned art from around the UK', arranged by an up-and-coming curator. Ring the bell and you're warmly welcomed by volunteers into a house with decor that combines sublime, extravagant craftsmanship with a thorough lack of interest in coherence: above porphyry tiles, the Three Musketeers adorn the banisters of a staircase; intricately carved literary characters crowd the first floor, mixing Shakespeare with Fenimore Cooper; the medieval-style Great Hall, with lovely stained glass, crams together 54 random busts – Voltaire and Marlborough, Anne Boleyn enjoying the company of Mary Queen of Scots.

ST PAUL'S & AROUND

St Paul's tube.

The towering dome of **St Paul's Cathedral** is, excluding the 'Big Ben' clocktower, probably the definitive symbol of traditional London and an architectural two fingers to the Nazi bombers that pounded the city in 1940 and 1941. North of the cathedral is the redeveloped **Paternoster Square**, a modern plaza incorporating a sundial that rarely tells the time. The name harks back to the days when priests from St Paul's walked the streets chanting the Lord's Prayer (*Pater noster*, Latin for 'Our Father').

Also of interest is Wren's statue-covered **Temple Bar**. It once stood at the intersection of Fleet Street and Strand, marking the boundary between the City of London and neighbouring Westminster; during the Middle Ages, the monarch was allowed to pass through the Temple Bar into the City only with the approval of the Lord Mayor of London. The archway was

EXPLORE

dismantled as part of a Victorian road-widening programme in 1878 and became a garden ornament for a country estate in Hertfordshire, before being installed in its current location, as the gateway between St Paul's and Paternoster Square, in 2004. The gold-topped pillar in the centre of the square looks as if it commemorates something important, but it's just an air vent for the Underground.

South of St Paul's, steps cascade down to the **Millennium Bridge**, which spans the river to Tate Modern (*see p57*) and now offers the main gateway to the City for tourists. The grand **St Lawrence Jewry Memorial Fountain** is another peripatetic monument: kept in storage since the 1970s after it was removed from the church (*see p182*), it was placed here in 2011. The structure dates to 1866. The stairs take you close to the 17th-century **College of Arms** (130 Queen Victoria Street, EC4V 4BT, 7248 2762, www.college-of-arms.gov.uk), official seat of British heraldry. Originally created to identify competing knights at medieval jousting tournaments, coats of arms soon became an integral part of family identity for the landed gentry of Britain. Scriveners still work here to create beautiful heraldic certificates, but only the Earl Marshal's Court is open to the general public.

East of the cathedral is the huge **One New Change** shopping mall and office development. Designed by French architect Jean Nouvel, its most interesting aspects are a gash that gives views straight through the building to St Paul's and, for a fine roof-level panorama, the sixth-floor public terrace and bar-restaurant. Meekly hidden among the alleys behind it, you'll find narrow Bow Lane. At one end sits **St Mary-le-Bow** (7248 5139, www.stmarylebow.co.uk; closed Sat, Sun), built by Wren between 1671 and 1680. The church bell's peals once defined anyone born within earshot as a true Cockney. At the other end of Bow Lane is **St Mary Aldermary** (7248 9902, www.moot.uk.net; closed Sat, Sun). With a pin-straight spire designed by Wren's office, this was the only Gothic church by him to survive World War II. Inside, there's a fabulous moulded plaster ceiling and original wooden sword rest (London parishioners carried arms until the late 19th century).

There are more Wren creations south of St Paul's. On Garlick Hill, named for the medieval garlic market, is **St James Garlickhythe** (7236 1719, www.stjamesgarlickhythe.org.uk, open 11am-3pm Thur). The official church of London's vintners and joiners, it was built by Wren in 1682. Hidden in the tower are the naturally mummified remains of a young man, nicknamed Jimmy Garlick, discovered in the vaults in 1855. The church was hit by bombs in both World Wars, and partly ruined by a falling crane in 1991, but the interior has been convincingly restored. Off

St Paul's Cathedral.

Victoria Street, **St Nicholas Cole Abbey** was the first church rebuilt after the Great Fire.

Built on the site of the infamous Newgate Prison to the north-west of the cathedral is the **Old Bailey**. A remnant of the prison's east wall can be seen in Amen Corner.

Sights & Museums

FREE **Old Bailey (Central Criminal Court)**
Corner of Newgate Street & Old Bailey, EC4M 7EH (7248 3277, www.cityoflondon.gov.uk). St Paul's tube. **Open** *Public gallery* 9.55am-12.40pm, 1.55-3.40pm Mon-Fri. **Admission** free. No under-14s; 14-16s only if accompanied by adults. **Map** p168 D4 ㉙
A gilded statue of blind (meaning impartial) justice stands atop London's most famous criminal court. The current building was completed in 1907; the site itself has hosted some of the most famous trials in British history, including that of Oscar Wilde. Anyone is welcome to attend a trial, but bags, cameras, dictaphones, mobile phones and food are banned (and no storage facilities are provided).
▶ *A blocked-up door in St Sepulchre Without, opposite the court, is the visible remains of a priest tunnel into the court; the Newgate Execution Bell is also there.*

★ **St Paul's Cathedral**
Ludgate Hill, EC4M 8AD (7246 8348, www. st pauls.co.uk). St Paul's tube. **Open** 8.30am-4.15pm Mon-Sat. *Galleries, crypt & ambulatory* 9.30am-4.15pm Mon-Sat. Special events may cause closure; check before visiting. *Tours of cathedral & crypt* 10am, 11am, 1pm, 2pm Mon-Sat.

EXPLORE

Admission *Cathedral, crypt & gallery* (incl tour)
£17; £7.50-£15 reductions; £41.50 family; free
under-6s. **Map** p168 D4 ⓩ

The first cathedral to St Paul was built on this site
in 604, but fell to Viking marauders. Its Norman
replacement, a magnificent Gothic structure with a
490ft spire (taller than any London building until the
1960s), burned in the Great Fire. The current church
was commissioned in 1673 from Sir Christopher
Wren as the centrepiece of London's resurgence
from the ashes. Modern buildings now encroach on
the cathedral from all sides, but the passing of three
centuries has done nothing to diminish the appeal of
London's most famous cathedral.

A £40m restoration project has removed most of
the Victorian grime from the outside walls and the
extravagant main façade looks as brilliant today
as it must have when the last stone was placed in
1708. The vast open spaces of the interior contain
memorials to national heroes such as Wellington
and Lawrence of Arabia. The statue of John Donne,
metaphysical poet and former Dean of St Paul's, is
often overlooked, but it's the only monument to have
been saved from Old St Paul's. There are also more
modern works, including a Henry Moore sculpture
and Bill Viola's video installation *Martyrs (Earth,
Air, Fire, Water)*. The Whispering Gallery, inside
the dome, is reached by 259 steps from the main hall;
the acoustics here are so good that a whisper can be
bounced clearly to the other side of the dome. Steps
continue up to first the Stone Gallery (119 tighter,
steeper steps), with its high external balustrades,
then outside to the Golden Gallery (152 steps), with
its giddying views.

Before leaving St Paul's, head down to the maze-
like crypt (through a door whose frame is decorated
with skull and crossbones), which contains a shop
and café, and memorials to such dignitaries as
Alexander Fleming, William Blake and Admiral
Lord Nelson, whose grand tomb (purloined from
Wolsey by Henry VIII but never used by him) is right
beneath the centre of the dome. To one side is the
small, plain tombstone of Christopher Wren himself,
inscribed by his son with the epitaph, 'Reader, if you
seek a monument, look around you'; at their request,
Millais and Turner were buried near him.

As well as tours of the main cathedral and self-
guided audio tours (which are free), you can join
special tours of the Triforium, visiting the library
and Wren's 'Great Model', at 11.30am and 2pm
Monday and Tuesday and at 2pm on Friday (pre-
book on 7246 8357, £25 incl admission).

Restaurants

Gordon Ramsay's fun brasserie **Bread Street
Kitchen** (10 Bread Street, EC4M 9AB, 3030 4050,
www.gordonramsay.com) is the best of several
eating options in One New Change.

Pull'd

*61 Cannon Street, EC4N 5AA (3752 0326, www.
howtopull.co.uk). Mansion House tube.* **Open**
7am-3.30pm Mon; 7am-9pm Tue-Fri. **Dishes**
£4.95-£6.45. **Map** p169 E5 ⓚ **American**
Pull'd cram a lot of stuff in their bread or rice: flavourful leaves, high-grade tomato salad, tasty coleslaw made with red cabbage, grated cheese… Plus
your choice of sauces, including a sprightly salsa
verde and a better-than-average barbecue sauce. It is
mainly a takeaway but you can also pull up a chair –
more precisely, a stool at the counters.

EXPLORE

Sweetings

39 Queen Victoria Street, EC4N 4SF (7248 3062, www.sweetingsrestaurant.com). Mansion House tube. **Open** 11.30am-3pm Mon-Fri. **Main courses** £15-£45. **Map** p169 E5 ㉛ Fish & seafood

Things don't change much at this enduring City classic, and that's the way everyone likes it. The walls remain covered with photos of old sports teams, and many of the staff have been here for years. Lobster and crab bisques preface a choice of fish and seafood dishes that read and taste like upmarket versions of a pub-side stall – smoked fish, whitebait, trout and so forth. Top-quality fish are then served fried, grilled or poached to order. The handful of more elaborate dishes includes an excellent fish pie.

Shops & Services

One New Change

New Change Road, EC4M 9AF (7002 8900, www.onenewchange.com). Mansion House or St Paul's tube or Bank tube/DLR. **Open** varies; check website for opening hours of individual shops. **Map** p169 E4 ㉜ Mall

This sprawling Jean Nouvel-designed development is opposite the east end of St Paul's Cathedral, and features a warren of high-street retailers, office buildings and restaurants (Jamie Oliver's Barbecoa, Wahaca, Ramsay's Bread Street Kitchen). Nicknamed the 'stealth building' due to its dark, low-slung design, the place is unsurprisingly popular with City workers on lunchbreaks or post-work spending sprees among predictable chain stores. Take the glass elevator up to the top floor, though, and you'll be rewarded with a surprising view – St

Paul's, yes, but on a level with its roof rather than above or below it. Enjoy it for free, or accompanied by a pricey drink or tapas.

NORTH TO SMITHFIELD

Barbican or St Paul's tube.

North of St Paul's Cathedral on Foster Lane is **St Vedast-alias-Foster** (7606 3998, www. vedast.org.uk), another finely proportioned Wren church, restored after World War II using spare trim from other churches in the area. Further west on Little Britain (named after the Duke of Brittany) is **St Bartholomew-the-Great**, founded along with **St Bartholomew's Hospital** in the 12th century. Popularly known as Bart's, the hospital treated air-raid casualties throughout World War II; shrapnel damage from German bombs is still visible on the exterior walls. Scottish nationalists now come here to lay flowers at the monument to William Wallace, executed in front of the church on the orders of Edward I in 1305.

Just beyond Bart's is the fine ironwork of **Smithfield Market**. The market – under almost constant threat of redevelopment, usually with associated promises to maintain historic façades – provides a colourful, not to say visceral, link to an age when the quality of British beef was a symbol of national virility and good humour. Meat has been traded here for a millennium; the current market, designed by Horace Jones, opened in 1868, though it's since been altered (in part thanks to World War II bombs). At weekends, one former cold storage warehouse

Pull'd. See p177.

opposite the market opens as the indefatigable superclub **Fabric** (*see p267*).

Sights & Museums

FREE Museum of St Bartholomew's Hospital

North Wing, St Bartholomew's Hospital, West Smithfield, EC1A 7BE (www.bartshealth.nhs.uk). Barbican tube or Farringdon tube/rail. **Open** 10am-4pm Tue-Fri. **Admission** free; donations appreciated. Tours £7; £6 reductions; children free. **Map** p168 D4 ㉝

Be glad you're living in the 21st century. Many of the displays in this small museum inside St Bart's Hospital relate to the days before anaesthetics, when surgery and carpentry were kindred occupations. Every Friday at 2pm, visitors can take a guided tour of the museum that takes in the Hogarth paintings in the Great Hall, the little church of St Bartholomew-the-Less, neighbouring St Bartholomew-the-Great and Smithfield.

▶ *Also in the hospital grounds, Barts Pathology Museum (3rd floor, Robin Brook Centre, 7882 8766, www.qmul.ac.uk/bartspathology) has a riveting collection of 5,000 human specimens (including the skull of PM Spencer Perceval's assassin in 1812), the tight regulation of which means it can only open infrequently to the public.*

St Bartholomew-the-Great

West Smithfield, EC1A 9DS (7600 0440, www. greatstbarts.com). Barbican tube or Farringdon tube/rail. **Open** 8.30am-5pm Mon-Fri (until 4pm Nov-Feb); 10.30am-4pm Sat; 8.30am-8pm Sun. **Admission** £4; £3 reductions; £10 family; free under-7s. **Map** p168 D3 ㉞

This atmospheric medieval church was built over the remains of the 12th-century priory hospital of St Bartholomew, founded by Prior Rahere, a former courtier of Henry I. The church was chopped about during Henry VIII's reign and the interior is now firmly Elizabethan, although it also contains donated works of modern art. You may recognise the main hall from *Shakespeare in Love* or *Four Weddings and a Funeral*.

▶ *If you need refreshment, the church has a bar-café in the 15th-century cloister, serving coffee, monastery beers and home-made weekday lunches.*

MUSEUM OF LONDON & THE BARBICAN

Barbican tube or Moorgate tube/rail.

From Bart's, the road known as London Wall runs east to Bishopsgate, following the approximate route of the old Roman wall. Tower blocks have sprung up here like daisies, but the odd lump of weathered stonework can still be seen poking up between the office blocks,

marking the path of the old City wall. You can patrol the remaining stretches of the wall, with panels (some barely legible) pointing out highlights (for our version of this walk, *see p324* **Walk**). The walk runs all the way to the Tower of London. Also of interest is peaceful **Postman's Park**, next to one of the exit staircases from the **Museum of London**.

The area north of London Wall was reduced to rubble by German bombs in World War II. In 1958, the City of London and London County Council clubbed together to buy the land for the construction of 'a genuine residential neighbourhood, with schools, shops, open spaces and amenities'. What Londoners got was the **Barbican**, a vast concrete estate of 2,000 flats that feels a bit like a university campus after the students have gone home. Casual visitors may get the eerie feeling they have been miniaturised and transported into a giant architect's model, but design enthusiasts will recognise the Barbican – with its landmark saw-toothed towers – as a prime example of 1970s Brutalism, softened a little by time and rectangular ponds of friendly resident ducks. Learn to love the place by taking one of the regular, 90-minute architectural tours of the complex (www.barbican.org.uk/education, £10, £8.40 reductions) – which will also help you to navigate its famously confusing layout.

The main attraction here is the Barbican arts complex, with its library, cinema, theatre and concert hall – each reviewed in the appropriate chapters – plus an art gallery (*see below*) and the **Barbican Conservatory** (open 11am-5pm Sun), a steamy greenhouse full of tropical plants, exotic fish and twittering birds. Marooned amid the towers is the only pre-war building in the vicinity: the restored 16th-century church of **St Giles Cripplegate** (7638 1997, www.stgilescripplegate.com; closed Sat, Suh), where Oliver Cromwell was married and John Milton buried.

North-east of the Barbican on City Road are **John Wesley's House** and **Bunhill Fields**, the nonconformist cemetery where William Blake, the preacher John Bunyan and novelist Daniel Defoe are buried.

Sights & Museums

Barbican Art Gallery

Barbican Centre, Silk Street, EC2Y 8DS (7638 8891, www.barbican.org.uk). Barbican tube or Moorgate tube/rail. **Open** 10am-6pm Mon-Wed, Sat; 10am-9pm Thur, Fri. **Admission** varies. **Map** p169 E3 ㉟

The art gallery on the third floor at the Barbican Centre isn't quite as 'out there' as it would like you to think, but the exhibitions on architecture, fashion, design and pop culture are usually pretty diverting, and accompanied by interesting events.

EXPLORE

IN THE KNOW
COMING ATTRACTIONS

For such an august area of London, the City is experiencing an extraordinary level of change at the moment. Tall buildings continue to sprout above it, the immense Crossrail boring machines have tunnelled beneath and there are several exciting new attractions on the way. The **British Postal Museum & Archive** (http://postalmuseum. org) should open, complete with its own functioning underground train, in 2016. The Charterhouse (see p170) looks likely to open regularly to the public in the same year, under the aegis of the **Museum of London** (see below), which is itself actively seeking to move into Smithfield Market.

▶ *On the ground floor, the Curve is a long, thin gallery (yes, it's curved) that commissions large-scale installations. They're free, and often superb.*

[FREE] John Wesley's House & the Museum of Methodism

Wesley's Chapel, 49 City Road, EC1Y 1AU (7253 2262, www.wesleyschapel.org.uk). Moorgate or Old Street tube/rail. **Open** 10am-4pm Mon-Sat; after the service until 1.45pm Sun; closed 12.45-1.30pm Thur for service. *Tours* arrangements on arrival; groups of 6 or more phone ahead. **Admission** free; donations appreciated. **Map** p169 F2 ❸

John Wesley (1703-91), the founder of Methodism, was a man of legendary self-discipline. You can see the minister's nightcap, preaching gown and personal experimental electric-shock machine on a tour of his austere home on City Road. The adjacent chapel has a small museum on the history of Methodism and fine memorials of dour, sideburn-sporting preachers. Downstairs (to the right) are some of the finest public toilets in London, built in 1899 with original fittings by Sir Thomas Crapper.

★ [FREE] Museum of London

150 London Wall, EC2Y 5HN (7001 9844, www. museumoflondon.org.uk). Barbican or St Paul's tube. **Open** 10am-6pm daily. **Admission** free; suggested donation £5. **Map** p169 E3 ❸

A five-year, £20m refurbishment came to completion in 2010 with the unveiling of a thrilling lower-ground-floor gallery that covers the city from 1666 to the present day. The new space features everything from an unexploded World War II bomb, suspended in a room where the understated and very moving testimony of ordinary Blitz survivors is screened, to clothes by the late Alexander McQueen. There are displays and brilliant interactives on poverty (an actual debtor's cell has been reconstructed, complete with graffiti), finance, shopping and 20th-century

fashion, including a recreated Georgian pleasure garden, with mannequins that sport Philip Treacy masks and hats. Some displays are grand flourishes – the suspended installation that chatters London-related web trivia in the Sackler Hall, a printing press gushing changing news-sheets, a grand new gallery for Thomas Heatherwick's delicate flower 'Cauldron' from the 2012 Olympics – others ingeniously solve problems: games to engage the kids, glass cases in the floors to maximise display space. The museum's biggest obstacle had always been its location: the entrance is two floors above street level, and hidden behind a dark and rather featureless brick wall. To solve this, a new space was created on the ground floor, allowing one key exhibit – the Lord Mayor's gold coach – to be seen from outside.

Upstairs, the social history of London is told in chronological displays that begin with 'London Before London', where artefacts include flint axes from 300,000 BC, found near Piccadilly, and the bones of an auroch, an extinct type of wild cattle. 'Roman London' includes an impressive reconstructed dining room complete with mosaic floor. Windows overlook a sizeable fragment of the City wall, whose Roman foundations have clearly been built upon many times over the centuries. Sound effects and audio-visual displays illustrate the medieval, Elizabethan and Jacobean city, with particular focus on the plague and the Great Fire.

▶ *The museum has issued a number of excellent free apps, including Streetmuseum and Streetmuseum Londinium (see p324 **Walk**). They offer archive images and information about historic sites, geolocated to where you're standing.*

[FREE] Postman's Park

Entrances from St Martin's Le-Grand, Aldersgate Street or King Edward Street. St Paul's tube. **Open** 8am-7pm (or dusk) daily. **Map** p168 D4 ❸

A soothing little park in itself, Postman's Park is best known for the Watts Memorial to Heroic Sacrifice: a wall of ceramic plaques, established in 1900, each of which commemorates a heroic but doomed act of bravery. Most date to Victorian times – pantomime artiste Sarah Smith, for example, who received 'terrible injuries when attempting in her inflammable dress to extinguish the flames which had engulfed her companion (1863)' – but the first new plaque for 70 years was added in 2009. It was dedicated to 30-year-old Leigh Pitt, who died while saving a child from drowning.

Restaurants

Dining options in the **Barbican** aren't inspiring, although the café-bar in the new Beech Street screens (see p256) is appealing, as is a French-style chain brasserie **Côte** (57 Whitecross Street, EC1Y 8AA, 7628 5724, http://cote-restaurants. co.uk) next door. The **Chiswell Street Dining Rooms** (56 Chiswell Street, EC1Y 4SA, 7614 0177, www.chiswellstreetdining.com) is an upscale alternative nearby, or there are a few cheap-and-cheerful options up Whitecross Street.

Shops & Services

★ F Flittner
86 Moorgate, EC2M 6SE (7606 4750, www. fflittner.com). Moorgate tube/rail. **Open** 8am-6pm Mon-Wed, Fri; 8am-6.30pm Thur. **Map** p169 F4 ③⑨
Health & beauty
In business since 1904, Flittner seems not to have noticed that the 21st century has begun. Hidden behind beautifully frosted doors (marked 'Saloon') is a simple, handsome room, done out with an array of classic barber's furniture that's older than your gran. Within these hushed confines, up to six black coat-clad barbers deliver straightforward haircuts (dry cuts £18-£20, wet cuts £25-£30) and shaves (£24 with hot towels).

BANK & AROUND

Mansion House tube or Bank tube/DLR.

Above Bank station, seven streets come together to mark the symbolic heart of the Square Mile, ringed by some of the most important buildings in the City. Constructed from Portland stone, the

Museum of London.

Bank of England, the Royal Exchange and Mansion House form a stirring monument to the power of money: most decisions about the British economy are still made within this small precinct. Few places in London have quite the same sense of pomp and circumstance.

Easily the most dramatic building is the **Bank of England**, founded in 1694 to fund William III's war against the French. It's a fortress, with no accessible windows and just one public entrance (leading to the **Bank of England Museum**). The outer walls were designed in 1788 by Sir John Soane, whose own museum can be seen in Holborn (**Sir John Soane's Museum**). Millions have been stolen from its depots elsewhere in London, but the bank itself has never been robbed. Today, it's responsible for printing the nation's banknotes and setting the base interest rate. On the south side of the junction is the Lord Mayor of London's official residence, **Mansion House** (7626 2500, www.cityoflondon.gov.uk), an imposing neoclassical building constructed by George Dance in 1753; there are tours at 2pm on Tuesday. It's the only private residence in the country to have its own court and prison cells for unruly guests. Just behind Mansion House is the superbly elegant church of **St Stephen Walbrook** (7626 9000, www.ststephenwalbrook. net; closed Sat, Sun), built by Wren in 1672. Its gleaming domed, coffered ceiling was borrowed from Wren's original design for St Paul's; other features include an incongruous modernist altar, sculpted by Sir Henry Moore and cruelly dubbed 'the camembert'. The Samaritans were founded here in the 1950s.

To the east of Mansion House is the **Royal Exchange**, flanked by statues of James Henry Greathead, who invented the machine that cut the tunnels for the London Underground, and Paul Reuter, who founded the Reuters news agency here in 1851. In 1972, the exchange shifted to offices on Threadneedle Street, thence to Paternoster Square in 2004, where it remains.

The period grandeur is undermined by the monstrosity on the west side of the junction, **No.1 Poultry**. The name fits: it's a turkey. A short walk down Queen Victoria Street is the Roman **Temple of Mithras** – discovered by accident in the 1950s, the little temple was a media sensation. Duly opened to the public, just a few scrubby courses of old brick remained, and no longer on the original site. Things have moved on since then: Museum of London Archaeology have re-excavated the site, and a better restoration of the Temple will reopen in due course – back where it was found.

Further south, turn left on to Cannon Street, where you can see the **London Stone**. Roughly opposite the Stone is the late Wren church of **St Michael Paternoster Royal** (7248 5202, closed Sat, Sun), the final resting place of Richard 'Dick'

EXPLORE

Whittington. Later transformed into a rags-to-riches pantomime hero, the real Dick Whittington was a wealthy merchant elected Lord Mayor of London four times between 1397 and 1420. The role of Dick Whittington's cat is less clear – many now believe that 'cat' was actually slang for a ship – but an excavation to find Whittington's tomb in 1949 did uncover a mummified medieval moggy. The happy pair are shown in the stained-glass windows.

Returning to Bank, stroll north along Prince's Street, beside the Bank of England's blind wall. Look right along Lothbury to find **St Margaret Lothbury** (7726 4878, www.stml.org.uk, closed Sat, Sun). The grand screen dividing the choir from the nave was designed by Wren himself; other works here by his favourite woodcarver, Grinling Gibbons, were recovered from various churches damaged in World War II. Lothbury also features a beautiful neo-Venetian building, now apartments, built by 19th-century architect Augustus Pugin, who worked with Charles Barry on the Houses of Parliament.

South-east of Bank on Lombard Street is Hawksmoor's striking, twin-spired church of **St Mary Woolnoth** (7626 9701, closed Sat, Sun), squeezed in between what were 17th-century banking houses. Only their gilded signboards now remain, a hanging heritage artfully maintained by the City's planners.

Further east on Lombard Street is Wren's **St Edmund the King** (7621 1391, www.spiritualitycentre.org, closed Sat, Sun), which now houses a centre for modern spirituality. Other significant churches in the area include Wren's handsome red-brick **St Mary Abchurch**, off Abchurch Lane, and **St Clement**, on Clement's Lane, immortalised in the nursery rhyme 'Oranges and Lemons'. Over on Cornhill are two more Wren churches: **St Peter-upon-Cornhill**, mentioned by Dickens in *Our Mutual Friend*, and **St Michael Cornhill**, which contains a bizarre statue of a pelican feeding its young with pieces of its own body – a medieval symbol for the Eucharist, it was sculpted by someone who had plainly never seen a pelican.

North-west of the Bank of England is the **Guildhall**, the City of London headquarters. 'Guildhall' can either describe the original banqueting hall or the cluster of buildings around it, of which the **Guildhall Art Gallery** and the church of **St Lawrence Jewry** (7600 9478, www.stlawrencejewry.org.uk, closed Sat, Sun), opposite the hall, are also open to the public. St Lawrence is another restored Wren, with an impressive gilt ceiling. Within, you can hear the renowned Klais organ at lunchtime organ recitals (usually from 1pm Tue).

Glance north along Wood Street to see the isolated tower of **St Alban**, built by Wren in 1685

IN THE KNOW NO PISS TAKE

One of many bits of Victorian arcana that Lee Jackson's fine sanitary history, *Dirty Old London,* revealed to us was the 'urine deflector'. Before public conveniences, to stop men relieving themselves in dark corners, sloping shelves were built into walls that would deposit any urine on the would-be urinator's shoes. We were delighted to discover one remains, in the wall of the **Bank of England** (*see below*) no less, near the corner of Lothbury and Bartholomew Lane. But Jackson himself found the finest array: a row on Clifford's Inn Passage, off Chancery Lane.

but ruined in World War II and now an eccentric private home. At the end of the street is **St Anne & St Agnes**, laid out in the form of a Greek cross, and now home to a music charity.

Sights & Museums

FREE Bank of England Museum

Entrance on Bartholomew Lane, EC2R 8AH (7601 5545, www.bankofengland.co.uk/museum). Bank tube/DLR. **Open** 10am-5pm Mon-Fri. **Admission** free. **Map** p169 F4 ⓓ

Housed inside the former Stock Offices of the Bank of England (there's a full-size recreation of Sir John Soane's Bank Stock Office from 1693), this surprisingly lively museum explores the history of the national bank. As well as ancient coins and original artwork for British banknotes, the museum offers a rare chance to lift nearly 30lbs of gold bar (you reach into a secure box, closely monitored by CCTV). After a three-month refurb in early 2014, the museum emerged with a new display of curious objects gathered from the vaults.

FREE Guildhall

Gresham Street, EC2P 2EJ (7606 3030, www.guildhall.cityoflondon.gov.uk). St Paul's tube or Bank tube/DLR. **Open** *May-Sept* 10am-5pm daily. *Oct-Apr* 10am-4.30pm Mon-Sat. Closes for functions; phone ahead. **Admission** free. **Map** p169 E4 ⓓ

The City of London and its progenitors have been holding grand ceremonial dinners in this hall for eight centuries. Memorials to national heroes line the walls, shields of the 100 livery companies grace the ceiling, and every Lord Mayor since 1189 gets a namecheck on the windows. Many famous trials have taken place here, including the treason trial of 16-year-old Lady Jane Grey, 'the nine days' queen', in 1553. Above the internal entrance to the Guildhall are statues of Gog and Magog, mythical giants who are said to protect the City. (Scholars say they're

EXPLORE

derived from a medieval legend concerning an exiled Trojan who wrestled the giant Briton Gogmagog, whose name over time was split into this pair of giants.) The current statues replaced 18th-century forebears that were destroyed in the Blitz.

▶ *The collection of the charming Clockmakers' Museum – which had been on the Guildhall site for more than a century – has been moved to the Science Museum (see p87), where it will open in late 2015.*

★ FREE Guildhall Art Gallery

Guildhall Yard, off Gresham Street, EC2V 5AE (7332 3700, www.cityoflondon.org.uk). St Paul's tube or Bank tube/DLR. **Open** 10am-5pm Mon-Sat; noon-4pm Sun. **Admission** free. *Temporary exhibitions* £5; £3 reductions; free under-16s. **Map** p169 E4 ❷

The City of London's gallery was always a favourite of ours, but few others seemed as keen. The recent comprehensive rehang – in celebration of the gallery's 15th anniversary in 2014 – should make it more popular. Upstairs, dull portraits of royalty and long-gone mayors have been replaced by the entertaining and informative thematic display of the Victorian Collection. Here, you'll find lushly romantic and superbly camp Pre-Raphaelite works by Frederic Leighton, Dante Gabriel Rossetti and John Everett Millais; you certainly wouldn't mess with John Collier's *Clytemnestra* of 1832. A few steps down from the entrance, a mezzanine gallery holds joyous, sun-filled abstracts by Matthew Smith; continuing to the Undercroft you'll find various London-themed pieces, some of historical and sociological more than artist merit, but fascinating nonetheless. There are also some neat heritage displays of Roman artefacts and medieval charters that explain the background to Dick Whittington, Gog and Magog and various other topics. Towering over the temporary exhibition spaces on this floor, John Singleton Copley's *Defeat of the Floating Batteries at Gibraltar* takes up two storeys of wall. Finally, a sub-basement contains the scant remains of London's 6,000-seat Roman amphitheatre, built around AD 70; *Tron*-like figures and crowd sound effects give a quaint inkling of scale.

▶ *When you're outside in the courtyard again, you'll notice a long, curved line in the paving: this indicates the perimeter of the amphitheatre 20ft beneath where you stand. See p324* **Walk**.

FREE London Stone

111 Cannon Street. Cannon Street tube/rail. **Map** p169 F5 ❸

Possibly a Roman milestone, mentioned by both Shakespeare and William Blake, this rather boring lump of rock – visible from the street through a slightly fancy grille in the wall at ankle level – was first written about in 1188. One ancient legend insists that, should it be moved, the City will founder. In fact, it has already been moved twice (in 1742 and again in 1798), and was in 1962 put back in place when the current office replaced Blitz-damaged St Swithin's church. And that ancient legend? It was first recorded in 1862.

Restaurants

City Càphê

17 Ironmonger Lane, EC2V 8EY (www.citycaphe. com). Bank tube/DLR. **Open** 11.30am-4pm Mon-Fri. **Main courses** £3.65-£6.50. **Map** p169 E4 ❹ Vietnamese

EXPLORE

Guildhall.

Long before you see this charming Vietnamese café, you'll smell enticing aromas wafting down the street. At lunchtime, you can expect to see a queue at the door; staff are calmly efficient, so don't baulk at the length – it disappears in next to no time. The menu is easy to follow and most options are available with beef, pork, chicken or tofu. Seating in the bright, modern interior is limited, so City Càphê is not the place for a long lunch, but it's perfect for a quick bite or a tasty takeaway.

Shops & Services

Royal Exchange

Cornhill, ED3V 3LR (www.theroyalexchange. co.uk). Bank tube/DLR. **Open** 10am-6pm daily. *Restaurants & bars* 8am-11pm daily. **Map** p169 F5
⑮ Mall

This Parthenon-like building is the former home of the London Stock Exchange, founded by ace financier Sir Thomas Gresham back in 1565 to facilitate the newly invented trade in stocks and shares with Antwerp. Destroyed by the Great Fire, and again in 1838, the current premises date to 1844, when they were opened by Queen Victoria, but stopped trading in 1939. The Exchange reopened in 2001 as a rather upmarket mall, with a grand champagne bar and

City Càphê. *See p183.*

expensive fashion and gift shops – if your desire for a fancy fountain pen or flash watch subsides, it's still worth a look to see City dwellers in repose.
▶ *The gilded grasshopper hanging over 68 Lombard Street is Gresham's heraldic emblem.*

MONUMENT & THE TOWER OF LONDON

Aldgate, Monument or Tower Hill tube, Liverpool Street tube/Overground/rail, or Tower Gateway DLR.

From Bank, King William Street runs south-east towards London Bridge, passing the small square containing the **Monument**. South on Lower Thames Street is the moody-looking church of **St Magnus the Martyr**; nearby are several relics from the days when this area was a busy port, including the old Customs House and **Billingsgate Market**, London's main fish market until 1982 (when it moved to east London).

North of the Monument along Gracechurch Street is the atmospheric **Leadenhall Market**, constructed in 1881 by Horace Jones (who also built the market at Smithfield; *see p178*). The vaulted roof was restored to its original Victorian finery in 1991, and City workers come here in droves to lunch at the pubs, cafés and restaurants, including the historic **Lamb Tavern**. Fantasy fans may recognise the market as Diagon Alley in *Harry Potter & the Philosopher's Stone*.

Behind the market is Lord Rogers' high-tech **Lloyd's of London** building, constructed in 1986, with all its ducts, vents, stairwells and lift shafts on the outside, like an oil rig dumped in the heart of the City. Rogers has a new building, 122 Leadenhall (the **Cheesegrater**) – the second-tallest building in the City – directly opposite. The original Lloyd's Register of Shipping, decorated with evocative bas-reliefs of sea monsters and nautical scenes, is on Fenchurch Street, where the next in the sequence of distinctive new City skyscrapers has emerged: Rafael Viñoly's 20 Fenchurch Street (www.20fenchurchstreet. co.uk), nicknamed the **Walkie Talkie** due to its distinctive top-heavy shape, and now providing wonderful views from the **Sky Garden**. South of Fenchurch Street, on Eastcheap (derived from the Old English *ceap,* meaning 'barter'), is Wren's **St Margaret Pattens**, with an original 17th-century interior.

Several more of the City's tallest buildings are nearby. To the north, the ugly and rather dated **Tower 42** (25 Old Broad Street) was the tallest building in Britain until the construction of One Canada Square in Docklands in 1990. And topped out at 755 feet (including a radio mast), **Heron Tower** (110 Bishopsgate, www.herontower.com) became the City's tallest building at the end of 2009. Its 46 storeys include bar-restaurants,

EXPLORE

Heron Tower, the Cheesegrater, the Gherkin and the Walkie Talkie.

complete with outdoor terraces and reached by an external, glass-sided lift. A rival, 945-foot monster called the **Pinnacle** was begun on Bishopsgate – having stalled, it looks like it will be reborn under a new design. Also on Bishopsgate, behind Tower 42, is **Gibson Hall**, the ostentatious former offices of the National Provincial Bank of England.

A block south, St Mary Axe is an insignificant street named after a vanished church that is said to have contained an axe used by Attila the Hun to behead English virgins. It is now known for Lord Foster's **30 St Mary Axe**, arguably London's finest modern building. The building is known as **'the Gherkin'**, for reasons that are obvious. On curved stone benches either side of 30 St Mary Axe are inscribed the 20 lines of Scottish poet Ian Hamilton Finlay's 'Arcadian Dream Garden', a curious counterpart to Lord Foster's building. Nearby are two medieval churches that survived the Great Fire: **St Helen's Bishopsgate** and **St Andrew Undershaft**. The latter, right at the foot of the Cheesegrater, contains a Hobbit-sized statue of John Stow, who wrote London's first guidebook, the *Survey of London*, in 1598. The quill his effigy holds is replaced by the Lord Mayor every three years (next in 2017).

The north end of St Mary Axe intersects with two interesting streets. The more northerly, Houndsditch, is where Londoners threw dead dogs and other rubbish in medieval times – the ditch ran outside the London Wall, dividing the City from the East End. The southerly one is Bevis Marks, home to the superbly preserved **Bevis Marks Synagogue** (7626 1274, closed Sat), founded in 1701 by Sephardic Jews fleeing the Spanish Inquisition. Services are still held in Portuguese as well as Hebrew.

South along Bevis Marks are **St Botolph's-without-Aldgate** and the tiny stone church of **St Katharine Cree** (7488 4318; closed Sat, Sun) on Leadenhall Street, one of only eight churches to survive the Great Fire. Inside is a memorial to Sir Nicholas Throckmorton, Queen Elizabeth I's ambassador to France, who was imprisoned for treason on numerous occasions, despite – or perhaps because of – his friendship with the temperamental queen.

Further south, towards the Tower of London, streets and alleys have evocative names: Crutched Friars, Savage Gardens, Pepys Street and the like. The famous diarist lived in nearby Seething Lane and observed the Great Fire of London from **All Hallows by the Tower**. Pepys is buried in the church of **St Olave** (7488 4318, www.sanctuaryinthecity.net) on Hart Street, nicknamed 'St Ghastly Grim' by Dickens due to the skulls above the entrance.

Marking the eastern edge of the City, the **Tower of London** was the palace of the medieval kings and queens of England. Home to the Crown Jewels and the Royal Armoury, it's one of Britain's best-loved tourist attractions and, accordingly, is mobbed by visitors seven days a week. Overlooking the Tower from the north, beside the tube station, **Trinity Square Gardens** contain a humbling memorial to the tens of thousands of merchant seamen killed in the two World Wars, as well as a set of four plaques commemorating more than 125 Catholics who were executed at the Tower Hill scaffold between 1381 and 1747. Across the road is the small square in which London's druids celebrate each spring equinox with an elaborate ceremony. Just beyond is one of the City's finest Edwardian buildings: the former **Port of London HQ** at 10

EXPLORE

Trinity Square, with a huge neoclassical façade and gigantic statues symbolising Commerce, Navigation, Export, Produce and Father Thames. Work is underway to turn this into a luxury hotel. Next door is **Trinity House**, the home of the General Lighthouse Authority, founded by Henry VIII for the upkeep of shipping beacons along the river.

At the south-east corner of the Tower is **Tower Bridge**, built in 1894 and still London's most distinctive bridge. Used as a navigation aid by German bombers, it escaped the firestorm of the Blitz. East across Bridge Approach is **St Katharine Docks**, the first London docks to be formally closed. The restaurants around the marina, slightly hidden behind modern office blocks, offer more dignified dining than those around the Tower.

Tower of London.

Sights & Museums

FREE All Hallows by the Tower
Byward Street, EC3R 5BJ (7481 2928, www.ahbtt. org.uk). Tower Hill tube or Tower Gateway DLR. **Open** 9am-5pm Mon-Fri; 10am-5pm Sat, Sun. *Tours* Apr-Oct 2-4pm most weekdays; donation requested. **Admission** free; donations appreciated. **Map** p169 G6 ⑯
Often described as London's oldest church, All Hallows is built on the foundations of a seventh-century Saxon church. Much of what survives today was reconstructed after World War II, but several Saxon details can be seen in the main hall, where the Knights Templar were tried by Edward II in 1314. The undercroft contains a museum with Roman and Saxon relics and a Crusader altar. William Penn, the founder of Pennsylvania, was baptised here in 1644.

★ Monument
Monument Street, EC3R 8AH (7626 2717, www. themonument.info). Monument tube. **Open** *Apr-Sept* 9.30am-6pm daily. *Oct-Mar* 9.30am-5.30pm daily. **Admission** £6; £2.70-£4 reductions; free under-5s. **Map** p169 F5 ⑰
One of 17th-century London's most important landmarks, the Monument is a magnificent Portland stone column, topped by a landmark golden orb with more than 30,000 fiery leaves of gold – it looks decidedly like the head of a thistle. The Monument was designed by Sir Christopher Wren and his (often overlooked) associate Robert Hooke as a memorial to the Great Fire. The world's tallest free-standing stone column, it measures 202ft from the ground to the tip of its golden flames, exactly the distance east to Farriner's bakery in Pudding Lane, where the fire is supposed to have begun on 2 September 1666. The viewing platform is surrounded by a lightweight mesh cage, but the views are great – you have to walk 311 steps up the internal spiral staircase to enjoy them, though. At least, everyone who makes it to the top gets a certificate.

FREE St Botolph's-without-Aldgate
Aldgate High Street, EC3N 1AB (7283 1670, www. stbotolphs.org.uk). Aldgate tube. **Open** 11am-3pm Mon; 9am-3pm Tue-Fri. *Eucharist* 1.05pm Tue, Thur; 10.30am Sun. **Admission** free; donations appreciated. **Map** p169 H4 ⑲
The oldest of three churches of St Botolph in the City, this handsome monument was built at the gates of Roman London as a homage to and to ask the intercession of the patron saint of travellers. The building was reconstructed by George Dance in 1744 and a beautiful ornamental ceiling was added in the 19th century by John Francis Bentley, who also created Westminster Cathedral.

FREE St Ethelburga Centre for Reconciliation & Peace
78 Bishopsgate, EC2N 4AG (7496 1610, www. stethelburgas.org). Bank tube/DLR or Liverpool Street tube/rail. **Open** 11am-3pm Wed, Fri. **Admission** free; donations appreciated. **Map** p169 G4 ⑱
Built around 1390, the tiny church of St Ethelburga was reduced to rubble by an IRA bomb in 1993 and rebuilt as a centre for peace and reconciliation. Behind the chapel is a Bedouin tent where events are held to promote dialogue between the faiths (phone or check the website for details), an increasingly heated issue in modern Britain.

FREE St Helen's Bishopsgate
Great St Helen's, off Bishopsgate, EC3A 6AT (7283 2231, www.st-helens.org.uk). Bank tube/DLR or Liverpool Street tube/rail. **Open** 9.30am-12.30pm Mon-Fri; afternoons by appt. **Admission** free. **Map** p169 G4 ⑳
Founded in 1210, St Helen's Bishopsgate is actually two churches knocked into one, which explains its unusual shape. The church survived the Great Fire

EXPLORE

and the Blitz, only to be partly wrecked by IRA bombs in 1992 and 1993. The hugely impressive 16th- and 17th-century memorials inside include the grave of Thomas Gresham, founder of the Royal Exchange (*see p184*).

FREE St Magnus the Martyr

Lower Thames Street, EC3R 6DN (7626 4481, www.stmagnusmartyr.org.uk). Monument tube. **Open** 10am-4pm Tue-Fri. *Mass* 12.30pm Tue-Fri; 11am Sun. **Admission** free; donations appreciated. **Map** p169 F6 ⑤

Downhill from the Monument, this looming Wren church marked the entrance to the original London Bridge. There's a scale model of the old bridge inside the church, and the porch has a timber from the original version. There's also a statue of axe-wielding St Magnus, the 12th-century Earl of Orkney. The church is mentioned at one of the climaxes of TS Eliot's *The Waste Land*: 'Where the walls/Of Magnus Martyr hold/Inexplicable splendour of Ionian white and gold.'

▶ *St Mary Woolnoth (see p182) is another star of* The Waste Land: *keeping 'the hours/With a dead sound on the final stroke of nine'.*

★ FREE Sky Garden

20 Fenchurch Street (entrance via Philpot Lane), EC3M 3BY (no phone, http://skygarden.london). Monument tube. **Open** *Apr-Sept* 10am-6pm Mon-Fri; 11am-9pm Sat, Sun. *Oct-Mar* 9.30am-5pm daily. **Admission** free. **Map** p169 G5 ⑤②

Although it's free to do so, visiting the City's newest attraction takes a bit of folderol: book ahead online – as soon as you arrive in London, perhaps before you leave home – and bring photo ID and the confirmation email. If no slots are available, book a table at the Sky Pod Bar (cocktails there cost around a tenner) or at one of the two restaurants (the Darwin Brasserie is cheaper): all three also give access to the viewing floors. *See p189* **Eyes in the Sky**.

Tower Bridge Exhibition

Tower Bridge Road, SE1 2UP (7403 3761, www. towerbridge.org.uk). Tower Hill tube or Tower Gateway DLR. **Open** *Apr-Sept* 10am-5.30pm daily. *Oct-Mar* 9.30am-5pm daily. **Admission** £9; £3.90-£6.30 reductions; £14.10-£22.50 family; free under-5s. **Map** p169 H6 ⑤③

Opened in 1894, this is the 'London Bridge' that wasn't sold to America. Originally powered by steam, the drawbridge is now opened by electric rams when big ships need to venture upstream (check when the bridge is next due to be raised on the bridge's website or follow the Twitter feed). The bridge looks resplendent after a three-year restoration that was completed in 2011. An entertaining exhibition on its history is displayed in the old steamrooms and the west walkway, which provides a crow's-nest view along the Thames. Since 2014, when glass panels were placed in the walkways, you've also been able to look directly down past your own feet at the river below – assuming you're not prone to vertigo.

★ Tower of London

Tower Hill, EC3N 4AB (0844 482 7777, www. hrp.org.uk). Tower Hill tube or Tower Gateway DLR. **Open** *Mar-Oct* 10am-5.30pm Mon, Sun; 9am-5.30pm Tue-Sat. *Nov-Feb* 10am-4.30pm Mon, Sun; 9am-4.30pm Tue-Sat. **Admission** £22; £11-£18 reductions; £59 family; free under-5s. **Map** p169 H6 ⑤④

If you haven't been to the Tower of London before, you should go now. Despite the exhausting crowds and long climbs up barely accessible, narrow stairways, this is one of Britain's finest historical attractions. Who wouldn't be fascinated by a close-up look at the crown of Queen Victoria or the armour (and prodigious codpiece) of King Henry VIII? The buildings of the Tower span 900 years of – mostly violent – history, and the bastions and battlements house a series of interactive displays on the lives of British monarchs, and the often excruciatingly painful deaths of traitors. There's easily enough to do here to fill a whole day, which makes the steep entry price pretty good value, and it's worth joining one of the highly recommended and entertaining free tours led by the Yeoman Warders (or Beefeaters).

Make the Crown Jewels your first stop, and as early in the day as you possibly can: if you wait until you've pottered around a few other things the queues are usually immense. Beyond satisfyingly solid vault doors, you get to glide along a set of travelators (each branded with the Queen's official 'EIIR' badge) past such treasures of state as the Monarch's Sceptre, mounted with the Cullinan I diamond, and the Imperial State Crown, which is worn by the Queen each year for the opening of Parliament.

The other big draw is the Royal Armoury in the central White Tower, with its swords, armour, poleaxes, morning stars (spiky maces) and other gruesome tools for separating human beings from their body parts. The recently reassembled Line of Kings, a collection of arms and armour (some belonging to monarchs), life-sized wooden horses and the carved heads of kings, is eccentric pro-monarchy propaganda that dates from the Restoration. Kids are entertained by swordsmanship games, coin-minting activities and even a child-sized longbow. The garderobes (medieval toilets) also seem to appeal.

Back outside, Tower Green – where executions of prisoners of noble birth were carried out (the last execution, of World War II German spy Joseph Jakobs, was in 1941) – is marked by a stiff glass pillow, sculpted by poet/artist Brian Catling. Overlooking the green, Beauchamp Tower, dating from 1280, has an upper floor full of intriguing graffiti by the prisoners who were held here. The Tower only ceased functioning as a prison in 1952

EXPLORE

City Social Bar.

and over the years counted Anne Boleyn, Rudolf Hess and the Krays among its inmates.

Towards the entrance, the 13th-century Bloody Tower is another must-see that gets overwhelmed by numbers later in the day. The ground floor is a reconstruction of Sir Walter Raleigh's study, the upper floor details the fate of the Princes in the Tower. In the riverside wall is the unexpectedly beautiful Medieval Palace, with its reconstructed bedroom and throne room, and spectacularly complex stained glass in the private chapel. The whole palace is deliciously cool if you've been struggling round on a hot summer's day.

Restaurants

Not long ago finding places where people could eat or drink in London with good views was surprisingly hard – and the quality wasn't always good. Nowadays, you're spoilt for choice in the City alone, with **Duck & Waffle** and

Sushisamba in Heron Tower; Darwin Brasserie, Fenchurch Seafood and the Sky Pod Bar in the Walkie Talkie, and **City Social** in Tower 42.

Duck & Waffle
Floor 40, Heron Tower, 110 Bishopsgate, EC2N 4AY (3640 7310, http://duckandwaffle.com). Liverpool Street tube/rail. **Open** 24hrs daily. **Food served** 6-10.30am, 11.30-3.30pm Mon-Fri; 9am-3.30pm Sat, Sun. **Dishes** £5-£32. **Map** p169 G4 🌐 **Modern European**
There's a dedicated entrance in Heron Tower from which a glass lift whizzes you up to Duck & Waffle on the 40th floor, or its glitzier sibling Sushisamba (*see right*) below. The views are stunning – if you're pointed the right way and, preferably, sitting at a window table (many of which are for couples). Food is an on-trend mix of pricey small plates, raw offerings (oysters, ceviche) and a few main courses (including the namesake duck confit and waffle), as well as sensational barbecue-spiced crispy pigs' ears (*see p131* **London's Best Dishes**). Service wavers between keen and offhand, and the acoustics are terrible. But Duck & Waffle is open 24/7 – which is unheard of in London.
▶ *Although food is served 24hrs a day, a limited menu is offered between midnight and 6am.*

Pubs & Bars

City Social Bar
Tower 42, 25 Old Broad Street, EC2N 1HQ (7877 7703, http://citysociallondon.com). Liverpool Street tube/Overground/rail. **Open** noon-midnight Mon-Sat. **Map** p169 G4 🌐
Chef-about-town Jason Atherton has taken over this 24th-floor restaurant, with an attached bar anyone can just show up to – having negotiated two lots of security, an escalator and at least one lift. In the bar, the food and drink is of a far higher standard than you might expect up a skyscraper. The cocktails are great, with just enough invention to make them worth the lofty prices: the Pea-lini, for example, comprises 'salted pea cordial', spearmint, absinthe, citric acid, prosecco – and an edible flower. Bar snacks aren't so decently priced, but are characteristically Atherton: a 'ploughman's basket' (£15) came with cheese, bread and things in little jars, picnic-style on a checked cloth.
▶ *The prolific Atherton's other restaurants include Pollen Street Social (see p118), Social Eating House (see p133), Berners Tavern (see p161) and Typing Room (see p212). They're all terrific.*

Draft House
14-15 Seething Lane, EC3N 4AX (7626 3360, www.drafthouse.co.uk). Tower Hill tube or Tower Gateway DLR. **Open** noon-11pm Mon-Wed, Fri, Sat; noon-midnight Thur. **Map** p169 G5 🌐
Pretty much the archetypal 'beers bars', the Draft House mini-chain focuses on serving a

brilliant range of superb beers, simple but relaxed surroundings, and eats that don't deviate far from the sausage/burger/hot dog booze-fodder axis. In addition to its handy location, this branch has a big screen for sporting events – which it shows with great verve and much audience advice to the players. **Other locations** throughout the city.

Sushisamba

Floors 38 & 39, Heron Tower, 110 Bishopsgate, EC2N 4AY (3640 7330, www.sushisamba.com). Liverpool Street tube/rail. **Open** 11.30am-11.30pm Mon, Sun; 2pm-12.30am Tue-Sat. **Map** p169 G4 ⑤⑧

Duck & Waffle (*see p188*) is a floor higher and has 24hr opening, but Sushisamba's two small bars and outdoor roof terrace bar have the edge for views; tell the door staff you don't have a meal reservation but are going to the bar, then take the lift to the 39th floor to avoid another volley of questions, and walk on in. The few cocktails are a little unimaginative – try the saké list instead. But this is a classic destination bar: views, a blinged-up crowd, and relatively easy access. If you do want to eat, the restaurant serves a fusion of Japanese, Brazilian and Peruvian cuisines. That's not an eye-opener these days, but then your eyes are bound to be elsewhere.

EYES IN THE SKY

London's newest viewing point is brilliant – and it's free.

The most thrilling thing you can do in London right now is completely free: a visit to the **Sky Garden** (*see p187*). The provision of a public space was a requirement of the 'Walkie Talkie' getting planning permission, so the fact that this square in the sky will sometimes be closed for private functions has aroused ire in some quarters. Ditto the requirement to book in advance. Whatever your stance on those matters, you're likely to find yourself knocked sideways when you do emerge into the soaring space. First, though, you'll need to clear the airport-style security in the unprepossessing lobby, which gives no hint of the glorious experience in store.

The 360° views take in pretty much every London landmark you can think of, including the **Shard** (*see p63*) and **London Eye** (*see p51*), where this new rival must be cause for anxiety, although the capital's high viewing points offer such different experiences that there's room for them all. The Shard's elegant, cathedral-like spire certainly has a

more positive impact on the skyline than this cartoon-like competitor across the Thames.

But once you're inside the Walkie Talkie looking out, you understand suddenly why it has that unsightly bulge. Up on the 35th floor – flanked by flights of steps rising through lush, leafy plants to a series of terraces – is a vast piazza that commands outstanding views of the capital.

It's a space that changes with the light, becoming more intimate as darkness falls. Although entirely enclosed, it's not warm – even in spring, the bar staff were wearing several layers topped with padded waistcoats. Our visit coincided with a sublime sunset and we lingered, enjoying our (pricey) drinks and mellow piped jazz, and taking endless pictures, until the city had completed its transformation from detailed panorama to impressionistic night scene. By which time we were quite chilly but entirely charmed. We left reluctantly, making plans to return soon, with bigger memory cards and warmer coats.

EXPLORE

Camden

Some parts of London loom large in legend: Camden is one such. Pretty much everybody who's spent any time in this city will have been to Camden Market – a melée of more than 700 shops and stalls, with the Regent's Canal cutting through it. Despite the East End's recent dominance of art, fashion and culture, Camden clings on to some residual cool. Perhaps this is in part due to the late Amy Winehouse, who presides over the place like a tutelary deity; certainly, plenty of energy is brought here by the legion of never-will-be bands that troop up looking for some rock 'n' roll magic to rub off on them. Whatever the reasons, the ramshackle is still ahead of the gentrified by a short head.

The reverse is true to the west: chichi and celebrity-heavy Primrose Hill, where life seems slower and smarter amid the chic cafés and gastropubs. To the east, in Kentish Town, there's a cluster of inventive restaurants and bars. And in the northern reaches of Regent's Park is one of London's top attractions – London Zoo.

EXPLORE

Roundhouse.

Don't Miss

1 **Camden Market** Crazy clothes, music, crafts and much more (p195).

2 **Jewish Museum** Britain's Jewish heritage explored (p192).

3 **ZSL London Zoo** More than 600 species and a new Tiger Territory (p197).

4 **Roundhouse** Railway turntable shed turned performance venue (p192).

5 **Regent's Park** Acres of green, rose gardens and an open-air theatre to boot (p197).

CAMDEN TOWN

Camden Town tube (no exit 1-5pm Sun: use Chalk Farm tube) or Camden Road Overground.

Despite the pressures of gentrification, Camden refuses to leave behind its grungy history as the cradle of British rock music. Against a backdrop of social deprivation, venues such as the **Electric Ballroom** (184 Camden High Street – but seemingly always under threat of redevelopment) and **Dingwalls** (Middle Yard, Camden Lock, 7428 5929, www.dingwalls.com) provided a platform for musical rebels. By the 1990s, the Creation label was based in nearby Primrose Hill (*see p197*), unleashing My Bloody Valentine and the Jesus & Mary Chain on the world, before making it big with Oasis. The Gallagher brothers were often seen trading insults with Blur at the **Good Mixer** (30 Inverness Street, 7916 7929). The music still plays at the **Roundhouse** (*see p273*) in the north, **Koko** (*see p269*) to the south, and any number of pubs and clubs between.

Before the Victorian expansion of London, this was no more than a watering stop on the highway to Hampstead, with two notorious taverns – the Mother Black Cap and Mother Red Cap – frequented by highwaymen and brigands. (The latter is now the **World's End/Underworld**, *see p276*.) After the gaps between the pubs were filled in with terraced houses, the borough became a magnet for Irish and Greek railway workers, many of them working in the engine turning-house that is now the Roundhouse. The area's squalor had a powerful negative influence on the young Charles Dickens, who lived briefly on Bayham Street – you can see a blue plaque that commemorates his residence there.

From the 1960s, things started to pick up, helped by an influx of students, lured by low rents and the growing arts scene that nurtured punk, then indie, then Britpop – and now any number of short-lived indie-electro and alt-folk hybrids, whose young protagonists will all tell you with great fervour about the Camden they knew before it went upmarket.

Parts of Camden still have a rough quality, but the hardcore rebellion of the rock 'n' roll years has been replaced by a more laid-back carnival vibe, as young shoppers join the international parade of counterculture costumes. Tourists travel here in their thousands for the sprawling mayhem of **Camden Market**, which stretches north from the tube along boutique-lined Camden High Street and Chalk Farm Road.

But there are unmistakable signs of gentrification: not least **Shaka Zulu** (Stables Market, Chalk Farm Road, 3376 9911, www.shaka-zulu.com), a hugely over-the-top Zulu-themed bar-restaurant, right beneath **Gilgamesh** (7428 4922, www.gilgameshbar.com), a hugely

Hook Camden Town.

over-the-top Sumerian-themed bar-restaurant. Drop in to **Proud** (*see p271*) if you want to reset your cultural compass.

Cutting through the market is **Regent's Canal**, which opened in 1820 to provide a link between east and west London for horse-drawn narrowboats loaded with coal. Today, the canal is used by the jolly tour boats of the London Waterbus Company (7482 2660, www.london waterbus.co.uk) and Walker's Quay (7485 6210, www.walkersquay.com), which run between Camden Lock and Little Venice in the warmer months. The canal towpath is a convenient walking route west to **Regent's Park** and **ZSL London Zoo**, or east to Islington.

Camden's single avowed 'sight' is west of Camden Town – the excellent **Jewish Museum** – but this remains a good bit of town for rough-and-ready gigs. As well as Koko and the Roundhouse, there are plenty of pub stages where this year's hopefuls try to get spotted: try the **Barfly** (*see p275*), **Underworld** (*see p276*) and the **Dublin Castle** (94 Parkway, 7485 1773, 07949 575 149), where Madness and, later, Blur were launched. The **Jazz Café** (*see p275*) and the **Blues Kitchen** (*see p277*) offer a different vibe.

Sights & Museums

Jewish Museum
Raymond Burton House, 129-131 Albert Street, NW1 7NB (7284 7384, www.jewishmuseum.org. uk). Camden Town tube. **Open** 10am-5pm

Mon-Thur, Sun; 10am-2pm Fri; 10am-9pm Thur during temporary exhibitions. **Admission** £7.50; £3.50-£6.50 reductions; free under-5s. **Map** p193 C3 ❶
This museum is a brilliant exploration of Jewish life in Britain since 1066, combining fun interactives – you can wield the iron in a tailor's sweatshop, sniff chicken soup, pose for a wedding photo or take part in some Yiddish theatre – with serious history. There's a powerful Holocaust section, using the testimony of a single survivor, Leon Greenman, to bring tight focus to the unimaginable horror of it all. Opposite, a beautiful room of religious artefacts, including a 17th-century synagogue ark and centrepiece chandelier of Hanukkah lamps, does an elegant job of introducing Jewish ritual. Access is free to the downstairs café, located beside an ancient ritual bath, and to the shop.

Restaurants

Hook Camden Town
63 Parkway, NW1 7PP (7482 0475, www.hook restaurants.com). Camden Town tube. **Open** noon-3pm, 5.30-10.30pm Tue-Thur; noon-10.30pm Fri, Sat; noon-9pm Sun. **Main courses** £10-£12. **Map** p193 C3 ❷ Fish & chips
Hook will make you feel as if you're at the seaside. The simple, maritime-themed furnishings are reminiscent of a beach hut. The walls are painted blue like sea and sky. And, as on any seaside visit, you'll be eating fish and chips. The menu changes daily: Hook gets some fish from Cornish day boats. Other fish are farmed, and Hook isn't afraid to use lesser-known species such as ling. Fish is served tempura as well as breaded, and there are some lovely home-made sauces alongside the usual tartare.

Made in Camden
Roundhouse, Chalk Farm Road, NW1 8EH (7424 8495, www.madeincamden.com). Chalk Farm tube. **Open** noon-3pm, 5-9pm Tue-Fri; 11am-3pm, 5-9pm Sat, Sun. **Main courses** £11-£16. **Set lunch** £6.50. **Map** p193 A1 ❸ Brasserie
This bar and restaurant in the Roundhouse concert venue has won much applause. The kitchen is capable of excellent fusion cooking, with memorable plates such as fennel with feta, pistachios, salted caramel, lemon zest and dill. Once the concertgoers have taken their seats, noise diminishes and the red and wood-toned room transforms into a chilled spot that makes an alternative to standalone restaurants.

Market
43 Parkway, NW1 7PN (7267 9700, www. marketrestaurant.co.uk). Camden Town tube. **Open** noon-2.30pm, 6-10.30pm Mon-Sat;

EXPLORE

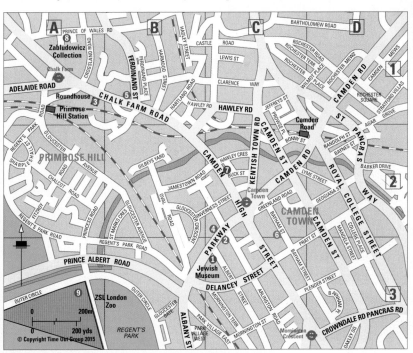

© Copyright Time Out Group 2015

THIS IS **Hard Rock** CAFE

THERE'S NO GREATER SALUTE TO ROCK 'N' ROLL HISTORY
THAN A HARD ROCK CLASSIC TEE.

Present this ad and receive a complimentary gift
with a £25 retail spend in the Rock Shop

Valid in London only. Expires 30/12/15

Rock Shop: Mon – Sat: 09.30 – 23.30 Sun: 09.30 – 23.00
Nearest Tube: Hyde Park Corner (Piccadilly Line) Green Park (Jubilee/Piccadilly/Victoria Line)
Bus: 9, 14, 19, 22, 38, C2

LONDON | 150 OLD PARK LANE | +44 0207 514 1700
HARDROCK.COM   f ⚘ ⚘ ⚘ You Tube #THISISHARDROCK

11am-3pm Sun. **Main courses** £14-£18. **Set lunch** (Mon-Sat) £10 2 courses. **Set dinner** (6-7pm) £17.50 2 courses; £20 3 courses. **Map** p193 C2 ❹ British

One of the best venues to eat in the area. 'Simple things, done well' is a phrase that could apply to the whole operation. The narrow space has been denuded back to its structural brick; specials are chalked on a blackboard. The proudly British and mainly meaty food is straightforward and effective too, such as a signature pie – chicken and leek, say – or the 'modern British' standard of onglet and chips.

Q Grill

29-33 Chalk Farm Road, NW1 8AJ (7267 2678, http://q-bbq.co.uk). Camden Town or Chalk Farm tube. **Open** noon-11.30pm Mon-Thur; noon-midnight Fri; 1pm-midnight Sat; 11am-10.30pm Sun. **Main courses** £9.50-£21. **Set lunch** (noon-4pm Mon-Fri) £10 1 course; £14 2 courses. **Map** p193 B1 ❺ American

Q updates American classics with skill and intelligence. The large, high-ceilinged room is edgy and sexy – dark walls, rusty girders and vintage wooden butchers' paraphernalia – with loud rock as the soundtrack, but make no mistake: Q is a slick operation. The polished, attentive service never misses a beat, even when the kitchen is on the point of combusting. Children's menu is £5.50.

Pubs & Bars

The **Lock Tavern** (*see p270*) and **Proud** (*see p271*) are excellent Camden DJ bars, while the **Blues Kitchen** (*see p277*) and scuzzy indie-den the **Dublin Castle** (*see p192*) supply live music.

BrewDog

113 Bayham Street, NW1 0AG (7284 4626, www.brewdog.com). Camden Town tube or Camden Road Overground. **Open** noon-11.30pm Mon-Thur; noon-midnight Fri, Sat; noon-10.30pm Sun. **Map** p193 C2 ❻

The Scottish craft brewery's Camden outpost is an initiation into the exciting world of craft beer, but never feels intimidating. The drinks list features BrewDog's own beers on keg draught (with guests), while fridges hold a selection of bottles from other microbreweries, mainly from the US.

Other locations 51-55 Bethnal Green Road, Shoreditch, E1 6LA (7729 8476); 15-19 Goldhawk Road, Shepherd's Bush, W12 8QQ (8749 8094); 11-13 Battersea Rise, Clapham, SW11 1HG.

Shops & Services

Camden Market

Camden Lock *Camden Lock Place, off Chalk Farm Road, NW1 8AF (7485 5511, www.camdenlock market.com).* **Open** 10am-6pm daily (note: there are fewer stalls Mon-Fri).

Q Grill.

Camden Lock Village *east of Chalk Farm Road, NW1 (www.camdenlock.net)*. **Open** 10am-6pm daily.

Camden Market *Camden High Street, at Buck Street, NW1 (www.camdenmarkets.org)*. **Open** 10am-5.30pm Thur-Sun.

Inverness Street Market *Inverness Street, NW1 (www.camdenlock.net/inverness)*. **Open** 8.30am-5pm daily.

Stables Market *off Chalk Farm Road, opposite Hartland Road, NW1 8AH (7485 5511)*. **Open** 10.30am-6pm Mon-Fri (reduced stalls); 10am-6pm Sat, Sun.

All *Camden Town or Chalk Farm tube.*
Map p193 C2 **❼ Market**
Camden's sprawling collection of markets offers a real smörgåsbord of street culture. Wander past loitering goths and punks to join the throng of tourists, locals and random celebs fighting it out at the vast and varied selection of shops and stalls. Saturdays are not for the faint-hearted – crowds craving lava lamps, skull rings, fashion, interiors, music and vintage swarm about. To avoid the rough and tumble, visit on a weekday, though weekends are better for variety and atmosphere. Camden Market proper (on the junction with Buck Street) is the place for cheapo jeans, T-shirts and accessories and the same goes for Canal Market, now happily reopened after being destroyed by a fire in 2008. Down the road, a multimillion-pound redevelopment project is in the midst of transforming the once boho Stables Market into something a little more sterile. However, vintage threads can still be found here alongside crafts, antiques and the now-sprawling

---

SIDE DISH

Some of Camden's best eating is – in unheralded Kentish Town.

Until recently, Kentish Town was just a cheap place to live. How things have changed. Now, members' club Soho House runs the **Dirty Burger** shack (79 Highgate Road, NW5 1TL, 3310 2010, www.eatdirtyburger.com). It's a little place made of corrugated iron, all salvaged wood and rusty chairs with barely room for 20 diners. The menu offers only cheeseburgers, fries, onion fries, a tiny breakfast menu and drinks – but what deliciously naughty burgers they are.

The foodies' noses twitched – and brought them here. They found plenty to enjoy. Keeping to the fast food theme, **E Mono** (287 Kentish Town Road, NW5 2JS, 7485 9779) is for kebabs that feel like they're worth a coronary and the **Arancini Factory** (115 Kentish Town Road, NW1 8PB, 3583 2242, www.arancinibrothers.com) serves Sicilian-style deep-fried risotto balls in various formats. Enough of snacking? Head to the **Shoe Shop** (122 Fortess Road, NW5 2HL, 7267 8444, www.shoeshoplondon.com), where the chef, Paul Merrony, produces magnificent modern European food, such as ox tongue with a parsley and lentil salad.

Forget the foodies, what about the hipsters? They'll be needing coffee – and craft beer. For the former: the **Fields Beneath** (52A Prince of Wales Road, NW5 3LN, 7424 8838) and **Two Doors Down** (73 Kentish Town Road, NW1 8HY). Both are tiny; both have a real neighbourhood feel. For the latter? **Camden Town Brewery** is actually based in Kentish Town and you can pop in to its brewery tap (55-59 Wilkin Street Mews, NW5 3NN, 7485 1671, www.camdentownbrewery.com).

Now we've had a couple of pints, another recommendation: go the the loo. Not any loo, but the public toilet that now operates as a bar **Ladies & Gentlemen** (2 Highgate Road, NW5 1NR, www.ladiesandgents.co). There are a few seats at the bar, but mostly it's table service – delivered with a smile and loads of enthusiasm. The cocktails are generally £8-£9 and mix the classics with the new. Or try basement bar **Knowhere Special** (296 Kentish Town Road, NW5 2TG, www.knowherespecial.com). It has low lighting, great music, and a resident jack russell named Otto. The effect is classic simplicity. Much like Kentish Town itself.

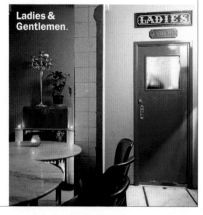

EXPLORE

Proud gallery and bar. Next door, at the pleasant, waterside Camden Lock, you'll find everything from corsets and children's clothes to Japanese tableware and multicultural street food.

▶ *From Camden Lock, it's a pleasant half-hour walk east then south on the Regent's Canal to Granary Square (see p158), passing the sweet little Camley Street Natural Park (www.wildlondon. org.uk) on the opposite bank.*

AROUND CAMDEN

Primrose Hill, to the west of Camden, is just as attractive as the celebrities who frequent the gastropubs and quaint cafés along **Regent's Park Road** and **Gloucester Avenue**. It's all rather spacious and slow-moving after the crowds in Camden proper, although the restaurants fill up fast enough. Try upmarket Greek bistro **Lemonia** (89 Regent's Park Road, 7586 7454). For a gastropub feed, head to Gloucester Avenue: both the **Engineer** (no.65, 7483 1890) and **Lansdowne** (no.90, 7483 0409) are here. On a clear day, the walk up the hill is a delight, with fabulous views back over London.

North-east of Camden, scruffy **Kentish Town** has quietly become a great place for eating and drinking – and it's just a tube stop or bus ride from the craziness of the market environs (*see p196* **Side Dish**).

Sights & Museums

FREE **Zabludowicz Collection**
176 Prince of Wales Road, Chalk Farm, NW5 3PT (7428 8940, www.zabludowiczcollection. com). Chalk Farm tube or Kentish Town West Overground. **Open** noon-6pm Thur-Sun. **Admission** free. **Map** p191 A1 ❽
This former Methodist chapel – a remarkable neoclassical building that makes a superb setting for art exhibitions – holds three shows a year, enabling artists to create experimental new work and curators to build exhibitions around the Collection's global emerging art in all media.

REGENT'S PARK

Baker Street or Regent's Park tube.

Regent's Park (open 5am-dusk daily) is one of London's most delightful open spaces. Originally a hunting ground for Henry VIII, it remained a royals-only retreat long after it was formally designed by John Nash in 1811; only in 1845 did it open to the public. Attractions run from the animal noises and odours of **ZSL London Zoo** to the enchanting **Open Air Theatre** (*see p288*); rowing-boat hire, beautiful rose gardens, ice-cream stands and the **Cow & Coffee Bean Café** (7935 5729, www.companyofcooks.com) complete

Regent's Park.

the postcard-pretty picture. West of Regent's Park rises the golden dome of the **London Central Mosque** (www.iccuk.org); exit to the south and you're in Marylebone (*see p107*).

Sights & Museums

★ **ZSL London Zoo**
Regent's Park, NW1 4RY (7722 3333, www.zsl.org/london-zoo). Baker Street or Camden Town tube then bus 274, C2. **Open** times vary; check website for details. **Admission** £22.50-£27; £16.65-£24.30 reductions; free under-3s. **Map** p191 A3 ❾
London Zoo has been open in one form or another since 1826. Spread over 36 acres and containing more than 600 species, it cares for many of the endangered variety – part of the entry price (pretty steep at £27 in peak season) goes towards the ZSL's projects around the world. Regular events include 'animals in action' and keeper talks. Exhibits are entertaining: look out, for example, for the re-creation of a kitchen overrun with large cockroaches. The latest big attraction, the fabulous 'In with the Lemurs', opened in 2015: you get to walk through jungle habitat with the long-tailed primates leaping over your head. Other major attractions are 'Tiger Territory', where Sumatran tigers can be watched through floor-to-ceiling windows, and 'Gorilla Kingdom'. The relaunched 'Rainforest Life' biodome and the 'Meet the Monkeys' attractions allow visitors to walk through enclosures that recreate the natural habitat of, respectively, tree anteaters and sloths, and black-capped Bolivian squirrel monkeys. Personal encounters of the avian kind can be had in the Victorian Blackburn Pavilion – as well as at Penguin Beach, where the black-and-white favourites are plainly visible as they swim underwater; responses to the snakes and crocodiles in the reptile house tend to involve a larger proportion of shudders. Bring a picnic and you could easily spend the day here.

The East End

Browse Instagram, and it's hard to believe how recently the East End was notorious for its slums and cursed with the smelliest and most unpleasant industries. Jack the Ripper stalked through Whitechapel; the presence of the docks – the sanitised remains of which can be enjoyably explored at Wapping and Limehouse – later attracted some of the most brutal bombing during the Blitz. How things change. The East End now comprises much of what is most vibrant about London: Spitalfields and Brick Lane, Shoreditch and Hoxton are all must-visits.

A word about geography: the boundaries of the East End are notoriously difficult to pin down. One neat definition would include everything east of the City from the Thames in the south, north all the way through Hackney, and everything east as far as the River Lea. For ease of navigation, we've gathered just the focal areas in this chapter. For more of east London (including Dalston), *see pp236-244.*

EXPLORE

White Lyan.

Don't Miss

1 Geffrye Museum Charming museum following domestic interiors through centuries (p206).

2 House of Hackney Fashion-forward Shoreditch store (p210).

3 Broadway Market Shop and people-watch in the heart of Hackney (p213).

4 White Lyan Pioneer of the new wave of London cocktail bars (p209).

5 Columbia Road Market Sunday flower power and a street packed with independent shops (p213).

SPITALFIELDS

Aldgate East tube or Liverpool Street tube/rail.

Approach this area from Liverpool Street Station, up Brushfield Street, and you'll know you're on the right track when the magnificent spiky spire of **Christ Church Spitalfields** comes into view. The area's other signature sight, **Spitalfields Market**, has emerged from redevelopment and the market stalls have moved back underneath the vaulted Victorian roof of the original building.

Outside, along Brushfield Street, the shops might look as if they're from Dickens' day, but most are recent inventions: the charming grocery shop **A Gold** (no.42, 7247 2487) was lovingly restored in the noughties; and the deli **Verde & Co** (no.40, 7247 1924) was opened by its owner, author Jeanette Winterson, inspired by the local food shops she found in – whisper it – France. This tendency will, after Mayor Boris Johnson overruled the council's objections, be made literal by the redevelopment of the **Fruit & Wool Exchange**, built in 1920 – only the façade will remain of a building that sheltered as many as 10,000 East Enders from the Blitz, and still bears graffiti from those days. Settle any anxieties about gentrification by heading a few streets south: on Sundays, the salt-of-the-earth **Petticoat Lane Market** hawks knickers and cheap electronics around Middlesex Street.

A block north of Spitalfields Market is **Dennis Severs' House**, while across from the market, on the east side of Commercial Street and in the shadow of Christ Church, the **Ten Bells** (84 Commercial Street, 0753 049 2986, www.tenbells.com) is where one of Jack the Ripper's victims drank her last gin. On the next corner, Sandra

Esqulant's **Golden Heart** pub (no.110, 7247 2158) has hosted every Young British Artist of note, ever since the day Gilbert & George decided to pop in on their new local.

The streets between here and Brick Lane to the east are dourly impressive, lined with tall, shuttered Huguenot houses; **19 Princelet Street** (7247 5332, www.19princeletstreet.org.uk) opens to the public a few times a year as the Museum of Immigration and Diversity. This unrestored 18th-century house was home first to French silk merchants and later to Polish Jews who built a synagogue in the garden; its spare exhibition now serves as a symbol of the many changes this area has witnessed.

Sights & Museums

FREE Christ Church Spitalfields

Commercial Street, E1 6QE (7377 6793, www.christchurchspitalfields.org). Liverpool Street tube/rail or Shoreditch High Street Overground. **Open** 11am-4pm Tue; 11am-4pm Mon, Wed-Fri phone for availability; 1-4pm Sun. **Tours** phone for details. **Admission** free. **Map** p202 C4 ❶
Built in 1729 by architect Nicholas Hawksmoor, this splendid church has in recent years been restored to its original state (tasteless alterations had been made to the building following a lightning strike in the 19th century). Most tourists get no further than cowering before the wonderfully overbearing spire, but the revived interior is impressive too, its pristine whiteness in marked contrast to its architect's dark reputation. The formidable 1735 Richard Bridge organ is almost as old as the church. Regular concerts are held here, notably during the two annual Spitalfields festivals (*see p33 and p40*).

Dennis Severs' House

18 Folgate Street, E1 6BX (7247 4013, www.dennissevershouse.co.uk). Liverpool Street tube/rail or Shoreditch High Street Overground.

Spitalfields Market.

Open noon-2pm, 5-9pm Mon; 5-9pm Wed; noon-4pmSun. **Admission** £10 Sun, noon-2pm Mon, £5 reductions; £15 Mon, Wed evenings. **Map** p202 C4 ➋
The ten rooms of this original Huguenot house have been decked out to recreate vivid snapshots of daily life in Spitalfields between 1724 and 1914. A tour through the compelling 'still-life drama', as American creator Dennis Severs dubbed it, takes you through the cellar, kitchen, dining room, smoking room and upstairs to the bedrooms. With hearth and candles burning, smells lingering and objects scattered apparently haphazardly, it feels as though the inhabitants have deserted the building only moments before you arrived.

Restaurants

Poppies
6-8 Hanbury Street, E1 6QR (7247 0892, www.poppiesfishandchips.co.uk). Liverpool Street tube/rail or Shoreditch High Street Overground. **Meals served** 11am-11pm Mon-Thur; 11am-11.30pm Fri, Sat; 11am-10.30pm Sun. **Main courses** £7.90-£15.90. **Map** p202 D4 ➌
Fish & chips
Poppies' pick and mix assortment of shiny British kitsch – including a jukebox, mini red telephone box and a monochrome photo of heart-throb Cliff Richard – makes it look like a simulation of a fish and chip shop. But the food on the plate is excellent, and offered grilled as well as fried. Extending beyond the staples of cod and haddock, the menu encompasses mackerel, seafood platters and jellied eels. The bill, however, gives the game away – Poppies is a cut above the average chippie. It's spawned a second branch in Camden: not surprising, since this is as good as fish and chips gets.
Other location 30 Hawley Crescent, Camden, NW1 8NP (7267 0440).

Rosa's
12 Hanbury Street, E1 6QR (7247 1093, www. rosasthaicafe.com). Liverpool Street tube/rail or Shoreditch High Street Overground. **Meals served** 11am-10.30pm Mon-Thur; 11am-11pm Fri, Sat; 10.30am-10.30pm Sun. **Main courses** £7.50-£16.50. **Map** p202 C4 ➍ Thai
The original branch of Rosa's plays host to a vibrant young crowd of visiting tourists and local hipsters. The dining room is clean and contemporary, and the usual Thai repertoire is executed competently: stir-fried slices of European aubergine coated in a sweet, salty soya and yellow-bean sauce, and laced with plenty of ginger and black pepper, or a salad of chargrilled beef strips in chilli dressing. Service is mostly quick and efficient.
Other locations 48 Dean Street, Soho, W1D 5BF (7494 1638); 23A Ganton Street, Soho, W1F 9BW (7287 9617); 1st floor, Westfield Stratford City, E15 1AA.

Pubs & Bars

Commercial Tavern
142 Commercial Street, E1 6NU (7247 1888). Liverpool Street tube/rail or Shoreditch High Street Overground. **Open** 11am-11pm Mon-Sat; noon-10.30pm Sun. **Map** p202 C4 ➎
The inspired chaos of retro-eccentric decor and warm, inclusive atmosphere make this landmark flat-iron corner pub very likeable. It seems to have escaped the attentions of the masses, perhaps because of the absence of wall-to-wall lager pumps in favour of some proper real ale. The bar is made up of colourful art deco tiles, and there's a decorative playfulness throughout; it's a great example of how a historic pub can be lit up with new life.

Mayor of Scaredy Cat Town
12-16 Artillery Lane, E1 7LS (7078 9639, www. themayorofscaredycattown.com). Liverpool Street tube/rail or Shoreditch High Street Overground. **Open** 5pm-midnight Mon-Thur; 3pm-midnight Fri; noon-midnight Sat; noon-10.30pm Sun. **Map** p202 C4 ➏
Part of the trend for 'secret' speakeasies, this one is a basement bar beneath the Breakfast Club. The entrance is the one that looks like a big Smeg fridge door. Go inside and you'll find a quirky, dimly lit cocktail bar clad in exposed brick and wood: it's all a bit like a cabin from Twin Peaks. The drinks menu makes an amusing mockery of more self-conscious 'underground' venues. The cocktails– classics and house specials – are well crafted on the whole.

Shops & Services

Mercantile London
17 Lamb Street, E1 6EA (7377 8926, www. themercantilelondon.com). Shoreditch High Street Overground. **Open** 11am-7pm Mon-Sat; 11am-6pm Sun. **Map** p202 C4 ➐ Fashion
This independent boutique, full of independent labels (not to mention an in-store dog called Robert), is enough to restore your faith in the future of London retail. Founder Debra McCann has a good eye for striking fashion that ordinary women will covet, so labels err on the side of tasteful rather than daft – think high-waisted jeans, batwing silk blouses and cool ankle boots at sensible prices (£70-100 for a silk top, £150 for well-made leather boots).
▶ Just round the corner is the Topman General Store (98 Commercial Street, E1 6LZ, 7377 2671).

BRICK LANE
Aldgate East tube or Shoreditch High Street Overground.

Join the crowds flowing east from Spitalfields Market along Hanbury Street at the weekend, and the direction you turn at the end determines

EXPLORE

EXPLORE

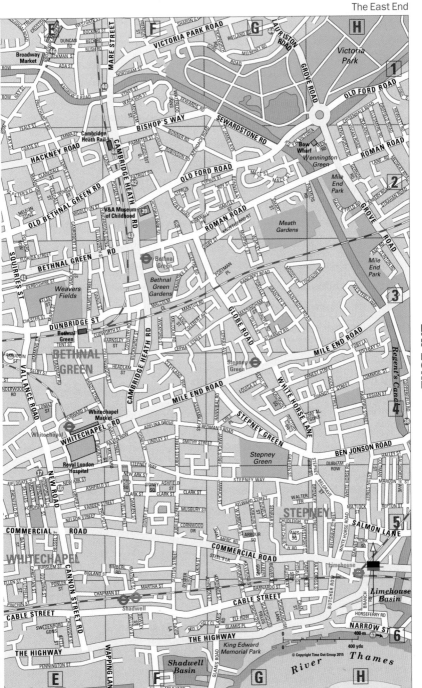

EXPLORE

which Brick Lane you see. Turn right and you'll know you're in 'Banglatown', the name adopted by the ward back in 2002: until you hit the bland modern offices beside the kitsch Banglatown arch, it's almost all Bangladeshi cafés, curry houses, grocery stores, money-transfer services and sari shops – plus the **Pride of Spitalfields** (3 Heneage Street, 7247 8933), an old-style East End boozer serving ale to all-comers.

Despite the street's global reputation for Indian food, most of the food on offer in the street is disappointing, but nearby are some good restaurants: try **Needoo Grill** or **Tayyabs**. Alternatively, opt for Bengali sweets from the **Madhubon Sweet Centre** at no.42.

Between Fournier Street and Princelet Street, **Jamme Masjid Mosque** is a key symbol of Brick Lane's hybridity. It began as a Huguenot chapel, became a synagogue and was converted, in 1976, into a mosque – in other words, immigrant communities have been layering their experiences on this street at least since 1572, when the St Bartholomew's Day Massacre forced many French Huguenots into exile.

The newest layer is boho gentrification. On Sunday, there's the lively street market, complemented by the trendier UpMarket and Backyard Market (for arts and crafts), both held in the **Old Truman Brewery** (nos.91-95). Pedestrianised Dray Walk, full of hip independent businesses, is crowded every day. Heading north on Brick Lane, you'll find bars, cafés and vintage fashion shops.

Restaurants

★ Brick Lane Beigel Bake

159 Brick Lane, E1 6SB (7729 0616). Shoreditch High Street Overground. **Open** 24hrs daily. **Bagels** £1.95-£5.95. **No credit cards.** Map p202 D3 ❽ Jewish

This little East End institution rolls out perfect bagels (egg, cream cheese, salt beef, at seriously low prices), good bread and moreish cakes. Even at 3am, fresh-baked goods are pulled from the ovens at the back; no wonder the queue for bagels trails out the door when the local bars and clubs close. Note that it's essentially a takeaway operation.

Chez Elles

45 Brick Lane, E1 6PU (7247 9699, www. chezellesbistroquet.co.uk). Aldgate East tube or Shoreditch High Street Overground. **Open** 5.30-10.30pm Tue, Sat; noon-3pm, 5.30-10.30pm Wed-Fri; 11am-5pm Sun. **Main courses** £12.50-£22.50. Map p202 D4 ❾ Bistro

Chez Elles narrowly misses being a parody of itself, saved by fantastic cooking and an unexpected location – somehow, the cutesy Parisian hipster vibe grates far less on Brick Lane than it would elsewhere. There's coffee and own-made cakes at

a counter propping up (French) regulars, and a disarming, heavily accented welcome. The menu is beyond reproach: smoky, spicy, peppery charcuterie with lots of bread; soft, nutty snails swimming in garlic butter; and a seriously good, tender bavette steak with triple-fried chips.

Lady Dinah's Cat Emporium

152-154 Bethnal Green Road, E2 6DG (7729 0953, http://ladydinahs.com). Shoreditch High Street Overground. **Open/main courses** check website for details. Map p202 D3 ❿ Café

A Taiwanese concept popularised in Tokyo, the cat café is finally arriving in London. Moggy-lover Lauren Pears crowdfunded £108,000 through IndieGoGo to provide urbanites with cats to pet while they enjoy tea and cakes, simultaneously giving lonely pussies a loving, comfortable home.

Shops & Services

Bernstock Speirs

234 Brick Lane, E2 7EB (7739 7385, www. bernstockspeirs.com). Shoreditch High Street Overground. **Open** 10am-6pm Mon-Fri; 11am-5pm Sat, Sun. Map p202 D3 ⓫ Accessories

Paul Bernstock and Thelma Speirs's unconventional hats for men and women have a loyal following, being both wearable and fashion-forward. Past ranges have included collaborations with Peter Jensen and Emma Cook.

Blitz

55-59 Hanbury Street, E1 5JP (7377 0730, www.blitzlondon.co.uk). Shoreditch High Street Overground. **Open** 11am-7pm Mon-Wed; 11am-8pm Thur-Sat; 11am-5pm Sun. Map p202 D4 ⓬ Fashion

Blitz puts the other vintage shops in the capital to shame. This is a vintage department store, covering all floors of a glorious old furniture factory. The building itself is jaw-dropping, and has been renovated beautifully by the Blitz team. There's a furniture selection from Broadway Market's the Dog & Wardrobe, an accessories floor, a book collection and rails and rails of neatly presented fashion. Buyers Jan Skinners and John Howlin look to nearby Brick Lane for inspiration, which means the selection is all killer and no filler – and cleaned, steamed and folded before it hits the shop floor.

▶ *Although overshadowed by Blitz, Beyond Retro (112 Cheshire Street, E2 6EJ, 7613 3636, www. beyondretro.com) is worth a rummage. It's off the north end of Brick Lane.*

★ Rough Trade East

Dray Walk, Old Truman Brewery, 91 Brick Lane, E1 6QL (7392 7788, www.roughtrade.com). Shoreditch High Street Overground. **Open** 8am-9pm Mon-Thur; 8am-8pm Fri; 10am-8pm Sat; 11am-7pm Sun. Map p202 D4 ⓭ Books & music

Brick Lane

Indie music label Rough Trade's 5,000sq ft record store, café and gig space offers a dizzying range of vinyl and CDs, spanning punk, indie, dub, soul, electronica and more. With 16 listening posts and a stage for live sets, this is close to musical nirvana. **Other location** 130 Talbot Road, Notting Hill, W11 1JA (7229 8541).

Tatty Devine

236 Brick Lane, E2 7EB (7739 9191, www.tatty devine.com). Shoreditch High Street Overground. **Open** 10am-6.30pm Mon-Fri; 11am-6pm Sat; 10am-5pm Sun. **Map** p202 D3 ⑭ **Jewellery**
Shoreditch pioneers Tatty Devine (AKA art-school pals Harriet Vine and Rosie Wolfenden) began making and selling their distinctive perspex jewellery from this bijou boutique in 2001. Since then, they've opened a store in Covent Garden's Monmouth Street (*see p106*), collaborated with everyone from Ashish to Rob Ryan, and seen their designs sold in over 200 shops worldwide. As well as now-classic perspex pieces such as the anchor and dinosaur necklaces and volume-control brooch, you'll find rings, cufflinks and earrings in enamel, wood and silver.

WHITECHAPEL

Aldgate East tube or Whitechapel tube/ Overground.

Not one of London's prettier thoroughfares, busy but anonymous Whitechapel Road sets the tone for this area. One bright spot is **Whitechapel Gallery**, west from the foot of Brick Lane, while a little to the east, the **Whitechapel Bell Foundry** (nos.32 & 34, 7247 2599,

www.whitechapelbellfoundry.co.uk) continues to manufacture bells, as it has since 1420. It famously produced Philadelphia's Liberty Bell and 'Big Ben'. To join one of the fascinating Saturday tours, you'll have to reserve a place (usually well in advance).

At Whitechapel's foremost place of worship, it isn't bells but a muezzin that summons the faithful each Friday: the **East London Mosque**, founded elsewhere in 1910 and now the focal point for the largest Muslim community in Britain, can accommodate 10,000 worshippers. Behind is Fieldgate Street and the dark mass of **Tower House**, a former doss house whose 700 rooms have, inevitably, been redeveloped into flats. This 'sought after converted warehouse building' was a dismal – but decidedly cheaper – proposition when Joseph Stalin and George Orwell (researching his book *Down and Out in Paris and London*) kipped here for pennies. The red-brick alleys give a flavour of what Victorian Whitechapel must have been like.

East again is the frontage of the Royal London Hospital – the hospital itself is now in that monstrous blue tower block – and behind it, in a small crypt on Newark Street, the **Royal London Hospital Archives & Museum** (7377 7608, closed Mon, Sat & Sun). Inside are reproduction letters from Jack the Ripper (including the notorious missive 'From Hell', delivered with an enclosed portion of human kidney) and information on Joseph Merrick, the 'Elephant Man', rescued by Royal London surgeon Sir Frederick Treves. Behind the hospital is the high-tech **Centre of the Cell** (4 Newark Street, 7882 2562, www.centreofthecell.org), which gives visitors a lively, interactive insight into cell biology in a purpose-built pod, suspended over labs investigating cancer and tuberculosis.

Sights & Museums

★ FREE Whitechapel Gallery

77-82 Whitechapel High Street, E1 7QX (7522 7888, www.whitechapelgallery.org). Aldgate East tube. **Open** 11am-6pm Tue, Wed, Fri-Sun; 11am-9pm Thur. **Admission** free. *Temporary exhibitions* vary. **Map** p202 D5 ⑮
This East End stalwart reopened in 2009, following a major redesign that saw the Grade II-listed building expand into the similarly historic former library next door – rather brilliantly, the architects left the two buildings stylistically distinct rather than trying to smooth out their differences. As well as nearly tripling its exhibition space, the Whitechapel gave itself a research centre and archives, plus a café/bar. It looks set to improve a stellar reputation as a contemporary-art pioneer built on shows of Picasso – *Guernica* was shown here in 1939 – Jackson Pollock, Mark Rothko and Frida Kahlo. With no permanent collection, there's a rolling programme

EXPLORE

of temporary shows. An increasing number of artists have contributed permanently to the fabric of the building: a few years back, Rachel Whiteread added a lovely frieze with gold vine leaves to a space on the front of the gallery.

Restaurants

Needoo Grill

85-87 New Road, E1 1HH (7247 0648, www. needoogrill.co.uk). Whitechapel tube/Overground. **Open** noon-11.30pm daily. **Main courses** £5.50-£15. **Map** p203 E5 ⑯ **Pakistani**

This squashed space doesn't suffer from the same problem of endless queues as its rival Tayyabs, though you will usually have a wait, but it is just as gaudy. Bright red walls, leather benches and blaring flatscreen TVs are the order of the day, yet with curries this good, the decor just fades into the background. What you get are succulent karahi dishes and specials that include nihari (lamb on the bone) and a very passable biriani. Service is swift and friendly, and it's hard to argue with the appeal of BYOB and curries of such high standard.

Tayyabs

83-89 Fieldgate Street, E1 1JU (7247 9543, www. tayyabs.co.uk). Aldgate East tube or Whitechapel tube/Overground. **Open** noon-11.30pm daily. **Main courses** £6-£14. **Map** p203 E5 ⑰ **Pakistani**

Tayyabs is a full-on, hectic, loud, in-and-out sort of place, and if you come here without booking, expect to wait up to an hour for a table. But we recommend this Punjabi stalwart because of the cheapness and unreserved boldness of the food. Fiery grilled lamb chops are a must. The rest of the menu is all about rich dhals and masala channa; unctuous, slow-cooked lamb curries; and good versions of North Indian staples – spice-rubbed tikka, hot, buttery breads and juicy kebabs. The corkage-free BYO policy doesn't do its popularity any harm either.

SHOREDITCH & HOXTON

Old Street tube/rail, or Hoxton or Shoreditch High Street Overground.

The story is familiar: in the 1980s, impecunious artists moved into the derelict warehouses in the triangle formed by Old Street, Shoreditch High Street and Great Eastern Street, and quickly turned it into the place to be. Rising rents have since driven many of the artists further east, but they've been replaced by the tech-hip denizens of 'silicon roundabout'. The area around Old Street roundabout has become a focus for digital start-ups, the beginning of **East London Tech City** (www.techcityuk.com).

Nightlife permeates the area (linking conveniently to Brick Lane), with centres on Curtain Road, the lower end of Kingsland Road

Geffrye Museum.

and around Hoxton Square. But the nature of the scene has changed dramatically: growing up in some people's eyes, losing its edge for others. New hotels and smart shops are opening, cocktail bars are more prevalent than bug-eyed rave holes, and there's commercial culture of a different type to come, following the discovery of the remains of the Curtain Theatre behind a pub on Plough Yard, south of Great Eastern Street. The Curtain, which opened in 1577, is intimately connected to Shakespeare's early career, probably hosting the première of *Romeo and Juliet*. Plans for the site – a 250-seat outdoor auditorium (managed by the people at the Globe; *see p57*) and a Shakespeare museum – are under way.

At present, apart from seemingly countless galleries – Wharf Road neighbours **Parasol Unit** (no.14, N1 7RW, 7490 7373, www.parasol-unit.org) and **Victoria Miro** (no.16, N1 7RW, 7336 8109, www.victoria-miro.com) and not-for-profit pioneer **Raven Row** (56 Artillery Lane, E1 7LS, 7377 4300, www.ravenrow.org) are notable – the area's sole bona fide tourist attraction is the exquisite **Geffrye Museum**, a short walk north up Kingsland Road. The surrounding area is dense with good, cheap Vietnamese restaurants (try **Sông Quê**).

To the east, it's a short walk to **Columbia Road flower market**.

Sights & Museums

★ FREE Geffrye Museum

136 Kingsland Road, E2 8EA (7739 9893, www. geffrye-museum.org.uk). Hoxton Overground.

Open 10am-5pm Tue-Sun. *Almshouse tours* 1st Sat, 1st & 3rd Tue, Wed of mth. **Admission** free; donations appreciated. *Almshouse tours* £3; free under-16s. **Map** p202 C2 ⑱

Housed in a set of 18th-century almshouses, the Geffrye Museum has for 100 years offered a vivid physical history of the English interior. Displaying original furniture, paintings, textiles and decorative arts, the museum recreates a sequence of typical middle-class living rooms from 1600 to the present. It's an oddly interesting way to take in domestic history, with any number of intriguing details to catch your eye – from a bell jar of stuffed birds to a particular decorative flourish on a chair. There's an airy restaurant overlooking the lovely gardens, which include a walled plot for herbs and a chronological series in different historical styles.

Restaurants

8 Hoxton Square

8 Hoxton Square, N1 6NU (7729 4232, www.8hoxtonsquare.com). Old Street tube. **Open** noon-11pm Mon-Fri; 10am-11pm Sat; 10am-5pm Sun. **Main courses** £16-£19. **Map** p202 B3 ⑲
Modern European

An outpost of the no-reservations 10 Greek Street (*see p124*), one of Soho's most popular restaurants, 8 Hoxton Square is targeted at those who are looking for something more interesting than beers and burgers, something that's more destination than pit stop. It combines great food, great wines and great service – a common goal, but hard to realise.

Albion

2-4 Boundary Street, E2 7DD (7729 1051, www.albioncaff.co.uk). Shoreditch High Street Overground. **Open** 8am-late daily. **Main courses** £8.75-£13. **Map** p202 C3 ⑳ **British**

Albion may describe itself as a 'caff', but no greasy spoon in London was ever designed and owned by Terence Conran. But, in spirit at least, it is something approaching a café for 21st-century Shoreditch – a place where locals can drop in for a casual breakfast, lunch or dinner, or a cup of tea and a slice of cake. Menu descriptions suggest dishes wouldn't seem out of place in your average caff too – ham and mustard sandwich, devilled kidneys, sausage and mash, fish and chips. They're all prepared with top-quality ingredients, great care and an eye for presentation. A new branch, Albion NEO (*see p58*), has opened near Tate Modern, and there's a swanky hotel upstairs (*see p361* **Boundary**).

Beagle

397-400 Geffrye Street, E2 8HZ (7613 2967, www.beaglelondon.co.uk). Hoxton Overground. **Open** *Bar* noon-midnight Mon-Fri; 11am-midnight Sat, Sun. *Restaurant* noon-3pm, 6-10.30pm Mon-Fri; 11am-3pm, 6-10.30pm Sat; 11am-5pm Sun. **Main courses** £13.50-£18. **Map** p202 C2 ㉑ **British**

Beagle is a smart café, bar and restaurant in the railway arches below Hoxton station. There's a bar, serving sophisticated cocktails, leading into a dining area with open kitchen. A back-to-basics British ethos governs the food. Grilled cuttlefish comes with new potatoes and a salsa-like coriander pesto. Pigeon terrine, made in-house, is well textured and has a slightly gamey flavour. Beagle deserves success for making E2 a culinary destination beyond the area's famous budget Vietnamese cafés.

★ Hoi Polloi

Ace Hotel, 100 Shoreditch High Street, E1 6JQ (8880 6100, www.hoi-polloi.co.uk). Shoreditch High Street Overground. **Open** 7am-midnight Mon-Wed, Sun; 7am-1am Thur-Sat. **Main courses** £14-£25. **Map** p202 C3 ㉒ **Brasserie**

EXPLORE

8 Hoxton Square.

You enter this restaurant via the tiny flower shop of the Ace Hotel (*see p361*), to find yourself amid retro and contemporary styling that wouldn't look out of place on a 1950s Scandinavian cruise ship. The casual and sneaker-clad service is notably smooth and well informed. The music (a mix of retro '80s pop and US alt electronic) for a mercy isn't too loud, allowing attention to focus on conversation – and on the food. Covering breakfast, lunch, snacks, cocktails and dinner, the dishes are British, seasonal and juxtapose flavours in modern but not outlandish ways that leave you craving more. The small bar is a destination in itself, with cocktails that bear the

usual silly names but in themselves are appealing combinations of modish spirits.

Lyle's
The Tea Building, 56 Shoreditch High Street, E1 6JJ (3019 2468, http://lyleslondon.com). Shoreditch High Street Overground. **Open** 8am-11pm Mon-Fri; 6-11pm Sat. *Food served* noon-2.30pm, 6-10pm. **Main courses** £.6.50-£17. **Map** p202 C3 ㉕
British
Dinner at Lyle's is a long, leisurely affair. You can book and stay as long as you like, as there's no turning tables. The pricing is fair: the no-choice menu

---

HE'S NOT LYAN

Ryan Chetiyawardana – Mr Lyan – runs two of London's finest cocktail bars.

When Ryan Chetiyawardana opened his first cocktail bar in 2013, **White Lyan** (*see p209*), the focus of the reviews was narrow: this is the bar that doesn't use ice. That shows how extraordinary it is to dispense altogether with such a time-honoured way of chilling drinks, but it's not even the most unusual thing about the bar. Not only has Chetiyawardana – in his mixologist persona as Mr Lyan – chucked out the frozen water, he also employs no citrus, sugar, fruit or other perishables, and next to no branded products. Here the flavour of the single red and white wine on offer can be modified by an 'oak distillate'; the only lager can be pepped up with a hop 'atomisation'.

This is a bar that functions through an arsenal of pre-made, custom products that represent hours of labour by Ryan and his team. This means there's almost total control of the flavour of every drink, something that's hard to achieve when ice is slowly dissolving water into your drink and even humble limes will vary considerably in taste and juiciness. The concoctions that arrive look surprisingly simple – no clouds of dry ice or outlandish decoration – leaving the wizardry packed into them to reveal itself to your palate rather than your eyes. And because the hard work has been done before opening, there's a lot less shaking and twizzling when you order. The bartenders are thus free to chat, which is something important for Chetiyawardana: he trained as a chef, but didn't like being locked in the kitchen away from his guests, so a career behind the bar beckoned.

After White Lyan's success, he pushed things a little further in 2014 when he opened his second bar, **Dandelyan** (*see p59*), in a classy central London hotel with a great Thameside location. The techniques were

the similar, but this time the emphasis was on the botanicals – everything has a hint of the garden, with versions of even classic drinks haunted by the countryside.

A typical White Lyan drink might be a Moby Dick Sazerac of rye whiskey, Peychaud's bitters, absinthe-soaked rice paper and, to add body, ambergris – yes, the sperm whale secretion; at Dandelyan, the Ford & Warner, a fruitily fearsome blend of gin, 'bittered blackcurrant', dandelion flower and lemon, garnished with a frozen cube of blackcurrant sorbet. If these don't pique any interest, then perhaps a Bloody Mary thrown together in the local pub would be more your style?

EXPLORE

costs £39, which gets you five small courses (plus bread, petits fours and filtered tap water), served in a drawn-out procession. The chef is James Lowe, one of the most talented cooks in town; the sweet staff know their food, and the semi-industrial setting (polished concrete floors, exposed girders, whitewashed brick walls) makes for a thoroughly relaxing setting. Set aside two and a half hours or so – then settle in and enjoy your meal.

Pizza East

56 Shoreditch High Street, E1 6JJ (7729 1888, www.pizzaeast.com). Shoreditch High Street Overground. **Open** noon-midnight Mon-Wed; noon-1am Thur; noon-2am Fri; 10am-2am Sat; 10am-midnight Sun. **Main courses** £8-£18. **Map** p202 C3 ㉔ Pizza

This huge warehouse space features sharing benches, industrial decor and more bare brick and concrete than your average multistorey car park. It's busy, noisy and dark. The regularly changing menu, however, remains inventive and original. Pizza bases are crusty around the outside and thin and gorgeously saturated in the middle, and toppings employ fresh, quality ingredients. Antipasti and salads are also good.
Other locations 310 Portobello Road, Ladbroke Grove, W10 5TA (8969 4500); 79 Highgate Road, Kentish Town, NW5 1TL (3310 2000).

Sông Quê

134 Kingsland Road, E2 8DY (7613 3222, www.songque.co.uk). Hoxton Overground. **Open** noon-3pm, 5.30-11pm Mon-Fri; noon-11pm Sat; noon-10.30pm Sun. **Main courses** £7.80-£15.20. **Map** p202 C2 ㉕ Vietnamese

This is still the undoubted star of the Kingsland Road Vietnamese scene. Big, light, buzzy (if slightly resembling a school canteen), Sông Quê is constantly packed with customers, including many families and a good showing of Vietnamese locals. Flavours are full and true, and textures perfect, bringing the best out of each dish. Fans claim the kitchen makes the best pho in London. It's very conveniently located for a meal after visiting the Geffrye Museum.

Pubs & Bars

Late-night hangout **Charlie Wright's International Bar** (*see p277*) is at least as much about drinking as it is about music, and there's music, food and booze at Concrete, beneath **Pizza East** (*see above*).

Book Club

100-106 Leonard Street, EC2A 4RH (7684 8618, www.wearetbc.com). Old Street tube/rail or Shoreditch High Street Overground. **Open** 8am-midnight Mon-Wed; 8am-2am Thur, Fri; 10am-2am Sat; 10am-midnight Sun. **Admission** *Club* free-£12. **Map** p202 B3 ㉖

Behind the sedate name is one of the most consistently creative cocktail bars in London. You could visit for the drinks alone: cocktails come with names like Don't Go To Dalston. Or – and this is what sets Book Club apart – you could visit for the packed timetable of events, which includes bands, DJs, ping-pong tournaments, life drawing and classic video-game nights. The young and laid-back crowd that packs into the spacious artwork-dotted space is here for a bit of everything.

Happiness Forgets

8-9 Hoxton Square, N1 6NU (7613 0325, www.happinessforgets.com). Old Street tube/rail or Shoreditch High Street Overground. **Open** 5-11pm daily. **Map** p202 B3 ㉗

From the moment you walk in, staff here know how to make you happy and endeavour to do so. The short list of original cocktails is unfailingly good: lots of nice twists on classic ideas but never departing from the essential cocktail principles of balance, harmony and drinkability. Star turns: Mr McRae, Perfect Storm and Tokyo Collins. But the classics are brilliantly handled too, and the food is fabulous, as is the service. This very special place is not very large and plenty of people know about it, so booking is a good idea.

★ Wenlock Arms

26 Wenlock Road, N1 7TA (7608 3406, www.wenlockarms.com). Old Street tube/rail. **Open** noon-11pm Mon-Wed, Sun; noon-midnight Thur; noon-1am Fri, Sat. **Map** p202 A2 ㉘

On an unremarkable backstreet, this old pub was the tap for a nearby brewery, and poured its first pint in 1836; it closed with its parent brewery in the 1960s, then reopened in 1994, whereupon it won awards for the quality of its real ale and plaudits for the toastiness of its real fire. In 2010, threats of redevelopment began, but a sympathetic Hackney Council included it in a conservation area and in 2011 new owners stepped in: cue quality paintjob, new furniture and even more beer fonts. Now, the Wenlock is again the quintessence of all that is good about pubs – minimal decor, minimal food (salt-beef sandwiches, own-made scratchings) and a great range of ace beer.

★ White Lyan

153-155 Hoxton Street, N1 6PJ (3011 1153, www.whitelyan.com). Hoxton Overground. **Open** 6pm-late daily. **Map** p202 C2 ㉙

Comparing White Lyan to your local boozer is like comparing Heston Blumenthal's Fat Duck to a greasy spoon. This former pub doesn't give much away from the outside, but it's a genuine pioneer in a new cocktail movement. It doesn't use ice, nor citrus, sugar, fruit or other perishables, and next to no branded products. You can't order off menu, and there's only one of each colour of wine and one lager. Big fridges hold the pre-made products of hours of labour by cocktailian Ryan Chetiyawardana and his team (*see p208* **He's Not Lyan**). Spirits are especially made to order, or refined and 'rebuilt' using filtered water and distillations. All this results in unusual – and amazing – cocktails.

▶ *Chetiyawardana's newest enterprise is Dandelyan (see p59) on the South Bank.*

Worship Street Whistling Shop
63 Worship Street, EC2A 2DU (7247 0015, www. whistlingshop.com). Old Street tube/rail. **Open** 5pm-midnight Mon, Tue; 5pm-1am Wed, Thur; 5pm-2am Fri, Sat. **Map** p202 C4 ➌⓪
This cellar cocktail bar is decked out in what seems to be a speakeasy/Victorian mash-up (dark wood and lots of eccentric decorative touches). It makes much of its experimental techniques; if your curiosity is tickled by the sound of 'enzymes, acids, proteins and hydrocolloids', you're all set. The list is mercifully short, and classics are well handled. There's an extensive selection of spirits, including their own barrel-aged ones. Staff are skilled, friendly and eager to please.

Shops & Services

Once a shabby cut-through, **Redchurch Street** has gone on to become a strong contender for London's most interesting shopping street, starting with Aesop and Sunspel at one end, then a parade including Hostem, Maison Trois Garçons and Labour & Wait.

Boxpark
2-10 Bethnal Green Road, E1 6GY (7033 2899, www.boxpark.co.uk). Shoreditch High Street Overground. **Open** 11am-7pm Mon-Wed, Fri, Sat; 11am-8pm Thur; noon-6pm Sun. **Map** p202 C3 ➌➊ **Mall**
Refitted shipping containers plonked underneath the elevated Shoreditch High Street Overground station make up this contemporary 'shopping mall'. Installed in 2011, the units of Boxpark are full of high-street labels (Puma, Nike), but also contain an impressive array of independents, cafés and pop-ups. The food stalls open from 8am (10am Sun).

Celestine Eleven
4 Holywell Lane, EC2A 3ET (7729 2987, www.celestineeleven.com). Shoreditch High Street Overground. **Open** 11am-7pm Mon-Sat; noon-5pm Sun. **Map** p202 C3 ➌➋ **Fashion/health**
Tena Strok was a stylist before launching this whopping lifestyle store on a quiet backstreet, and her background shows in individualistic and exclusive buys that are a perfect fit for her earthy aesthetic. Talented London designers such as J.W. Anderson and Atalanta Weller are here, but so are amazing new finds like it-label-of-the-future Niels Peeraer. A library of beautiful coffee-table books and holistic treatment rooms cater for body and soul.

Goodhood Store
41 Coronet Street, N1 6HD (7729 3600, www.goodhood.co.uk). Old Street tube/rail. **Open** 10am-6pm Mon-Sat; 11am-5pm Sun. **Map** p202 B3 ➌➌ **Fashion**
A first stop for East End trendies, Goodhood is owned by streetwear obsessives Kyle and Jo. Japanese independent labels are well represented, while other covetable brands include Pendleton, Norse Projects and Wood Wood.

★ House of Hackney
131 Shoreditch High Street, E1 6JE (7739 3901, www.houseofhackney.com). Old Street tube/rail or Shoreditch High Street Overground. **Open** 10am-7pm Mon-Sat; 11am-5pm Sun. **Map** p202 C3 ➌➍ **Homewares**
House of Hackney has the makings of a new Liberty: buy your future design classics now, we say. This is one of the most gorgeous retail establishments to land in London in years – bedecked in the deliberately over-the-top juxtapositions of print-on-print-on-print that have made the brand's name, and with the entrance full of flowers. Upstairs, you'll find rolls of gorgeous paper, fabric, trays, mugs, fashion and collaborative designs with brands such as Puma; downstairs are generously proportioned sofas and plump armchairs in more-is-more combinations of print and texture.

★ Hoxton Street Monster Supplies
159 Hoxton Street, N1 6PJ (7729 4159, www.monstersupplies.org). Hoxton Overground. **Open** 1-5pm Tue-Fri; 11am-5pm Sat. **Map** p202 C2 ➌➎ **Children**
Purveyor of quality goods for monsters of every kind, this curious little shop stocks jars of Thickest Human Snot and pots of Salt Made From Tears of Anger – oddly reminiscent of lemon curd and of smoked sea salt. Follow the creepy music past a pinboard plastered with notices for missing brains and gravestone engravers, and you'll find a wall of cabinets piled high with Milk Tooth chocolate bars, Witches' Brew tea and Tinned Fear (a can of stories courtesy of Zadie Smith, Joe Dunthorne and Meg Rosoff). Proceeds support the Ministry of Stories' creative writing and mentoring centre for local children. Mind the invisible cat on your way out.

★ Labour & Wait
85 Redchurch Street, E2 7DJ (7729 6253, www.labourandwait.co.uk). Shoreditch High Street Overground. **Open** 11am-6pm Tue-Sun. **Map** p202 C3 ➌➏ **Homewares**
This retro-stylish store, on London's ultra-trendy Redchurch Street, sells the sort of things everybody would have had in their kitchen or pantry 60 years ago: functional domestic goods that have a timeless style. For the kitchen, there are some great simple classics such as enamel milk pans in retro pastels, and lovely 1950s-inspired Japanese teapots, and you

Boxpark.

can garden beautifully with ash-handled trowels.
Vintage Welsh wool blankets, classic toiletries,
and some great old-fashioned gifts, such as a
pinhole-camera kit and a lovely range of handmade
notebooks from Portugal, all conspire to make it
hard to leave empty-handed.

Sunspel

*7 Redchurch Street, E2 7DJ (7739 9729, www.
sunspel.com). Shoreditch High Street Overground.*
Open 11am-7pm Mon-Sat; noon-5pm Sun. **Map**
p202 C3 ⑨ **Fashion**
It may look like a trendy east London newcomer,
but Sunspel is actually a classic British label, which
has been producing quality menswear for over 150
years. It even claims to have introduced boxer shorts
to the UK. This corner space showcases the range of
underwear, T-shirts, merino wool knitwear and polo
shirts, as well as the smaller line of equally pared-
down womenswear.
Other locations 13-15 Chiltern Street,
Marylebone, W1U 7PG (7009 0650); 21A Jermyn
Street, St James's, SW1Y 6LT (7434 0974); 40 Old
Compton Street, Soho, W1D 4TU (7734 4491).

BETHNAL GREEN

*Bethnal Green tube/Overground, Cambridge
Heath Overground, or Mile End tube.*

Once a gracious suburb of spacious townhouses,
by the mid 19th century Bethnal Green was one
of the city's poorest neighbourhoods. As in
neighbouring Hoxton, a recent upturn in
fortunes has in part been occasioned by Bethnal
Green's adoption as home by a new generation
of artists, attracted by the low rents resulting
from the area's longstanding misfortunes. The
Maureen Paley gallery in Herald Street (no.21)
remains the key venue, but the new Bethnal
Green is typified by places such as **Herald
Street** (no.2), just down the road, and the arrival
of the ambitious **Town Hall Hotel** (*see p361*)
and its **Typing Room** restaurant. Then take a

seat at **E Pellicci**, the exemplary traditional
London caff, for a taste of the old Bethnal Green.
    The **V&A Museum of Childhood** is close
to Bethnal Green tube station, but the area's other
main attraction is a bit of a walk away (almost
in Shoreditch). Nonetheless, a visit to the weekly
Columbia Road flower market is a lovely
way to fritter away a Sunday morning. A
microcosmic retail community has grown up
around the market: try **Treacle** (nos.110-112,
7729 0538) for groovy crockery and cupcakes;
Angela Flanders (no.96, 7739 7555) for
perfume; and **Marcos & Trump** (no.145,
7739 9008) for vintage fashion.

Sights & Museums

FREE Ragged School Museum
*46-50 Copperfield Road, E3 4RR (8980 6405,
www.raggedschoolmuseum.org.uk). Mile End tube.*
Open 10am-5pm Wed, Thur; 2-5pm 1st Sun of mth.
Tours by appt. **Admission** free; donations
appreciated. **Map** p203 H4 ㊳
Ragged schools were an early experiment in public
education: they provided tuition, food and clothes
for destitute children. This one was the largest in
London, and Dr Barnardo himself taught here. It's
now a sweet local museum that contains complete
mock-ups of a ragged classroom and Edwardian
kitchen, with displays on vanished local history.

★ FREE V&A Museum of Childhood
*Cambridge Heath Road, E2 9PA (8983 5200, www.
vam.ac.uk/moc). Bethnal Green tube/Overground or
Cambridge Heath Overground.* **Open** 10am-5.45pm
daily. **Admission** free; donations appreciated.
Map p203 F2 ㊴
Home to one of the world's finest collections of
children's toys, dolls' houses, games and costumes,
the Museum of Childhood shines brighter than ever
after extensive refurbishment, which has given
it an impressive entrance. Part of the Victoria &
Albert Museum, the museum has been amassing
childhood-related objects since 1872 and continues

to do so, with *Incredibles* figures complementing bonkers 1970s puppets, Barbie dolls and Victorian praxinoscopes. The museum has lots of hands-on stuff for kids dotted about the many cases of historic artefacts. Regular exhibitions are held upstairs, while the café helps to revive flagging grown-ups.

Viktor Wynd Museum of Curiosities

11 Mare Street, E8 4RP (7998 3617, www. thelasttuesdaysociety.org). Bethnal Green tube/ Overground. **Open** 11am-10pm Wed-Sun. **Admission** varies; check website for details. **Map** p203 F1 ⑩

This oddity is both on the art circuit and determinedly off any beaten track. Peek through the windows and you'll see a world in which velvet-cloaked Victorians might reside. Entering the shop, which is also the spiritual home of the esoterically minded Last Tuesday Society, reveals a wunderkammer of shells, skulls, taxidermy specimens and assorted weirdness. Art gets a designated space in the first-floor gallery, where the shows tend towards the eerily surreal. There's a cocktail bar and café if you need bracing up again.

Restaurants

★ E Pellicci

332 Bethnal Green Road, E2 0AG (7739 4873). Bethnal Green tube/Overground or bus 8. **Open** 7am-4pm Mon-Sat. **Main courses** £5.50-£8.20. **No credit cards. Map** p203 E3 ㉑ **Café**

You go to Pellicci's as much for the atmosphere as for the food, although the food is more than edible. Opened in 1900, and still in the hands of the same family, this Bethnal Green landmark has chrome and Vitrolite outside, wood panelling with deco marquetry, Formica tabletops and stained glass within – it earned the café a Grade-II listing in 2005. Fry-ups are first rate, and the fish and chips, daily grills and Italian specials aren't half bad either.

★ Typing Room

Town Hall Hotel, Patriot Square, E2 9NF (7871 0461, www.typingroom.com). Bethnal Green tube/ Overground or Cambridge Heath Overground. **Open** 6-10pm Tue; noon-2.30pm, 6-10pm Wed-Sat. **Tasting menu** £60 5 courses; £75 7 courses. **Map** p203 F2 ㉒ **Modern European**

Jason Atherton has opened a surprising number of London's best new restaurants and bars, Pollen Street Social (*see p118*) and City Social Bar (*see p188*) among them. Could Typing Room become the best of all? It has the right ingredients. Under the careful eyes of executive chef Lee Westcott, dishes are so exquisitely intricate that it almost seems a pity to eat them. Service is warm and professional. The setting, too, is quietly stylish: teal walls, muted greys, touches of elegant white marble in a hotel (*see p361*) that's surprisingly refined for the location. This is the best restaurant in east London just now.

Typing Room.

Pubs & Bars

Mission

250 Paradise Row, E2 9LE (7613 0478, www. missione2.com). Bethnal Green tube/Overground. **Open** 6pm-midnight Mon; noon-midnight Tue-Fri; 10am-midnight Sat, Sun. **Map** p203 F2 ㊸

The Mission lies in a railway arch, low lit in the evenings, with a cathedral-like vaulted ceiling the colour of Carrara marble. The walls are wood-panelled, a real palm tree soars to the roof, and a spacious courtyard faces the traffic-free road. The wine list has a score of wines daily, but they change frequently, so there's always something new served by the glass on each visit. Mission places as much emphasis on the kitchen as the grape, with chef James de Jong turning out sunny dishes (£13-£19 mains) that match the Californian wine country bottles.

Satan's Whiskers

343 Cambridge Heath Road, E2 9RA (7739 8362). Bethnal Green tube/Overground or Cambridge Heath Overground. **Open** 5pm-midnight daily. **Map** p203 F2 ㊹

Satan's Whiskers might sound like a Captain Haddock curse, but it refers to a classic cocktail containing gin, orange and vermouth topped with Grand Marnier and orange bitters. It's a staple on the otherwise daily changing menu here, along with seductive alternatives – this tiny bar was set up by three bartenders, and they really know their stuff. Leather booths, an illuminated ice box and taxidermy for decor all add to the atmosphere.

Shops & Services

★ Columbia Road Market
Columbia Road, Hoxton, E2 (www.columbiaroad. info). Hoxton Overground or bus 26, 48, 55. **Open** 8am-3pm Sun. **Map** p202 D2 ⓯ **Market**
On Sunday mornings, this unassuming East End street is transformed into a swathe of fabulous plant life and the air is fragrant with blooms and the shouts of old-school Cockney stallholders (most offering deals for 'a fiver'). But a visit here isn't only about flowers and pot plants: alongside the market is a growing number of shops selling everything from pottery and arty prints to cupcakes and perfume; don't miss Ryantown's delicate paper cut-outs at no.126 (7613 1510). Refuel at Jones Dairy (23 Ezra Street, 7739 5372, www.jonesdairy.co.uk).

NORTH OF REGENT'S CANAL

The area of London Fields, just over the canal, demonstrates Hackney's changing demographics. Once a failing fruit and veg market, **Broadway Market** is now brimming with young urbanites and trendy families.

From the south end of Broadway Market, you can walk east along the Regent's Canal to **Victoria Park**. Opened in 1845 to give the impoverished working classes access to green space, this sprawling, 290-acre oasis was designed by Sir James Pennethorne, a pupil of John Nash; its elegant landscaping (with rose garden and waterfowl lake) is reminiscent of Nash's Regent's Park (*see p197*). There's also a terrific lakeside café. At the eastern end of the park, across a nasty dual carriageway, is the mish-mash of artist-colonised post-industrial buildings that makes up **Hackney Wick**.

If you head west from Broadway Market, you'll soon find yourself under the Kingsland Road bridge, shortly followed by the 'Haggerston Riviera' – some cafés and restaurants fronting a surprisingly pleasant stretch of the Regent's Canal – and such Dalston favourites as the **Towpath** café (*see p237*).

Shops & Services

Broadway Market
E8 4QL (www.broadwaymarket.co.uk). London Fields Overground or bus 394. **Open** 9am-5pm Sat. **Map** p203 E1 ⓯ **Market**
The talk of summer 2014 was that we'd reached 'peak beard' – the moment when the trend of crazy facial hair went mainstream – but the hipsters of Broadway Market had been operating in that vicinity for years. The coolest and most ridiculous

of east London's young trendies can be found at this endearing market, where fruit-and-veg sellers trade alongside vintage clothes 'specialists'. It's as busy as a beehive, but the slew of cafés, pubs, restaurants and boutiques along the street – plus the market itself, plus the nearby Netil Market for further streetfood, plus Saturday's School Yard Market, plus the overspill of drunks and slumming may-do-wells on London Fields on anything that looks like a sunny day – is an education in new London.

▶ *If your tastes extend to the old East End, dig into some eels at F Cooke (9 Broadway Market, 7254 6458), a pie and mash place that's been in operation since the early 1900s.*

WAPPING & LIMEHOUSE

Just a few stops from where the DLR starts at Bank station is Shadwell, south of which is **Wapping**. In 1598, John Stowe described Wapping High Street as 'a filthy strait passage, with alleys of small tenements or cottages, inhabited by sailors' victuallers.' This can still just about be imagined as you walk along it now, flanked by tall Victorian warehouses. The historic **Town of Ramsgate** pub (no.62, 7481 8000), dating from 1545, helps. Here, 'hanging judge' George Jeffreys was captured in 1688, trying to escape to Europe in disguise as a woman. Privateer Captain William Kidd was executed in 1701 at Execution Dock, near Wapping New Stairs; the bodies of pirates were hanged from a gibbet until seven tides had washed over them. Further east, the touristy but atmospheric **Prospect of Whitby** (57 Wapping Wall, 7481 1095) dates from 1520 and counted Pepys and Dickens among its regulars. It has a riverside terrace and balcony outside, and a handsome pewter bar counter and flagstone floor within.

Pubs & Bars

Grapes
76 Narrow Street, E14 8BP (7987 4396, www. thegrapes.co.uk). Limehouse or Westferry DLR. **Open** noon-3pm, 5.30-11pm Mon-Wed; noon-11.30pm Thur-Sat; noon-10.30pm Sun. *Food served* noon-2.30pm, 6.30-9.30pm Mon-Fri; noon-9.30pm Sat; noon-3.30pm Sun. **Map** p203 H6 ⓱
If you're trying to evoke the feel of the Thames docks before their Disneyfication into Docklands, these narrow, ivy-covered and etched-glass 1720 riverside premises in Limehouse are a good place to start: the downstairs is all wood panels and nautical jetsam; upstairs is plainer, but it's easier to find seats for Sunday lunch. Expect good ales and a half-dozen wines of each colour by glass and bottle.

▶ *Nearby, Gordon Ramsay's gastropub, the Narrow (44 Narrow Street, E14 8DQ, 7592 7950, www.gordonramsay.com) has a good Thameside terrace as well as a wraparound conservatory.*

EXPLORE

Greenwich

Riverside Greenwich is an irresistible mixture of maritime, royal and horological history, a combination that earned it recognition as a UNESCO World Heritage Site, and in 2012 it was elevated to the status of a Royal Borough as part of the Queen's Jubilee celebrations.

Following a near catastrophic fire and many years of careful renovation, the beautiful tea clipper *Cutty Sark* is open again to the public. Just as much work has gone into the new galleries at the National Maritime Museum and they have brought this wonderful attraction back to prominence. Together with the *Cutty Sark*, the NMM is now one of a proud cluster of venues collectively known as the Royal Museums Greenwich. Also here is glorious Greenwich Park, home to the Royal Observatory & Planetarium, as well as the charming Queen's House. The views from the top of the hill are splendid and far-reaching. And few can resist the chance to straddle the prime meridian.

EXPLORE

National Maritime Museum.

Don't Miss

1 **National Maritime Museum** Now bigger and better than ever (p217).

2 **Cutty Sark** See the fully restored tea clipper from all angles (p216).

3 **O2 Arena** See your gig – then take a stroll right over the dome (p219).

4 **Royal Observatory & Planetarium** Two marvels on one site, plus a Prime photo-op (p218).

5 **Thames Clipper** Arrive at Maritime Greenwich in style – with regular services from central London (p216).

IN THE KNOW FANS OF TEA

The **Fan Museum** has a small tearoom, the Orangery. English cream teas are served here on Tuesdays and Sundays (2.15pm and 3.45pm, booking essential). The room overlooks a pretty garden, replete with Japanese themed paintings and fan-shaped flowerbeds.

ROYAL GREENWICH

Cutty Sark for Maritime Greenwich DLR or Greenwich DLR/rail.

Royalty has stalked this area since 1300, when Edward I stayed here. Henry VIII was born in Greenwich Palace; the palace was built on land that later contained Wren's Royal Naval Hospital, now the **Old Royal Naval College**. The college is now a very handy first port of call. Its Pepys Building not only contains the **Greenwich Tourist Information Centre** (0870 608 2000, www.greenwich.gov.uk), but is also the home of **Discover Greenwich**, which provides a great overview of the area's numerous attractions. Just opposite, shoppers swarm to **Greenwich Market**, a handsome 19th-century building sheltering a mixture of shops and stalls.

Near the DLR stop is Greenwich Pier; every 15 minutes (peak times), the popular and speedy **Thames Clipper** boats (0870 781 5049, www.thamesclippers.com) shuttle passengers to and from central London. This is where you'll find the *Cutty Sark*, as well as a domed structure that is the entrance to a Victorian **pedestrian tunnel** that emerges on the far side of the Thames in Island Gardens. The tunnel is rather dingy, due to incomplete repair work, but it's still fun to walk beneath the river.

At the north end of Greenwich Park are the **Queen's House** and **National Maritime Museum**, beyond which it's a ten-minute walk (or shorter shuttle-bus trip) up the steep slopes of Greenwich Park to the **Royal Observatory**. The building looks even more stunning at night, when the bright green Meridian Line Laser illuminates the path of the Prime Meridian across the London sky.

Sights & Museums

Cutty Sark

King William Walk, SE10 9HT (8858 2698, www.rmg.co.uk/cuttysark). Cutty Sark DLR. **Open** 10am-5pm daily. **Admission** £13.50; £7-£11.50 reductions; £24-£35 family; free under-5s. **Map** p217 B2 ❶

Built in Scotland in 1869, this tea clipper was the quickest in the business when she was launched in 1870 – renovation after the *Cutty Sark* went up in flames in 2007 was rather slower. But you can visit her once more (by timed tickets) in her permanent berth in a purpose-built dry dock beside the Thames. The ship is now raised three metres off the ground and surrounded by a dramatic glass 'skirt', which allows visitors to admire the hull from underneath for the first time – while sipping a cup of tea from the museum café, should they desire. Critics have objected that the glazed canopy obscures the elegant lines of the *Cutty Sark's* hull – as well as raising fears about the stresses that are being put on the elderly ship – but the visitor experience is much improved, with interactives giving context to a story of reckless, high-speed trade in tea, wine, spirits, beer, coal, jute, wool and castor oil. The sailing clippers were gradually put out of business by steamships: by 1922, the *Cutty Sark* was the last of her breed afloat. The space beneath the ship displays another lost tradition: an exhibit of more than 80 figureheads, including Florence Nightingale, William Wilberforce, Hiawatha and Sir Lancelot. ▶ *In a move not likely to win over the critics, the Cutty Sark Studio Theatre hosts comedy and other events in the ship's hull.*

★ FREE Discover Greenwich & the Old Royal Naval College

2 Cutty Sark Gardens, SE10 9NN (8269 4799, www.ornc.org). Cutty Sark DLR or Greenwich DLR/rail. **Open** 10am-5pm daily. *Tours* noon daily; other times by appt. **Admission** free. *Tours* £7.50. **Map** p217 B1 ❷

The block of the Old Royal Naval College nearest to the *Cutty Sark* is now the excellent Discover Greenwich. It's full of focused, informative exhibits on architecture and the building techniques of the surrounding buildings, the life of Greenwich pensioners, Tudor royalty and so forth, delivered with a real sense of fun: while grown-ups read about coade stone or scagliola (popular fake-stone building materials), for example, children can build their own chapel with soft bricks or try on a knight's helmet. There's also a well-stocked shop and a Tourist Information Centre.

It's a perfect introduction to the superb collection of buildings that make up the Naval College. Designed by Wren in 1694, with Hawksmoor and Vanbrugh helping to complete the project, it was originally a hospital for the relief and support of seamen and their dependants, with pensioners living here from 1705 to 1869, when the complex became the Royal Naval College. The Navy left in 1998, and the neoclassical buildings now house part of the University of Greenwich and Trinity College of Music. The public are allowed into the impressive rococo chapel, where there are free organ recitals, and the Painted Hall, a tribute to William and Mary that took Sir James Thornhill 19 years to complete. Nelson lay in state in the Painted Hall for three days in 1806, before being taken, in grand river procession, to St Paul's Cathedral for his funeral.

There's a lively events programme in the grounds, ranging from comedy shows and early music to weekend appearances from historic figures – costumed actors – ranging from Pepys and Sir James to the 'pirate queen' Grace O'Malley and Joe Brown, veteran of the Battle of Trafalgar.

Fan Museum
12 Crooms Hill, SE10 8ER (8305 1441, www. thefanmuseum.org.uk). Cutty Sark DLR or Greenwich DLR/rail. **Open** 11am-5pm Tue-Sat; noon-5pm Sun. **Admission** £4; £3 reductions; £10 family; free under-7s. **Map** p217 B2 ❸

The world's most important collection of hand-held fans is displayed in a pair of Georgian townhouses. There are about 3,500 fans, including some beauties in the Hélène Alexander collection, but not all are on

display at any one time. For details of fan-making workshops and exhibitions, see the website. There's also a lovely orangery serving afternoon tea.

★ FREE National Maritime Museum
Park Row, SE10 9NF (8858 4422, information 8312 6565, www.nmm.ac.uk). Cutty Sark DLR or Greenwich DLR/rail. **Open** 10am-5pm daily. *Tours* phone for details. **Admission** free; donations appreciated. *Temporary exhibitions* vary; check website for details. **Map** p217 B2 ❹

The world's largest maritime museum contains a huge store of creatively organised maritime art, cartography, models, interactives and regalia – and is even bigger since the impressive expansion in 2011 into the new Sammy Ofer Wing. Centred on Voyagers: Britons and the Sea – a collection of 200 artefacts, accompanied by an impressive audio-visual installation called the Wave – this extension also has the Compass Lounge (with

EXPLORE

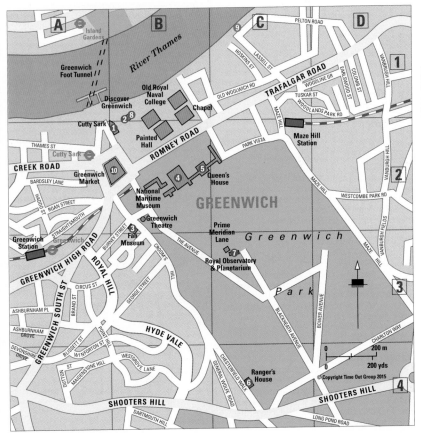

free Wi-Fi), where you can explore the collection using computers, and a brasserie, café and shop. Downstairs, the temporary gallery is building a reputation for compelling – and varied – exhibitions of historic art (Ansel Adams and Turner have both appeared here).

Ground-level galleries include Explorers, which covers great sea expeditions back to medieval times, and Maritime London, which concentrates on the city as a port. Upstairs is the Environment Gallery, which reveals our dependence on the health of the world's oceans. Level two holds the interactives: the Bridge has a ship simulator, All Hands lets children load cargo, and you can even try your hand as a ship's gunner. The Ship of War is the museum's superb collection of models, dating from 1660 to 1815, and the Atlantic: Slavery, Trade, Empires gallery looks at the transport of goods between Britain, Africa and the Americas during the 17th to 19th centuries.

More recent additions are the Great Map, a large interactive floor map of the oceans, and a Nelson, Navy, Nation gallery, which recalls the seaborne battles of the 18th century, and the glamour and gore of life as a naval officer at the time. Here, you'll find Nelson's Trafalgar uniform, blood-stained and with fatal bullet-hole, as well as a 3D reconstruction of him, as if laid in a coffin.

▶ *The main entrance (from Greenwich Park) is now overlooked by Yinka Shonibare's playful* Nelson's Ship in a Bottle, *formerly on show on the Fourth Plinth in Trafalgar Square; see p68.*

FREE Queen's House
Romney Road, SE10 9NF (8858 4422, www. nmm.ac.uk). Cutty Sark DLR or Greenwich DLR/ rail. **Open** *10am-5pm daily.* **Admission** *free.* **Map** p217 B2 ❺

The art collection of the National Maritime Museum is displayed in what was formerly the summer villa of Charles I's queen, Henrietta Maria. Completed in 1638 by Inigo Jones, the house has an interior as impressive as the paintings on the walls. As well as the stunning 1635 marble floor, look for Britain's first centrally unsupported spiral stair, fine painted woodwork and ceilings, and the proportions of the Great Hall – it is a perfect cube. The collection includes portraits of famous maritime figures and works by Hogarth and Gainsborough, as well as some arresting wartime art from the 20th century.

▶ *Among all the pictures of bluff seamen and naval cannonades, check out the exotic paintings from Captain Cook's explorations – mysterious creatures lurk in the depths.*

Ranger's House
Chesterfield Walk, SE10 8QX (8853 0035, www. english-heritage.org.uk). Blackheath rail, Cutty Sark DLR or bus 53. **Open** *Apr-Sept guided tours only. Tours 11.30am, 2.30pm Mon-Wed, Sun. Closed Oct-Mar.* **Tickets** *£6.90; £4.10-£6.20 reductions; free under-5s.* **Map** p217 C4 ❻

The house of the 'Ranger of Greenwich Park' (a post held by George III's niece, Princess Sophia Matilda, from 1815) now contains the treasure – medieval and Renaissance art, jewellery, bronzes, tapestries, furniture, porcelain, paintings – amassed by Julius Wernher, a German who made his considerable fortune trading in South African diamonds. His booty is displayed through a dozen lovely rooms in this red-brick Georgian villa, the back garden of which is the fragrant Greenwich Park rose collection.

★ FREE Royal Observatory & Planetarium
Blackheath Avenue, SE10 8XJ (8312 6565, www. rmg.co.uk/royal-observatory). Cutty Sark DLR or Greenwich DLR/rail. **Open** *10am-5pm daily. Tours phone for details.* **Admission** *prices vary; check website for full details.* **Map** p217 C3 ❼

The northern section of this two-halved attraction chronicles Greenwich's horological connection.

Up at the O2.

Flamsteed House, the observatory built in 1675 on the orders of Charles II, contains the apartments of Sir John Flamsteed and other Astronomers Royal, as well as the instruments used in timekeeping since the 14th century. John Harrison's four timekeepers, used to crack the problem of longitude, are here, while the onion dome houses the country's largest (28-inch) refracting telescope – it was completed in 1893. The courtyard is where tourists gather for their Prime Meridian Line photo-opportunity, and you must pay for entry for this whole section of the attraction (£5-£9.50).

The south site houses the Astronomy Centre (free admission), which is also home to the Peter Harrison Planetarium and the Astronomy & Time Galleries, where daily and weekend star shows cost £5.50-£7.50. The 120-seat planetarium's architecture cleverly reflects its astronomical position: the semi-submerged cone tilts at 51.5 degrees, the latitude of Greenwich, pointing to the north star, and its reflective disc is aligned with the celestial equator.

Restaurants

Old Brewery
Pepys Building, Old Royal Naval College, SE10 9LW (3327 1280, www.oldbrewerygreenwich.com). Cutty Sark DLR. **Open** 11am-midnight daily. **Main courses** £12.50-£28.50. **Map** p217 B2 ❽ **British**
The flagship of the Greenwich-based Meantime Brewery: by day, it's a café; by night, a restaurant. There's a small bar, with tables outside in a large walled courtyard – a lovely spot in which to test the 50-strong beer list – but most of the action is in the vast, high-ceilinged main space. Dishes, such as Barnsley lamb chop and black-pudding hash, come with matching beers.
▶ *In the unimaginable days before every railway arch in the city was a microbrewery (1999, nostalgia fans), Alastair Hook set up Meantime in Greenwich. He has now opened a fine brewery tap, the Tasting Rooms (Blackwall Lane, SE10 0AR, 3384 0582, www.meantimebrewing.com/tasting-rooms).*

Pubs & bars

As well as the rather civilised **Old Brewery**, Meantime also runs a proper pub that's pretty handy for the attractions: the **Greenwich Union** (56 Royal Hill, SE10 8RT, 8692 6258, www.greenwichunion.com).

Cutty Sark Tavern
4-6 Ballast Quay, SE10 9PD (8858 3146, www.cuttysarkse10.co.uk). Cutty Sark DLR. **Open/food served** 11am-10pm Mon-Sat; noon-9pm Sun. **Map** p217 C1 ❾
Were it a couple of miles inland, the Cutty Sark would be a charming but unremarkable pub, the recipient of the Youngs brewery's current style of makeover: a lot of Farrow & Ball paint, better-than-average grub

and a decent, if unadventurous, selection of ales and wine. But add the mighty Thames and it becomes three floors of bow-fronted Georgian magic, with the top-level room in particular giving fantastic river views up- and downstream. Secure a window seat, or a table on the cobbled street outside, and imagine yourself in a scene from *Our Mutual Friend*.

Shops & Services

Greenwich Market
King William Walk, SE10 9HZ (8269 5090, www.greenwichmarketlondon.com). Cutty Sark DLR. **Open** 10am-5.30pm Thur-Sun. **Map** p217 B2 ❿ **Market**
Reprieved in late 2012 from the long-running threat of redevelopment, Greenwich Market can trace its origins to 1737 – although the current covered building dates only to the 19th century. On Thursdays and Fridays, up to 120 stalls are dominated by antiques (including classic 20th-century pieces); the weekends are for the craftier end of things. There is also a cluster of shops dedicated to art, fashion and jewellery. If you're flagging, there is plenty of street food.

GREENWICH PENINSULA

The riverside Thames Path leads north from the main attractions of Greenwich, past rusting piers and boarded-up factories, on to the **Greenwich Peninsula**, now dominated by the **O2 Arena** (*see p273*). Designed by the Richard Rogers Partnership as the Millennium Dome, this once-maligned structure's fortunes have improved considerably since its change of use. Alongside the concerts and sporting events in the huge auditorium, and movies in the cineplex, attractions include chain restaurants and big temporary exhibitions – you can now even book **Up at the O2** tickets (www.theo2.co.uk/upattheo2) to walk right over the top of the Dome, safely attached to a security line. A rather elegant (but, for public-transport purposes, almost entirely useless) cable car, the **Emirates Air Line** (*see p243*), runs from the east flank of the peninsula right across the Thames.

The Dome and its eastern environs are the site of a vast redevelopment (www.greenwichpeninsula.co.uk), which is adding to the lovely **Greenwich Peninsula Ecology Park** (www.tcv.org.uk) the **Peninsula Garden**, designed by Tom Dixon's studio. The riverside walk affords broad, flat, bracing views and works of art; you could hardly miss *Slice of Reality*, a rusting ship cut in half by Richard Wilson, or Antony Gormley's 100-foot-tall *Quantum Cloud*, which consists of a seemingly random cloud of steel sections, but look into it from a distance and you'll see a denser area at the centre in the shape of a human body.

EXPLORE

Notting Hill & Holland Park

For a cadre of right-wing politicians and a certain range of celebs, Notting Hill is the coolest address in London, with Portobello Market surrounded by some of the most expensive addresses in west London – as well as the inimitable Museum of Brands, Packaging & Advertising. As in so many parts of London, any patina of funkiness is down to previous generations of residents – poor working class and immigrants mostly – who made the place in their own image. The huge **Notting Hill Carnival** (*see p37*) gives the best flavour of this community. More high-end, elegant housing is found to the south in Holland Park and Kensington, where there are said to be more millionaires per square mile than in any other part of Europe. Apart from rubbernecking the rich, visitors will soon be able to enjoy the opening of ambitious new premises for the Design Museum.

Portobello Market

Don't Miss

1 **Portobello Road Market** Antiques and fruit and veg market (p225).

2 **Leighton House** Art and oriental decor (p226).

3 **Design Museum** New premises destined to be a design classic (p226).

4 **Ledbury** One of the city's enduringly great restaurants (p224).

5 **Museum of Brands, Packaging & Advertising** The stuff we throw away (p222).

NOTTING HILL

Ladbroke Grove, Notting Hill Gate or Westbourne Park tube.

Head north up Queensway from Kensington Gardens, then west along **Westbourne Grove**, and the road gets posher the further you go; cross Chepstow Road and you're in upmarket **Notting Hill**. Fashionable restaurants and bars exploit the lingering street cred of the fast-disappearing black and working-class communities. **Notting Hill Gate** isn't a pretty street, but the leafy avenues to the south are; so is **Pembridge Road**, to the north, leading to the boutique-filled streets of Westbourne Grove and Ledbury Road, and to **Portobello Road** and its renowned market.

Halfway down the road, **Blenheim Crescent** has a couple of independent booksellers, but the Travel Bookshop (nos.13-15), on which the movie *Notting Hill* focused its attention, has gone. Under the Westway, that elevated section of the M40 motorway linking London with Oxford, is the small but busy **Portobello Green Market**.

North of the Westway, Portobello's vitality fizzles out. It sparks back to life at **Golborne Road**, the heartland of London's North African community. Here, too, is a fine Portuguese café-deli, the **Lisboa Pâtisserie** (no.57, 8968 5242). At the north-eastern end of the road stands **Trellick Tower**, an architecturally significant, like-it-or-loathe-it piece of Ernö Goldfinger modernism. At its western end, Golborne Road connects with Ladbroke Grove, which can be followed north to **Kensal Green Cemetery**.

Sights & Museums

FREE **Kensal Green Cemetery**
Harrow Road, Kensal Green, W10 4RA (8969 0152, www.kensalgreencemetery.co.uk). Kensal Green tube/Overground. **Open** *Apr-Sept* 9am-6pm Mon-Sat; 10am-6pm Sun. *Oct-Mar* 9am-5pm Mon-Sat; 10am-5pm Sun. **Tours** *Mar-Oct* 2pm Sun. *Nov-Feb* 2pm 1st & 3rd Sun of mth. **Admission** free. *Tours* £7; £5 reductions. **No credit cards. Map** p223 C1 ❶
Behind a neoclassical gate is a green oasis of the dead. It's the resting place of the Duke of Sussex, sixth son of George III, and his sister, Princess Sophia; also buried here are Wilkie Collins, Anthony Trollope and William Makepeace Thackeray.

★ **Museum of Brands, Packaging & Advertising**
2 Colville Mews, Lonsdale Road, W11 2AR (7908 0880, www.museumofbrands.com). Notting Hill Gate tube. **Open** 10am-6pm Tue-Sat; 11am-5pm Sun. **Admission** £7.50; £3-£5 reductions; £20 family; free under-7s. **Map** p223 B2 ❷

Robert Opie began collecting the things others throw away when he was 16. His collection now includes anything from milk bottles to vacuum cleaners and cereal packets. The emphasis is on the last century of British consumerism, design and domestic life, but there are also some older items, such as an ancient Egyptian doll.
▶ *Due to visitor numbers increasing, the museum will open in bigger premises (London Lighthouse, 111-117 Lancaster Road, W11 1QT), probably by September 2015. Check the website for details.*

Restaurants

Electric Diner
191 Portobello Road, W11 2ED (7908 9696, www.electricdiner.com). Ladbroke Grove tube. **Open** 8am-midnight Mon-Wed; 8am-1am Thur-Sat; 8am-11pm Sun. **Main courses** £7-£19. **Map** p223 B2 ❸ America
The unfinished brick and concrete walls, low lighting, french grey-painted plank ceiling, red leather banquettes and lively open kitchen evoke a sort of chic US railway car diner. The hip vibe extends to the menu, which features artery-unfriendly American classics: cheeseburgers, hot dogs, milkshakes. Each dish is well-thought-out and uses good ingredients: french fries are thin and crispy, and even a simple bibb lettuce and avocado salad was enlivened with chives and tarragon.

Galicia
323 Portobello Road, W10 5SY (8969 3539). Ladbroke Grove tube. **Open** noon-3pm, 7-11.30pm Tue-Sat; noon-3pm, 7-10pm Sun. **Tapas** £3.75-£8.90. **Map** p223 A1 ❹ Tapas
'If it ain't broke, don't fix it' seems to be the philosophy of Galicia, which has changed little in its many years of serving tapas. The grudging effort at décor, the rarely smiling (but still efficient and personable) service, the cooking – all emphatically reject food fashion. Go elsewhere for cutting-edge culinary creations; come here for excellent renditions of standard dishes. Even better, with a glass of house wine, two people can eat a hearty meal for around £30.

Portobello Road.

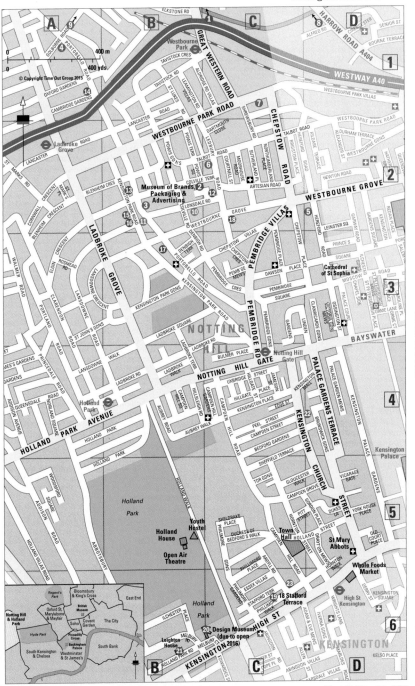

★ Hereford Road

3 Hereford Road, W2 4AB (7727 1144, www. herefordroad.org). Bayswater tube. **Open** noon-3pm, 6-10.30pm Mon-Sat; noon-4pm, 6-10pm Sun. **Main courses** £10-£16.50. **Map** p223 D2 ❺
British

This restaurant makes its intentions clear: the first thing you see upon entering the long, narrow space is the kitchen; if it were any more open, you'd be eating off the chefs' laps. Sit and wonder how the restaurant can manage to serve two marvellous courses for £13.50 at lunch as you tuck into hearty dishes such as devilled duck livers with shallots, brill with roasted cauliflower, or onglet and chips. The slightly fancier à la carte menu includes the likes of pot roast rabbit, turnips and bacon.

★ Ledbury

127 Ledbury Road, W11 2AQ (7792 9090, www. theledbury.com). Westbourne Park tube. **Open** 6.30-9.45pm Mon, Tue; noon-2pm, 6.30-9.45pm Wed-Sat; noon-2pm, 6.45-9.45pm Sun. **Set lunch** £85 4 courses. **Set dinner** £95 4 courses. **Tasting menu** £115. **Map** p223 C2 ❻ French

Few haute establishments have the hospitable hum of the Ledbury; this former pub remains top-tier for gustatory good times. British ingredients – smoked eel, Cumbrian lamb – line up alongside delicacies such as Tokyo turnips, Bresse chicken and black truffle, but it's chef Brett Graham's clever contemporary treatment of them that sets the place apart. Ledbury signatures are consistently thrilling – particularly the flame-grilled mackerel with pickled cucumber, celtic mustard and shiso; and, well, all the desserts.

Lucky 7

127 Westbourne Park Road, W2 5QL (7727 6771, www.lucky7london.co.uk). Royal Oak or Westbourne Park tube. **Open** noon-11pm Mon; 10am-11pm Tue-Thur; 9am-11pm Fri, Sat; 9am-10.30pm Sun. **Main courses** £6.95-£14.75. **Map** p223 C1 ❼ American

Lucky 7's American-retro decor is a smile from floor to ceiling, with outsized, wildly kitsch figurines stealing the show. The menu is 90% breakfast, burgers and outlandishly rich desserts, with craft beer, some cocktails and many shakes to ease it down. The place's only drawback is size – seating capacity is just a couple of dozen – which, combined with the no-bookings policy, means you'll often have to queue. But quality is high enough to merit a wait.

Mosob

339 Harrow Road, W9 3RB (7266 2012, http:// mosob.co.uk). Westbourne Park tube. **Open** 6-11.30pm Mon-Fri; 3pm-midnight Sat, Sun. **Main courses** £8.95-£13.95. **Map** p223 D1 ❽ Eritrean

A *mosob* is a handwoven table around which people eat. This is one of the many facts about Eritrean cuisine we learned at this welcoming restaurant

(romantics should try eating *koloso*-style, when a scoop of food is placed in another's mouth as a sign of affection) – the people who run it are on a mission to promote their homeland. But the main event is the cooking, especially the gloriously diverse vegetarian choices (pulses and green chillies feature heavily). Meat-eaters also fare well, though, and everything is served on spongy, yeasty injera: the traditional bread, which is also used to scoop up your food.

Snaps & Rye

93 Golborne Road, W10 5NL (8964 3004, www.snapsandrye.com). Westbourne Park tube. **Open** 8am-5pm daily. **Main courses** £2.70-£3.90. **Map** p223 A1 ❾ Danish

Snaps (alcohol infusions) & Rye (the accompanying food) embodies all that's best about Scandinavian design: simple and functional, but every detail designed or chosen with aesthetic pleasure in mind. The owners have also taken great pains to make their food, prepared by British chef Tania Steytler, as good as it can possibly be. While Denmark's famous open-faced sandwiches (smørrebrød) are simple in concept, Steytler raises them to great heights through the use of superb ingredients, masterly cooking skills and attention to detail. Other options are meatballs, herring, cured salmon and apple cake. Feeling the cold but don't fancy snaps? Try cocio, a Nordic hot chocolate.

Pubs & Bars

Lonsdale

48 Lonsdale Road, W11 2DE (7727 4080, www. thelonsdale.co.uk). Ladbroke Grove or Notting Hill Gate tube. **Open** 6pm-midnight Tue-Thur; 6pm-1am Fri, Sat. **Map** p223 B2 ❿

The scholarliness of the cocktail list here breeds confidence. Nearly every drink is given a time and place of creation, and in most cases, the bartender responsible is named. This makes for informative, sometimes amusing reading, and anything you order will be first rate. Classics like Martinis are always very proper. Sitting at the incredibly long and atmospherically lit bar, and watching the bartenders work is entertainment in itself. There's a restaurant too, specialising in top-quality meat.

Portobello Star

171 Portobello Road, W11 2DY (3588 7800, www.portobellostarbar.co.uk). Ladbroke Grove or Notting Hill Gate tube. **Open** 11am-11.30pm Mon-Thur, Sun; 11am-12.30am Fri, Sat. **Map** p223 B2 ⓫

This 'cocktail tavern' deftly blends discerning bar and traditional boozer. The well-stocked bar is manned by friendly staff thoroughly educated in the art of adult refreshment. Mixologist Jake Burger's impeccable, approachable directory of drinks is the last word on sophisticated intoxication. Ginger Pig pies are on hand to soak up the alcohol.

EXPLORE

Snaps & Rye.

Shops & Services

Ben Day
3 Lonsdale Road, W11 2BY (3417 3873, www. benday.co.uk). Ladbroke Grove or Notting Hill Gate tube. **Open** 11am-6pm Mon-Sat; 11am-5pm Sun. **Map** p223 C2 ⓬ **Jewellery**
Everything here is handmade in the studio below the shop and, although you can buy off the shelf, bespoke is what Ben Day does best. Love the green chrysoprase cocktail ring but have your heart set on purple? No problem. Thirty years of sourcing rare stones ensures there's no one better placed to track it down. Best of all, whether you're a jewellery novice or a gem collector with a sky's-the-limit budget, Day's discretion, enthusiasm and down-to-earth manner make shopping here a pleasure.

Couverture & the Garbstore
188 Kensington Park Road, W11 2ES (7229 2178, www.couvertureandthegarbstore.com). Ladbroke Grove tube. **Open** 11am-6pm Mon-Sat. **Map** p223 B2 ⓭ **Fashion/homewares**
Cult shop Couverture & The Garbstore sticks it to The Man with an under-the-radar collection of independent labels and up-and-coming designer fashion (sell out and you're out, basically). On the lower level of this slick three-storey boutique is designer Ian Paley's menswear label, The Garbstore. The ground and upper levels house Emily Dyson's much-admired lifestyle concept Couverture, where you'll find an enticing array of homewares and beautiful women's and children's fashion.

Honest Jon's
278 Portobello Road, W10 5TE (8969 9822, www. honestjons.com). Ladbroke Grove tube. **Open** 10am-6pm Mon-Sat; 11am-5pm Sun. **Map** p223 A1 ⓮ **Books & music**
Honest Jon's found its way to Notting Hill in 1979, and the shop's owner helped James Lavelle to set up Mo'Wax records. Here you'll find jazz, hip hop, soul, broken beat, reggae and Brazilian music, as well as the label's own brilliant compilations – the first volumes of the *London is the Place for Me* series, detailing calypso, Afro-jazz and highlife in the post-war years, were a revelation.

Lutyens & Rubinstein
21 Kensington Park Road, W11 2EU (7229 1010, www.lutyensrubinstein.co.uk). Ladbroke Grove tube. **Open** 10am-6pm Mon, Sat; 10am-6.30pm Tue-Fri; 11am-5pm Sun. **Map** p223 B2 ⓯ **Books & music**
Lutyens & Rubinstein sells a beautifully arranged selection of literary fiction and general non-fiction. The core stock was put together by the owners canvassing hundreds of readers on the books they'd most like to find in a bookshop; thus every book stocked is sold because somebody has recommended it. The result is an appealing alternative to the homogeneous chain bookshops, with some unusual titles available. As well as books, the shop stocks a small range of stationery, greetings cards, paperweights, local honey and literary-inspired scents from CB I Hate Perfume.

Merchant Archive
19 Kensington Park Road, W11 2EU (7229 9006, www.merchantarchive.com). Ladboke Grove or Notting Hill Gate tube. **Open** 10am-6.30pm Mon-Sat; noon-5pm Sun. **Map** p223 B2 ⓰ **Fashion/homewares**
Carrying an edited selection of its own label, new designer duds, homewares and fine vintage, Merchant Archive is a Notting Hill treasure. On the main floor brands such as Mother of Pearl and Studio Nicholson are shown against a backdrop of glass tables and artwork, with the odd 1920s feathered headpiece tossed atop a rack. Head downstairs to discover most of the vintage stuff.

★ Portobello Road Market
Portobello Road, W10 (www.portobelloroad.co.uk). Ladbroke Grove or Notting Hill Gate tube. **Open** *General* 9am-6pm Mon-Wed; 9am-1pm Thur; 7am-7pm Fri, Sat. *Antiques* 7am-4pm Sat. **No credit cards. Map** p223 B3 ⓱ **Market**
Best known for antiques and collectibles, this is actually several markets rolled into one: antiques start at the Notting Hill end; further up are food stalls; under the Westway and along the walkway to Ladbroke Grove are emerging designer and vintage clothes on Fridays (usually marginally less busy) and Saturdays (invariably manic).

EXPLORE

There are more than 2,000 specialist antiques dealers squeezed tightly into any available space along Portobello Road, with bargain-hunters jostling with camera-laden tourists to the soundtrack of live jazz. Pickings around Elgin Crescent are meagre, so push on to explore the fashion market under the Westway flyover. Best visited on a less-frantic Friday morning, it's here you'll find fashionistas and trendy teens delving through troves of prized vintage, boutique fashion and retro memorabilia. And don't stop there: continue up to Golborne Road for bargains away from the masses, helped by the presence of eccentric second-hand interiors stalls.

▶ *Bring plenty of cash: the few cashpoints attract ridiculous queues.*

Wolf & Badger

46 Ledbury Road, W11 2AB (7229 5698, www. wolfandbadger.com). Notting Hill Gate tube. **Open** 10am-6pm Mon-Fri; 10am-6.30pm Sat; 11am-5pm Sun. **Map** p223 C2 ⓰ **Fashion/homewares**
A hotbed of emerging design talent, this innovative boutique champions the work of up-and-coming (mostly) British fashion and homewares designers by offering them retail space and a sizeable return (over 75 percent) on anything they sell. New designers are introduced every three months, giving the space a constantly evolving, one-step-ahead vibe that makes it a first port of call for show-stopping dresses, edgy tees and statement accessories.

KENSINGTON & HOLLAND PARK

High Street Kensington or Holland Park tube.

Just off **Kensington High Street**, a smart but rarely intoxicating shopping drag, an array of handsome squares are lined with grand 19th-century houses, many of which still serve as single-family homes for the wealthy. Linking with Notting Hill to the north, **Kensington Church Street** has many antiques shops selling furniture so fine you would probably never dare use it. **St Mary Abbots** (http://smanews.weebly.com), at the junction of Church Street and High Street, is a Victorian neo-Gothic church. It was built – on the site of the 12th-century original – by Sir George Gilbert Scott between 1869 and 1872. Past worshippers have included Isaac Newton and William Wilberforce. As well as beautiful stained-glass windows, it has London's tallest spire (278 feet).

Across the road, in a striking art deco building, is organic-food giant **Whole Foods Market**. South down Derry Street, past the entrance to the **Roof Gardens** – a restaurant and private members' club with flamingos and a stream, 100 feet above central London – is Kensington Square, which has a mighty concentration of blue plaques. The writer William Thackeray lived at no.16 and the painter Edward Burne-Jones

at no.41; at no.18, John Stuart Mill's maid made her bid for 'person from Porlock' status by using Carlyle's sole manuscript of *The French Revolution* to light the fire. The houses, though much altered, date from the development of the square in 1685, and were surrounded by fields until 1840.

Further west is one of London's finest green spaces: **Holland Park**. Along its eastern edge, Holland Walk is one of the most pleasant paths in central London, but the heart of the park is the Jacobean **Holland House**. Left derelict after World War II, it is now an exhibition space. In summer, open-air theatre and opera are staged on the front terrace, and there are three lovely formal gardens laid out close to the house. A little further to the west, the Japanese-style Kyoto Garden has huge koi carp and a bridge at the foot of a waterfall.

To the south of the park are another two historic houses: **18 Stafford Terrace** and, extensively refurbished, **Leighton House**, as well as the Commonwealth Institute, soon to be home to the **Design Museum**.

Sights & Museums

18 Stafford Terrace

18 Stafford Terrace, W8 7BH (tours 7602 3316 Mon-Fri, 7938 1295 Sat, Sun, www.rbkc.gov.uk). High Street Kensington tube. **Tours** (pre-booked only) *Mid Sept-mid June* 11.15am, 2.15pm Wed; 11.15am, 1pm, 2.15pm, 3.30pm Sat, Sun. **Tickets** £8; £3-£6 reductions. **Map** p223 C6 ⓳
The home of cartoonist Edward Linley Sambourne was built in the 1870s and has almost all of its original fittings and furniture. At the weekend, tours (except the one at 11.15am) are led by an actor in period costume.

Design Museum

Kensington High Street, W14 8ND (7403 6933, http://designmuseum.org). High Street Kensington tube. **Map** p223 C6 ⓴
The museum, in the old Commonwealth Institute, should open in 2016. *See right* **The Future of Design**.

★ Leighton House

12 Holland Park Road, W14 8LZ (7602 3316, www.rbkc.gov.uk). High Street Kensington tube. **Open** 10am-5.30pm Mon, Wed-Sun. *Tours* 11am, 2pm Mon, Wed-Fri. **Admission** £10; £3 reductions. **Tours** £12. **Map** p223 B6 ㉑
In the 1860s, artist Frederic Leighton commissioned a showpiece house. Behind the sternly Victorian red-brick façade, he made sure it was full of treasures from all over the world, as well as his own works and those of his contemporaries. The house is decorated in high style: magnificent downstairs reception rooms designed for lavish entertaining; a dramatic staircase leading to a light-filled studio that takes

up most of the first floor; and, above all, the Arab Hall, which showcases Leighton's huge collection of 16th-century Middle Eastern tiles. The only private space in the whole house is a tiny single bedroom.

▶ Note that tickets are for timed slots only and that advance booking is highly recommended.

Restaurants

For gourmet grazing, try **Whole Foods Market** (63-97 Kensington High Street, W8 5SE, 7368 4500, www.wholefoodmarket.com), London flagship of the US health-food supermarket chain, which occupies the handsome building that was once Barkers department store.

Clarke's

124 Kensington Church Street, W8 4BH (7221 9225, www.sallyclarke.com). Notting Hill Gate tube. **Open** 8-11am, 12.30-2pm, 6.30-10pm Mon-Fri; 8-11am, noon-2pm, 6.30-10pm Sat. **Main courses** £20-£27.50. **Map** p223 D4 ② Modern European

At Clarke's, that overused 'best ingredients, simply prepared' phrase is true; a salad of peas, baby broad beans, spinach and grilled courgette looks like spring on a plate, while roast salmon is a gorgeous deep pink, set off by sweet baked tomatoes and olives. Chef-proprietor Sally Clarke has been espousing the 'seasonal and local' ethic since the 1980s.

Yashin

1A Argyll Road, W8 7DB (7938 1536, www. yashinsushi.com). High Street Kensington tube. **Open** noon-3pm, 6-11pm daily. **Dishes** £3.80-£60. **Map** p223 C6 ② Sushi

The centrepiece sushi counter gives the game away. Set on the dark green tiles behind the team of itamae (sushi chefs), a neon sign reads 'without soy sauce', and this is how the chefs ask you to eat your artfully crafted sushi. In place of a dunking, each piece is finished with its own flavourings or even a quick blast from a blowtorch.

Other location 117-119 Old Brompton Road, South Kensington, SW7 3RN (7373 3990).

THE FUTURE OF DESIGN
How the Design Museum plans to go forward by looking back.

Throughout his career, Terence Conran has been a pioneer of great design in everyday life; it was he who decided, more than a quarter of a century ago, that London must have a **Design Museum**. The museum opened in 1989, in a dilapidated warehouse on Shad Thames. The premises were soon unrecognisable, as a clean-lined white building emerged from the fabric of a 1940s banana warehouse. Currently, some 200,000 visitors a year come to see changing exhibitions such as global architect Zaha Hadid's debut solo show, and the ever-popular Designs of the Year – approaching a decade of nominations and awards.

With the arrival of a new director, Deyan Sudjic, in 2006, ambitious plans began to be hatched: for one thing, there had never been enough room to show off the museum's own design collection. Eyes turned to the Grade II*-listed former Commonwealth Institute on Kensington High Street. Opened in 1962, but closed since 2002, the Institute is a distinctive place, built to look like a tent, with a remarkable hyperbolic paraboloid roof (made of 25 tonnes of copper mined in what was then Rhodesia).

The new museum has been designed by John Pawson and will cost £80 million (£17 million of which is coming from Conran). As well as bringing a classic modernist building

back into use, there will be three times as much gallery space. Visitors will enter a dramatic atrium, with an exhibition gallery, café and shop on the ground floor, before descending to a further gallery space and an auditorium in the basement, or climbing to the top-floor restaurant and events space. There, too, will be the permanent collection, liberated from storage and not just open to the public, but open to the public for free.

The new Design Museum is due to open in 2016. Until then, it remains to visitors at its old premises on Shad Thames, SE1 2YD, 7403 6933, https://designmuseum.org.

EXPLORE

Further Afield

London is an old city – there are Bronze Age remains on the Vauxhall foreshore – and one that industrialised early, opening the world's first underground railway in 1863. Thus it is both large (600 square miles) and dense in historic attractions. In this chapter, we try to gather the most interesting self-contained areas of the city, and round up the single attractions worthiest of your attention.

Sigmund Freud, Karl Marx and John Keats all settled in north London: find out why among the grand squares of Islington or in villagey Hampstead and Highgate; Camden has its own chapter (see pp192-197). In east London – not at all the same thing as the East End (see pp198-213) – we highlight Docklands and the Olympic Park, as well as hipster Dalston and rapidly gentrifying Hackney, on the northern fringe of the East End proper. After that, head 'south of the river' – where, apocryphally, black cabbies refuse to go – for Greenwich (in its own chapter, see pp214-219) and Brixton.

William Morris Gallery.

Don't Miss

1 Kenwood House
A 17th-century manor house (p231).

2 William Morris Gallery
Home of the man behind the fabric (p233).

3 Highgate Cemetery
Victorian tombs and Karl Marx's grave (p232).

4 Towpath Have brekkie on the 'Haggerston Riviera' (p234).

5 Queen Elizabeth Olympic Park Flowers, waterways and art (p241).

HAMPSTEAD

Hampstead tube, or Gospel Oak or Hampstead Heath Overground.

It may have been absorbed into London during the city's great Victorian expansion, but hilltop Hampstead still feels like a Home Counties village. It has long been a favoured roost for literary and artistic types: Keats and Constable lived here in the 19th century, and sculptors Barbara Hepworth and Henry Moore took up residence in the 1930s. However, the area is now popular with City workers, who are among the only people able to afford what is some of London's priciest property.

The undisputed highlight of the district is **Hampstead Heath**, the vast and in places wonderfully overgrown tract of countryside between Hampstead village and Highgate that is said to have inspired CS Lewis's Narnia. The heath covers 791 acres of woodland, playing fields, swimming ponds and meadows of tall grass that attract picnickers and couples in search of privacy.

The south end of the heath is where you'll find dinky Hampstead village, all genteel shops and cafés, restaurants and lovely pubs such as the **Holly Bush**. While you're there, tour the gorgeous sunken gardens and antique collection at **Fenton House** or gaze at the stars from the **Hampstead Scientific Society Observatory** (Lower Terrace, www.hampsteadscience.ac.uk/astro), open on clear Friday and Saturday evenings and Sunday lunchtimes from October to May. A stroll along nearby Judges Walk reveals a line of horse chestnuts and limes virtually unchanged since they appeared in a Constable painting in 1820. Constable was buried nearby at **St John-at-Hampstead Church** (7794 5808, www.hampsteadparishchurch.org.uk), as was the comedian Peter Cook. At the top of Hampstead, North End Way divides the main heath from the wooded West Heath, one of London's oldest gay cruising areas (but perfectly family-friendly by day). Just off North End Way is Hampstead's best-kept secret, the secluded and charmingly overgrown **Hill Garden & Pergola** (open 8.30am-dusk daily), which was built by Lord Leverhulme using soil from the excavation of the Northern line's tunnels.

East of Hampstead tube, a maze of postcard-pretty residential streets shelters **Burgh House** (New End Square, 7431 0144, www.burghhouse.org.uk), a Queen Anne house with a small local-history museum and gallery. Also in the area are **2 Willow Road**, architect Ernö Goldfinger's self-designed 1930s residence, and **40 Well Walk**, Constable's home for the last ten years of his life. Downhill towards Hampstead Heath Overground station is **Keats House**.

Camden Arts Centre.

Further west, and marginally closer to Finchley Road tube, is the **Freud Museum**, while the contemporary art exhibitions of **Camden Arts Centre** are almost opposite Finchley Road & Frognal Overground station.

Sights & Museums

2 Willow Road

2 Willow Road, NW3 1TH (7435 6166, www.nationaltrust.org.uk). Hampstead tube or Hampstead Heath Overground. Open Mar-Oct 11am-5pm Wed-Sun. Closed Nov-Feb. Tours 11am, noon, 1pm, 2pm Wed-Sun. Admission £6; £3 children; £15 family; free under-5s. Joint ticket with Fenton House £9.

A surprising addition to the National Trust's collection of historic houses, this small modernist building was designed by Hungarian-born architect Ernö Goldfinger. The house was made to be flexible, with ingenious movable partitions and folding doors. Home to the architect and his wife until their deaths, it contains a fine, idiosyncratic collection of art by the likes of Max Ernst and Henry Moore. Goldfinger also designed Notting Hill's Trellick Tower. Ian Fleming despised the architect and named a James-Bond villain after Goldfinger.

★ FREE Camden Arts Centre

Arkwright Road, NW3 6DG (7472 5500, www.camdenartscentre.org). Finchley Road tube or Finchley Road & Frognal Overground. Open 10am-6pm Tue, Thur-Sun; 10am-9pm Wed. Admission free.

Under director Jenni Lomax, this 50-year-old gallery eclipses larger, younger venues. The annual artist-curated shows – sculpture, automata, film works – have been among the most memorable in recent history. The Centre also hosts a comprehensive programme of talks, events and workshops and boasts a good bookshop and a great café, which opens on to a surprisingly tranquil garden.

Fenton House

3 Hampstead Grove, NW3 6RT (7435 3471, www. nationaltrust.org.uk). Hampstead tube. **Open** *Mar-Oct* times vary; check website for details. Closed *Nov-Feb.* **Admission** *House & gardens* £6.50; £3 reductions; £16 family; free under-5s. *Gardens* £2. *Joint ticket with 2 Willow Road* £9.

Set in a gorgeous garden, with a 300-year-old apple orchard, this manor house is notable for its 17th- and 18th-century harpsichords, virginals and spinets, which are still played at lunchtime and evening concerts (usually Wed; phone for details). Also on display are European and Chinese porcelain, Chippendale furniture and some artful and intricate 17th-century needlework.

Freud Museum

20 Maresfield Gardens, NW3 5SX (7435 2002, www.freud.org.uk). Finchley Road tube. **Open** noon-5pm Wed-Sun. **Admission** £7; £4-£5 reductions; free under-12s.

Driven from Vienna by the Nazis, Sigmund Freud lived in this quiet house in north London with his wife Martha and daughter Anna until his death in 1939. Now a museum with temporary exhibitions, the house displays Freud's antiques, art and therapy tools, including his famous couch. Unusually, the building has two blue plaques, one for Sigmund and another for Anna, a pioneer in child psychiatry.

Keats House

Keats Grove, NW3 2RR (7332 3868, www. cityoflondon.gov.uk/keatshousehampstead). Hampstead tube, Hampstead Heath Overground or bus 24, 46, 168. **Open** *Mar-Oct* 1-5pm Tue-Sun. *Nov-Feb* 1-5pm Fri-Sun. **Admission** £5.50; £3.50 reductions; free under-18s.

Keats House was the Romantic poet's last British home before tuberculosis forced him to Italy and death at the age of only 25. A leaflet guides you through each room, starting from the rear, as well as providing context for Keats's life and that of his less famous friend and patron, Charles Brown. Painstaking renovation has ensured the decorative scheme is entirely accurate, down to pale pink walls in Keats's humble bedroom. The garden, in which he wrote 'Ode to a Nightingale', is particularly pleasant.

★ FREE Kenwood House/ Iveagh Bequest

Hampstead Lane, NW3 7JR (8348 1286, www. english-heritage.org.uk). Hampstead tube, or Golders Green tube then bus 210. **Open** 9am-5pm daily. **Admission** free.

Set in lovely grounds at the top of Hampstead Heath, Kenwood House is every inch the country manor house. Built in 1616, the mansion was remodelled in the 18th century for William Murray, who made the pivotal court ruling in 1772 that made it illegal to own slaves in England. The house was purchased by brewing magnate Edward Guinness, who was kind enough to donate his art collection to the nation in 1927. It reopened in 2014 after extensive, splendid renovations, returning the interiors to a state that enhances such highlights of the collection as Vermeer's *The Guitar Player*, Gainsborough's *Countess Howe*, and one of Rembrandt's finest self-portraits (dating to c1663).

EXPLORE

Kenwood House.

Restaurants

★ Bull & Last
168 Highgate Road, NW5 1QS (7267 3641, www. thebullandlast.co.uk). Kentish Town tube/rail then bus 214, C2, or Gospel Oak Overground then bus C11. **Open** noon-11pm Mon-Thur; 9am-midnight Fri, Sat; 9am-10.30pm Sun. **Main courses** £14.50-£23. Gastropub
For a place with such a good reputation for its food, the Bull & Last is refreshingly pubby: heavy wooden furniture, velvet drapes, stuffed animals and old prints decorate both the bar and the upstairs dining room. The latter is a calmer and cooler place to eat than the ground-floor bar, and allows diners to focus on dishes such as pig's cheek with watermelon pickle, basil and sesame. There are (big) roasts at weekends, a changing selection of beers and ciders from small breweries and a decent wine list.

Wells
30 Well Walk, NW3 1BX (7794 3785, www. thewellshampstead.co.uk). Hampstead tube or Hampstead Heath Overground. **Open** *Food served* noon-3pm, 6-10pm Mon-Fri; noon-4pm, 7-10pm Sat; noon-4pm, 7-9.30pm Sun. **Main courses** £9.95-£18.75. Gastropub
The dining rooms above this very soigné Georgian pub are a useful addition to Hampstead's relatively limited restaurant scene. The menu is appealing without being faddish or daring. Perfectly grilled scallops with crisp bacon, samphire and shallot and

rocket purées might be followed by crisp-skinned sea bass; there's also a section of the menu devoted to steaks. Add solicitous service and well-chosen wines at friendly prices and the Wells is a winner.

Pubs & Bars

The **Horseshoe** (28 Heath Street, NW3 6TE, 7431 7206) in Hampstead is an excellent gastropub, with fine own-brewed ale.

★ Holly Bush
22 Holly Mount, NW3 6SG (7435 2892, www. hollybushhampstead.co.uk). Hampstead tube or Hampstead Heath Overground. **Open** noon-11pm Mon-Sat; noon-10.30pm Sun. *Food served* noon-3pm, 6-10pm Mon-Fri; noon-4pm, 6-10pm Sat; noon-9pm Sun.
As the trend for gutting old pubs claims yet more Hampstead boozers, this place's cachet increases. Located on a quiet hilltop backstreet, this Grade-II listed building was originally built as a house in the 1790s and used as the Assembly Rooms in the 1800s, before becoming a pub in 1928. A higgledy-piggledy air remains, with three low-ceilinged bar areas and one bar counter at which decent pints are poured. Sound food and a good choice of wines by the glass are further draws.

HIGHGATE
Archway or Highgate tube.

Taking its name from the tollgate that once stood on the High Street, Highgate is inexorably linked with London's medieval mayor, Richard 'Dick' Whittington. As the story goes, the disheartened Whittington, having failed to make his fortune, fled the City as far as Highgate Hill, but turned back when he heard the Bow bells peal out 'Turn again, Whittington, thrice Mayor of London'. Today, the area is best known for the atmospheric grounds of **Highgate Cemetery**. Adjoining the cemetery is pretty **Waterlow Park**, created by low-cost housing pioneer Sir Sydney Waterlow in 1889, with ponds, a mini-aviary, tennis courts, and a cute garden café in 16th-century **Lauderdale House** (8348 8716, www.lauderdalehouse.co.uk), former home of Charles II's mistress, Nell Gwynn. North of Highgate tube, shady **Highgate Woods** are preserved as a conservation area, with a nature trail, an adventure playground and a café that hosts live jazz during the summer.

Sights & Museums

★ Highgate Cemetery
Swains Lane, N6 6PJ (8340 1834, www.highgate-cemetery.org). Archway tube. **Open** *East Cemetery* Mar-Oct 10am-5pm Mon-Fri; 11am-5pm Sat, Sun.

Bull & Last.

EXPLORE

ONE-OF-A-KIND HISTORIC HOUSES

Homes of the high and mighty.

Chiswick House.

Chiswick House

Burlington Lane, Chiswick, W4 2RP (8995 0508, www.chgt.org.uk). Hammersmith tube then bus 190, or Chiswick rail. **Open** *Apr-Oct* 10am-6pm Mon-Wed, Sun. *Nov* 10am-5pm Mon-Wed, Sun. Closed Dec-Mar. **Admission** £6.10; £3.70-£5.50 reductions; £15.90 family; free under-5s.

Richard Boyle, third Earl of Burlington, designed this Palladian villa in 1725 as a place to entertain the artistic and philosophical luminaries of his day. The Chiswick House & Gardens Trust has restored the gardens (free entry) to the original design. The restoration was helped by details from a painting by Dutch landscape artist Pieter Andreas Rysbrack (c1685-1748), which can be seen here. There's an impressive café too (8995 6356, www.chiswickhousecafe.co.uk).

Ham House

Ham Street, Richmond, Surrey, TW10 7RS (8940 1950, www.nationaltrust.org.uk/hamhouse). Richmond tube/rail then bus 371. **Open** varies. **Admission** £10; £5 reductions; £25 family; free under-5s.

Built in 1610 for one of James I's courtiers, Thomas Vavasour, this lavish red-brick mansion is full of period furnishings, rococo mirrors and ornate tapestries. The restored formal grounds have a lovely trellised cherry garden and some lavender parterres. The tearoom turns out historic dishes using ingredients from the kitchen gardens.

Hogarth's House

Hogarth Lane, Great West Road, Chiswick, W4 2QN (8994 6757). Turnham Green tube or Chiswick rail. **Open** noon-5pm Tue-Sun. **Admission** free; donations appreciated.

Recently reopened after refurbishment, this was the country retreat of the 18th-century artist and social commentator William Hogarth. On display are some famous engravings, including 'Gin Lane', 'Marriage à la Mode' and a copy of 'Rake's Progress', and plenty of biographical information. Despite the setting on a horrid main road, the garden is charming – and amazingly tranquil.

Strawberry Hill

268 Waldegrave Road, Twickenham, Middx, TW1 4ST (8744 1241, www.strawberryhillhouse.org.uk). Richmond tube/Overground/rail then bus R68, or Strawberry Hill rail. **Open** Mar-Nov 1.40-5.30pm Mon-Wed; noon-5.30pm Sat, Sun. Closed Dec-Feb. **Admission** £11.80; £5.40 reductions; free under-16s.

Antiquarian Horace Walpole, who created the Gothic novel with his book *The Castle of Otranto* (the study in which he wrote it opened to the public for the first time in 2015), laid the groundwork for the Gothic Revival in Victorian times as early as the 1700s. Pre-booked tickets, at 20-minute intervals, allow you to explore the crepuscular nooks and crannies of his 'play-thing house', this 'little Gothic castle'.

William Morris Gallery

Lloyd Park, Forest Road, Walthamstow, E17 4PP (8496 4390, www.wmgallery.org.uk). Walthamstow Central tube/rail or bus 34, 97, 215, 275. **Open** 10am-5pm Wed-Sun. **Admission** free; donations appreciated.

Artist, poet, novelist, socialist and source of flowery wallpaper, William Morris lived here between 1848 and 1856. There are plenty of designs in fabric, stained glass and ceramic on show, produced by Morris and his associates in the Arts and Crafts Movement. Excellent refurbishments improved the displays (which show off the medieval-style helmet and sword Morris used as props for murals, and the satchel from which he distributed political tracts) and created a popular tearoom.

EXPLORE

Nov-Feb 10am-4pm Mon-Fri; 11am-4pm Sat,
Sun. *West Cemetery* by tour only. **Admission**
£4; free 7-18; under-7s not admitted. *Tours £12;*
£6 reductions.

The final resting place of some very famous
Londoners, Highgate Cemetery is a wonderfully
overgrown maze of ivy-cloaked Victorian tombs
and time-shattered urns. Visitors can wander at
their own pace through the East Cemetery, with its
memorials to Karl Marx, George Eliot and Douglas
Adams, but the most atmospheric part of the
cemetery is the foliage-shrouded West Cemetery,
laid out in 1839. Only accessible on an organised
tour (book ahead, dress respectfully and arrive 30
minutes early), the shady paths wind past gloomy
catacombs, grand Victorian pharaonic tombs,
and the graves of notables such as poet Christina
Rossetti, scientist Michael Faraday and poisoned
Russian dissident Alexander Litvinenko.
▶ *The cemetery closes during burials, so call ahead*
before you visit.

Pubs & Bars

Bull

13 North Hill, N6 4AB (8341 0510, www.
thebullhighgate.co.uk). Highgate tube. **Open** noon-
11.30pm Mon-Thur, Sun; noon-midnight Fri, Sat.
Food served noon-10pm Mon-Sat; noon-9pm Sun.
First impressions would suggest the Bull is just
another suburban gastropub, but note the enamelled
beer memorabilia on the walls and garlands of
hop flowers: this pub holds beer in extremely high
esteem. You might catch a glimpse of the Willy
Wonka tubing and brass vats of the brewing
equipment, and the beer taps reveal almost nothing
recognisable from the average high-street chain pub.
Five of the pumps dispense the fine products of the
London Brewing Company, made on the premises,
and keg fonts advertise the likes of Sierra Nevada
Torpedo and Veltins Pils.

ISLINGTON

Angel tube or Highbury & Islington tube/
Overground.

Islington started life as a country village beside
one of Henry VIII's expansive hunting reserves.
It soon became an important livestock market,
supplying the Smithfield meat yards, before
being enveloped into Greater London. The 19th
century brought industrial development along
the Regent's Canal and later industrial decay, but
locals kept up their spirits at the area's music
halls, launchpads for such working-class heroes
as Marie Lloyd, George Formby and Norman
Wisdom. From the 1960s, there was an influx of
arts and media types, who gentrified the Georgian
squares and Victorian terraces, and opened cafés,
restaurants and boutiques around Upper Street

and Essex Road. It is now a suburban bower
of the *Guardian*-reading middle classes.

Close to Angel station on Upper Street, the
Camden Passage antique market bustles with
browsing activity on Wednesdays and Saturdays.
The music halls have long gone, but locals still
take advantage of the celluloid offerings at the
Screen on the Green (*see p256* **Everyman**
& Screen Cinemas) and the stage productions
at the **Almeida** theatre (*see p290*).

North of Angel, Regency-era **Canonbury**
Square was once home to George Orwell
(no.27) and Evelyn Waugh (no.17A). One of
the handsome townhouses now contains the
Estorick Collection of Modern Italian Art.
Just beyond the end of Upper Street is **Highbury**
Fields, where 200,000 Londoners fled in 1666 to
escape the Great Fire. The surrounding district is
best known as the home of Arsenal Football Club,
who abandoned the charming Highbury Stadium
in 2006 for the gleaming 60,000-seat behemoth
that is the **Emirates Stadium** (Hornsey Road,
N7 7AJ). Fans can either take a fine self-guided
audio tour of the stadium or check out the
memorabilia at the **Arsenal Museum** (7619
5000, www.arsenal.com). Dedicated football fans
will enjoy walking a couple of blocks east to
Avenell Road, where Archibald Leitch's palatial
East Stand has been preserved as offices; on
parallel Highbury Hill, a single painted house
marks the entrance to the vanished West Stand.

Sights & Museums

Estorick Collection of
Modern Italian Art

39A Canonbury Square, N1 2AN (7704 9522,
www.estorickcollection.com). Highbury & Islington
tube/Overground or bus 271. **Open** 11am-6pm
Wed-Sat; noon-5pm Sun. **Admission** £5; £3.50
reductions; free under-16s, students.
Originally owned by American political scientist
and writer Eric Estorick, this is a wonderful repository of early 20th-century Italian art. It is one of
the world's foremost collections of futurism, Italy's
brash and confrontational contribution to international modernism. The four galleries are full of
movement, machines and colour, while the temporary exhibits meet the futurist commitment to fas-
cism full on. There is also a shop and café.

Restaurants

Ottolenghi

287 Upper Street, N1 2TZ (7288 1454, www.
ottolenghi.co.uk). Angel tube or Highbury &
Islington tube/Overground. **Open** 8am-10.30pm
Mon-Sat; 9am-7pm Sun. **Main courses** £9-£13.
Café
Hit cookbooks have made this flagship branch of the
burgeoning Ottolenghi empire a point of pilgrimage

EXPLORE

69 Colebrooke Row.

for foodies the world over. French toast made from brioche and served with crème fraîche and a thin berry and muscat compote makes a heady start to the day. Or there's welsh rarebit, scrambled eggs with smoked salmon or a lively chorizo-spiked take on baked beans served with sourdough, fried egg and black pudding. In the evening (when bookings are taken), the cool white interior works a double shift as a smart and comparatively pricey restaurant serving elegant fusion dishes for sharing.

Other locations 63 Ledbury Road, Notting Hill, W11 2AD (7727 1121); 13 Motcomb Street, Belgravia, SW1X 8LB (7823 2707); 50 Artillery Lane, Spitalfields, E1 7LJ (7247 1999).

▶ *Yotam Ottolenghi also runs Nopi (21-22 Warwick Street, W1B 5NE, 7494 9584).*

Smokehouse
63-69 Canonbury Road, N1 2DG (7354 1144, www.smokehouseislington.co.uk). Highbury & Islington tube/Overground. **Open** 6-10pm Mon-Fri; 11am-4pm, 6-10pm Sat; noon-9pm Sun. **Main courses** £13.50-£18. Barbecue
In the Big Smoke, chef Neil Rankin has become a high priest of barbecue. Trendy though the menu seems – it includes French bistro dishes, carefully sourced British produce and even Korean flavours – the mutton chops come from the grill, not the barman's cheeks, and they come fatty and full-flavoured. Mullet is smoked, cut into translucent slivers and served with white pickled clams, radishes and sea purslane. Pit-roasted corn on the cob, slathered with buttery smoked béarnaise sauce, shows that a barbecue expert doesn't just cook flesh.

★ Trullo
300-302 St Paul's Road, N1 2LH (7226 2733, www.trullorestaurant.com). Highbury & Islington

tube/Overground. **Open** 12.30-2.45pm, 6-10pm Mon-Sat; 12.30-3pm Sun. **Main courses** £14-£30. Italian
While evenings are still busy-to-frantic in this two-floored contemporary trattoria, lunchtime finds Trullo calm and the cooking relaxed and assured. A bargain £15 set menu gleans two courses (primi plus either antipasti or dessert) from a daily-changing menu. Grills and roasts from the carte might include Black Hampshire pork chop and cod with cannellini beans and mussels, while pappardelle with beef shin ragù has been a staple since Trullo's early days and remains a silky, substantial delight.

Pubs & Bars

The **Old Queen's Head** (*see p270*) is a boisterous and lively pub.

★ 69 Colebrooke Row
69 Colebrooke Row, N1 8AA (07540 528 593, www.69colebrookerow.com). Angel tube. **Open** 5pm-midnight Mon-Wed, Sun; 5pm-1am Thur; 5pm-2am Fri, Sat.
It's not easy to get a seat in this flagship of bar supremo Tony Conigliaro without booking. Punters come for the outstanding cocktails; some of them may push the boundaries of what can be put in a glass, but they always maintain the drinkability of the classics. Take the Terroir, for instance, which lists as its ingredients 'distilled clay, flint and lichen', and tastes wonderfully like a chilled, earthy, minerally vodka. It's made in Conigliaro's upstairs laboratory, which also produces bespoke cocktail ingredients such as Guinness reduction, paprika bitters, rhubarb cordial and pine-infused gin. There's a subtle jazz-age vibe and – on certain nights – a pianist belts out swinging standards.

EXPLORE

EXPLORE

Shops & Services

Islington isn't the shopping area it once was – many of the boutiques have been replaced by chains – but Upper Street still rewards a stroll.

Aria

Barnsbury Hall, Barnsbury Street, N1 1PN (7704 6222, www.ariashop.co.uk). Angel tube or Highbury & Islington tube/Overground. **Open** 10am-6.30pm Mon-Sat; noon-5pm Sun. **Homewares**
Housed in an impressive Victorian-era former concert hall, Aria is one of London's best design destinations. As well as mid-range contemporary designed kitchenware, clocks and lighting by Alessi, Marimekko and Kartell, there are quirkier international treasures, including vintage Indian trestle market tables and Finnish folklore cushions from Klaus Haapaniemi.

Cass Art

66-67 Colebrooke Row, N1 8AB (7619 2601, www. cassart.co.uk). Angel tube. **Open** 10am-7pm Mon-Wed, Fri, Sat; 10am-8pm Thur; 11am-5.30pm Sun. **Art supplies**
This cavernous store, hidden down a back street, houses a dazzling array of art materials. Everything is here, from sable brushes and oil paints to Winsor & Newton inks and artists' mannequins. You'll find all you need for crafting too, with full accessories for screen printing, calligraphy and découpage. It's absolutely brilliant for kids, with stickers, origami and paper-doll sets from hip French brand Djeco, art toys like Etch-a-Sketch and more felt-tip pens and glitter pots than you can shake a glue stick at.

twentytwentyone

274-275 Upper Street, N1 2UA (7299 1996, www. twentytwentyone.com). Angel tube or Highbury & Islington tube/Overground. **Open** 10am-6pm Mon-Sat; 11am-5pm Sun. **Homewares**
There's a definite Scandi-slant to north London furniture store twentytwentyone. Set over two spacious floors, its sleek lines, muted colours and clean outlines display minimalistic furniture, accessories and ceramics at their most appealing. We love the functionality of the Lonneberga Wood stacking beds, which will transform a study into a guest room, and the off-kilter angles of Martino Gamper's colourful Arnold Circus stool. The El Baúl golf-ball-like storage box is perfect for hiding kids' toys somewhere chic. You can also find the world's most stylish smoke alarm here – a tactile pastel ingot that simply sticks to the ceiling.

DALSTON & HACKNEY

Dalston Junction, Dalston Kingsland, Hackney Central or London Fields Overground.

The opening of the Overground leaves even bus-averse visitors few excuses to ignore this part of town. Occupying the area around the junction of Balls Pond Road and Kingsland Road, scruffy Dalston may be summed up these days by African-flavoured Ridley Road market: routinely praised by hipsters for its authentic cultural mix, it's still 'real' enough that some stallholders were caught selling 'illicit' meat in 2012. Safer to head to one of the delicious Turkish *ocakbaşı* (grill restaurants) along Stoke Newington Road,

Mangal 1 Ocakbaşı.

although the throngs of hipsters OMGing over sharing plates and the latest 'dirty' food pop-up are the current zeitgeist. In truth, even as the brand managers descend, Dalston remains a cool and lively part of London – with several establishments now well established. All tribes play together happily enough at the appealingly urban **Dalston Jazz Bar** (4 Bradbury Street, 7254 9728), and the brilliant **Vortex Jazz Club** (*see p279*) and **Café Oto** (*see p277*). Also nearby is an appealing 'micropark', the delightfully urban **Dalston Eastern Curve Garden** (3 Dalston Lane, E8 3DF, http://dalstongarden.org).

Neighbouring **Stoke Newington** is the richer cousin of Dalston and poorer cousin of Islington. At weekends, pretty **Clissold Park** (www.clissoldpark.com) is overrun with picnickers and mums pushing prams. Most visitors head here for bijou **Church Street**. This curvy road is lined with second-hand bookshops, cute boutiques and kids' stores, and superior cafés and restaurants – Keralan vegetarian restaurant **Rasa** (no.55, 7249 0344) is probably the best of them. Another local highlight is **Abney Park Cemetery** (www.abney-park.org.uk), a wonderfully wild, overgrown Victorian boneyard and nature reserve.

Alongside Stoke Newington to the east, Hackney has few blockbuster sights, but is one of London's fastest changing areas – a pioneer in the current wave of gentrification. Its administrative centre is Town Hall Square on Mare Street, where you'll find a century-old music hall, the **Hackney Empire** (291 Mare Street, 8985 2424, www.hackneyempire.co.uk); an art deco town hall; a multi-screen cinema in the old Victorian library; and the fine little **Hackney Museum** (1 Reading Lane, 8356 3500, www.hackney.gov.uk/cm-museum.htm), in the 21st-century library. Opposite, an ambitious failed music venue has become a successful cinema (**Hackney Picturehouse**; *see p258*). Within walking distance to the east is the historic **Sutton House**.

Sights & Museums

Sutton House

2-4 Homerton High Street, E9 6JQ (8986 2264, www.nationaltrust.org.uk). Bethnal Green tube then bus 254, 106, D6, or Hackney Central Overground. **Open** times vary; check website for details. **Admission** £3.90; £1.10 reductions; £7 family; free under-5s.

Built in 1535 for Henry VIII's first secretary of state, Sir Ralph Sadleir, this red-brick Tudor mansion is east London's oldest home. Now beautifully restored in authentic original decor, with a real Tudor kitchen to boot, it makes no secret of its history of neglect: even some 1980s squatter graffiti has been preserved. The house closes for January each year.

Restaurants

Mangal 1 Ocakbaşı

10 Arcola Street, E8 2DJ (7275 8981, www.mangal1.com). Dalston Kingsland Overground. **Open** noon-midnight daily. **Main courses** £6.50-£17.50. **Turkish**

For more than 20 years, this restaurant has excelled at grilling meat; the enormous mangal by the entrance, which pumps smoke halfway down Arcola Street, has never failed us yet. Don't bother with starters: tuck straight into *cop sis* (rich and succulent grilled lamb) and *tavuk beyti* (a delicately garlicky kebab of minced chicken). There are no frills – in decor or service – but that's not why you come here.

Tina, We Salute You

47 King Henry's Walk, N1 4NH (3119 0047, www.tinawesaluteyou.com). Dalston Kingsland Overground. **Open** 8am-6pm Mon-Fri; 10am-6pm Sat, Sun. **Main courses** £4-£6. **No credit cards**. Café

Tina's puts you instantly at ease: the large communal table in the middle (sofas and a handful of pavement tables also available for early arrivers) – populated with help-yourself jars of Marmite and jam, and locals helping each other with the *Guardian* crossword – feels like your best friend's kitchen table. Owners Danny and Steve make all the cakes at home, but there's also a comforting breakfast menu (poached eggs, pancakes with berries, porridge) that eases itself into lunch (toasted sandwiches, bagels, ploughman's). Tina's also serves good coffee; expand your tastes beyond the usual latte with a Gibraltar (between a mini latte and a large macchiato).

★ Towpath

Regent's Canal towpath, between Whitmore Bridge and Kingsland Road Bridge, N1 5SB (no phone). Haggerston Overground. **Open** *Mar-Nov* 8am-dusk Tue-Fri; 9am-dusk Sat, Sun. Closed Dec-Feb. **Main courses** £3-£8. **No credit cards**. Café

This simple operation on Regent's Canal towpath was a novelty when it opened in 2010. Its four shallow units continue to lure passing walkers and cyclists with its original setting and enticing food and drink, even with a couple of more elaborate restaurants now on the same block. Grab a table in the sunshine on a summer's day, and you might end up staying for hours. Relaxed entertainment is provided by coots tending their nests and passing bikes whizzing by, as you tuck into delicious grilled cheese sandwiches and decent coffee.

Pubs & Bars

Cock Tavern

315 Mare Street, E8 1EJ (no phone, www.the cocktavern.co.uk). Hackney Central Overground. **Open** from noon daily.

EXPLORE

ONE-OF-A-KIND ATTRACTIONS

Sightseeing treats off the beaten track.

Bethlem Gallery & Museum of the Mind

Bethlem Royal Hospital, Monks Orchard Road, Beckenham, BR3 3BX (http:// museumofthemind.org.uk, 3228 4227). Eden Park rail, then 15mins walk or 356 bus, or East Croydon rail, then 119 or 198 bus. **Open** 10am-5pm Wed-Fri, 1st & last Sat of mth. **Admission** free.

Opened in 2015, this museum is a fascinating insight into mental illness and creativity, stretching back to the origins of Bethlem hospital (which became notorious as 'Bedlam') in 1247. It has an extraordinary collection of art – key works include Richard Dadd's *Sketch of an idea for Crazy Jane* (1855) and Louis Wain's *Phrenology* (1911) – as well as manacles and straitjackets, while the statues that flanked the gates of 17th-century 'Bedlam' guard the stairs.

Dulwich Picture Gallery

Gallery Road, Dulwich, SE21 7AD (8693 5254, www.dulwichpicturegallery.org.uk). North Dulwich or West Dulwich rail. **Open** 10am-5pm Tue-Fri; 11am-5pm Sat, Sun. **Admission** £6; free-£5 reductions. *Special exhibitions* £11; free-£10 reductions.

This bijou attraction was designed by Sir John Soane in 1811 as the first purpose-built gallery in the UK. It's a beautiful space that shows off Soane's ingenuity with lighting effects. The gallery displays a small but outstanding collection of work by Old Masters, offering a fine introduction to the Baroque era through works by Rembrandt, Rubens, Poussin and Gainsborough.

Horniman Museum

100 London Road, Forest Hill, SE23 3PQ (8699 1872, www.horniman.ac.uk). Forest Hill rail or bus 122, 176, 185, 363, P4, P13. **Open** 10.30am-5.30pm daily. **Admission** free; donations appreciated. *Temporary exhibitions vary. Aquarium* £3; £1.10 reductions; £7 family; free under-3s.

The Horniman is an eccentric-looking art nouveau building with extensive gardens. The Natural History Gallery is dominated by an ancient walrus (overstuffed by Victorian taxidermists, who thought they ought to get the wrinkles out of the animal's skin) and ringed by glass cabinets containing pickled animals, stuffed birds and insect models.

Other galleries include African Worlds and the Centenary Gallery, which focuses on world cultures. The Music Gallery contains hundreds of instruments: their sounds can be unleashed via touch-screen tables. The museum's popular showpiece Aquarium is a series of tanks and rockpools covering seven distinct aquatic ecosystems.

London Museum of Water & Steam

Green Dragon Lane, Brentford, Middx, TW8 0EN (8568 4757, www.kbsm.org). Gunnersbury tube/Overground or Kew Bridge rail. **Open** 11am-4pm daily. **Admission** £11.50; £5-£10 reductions; free under-5s.

This Victorian pumping station is a reminder that steam wasn't just used for powering trains but also for supplying water to the citizens of an expanding London. Home to an extraordinary collection of engines, it now has a great array of new interactives, a dressing-up box and even a miniature steam train. The engines crank into action at weekends and bank holidays.

Lord's Tour & MCC Museum

St John's Wood Road, St John's Wood, NW8 8QN (7616 8500, www.lords.org). St John's Wood tube. **Tours** times vary. **Tickets** £18; £12 reductions; £49 family; free under-5s.

Lord's is more than just a cricket ground. As the headquarters of the Marylebone Cricket Club (MCC), it is the official guardian of the sport's rules. The museum's highlight is the tiny urn containing the Ashes (the coveted trophy never leaves Lord's, so it's still here despite England's pitiful capitulation in 2013/14; we await the 2015 series with some trepidation). There's also memorabilia celebrating legends of the game.

South London Gallery

65 Peckham Road, Peckham, SE5 8UH (7703 6120, www.southlondongallery.org). Oval tube then bus 436, or Elephant & Castle tube/rail then bus 12, 171. **Open** 11am-6pm Tue, Thur-Sun; 10am-9pm Wed. **Admission** free; temporary exhibitions vary.

In 1891, William Rossiter opened the pioneering South London Fine Art Gallery. A century later, renamed the South London Gallery, it found new renown as first exhibitor of 'Everyone I Have Ever Slept With 1963-1995', Tracey Emin's infamous tent. A

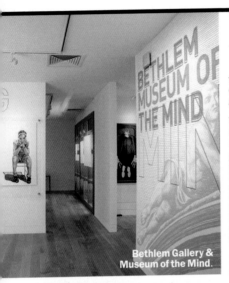

Bethlem Gallery & Museum of the Mind.

their only World Cup in 1966, and the crossbar from which Hurst's disputed goal bounced is in one of the cafés.

Wimbledon Lawn Tennis Museum
Museum Building, All England Lawn Tennis Club, Church Road, Wimbledon, SW19 5AE (8946 6131, www.wimbledon.org/museum). Southfields tube. **Open** 10am-5pm daily; ticket holders only during championships. **Admission** (incl tour) £22; £13-£19 reductions; free under-5s.
Highlights at this popular museum on the history of tennis include a 200° cinema screen that allows you to find out what it's like to play on Centre Court, and a re-creation of a 1980s men's dressing room, complete with a 'ghost' of John McEnroe. Visitors can also enjoy a behind-the-scenes tour.

World Rugby Museum/ Twickenham Stadium
Twickenham Rugby Stadium, Whitton Road, Twickenham, Middx, TW2 7BA (8892 8877, www.rfu.com). Hounslow East tube then bus 281, or Twickenham rail. **Open** *Museum* 10am-5pm Tue-Sat; 11am-5pm Sun. *Tours* times vary. **Admission** £16; £10 reductions; free under-5s.
Twickenham Stadium is the home of English rugby union. Guided tours take in the England dressing room, the players' tunnel and the Royal Box. Memorabilia charts the game's development from the late 19th century, and there's a scrum machine.

WWT Wetland Centre
Queen Elizabeth's Walk, Barnes, SW13 9WT (8409 4400, www.wwt.org.uk). Hammersmith tube then bus 283, Barnes rail. **Open** *Apr-Oct* 9.30am-6pm daily. *Nov-Mar* 9.30am-5pm daily. **Admission** £12.35; £6.90-£9.20 reductions; free under-4s.
The 43-acre Wetland Centre is four miles from central London, but feels a world away. Quiet ponds, rushes, rustling reeds and wildflower gardens all teem with bird life – some 150 species. There are over 300 varieties of butterfly, 20 types of dragonfly and four species of bat. You can explore water-recycling in the Rain Garden or try the interactive section: pilot a submerged camera around a pond, learn the life-cycle of a dragonfly or make waves in a digital pool.

£1.8m-extension in 2010 added a great café, two exhibition spaces and a resident artist's flat, and helps to keep it on the cutting edge as a contemporary-art venue.

Thames Barrier
1 Unity Way, Woolwich, SE18 5NJ (8305 4188, www.environment-agency.gov.uk/ thamesbarrier). Woolwich Dockyard rail, or North Greenwich tube then bus 472. **Open** 10.30am-5pm Thur-Sun. **Admission** £3.75; £2.25-£3.25 reductions; free under-5s.
This adjustable dam came into its own in the terrible floods of 2014. The shiny silver fins, lined up across Woolwich Reach, are an impressive sight. Built in 1982 at a cost of £535m, the barrier is regularly in action for maintenance purposes; check the website for a current timetable. To learn more, look around the learning centre, where you'll find an account of the 1953 flood that led to the barrier's construction, as well as displays on Thames wildlife. There's a pleasant café.

Wembley Stadium
Stadium Way, Wembley, Middx, HA9 0WS (0844 980 8001, www.wembleystadium. com). Wembley Park tube or Wembley Stadium rail. **Tours** £19; £11 reductions; free under-5s.
Lord Foster's 2007 Wembley redesign is impressive, and the guided tours of the 90,000-seat stadium give a fantastic flavour of the venue's history: here, England won

EXPLORE

Pond Dalston

The Cock Tavern is the sort of place you walk into and think: this is a bloody good pub. It's dark, uncomplicated and resonant with merry conversation. Put simply, it's a room for grown-ups to stand in and drink beer. It's timelessly classic: aside from the Victorian beards on the bar staff, it could be any era between 1920 and 2015. It's usually rammed, which is mainly down to the fabulous beer and cider: the pub cellar is now home to the Howling Hops microbrewery, whose output is mostly drunk in the Cock. A few guests pop up too among the 22 taps, but with a home-brewed selection this good, you might not need them. To fill you up, there's simple food. A bartop cabinet displays scotch eggs and pork pies, and there's a jar of pickled eggs.

Pond Dalston

Unit G2, Stamford Works, 3 Gillett Street, N16 8JH (3772 6727, http://pond-dalston.com). Dalston Kingsland Overground. **Open** 5-11pm Mon-Sat.
Sizeable former industrial premises aren't the first place you'd think to look for 'New Hawaiian Cuisine' – and we suggest you don't. Instead, pull up to the smart, long bar and say 'aloha' to terrific cocktails, which have a tropical twist that stops long before the kitsch clichés of tiki. Try a Luscious Lanai that melts pineapple sorbet into the glass with prosecco and St Germain elderflower liqueur, or the Kamm On Baby Light My Fire, which mixes Kamm & Sons ginseng spirit with pisco, fresh lime and tiki bitters.

Shops & Services

For a fashion show and farmers' market, head to Hackney's **Broadway Market** on Saturday.

Hackney Fashion Hub
Morning Lane, E9. Hackney Central or Homerton Overground. **Fashion**
Is there a more unlikely part of town for a fashion nexus? From Hackney Central station, you stroll past junkyards, a supermarket, tower blocks and takeaways. But the Hackney Fashion Hub initiative (www.hackneyfashionhub.co.uk) has earmarked this bit of land for a 6,250sq m shopping mall. The developer (Manhattan Loft Corporation, which was behind the rebirth of St Pancras International) capitalised on footfall to the nearby Burberry factory outlet (29-31 Chatham Place, E9 6LP, 8328 4287) by renting neighbouring property to Aquascutum (7-8 Ram Place, E9 6LT, 3096 1863, www.aquascutum. co.uk) and, in a converted pub, Pringle (90 Morning Lane, E9 6NA, 8533 1158, www.pringlescotland. com); there are monster bargains to be had at all three. Due to open in 2016, the mall will house discount outlets for designer brands, workshops and pop-up spaces for up-and-coming local designers. The pop-up aspect is already being trialled at a pocket-sized boutique a few strides from Burberry: the Hackney Shop (99 Morning Lane, E9 6ND, www. thehackneyshop.com) has rails of gorgeous catwalk fashion by designers who dress red-carpet celebs and models in glossy magazines – Roksanda Ilincic and Jonathan Saunders have both been here – but it's a not-for-profit enterprise that also offers rent-free space by the week to local designers.

Hub
49 & 88 Stoke Newington Church Street, N16 0AR (no.49: 7524 4494, no.88: 7275 8160, www. hubshop.co.uk). Stoke Newington Overground. **Open** 10.30am-6pm Mon-Sat; 11am-5pm Sun. **Fashion**
With its edited selection of mid-market heritage and emerging labels, Stoke Newington boutique Hub is the ideal place to cultivate that casual, not-trying-too-hard look. At no.49, ladies snap up Sessùn coats, Petit Bateau shirts, jeans by Dr Denim and holdalls by Great Plains from a decidedly un-feminine shop, while gents stock up on Barbour jackets, Herschel backpacks and Wolsey hats at no.88.

Kristina Records
44 Stoke Newington Road, N16 7XJ (7254 2130, www.kristinarecords.com). Dalston Kingsland Overground. **Open** noon-8pm Mon-Sat; noon-7pm Sun. **Books & music**
It's easier to buy your vinyl online, of course, but Kristina proves that convenience doesn't always equal satisfaction. This shop is a living, breathing experience for living, breathing music fans, with a clean and uncluttered layout that makes Kristina's

platters matter far more than a website ever could. For the dedicated dance-music fan, the racks of new house and techno are a goldmine, while expertly chosen oldies of a soul and jazz bent are represented too.

★ LN-CC

18-24 Shacklewell Lane, E8 2EZ (7275 7265, www.ln-cc.com). Dalston Kingsland Overground. **Open** by appt. **Fashion, books & music** LN-CC, otherwise known as the Late Night Chameleon Club, is as mysterious as its name suggests. Accessed by appointment via a basement-level door in an unlikely Shacklewell warehouse building, the store is a Tim Burton-like wonderland rendered in natural wood with a secret dancefloor, tree house, listening library and London's most unique edit of super-rare fashion. Ostensibly a showroom for internet boutique LN-CC.com, the space is a gallery for upscale design, selling super-posh brands such as Rik Owens, Givenchy, Lanvin and any number of hard-to-pronounce rarities. With vinyl, art books and eyewear, and stock in different themed zones, LN-CC is a shop like no other.

OLYMPIC PARK

Stratford tube/DLR/Overground.

The Olympic Park, scene of the 2012 Games, is a square mile of the Lower Lea Valley in east London. Closed between the end of the Paralympics and spring 2014, it is now fully open. After a sporting summer that exceeded most predictions – and won over many critics – the Games are long gone and only the contentious business of 'legacy' remains: arguments over what benefits have been brought to Londoners by the £8.77 billion spent on the Games may continue for generations, but the physical legacy of the post-Games Olympic Park – officially renamed the **Queen Elizabeth Olympic Park** (www.queenelizabetholympicpark.co.uk) in January 2013 – is becoming clear.

The immaculate parklands to the north had already been launched in summer 2013, their paths and waterways enhanced by the new Timber Lodge with its café. Next came the Zaha Hadid-designed **Aquatics Centre** (£3.50-£4.50, £2-£2.50 reductions), open for public swimming and diving, followed by the **VeloPark**, home to road, track, BMX and mountain biking, and the southern section of the park. The latter comprises all the remaining parkland, including children's play areas, four walking trails, a couple of dozen public artworks, plus the **ArcelorMittal Orbit**. All that remains is the Olympic Stadium, which is currently being retooled (including the addition of a roof over the seats). It is due to reopen for the Rugby World Cup in 2015, before West Ham football club take up residence in 2016. In the meantime, it will host music events Hard Rock Calling and the Wireless Festival. There are also ambitious plans to create an 'Olympicopolis' by 2018 – combining spaces for the V&A, UCL, Sadler's Wells and even the Smithsonian in a cultural hub to rival South Ken. For a good vantage point on the park, head to **Moka East** in the View Tube. And if you've a little time on your hands, stroll south along the Lea towards the Thames to **Three Mills Island**, or north.

EXPLORE

Aquatics Centre.

Sights & Museums

ArcelorMittal Orbit

Queen Elizabeth Olympic Park (www.queenelizabeth olympicpark.co.uk). Stratford tube/DLR/Overground or West Ham tube/Overground. **Open** varies; check website for details. **Admission** £15; £7-£12 reductions; £40 family.

Perhaps the most dramatic structure in the Olympic Park, overlooking the Olympic Stadium, is the Orbit. Designed by sculptor Anish Kapoor and engineer Cecil Balmond, it is red, 374 feet tall and not much loved by locals. The peripheral location – compared to both Shard (*see p63*) and Eye (*see p51*) – makes the view interesting rather than breathtaking, but Kapoor's arty mirrors inside are fun.

Three Mills Island

Three Mill Lane, E3 3DU (08456 770 600, www. visitleevalley.org.uk). Bromley-by-Bow tube. **Tours** *May-Oct* 11am-4pm Sun; 1st Sun Mar, Apr, Dec. **Admission** £3; £1.50 reductions; free under-16s. **No credit cards**.

Just south of the Olympic Park, this island on the River Lea takes its name from the three mills that ground flour and gunpowder here. The House Mill, built in 1776, is the oldest and largest tidal mill in Britain and is occasionally opened to the public (www.housemill.org.uk, £3, £1.50 reductions, free under-16s). Even when that's closed, the island provides pleasant walks that can feel surprisingly rural – and the new Wild Kingdom children's playground is a joy. Victorian sewer engineer Sir Joseph Bazalgette's extraordinary, Byzantine-style Abbey Mills Pumping Station can be seen nearby.

Restaurants

Moka East

View Tube, Marshgate Lane, E15 2PJ (no phone, www.theviewtube.co.uk). Pudding Mill Lane DLR. **Open** 9am-5pm daily. **Café**.

Set up as a viewing point during the construction of the Olympic Park, this café is housed in stacked-up acid-green shipping containers. It's now run by the family behind Mario's Cafe – sung about by St Etienne, and one of London's proper old-fashioned caffs. Breakfast options include standard bacon, sausage and eggs, muesli with yoghurt and berries, and kippers. The café is right in front of the Olympic Stadium – Anish Kapoor's ArcelorMittal Orbit sculpture is directly opposite.

DOCKLANDS

Canary Wharf tube and numerous DLR stations.

London's docks were fundamental to the prosperity of the British Empire. Between 1802 and 1921, ten separate docks were built between Tower Bridge in the west and Woolwich in the east. These employed tens of thousands of people. Yet by the 1960s, the shipping industry was changing irrevocably. The new 'container' system of cargo demanded larger, deep-draught ships, as a result of which the work moved out to Tilbury, from where lorries would ship the containers into the city. By 1980, the London docks had closed.

The London Docklands Development Corporation (LDDC), founded in 1981, spent £790 million of public money on redevelopment during the following decade, only for a country-wide property slump in the early 1990s to leave the shiny new high-rise offices and luxury flats unoccupied. Nowadays, though, as a financial hub, Docklands is a booming rival to the City, with an estimated 90,000 workers commuting to the area each day, on improved transport links. For visitors, regular **Thames Clippers** (7001 2200, www.thamesclippers.com) boat connections with central London and the **Docklands Light Railway** (DLR) make the area easily accessible.

The **Isle of Dogs** is where you'll find Canary Wharf. The origin of the name 'Isle of Dogs' remains uncertain, but the first recorded use is on a map of 1588; one theory claims Henry VIII kept his hunting dogs here. In the 19th century, a huge system of docks and locks transformed what had been just drained marshland; in fact, the West India Docks cut right across the peninsula, so the Isle of Dogs did eventually become an island.

Almost all the interest for visitors is to be found in the vicinity of Cesar Pelli's dramatic **One Canada Square**, which was the country's tallest habitable building between 1991 and 2012, when it was topped by the Shard (*see p63*). The only slightly shorter HSBC and Citigroup towers joined it in the noughties, and clones are springing up thick and fast. Shopping options are limited to the mall beneath the towers (www.mycanary wharf.com), but you'll find a calm but crisp Japanese garden beside Canary Wharf tube station. Across a floating bridge over the basin to the north, there's the brilliant **Museum of London Docklands**.

It's also well worth hopping on the DLR and heading south to **Island Gardens** station at the tip of the Isle of Dogs. From narrow Island Gardens park, there's a famous Greenwich view – and the entrance to the Victorian pedestrian tunnel. Nearby to the north, at **Mudchute Park & Farm** (Pier Street, 7515 5901, www.mudchute. org), a complete farmyard of animals ruminate in front of the skyscrapers.

Further east (get off at East India DLR), the Lea River empties into the Thames at **Bow Creek**, almost directly opposite the white, deflated balloon of the O2 Arena (*see p273*). Here, **Trinity Buoy Wharf** (64 Orchard Place, E14 0JW, www. trinitybuoywharf.com) is pure incongruity. Built

EXPLORE

Emirates Air Line.

Barrier (*see p239*). If you don't fancy walking, enter the park from Pontoon Dock DLR.

Unless you're checking in at **London City Airport** (*see p367*), keep on the DLR as far as King George V to get a free ferry (every 15mins daily, 8853 9400) that chugs pedestrians and cars across the river, or stay in your carriage as the DLR passes under the river all the way to its final stop at Woolwich Arsenal.

Sights & Museums

FREE Crystal
Royal Victoria Dock, 1 Siemens Brothers Way, E16 1GB (7055 6400, http://thecrystal.org). Royal Victoria DLR. **Open** 10am-5pm Tue-Sat; 10am-7pm Sun. *Café* 8.30am-5pm daily. **Admission** free. Exhibitions vary.
The Crystal attempts to explain in an engaging fashion how cities work, and how they might meet the challenges of global warming, population growth, ageing and the shortage of key resources, especially water. The two floors of interactives are slick and fun: beat the computer at face recognition, or plan the transport for different cities. There's a good café too.

★ Emirates Air Line
North terminal *27 Western Gateway, E16 4FA. Royal Victoria DLR.*
South terminal *Edmund Halley Way, SE10 0FR. North Greenwich tube.*
Both *0343 222 1234, www.tfl.gov.uk/modes/ emirates-air-line.* **Open** *Summer* 7am-9pm Mon-Fri; 8am-9pm Sat; 9am-9pm Sun. *Winter* 7am-8pm Mon-Fri; 8am-8pm Sat; 9am-8pm Sun. **Tickets** £4.80 single; £2.40 reductions, free under-5s.
Arguments for a cable car across the Thames as a solution to any of London's many transport problems are, at best, moot, but its value as a tourist thrill is huge. The comfy pods zoom 295ft up elegant stanchions at a gratifying pace. Suddenly there are brilliant views of the expanses of water that make up the Royal Docks, the ships on the Thames, Docklands and the Thames Barrier. Good fun and good value – but note that the cable car may not run in high winds.
▶ *Tickets are cheaper if you use an Oyster card, and you'll avoid any ticket desk queues.*

★ FREE Museum of London Docklands
No.1 Warehouse, West India Quay, Hertsmere Road, E14 4AL (7001 9844, www.museumof londonindocklands.org.uk). Canary Wharf tube/ DLR or West India Quay DLR. **Open** 10am-6pm daily. **Admission** free. *Temporary exhibitions vary.*
Housed in a 19th-century warehouse (itself a Grade I-listed building), this museum explores the complex history of London's docklands and the river over two millennia. Displays spreading over three storeys

in the early 1800s, it was a depot and repair yard for shipping buoys, and it was here, in the 1860s, that James Douglass – later designer of the fourth Eddystone Lighthouse – built London's only lighthouse. Open every weekend from 11am to 4pm (5pm in summer), the lighthouse is the perfect setting for the haunting *Longplayer* sound installation (http://longplayer.org).

A couple more stops east give you access to the **Royal Docks** – get off at Royal Victoria or Royal Albert – as well as the ExCeL conference centre, a docked steamship and a new attraction, the black and pointy **Crystal**. You can also cross the slightly hair-raising, high white bridge from ExCeL to find two historic ships: a red lightship and, floating on a raft to preserve it, **SS Robin** (www.ssrobin.org), a steamship so rare it is included (with the *Cutty Sark* and HMS *Belfast*) in the National Historic Fleet. Head south towards the Thames and you'll find the beautiful **Thames Barrier Park**. Opened in 2001, this was London's first new park in half a century. It has a lush sunken garden of waggly hedges and offers perhaps the best views from land of the Thames

EXPLORE

take you from the arrival of the Romans all the way to the docks' 1980s closure and the area's subsequent redevelopment. The Docklands at War section is very moving, while a haunting new permanent exhibition sheds light on the dark side of London's rise as a centre for finance and commerce, exploring its involvement in the slave trade. You can also walk through full-scale mock-ups of a quayside and a dingy riverfront alley. Temporary exhibitions are set up on the ground floor, where you'll also find a café and a docks-themed play area. Just like its elder brother, the Museum of London (*see p180*), the MoLD has a great programme of special events.

Restaurants

Jamie's Italian

Unit 17, 2 Churchill Place, Canary Wharf, E14 5RB (3002 5252, www.jamieoliver.com). Canary Wharf tube/DLR. **Open** 11.30am-11pm Mon-Fri; noon-11pm Sat; noon-10.30pm Sun. **Main courses** £9.95-£24. Italian
The vivacity and personality of the cooking makes Jamie Oliver's most successful concept an appealing choice. This likeable chain serves dishes such as grilled free-range chicken with garlic and rosemary; spaghetti alla norma, with aubergines, oregano, chilli and basil in a tomato sauce. All are punchily flavoured, well sourced and served with panache. **Other locations** throughout the city.

Yi-Ban

London Regatta Centre, 1010 Dockside Road, E16 2QT (7473 6699, www.yi-ban.co.uk). Royal Albert DLR. **Open** noon-11pm Mon-Sat; 11am-10.30pm Sun. **Main courses** £8-£45. Chinese
Visiting Yi-Ban by public transport can be a disconcerting experience, involving a trip on the DLR to Royal Albert station, then a walk along a deserted road and across a large car park to the first floor of the grey concrete box that is the London Regatta Centre. Once inside, you're greeted by a spacious room lined with floor-to-ceiling windows offering striking views across the dock of planes taking off and landing at City Airport. The menu is extensive, with Vietnamese as well as Chinese dishes, a particularly good selection of seafood and a dozen hotpots. Note that the restaurant gets very busy at weekends, so it's wise to book.

VAUXHALL & BRIXTON

Stockwell tube, or Brixton or Vauxhall tube/rail.

The area now known as Vauxhall was, in the 13th century, home to a house owned by one Falkes de Bréauté, a soldier rewarded for carrying out King John's dirtier military deeds. Over time, Falkes' Hall became Fox Hall and finally Vauxhall. Vauxhall's heyday was in the 18th century when the infamous Pleasure Gardens, built back in 1661, reached the height of their popularity: a mingling of wealthy and not-so-wealthy, with everyone getting into trouble on 'lovers' walks'. When the Gardens closed in 1859, the area became reasonably respectable – all that remains is Spring Garden, behind popular gay haunt the Royal Vauxhall Tavern (aka **RVT**; *see p261*). For a glimpse of old Vauxhall, head to **Bonnington Square**. Down on the river is the cream and emerald ziggurat designed by Terry Farrell for the Secret Intelligence Service (formerly MI6).

At the top end of the South Lambeth Road, **Little Portugal** – a cluster of Portuguese cafés, shops and tapas bars – is an enticing oasis. At the other end, **Stockwell** is commuter territory, with little to lure visitors except some charming Victorian streets: Albert Square, Durand Gardens and Stockwell Park Crescent; van Gogh was briefly resident at 87 Hackford Road.

South of Stockwell is **Brixton**, a lively hub of clubs and music. The town centre has been enjoying significant redevelopment, with Windrush Square completed at the end of Coldharbour Lane in 2010. The square's name is significant: HMS *Windrush* was the boat that brought West Indian immigrants from Jamaica in 1948. They were hardly welcomed, but managed to make Brixton a thriving community. As late as the 1980s, tensions were still strong, as the Clash song 'Guns of Brixton' famously illustrates. The rage of the persecuted black community, still finding themselves isolated and under suspicion decades after arriving, is better expressed by dub poet Linton Kwesi Johnson – try 'Sonny's Lettah' (Anti-Sus Poem)' for starters. The riots of 1981 and 1985 around Railton Road and Coldharbour Lane left the district scarred for years.

Now, most visitors come to Brixton for Brixton Village (*see p245*). The two covered arcades date to the 1920s and '30s and have been – with Market Row – Grade II listed. The district's main roads are modern and filled with chain stores, but there's also some attractive architecture – check out the **Ritzy Cinema** (Brixton Oval, Coldharbour Lane, 0871 902 5739, www.picturehouses.co.uk), dating to 1911. Brixton's best-known street, **Electric Avenue**, got its name when, in 1880, it became one of the first shopping streets to get electric lights.

Minutes south of Brixton's hectic centre, flanked by Tulse Hill and Dulwich Road, **Brockwell Park** (www.brockwellpark.com) is one of London's most underrated green spaces. Landscaped in the early 19th century for a wealthy glass-maker, the park contains his Georgian country house – now a café – an open-air swimming pool, bowling green, walled rose garden and miniature railway. Each July, there's an enjoyable country fair. If that doesn't seem bucolic enough, visit **Brixton Windmill** just off Brixton Hill a little further west.

EXPLORE

Sights & Museums

FREE Brixton Windmill
Windmill Gardens, off Blenheim Gardens, SW2 5BZ (www.brixtonwindmill.org). Brixton tube. **Tours** *Apr-Oct* times vary; see website for details. Closed Nov-Mar. **Admission** free.

Built in 1816 and in service until 1934, Brixton Windmill reopened to the public in 2011, and had already won several tourism and heritage awards by 2012. There are about 20 open days a year, during which you can visit without booking (but may have to queue: there isn't much room in the windmill), but the 30-45min pre-booked guided tours give access to the upper floors – and are a fascinating glimpse into a lost London industry.

Restaurants

Brunswick House Café
30 Wandsworth Road, Vauxhall Cross, SW8 2LG (7720 2926, www.brunswickhouse.co). Vauxhall tube/rail. **Open** 9.30am-midnight Mon-Fri; 10am-midnight Sat; noon-5pm Sun. **Main courses** £14-£18.60. **Brasserie**

This Georgian mansion, a tiny beacon of classic calm amid the high-rise apartments and noisy chaos of Vauxhall Cross, has no trouble packing in a young, high-spending clientele. Some are simply stopping by for a cocktail while perusing the desirable bric-a-brac on offer from architectural salvage company Lassco, but most are here to meet, drink, eat and

generally enjoy the place's markedly non-corporate hospitality. It's an appealing combination of boho-chic comfort and minimalist menu presentation.

★ Franco Manca
Unit 1, 4 Market Row, Electric Lane, SW9 8LD (7738 3021, www.francomanca.co.uk). Brixton tube/rail. **Open** noon-5pm Mon; noon-11pm Tue-Sat; noon-10.30pm Sun. **Main courses** £4.50-£7.50. **Pizza**

With its top-notch, UK-sourced (when possible) ingredients, speedy and friendly service, and rapid turnover, the original Brixton branch of Franco Manca remains, for our money, the best pizza joint in London. Here, you can sate a craving for genuine, Neapolitan-style pizza, with a flavourful slow-rise sourdough crust and a variety of traditional and innovative toppings. **Other locations** throughout the city.

Pubs & Bars

Crown & Anchor
246 Brixton Road, SW9 6AQ (7737 0060, www.crownandanchorbrixton.co.uk). Stockwell tube or Brixton tube/rail. **Open** 4.30pm-midnight Mon-Thur; 4.30pm-1am Fri; noon-1am Sat; noon-11pm Sun. *Food served* 5-10pm Mon-Fri; noon-10pm Sat; noon-8pm Sun

The most exciting feature of this pub, after a back-to-basics restoration, is the lengthy bar with its endless fonts: seven cask ales, 14 keg beers and ciders. It's a friendly place, devoted to great beer.

Shops & Services

★ Brixton Village
Corner of Coldharbour Lane & Brixton Station Road, SW9 8PR (7274 2990, http://brixtonmarket.net). Brixton tube/rail. **Open** 6am-6pm Mon; 6am-11.30pm Tue-Sun; check website for opening hours of individual shops. **Mall**

Once almost forgotten, Granville Arcade has found a new lease of life. It originally opened in 1937, when it was proclaimed 'London's Largest Emporium', and in the 1960s became a Caribbean market. But by the 1990s, many of the arcade's units were unoccupied and its old art deco avenues were falling into a dilapidated state. In 2009, Lambeth Council called in urban-regeneration agency Space Makers, which launched a competition for local entrepreneurs to apply for a unit. It then awarded the best initiatives a place on site, and renamed the space Brixton Village, in line with its eclectic, locally minded new contents – from bijoux bakeries and vintage boutiques to international eateries and fledgling fashion labels. Highlights here include Margot Waggoner's Leftovers (unit 71), with its Marseille lace and vintage sailor dresses, and Binkie and Tabitha's Circus (unit 70), which juxtaposes retro glassware with an assortment of socialist literature.

Brixton Village.

EXPLORE

Arts & Entertainment

Children

London has a lot to offer young visitors. Its museums go out of their way to engage the minds of children with enjoyable events, there are gorgeous parks and playgrounds, brilliant theatres with child-oriented productions, and world-famous attractions. Many of these, such as the Natural History Museum and the Science Museum, are free; many of those that aren't, such as the Tower of London, give you a lot of fun for your entry fee. Plan carefully, but it is essential not to cram too much into one day. Sometimes, the most fun happens in the gaps between the official itinerary – lots of kids get a big kick just from using public transport. For children's festivals (and the many more events that aren't specifically for children but will be enjoyed by them), see *pp30-41*.

WHERE TO GO

There are few secrets for parents in London these days – in other words, anywhere that's any good is likely to be busy. To help you with your planning, *see p251* **Timing is Everything**.

South Bank

This is one of the all-time favourite spots for a family day out in London. Just strolling along the wide riverside promenade will lead you past skateboarders, installations, street artists, book stalls and, often, free performances. The expensive end is around **London Eye** (*see p54*), **London Aquarium** (*see p54*) and the **London Dungeon** (*see p51*). Moving east, visit the **Southbank Centre** (*see p50 and p287*), where free shows and workshops take place during holidays and on weekends in the Clore Ballroom. Don't miss Jeppe Hein's *Appearing Rooms* play-fountains in summer. Next, the **National Theatre** (*see p289*) usually offers free entertainment outside during the summer.

Keep going along the riverbank, past Gabriel's Wharf, a riverside cluster of restaurants and shops, to reach **Tate Modern** (*see p57*). Tate Modern is a day out in itself, with its dramatic Turbine Hall, free family trails and the Bloomberg

Learning Zone on Level 5. At weekends and in school holidays, age-appropriate activity packs are available from Level 3. (There's a boat service from here to **Tate Britain**; *see p77*.)

Once you've emerged, pick up the Bankside Walk, ducking under the southern end of Southwark Bridge. Walk down cobbled Clink Street towards the **Golden Hinde** (*see p59*) and **Southwark Cathedral** (*see p60*), having passed the **Clink Prison Museum** (1 Clink Street, SE1 9DG, 7403 0900, www.clink.co.uk), a cheaper alternative to the London Dungeon. From Tooley Street, march through Hays Galleria to regain the riverside path, which takes you to the excellent warship museum **HMS Belfast** (*see p63*) and on, past the dancing fountains, to **City Hall** and the southern end of **Tower Bridge** (*see p187*). Kids love watching the bridge being lifted: the timings are at www.towerbridge.org.uk/lift-times/.

Trafalgar Square

London's central square (www.london.gov.uk/trafalgarsquare) has been a free playground for children since time immemorial – chasing pigeons can be encouraged; climbing on lions and jumping in fountains should not. Look out for the sculpted skeleton of a horse (*Gift Horse*) on the Fourth Plinth (it will be replaced by *Really Good*, an overextended thumbs-up, in 2016). Festivals take place most weekends. Even if all is quiet in the square, the **National Gallery** (*see p68*) has paper trails and audio tours, as well as workshops for teens and three- to five-year-olds. For five- to 11-year-olds, the **National Portrait Gallery** (*see p69*) runs Family Art Workshops at weekends and during the school holidays.

Just nearby, **St Martin-in-the-Fields** (*see p69*) has London's only brass-rubbing centre, as well as a fine café that does plenty of the type of food that goes down well with children.

South Kensington

Top of any Grand Day Out itinerary is this cultural goldmine. The **Science Museum** (*see p87*) offers heaps of excitement for all ages, from the Garden in the basement for under-sixes to the Pattern Pod on the ground floor and Launchpad upstairs, where children can play with all manner of science experiments. Dinosaur fans won't rest until they've visited the **Natural History Museum** (*see p87*) and seen the animatronic beasties in action. An ice rink in winter and the 'Sensational Butterflies' tent in summer also draw the crowds. The **Victoria & Albert Museum** (*see p90*) marks interactive displays on its floorplan. Its free weekend and school-holiday drop-in family events (featuring trails, activity backpacks, and interactive workshops) provide great ways of focusing on the collection. (Its sister gallery, Bethnal Green's **V&A Museum of Childhood**, *see p211*, has an excellent programme of events for children.)

Covent Garden

At the lively **London Transport Museum** (*see p140*), children can make believe they are driving a bus or riding in a horse-drawn carriage. They love the numbered stamp trail too; a dedicated play area opened early in 2015 – a small one, so it gets busy. The museum also has a programme of school-holiday events. Across the Piazza, the acts in front of **St Paul's Covent Garden** (*see p140*) are worth watching. On the south side of Strand, **Somerset House** (*see*

V&A Museum of Childhod.

p147) allows kids to play outside among the fountains in summer and skate on the winter ice rink. There are also regular art workshops.

Bloomsbury & King's Cross

Children are captivated by the mummies at the **British Museum** (*see p150*). However, the size of the collection can make it overwhelming. The beautifully produced and well-conceived free trails for different ages take a theme and lead families around an edited selection (available in the Paul Hamlyn Library). Alternatively, there are regular events and workshops or free backpacks for kids, filled with puzzles and games. For weekends and school holidays, the Ford Centre for Young Visitors provides a picnic-style eating area.

Central London's best playground, **Coram's Fields** (*see p253*), is close to the British Museum, and the nearby **Foundling Museum** (*see p151*) is also well worth a visit to learn how orphans and foundlings used to be treated.

Further play opportunities are to be found a 15-minute walk north at King's Cross, where the lovely illuminated fountains of **Granary Square** (*see p158*) can be frolicked through, and there's the green tranquillity of **Camley Street** nature reserve (*see p252*) just across the canal.

IN THE KNOW ON THE BUS

Tours too expensive? An economical way to see London as a family is by bus, since under-16s travel free (over-11s need special ID; see p368). Good routes for sightseeing are the 7, 8, 11 and 12 (all double-deckers). For a riverside route, the RV1 goes from Tower Hill to South Bank. Routemaster 15 is a Heritage Route (see p69 **In the Know**).

ARTS & ENTERTAINMENT

The City

It seems pricey, but the **Tower of London** (*see p186*) is a top day out for all ages. If it's free stuff you're after, though, the **Museum of London** (*see p180*) is superb. Its Galleries of Modern London put interactivity and drama at the heart of exciting exhibits, but there are dressing-up boxes throughout, and lots of storytelling sessions and workshops. Nearby, in the **Bank of England Museum** (*see p182*), kids can try to lift a gold bar – by reaching into an otherwise sealed box, so no bank heist is possible.

Greenwich

Magical Greenwich provides a lovely day out away from the mayhem of the West End. Arrive by boat to appreciate its riverside charms, then take time to check out the restored **Cutty Sark** (*see p216*) and excellent **Discover Greenwich** (*see p216*). Next, head to the very child-friendly **National Maritime Museum** (*see p217*), where there's a boat simulator to pilot and a whole room of interactives. From here, it's a pleasant walk in the Royal Park for views from the top of the hill, crowned by the **Royal Observatory & Planetarium** (*see p218*). When the stars come out, watch for the luminous green Meridian Line that cuts across the sky towards the city.

Further north, the **Emirates Air Line** cable car (*see p243*) is an exciting way to cross the river. It runs from North Greenwich tube to the Royal Victoria Dock DLR.

Olympic Park

On a clear day, an excursion to the **Olympic Park** (*see p241*) is a fine adventure for children. There are superb facilities (the Tumbling Bay Playground next to Timber Lodge Café is especially good), as well as rivers for spotting wildlife and some engaging public art, and the fabulous reflecting bridge near Carpenters Lock. An excellent children's trail (including stamping points) can be downloaded from http://queen elizabetholympicpark.co.uk. The **Discover** (*see p253*) story centre is within easy walking distance, beyond the Westfield shopping centre exit from the park.

Enthusiastic walkers and parents with children who are docile in their pushchairs can explore south down the River Lea to **Three Mills Island** (*see p241*), which also has an impressive new playground.

EATING & DRINKING

Few but the very poshest London restaurants are unsuitable for children, although many pubs close even to accompanied children in the evenings.

During the day, however, pretty much any pub that serves food will welcome families; many have high chairs and children's menus. The following are especially enjoyable or solicitous destinations.

Big Red Bus

30 Deptford Church Street, Deptford, SE8 4RZ (3490 8346, www.bigredpizza.co.uk). Deptford Bridge DLR. **Open** noon-10.30pm Tue, Wed; noon-11pm Thur; noon-midnight Fri, Sat; noon-8.30pm Sun. **Main courses** £6.50-£11.

Kids love this pizzeria – in part, because it is inside an old double-decker bus. You can either sit inside, or on the pretty decked terrace. It's beside the DLR, so travel is easy, and the nearby Creekside Centre (*see p252*) makes a good excursion.

Frizzante@Hackney City Farm

1A Goldsmith's Row, Hackney, E2 8QA (7739 2266, www.frizzanteltd.co.uk). Hoxton Overground. **Open** 10am-4.30pm Tue, Wed, Fri-Sun; 10am-4.30pm, 7-10pm Thur. **Main courses** £6-£18.

Trot around the pigs, poultry and sheep outside, then settle down to eat their relatives (or stick to vegetarian options). The oilcloth-covered tables always heave with families tucking into healthy nosh, including big farm breakfasts.

Mudchute Kitchen

Mudchute Park & Farm, Pier Street, Isle of Dogs, Docklands, E14 3HP (3069 9290, www.mudchute. org). Mudchute DLR. **Open** 9.30am-3pm Tue-Fri; 9.30am-5pm Sat, Sun. **Main courses** £2.50-£9.

A farm fenced in by skyscrapers is an amusing place for anyone to eat lunch, but Mudchute is ideal for families. You can eat at farmhouse kitchen tables in the courtyard, while your babies roll around on a big futon in the spacious interior, or in the toy corner.

Rainforest Café

20 Shaftesbury Avenue, Piccadilly, W1D 7EU (7434 3111, www.therainforestcafe.co.uk). Piccadilly Circus tube. **Open** noon-10pm Mon-Fri; 11.30am-10.30pm Sat; 11.30am-10pm Sun (from 11.30am during school holidays). **Main courses** £16.20-£25. **Map** p401 K7.

This themed and handily located restaurant is designed to thrill children with animatronic wildlife, cascading waterfalls and jungle sound-effects. The menu has lots of family-friendly fare, from 'paradise pizza' and 'Maya's meatballs' to amusing dishes for grown-ups. The children's menu costs £12.95 for two courses and a drink.

★ Tate Modern Café

Tate Modern, Sumner Street, Bankside, SE1 9TG (7887 8888, www.tate.org.uk). Southwark tube or London Bridge tube/rail. **Open** 10am-5.30pm Mon-Thur, Sun; 10am-8.30pm Fri; 10am-6.30pm Sat. **Main courses** £6.40-£12.75. **Map** p404 O7.

TIMING IS EVERYTHING

How to skip the crowds at London's key attractions.

London's a great city for children – but you won't be the only parents who've noticed. So expect crowds and plan accordingly.

EARLY... AND LATE

The simplest advice is to arrive at opening time – a breakfast-friendly 10am at most of the key London attractions. You'll be amazed how much difference even an hour can make at a busy museum. After your visit, avoid rush hour (5-7pm, peaking around 6pm): even expert pushchair-wranglers survive rush hour on public transport only with a combination of assertiveness and strained politeness. Instead, have a relaxed evening meal near the attraction and return to your hotel a bit later, when the commuters have gone and the Underground becomes part of the fun.

SCHOOLING YOURSELF

If your kids aren't yet of school age, avoid the holidays – these vary somewhat but www.rbkc. gov.uk gives term dates that are indicative of what's happening in the rest of London. If you can't avoid the holidays entirely, avoid weekends, when working parents join tourist parents and the unwise unchilded to form unconscionable crowds.

There is an exception to the holiday rule: Christmas is quieter in London than either Easter or the summer holidays.

During term time, London's more serious-minded attractions (especially the Science Museum, Natural History Museum and Museum of London) attract great crocodiles of kids on school outings: they rarely arrive first thing and usually depart early afternoon.

TOILET TRAINING

Another piece of helpful advice: go before you go. Public loos aren't as common as they should be, so use the toilets before you leave an attraction. If your nippers do get caught out, rail stations are often a better bet than the tube or buy the family a round of babyccinos in the nearest coffee chain.

THE SECRET OF ATTRACTIONS

Merlin Entertainments has made queue-jumping at their stable of sights – **Madame Tussauds** (*see p109*), **London Eye** (*see p54*),

Sea-life London Aquarium (*see p54*), **London Dungeon** (*see p51*) – pretty straightforward: book online in advance. You'll not only get a timed ticket – but a cheaper one. (If you plan to visit more than one of their attractions, look at combination tickets.)

FIGHT AT THE MUSEUM

Key choke points at the **British Museum** (*see p150*) are around the Egyptian mummies (first floor, Rooms 62 and 63) and Egyptian sculpture (ground floor, Room 4) – visit as soon as you arrive. If the kids are interested in the Rosetta Stone, there's a perfect, crowd-free replica in Room 1.

In South Ken, the **V&A** (*see p90*) is quieter than either the NHM or the Science Museum, but more suitable for older kids. If you arrive mid morning during the holidays at the **Natural History Museum** (*see p87*), even on a weekday, you will queue. The Exhibition Road side entrance used to be quieter, but at peak times nowadays entering there is hardly quicker. Afternoons tend to be quieter, but Fridays are often mobbed all day. For the **Science Museum** (*see p87*) don't merely arrive for opening time: go straight up to the third floor. There, you'll find Launchpad, with its free interactive experiments, as well as the flight simulators (for which you pay extra). Within an hour, Launchpad will be packed with kids.

At the **Tower of London** (*see p187*), too, the trick is just to arrive early, but to prioritise: head straight to the Crown Jewels, where the queue will be out of the door by mid morning. Second is probably the prisoner graffiti in the Beauchamp Tower – incredibly moving for older kids, but best experienced without a paparazzi mob of flashing cameraphones.

An early start also really pays off at **St Paul's Cathedral** (*see p176*). If you manage to arrive by the unusually early opening time of 8.30am, you'll have the Whispering Gallery pretty much to yourselves.

And finally, the best way to skip the crowds at **Tate Modern** (*see p57*)? Go to **Tate Britain** (*see p77*). We're being naughty, but it is much quieter, yet just as child-friendly, with pick-up activities at the information desks, and is packed with amazing art.

ARTS & ENTERTAINMENT

Unicorn Theatre

In addition to views from the windows framing the busy River Thames, there are literacy and art activities on the junior menu, which is handed out with an accompanying pot of crayons. Children can choose haddock fingers with chips, pasta bolognese with parmesan, or a ham and cheese bake with focaccia, finished off with ice-cream or a fruit salad; a free children's main is offered when an adult orders a regular main. There is also a 'teen menu' of reduced-price dishes from the adult menu.

ENTERTAINMENT
City Farms & Zoos

There's always something new at **ZSL London Zoo** (*see p197*); the admission charge seems high, but it's a guaranteed winner. Easier on the budget is the adorable **Battersea Park Children's Zoo** (www.batterseaparkzoo.co.uk), where ring-tailed lemurs, giant rabbits, inquisitive meerkats and kune kune pigs are among the inhabitants.

City farms all over London charge nothing to get in. Try **Freightliners City Farm** (www.freightlinersfarm.org.uk) and **Kentish Town City Farm** (http://ktcityfarm.org.uk) or, in the east, **Mudchute City Farm** (www.mudchute.org) and **Hackney City Farm** (www.hackneycityfarm.co.uk), both of which have the added bonus of terrific cafés.

Puppets

★ Little Angel Theatre
14 Dagmar Passage, off Cross Street, Islington, N1 2DN (7226 1787, www.littleangeltheatre.com). Angel tube or Highbury & Islington tube/ Overground/rail. **Box office** 10am-5pm daily. **Tickets** £5-£14. **Map** p402 O1.
London's only permanent puppet theatre is set in a charming old Victorian temperance hall. All aspects of puppetry are covered, with themes, styles and stories drawn from a broad array of traditions. There's a Saturday Puppet Club and a youth puppet theatre. Shows are often for fives and above.

Puppet Theatre Barge
Opposite 35 Blomfield Road, Little Venice, W9 2PF (summer 07836 202745, winter 7249 6876, www.puppetbarge.com). Warwick Avenue tube. **Box office** 10am-6pm daily. **Tickets** £12; £8.50; £10 reductions.
This intimate waterborne stage is the setting for quality puppet shows that put a modern twist on traditional tales, such as *Mr Rabbit Meets Brer Santa Claus* and *The Flight of Babuscha Baboon*. The barge is moored here between October and July; shows themselves are held at 3pm on Saturday and Sunday, and daily during school holidays, plus some matinées. During the summer (Aug-Sept), the barge also holds performances in Richmond.

Science & Nature

If you can get children past the giant snakes-and-ladders game (complete with giant dice) at the **WWT Wetland Centre** (*see p239*), there are 104 acres in which to stretch their legs, including one of the best playgrounds in London.

FREE Camley Street Natural Park
12 Camley Street, King's Cross, N1C 4PW (7833 2311, www.wildlondon.org.uk). King's Cross St Pancras tube/rail. **Open** 10am-5pm daily (closes at 4pm in winter). **Admission** free.
A small but thriving green space on the site of a former coal yard, Camley Street is near the heart of the renovated King's Cross. London Wildlife Trust's flagship reserve, it hosts pond-dipping and nature-watching sessons for children, and its wood-cabin visitor centre is used by the Wildlife Watch Club.

FREE Creekside Centre
14 Creekside, Deptford, SE8 4SA (8692 9922, www.creeksidecentre.org.uk). Deptford Bridge or Greenwich DLR, or bus 53, 177, 188. **Open** varies. **Admission** free. **Events** varies.
Deptford Creek is a tributary of the Thames, and this centre allows visitors to explore its surprisingly diverse wildlife and rich heritage. Low-tide walks take place on selected weekend days for

accompanied eight-year-olds and above and there's also a programme of puppet theatre and puppet-making. Events vary (and some charge a fee), so phone ahead for the programme.

Theatre

Polka Theatre
240 Broadway, Wimbledon, SW19 1SB (8543 4888, www.polkatheatre.com). South Wimbledon tube or Wimbledon tube/rail, then bus 57, 93, 131, 219. **Box office** 9.30am-5.30pm Mon-Fri; 10am-4.30pm Sat; noon-4.30pm Sun. **Tickets** £10-£13.50.
This children's-theatre pioneer has been up and running since 1979. Daily shows are staged by touring companies in the main auditorium, while shorter works for babies and toddlers take over at the Adventure Theatre once a week.

Unicorn Theatre
147 Tooley Street, Bankside, SE1 2HZ (7645 0560, www.unicorntheatre.com). London Bridge tube/rail. **Box office** 9am-6pm Mon-Sat; 10am-4pm Sun. **Tickets** £9-£22; £7-£13 reductions. **Map** p405 Q8.
This light, bright building, with a huge white unicorn in the foyer, has two performance spaces. Its small ensemble company performs in all shows and focuses on an outreach programme for local children.

Theme Parks

There are several theme parks within easy reach of London. Heading out west, **Legoland** (Winkfield Road, Windsor, Berkshire, SL4 4AY, 0871 222 2001, www.legoland.co.uk) has rides including the wet 'n' wild Viking's River Splash, and the extraordinary Miniland London, made of 13 million Lego bricks. **Thorpe Park** (Staines Road, Chertsey, Surrey, KT16 8PN, 0871 663 1673, www.thorpepark.com) has the fastest rollercoaster in Europe, called Stealth, and the terrifying horror-movie ride, Saw; it's best for older kids and teens. **Chessington World of Adventures** (Leatherhead Road, Chessington, Surrey, KT9 2NE, 0871 663 4477, www. chessington.com) is a gentler option. This theme park is partly a zoo, and children can pay to be zoo keeper for a day.

Likely to be on any child's wishlist is the new Harry Potter studio tour near Watford, a short journey north of town; *see p303* **Warner Bros Studio Tour**.

For a day with less of an adrenaline rush, try **Bekonscot Model Village** (Warwick Road, Beaconsfield, Buckinghamshire, HP9 2PL, 01494 672919, www.bekonscot.com), a haven of vintage miniature villages with a ride-on train. To the north, **Butterfly World** (Miriam Lane, Chiswell Green, Hertfordshire, AL2 3NY, 01727 869203, www.butterflyworldproject.com) is designed to look like a huge butterfly head from the air, with a 330-foot diameter walk-through biome (the butterfly's eye). There's also a walk-through butterfly tunnel and butterfly breeding house.

SPACES TO PLAY

London's parks are lovely. **Hyde Park** (*see p92*) and **St James's Park** (*see p89*) are very central, but it isn't much further to **Regent's Park** (*see p197*), and **Greenwich Park** (*see p219*) is easily reached by river.

★ FREE Coram's Fields
93 Guilford Street, Bloomsbury, WC1N 1DN (7837 6138, www.coramsfields.org). Russell Square tube. **Open** 9am-dusk daily. **Admission** free; adults admitted only if accompanied by under-16s. **No credit cards. Map** p399 L4.
This historic site dates to 1747, when Thomas Coram established the Foundling Hospital (now a museum; *see p151*), but only opened as a park in 1936. It is now probably the best playground in London. It has sandpits, a small petting zoo, ride-on toys and several well-designed playgrounds for different age groups, with the most challenging including a zip wire and some superb spiral slides.

FREE Diana, Princess of Wales Memorial Playground
Near Black Lion Gate, Broad Walk, Kensington Gardens, South Kensington, W8 2UH (0300 061 2001, www.royalparks.gov.uk). Bayswater or Queensway tube. **Open** *Summer* 10am-7.45pm daily. *Winter* 10am-dusk daily. **Admission** free; adults admitted only if accompanied by under-12s. **Map** p395 E8.
Bring buckets and spades, if you can, to this superb playground: the focal attraction is a huge pirate ship, moored in a sea of sand. Other attractions include a tepee camp and a treehouse encampment with walkways, ladders, slides and 'tree phones'. Many of the playground's attractions appeal to the senses (scented shrubs, whispering willows and bamboo are planted throughout), and much equipment has been designed for use by children with special needs.
▶ *The playground often has queues to get in. If you get bored, head to the south of the park and the Hyde Park Playground. Refurbished in 2014, it has a slide, nest swing and 'jungle area' for nature quests.*

Discover Children's Story Centre
383-387 High Street, Stratford, E15 4QZ (8536 5555, www.discover.org.uk). Stratford tube/rail/ DLR. **Open** 10am-5pm Mon-Fri; 11am 5pm Sat, Sun. Closed Mon in term time. **Admission** £5; £18 family of 4; free under-2s.
The UK's first creative-learning centre offers all sorts of imaginative exploration, while downstairs houses temporary interactive exhibitions. The garden is good fun too.

Film

Londoners still seem to have a feel for the romance of film that suburban multiplexes just can't satisfy. Perhaps that's why there's such a lively and varied range of screenings in the capital. Giant picture palaces hosting red-carpet premières attended by A-list actors? Check out the Odeon Leicester Square. Cheap-as-chips repertory cinema? The Prince Charles is right around the corner. Refurbished art deco gems? Try the gorgeous, historic Phoenix or the Rio in Dalston. A world-class film festival? Happens every autumn. Outdoor screenings in remarkable settings, ciné clubs, film seasons devoted to every genre and national cinema under the sun? Yes, yes and yes. So get some popcorn and sit yourself down.

WHERE TO GO

Leicester Square underwent a major and much-needed facelift in 2011, and has the biggest first-run cinemas and stages most of the big-budget premières – but it also has the biggest prices. By contrast, the independents provide a cheaper night out and they often show films that wouldn't come within a million miles of a red carpet.

Outside the mainstream, the British Film Institute's flagship venue gets top billing. **BFI Southbank** screens seasons exploring and celebrating various genres of cinema and TV. It also has a brilliant bar. After the BFI, the **Curzon** group (*see p255* **Indie Takeover**) is the favoured choice for most cineastes, but London has a growing number of arthouse cinemas – and in increasingly unlikely places, such as Kensal Green (**Lexi**) and Crouch End (**ArtHouse**).

There's a vogue for having screening rooms in unusual venues. These include the refurbished **Imperial War Museum** (*see p56*) and the Tanks, a multimedia space in the **Tate Modern** extension (*see p57*). Several luxury hotels are in on the act too: long-term favourites **Soho Hotel** (*see p351*), **Charlotte Street Hotel** (*see p356*), **Covent Garden Hotel** (*see p352*) and **One Aldwych** (*see p354*) have been joined by **Ham Yard** (*see p351*) and the **Mondrian** (*see p340*). Outdoor summertime screens have popped up across the capital: these are listed on p258.

And film lovers have two options: the **London Film Museum** (*see p140*) is the one for fans of memorabilia, with its current show exhibiting cars from the Bond movies; film buffs should book a tour of the **Cinema Museum** (The Master's House, 2 Dugard Way, SE11 4TH, 7840 2200, www.cinemamuseum.org.uk, £7, £5 reductions), its cinema seats and signs, stills and posters, projectors and other machinery telling cinema's history from the 1890s.

Information

Consult *Time Out* magazine's weekly listings or visit www.timeout.com/film for full details of what's on and performance times; note that the programmes change on a Friday. Films released in the UK are classified as follows: **U** – suitable for all ages; **PG** – open to all, parental guidance is advised; **12A** – under-12s only admitted with an over-18; **15** – no one under 15 is admitted; **18** – no one under 18 is admitted.

GIANT SCREENS & MULTIPLEX CINEMAS

BFI IMAX
1 Charlie Chaplin Walk, South Bank, SE1 8XR (0330 333 7878, www.bfi.org.uk/imax). Waterloo tube/rail. **Tickets** £16.60-£20.80; £11.20-£16.40 reductions. **Screens** 1. **Map** p401 M8.

London's biggest screen mixes made-for-IMAX fare and scenery-heavy documentaries with mainstream blockbusters, such as the Harry Potter films.

Cineworld at the O2

The O2, Peninsula Square, Greenwich, SE10 0DX (0871 200 2000, www.cineworld.co.uk). North Greenwich tube. **Tickets** £11; £8-£8.50 reductions. Extra for 3D, D-BOX, IMAX. **Screens** 11.

People don't just come to the O2 Arena (*see p273*) for gigs: this 11-screen multiplex from the Cineworld chain supersizes everything, from the jaw-dropping dimensions of the Sky Superscreen – the widest in Europe – down to the jam-packed programme.

Empire Leicester Square

5-6 Leicester Square, WC2H 7NA (0871 471 4714, www.empirecinemas.co.uk). Leicester Square tube. **Tickets** £9.95-£12.95 adult; £9.95 reductions. *Impact* £15.50-£18; £9.95-£12.50. *IMAX* £16-£18; £9.95-£12.95. **Screens** 9. **Map** p401 K7.

One of London's oldest cinemas (it opened as a theatre in 1884, as a cinema after World War II), the Empire was until recently home to London's biggest non-IMAX cinema screen (that's now at the O2 Cineworld; *see above*). Its massive main auditorium is these days separated into a full IMAX screen and smaller (but still impressive) 400-seat Impact theatre, with seven smaller screens tucked away elsewhere in the building. The programme is mainstream and prices reflect the central location.

★ Odeon Leicester Square

Leicester Square, WC2H 7LQ (0333 006 7777, www.odeon.co.uk). Leicester Square tube. **Tickets** £14-£22; £7-£19.50 reductions. **Screens** 5. **Map** p401 K7.

London's number-one destination for red carpet premières. Not only do you get blockbuster bangs in the huge 1,683-seat auditorium, you get them in splendour: the Odeon Leicester Square still has a fully operational 1937 pipe organ (occasionally used to soundtrack silent films) and gorgeous 1930s art-deco nymph motifs on the walls. It's also one of the few remaining cinemas to still have its circle – from which the view (at extra cost) is pretty spectacular.

★ Prince Charles

7 Leicester Place, off Leicester Square, WC2H 7BY (7494 3654, www.princecharlescinema.com). Leicester Square tube. **Tickets** £8-£11.50. **Screens** 2. **Map** p401 K7.

This is the only cinema where no one is going to shush you. In fact, it's all about audience participation: sing along to *Frozen* or settle in for a marathon all-night pyjama party. Having started life screening porn, the Prince Charles is still central London's wildcard cinema, providing a fantastic blend of new-ish blockbusters and arthouse titles, with heaps of horror, sci-fi and teen-flick all-nighters, double bills and short seasons. It's comfy, cheap and cheerful.

INDIE TAKEOVER

The Curzons keep right on coming.

In spring 2015, we were hugely excited about the return of the much-loved Renoir, near Russell Square tube, which reopened as the **Curzon Bloomsbury** (The Brunswick Centre, WC1N 1AW; for contact details, *see p256*). The cinema's two screens have become six, one of which is – winningly – dedicated to documentaries. The inaugural week was promising, with its focus on auteur movies, including Jean Renoir's brilliant comedy *La Regle du Jeu*.

It's starting to feel like Curzon know something about the supposedly defunct notion of 'cinema' that other arthouses don't. The group's key venues are well established – the perennially hip **Soho** and the Grade II-listed **Mayfair**, so classy it's the only cinema where we've been told off by a fellow movie-goer for eating popcorn too loudly – but recent years have seen vigorous expansion. Curzon opened the five-screen, purpose-built **Victoria** (58 Victoria Street, SW1E 6QW) in 2014, but has also entered an intriguing partnership to open an in-store cinema, **hmvcurzon** (23 The Broadway, SW19 1RE), at the Wimbledon branch of the record-selling behemoth. Curzon is also in charge of films at two hotels – programming movies at **Ham Yard** (*see p351*) and operating the cinema at the new **Mondrian at Sea Containers** (*see p340*). And the group even pitches in at another London independent: **ArtHouse Crouch End** (*see p256*).

ARTHOUSE CINEMAS

There are plenty of central London arthouses, but some of the most atmospheric are in the suburbs.

ArtHouse Crouch End

159A Tottenham Lane, Crouch End, N8 9BT (8245 3099, www.arthousecrouchend.co.uk). Bus 41, 91, N41, N91, W3. **Tickets** £7-£11; £4 reductions. **Screens** 2.

Voted London's best cinema by *Time Out* readers, this two-screen independent in a former Salvation Army Hall opened its doors in spring 2014 and quickly became a favourite with locals. The ArtHouse prides itself on being not just a cinema but also a venue offering music, comedy and theatre. Its programme leans towards independent and foreign movies, and there's a welcoming foyer bar and café.

Barbican

Silk Street, the City, EC2Y 8DS (7638 8891, www.barbican.org.uk). Barbican tube or Moorgate tube/rail. **Tickets** £11.50; £6 Mon; £6-£10.50 reductions. **Screens** 3. **Map** p402 P5.

Two new (small) screens have been added – at the corner of Beech Street and Whitecross Street – bringing the Barbican Centre's total number of screens back to three (the excellent Cinema 1 remains within the Barbican Centre proper). Expect quality world and independent films.

★ BFI Southbank

South Bank, SE1 8XT (7928 3232 tickets, www.bfi.org.uk). Embankment tube or Waterloo tube/rail. **Tickets** £8.25-£12.10; £8.25-£9.35 reductions. **Screens** 4. **Map** p401 M8.

The BFI's success is still built on its core function: thought-provoking seasons giving film fans the chance to enjoy rare and significant British and foreign films. A terrific place to enjoy movies.

▶ *The BFI's Mediatheque gives you free access to its huge film and documentary archive.*

Ciné Lumière

Institut Français, 17 Queensberry Place, South Kensington, SW7 2DT (7871 3515, www.institut-francais.org.uk). South Kensington tube. **Tickets** £7-£9; £5-£7 reductions. **Screens** 1. **Map** p397 D10.

Ciné Lumière reopened in 2009 with better seating and a refreshed art-deco interior. No longer screening French films only (there are still, however, regular French previews and classics), the Lumière is a standard-bearer for world cinema in the capital.

Curzon

Chelsea *206 King's Road, SW3 5XP. Sloane Square tube then bus 11, 19, 22, 319.* **Screens** 1. **Map** p397 E12.

Mayfair *38 Curzon Street, W1J 7TY. Green Park or Hyde Park Corner tube.* **Screens** 2. **Map** p400 H8.

★ **Soho** *99 Shaftesbury Avenue, W1D 5DY. Leicester Square tube.* **Screens** 3. **Map** p401 K6.
All *0330 500 1331, www.curzoncinemas.com.* **Tickets** £8.50-£18.50; £6.50-£11.50 reductions.

Expect a superb range of shorts, rarities, double-bills and seasons along with new international releases across the Curzon chain. There's '70s splendour in Mayfair (sometimes used for premières), while Chelsea is perfect for a Sunday screening after a brunch on the King's Road. But the Soho outpost is the coolest, with its buzzing café and decent basement bar. *See also p255* **Indie Takeover**.

Electric

Portobello *191 Portobello Road, Notting Hill, W11 2ED (7908 9696, www.electriccinema.co.uk). Ladbroke Grove or Notting Hill Gate tube.* **Tickets** £15.50-£18 adult; £10 children. **Screens** 1.

★ **Shoreditch** *64-66 Redchurch Street, E2 7DP (3350 3490, www.electriccinema.co.uk/shoreditch). Shoreditch High Street Overground or Old Street tube/rail.* **Tickets** £18; £8. **Screens** 1. **Map** p403 S4.

Once a past-it fleapit, the Electric Portobello was a pioneer of the 'boutique' cinema trend: a luscious destination with leather seats and sofas, footstools and a bar inside the auditorium. Further improved after fire damage in 2012 (six date-perfect luxurious, velvet-lined double beds were put in), the Electric has now taken over a snug little screen in the East End. Formerly the Aubin, the Electric Shoreditch exudes luxury, from the leather armchairs and footstools to the cashmere blankets and chic little tables to hold your drinks.

Everyman & Screen Cinemas

Everyman *5 Hollybush Vale, Hampstead, NW3 6TX. Hampstead tube.* **Tickets** £11.95-£14.50; £9.50 reductions. **Screens** 2.

Screen on the Green *83 Upper Street, Islington, N1 0NP. Angel tube.* **Tickets** £14-£16; £9.50-£11 reductions. **Screens** 1. **Map** p402 O2.

Both *0871 906 9060, www.everymancinema.com.*

London's most elegant cinema, the Everyman has a glamorous bar and two-seaters (£35) in its 'screening lounges', complete with foot stools and wine coolers. Everyman now also owns three former Screen cinemas, of which Screen on the Green is the best – carefully refurbished in 2009, it lost seats to make space for the more comfortable kind, gained a bar and a stage for gigs, but kept its lovely neon sign.

Genesis Cinema Whitechapel

93-95 Mile End Road, Stepney, E1 4UJ (7780 2000, www.genesiscinema.co.uk). Whitechapel tube/Overground or Stepney Green tube. **Tickets** £7-£8.50; £4 Mon, Wed; £3.50-£6 reductions. *Studio 5* £11-£13; £8. **Screens** 6.

Not only is the Genesis cheap, it's also beautifully renovated – by guys who design film sets for a living (try knocking on the bricks on the mezzanine).

ESSENTIAL LONDON FILMS
We pick out six of the capital's star turns.

Frenzy.

BLOWUP
MICHELANGELO
ANTONIONI (1966)
It's Swinging London, and a fashion photographer (David Hemmings) is at a loose end, having ditched his jobs for the day. He wanders into Maryon Park and when he develops the pictures he takes there, they appear to show a murder. Music from the Yardbirds, with Jimmy Page and Jeff Beck playing guitar (and Beck smashing his).

FRENZY
ALFRED HITCHCOCK
(1972)
Covent Garden was still a fruit and veg market when this was made, and a serial killer is on the loose in the area, raping and strangling women. Fruit merchant Robert Rusk is revealed to viewers as the murderer, but suspicion falls on his friend, Richard Blaney. Will the real culprit be uncovered?

LONDON
PATRICK KEILLER (1994)
Lying at the point where documentary meets fiction, this film follows the travels of an unseen narrator around London with his friend/ex-lover to research English Romanticism. But events soon distract the pair from their planned focus. A fascinating study of early 1990s London.

PADDINGTON
PAUL KING (2014)
This first movie take on Peru's furriest export is a cuddly, thoughtful triumph – but not too cuddly. Charmingly simple, it also offers a sharp modern spin on Michael Bond's London-set stories about a small bear with a marmalade habit who is adopted by a nice middle-class family. For kids, it's fun, fast and sweet; for adults, it's a parable of London immigration.

PASSPORT TO PIMLICO
HENRY CORNELIUS
(1949)
An antidote to the grimness and depression of the post-war years of austerity, cosy Ealing comedy *Passport to Pimlico* sees the citizens of that area of London discover that they are really Burgundians and declare independence. So it's out with the ration books and in with free-for-all shopping, boozing and jollity.

PERFORMANCE
NICOLAS ROEG (1970)
Roeg's complex visual kaleidoscope sees an enforcer for a protection racket (James Fox) involved in murder and forced to hide from retribution in a Notting Hill basement. There, as he waits to escape abroad, he gets involved with a fading pop star (Mick Jagger) brooding over the loss of his powers of incantation.

ARTS & ENTERTAINMENT

The end result is a perfect local cinema, with proper old East End ladies drinking coffee in the café next to cool kids on their laptops. There's a bar upstairs, where snacks include crodoughs from 100-year-old Rinkoffs bakery. For a date, book seats in the Studio 5 boutique screening room, with its armchairs.

Hackney Picturehouse

270 Mare Street, Hackney, E8 1HE (0871 902 5734, www.picturehouses.com). Hackney Central or London Fields rail. **Tickets** £7-£11.60; £4-£10.60 reductions. **Screens** 4.

This branch of the Picturehouse chain only opened in 2011, but it's impossible to remember Hackney without it. The buzzy ground-floor bar/café serves good burgers, and bang-on programming mixes top-of-the-range mainstream with artier films – for the former, book Screen 1, with its beast of a screen, big sound and steep incline for uninterrupted viewing. On the top floor, the Hackney Attic is home to music quizzes, open-mic nights and other live events.

★ Lexi

Pinkham Lighthouse, 194B Chamberlayne Road, Kensal Rise, NW10 3JU (0871 704 2069, https:// thelexicinema.co.uk). Kensal Green tube or Kensal Rise Overground. **Tickets** £7.50-£11; £7-£7.50 reductions. **Screens** 1.

One of London's friendliest cinemas, the Lexi is run mostly by enthusiastic local volunteers, with every penny of profits going to charity. You might see anything from recent blockbusters to arthouse and foreign films, with the programme filled out by special events, Q&As and classic-movie seasons (a run of Truffaut oldies was accompanied by cheese and wine tastings). The chairs are comfy, the sound system is great and the bar is cosy. The Lexi team is also responsible for the peripatetic outdoor cinema screen Nomad (www.whereisthenomad.com).

★ Phoenix

52 High Road, East Finchley, N2 9PJ (8444 6789, www.phoenixcinema.co.uk). East Finchley tube. **Tickets** £7-£9.50; £5-£7 reductions. **Screens** 1.

This gorgeous single-screen cinema can fairly claim to be London's oldest continuously operating cinema: it was completed in 1910 and opened in 1912. Since 1985, it has been run as a charitable trust. The programme mixes independent and foreign films, and the auditorium is one of the most beautiful places to watch a film in London. This is also a great place to catch directors introducing their work, late-night films and special events.

Rio Cinema

107 Kingsland High Street, Dalston, E8 2PB (7241 9410, www.riocinema.org.uk). Dalston Kingsland Overground. **Tickets** £6-£10; £4-£8 reductions. **Screens** 1.

Another great deco survivor, restored to its original sleek lines, the Rio is east London's finest independent. Alongside mainstream releases, the Rio is well known for its programme of Turkish and Kurdish films and documentaries.

FESTIVALS & OUTDOOR SCREENINGS

The best known open-air screenings are those in the lovely neoclassical courtyard of **Somerset House** (Strand, WC2R 1LA, 7845 4600, www. somersethouse.org.uk). Book well ahead – and bring your own picnic and cushions. There are plenty of other alfresco opportunities, however. **Free Film Festivals** (www. freefilmfestivals.org) puts on free outdoor screenings in interesting public spaces in south-east London. The Scoop (*see p62*) is the location for summer screenings as part of **More London Free Festival** (www.morelondon.com), while **Pop Up Screens** (www.popupscreens.co.uk) shows popular films in parks in west London.

There's also a film festival in the capital on pretty much any given week during the year, but the **London Film Festival** (www.bfi.org.uk/lff, Oct) is far and away the most prestigious. Nearly 200 new British and international features are screened, mainly at the BFI Southbank and Leicester Square's Vue West End. It's preceded by the leftfield **Raindance Festival** (www. raindance.co.uk), with a terrific shorts programme. Highlighting the importance of the city's lesbian, gay and transgender communities, the **BFI Flare** (7928 3232, www.bfi.org.uk/llgff, late Mar) is the UK's third largest film festival.

In spring there is the **Human Rights Watch International Film Festival** (7713 1995, www. hrw.org/iff, mid-late Mar). The **East End Film Festival** (www.eastendfilmfestival.com, early July) has a fondness for films starring London. Short films hog the limelight at the **London Short Film Festival** (www.shortfilms.org.uk, Jan), while the **London International Animation Festival** (www.liaf.org.uk, Mar) screens 300 or more animated shorts. The **Portobello Film Festival** (www.portobello filmfestival.com, early Sept) offers an eclectic programme of free screenings, while the **Open City London Documentary Festival** (www. opencitylondon.com, June) focuses on non-fiction.

In summer (May-Sept), the **Rooftop Film Club** offers a more relaxed take on filmgoing, screening five movies a week in the rooftop garden of the bar/club/arts collective the Queen of Hoxton (1-5 Curtain Road, EC2A 3JX, 7635 6655, www.rooftopfilmclub.com, £13), while the hugely popular **Secret Cinema** (www. secretcinema.org) takes things to another level. Effectively building huge film sets for their costumed screenings, Secret Cinema is the apotheosis of 'event screening': their *Back to the Future* screenings reconstructed a town square.

Gay & Lesbian

Acceptance of gay lifestyles in London feels broader than ever, with many clubs in Dalston no longer bothering much about sexual orientation – gay, bi-, polysexual, hetero- even – whatever, just so long as everyone gets to have a good time. It's a golden time for diversity of entertainment, yet for all the cabaret, soulful disco and plain weird nights out there, there's anxiety about the health of the gay scene in central London. The closure of key venues has caused plenty of soul-searching. Has Grindr killed the gay bar? Rising rents? Noise complaints?

Some things remain the same: London's headline homo event, Pride, is still surrounded throughout the year by smaller, more DIY goings-on. Whatever your taste in music, you'll find somewhere that specialises in it, in a nightlife scene that runs around the clock. Off the dancefloor, the scene is more varied still, with cabaret nights, literary salons and plays, and a major gay and lesbian film festival.

SCENE

Roughly speaking, London's gay scene is split into three distinct zones: **Soho**, **Vauxhall** and **east London**. Each of these three districts has its own character: in a nutshell, Soho is the most mainstream, Vauxhall is the most decadent and east London is the most outré.

Centred on **Old Compton Street**, the Soho scene continues to attract the crowds, with pretty boys sipping espresso martinis at pavement café tables as unfeasibly tanned chaps in muscle vests stroll past. But all is not well in London's historic gay heartland: around the New Year, cabaret venue Madame JoJo's was shut down by the council, Manbar closed down, **Green Carnation** announced it would reopen in an entirely new format and the **Yard** began an ongoing battle with the developers; ever imaginative, the cabaret community paraded coffins through the streets to protest the death of the area's nightlife. Gay Soho has been caught between the rising rents that now stalk central London and a council that, while friendly to the pink pound, is intolerant of nightlife that might upset increasingly affluent

residents. At least the party continues down the road at the legendary **Heaven**, home to **G-A-Y**, close to Charing Cross Station. If your dream has always been to see Madonna or Kylie in a club, here's your chance – the list of singers who've done PAs here reads like a *Who's Who* of squeal-tastic gay pop icons.

Down south, Vauxhall is also looking fearfully at the major redevelopment of the area, led by the arrival of the US Embassy (probably in 2017). Concerns have been raised that the refurbishment of long-standing alt-cabaret venue **RVT** is a bad omen – although not everyone is upset by the prospect of a champagne bar. For now, the hedonists can console themselves: arrive in London on a Friday evening and you can still dance non-stop here for an entire weekend before flying out of town again. Venues such as RVT and the Eagle (home to the superb **Horse Meat Disco**) provide alternatives to the standard Vauxhall throngs of shirtless, sweaty chaps.

The most alternative, creative and vibrant of the capital's queer scenes is in east London, although the closure of queer Shoreditch

ARTS & ENTERTAINMENT

institution the Joiners Arms, followed shortly afterwards by the Nelson's Head near Columbia Road, has undermined any sense of complacency. (The Joiners is set to remain some kind of gay community centre after Tower Hamlets council refused to allow a change of use to residential property, but details are yet to be fleshed out.) Still, in the likes of the **George & Dragon**, **Dalston Superstore** and now the **Glory** (*see p263* **Welcome to Faggerston**), you'll be rubbing shoulders with fashion and music's movers and shakers (plus assorted straight folk), to soundtracks built by ferociously underground DJs. With so much coolness, it can get a little snooty, but a lot of the bars and clubs round Shoreditch and Dalston are also properly mixed, which makes the area ideal for a night out with straight mates.

Keen to cut to the chase? **Chariots** is the sauna chain of choice, although **Vault 139** also has its followers. Most regular bars don't have backrooms, but some club nights in Vauxhall can get raunchy. The monthly **Hard On** (www. hardonclub.co.uk) is the top pick on the calendar for lovers of fetish and leather.

It was a blow for London's lesbian scene when the Candy Bar – the city's first full-time drinking den for lesbians – closed in 2014, though rumour has it that **Ku** may open a women's bar as a replacement. Until then, try the basement venue **She Soho** (23A Old Compton Street, W1D 5LB, http://she-soho.com); Monday and Wednesday nights at **Retro**; or the monthly R&B night **R&She** at **Vogue Fabrics** and basement bar **Tipsy** (20 Stoke Newington Road, N16 7XN, www.tipsybar.co.uk). The women-only **Glass Bar** (www.theglassbar.org.uk), which lost its own premises a few years ago, now runs various events, and there's also the glam **Bijou Cocktail Social** on the second Saturday of the month at Rudds bar (148 Queen Victoria Street, EC4V 4BY, www.elysionevents.co.uk).

New stand-alone nights for clubbing, cabaret and entertainment of all kinds pop up all the time, but **Bird Club** at the **Bethnal Green Working Men's Club** (*see p280*) and Ruby Tuesdays at **Ku** are recommended. Queer performance nights Duckie (hosted by Amy Lamé) and Bar Wotever at **RVT** are popular with the girls and the boys.

Lastly, special mention should go to the **NYC Downlow** (http://thedownlowradio.com/the-downlow), a travelling homo disco straight out of 1970s New York that you can catch at festivals such as **Lovebox** (*see p35*), the Sunday of which competes with **Summer Rites** (http:// summerritesevents.com) in Shoreditch Park for the title of London's gayest dance festival. In **BFI Flare** (www.bfi.org.uk/flare), London also has its own LGBT film festival – one of the largest film festivals in the country, gay or straight, held each spring. But the daddy on the queer calendar is always **Pride** festival (*see p34*), which now attracts around 800,000 LGBT people and their straight friends. No longer billed as a protest, but a celebration, it's one day in June every year when LGBT people from all over the country descend on London for a massive street party.

RESTAURANTS & CAFÉS

More or less every café and restaurant in London welcomes gay custom. Certainly nowhere in or around Soho will so much as bat an eyelid at you and your other half having a romantic dinner. For thirtysomething lesbians, there are fun cocktail evenings and the mom-and-pop Italian vintage decor of **Star at Night** (22 Great Chapel Street, Soho, W1F 8FR, 7494 2488, www.thestaratnight.com, closed Mon, Sun) – by day, it's a greasy spoon.

Balans

60-62 Old Compton Street, Soho, W1D 4UG (7439 2183, www.balans.co.uk). Leicester Square or Piccadilly Circus tube. **Open** 7.30am-5am Mon-Thur; 7.30am-6am Fri, Sat; 7.30am-2am Sun. **Main courses** £11.50-£17.95. **Admission** £2.50 after midnight Mon-Sat. **Map** p399 K6.
The gay café-restaurant of choice for many years, Balans is all about location, location, location (plus hot waiters, decent food and ridiculous opening hours). Situated across from Compton's bar and next door to Clone Zone, it's the beating heart of the Soho scene. The nearby Balans Café (no.34) serves a shorter version of the menu. Both are open almost all night and are good for a post-club bite.
Other locations throughout the city.

CLUBBING

London's club scene is particularly subject to change: venues close, nights end and new soirées start. Check *Time Out* magazine or www.timeout. com for details of what's on when you're here.

If you want to stay up all night and next day as well, head to **Vauxhall**. At **Fire** (South Lambeth Road, SW8 1RT, www.fireclub.co.uk), popular nights include Orange, a Sunday staple. Still in Vauxhall, on the Albert Embankment, try **Union** (no.66, www.clubunion.co.uk) and **Area** (nos.67-68, www.arealondon.net). If you're near Old Street, there's late-night dancing at **East Bloc** (217 City Road, EC1V 1JN, www.eastbloc.co.uk).

Club Kali

Dome, 1 Dartmouth Park Hill, Tufnell Park, N19 5QQ (7272 8153, http://clubkali.com). Tufnell Park tube. **Admission** 10pm-3am 3rd Fri of mth. **Admission** £8; £5 reductions.
The world's largest LGBT Asian dance club offers Bollywood, bhangra, Arabic tunes, R&B and dance classics spun by DJs Ritu, Dilz Riz & Qurra.

Horse Meat Disco.

★ Dalston Superstore
*117 Kingland High Street, Dalston, E8 2PB
(7254 2273, http://dalstonsuperstore.com).
Dalston Kingsland rail.* **Open** 11.45am-2am
Mon-Wed; 11am-2.30am Thur; 11am-4am Fri;
10am-4am Sat; 10am-2.30am Sun.

The opening of this club-bar in 2009 cemented
Dalston's status as the final frontier of the East
End's gay scene. A café during the day, at night you
can expect queues for a hugely impressive roster of
guest DJs spinning a typically east London mix of
of pop and dance tunes to a dance floor that's pitch-
black and intense. Regular dates, such as Sunday's
Tutti Frutti (soul, disco and house), are well worth
putting in the diary. Upstairs, alt-cabaret drag stars
whip revellers into shape with sharp one-liners.

Exilio Latin Dance Club
*Venues vary; see website for details (07956 983230,
www.exilio.co.uk). Open 9.30pm-4am every other
Sat.* **Admission** £6-£12. **No credit cards.**

This is London's principal queer Latino club, held
in various locations, with girls and guys getting
together for merengue, salsa, cumbia and reggaeton.

★ Glory
*281 Kingsland Road, Dalston, E2 8AS (7684
0794, www.theglory.co). Haggerston Overground.*
Open 5pm-midnight Tue-Thur; 5pm-2am Fri, Sat;
5-10.30pm Sun. **Admission** varies.
See p263 **Welcome to Faggerston.**

Heaven
*Underneath the Arches, Villiers Street, Covent
Garden, WC2N 6NG (7930 2020, www.heaven
nightclublondon.com). Embankment tube or*
Charing Cross tube/rail. **Open** 11pm-5.30am
Mon; 11pm-4am Thur, Fri; 10.30pm-5am Sat.
Admission varies. **No credit cards.**
Map p401 L7.

London's most famous gay club is a bit like *Les
Misérables* – it's camp, it's full of history, and tourists
love it. Popcorn (Mon) has long been a good bet, but
it's really all about G-A-Y (Thur-Sat). For years,
divas with an album to flog (Madonna, Kylie, Girls
Aloud) have turned up to play here at the weekend.

★ Horse Meat Disco
*Eagle London, 349 Kennington Lane, Vauxhall,
SE11 5QY (7793 0903, www.eaglelondon.com).
Vauxhall tube/rail.* **Open** 9pm-2am Mon-Wed;
9pm-3am Thur, Fri, Sun; 9pm-4am Sat.
Admission £6. **No credit cards.**

Not your average gay club. Skinny Soho boys and
fashionistas rub shoulders with scally lads and
bears in a traditional old boozer. The hip soundtrack
is an inspired mix of Studio 54, New York punk and
new wave. As one *Time Out* critic put it: 'If you ever
wished you could hang out in a club like the one in
Beyond the Valley of the Dolls or *Scarface*, you'll love
Horse Meat Disco.' A must.
▶ *When Horse Meat isn't in residence, the Eagle is a
hub for those wishing to try a bit of leather.*

★ RVT
*Royal Vauxhall Tavern, 372 Kennington Lane,
Vauxhall, SE11 5HY (7820 1222, www.rvt.org.uk).
Vauxhall tube/rail.* **Open** 6pm-midnight Mon-Thur;
6pm-midnight Tue; 7pm-2am Fri; 9pm-2am Sat;
3pm-midnight Sun. **Admission** £5-£8.

This pub turned legendary gay cabaret venue,
a much-loved stalwart on the scene for years,

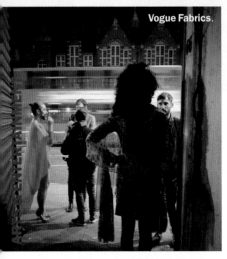

Vogue Fabrics.

operates an anything-goes booking policy. The most famous fixture is Saturday's queer performance night Duckie (www.duckie.co.uk), with Amy Lamé hosting acts at midnight that range from strip cabaret to porn puppets. On Sundays, there's S.L.A.G.S/Chill-out, with house spun by DJ Simon Le Vans at 3pm, followed by cabaret from Charlie Hides at 5.30pm and guest DJs from 7.30pm. The aim is to please the crowd of regulars. Punters verge on the bear, but the main dress code is 'no attitude'.

▶ *RVT was taken over by new owners in late 2014. It is understood they plan a top-to-toe refurb, which will give the pub a first-floor champagne bar and new toilets, but will maintain the place's character. But as we go to press, it's business as usual.*

★ Savage
Metropolis, 234 Cambridge Heath Road, Bethnal Green, E2 2NN (http://sinkthepink.co.uk). Cambridge Heath Overground. **Open** 11pm-5am Sat. **Admission** £6. **No credit cards.**

The restless polysexual party animals Sink the Pink launched their new weekly night of disco tunes and filthy fun in spring 2015 – in an East End strip club. For only a fiver, you can roam around three floors of naughtiness. We're promised pure Vegas decor, a dancing pole running through two floors, a jeep in a wet room and top London DJs (including Horse Meat Disco's Severino and the 2 Bears' Raf Daddy) on rotation, playing deliciously dirty disco, house and party bangers until 5am.

Vogue Fabrics
66 Stoke Newington Road, Dalston, N16 7XB (http://voguefabricsdalston.com). Dalston Junction or Dalston Kingsland Overground. **Open** 10pm-3am Fri. **Admission** £5-£6. **No credit cards.**
Small, sweaty and seemingly illegal (but in fact perfectly legitimate), Vogue Fabrics is the place to come if you like your nights messy and your men of the bear and otter variety. While the regular parties come and go, the recently departed electro-, disco-, Italo-pumpin' Dirtbox remains the archetype.

XXL
1 Invicta Plaza, South Bank, SE1 9UF (www.xxl-london.com). Southwark tube. **Open** 10pm-3am Wed; 10pm-7am Sat. **Admission** £15. **No credit cards. Map** p404 O7.
XXL has moved from its longstanding home in Vauxhall, but it's still the world's biggest club – naturally! – for bears and their friends. XXL is nirvana for chubbier, hairier and blokier gay men and their twinky admirers.

PUBS & BARS

Unless otherwise stated, the pubs and bars listed here are open to both gay men and lesbians. If you're in east London, it's worth visiting **Dalston Superstore** (*see p261*) during the day for café grub: the food's good (with breakfast quite a trendy scene) and there are Wi-Fi and art displays.

Barcode Vauxhall
Arch 69, Albert Embankment, Vauxhall, SE11 5AW (7582 4180, www.bar-code.co.uk). Vauxhall tube/rail. **Open** 10pm-4am Thur; 8pm-8am Fri, Sat; 8pm-late Sun. **Admission** £6; £8 after midnight.
Prior to the arrival of Barcode, Vauxhall was mostly for clubbing, with those oh-so-necessary pre-dance drinks to be enjoyed anywhere else but here. But despite the shiny, sparkly surfaces at this lavish, massive venue, the crowd trends toward blokey-ish pre-dancing punters and folks who are just after a drink.

Freedom Bar
66 Wardour Street, Soho, W1F 0TA (7437 3490, www.freedombarsoho.com). Leicester Square or Piccadilly Circus tube. **Open** 4pm-3am Mon-Thur;

WELCOME TO FAGGERSTON

Jonny Woo opens a fabulous new cabaret venue in Dalston.

If you're wondering where all the fun went from Soho, Jonny Woo hopes he has the answer: the arid stretch of the Kingsland Road south of Dalston. It is, as he puts it himself, just 'a clutch bag's throw away from Haggerston station… and one-and-a-half-songs-on-an-iPod's stroll from Shoreditch High Street'. Here, Woo and his co-founders – among them Zoe Argiros, a mover and shaker in the early days of trendy Dalston – have established the **Glory** (*see p261*).

While a major aspect of the Glory's existence will revolve around cabaret, calling it a 'cabaret venue' is probably misleading. This is no velvet curtain and brocade burlesque joint, where blokes who feel they're too sophisticated for a strip joint get to ogle a lady in an expensive basque. Instead, it follows the Dalston pattern of adapting a pub, in this case the 200-year-old Victory, into, well, a pub – just with the addition of cocktails, and opportunities for late-night disco dancing and various alt-cabaret antics.

Woo's own career might give a flavour of what to expect from the performances. If one axis is the old-school disco NYC Downlow that became the first gay tent at Glastonbury (you can have a listen at http://thedownlowradio.com/the-downlow/), the other axis is Woo's indescribable Gay Bingo party – which he runs with another of his co-founders here, John Sizzle – and the tranny talent and lip-synching shows he ran during his nearly decade-long residency at Bethnal Green's Bistrotheque (23-27 Wadeson Street, E2 9DR, 8983 7900, www.bistrotheque.com). There will certainly be drag on the programme – of all varieties, but often of the man-in-a-beard-and-a-dress and tranny-with-a-fanny type, but the rest of the performances will mix dance, stand-up, theatre and music into a heady brew.

The venue's structure is straightforward – ground-floor bar with a stage, basement for dancing and more performances, and the obligatory yard outside for smokers – and it is perfect for what Woo clearly regards as something of a crusade: to keep gender-ambiguous and adventurous alternative cabaret thriving. Prepare to be glorious.

ARTS & ENTERTAINMENT

2pm-3am Fri, Sat; 2-10.30pm Sun. **Admission** free;
£5 after 10pm Fri, Sat. **Map** p398 J6.

A glitzy cocktail lounge and DJ bar, spread over
two floors. The glam ground-floor bar attracts a
fashion-conscious crowd, who sip cocktails among
chandeliers, zebra-print banquettes and Venetian
mirrors. A few 'strays' and dolled-up gal pals add
colour. The large basement club and performance
space hosts weekday cabaret and gets busy with the
gay party crowd over the weekend.

G-A-Y Bar

*30 Old Compton Street, Soho, W1D 4UR (7494
2756, www.g-a-y.co.uk). Leicester Square or
Tottenham Court Road tube.* **Open** noon-midnight
daily. **Map** p399 K6.

The G-A-Y night at Heaven (*see p261*) gets the
celebrity cameos, but this popular bar is still a shrine
to queer pop idols, with nightly drinks promos every
time they play a video from the current diva du jour.
There's also a women's bar in the basement, called
(delightfully) Girls Go Down – popular with flirty,
studenty lesbians, loathed by most older women.

▶ *G-A-Y bar's plush late-night sibling, G-A-Y Late,
is round the corner at 5 Goslett Yard.*

George & Dragon

*2 Hackney Road, Shoreditch, E2 7NS (7012 1100).
Old Street tube/rail or Hoxton Overground.* **Open**
6pm-midnight daily. **Map** p403 S3.

The location of this mini-pub ensures a stylish and
up-for-it clientele, while the decor (a wall-mounted
horse's head, creepy puppets, random garbage)
keeps the vibe fun. The music – pop, indie and
electronica – is often delivered with a sense of
humour. Gay or not, it's one of London's best boozers.

Hoist

*Arches 47B & 47C, South Lambeth Road, Vauxhall,
SW8 1SR (7735 9972, www.thehoist.co.uk).
Vauxhall tube/rail.* **Open** 5pm-1am Wed; 10pm-3am
Fri; 10pm-4am Sat; 2pm-1am Sun. **Admission** £6
Fri, Sun; £2-£10 Sat. **No credit cards**.

One of only two genuine leather bars in town, this
club sits under the arches and makes the most of its
underground and industrial setting. The Saturday
night event SBN (Stark Bollock Naked) gives you the
tone of the place; leather, uniforms, rubber, skinhead
or boots are the usual dress code. Strictly no trainers.

★ Ku

*30 Lisle Street, Chinatown, WC2H 7BA (7437
4303, www.ku-bar.co.uk). Leicester Square or
Piccadilly Circus tube.* **Open** noon-3am Mon-Sat;
noon-midnight Sun. **Map** p401 K7.

With a string of awards to its name, Ku must be
doing something right. Formerly known as West
Central, it has morphed from a mediocre space into
a popular bar and club that offers everything
from film nights to comedy. The sheer variety of
club nights (which are held in the basement) is

Ku.

impressive. The choice ranges from Sandra D's
Ruby Tuesdays for lesbians, to drag queen Vicki
Vivacious on Wednesdays and the Ku DJs Rodrigo
and Prince Persona on Saturday nights.

▶ *Ku also runs a two-floor bar-club in the heart of
Soho, on the corner of Frith and Old Compton
streets. Serious competition for G-A-Y, then.*

KW4

*77 Hampstead High Street, Hampstead, NW3 1RE
(7435 5747, www.kingwilliamhampstead.co.uk).
Hampstead tube or Hampstead Heath Overground.*
Open 11am-11pm Mon-Thur; 11am-midnight
Fri-Sun.

The perfect evening ending (or beginning) to time
spent on the Heath, this fabulous old local – the
King William IV, or King Willy to those with longer
memories – attracts a very Hampstead crowd (read:
well-off and ready for fun). On summer weekends,
the cute little beer garden tends to fill up with a
mix of gay and straight punters keen to put down
their shopping bags. The pub is more popular with
lesbians in summer too, as a stop-off after a dip in the
Heath's women's bathing pond.

Retro Bar

*2 George Court, off Strand, Covent Garden, WC2N
6HH (7839 8760, www.retrobarlondon.co.uk).*

Charing Cross tube/rail or Embankment tube.
Open noon-11pm Mon-Fri; 2-11pm Sat; 2-10.30pm
Sun. **Map** p401 L7.
Iggy Pop and Kate Bush are on the walls of this bar,
where nights are dedicated to punk, glam, slutty pop
and electronica (Retro-normative on Thursdays).
The crowd is mixed in every sense: gay/straight,
gay/lesbian and scene queen/true eccentric. Quiz
nights (Tuesday) are popular, too, and the bar on
occasion even relinquishes control of the music and
lets punters be the DJ – bring your iPod.

Shadow Lounge
*5 Brewer Street, Soho, W1F 0RF (7317 9270,
www.theshadowlounge.co.uk). Leicester Square or
Piccadilly Circus tube.* **Open** 9pm-3am Mon-Sat.
Admission free Mon; £5 Tue-Thur; £10 Fri, Sat.
Map p401 K6.
For celebrity sightings, suits, cutes and fancy boots,
this is your West End venue. Expect a hefty cover
charge and a queue at the weekends, but there's often
a sublime atmosphere inside.

Yard
*57 Rupert Street, Soho, W1D 7PL (7437 2652,
www.yardbar.co.uk). Leicester Square or Piccadilly
Circus tube.* **Open** 4-11.30pm Mon-Wed; 3-11.30pm
Thur; 2pm-midnight Fri, Sat; 2-10.30pm Sun. **Map**
p401 K6.
Assuming it manages to hold off the developers,
who began circling in early 2015, the Yard is set to
remain one of the most reliable gay bars in Soho:
come for the courtyard in summer, stay for the Loft
Bar in winter. This unpretentious bar offers a great
open-air courtyard in a central location, attracting
pretty boys, blokes and lesbians in equal numbers.

ADULT CLUBS & SAUNAS

Chariots
*1 Fairchild Street, Shoreditch, EC2A 3NS (7247
5333, www.chariots.co.uk). Liverpool Street tube/
rail or Shoreditch High Street Overground.* **Open**
noon-8am Mon-Fri; noon-9am Sat, Sun.
Admission £19; £17 reductions. **Map** p403 R4.
Chariots is a sauna chain with outlets all over town.
The original is this one in Shoreditch, the biggest
and busiest, although not necessarily the best. That
accolade probably goes to the one on the Albert
Embankment at Vauxhall (nos.63-64, 7247 5333).
The Waterloo branch (101 Lower Marsh, 7401 8484)
has the biggest sauna in the UK.

★ Sweatbox
*Ramillies House, 1-2 Ramillies Street, Soho, W1F
7LN (3214 6014, www.sweatboxsoho.com). Oxford
Circus tube.* **Open** 24hrs daily. **Admission** £16/
day; £10 under-25s. **Map** p398 J6.
Sweatbox Soho looks more like a nightclub than a
typical gym, with the sleek design offset by friendly
staff. Though small, the space is well laid out, with
a multigym and a free-weights room. Qualified
masseurs offer treatments. If that doesn't do the
trick, there's a sauna downstairs.

Vault 139
*139-143 Whitfield Street, Fitzrovia, W1T 5EN
(7388 5500, www.vault139.com). Warren Street
tube.* **Open** 1pm-1am daily. **No credit cards**.
Map p398 J4.
Hidden away on a quiet backstreet, Vault 139 is
London's most central cruise bar – and it's classy too,
with plush sofas, TV screens and a DJ booth.

ARTS & ENTERTAINMENT

Shadow Lounge.

Nightlife

To say London has brilliant and diverse nightlife is an understatement, whether it's clubbing, live music, cabaret or comedy. These days, though, big is rarely best. We have one of the world's largest and most influential nightclubs, Fabric, and another fine superclub in Studio 338, but it's the smaller venues that really buzz. In particular, good clubbing is easy to come by along the Kingsland Road strip in Dalston, where you'll find the Dance Tunnel, Nest and a range of party bars. There's more new music from the edge at places such as XOYO and the Shacklewell Arms, the latter proving that the London cliché of indie bands in sticky dives endures. London also has more than 250 comedy gigs a week, ranging from pub open-mics to arena shows; the Comedy Store is a good place to start. And the key venues on the alt cabaret scene are Bethnal Green Working Men's Club and RVT.

Clubs

In this era of boutique clubbing, London has all the variety you could possibly wish for – you don't even always have to go to a club to have the club experience. Try bowling and boogieing at **Bloomsbury Bowling Lanes** (*see p157*), for example, or dress up for one of the city's burgeoning number of 'vintage'-themed parties. And these days, some of the best events happen in warehouse locations, usually in east or south London – **The Hydra** (http://the-hydra.net) and **London Warehouse Events** (http://londonwarehouseevents.co.uk) are usually worth checking out for a fix of big-name electronica.

Still, some things remain constant. Since the arrival of jungle in the mainstream way back in the 1990s, big, beefy, speakerstack-destroying bass has always been hot in London. Dubstep is huge – and heavy – its reverberating beats sending dancefloors wild across the capital as it continues to morph through urban genres such as funky, future house, bassline, dancehall and 2step – all characterised as UK bass. But revivalists continue to mine any number of genres – disco, psychsoul, UKG (UK Garage) – anything that will get you dancing.

In fact, the days of epoch-defining megaraves is gone, shattered into a thousand microscenes and sound systems that are fleet of foot and quick to respond to the passions of their audience. Upstairs rooms in pubs and the basements of abandoned shops – still especially in east London – are the birthing ground for DJs and promoters who might graduate to more permanent venues, or might vanish without a trace. It's a bewildering scene, but thrilling too.

WHERE IT'S AT

Shoreditch was the hub of the capital's nightlife scene for a long time. It has, however, become increasingly commercialised in recent years (witness the weekend trails of hen and office parties between Old Street and Spitalfields), despite the groovy work still being done at live space and club **XOYO** (*see p271*). The closure of **Plastic People** at the start of 2015, after 20 years at the cutting edge, had the feel of the end of an era. Nights at **Book Club** (*see p269*), which range from disco to science drink-and-thinks, show a newer kind of Shoreditch nightlife.

The city's cool kids now routinely take the bus north up the Kingsland Road from Shoreditch into

Dalston and beyond into Stoke Newington. The former has much-improved transport connections since the London Overground arrived at Dalston Junction station, but it can be difficult to find the clubs – even more so what's happening in them. Spend a few moments checking *Time Out* magazine (www.timeout.com/clubs) or hunting on Facebook and you'll unearth fabulous happenings at the likes of **Dalston Superstore** (*see p261*) and **Dance Tunnel** (*see p270*).

The appeal of clubbing in the **West End** has steeply declined in recent years; there's little here beside bars, pubs and a lively – but not especially adventurous – gay scene. The best remaining option is the excellent **Blow Up** (www.blowup club.com) on Friday nights, which celebrated its 21st birthday with a new residency in the club under the St Moritz fondue restaurant (159 Wardour Street, Soho, W1F 8WL, www. stmoritz-restaurant.co.uk).

To the north, up in **King's Cross**, little remains of the former clubbing nexus lost to the redevelopment that is now King's Cross Central. There are some good nights at **Egg** (200 York Way, N7 9AP, 7871 7111, www.egglondon.net) and the **Big Chill House** (257-259 Pentonville Road, N1 9NL, 7427 2540, www.wearebigchill.com/ venues), while the **Star of Kings** pub-club (126 York Way, N1 0AX, 7458 4218, www.starofkings. co.uk), with its late weekend licence and killer sound system, gives the area further hedonistic potential. East, on the way into Islington, the upstairs room at the **Lexington** (*see p275*) is known for rough and ready nights with a casual, studenty feel.

Further north, **Camden** is still very popular – especially with tourists. Indie student hangout **Proud** (*see p271*), teeny pub-rave spot the **Lock**

Tavern (*see p270*) and bourbon-soaked gig haunt the **Blues Kitchen** (*see p277*) offer credible nights for London party people too. And **Koko** (*see p272*) runs some of the biggest student nights around – Club NME and Annie Mac Presents.

There's more of interest to the south. The gay village in **Vauxhall** is just as welcoming to open-minded, straight-rolling types, with club promoters looking towards south-of-the-river venues such as **Fire** (South Lambeth Road, SW8 1RT, 3242 0040, www.firelondon.net), which has some big line-ups, and **Hidden** (100 Tinworth Street, SE11 5EQ, 7820 6613) as occasional homes for their (largely drum 'n' bass and electronica) parties. The calendar is even fuller at **Corsica Studios** (*see p269*), at Elephant and Castle.

Major Venues

Electric Brixton
Town Hall Parade, Brixton, SW2 1RJ (7274 2290, www.electricbrixton.uk.com). Brixton tube/rail. **Open** Thur-Sun; times vary. **Admission** £10-£35. The Fridge in Brixton was a legendary rave paradise in the early '90s, a stomping ground for the rare groove scene, funky jazz-house and, later, hard dance and psy-trance beats. In 2011, however, it underwent a £1m refit, with new management in place, and was reborn as Electric Brixton, with a mix of club nights – the likes of Skreamizm with Skream, featuring dubstep with forays into jungle, drum 'n' bass and disco – and live music.

★ Fabric
77A Charterhouse Street, Clerkenwell, EC1M 6HJ (7336 8898, www.fabriclondon.com). Farringdon tube/rail. **Open** 11pm-6am Fri, Sun; 11pm-8am Sat. **Admission** £5-£24. **Map** p402 O5.

Fabric.

Fabric is the club that most party people come to see in London – with good reason. Located in a former meatpacking warehouse, it has a well-deserved reputation as the capital's biggest and best club. The line-ups are legendary. Fridays belong to the bass: guaranteed highlights include DJ Hype, with his drum 'n' bass and dubstep night Playaz, plus Andy C's Ram Records takeover and Caspa's Dub Police label nights. Saturdays descend into techy, minimal, deep house territory, with the world's most famous DJs regularly making appearances. Be warned: the queues are also legendary. Blag on to the guestlist or buy tickets in advance to avoid a two-hour wait.

Ministry of Sound

103 Gaunt Street, off Newington Causeway, Elephant & Castle, SE1 6DP (7740 8600, www.ministryofsound.com). Elephant & Castle tube/rail. **Open** 10.30pm-6am Fri; 11pm-7am Sat. **Admission** £10-£20. **Map** p404 O10.
Ministry of Sound was once the epitome of warehouse cool and is still the UK's best-known clubbing venue. Laid out across four bars, five rooms and three dancefloors, there's lots to explore. Trance night the Gallery has made its home here on Fridays, while Saturday nights are for big-name DJ takeovers from the likes of Roger Sanchez and Erick Morillo.

★ Oval Space

29-32 The Oval, Bethnal Green, E2 9DT (www. ovalspace.co.uk). Bethnal Green tube/Overgound. **Open** varies. **Admission** varies.
Located at the base of a disused gasworks off Hackney Road, this hangar-style space is 6,000sq ft of fun, and one of the most impressive and exciting recent additions to London nightlife. A mix of ace one-off parties and regular events mark Oval Space out as one of the most innovative venues around: DJs regularly play spacey techno, twisted electronica, alt hip hop and glitchy house, while on-point events such as Secretsundaze are regulars.
▶ *Oval Space has one of the best terrace spaces in town, put to full use for parties during the summer.*

★ Studio 338

338 Boord Street, Greenwich, SE10 0PF (8293 6669, www.studio338.co.uk). North Greenwich tube. **Open/admission** varies.
This sprawling club combines the best elements of Berlin's cool industrial venues with slicker super-club vibes. It attracts dedicated dancers with world-class house and techno DJs from the underground side of things, such as Kevin Saunderson and Marc 'MK' Kinchen. Another big draw is the all-night covered terrace, which allows punters to do Ibiza-style outdoor raving even in the unlikely event of rain.

Club & Pub Venues

If you're clubbing in Camden, the gig venues **Koko** (*see p272*) and **Barfly** (*see p275*) also host some feisty club nights. In addition to the east London venues listed below, check out gay hangout the **Dalston Superstore** (*see p261*) and the excellent **Village Underground** (*see p276*) and **Shacklewell Arms** (*see p276*).

Book Club

100 Leonard Street, Shoreditch, EC2A 4RH (7684 8618, www.wearetbc.com). Old Street tube/rail. **Open** 8am-midnight Mon-Wed; 8am-2am Thur, Fri; 10am-2am Sat; 10am-midnight Sun. **Admission** free-£5. **Map** p403 Q4.
The Book Club aims to fuse lively creative events, table tennis (there's a ping pong table and regular tournaments) and late-night drinking. Events range from Electro-Swing, the night that started a huge trend in mashing up vintage sounds with electro, to arty think-and-drink workshops and, our current fave, Crap Film Club (www.crapfilmclub.org.uk).

★ Bussey Building (CLF Art Cafe)

133 Rye Lane, Peckham, SE15 4ST (7732 5275, www.clfartcafe.org). Peckham Rye Overground. **Open** varies. **Admission** varies.
This post-industrial building is surely London's best all-round venue. Saved from demolition in 2007 by community group Peckham Vision, the CLF Art Cafe (known by pretty much everyone as the Bussey Building) is a multi-floored concrete block that thrives as a warehouse-style club at night and an arts venue during the day. Top promoters consistently bring in the best names on the underground and alternative dance scenes, across most genres, but leaning towards house, deep techno, garage and disco. The Bussey also hosts regular nights that offer more accessible sounds: the likes of Zonk Disco and the South London Soul Train make it one of London's best spaces for funk and soul club nights as well. In the summer, the roof gets thrown open for alfresco parties.
▶ *For the Bussey Building's role as a theatrical venue, see p290* **In the Know**.

Corsica Studios

4-5 Elephant Road, Elephant & Castle, SE17 1LB (7703 4760, www.corsicastudios.com). Elephant & Castle tube/rail. **Open** times vary Mon-Wed; 8pm-3am Thur; 10pm-6am Fri, Sat; 7am-3pm Sun. **Admission** free-£15.
An independent, not-for-profit arts complex, Corsica Studios seeks to breed a culture of creativity. The flexible warehouse space is one of London's most adventurous, supplementing the DJs that play here with bands, poets, painters and lunatic projectionists. Sure, it's rough around the edges, with makeshift bars and toilets, but the events are second to none. The flagship night is Trouble Vision, which boasts the very best of bass, while Sunday sees daytime house and techno events. The live-music roster has included gigs from Silver Apples, Acoustic Ladyland and Lydia Lunch.

ARTS & ENTERTAINMENT

Oval Space. See p269.

★ Dance Tunnel

95 Kingsland High Street, Dalston, E8 2PB (7249 7865, www.dancetunnel.com). Dalston Junction Overground. **Open** 9pm-3am Thur; 10pm-3am Fri, Sat. **Admission** £5-£8.

Under Voodoo Ray's pizza parlour (try a 'Giorgio Moroder' for the ultimate disco snack), an anonymous black door leads you to a dimly lit space that's tailor-made for dedicated dancers, unforgiving to wallflowers. As you'd expect from a club run by Dalston Superstore (*see p261*), excellent promoters bring a bevy of cutting-edge deep house and techno one-off nights, supplied by outstanding globally renowned DJs and producers. The acquisition of seminal bass night FWD>> added to an already glistening roster of regulars – check out Dance Tunnel Presents… and Comm.Une.

Lock Tavern

35 Chalk Farm Road, Camden, NW1 8AJ (7482 7163, www.lock-tavern.com). Chalk Farm tube. **Open** noon-midnight Mon-Thur; noon-1am Fri, Sat; noon-11pm Sun. **Admission** free.

A favourite of artfully distressed rock urchins, it teems with aesthetic niceties inside (cosy black couches and warm wood panels downstairs; open-air terrace on the first floor), but it's the unpredictable after-party vibe that packs in the punters, with big-name DJs regularly providing the tunes.

★ Nest

36 Stoke Newington Road, Dalston, N16 7XJ (7354 9993, www.ilovethenest.com). Dalston Junction Overground. **Open** 9pm-3am Thur; 9pm-4am Fri, Sat. **Admission** free-£10.

Formerly the hipster institution Bardens Boudoir, the 350-person capacity Nest retains much of its predecessor's eclectic, forward-looking booking policy, but with the benefit of a big money 'distressed industrial' refurbishment and, absolutely crucially for those who suffered here before, much-improved toilets. It's a bit like a corridor, but the line-ups are usually great, with music that hangs out at the dancefloor-focused disco, electro and house end of the spectrum. One of Dalston's finest.

Notting Hill Arts Club

21 Notting Hill Gate, Notting Hill, W11 3JQ (7460 4459, www.nottinghillartsclub.com). Notting Hill Gate tube. **Open** hours vary, but around 7pm-2am Wed-Thur; 6pm-2am Fri; 4pm-2am Sat; 6pm-1am Sun. **Admission** free-£8.

Notting Hill Arts Club almost single-handedly keeps this side of town on the radar thanks to nights such as Juicebox (electro) and NHAC Presents (DJ sets).

Old Queen's Head

44 Essex Road, Islington, N1 8LN (7354 9993, www.theoldqueenshead.com). Angel tube. **Open** noon-midnight Mon-Wed, Sun; noon-1am Thur; noon-2am Fri, Sat. **Admission** free; £5 after 8pm Fri, Sat. **Map** p402 O1.

Pulling in fun-seekers since its relaunch way back in 2006, the Old Queen's Head is another place with long queues at the weekends. There are two floors and outside seating front and back, and during the week you can lounge on battered sofas. Weekends are for dancing, minor-league celeb-spotting and chatting up the bar staff, or trying out the private karaoke room.

Paradise

19 Kilburn Lane, Kensal Green, W10 4AE (8969 0098, www.theparadise.co.uk). Kensal Green tube/ Overground or Kensal Rise Overground. **Open** 4pm-midnight Mon-Wed; 4pm-1am Thur; 4pm-2am Fri; noon-2am Sat; noon-11.30pm Sun. **Admission** free-£8.

This is a star among the legion of pub-clubs, thanks to its alternative programme of art auctions,

burlesque life drawing and late-night club nights, making it more than just a good local hangout. Also great for wild supper parties with friends.

Plan B
418 Brixton Road, Brixton, SW9 7AY (7733 0926, www.plan-brixton.co.uk). Brixton tube/rail. **Open** Fri-Sun; times vary. **Admission** £5-£20.
The decor is industrial chic (exposed brickwork, metal pillars, geometric furnishings) and the music programme rampantly eclectic. This, plus a late licence, happy hour every evening and student discounts, ensures the place is very often brimming. Watch out for irregular '90s R&B nights.

Proud Camden
Horse Hospital, Stables Market, Chalk Farm Road, Camden, NW1 8AH (7482 3867, www. proudcamden.com). Chalk Farm tube. **Open** 11am-1.30am Wed; 11am-2.30am Thur-Sat; 11am-12.30am Sun. **Admission** free-£10.
The north London guitar-slingers have given way to dubstep, rock 'n' rave and drum 'n' bass, but the action at this former equine hospital is still rock 'n' roll. Drape yourself – cocktail in hand – over the luxurious textiles in the individual stable-style booths (you must book in advance), sink into deckchairs on the outdoor terrace, or spin around in the main band room at its naughtily themed nights.
▶ *For spring 2015, Proud opened the Secret Garden, a roof space for alfresco revelling.*

★ XOYO
32-37 Cowper Street, Shoreditch, EC2A 4AP (7354 9993, www.xoyo.co.uk). Old Street tube/rail. **Open/ admission** varies. **Map** p403 Q4.
There's live music during the week at this 800-capacity venue, but XOYO is first and foremost a club. The former printworks is a bare concrete shell, defiantly taking the 'chic' out of 'shabby chic',

but the open space means the atmosphere is always buzzing, as the only place to escape immersion in the music is the small smoking courtyard outside. The Victorian loft-style space provides effortlessly cool programming and high-profile DJs, while the return of longer residencies – a 12-week stint for Skream in 2015, for instance – is the best kind of old-school.

Music
ROCK & POP
The rest of the country might not like it, but every musician is going to have to come to London: you might find yourself watching a US country star in a tiny basement, an African group under a railway arch or a torch singer in a church – all in one night, if you've any stamina.

While corporations have invested in venues, resulting in positives (improved facilities and sound systems) and negatives (overpriced bars), there's still rough and ready individuality to be found – as well as the newest sounds – in venues such as **XOYO** (*see below*) and the **Shacklewell Arms** (*see p276*).

There's often a huge disparity between door times and stage times; doors may open at 7pm, for instance, but the gigs often don't start until after 9pm. Some venues run club nights after the gigs, which means the show has to be wrapped up by 10.30pm; but at other venues, the main act won't even start until 11pm. If in doubt, call ahead.

Major Venues

In addition to the venues listed below, the **Barbican Centre** (*see p179*), the **Southbank Centre** (*see p287*) and the **Royal Albert Hall** (*see p285*) also stage regular events.

Alexandra Palace
Alexandra Palace Way, N22 7AY (8365 2121, www.alexandrapalace.com). Alexandra Palace rail or W3 bus. **Tickets** vary; the promoters rather than the venue sell tickets.
This hilltop landmark venue, adorned with sculptures and frescoes, opened in 1873 as the People's Palace and was devastated by fire twice – once only 16 days after opening, and the second time in 1980. Bar and toilet provision for some of the big shows remains patchy thanks to the layout, but the sound system is beloved of audiophiles – the Pixies chose it for their first London shows when they reformed, and James Murphy for the last UK appearances of LCD Soundsystem.

Eventim Apollo
45 Queen Caroline Street, Hammersmith, W6 9QH (information 8563 3800, tickets 0844 249 4300, www.eventimapollo.com). Hammersmith tube.

GORGEOUS GEORGE

A London-born rapper who's destined for greatness.

'I'm from Raph's/Home of guns and staffs/ Shooters running up on dons in caffs.'

Raph's is St Raphael's Estate near Neasden, north-west London, where George Mpanga grew up. Google it, and you're presented with three suggested searches: 'gangs', 'shooting' and 'crime'. But none of these say much about George. At 23, **George The Poet** has been shortlisted for a Brit Award, supported rap greats like Nas, graduated with a degree in politics from Cambridge University and, in February 2015, published a collection of poems, *Search Party*, as the follow-up to his critically acclaimed *The Chicken and the Egg EP*, which tackles the radio-unfriendly topic of becoming a parent too young – yet got its release on credible major Island. Turns out dreams are still made in London.

Mpanga's debut album looks set to build on the hyper-literate, attention-grabbing hip hop of songs like 'Grinding', which uses a prosaic iPhone ringtone as its melody. But in a way, the tunes are only half the appeal.

It's a basic question, but are you a poet or a rapper?
'I'm a spoken word artist who uses music to get social message across. But I don't feel there should be any distinction. Rap is just a specialist form of poetry.'

How important is music to you?
'We didn't have a TV when I was a child, so music was my escape. It's always been my favourite form of imagination. I write rhymes as a way to document my self-discovery.'

What do you think are the main challenges facing young Londoners?
'The biggest challenge is representation. It plagues us all, because we want things for ourselves, and we're separated from the means of achieving them.

'Those who need the most help are the most disempowered and the least able to do anything about it.'

How are you enjoying your new star status?
'It's a dream come true. I need the biggest platform I can get to share my ideas.'

Box office *In person* 4.30-8pm performance days. *By phone* 8am-10pm daily. **Tickets** £10-£65. This 1930s cinema doubles as a 3,600-capacity all-seater theatre (popular with big comedy acts and children's shows) and a 5,000-capacity standing-room-only gig space, hosting shows by major rock bands and others not quite ready for the O2. The venue scored a sensational coup at the end of 2014 when Kate Bush's 'Before the Dawn' was performed here – her first gigs since 1979.

Forum
9-17 Highgate Road, Kentish Town, NW5 1JY (information 7428 4080, 0844 847 2405, www. mamacolive.com/theforum). Kentish Town tube/ rail. **Box office** *In person* 4-8pm performance days. *By phone* 8am-10pm daily. **Tickets** £10-£30. **Map** p402 N2.
Originally constructed as part of a chain of art deco cinemas with a spurious Roman theme (hence the name, the incongruous bas relief battle scenes and imperial eagles flanking the stage), the 2,000-capacity Forum became a music venue

back in the early 1980s. Since then, it's been vital to generations of gig-goers, whether they cut their teeth on the Velvet Underground, Ian Dury & the Blockheads, The Pogues, Les Negresses Vertes, Duran Duran, Killing Joke or the Wu-Tang Clan, all of whom have played memorable shows here.

★ Koko
1A Camden High Street, Camden, NW1 7JE (information 7388 3222, tickets 0844 847 2405, www.koko.uk.com). Mornington Crescent tube. **Box office** *In person* noon-5pm Mon-Fri (performance days only). *By phone* 24hrs daily. **Tickets** £5-£30.
Koko has had a hand in the gestation of numerous styles over the decades. As the Music Machine, it hosted a four-night residency with the Clash in 1978; the venue changed its name to Camden Palace in the '80s, whereupon it became home to the emergent new romantic movement and saw Madonna's UK debut. Later, it was one of the first 'official' venues to host acid-house events. Since a spruce-up in the early noughties, it has hosted acts as diametrically opposed as Joss Stone and Queens of the Stone

Age, not to mention one of Prince's electrifying 'secret' gigs in 2014. Nonetheless, the 1,500-capacity hall majors on weekend club nights – Annie Mac Presents and Club NME – and gigs by indie rockers, from the small and cultish to those on the up.

★ 02 Academy Brixton

211 Stockwell Road, Brixton, SW9 9SL (information 7771 3000, tickets 0844 477 2000, www.o2academybrixton.co.uk). Brixton tube/rail. **Box office** *In person* 2hrs before doors on performance days. *By phone* 24hrs daily. **Tickets** £10-£40.

Brixton is still the preferred venue for metal, indie and alt-rock bands looking to play their triumphant 'Look, ma, we've made it!' headline show. Built in the 1920s, this ex-cinema is the city's most atmospheric big venue. The 5,000-capacity art deco gem straddles the chasm between the pomp and volume of a stadium show and the intimate (read: sweaty) atmosphere of a club. Since becoming a full-time music venue in the '80s, it's hosted names from James Brown to the Stones to Springsteen, Dylan, Prince and Madonna, via the Red Hot Chili Peppers and Run DMC with the Beastie Boys. And with its raked dancefloor, everyone's guaranteed a decent view.

02 Academy Islington

N1 Centre, 16 Parkfield Street, Islington, N1 0PS (information 7288 4400, tickets 0844 477 2000, www.o2academyislington.co.uk). Angel tube. **Box office** *In person* noon-4pm Mon-Sat. *By phone* 24hrs daily. **Tickets** £5-£25. **Map** p402 N2.

Located in a shopping mall, this 800-capacity room was never likely to be London's edgiest venue. Still, as a stepping stone between the pubs of Camden and the city's larger venues, it's a good place to catch fast-rising indie acts and re-formed '80s bands on nostalgia tours, not least because of the great sound system. The adjacent Bar Academy plays host to smaller bands, and also hosts club nights.

★ 02 Arena & Indig02

Peninsula Square, North Greenwich, SE10 0DX (information 8463 2000, tickets 0844 856 0202, www.theo2.co.uk). North Greenwich tube. **Box office** *In person* noon-7pm daily. *By phone* 8am-8pm daily. **Tickets** £10-£65.

The national embarrassment that was the Millennium Dome has been transformed into the city's de facto home of the mega-gig. This 20,000-seater has outstanding sound, unobstructed sightlines and the potential for artists to perform 'in the round'. Shows from even the world's biggest acts (U2, Beyoncé, the reformed Led Zep, the mostly reformed Monty Python) don't feel too far away, and the venue seems to handle music, comedy and even sport (international tennis, boxing, basketball) with equal aplomb.

On the same site, Indig02 is the Arena's little sister – but 'little' only by comparison. It has an impressive

IN THE KNOW
TICKETS & PLANNING

Before even arriving in London, your first stop should be www.timeout.com, which lists hundreds of gigs every week, with the key highlights featured in the weekly free magazine. We've included the websites for each venue here: these detail upcoming shows. But do check ticket availability before you set out: venues large and small can sell out weeks in advance. The main exception to this rule are pub venues, which normally sell tickets only on the day. Many venues offer tickets online via their websites, but beware: most online box offices are operated by ticket agencies, which add booking fees that can raise the ticket price by as much as 30 per cent. Try to pay cash in person if possible.

capacity of 2,350, arranged as part-standing room, part-amphitheatre seating and, sometimes, part-table seating. Indig02's niche roster of MOR acts is dominated by soul, funk, pop-jazz and old pop acts, but it does also host after-show parties for headliners from the Arena.

▶ *Also here, Brooklyn Bowl (7412 8778, http://london.brooklynbowl.com) provides surprisingly high-quality gigs – as well as Southern-style eats and, yes, bowling alleys.*

02 Shepherd's Bush Empire

Shepherd's Bush Green, Shepherd's Bush, W12 8TT (information 8354 3300, tickets 0844 477 2000, www.o2shepherdsbushempire.co.uk). Shepherd's Bush Market tube or Shepherd's Bush tube/Overground/rail. **Box office** *In person* 4-6pm performance days. *By phone* 24hrs daily. **Tickets** £10-£40.

Once a BBC television theatre, the Empire's baroque interior exudes a grown-up glamour few venues can match. The environment lends a gravitas to the chirpiest of performance, as Lily Allen demonstrated in the flush of her fame. So you can imagine the sensation of seeing the likes of David Bowie or Bob Dylan here. It holds 2,000 standing or 1,300 seated; sightlines are good; the sound is decent (with the exception of the alcove behind the stalls bar and the scarily vertiginous top floor); and the roster of shows is quite varied, with acts at the poppier end of the scale joined by everyone from folkies to grizzled '70s rockers.

★ Roundhouse

Chalk Farm Road, Camden, NW1 8EH (information 7424 9991, tickets 0300 678 9222, www.roundhouse.org.uk). Chalk Farm tube. **Box office** *In person* 9.30am-5pm Mon, Sat, Sun;

ARTS & ENTERTAINMENT

9.30am-9pm Tue-Fri. *By phone* 9am-7pm Mon-Fri; 9am-4pm Sat; 9.30am-4pm Sun. **Tickets** £5-£25. The main auditorium's supporting pillars mean there are some poor sightlines at the Roundhouse, but this one-time railway turntable shed (hence the name), which was used for hippie happenings in the 1960s before becoming a famous rock (and punk) venue in the '70s, has been a fine addition to London's music venues since its reopening in 2006. Expect a mix of arty rock gigs (the briefly re-formed Led Zeppelin played here), dance performances, theatre and multimedia events.

Scala

275 Pentonville Road, King's Cross, N1 9NL (information 7833 2022, tickets 0844 477 1000, www.scala-london.co.uk). King's Cross tube/rail. **Box office** 10am-6pm Mon-Fri. **Tickets** free-£25. **Map** p399 L3.

Although the venue has vacillated between use as a picturehouse and concert hall, the Scala's one consistent trait has been its lack of respect for authority: its stint as a cinema was ended after Stanley Kubrick sued it into bankruptcy for showing *A Clockwork Orange*. Nowadays, it's one of the most rewarding venues to push your way to the front for those cusp-of-greatness shows by big names in waiting – names as varied as the Chemical Brothers and Joss Stone.

SSE Arena, Wembley

Arena Square, Engineers Way, Wembley, Middlesex, HA9 0DH (information 8782 5500, tickets 0844 815 0815, www.livenation.co.uk/ wembley). Wembley Park tube or Wembley Stadium rail. **Box office** *In person* (performance days only) 10.30am-4.30pm Mon-Fri; noon-4.30pm Sat; 1hr before performance Sun. *By phone* 8.30am-8pm Mon-Fri; 8am-6pm Sat; 9am-6pm Sun. **Tickets** £15-£230.

Wembley Arena may have seen its commercial heyday end with the arrival of the O2 Arena (*see p273*), although it has carved out something of a niche for soul. Still, it's hardly anyone's favourite venue, not least because the food and drink could be better, but most Londoners have warm memories of at least one Arena megagig, and a £30 million refurbishment did much to improve this 12,500-capacity venue.

Club & Pub Venues

In addition to the venues listed below, several London nightclubs multitask, staging regular gigs as well as club nights. This tendency is well represented by **Corsica Studios**, the **Notting Hill Arts Club**, **Proud Camden** (for all, *see pp269-271*), as well as the **ICA** (*see p80*), but Dalston's **Nest** (*see p270*) is a particularly fine exponent of the art. **Borderline** (*see p277*) specialises in country and folk, but does also host indie bands.

93 Feet East

150 Brick Lane, Old Truman Brewery, Spitalfields, E1 6QL (7770 6006, www.93feeteast.co.uk). Shoreditch High Street Overground. **Open** 5-11pm Mon-Thur; 5pm-1am Fri, Sat; 3-10.30pm Sun. *Shows* vary. **Admission** free-£10. **Map** p403 S5.

With three rooms, a balcony and a wraparound courtyard that's great for barbecues, 93 Feet East keeps ticking by maintaining an incredibly broad programme: swing dance classes in the main bar, tech-house DJs and a mix of indie-dance bands and various art-rockers, plus short films, ping pong and cocktails nights, and a variety of arty happenings.

★ 100 Club

100 Oxford Street, Soho, W1D 1LL (7636 0933, www.the100club.co.uk). Oxford Circus or

Koko. *See p272.*

ARTS & ENTERTAINMENT

Tottenham Court Road tube. **Shows** times vary. **Tickets** £7-£20. **Map** p416 V1.

The 100 Club is synonymous with punk, having hosted shows by the Sex Pistols, the Clash, Siouxsie and the Banshees, and the Buzzcocks. One historic show, in September 1976, featured the Sex Pistols, the Clash and the Damned. These days, though, the famous, 350-capacity basement room is more of a hub for pub rockers, blues rockers and trad jazzers, coming into its own for the odd secret gig by A-list bands such as Primal Scream and Oasis.

Barfly

49 Chalk Farm Road, Camden, NW1 8AN (information 7424 0800, tickets 0844 847 2424, www.mamacolive.com/thebarfly). Chalk Farm tube. **Open** 3pm-2am Mon, Thur; 3pm-1am Tue, Wed; 3pm-3am Fri, Sat; 3pm-midnight Sun. *Shows* from 7pm daily. **Admission** free-£15.

A rock 'n' roll institution, this 200-capacity venue is part of London's indie-rock fabric, a key player in the fusion of indie guitars and electro into an unholy, danceable row. It hosts up-and-coming new bands as well as club nights and quizzes.

Bloomsbury Bowling Lanes

Basement, Tavistock Hotel, Bedford Way, Bloomsbury, WC1H 9EU (7183 1979, www. bloomsburybowling.com). Russell Square tube. **Open** 4pm-midnight Mon, Tue; 4pm-2am Wed; noon-2am Thur; noon-3am Fri, Sat; noon-midnight Sun. **Admission** varies. **Map** p399 K4.

Offering a late-night drink away from Soho, BBL has been putting on bands and DJs for ages – and the range of activities make it a playground for grown-ups. As well as the eight lanes for bowling, there's pool by the hour, table football, karaoke booths and, beside the entrance, a small cinema. Music includes Funk and Bowl Club's 'bowl' parties.

Bush Hall

310 Uxbridge Road, Shepherd's Bush, W12 7LJ (8222 6955, www.bushhallmusic.co.uk). Shepherd's Bush Market tube. **Open** varies. *Shows* from 7.30pm. **Tickets** £5-£8.

This handsome room has been a dance hall, soup kitchen and snooker club. Now, with original fittings intact, it plays host to big bands performing stripped-down shows and rising indie rockers, as well as top folk acts.

Garage

20-22 Highbury Corner, Highbury, N5 1RD (information 7619 6721, tickets 0844 847 1678, www.mamacolive.com/thegarage). Highbury & Islington tube/Overground/rail. **Box office In person** 5pm-close of venue. *By phone* 24hrs daily. **Tickets** free-£20.

This 650-capacity alt-rock venue books an exciting and surprisingly wide-ranging calendar of indie and art-rock gigs, from ancient punk survivors such

as the Pop Group and Sham 69 to the poppier end of the indie singer-songwriter scale (Fran Healy in the smaller Upstairs, for example).

Hoxton Square Bar & Kitchen

2-4 Hoxton Square, Shoreditch, N1 6NU (information 7613 0709, tickets 0844 847 2316, www.mamacolive.com/hoxton). Old Street tube/rail or Shoreditch High Street Overground. **Open** noon-midnight Mon; noon-1am Tue-Thur; noon-2am Fri, Sat; 11am-12.30am Sun. **Tickets** free-£14.50 after 10pm Fri, Sat. **Map** p403 R3.

This 450-capacity venue is more than just a place to be seen: the line-ups are always cutting edge and fun, with the HSB&K often hosting a band's first London outing. Get there early or be prepared to queue.

Jazz Café

5 Parkway, Camden, NW1 7PG (information 7485 6834, tickets 0844 847 2514, www.mamacolive. com/thejazzcafe). Camden Town tube. **Box office** *In person* 10.30am-5.30pm Mon-Sat. *By phone* 24hrs daily. **Tickets** £5-£30.

Back when the Jazz Café first opened in 1990, the support pillars famously commanded the audience to 'STFU' – this was a venue that took music seriously. These days, though, the interpretation of jazz is pretty loose, stretching to intimate shows by US hip hop legends (such as De La Soul) and racing certainties (such as rapper Aloe Blacc's incredible UK debut), as well as funk, soul and R&B legends such as Marlena Shaw and Mary J Blige.

★ Lexington

96-98 Pentonville Road, Islington, N1 9JB (7837 5371, www.thelexington.co.uk). Angel tube. **Open** noon-2am Mon-Wed, Sun; noon-3am Thur; noon-4am Fri, Sat. **Tickets** free-£15. **Map** p402 N2.

Effectively the common room for the music industry's perennial sixth form, this 200-capacity venue has a superb sound system in place for the leftfield indie bands that dominate the programme. It's where the hottest US exports often make their London debut: indie greats such as the Drums and Sleigh Bells have cut their teeth here in front of London's most receptive crowds. Downstairs, there's a lounge bar with a vast array of US beers and bourbons, above-par bar food and a Rough Trade music quiz (every Monday).

Oslo

1A Amhurst Road, Hackney, E8 1LL (3553 4831, www.oslohackney.com). Hackney Central Overground. **Open** varies. **Admission** varies.

In an old rail station, Oslo is a busy and rather fancy Scandinavian restaurant downstairs, with a more relaxed area for bar food. But head upstairs and you'll find all sorts of musical happenings, including-of-the-moment bands and some club nights. The decent-sized stage and proper sound system and lighting rig ensure a roster of good acts.

★ Shacklewell Arms

71 Shacklewell Lane, Dalston, E8 2EB (7249 0810, www.shacklewellarms.com). Dalston Junction Overground. **Open** 5pm-midnight Mon-Thur; 5pm-3am Fri; noon-3am Sat; noon-midnight Sun. **Admission** free-£8.

The Shacklewell Arms is a magnet for leftfield music. While the bands who have played here include the Horrors, Toy and Haim, DJs tend to come from the electronic, lo-fi, chillwave and post-dubstep arenas, all of which genres contrast brilliantly with the quirkily decorated interior – this former Afro-Caribbean hotspot has had its array of tropical-themed murals and signs pointing to 'the dancehall' updated. Thank goodness.

Underworld

174 Camden High Street, Camden, NW1 0NE (7482 1932, www.theunderworldcamden.co.uk). Camden Town tube. **Box office** *By phone* 24hrs daily. **Shows** times vary. **Admission** £5-£17.50.

A dingy maze of pillars and bars below Camden, this subterranean oddity is an essential for metal and hardcore fans who want their ears bludgeoned by bands with names such as Bitchwax, Skeletonwitch and Decrepit Birth. Tickets are purchased from the World's End pub upstairs.

★ Union Chapel

Compton Terrace, off Upper Street, Islington, N1 2UN (7226 1686, www.unionchapel.org.uk). Highbury & Islington tube/Overground/rail. **Open** varies. **Tickets** free-£35.

In 2012, readers of *Time Out* magazine voted Union Chapel their top music venue. The Grade I-listed Victorian Gothic church still holds services and runs a homeless centre, while doubling as an atmospheric gig venue. It made its name hosting acoustic events and occasional jazz shows, becoming a magnet for thinking bands and their fans. These days, you'll also find classy intimate shows from bigger artists such as Paloma Faith. Watch out for the Daylight Music free afternoon concerts.

Village Underground

54 Holywell Lane, Shoreditch, EC2A 3PQ (7422 7505, www.villageunderground.co.uk). Shoreditch High Street Overground. **Open** varies. **Admission** varies. **Map** p403 R4.

You can't miss Village Underground: four graffiti-covered tube carriages are perched on its roof. These and a series of shipping containers accommodate artists, writers, designers, filmmakers and musicians, while a Victorian warehouse space hosts exhibitions, concerts, plays, live art and club nights.

★ Windmill

22 Blenheim Gardens, Brixton, SW2 5BZ (8671 0700, http://windmillbrixton.co.uk). Brixton tube/rail. **Shows** 8-11pm Mon-Thur; 8pm-1am Fri, Sat; 2-11pm Sun. **Admission** free-£12.

There's a barbecue every Sunday afternoon in summer; a somewhat scary dog lives on the roof, frightening unsuspecting smokers; and an actual windmill stands in the adjacent park. The Windmill is certainly not your average music venue, but it's been revelling in its rough-around-the-edges eccentricity for years, its unprepossessing exterior a cloak for its dedication to new leftfield music. The Vaccines played here in 2013, though generally the programming is biased towards alt country, alt folk and alt punk. It's worth a visit just to pick up an 'I Believe in Roof Dog' T-shirt.

JAZZ, COUNTRY, FOLK & BLUES

The international big hitters keep on visiting London, but these are exciting times, too, for the homespun jazz scene. Inspired by freewheeling attractions at the **Vortex** (*see p279*) and the sporadic, unhinged **Boat-Ting Club** nights (www.boat-ting.co.uk), acts such as Portico Quartet, Led Bib and Kit Downes Trio have won Mercury Prize nominations in the last few years, and the F-IRE and Loop Collectives continue to nurture future stars.

In addition to the venues below, the **100 Club** (*see p274*) hosts blues rock and trad groups, **Bush Hall** (*see p275*) is a great setting for leading folk groups, and the **Spice of Life** at Cambridge Circus (6 Moor Street, W1D 5NA,

7437 7013, www.spiceoflifesoho.com) has solid mainstream jazz. In Hoxton, **Charlie Wright's International Bar** (45 Pitfield Street, N1 6DA, 7490 8345, www.charliewrights.com) usually has a fine jazz programme, but has closed for refurbishment until 2016. The **Jazz Café** (*see p275*) lives up to its name from time to time; there's a lot of very good jazz at the excellent **Kings Place** (*see p284*); and both the **Barbican** (*see p179*) and the **Southbank Centre** (*see p287*) host dozens of big names. For the admirable **London Jazz Festival**, *see p39*.

606 Club

90 Lots Road, Chelsea, SW10 0QD (7352 5953, www.606club.co.uk). Imperial Wharf Overground/rail or bus 11, 211. **Shows** 8.30-11.15pm Mon, Thur; 8-9.30pm, 9.45-11.15pm Tue, Wed; 9.30pm-12.45am Fri, Sat; 1.30-3.30pm, 8.30-11.15pm Sun. **Admission** (non-members) £10-£12.
Since 1976, Steve Rubie has run this spot, which relocated to this 150-capacity club in 1987. Alongside its Brit-dominated bills, expect informal jams featuring musos who've come here to wind down from gigs elsewhere. There's no entrance fee as such; bands are funded from a music charge added to bills at the end of the night.

Blues Kitchen

111-113 Camden High Street, Camden, NW1 7JN (7387 5277, www.theblueskitchen.com). Camden Town or Mornington Crescent tube. **Open** noon-midnight Mon, Tue; noon-1am Wed, Thur; noon-3am Fri; 10am-3.30am Sat; 10am-1am Sun. **Admission** free; £5 after 9.30pm Fri; £6 after 9pm Sat.
The Blues Kitchen combines credible live music of the earthier variety (roots, blues, rockabilly and so on) with a rather smart interior. The food is spicy New Orleans fare and there's a huge range of American bourbon for sippin'. All in all, it makes for a pleasant Sunday afternoon hangout as well as a late-opening gig venue.

★ Borderline

Orange Yard, off Manette Street, Soho, W1D 4JB (information 7734 5547, 0844 847 2465, www.theborderline.com). Tottenham Court Road tube. **Open** varies. **Admission** £3-£20. **Map** p416 W2.
A small, sweaty dive bar and juke joint right in the heart of Soho, the Borderline has long been a favoured stop-off for touring American bands of the country and blues varieties, though you'll also find a range of indie acts and singer-songwriters going through their repertoire here. Be warned, though: it can get very cramped.

Bull's Head

373 Lonsdale Road, Barnes, SW13 9PY (8876 5241, www.geronimo-inns.co.uk). Barnes Bridge rail. **Open** 11am-11pm Mon-Fri; noon-11pm Sat;

noon-10pm Sun. *Jazz Club* 8-11pm Mon-Sat; 1-3.30pm, 8.30-11pm Sun. **Admission** £5-£12.
This venerable Thames-side pub won a reputation for hosting modern jazz in the 1960s but today specialises in mainstream British jazz and swing, with guests such as the Humphrey Lyttelton band. A facelift added posh pub food and appealing decor.

★ Café Oto

18-22 Ashwin Street, Dalston, E8 3DL (7923 1231, www.cafeoto.co.uk). Dalston Junction or Dalston Kingsland Overground. **Open** *Café* 8.30am-5.30pm Mon-Fri; 9.30am-5.30pm Sat; 10.30am-5.30pm Sun. *Shows* 8pm. **Admission** free-£20.
Opened in 2008, this 150-capacity café and music venue can't easily be categorised, though its website offers the tidy definition that it specialises in 'creative new music that exists outside of the mainstream'. That means Japanese noise rockers ('Oto' is Japanese for 'sound'), electronica pioneers, improvising noiseniks and artists from the stranger ends of the rock, folk and classical spectrums.

★ Cecil Sharp House

2 Regent's Park Road, Camden, NW1 7AY (7485 2206, www.cecilsharphouse.org). Camden Town tube. **Open/admission** varies.

Shacklewell Arms.

ESSENTIAL LONDON ALBUMS

Songs of the city.

SOMETHING ELSE
THE KINKS (1967)
Early evidence of Ray Davies' melancholy romanticism lies in the most enduring track on the album that propelled a million moony couples to watch their very own 'Waterloo Sunset'. Listen too for the careful blend of self-deception, veiled homoeroticism and waspish irony on 'David Watts'.

PLEASE
PET SHOP BOYS (1986)
'I love London and I'm inspired by it,' said Neil Tennant, discussing this album's 'West End Girls' with us. The Pet Shop Boys sounded modern from the off, but the seminal electropop hits on *Please* – 'Opportunities (Let's Make Lots of Money)', 'Suburbia' – also sound like London.

ARULAR
MIA (2003)
Few albums are as representative of London's multiculturalism as this. Not just for its estates-by-way-of-Jamaica slang, nor MIA's Sri Lankan/west London heritage, but also by including carnival-electro-bashment anthems co-written by such indie stars as Steve Mackey.

NEW BOOTS AND
PANTIES!!
IAN DURY (1977)
The title refers to the only clothes a thrifty Dury wouldn't buy from charity shops, and the cover shows him with his son, Baxter. Classic tracks such as 'Wake Up and Make Love to Me' and 'Billericay Dickie' make this some of the finest work by the Essex pub-rock maestro.

PARKLIFE
BLUR (1994)
Launched at the defunct Walthamstow Dog Track, *Parklife* was a hymn to the East End, with the laddish Britpoppers on cheekily good form. 'Girls and Boys', 'End of a Century' and 'To the End' join the iconic 'Parklife' on an album that came to epitomise the emerging 1990s Britpop scene.

EVERYBODY DOWN
KATE TEMPEST (2015)
This Mercury award-nominated poet and spoken-word artist from Peckham in south London gets right into the grit of London life. Halfway between rap and spoken word, her tales of urban malaise and hope create a portrait of a lonely city of screens, police lights and concrete.

ARTS & ENTERTAINMENT

Headquarters of the British Folk Dance and Song Society, Cecil Sharp House is a great place to visit, even when there isn't any music playing – there's a folk-arts education centre and archive open during the day. But the Kennedy Hall performance space has a comfortably sprung floor and a well-informed and enthusiastic team of bookers ensuring all angles of trad music are well represented without being preserved in aspic. Events range from regular Scottish ceilidhs to more-contemporary alt folk.

Forge & Foundry

3-7 Delancey Street, Camden, NW1 7NL (7383 7808, www.forgevenue.org). Camden Town or Mornington Crescent tube. **Open** *varies.* **Shows** from 7.30pm. **Admission** free-£16.

Run by a non-profit community organisation, this innovative music/restaurant space incorporates a stunning atrium, and hosts concerts of various sizes and formalities. The programme is skewed heavily to jazz, but also features a carefully curated selection of roots and classical shows. There's an on-site restaurant, the Foundry; you can dine while you listen on a Friday, and there's an interesting weekend brunch programme.

Green Note

106 Parkway, Camden, NW1 7AN (7485 9899, www.greennote.co.uk). Camden Town tube. **Open** 7-11pm Mon-Thur, Sun; 7pm-midnight Fri, Sat. **Shows** 8.30pm daily. **Admission** £2-£15.

A stone's throw from Regent's Park, this cosy little venue and vegetarian café-bar was a welcome addition to the city's roots circuit back in 2005. Singer-songwriters, folkies and blues musicians make up the majority of the gig roster, with a handful of big names in among the listings.

Pizza Express Jazz Club

10 Dean Street, Soho, W1D 3RW (0845 602 7017, www.pizzaexpresslive.com). Tottenham Court Road tube. **Shows** times vary. **Admission** £15-£25. **Map** p416 W2.

The upstairs restaurant (7437 9595) is jazz-free, but the 120-capacity basement is one of the best mainstream jazz venues in town. Singers such as Kurt Elling and Lea DeLaria join instrumentalists from home and abroad on the nightly bills.

★ Ronnie Scott's

47 Frith Street, Soho, W1D 4HT (7439 0747, www.ronniescotts.co.uk). Leicester Square or Tottenham Court Road tube. **Shows** 6pm-3am Mon-Sat; noon-4pm, 6.30pm-midnight Sun. **Admission** free-£50. **Map** p416 W2.

Opened (on a different site) by the British saxophonist Ronnie Scott in 1959, this jazz institution – the setting for Jimi Hendrix's final UK performance, among many other distinctions – was completely refurbished in 2006. The capacity was expanded to 250, the food got better and the bookings

became drearier. Happily, though, Ronnie's has got back on track, with jazz heavyweights dominating once more – from trad talents such as Chick Corea to hotly tipped purists such as Kurt Elling to futuristic mavericks such as Robert Glasper. Perch by the rear bar, or get table service at the crammed side-seating or at the more spacious (but noisier) central tables in front of the stage.

★ Vortex Jazz Club

Dalston Culture House, 11 Gillett Street, Dalston, N16 8JN (7254 4097, www.vortexjazz.co.uk). Dalston Junction Overground. **Open** 4pm-midnight Mon-Thur; noon-midnight Fri, Sat; 2pm-1am Sun. **Shows** 8pm daily. **Admission** £5-£18.

One of the few venues in the city you could visit on spec and be guaranteed to hear something interesting. Along with the nearby Café Oto (*see p277*), the Vortex is one of London's most lovingly curated venues. Jazz is the order of the day, but the Vortex serves it up in kaleidoscopic variety. For the less daring, there's a regular calendar of big band, piano trio, vocal, free improv, world music and folk-oriented sounds, as well as some poetry gigs. The Vortex hosts its own strand of the London Jazz Festival and various other forward-thinking events.

▶ *Also at Gillett Square, the Servant Jazz Quarters cocktail dive (10A Bradbury Street, N16 8JN, 7684 8411, www.servantjazzquarters.com) serves cocktails and programmes gigs – sometimes jazz.*

Cabaret

To see the best cabaret, head to the always interesting **Bethnal Green Working Men's Club** (*see p280*) or the even more alternative **RVT** (*see p261*). The comedy and cabaret room downstairs at the multi-talented **Soho Theatre** (*see p294*) is a little on the cramped and clattery side, but that doesn't detract from the calibre of the performers: there's confident international scope and formal breadth to the programming, which ranges from home-grown sensations such as Bourgeois & Maurice to smoky chanteuses such as Lady Rizo and hysterical alt-drag acts such as Dina Martina. There have been some bitterly mourned closures over the last year: the loss of **Madame JoJo's** in Soho and of Camden drag pub the **Black Cap** within a few months of each other raised concerns about the future of cabaret in central London, which were somewhat calmed by the opening of the **Glory** (*see p261*) in Dalston. There's also a steady increase in cabaret in posh venues: the **Savoy** (*see p355*) hosts evenings in the Beaufort Bar that mix burlesque, variety and song; **Brasserie Zédel** (*see p114*) puts on shows at its Crazy Coqs venue and the **Hippodrome** (www.hippodromecasino.com), primarily a casino, also has a venue for music and cabaret. Many of the best nights are one-off

Invisible Dot Ltd.

parties in a range of formal and informal venues. But wherever you choose to party in London, be sure to bring an open mind.

★ Bethnal Green Working Men's Club

42-44 Pollard Row, Bethnal Green, E2 6NB (7739 7170, www.workersplaytime.net). Bethnal Green tube. **Open** varies. **Admission** free-£10.

Sticky red carpet and broken lampshades perfectly suit the programme of quirky lounge, retro rock 'n' roll and fancy-dress burlesque parties here. You might get to watch a spandex-lovin' dance duo or get hip with burlesque starlets on a 1960s dancefloor. The mood is friendly, the playlist upbeat and the air full of artful, playful mischief.

CellarDoor

Zero Aldwych, Covent Garden, WC2E 7DN (7240 8848, www.cellardoor.biz). Covent Garden tube. **Open** varies. **Admission** varies. **Map** p401 L7.

Some staggeringly clever design means that although there's room for just 60 in this subterranean converted Victorian loo, CellarDoor never feels claustrophobic. Musical-theatre cabaret crooners and drag queens are the order of the day, giving this sleek establishment a vintage feel. Nearly all shows are free and often great fun – EastEnd Cabaret regularly appears and Champagne Charlie's Trash Tuesday open-mic night is an institution.

Pheasantry

152-154 King's Road, Chelsea, SW3 4UT (0845 602 7017, www.pizzaexpresslive.com). Sloane Square tube. **Shows** 6.30pm; days vary. **Admission** varies. **Map** p397 F11.

The successor to the institution that was Pizza on the Park, this jazz and cabaret venue is also part of the Pizza Express stable. The bright, spacious basement space has something of a cruise-ship feel (where does that staircase actually go to?) and the sightlines aren't always that great, but it's the city's premier platform for New York-style jazz singing and

musical-theatre-influenced cabaret work, often managing to attract big names both from the West End and across the Atlantic.

St James Studio

12 Palace Street, Victoria, SW1E 5JA (0844 264 2140, www.stjamestheatre.co.uk). Victoria tube/rail. **Open** varies. **Admission** £8-£25. **Map** p400 J9.

When it opened in 2012, an integral part of St James Theatre was its downstairs Studio space, a cosy room that plays host to a range of work towards the classic end of the cabaret spectrum, as well as comedy, music and fringe work. Recent highlights have included runs from the sensational interpreter of song Barb Jungr and Peter Straker's barnstorming tribute to the songs of Jacques Brel.

Comedy

While the big stadiums – especially the **O2 Arena** (*see p273*) – host the massive shows (both TV star stand-ups and gigs such as the Monty Python 'alimony-payment' reunion of 2014), it's the circuit of pubs and smaller clubs that defines London's comedy scene. Over the last few years, in addition to its stellar role as a venue for plays and cabaret, the **Soho Theatre** (*see p294*) has become one of the best places to see comics breaking free from abbreviated club-circuit sets to present more substantial solo shows. Usually programming hour-long solo shows rather than the multi-act bills common elsewhere, it's currently the best venue in London for interesting, innovative and downright funny comedy. Another multi-tasking venue is the **Union Chapel** (*see p276*), whose monthly Live at the Chapel night provides line-ups of big guns (Noel Fielding and Stewart Lee, for example) supported by comics who are headliners in their own right, plus a terrific live band.

For the week's best line-ups, have a look at the free *Time Out* magazine; for comprehensive comedy listings, see www.timeout.com.

99 Club Leicester Square
Storm Nightclub, 28A Leicester Square, WC2H 7LE (07760 488119, www.99clubcomedy.com). Leicester Square tube. **Shows** 7.30pm Tue-Sat. **Admission** £8-£18. **Map** p401 K7.
The general rule when you get a flyer as you walk through Leicester Square is to stick it in the nearest recycling bin – but make an exception for this one. The 99 Club gang have been in the business for more than a decade, and this is their flagship venue. It offers quality line-ups five nights a week – recently the bills have been particularly impressive. Tickets are remarkably good value, but expect a hike in prices around Christmas.

★ Angel Comedy
Camden Head, 2 Camden Walk, Islington, N1 8DY (www.angelcomedy.co.uk). Angel tube. **Shows** 8pm daily. **Admission** free; donations appreciated.
Angel Comedy is one of the best comedy nights in London – and is certainly the best free night. That means long queues tend to form outside, with the promoters having to turn folk away every weekend. On Fridays and Saturdays, you can catch rising stars and a few professional comics performing their funniest sets, and weekdays feature either new material spots, improv troupes or solo shows. But the night's biggest sell is the inclusive, welcoming atmosphere – despite being free, punters come for the comedy rather than a cheap night out. Donations are encouraged at the end of the night.

★ Comedy Store
1A Oxendon Street, Soho, SW1Y 4EE (0844 871 7699, www.thecomedystore.co.uk). Leicester Square or Piccadilly Circus tube. **Admission** £5-£23.50. **Map** p416 W4.
It's true, the Comedy Store is still the daddy of all comedy clubs. Seemingly as old as London itself (it actually started in 1979, above a strip club), the Store has been instrumental in the growth of alternative comedy, and still to this day hosts stunning shows most nights of the week. The live room was created specifically for stand-up and it shows, with 400 chairs hugging the stage to keep each show intimate. Veteran improvisers the Comedy Store Players perform every Wednesday and Sunday. Don't miss the raucous King Gong new-act night on the last Monday of the month.

★ Invisible Dot Ltd
2 Northdown Street, King's Cross, N1 9BG (7424 8918, www.theinvisibledot.com). King's Cross tube/rail. **Shows/admission** varies. **Map** p399 M2.
This 100-capacity venue is a hipster's paradise. Plain white walls are adorned with stylish posters for upcoming shows from leftfield acts, and the audience is about 70% beard. But they aren't laughing to look cool: the Dot's shows are spectacular. The 'Saturday Night Show' has superb line-ups of alt talent; themed gigs for Christmas, Valentine's and Halloween put a strange twist on big calendar dates; and there are tons of work-in-progress gigs from the likes of Adam Buxton and Tim Key. London's trendiest comedy venue – and one of the best.

Knock2Bag
West *Bar FM, 184 Hopgood Street, Shepherd's Bush, W12 7JU. Shepherd's Bush tube/Overground.* **Shows** 7.30pm 3rd Wed of the month.
East *Rich Mix, 35-47 Bethnal Green Road, Shoreditch, E1 6LA. Liverpool Street tube/Overground/rail or Shoreditch High Street Overground.* **Shows** 8.30pm last Sat of the month.
Both *07870 212189, http://knock2bag.co.uk.* **Admission** £8-£12.
For variety, stunning line-ups and sheer value for money (the bills cram in seven or more top-class acts), it's hard to beat Knock2Bag. There is always a mix of inventive sketch troupes, weirdo character acts and slick stand-up, from household names to the finest newbies. And with clubs in both east and west, they're easy to visit wherever you're staying in town.

Leicester Square Theatre
6 Leicester Place, Leicester Square, WC2H 7BX (7734 2222, www.leicestersquaretheatre.com). Leicester Square tube. **Shows** times vary. **Admission** £5-£47. **Map** p416 X4.
Not strictly a comedy venue (it hosts music and theatre too), the Leicester Square Theatre's basement space is nonetheless home to enjoyable regular comedy nights and Edinburgh Fringe previews, while the 400-seat main house is a favourite room for big names (Stewart Lee, Jerry Sadowitz and Doug Stanhope often play long runs). Highlights from the studio space include an ongoing residency from professional underachiever Lewis Schaffer.
▶ *The same people run the Museum of Comedy (see p154), which has its own performance space for stand-up and comedy-themed plays.*

Up the Creek
302 Creek Road, Greenwich, SE10 9SW (8858 4581, www.up-the-creek.com). Cutty Sark DLR. **Shows** 9pm Fri, Sat; 8.30pm Sun. **Admission** £8-10 Fri; £12-£14 Sat; £4-£7 Sun.
Set up by the late and legendary alt-comedian Malcolm Hardee in the 1990s, this purpose-built comedy club is still one of the capital's best. The atmosphere is lively: it's less of a bearpit than it used to be, but the locals aren't afraid to torment comics – if a punter thinks of something funnier than what's being said on stage, they will shout it out.
▶ *The Sunday Special (www.sundayspecial.co.uk) has a more relaxed vibe, cheap tickets and often features arena-filling names testing new material.*

ARTS & ENTERTAINMENT

Performing Arts

London's classical musicians seem unusually open-minded, with classical nights in pubs and jazz strands at august classical auditoriums. But as well as this mix-and-match aesthetic, passionate purists remain – the Barbican and Royal Festival Hall still deliver a big orchestral punch with the traditional repertoire. Music of a different stripe dominates the West End theatres too: the biggest attractions remain the musicals.

That's not to say there's no 'proper' drama, with a string of recent successes having begun life in the National Theatre, the city's flagship publicly funded theatre, as well as at smaller venues such as the Donmar and the Young Vic.

Although there are some concerns about a lack of home-grown talent in the ranks of stellar performers in London, the city remains a hub for dance in a way few other cities can match. Even the 80-year-old Royal Ballet produces groundbreaking new work.

Classical Music & Opera

London's classical scene has never looked or sounded more current, with the **Southbank Centre** (*see p287*), the **Barbican Centre** (*see p283*) and **Kings Place** (*see p284*) all working with strong programmes – although, arguably, less impressive acoustics (*see p283* **Feeling Rattled**). Even the once-stuffy **Royal Opera House** now leavens its programme with occasional commissions, such as Mark-Anthony Turnage's opera *Anna Nicole*, the tragic tale of a Playboy model and her ancient sugar-daddy. And it will be interesting to see how the **English**

National Opera builds on Edward Gardner's adventurous legacy when Mark Wigglesworth succeeds him in October 2015. Tansy Davies' *Between Worlds*, an opera about the events of 9/11 that saw its debut at the Barbican in 2015, was a bold parting shot.

TICKETS & INFORMATION

Tickets for most classical and opera events are available direct from the venues, online or by phone. It's advisable always to book ahead. Several venues, such as the Barbican and the Southbank Centre, operate standby schemes, offering unsold tickets at cut-rate prices just before the show. They also have reduced-price tickets for under-26s.

CLASSICAL VENUES

In addition to the major venues below, you can hear what tomorrow's classical music might sound like at the city's music schools, which stage regular concerts by pupils and visiting professionals. Check the websites of the **Royal College of Music** (7591 4314, www.rcm.ac.uk)

IN THE KNOW DO MORE

Check the free *Time Out* magazine for the performing arts highlights of the week, or visit www.timeout.com for comprehensive cultural listings.

– which is planning to spend £25 million on two new performance spaces – the **Royal Academy of Music** (7873 7373, www.ram.ac.uk), the **Guildhall School of Music & Drama** (7628 2571, www.gsmd.ac.uk) and **Trinity Laban Conservatoire of Music & Dance** (8305 4444, www.trinitylaban.ac.uk). There's also a trend for top-class classical and contemporary classical music in relaxed – for which read 'alcohol-friendly' – settings (*see p285* **Cool Old-School**).

★ **Barbican Centre**

Silk Street, the City, EC2Y 8DS (information 7638 4141, tickets 7638 8891, www.barbican.org.uk). Barbican tube or Moorgate tube/rail. **Box office** 10am-9pm Mon-Sat; 11am-8pm Sun. **Tickets** £8-£65. **Map** p402 P5.

Europe's largest multi-arts centre is easier to navigate after a renovation – although 'easier' still isn't quite the same as 'with ease', so allow a little extra time to get to your seat. The programming remains as rich as ever, and the London Symphony Orchestra, guided by principal conductor Valery Gergiev, remains in residence. The BBC Symphony Orchestra also performs an annual series of concerts, and there's a laudable amount of contemporary classical music, not least an ambitious ENO production in 2015 covering the events of 9/11. Beyond classical, programming falls into a wide range of genres: from Sufi music to New York rock legends.

▶ *A brand-new concert hall opened in 2013 barely 100 yards from the main external entrance to the Barbican. Milton Court (1 Milton Street, EC2Y 9BH, 7638 8891, www.gsmd.ac.uk) is run by the Guildhall*

FEELING RATTLED

Has a star conductor's return ruffled feathers?

Now that Sir Simon Rattle has signed on the dotted line for the London Symphony Orchestra, one wonders if the superstar conductor will sheepishly try to avoid eye contact with Barbican management in the lift following his comments that the acoustic of the complex's concert hall (and LSO base) is merely 'serviceable'. And yet, while a new world-class symphony hall for London has not been a precondition of his tenure, the current Government has promised to look into the possibility.

The news of Rattle's homecoming in 2017 came at the end of his long-ago sold-out Berlin Philharmonic concerts at the **Barbican** (see above) and **Royal Festival Hall** (see p287). The series made front page news and created a buzz that rarely spreads beyond classical music circles. His appointment, too, generated the sort of media excitement that once surrounded the activities of his illustrious conducting forebears. He is, therefore, exactly what the sector needs to reassert the prominence of classical music as a prestigious cultural force.

So are London's concert halls just serviceable? Well, yes. Barbican Hall owns the best, albeit flat, orchestral acoustic, followed by the RFH's uneven one, but neither are a match for Berlin's Philharmonie or even Birmingham's Symphony Hall (built

to accommodate Rattle and his sharply honed CBSO in 1991). The BBC Proms, for instance, take place at the **Royal Albert Hall** (see p285), which is suitable for large orchestras and solo pianists, but not for medium-sized bands or Baroque music. Other colossi include **St Paul's Cathedral** (see p176), which hosts the LSO opening concerts of the City of London Festival, but with a delay of over nine seconds and a transcept-shaped auditorium, it is far from ideal.

The city is much better served for smaller-scale spaces. **Wigmore Hall** (see p287) is the pre-eminent chamber venue and the only one (along with the **Royal Opera House**, see p288) to hold its own internationally; although, since 2008, a runner-up can now be found in Hall One at **Kings Place** (see p284). Meanwhile, **Cadogan Hall** (see p284), a former church, is the right size for Baroque music, though is curiously home to the mighty Royal Philharmonic Orchestra. Mercifully, the Queen Elizabeth Hall and Purcell Room (for both, see p287) are closing for refurbishment from September 2015 and should re-emerge with warmer acoustics, while the most recent addition to the performance circuit, **Milton Court Hall** at the Barbican (see above), is a 600-seat auditorium with a bright response.

So, it is worth choosing concerts not just on the basis of the ensemble and its repertoire, but also the compatibility of the venue.

ARTS & ENTERTAINMENT

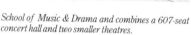
Wigmore Hall. See p287.

ARTS & ENTERTAINMENT

School of Music & Drama and combines a 607-seat concert hall and two smaller theatres.

Cadogan Hall

5 Sloane Terrace, off Sloane Street, Chelsea, SW1X 9DQ (7730 4500, www.cadoganhall.com). Sloane Square tube. **Box office** *Non-performance days* 10am-8pm Mon-Sat. *Performance days* 10am-6pm Mon-Sat; noon-6pm Sun. **Tickets** £15-£50. **Map** p400 G10.
Jazz groups and rock bands have been attracted by the acoustics in this renovated former Christian Science church, but the programming at the austere yet comfortable 900-seat hall is dominated by classical. The Royal Philharmonic are resident; other orchestras also perform, and there's regular chamber music.

★ Kings Place

90 York Way, King's Cross, N1 9AG (7520 1490, www.kingsplace.co.uk). King's Cross-St Pancras tube/rail. **Box office** noon-7pm Mon; 10am-6pm Tue; noon-8pm Wed-Sat; 10am-7pm Sun. **Tickets** £9.50-£51.50. **Map** p399 L2.
Once a lone pioneer in the revival of King's Cross, Kings Place suddenly finds itself part of the King's Cross Central cultural hub. Beneath seven office floors and a ground-floor restaurant-bar (with prized seats on the canal basin outside, the 400-seat main hall is a beauty, dominated by wood carved from a single, 500-year-old oak tree and ringed by invisible rubber pads that kill unwanted noise that might interfere with the immaculate acoustic. There's also a versatile second hall and a number of smaller rooms for workshops and lectures. The programming is tremendous and includes curated weeks featuring artists as wide-ranging as Schönberg and jazzer Kit Downes. Other strands include chamber music and experimental classical, and there are spoken-word events too.

LSO St Luke's

161 Old Street, the City, EC1V 9NG (information 7490 3939, tickets 7638 8891, www.lso.co.uk/lsostlukes). Old Street tube/rail. **Box office** (at Barbican box office) 10am-9pm Mon-Sat; 11am-8pm Sun. **Tickets** free-£40. **Map** p402 P4.
Built by Nicholas Hawksmoor in the 18th century, this Grade I-listed church was beautifully converted into a performance and rehearsal space by the LSO several years ago. The orchestra occasionally welcomes the public for open

rehearsals (book ahead); the more formal side of the programme takes in global sounds alongside classical music, including lunchtime concerts every Thursday that are broadcast on BBC Radio 3.
▶ *Intrigued by St Luke's obelisk spire? Hawksmoor also designed the brutal spike of Christ Church Spitalfields (see p200) and the mini-ziggurat atop St George's Bloomsbury (see p154).*

Royal Albert Hall
Kensington Gore, South Kensington, SW7 2AP (tickets 0845 401 5045, www.royalalberthall.com). South Kensington tube or bus 9, 10, 52, 452. **Box office** 9am-9pm daily. **Tickets** £13-£275. **Map** p397 D9.
In constant use since opening in 1871, with boxing matches, motorshows and Allen Ginsberg's 1965 International Poetry Incarnation among the headline events, the Royal Albert Hall continues to host a very broad programme. The classical side is dominated by the superb BBC Proms (*see p35*), which runs every night for two months in summer and sees a huge array of orchestras and other ensembles battling the difficult acoustics. It's well worth catching a concert that features the thunderous Grand Organ.

St James's Piccadilly
197 Piccadilly, Piccadilly, W1J 9LL (7381 0441, www.sjp.org.uk). Piccadilly Circus tube. **Box office** 10am-5pm Mon-Sat; 10am-6pm performance days. **Tickets** free-£28. **Map** p400 J7.
This community-spirited Wren church holds free lunchtime recitals (1.10pm Mon, Wed, Fri) and offers regular evening concerts covering a variety of musical styles.

St John's, Smith Square
Smith Square, Westminster, SW1P 3HA (7222 1061, www.sjss.org.uk). Westminster tube. **Box office** *Non-performance days* 10am-5pm Mon-Fri. *Performance days* 10am-6pm Mon-Fri. **Tickets** free-£28. **Map** p401 K10.
St John's is a curiously shaped 18th-century church – it is said that the four-turret design was the result of Queen Anne's demand that architect Thomas Archer make it look like a footstool that she had kicked over – which hosts concerts more or less nightly, and Thursday lunchtime recitals too. Everything from symphony orchestras to solo recitals make the most of its good acoustics. Down in the crypt are two bars for interval drinks and the Smith Square Bar & Restaurant.

St Martin-in-the-Fields
Trafalgar Square, Westminster, WC2N 4JJ (7766 1100, www.stmartin-in-the-fields.org). Charing Cross tube/rail. **Box office** *In person* 8am-5pm Mon, Tue; 8am-9.45pm Wed; 8am-8.30pm Thur-Sat. *By phone* 10am-5pm Mon-Sat. **Tickets** free-£30. **Map** p401 L7.

COOL OLD-SCHOOL
Classical music, but without the frosty penguin suits.

The vibrancy of London's classical music scene can hardly be doubted, but when you find yourself among reverent octogenarians at some London venues, you may feel you have to be on your best behaviour. Not so at the Orchestra of the Age of Enlightenment's popular series of **Night Shift** concerts (www. oae.co.uk/thenightshift), at which you'll see a far younger audience, perhaps belting out drinking songs by Purcell – with lyrics not fit for publication in a family guidebook. The idea is to gather a small group of performers in the relaxed setting of a pub – the Old Queen's Head (*see p270*) and George Tavern (373 Commercial Road, Stepney, E1 0LA, 7790 7335, www.thegeorgetavern.co.uk) are regular hosts – to perform canonical composers such as Mozart, Haydn and Handel. There's no shying away from difficult pieces: the professional and seriously talented performers trust that the combination of their skill and enthusiasm with the familiar setting to win new audiences to the classical music they love.

Arguably the pioneer of this informal classical scene is one Gabriel Prokofiev, grandson of the Russian composer. He founded **Nonclassical** (www.nonclassical. co.uk), which mixes contemporary classical music and DJs in a combination of 'proper' classical venues (Kings Place, *see p284*), clubs (XOYO, *see p271;* Hoxton Square Bar & Kitchen, *see p275*) and, yes, pubs (Shacklewell Arms, *see p276*). Keep an eye out too for occasional London concerts from Berlin-based **Yellow Lounge** (http://yellowlounge.co.uk), a club night set up by record label Deutsche Grammophon to bring classical music up to date with performances in urban spaces.

Night Shift

ARTS & ENTERTAINMENT

THE BEST OF THE WEST END

A selection of shows from London's theatreland.

SEEN THE FILM?

London's great film spin-off musical success has been… not *Ghost*, not *Dirty Dancing*, not *The Full Monty*, not Tim Rice's huge-budget *From Here to Eternity*, not even *Made in Dagenham* with the winsome Gemma Arterton… no, it's the tale of a humble miner's son who only wants to dance: **Billy Elliot** (*see p292*) has kept on high-kicking long after the other contenders have been hoofed off stage. We're not entirely convinced by a new adaptation of Pedro Almodóvar's 1988 indie classic *Women on the Verge of a Nervous Breakdown* (www.womenon thevergemusical.com), but Tamsin Greig is excellent in her musical-theatre debut as Pepa, a Madrid TV actor having a trying day: her lover Ivan dumps her by voicemail and she slowly discovers he's been hiding a son and crazy wife, Lucia. Also worthy of your time are the high-camp *Mamma Mia!* (www. delfontmackintosh.co.uk), *The Commitments* (www.palacetheatrelondon.org) and, built on an absolutely stunning opening sequence, *The Lion King* (www.lyceum-theatre.co.uk).

READ THE BOOK?

Want your heartstrings plucked? Two very different tales of oppressed but gifted children (**Matilda** and **The Curious Incident of the Dog in the Night-Time**; *pictured*; for both, *see p292*) did it for us, combining soul-expanding warmth with a sense of real peril. Tear-ducts need tickling? **War Horse** (*pictured*; *see p293*) is for you, then. For sheer spectacle, the Sam Mendes-directed *Charlie & the Chocolate Factory* (www.charlieandthe chocolatefactory.com) takes some beating, and we remain big fans of *Wizard of Oz* prequel *Wicked* (www.wickedthemusical.co.uk) too.

JUKEBOX MUSICALS

For a decade or more, the jukebox musical has been a West End staple. At their worst, they're just a roughly bolted together greatest-hits set not even performed by the original band. And at their best? You've got **Jersey Boys** (*see p292*). Instead of torturously extrapolating a zany plot out of the lyrics, *Jersey Boys* simply puts the story of the Four Seasons in the hands of a director who won't let extended song-and-dance routines get in the way of an incident-packed story. But fans are currently well-treated by musicals built from the back catalogues of the Kinks (*Sunny Afternoon*, www.atgtickets. com), Michael Jackson (*Thriller Live*, www. nimaxtheatres.com) and Carole King (*Beautiful*, http://beautifulmusical.co.uk).

OLD FAITHFULS AND REVIVALS

Les Misérables (*see p292*) continues its indefatigable run, unbroken since the 1980s, with *Phantom of the Opera* (www.reallyuseful. com) not far behind it, but the tang of the Cameron Mackintosh/Andrew Lloyd Webber West End can be savoured more widely: *Miss Saigon* (www.delfontmackintosh.co.uk) is back – in a magnificent-looking production that runs from a Vietnamese go-go bar to the Statue of Liberty itself – as is a revival of *Cats* (www.reallyuseful.com) that's every bit as odd as the original. You have to set the time-machine dial 30 years further into history to catch the première of the **Mousetrap** (*see p292*), which might make it feel quite at home with *Gypsy* (www.atgtickets.com). Not seen in London for 40 years, Jonathan Kent's revival of this 1959 Sondheim musical purrs along with a full, jazzy orchestra and some beautifully Gene Kelly-ish choreography. Imelda Staunton stars as hilarious, tragic, monstrous impresario Momma Rose in the best performance of her career. Which is what we seem to say after every one of her performances. But this one, really.

ARTS & ENTERTAINMENT

One of the capital's most amiable venues, St Martin's hosts populist performances of the likes of Bach, Mozart and Vivaldi by candlelight, jazz in the crypt's improved café and lunchtime recitals (1pm Mon, Tue, Fri) from young musicians. There's a fine atmosphere in the beautifully restored interior.

▶ *For more on the church, see p69.*

★ Southbank Centre

Belvedere Road, South Bank, SE1 8XX (information 7960 4200, tickets 0844 875 0073, www.southbankcentre.co.uk). Embankment tube or Waterloo tube/rail. **Box office** *In person* 10am-8pm daily. *By phone* 9am-8pm daily. **Tickets** £7-£75. **Map** p401 M8.

The centrepiece of the cluster of cultural venues collectively known as the Southbank Centre is the 3,000-seat Royal Festival Hall, which was renovated acoustically and externally to the tune of £90m back in 2007; now the neighbouring 900-seat Queen Elizabeth Hall and attached 365-seat Purcell Room are getting a little TLC – they should reopen after refurbishment in late 2015. All three programme a wide variety of events – spoken word, jazz, rock and pop gigs – but classical is very well represented. The RFH has four resident orchestras (the London Philharmonic and Philharmonia Orchestras, the London Sinfonietta and the Orchestra of the Age of Enlightenment), and hosts music from medieval motets to Messiaen via Beethoven and Elgar. Beneath this main hall, facing the foyer bar, a stage puts on hundreds of free concerts each year.

▶ *For the Hayward Gallery, also part of the Southbank Centre, see p51.*

★ Wigmore Hall

36 Wigmore Street, Marylebone, W1U 2BP (7935 2141, www.wigmore-hall.org.uk). Bond Street tube. **Box office** *Non-performance days* 10am-5pm Mon-Sat; 10am-2pm Sun. *Performance days* 10am-7pm daily. **Tickets** £5-£35. **Map** p398 G6.

Built in 1901 as the display hall for Bechstein pianos, this world-renowned, 550-seat concert venue has perfect acoustics for the 400 concerts that take place each year. Music from the classical and romantic periods are mainstays, usually performed by major classical stars to an intense audience, but under artistic director John Gilhooly there has been a broadening in the remit: more baroque and increased jazz (included heavyweights like Brad Mehldau, including late-night gigs. Monday lunchtime recitals are broadcast live on BBC Radio 3. *Photo p284.*

▶ *The nearby Steinway showroom (44 Marylebone Lane, W1U 2DB, 7487 3391, www.steinway.co.uk/concerts-events) hosts regular recitals.*

OPERA VENUES

In addition to the two big venues listed below, look out for performances at the **Linbury Studio**, downstairs at the Royal Opera House; **Cadogan**

Royal Opera House *See p288.*

Hall (*see p284*); summer's **Opera Holland Park** (*see p33*); sporadic appearances by **English Touring Opera** (www.englishtouringopera.org. uk); and much promising work, often directed by big names, at the city's music schools. A small but lively fringe opera scene has sprung up, with **OperaUpClose** (www.operaupclose.com) branching out from its King's Head Theatre base in Islington (www.kingsheadtheatre.com) to play up west at the Soho and Charing Cross Theatres; the **Charles Court Opera** company (www. charlescourtopera.com) doing fine operetta in various small theatres; and the annual **Tête à Tête** (www.tete-a-tete.org.uk), now settled in King's Cross and claiming to be 'the world's largest festival of new opera', programming 80 performances over a fortnight of song.

English National Opera, Coliseum

St Martin's Lane, Covent Garden, WC2N 4ES (tickets 7845 9300, www.eno.org). Leicester Square tube or Charing Cross tube/rail. **Box office** *In person* 10am-6pm Mon-Sat. *By phone* 24hrs daily. **Tickets** £20-£155. **Map** p401 L7.

Built as a music hall in 1904, the home of the English National Opera (ENO) was put under 'special funding arrangements' in early 2015; new music director Mark Wigglesworth, ten years the junior of his respected predecessor Edward Gardner, will find things tough when he takes over in late 2015 – but an announcement that prices will be reduced to £20 and under on 60,000 seats for his first season has already made headlines. The ENO has offered some fascinating collaborations over the last few years: physical theatre troupe

Complicité and Blur's Damon Albarn on *Doctor Dee*, for instance, and Bryn Terfel with Emma Thompson in Sondheim's *Sweeney Todd*. There have also been stagings of rare contemporary works (Ligeti's *Le Grand Macabre*, Glass's *Satyagraha*). But Gardner's 'Undress for the Opera', encouraging new, younger audience members to attend some classic operas in their everyday clothes, may yet prove to be his most important initiative. All works are in English, and prices are cheaper than at the Royal Opera.

▶ *The £20 Secret Seat offer allows you to book an unallocated seat online – the secret lies in its location in the auditorium. Wherever it turns out to be, your seat will always be worth at least £25.*

★ Royal Opera, Royal Opera House

Bow Street, Covent Garden, WC2E 9DD (7304 4000, www.roh.org.uk). Covent Garden tube. **Box office** 10am-8pm Mon-Sat. **Tickets** £4-£200. **Map** p401 L7. Thanks to a refurbishment at the start of the century, the Royal Opera House has once again taken its place among the ranks of the world's great opera houses – but it isn't enough: the £27m 'Open Up' redevelopment will make further infrastructural changes. Critics suggest that the programming at the Opera House can be a little spotty – especially so given the famously elevated ticket prices – but there is a solid spine to the programme: fine productions of the classics, often taking place under the baton of Antonio Pappano. Productions take in favourite traditional operatic composers (Donizetti, Mozart, Verdi) and some modern (Benjamin Britten, Harrison Birtwistle), while the annual month-long Deloitte Ignite festival fills the opera house with a wide range of free and ticketed events. *Photo p287.*

▶ *It's not just singing at the Opera House: the Royal Ballet is also based here; see p295.*

Theatre

The West End has managed to ride out the recession on a tide of song – in other words, those big-production musicals. The most ancient of these (**Les Misérables**) has been hoofing it on the London stage since the mid 1980s. Despite frequent revivals from the era (including a huge-budget *Miss Saigon*), its contemporaries have mostly gone, leaving the format to be brought up to date by a bunch of lively, thoroughly modern new musicals – including Broadway smash **The Book of Mormon**. Drama is making a very real comeback too, led by the colossal success of National Theatre transfers **War Horse** and **The Curious Incident**, and a spate of excellent Shakespeare productions, but also increasingly showing a fascination with making entertaining theatre out of challenging topics: the royal succession in the case of *Charles III*, virtual paedophilia in *The Nether*. Even Kenneth Branagh is returning to the West End with a three-month season in 2015/16.

The **Donmar Warehouse** (*see p293*) traditionally lures high-profile film stars to perform at its tiny Earlham Street home, while Kevin Spacey's term as artistic director brought his stellar chums to do turns at the **Old Vic** (*see p289*) – will his departure in autumn 2015 see a decline in the venue's celebrity pull?

On a smaller scale, Off-West End houses such as the **Young Vic** (*see p294*) – winner of the 2015 Olivier awards for best director, actor and revival for *A View from the Bridge* – and the **Almeida** (*see p293*) continue to produce some of London's most exciting, best-value theatre, while the **Barbican Centre** (*see p283*) programmes visually exciting and physically expressive work from around the world.

THEATRE DISTRICTS

In strictly geographical terms, the **West End** refers to London's traditional theatre district, a busy area bounded by Shaftesbury Avenue, Drury Lane, the Strand and the Haymarket. Most major musicals and big-money dramas run here, alongside transfers of successful smaller-scale shows. However, the 'West End' appellation is now routinely applied to major theatres elsewhere in town, including subsidised venues such as the Barbican (in the City), the National Theatre (on the South Bank) and the Old Vic (near Waterloo).

IN THE KNOW CHEAP SEATS

The **TKTS** booth (Clocktower Building, Leicester Square, Soho, WC2H 7NA, www.tkts.co.uk) sells tickets for big shows at much-reduced rates, either on the day or up to a week in advance. It opens at 9am (11am on Sundays); you can check which shows are available on the website. Before buying, be sure you're at the correct booth, in a stand-alone building on the south side of Leicester Square – the square is ringed with other ticket brokers, where the seats are worse and the prices are higher.

Many West End theatres also offer their own reduced-price tickets for shows that haven't sold out on the night; these are known as 'standby' seats. Some standby deals are limited to those with student ID. The time these tickets go on sale varies from theatre to theatre: check before setting out. Our website has a round-up of West End deals: www.timeout.com/london/theatre/cheap-west-end-theatre-tickets.

Watch out ,too, for cut-price Travelex tickets and the Friday Rush at the **National** (see p289), for 'groundling' tickets (standing) at the **Globe** (see p290) and for 'Secret Seats' at the **Coliseum** (see p287).

ARTS & ENTERTAINMENT

Old Vic.

Off-West End denotes theatres with smaller budgets and smaller capacities. These venues, many of them sponsored or subsidised, push the creative envelope with new writing, often brought to life by the best young acting and directing talent. The Almeida and Donmar Warehouse offer elegantly produced shows with the odd big star, while the new, purpose-built Park Theatre has already made a bit of a stir.

THE FRINGE

The best places to catch next-generation talent include Battersea's **Theatre 503** (503 Battersea Park Road, SW11 3BW, 7978 7040, http//:theatre 503.com), above the Latchmere pub. The theatre above the **Finborough** (118 Finborough Road, SW10 9ED, 0844 847 1652, www.finborough theatre.co.uk), a pub in Earl's Court, attracts national critics with its small but perfectly formed revivals of forgotten classics. Other venues worth investigating include the **Yard** (Unit 2A, Queen's Yard, Hackney Wick, E9 5EN, 07548 156266, www.theyardtheatre.co.uk), a 130-seat venue near the Olympic Park, made from recycled materials and playing to a house of local hipsters; the **Southwark Playhouse** (77-85 Newington Causeway, Southwark, SE1 6BD, 7407 0234, www.southwarkplayhouse. co.uk); and the **Menier Chocolate Factory** (53 Southwark Street, Southwark, SE1 1RU, 7378 1713, www.menierchocolatefactory.com), which, like the **Union Theatre** (204 Union Street, Southwark, SE1 0LX, 7261 9876, www.union theatre.biz) has a knack for musicals up-close.

BUYING TICKETS

If there's a specific show you want to see, aim to book ahead. And, if possible, always try to do so at the theatre's box office, at which booking fees are generally smaller than they are with agents such as **Ticketmaster** (0333 321 9999, www.ticketmaster.co.uk). Shop around: different agencies offer different prices and discounts.

If you're more flexible about your choice of show, consider buying from the **Tkts** booth or taking your chances with standby seats (for both, *see p288* **In the Know**).

THE WEST END
Major theatres

The **Barbican Centre** (*see p283*) continues to cherry-pick exciting and eclectic theatre companies from around the globe. Watch out, too, for imaginatively leftfield family-friendly theatre and installations during the school holidays.

★ National Theatre

South Bank, SE1 9PX (7452 3400, www.national theatre.org.uk). Embankment or Southwark tube, or Waterloo tube/rail. **Box office** 9.30am-8pm Mon-Sat; noon-6pm Sun (performance days only). **Tickets** £5-£50. **Map** p401 M8.
Celebrating its 50th birthday in 2013, this concrete monster is the flagship venue of British theatre, and no theatrical tour of London is complete without a visit. It is currently coming through some of the most dramatic changes of its five-decade history, with a major physical renovation and improvement having come to fruition in time to welcome a new artistic director, Rufus Norris (*see p291* **Grand National**).

The National's various auditoriums have always allowed for different kinds of performance: in-the-round, promenade, even classic proscenium arch. Under the artistic directorship of Norris's predecessor Nicholas Hytner, landmark successes such as Alan Bennett's *The History Boys* and *War Horse* showed that the state-subsidised home of British theatre could turn out quality drama at a profit, furnishing an array of West End hits. Productions range from top-notch Shakespeare and new plays to reworked foreign classics and British revivals.

The Travelex season ensures a widening audience by offering tickets for £15, as does the free outdoor performing arts stage, Watch This Space, each summer – although it's currently an itinerant festival, while the Temporary Theatre is in its spot.
▶ *The NT launched a new initiative in 2015: Friday Rush. At 1pm each Friday, a small number of £20 tickets for the next week's performances in the Olivier, Lyttelton, Dorfman and Temporary Theatre are released for purchase online.*

Old Vic

The Cut, Waterloo, SE1 8NB (0844 871 7628, www.oldvictheatre.com). Southwark tube or Waterloo tube/rail. **Box office** *In person* 10am-6pm Mon, Sun; 10am-7pm Tue-Sat. *By phone* 9am-7.30pm

Mon-Fri; 9am-4pm Sat; 9.30am-4pm Sun. **Tickets** £10-£90. **Map** p404 N9.

Artistic director here since 2003, Oscar-winner Kevin Spacey is moving on in autumn 2015, having put in a final barnstorming performance in a one-hander as civil liberties lawyer Clarence Darrow. Spacey leaves the theatre after a series of commercially successful plays – and some critical hits as well, especially when he or one of his stellar Hollywood chums took the stage; his successor, Matthew Warchus, will have is work cut out. The Old Vic is a beautiful venue, where programming runs from grown-up Christmas pantomimes to serious drama.

Open Air Theatre

Regent's Park, Inner Circle, Marylebone, NW1 4NR (0844 826 4242, www.openairtheatre.com). Baker Street tube. **Box office** *Non-performance days* 11am-6pm daily. *Performance days* 11am-8pm daily. **Tickets** £20-£60. **Map** p398 G3.

The verdant setting of this alfresco theatre lends itself perfectly to summery Shakespeare romps – *A Midsummer Night's Dream* is a regular. But it's not just the Bard – you'll also find an idiosyncratic mix of light-as-a-feather classic American musicals, such as *Seven Brides for Seven Brothers,* and dark dramas like Arthur Miller's *All My Sons* and Chekhov's *The Seagull.*

▶ *If you don't want to bring a picnic, book one at the venue, which can be pre-set with reserved seating (£45 for two people). Alternatively, good-value, tasty food can be bought at the Garden Café.*

★ Royal Court Theatre

Sloane Square, Chelsea, SW1W 8AS (7565 5000, www.royalcourttheatre.com). Sloane Square tube. **Box office** 10am-6pm Mon-Sat. **Tickets** £10-£35. **Map** p400 G11.

From John Osborne's *Look Back in Anger*, staged in the theatre's opening year of 1956, to the numerous discoveries of the past decade – among them Sarah Kane, Joe Penhall and Conor McPherson – the emphasis at the Royal Court has always been on new voices in British theatre. Since Vicky Featherstone took over as artistic director (the first woman in the role) in 2013, plenty of politics has been injected into the programme, successfully lowering the age of the

audiences in the process (*see below* **In the Know**). Expect to find rude, lyrical new work by first-time playwrights, as well as better established American and European writers with a message. Look out for quality shorts and more of the usual vividly produced British and international work by young writers.

Royal Shakespeare Company

Information 01789 403444, tickets 0844 800 1110, www.rsc.org.uk. **Box office** By phone 10am-6pm Mon-Sat. **Tickets** £2.50-£70.

Britain's flagship company hasn't had a London base since it quit the Barbican in 2002, although it is turning its mind towards finding one now that the £100m redevelopment of its home theatres in Stratford-upon-Avon has reached completion. In the meantime, it continues its itinerant existence in London, regularly staging Shakespeare (Antony Sher plays Falstaff in both *Henry IV*s in 2015, before David Tennant reprises his *Richard II* in early 2016), sometimes popping up in smaller venues with new writing, and increasingly feeding West End stages with eye-popping new shows: *Matilda* and, most recently, *Oppenheimer* (for both, *see p292*).

★ Shakespeare's Globe

21 New Globe Walk, Bankside, SE1 9DT (information 7902 1400, tickets 7401 9919, www.shakespearesglobe.com). Southwark tube or London Bridge tube/rail. **Box office** *In person* 10am-8pm Mon-Sat; 10am-4pm Sun. *By phone* 10am-8pm Mon-Sat; 10am-5pm Sun. **Tickets** £5-£100. **Map** p404 O7.

Sam Wanamaker's dream to recreate the theatre where Shakespeare first staged many of his plays has become a fabulously entertaining reality. Comedy quickly became the Globe's forte, but the venue has been on great form all round under artistic director Dominic Dromgoole, with the Shakespeare classics paralleled by new plays on similar themes; Dromgoole will be greatly missed when he leaves his role in April 2016. The open-air, standing-room Pit tickets are excellent value (if occasionally marred by low-flying aircraft), but the Globe's indoor Jacobean theatre, the Sam Wanamaker Playhouse, is arguably even more atmospheric. The 340-seat space is made entirely out of wood, exquisitely decorated and lit by candles, just as the Blackfriars theatre that Shakespeare and his King's Men troupe moved to in 1609 would have been. It is the perfect setting for weird Jacobean tragedies such as Webster's *Duchess of Malfi*, as well as a fine series of concerts. For tours, *see p57*.

Long-runners & musicals

It's a perilous task predicting which West End shows will run and which ones will close: we loved *Made in Dagenham*, starring Gemma Arterton, but it closed after only six months. Still, we reckon the following will hang around – though probably none as long as the weary but

GRAND NATIONAL

Taking the odds on London's theatrical thoroughbred.

Having passed its 50th anniversary in 2013, the **National Theatre** (for listings, *see p289*) first completed a major programme of renovations, then waved goodbye to its hugely appreciated artistic director, Nicholas Hytner, who had been in the post since 2003. Then, just as the NT might expect to be settling back into its stride, Hytner's successor, Rufus Norris, saw his 'dream team' artistic/commercial pairing consciously uncoupled: Tessa Ross, previously responsible for the hit movies *Slumdog Millionaire* and *12 Years a Slave* as Channel 4's director of film and drama, lasted just six months before she decided that the two-leader model with Norris wasn't working – no hard feelings, though.

Norris has been left with a theatre that's in terrific shape. The renovations have opened up the entrance to what had been a bit of a bunker of a building, as well as improving both the in-house catering (there's now a bar that serves craft beers, as well as cafés and a fine-dining restaurant) and the smallest of the theatres (the Cottesloe, now called the Dorfman after the NT's principal benefactor). But the NT also allowed itself to have some fun: there's the Sherling High-Level Walkway (closed Sun), which gives theatre-goers a chance to peer into the production workshops while props, staging and costumes are being made, while the riverside courtyard now contains a big red Temporary Theatre. Opened while the Cottesloe was shut for its improvements, the Shed – as it was initially known – stages experimental work and plays by young writers, with tickets priced at a bargain £15 or £20.

Ross's departure was the first time for a while that London's theatrical thoroughbred has put a hoof on anything less than solid turf, and this stumble comes from a theatre that is now a very complicated animal. The wildly successful NT Live programme (live streaming of plays to cinemas) and the *War Horse* juggernaut – an international hit play (*see p293*) and Spielberg movie, a generator, one must assume, of invaluable revenue in these days of falling government subsidy – will have to be managed. Norris will also have to match his predecessor's sure touch for shows that are at once popular and critically acclaimed: the NT's reduced presence at the 2015 Olivier awards was noted with relish in some quarters.

Still, the 2015-16 season has promise: solid Russian realism from Turgenev, a *Jane Eyre* that might have been purpose-built to pull in A-level students and, in case you'd got bored, a wild card: Damon Albarn's *Wonder.land*, a 150th anniversary take on *Alice's Adventures in Wonderland*. Giddy-up!

never bowed *Mousetrap* (St Martin's Theatre, West Street, Cambridge Circus, WC2H 9NZ, 0844 499 1515, www.the-mousetrap.co.uk), the Agatha Christie drawing-room whodunnit that has been running continuously in the West End since 1952. For a quick tour round other shows, *see p286* **The Best of the West End**.

★ Billy Elliot the Musical

Victoria Palace Theatre, Victoria Street, Victoria, SW1E 5EA (0844 248 5000, www.billyelliotthe musical.com). Victoria tube/rail. **Box office** 10am-7.45pm Mon-Sat. **Tickets** £22.50-£102. **Map** p400 H10.

The combination of Elton John's music and a heart-melting yarn about a northern working-class lad with a talent for ballet has scooped more awards internationally than any other British musical and launched the careers of dozens of young Billies.

The Book of Mormon.

The Book of Mormon

Prince of Wales Theatre, Coventry Street, Soho, W1D 6AS (0844 482 5110, www.book ofmormonlondon.com). Piccadilly Circus tube. **Box office** 10am-8pm Mon-Sat. **Tickets** £37.50-£152. **Map** p401 K7.

South Park creators Trey Parker and Matt Stone's smash musical about the absurdities of Mormonism is not as shocking as you might expect. There's lots of swearing and close-to-the-bone jokes, but beneath it all, this is a big-hearted affair that pays note-perfect homage to the spirit and sounds of Broadway's golden age. And it's very, very funny.

★ The Curious Incident of the Dog in the Night-Time

Gielgud Theatre, 35 Shaftesbury Avenue, Soho, W1D 6AR (7492 1548, 0844 482 5118, www. delfontmackintosh.co.uk). Piccadilly Circus tube. **Box office** 10am-8pm Mon-Fri; 9am-7pm Sat. **Tickets** £32-£125. **Map** p399 L6.

Another hit West End transfer from the National Theatre (*see p289*), this adaptation of Mark Haddon's best-selling novel about a boy with Asperger's syndrome is illuminating, touching and consistently surprising. With a wonderful graph-paper set, imaginative choreography and a strong young cast, it's deservedly garnered seven Oliviers and heaps of critical praise.

Jersey Boys

Piccadilly Theatre, 16 Denman Street, Soho W1D 7DY (0844 412 6666, www.jerseyboyslondon. com). Piccadilly Circus tube. **Box office** *In person* 10am-8pm Mon-Sat. *By phone* 24hrs daily. **Tickets** £22.50-£114. **Map** p400 J7.

This Broadway import had the critics singing praise of its Frankie Valli & the Four Seasons' doo-wop standards. The well-trodden storyline of early struggle, success and break-up is elevated by pacy direction.

★ Matilda the Musical

Cambridge Theatre, 32-34 Earlham Street, Covent Garden, WC2H 9HU (0844 412 6542, www.matildathemusical.com). Covent Garden tube or Charing Cross tube/rail. **Box office** *In person* 10am-8pm Mon-Sat. *By phone* 10am-6pm Mon-Sat. **Tickets** £5-£121. **Map** p399 L6.

Adapted from Roald Dahl's riotous children's novel, with songs by superstar Aussie comedian Tim Minchin, this RSC transfer received rapturous reviews on its first outing in Stratford-upon-Avon and has been going strong ever since, winning multiple Olivier awards.

Les Misérables

Queen's Theatre, 51 Shaftesbury Avenue, Soho, W1D 6BA (0844 482 5160, www.lesmis.com). Leicester Square or Piccadilly Circus tube. **Box office** *In person* 10am-8pm Mon-Sat. *By phone* 24hrs daily. **Tickets** £14.50-£97.25. **Map** p401 K7.

The RSC's version of Boublil and Schönberg's musical first came to the London stage in 1985 – and no fewer than three celebratory versions ran simultaneously on one October night in 2010. The version currently at the Queen's should manage a few more anniversaries, which has good and bad consequences. When actors have been singing these songs since their first audition, it's easy to take it that half-inch too far. Still, the voices remain lush, the revolutionary sets are film-fabulous, and the lyrics and score (based on Victor Hugo's novel) will be considerably less trivial than whatever's on next door.

★ Oppenheimer

404 the Strand, Covent Garden, WC2R 0NH (0844 482 9675, www.nimaxtheatres.com). Charing Cross tube/rail. **Tickets** £10-£65. **Map** p401 L7.

Arriving from Stratford-upon-Avon on a mushroom cloud of acclaim, the RSC's freewheeling bio-drama about the mastermind of the atomic bomb is unashamedly vast. Its huge cast relates not only the story of the atomic bomb, but also the lives and loves of the left-leaning intellectuals who made it, while addressing the rise and fall of Communism in 20th-century America, in a pacy, jazz-soaked production that's a hoot from start to finish.

War Horse

New London Theatre, Drury Lane, Covent Garden, WC2B 5PW (0844 412 2708, www.national theatre.org.uk/warhorse). Covent Garden tube. **Box office** *In person* 10am-7.30pm Mon-Sat; 10am-6pm Sun. *By phone* 24hrs daily. **Tickets** £15-£95. **Map** p399 L6.

Transferred from the National Theatre (*see p289*), *War Horse* is an incredibly moving piece of theatre (and a massive critical and popular hit). The play is based on Michael Morpurgo's children's novel about a horse separated from his young master and spirited off to World War I. Bereft Albert duly signs up, to seek Joey in the mud and carnage of the Flanders front. The real stars are the extraordinary puppet horses. Each visibly manipulated by three actors, who make them gallop, pant and emote as clearly as any human actor, these plywood and leather frames become astonishingly expressive beasts.

OFF-WEST END THEATRES

Almeida

Almeida Street, Islington, N1 1TA (information 7288 4900, tickets 7359 4404, www.almeida.co.uk). Angel tube. **Box office** 10am-7.30pm Mon-Sat. **Tickets** £10-£38. **Map** p402 O1.

Matilda the Musical.

Well groomed and with a rather funky bar, the Almeida turns out thoughtfully crafted theatre for grown-ups. Rupert Goold took over as artistic director in 2013 and immediately made his mark with *American Psycho*, a musical adaptation of the Bret Easton Ellis novel starring *Doctor Who*'s Matt Smith. He's carried on scoring big critical hits, not least *Chimerica*, Lucy Kirkwood's exhilarating political thriller about China and America, while also accepting serious challenges, such as running Almeida Greeks, three classical tragedies, in 2015. Each summer, the month-long Almeida Festival fills the building with 50 new works, even taking over the bar and dressing rooms.

★ Battersea Arts Centre (BAC)

Lavender Hill, Battersea, SW11 5TN (7223 2223, www.bac.org.uk). Clapham Common tube, Clapham Junction rail/Overground or bus 77, 77A, 345. **Box office** 10am-6pm Mon-Sat. **Tickets** £5-£25; pay what you can.

Housed in the old Battersea Town Hall, the forward-thinking BAC hit the headlines for the wrong reasons in 2015, when it suffered a major fire. Fund-raising efforts showed the esteem felt for the theatre, which has been able to continue its programme of quirky, fun and physical theatre from young companies and more-established names pursuing new directions.

★ Donmar Warehouse

41 Earlham Street, Covent Garden, WC2H 9LX (0844 871 7624, www.donmarwarehouse.com). Covent Garden or Leicester Square tube. **Box office** 9am-10pm Mon-Sat; 10am-8pm Sun. **Tickets** £7.50-£35. **Map** p399 L6.

The Donmar is less a warehouse than a boutique chamber. Through the noughties, artistic director Michael Grandage kept the venue on the fresh, intelligent path established by Sam Mendes; his successor, Josie Rourke, has continued the good work, with *My Night with Reg* getting a West End transfer. The Donmar's combination of artistic integrity and intimate size, with its audience right alongside the stage, has proved hard to resist, with many high-profile film actors appearing: Tom Hiddleston won awards and nominations for his *Coriolanus* in 2014.

Gate Theatre

Prince Albert, 11 Pembridge Road, Notting Hill, W11 3HQ (7229 0706, www.gatetheatre.co.uk). Notting Hill Gate tube. **Box office** *By phone* 10am-6pm Mon-Fri. *In person* 6.30-8pm Mon-Fri; 2-4pm, 6.30-8pm Sat. **Tickets** £20; £10 reductions. A doll's house of a theatre (only 70 seats), with rickety wooden chairs, the Gate is the only producing theatre in London dedicated to international work.

Lyric Hammersmith

Lyric Square, King Street, Hammersmith, W6 0QL (8741 6850, www.lyric.co.uk). Hammersmith tube. **Box office** 10am-6pm Mon-Fri; 10am-5pm Sun. **Tickets** £15-£40.

Reopening in spring 2015 after a major facelift and the creation of an entirely new wing, the Lyric decided to launch with a new all-child-cast production of Alan Parker's *Bugsy Malone*, directed by artistic director Sean Holmes. In fact, the relaunch programme was typically busy: along with *Bugsy* there would be an immersive site-specific show, and more new writing for the alfresco Theatre in the Square strand. The new two-storey extension to the hybrid modern/Victorian theatre adds drama, dance and recording studios, a new café and bar, and even a cinema. Holmes had pledged to bring writers back into the building when he took over in 2009, and has already brought neglected modern classics and new plays to the stage alongside the cutting-edge physical and devised work for which the Lyric had become known.

Park Theatre

Clifton Terrace, Finsbury Park, N4 3JP (7870 6876, www.parktheatre.co.uk). Finsbury Park tube/rail. **Box office** 8am-5pm Tue-Fri. **Tickets** £12.50-£25.

Opened in 2013 in a former office building, this commercial, non-subsidised venue offers a credible off-West End programme across two spaces (a 200 seat main house and 90-seat studio), with a pleasant bar-café on the ground floor in which to chew over what you've just seen. It isn't afraid of challenging subjects: as we went to press, TV impressionist Alistair McGowan was due to star as Jimmy Savile in the first play to tackle the paedophile scandal.

★ Soho Theatre

21 Dean Street, Soho, W1D 3NE (7478 0100, www.sohotheatre.com). Tottenham Court Road tube. **Box office** 10am-10pm Mon-Sat; 10am-1hr before performance Sun. **Tickets** £5-£45. **Map** p397 K6.

Since it opened in 2000, the Soho Theatre has built a terrific reputation – meriting its red star here for excellence across three inter-related genres: cabaret, comedy and, yes, theatre. It attracts a younger, hipper crowd than most London spaces, and brings on aspiring writers and youth theatre companies. Productions tend to be issue-heavy, but leftfield promenade work and scabrous comedy add a daring sparkle. British and international talent has included Russell Brand, Michael McIntyre, Kristen Schaal and Doug Stanhope. The hard lines, low stage and packed table seating favour comedy over cabaret in the theatre's basement space, but the Soho consistently books outstanding talent from the international cabaret circuit for the room, from Meow Meow and Caroline Nin to our own David Hoyle, Bourgeois & Maurice and the Tiger Lillies.

Theatre Royal Stratford East

*Gerry Raffles Square, Stratford, E15 1BN (8534 0310, www.stratfordeast.com). Stratford tube/*rail/DLR.* **Box office** *In person & by phone* 10am-6pm Mon-Sat. **Tickets** £5-£24.

This is a community theatre, with many shows written, directed and performed by black or Asian artists. Musicals are big here – *The Harder They Come* went on to West End success a few years ago and, fittingly, the theatre restaged *Oh What a Lovely War* in early 2014 to mark the triple anniversary of the birth of the play (in this theatre), of its creator (iconoclastic director Joan Littlewood) and of the very war it satirises – but there is also a fine annual Christmas pantomime and harder-hitting fare.

Tricycle

269 Kilburn High Road, Kilburn, NW6 7JR (information 7372 6611, tickets 7328 1000, www.tricycle.co.uk). Kilburn tube. **Box office** 10am-9pm Mon-Sat; 2-9pm Sun. **Tickets** £9-£29.

Passionate and political, the Tricycle consistently finds original ways into difficult subjects. It has pioneered its own genre of 'tribunal' docu-dramas.

★ Wilton's Music Hall

Graces Alley, off Ensign Street, Whitechapel, E1 8JB (7702 2789, www.wiltons.org.uk). Aldgate East or Tower Hill tube. **Box office** noon-6pm Mon-Fri. **Tickets** £6-£25. **Map** p405 S7.

One of London's last surviving examples of the giant music halls that flourished in the mid 19th century, Wilton's once entertained the masses with acts ranging from Chinese performing monkeys to acrobats, and from contortionists to opera singers. It was here that the can-can first scandalised London. Roughly 150 years later, Wilton's is Grade II*-listed but again operating as a theatre, offering an atmospheric stage for everything from immersive theatre to situation-specific performances of Bach, cinema screenings and magic shows. There's a major ongoing restoration programme, but the programme remains as packed as ever – and the bar is lively.

★ Young Vic

66 The Cut, Waterloo, SE1 8LZ (7922 2922, www.youngvic.org). Waterloo tube/rail. **Box office** 10am-6pm Mon-Sat. **Tickets** £10-£59.50. **Map** p404 N8.

As the name suggests, this Vic (actually now in its forties) has more youthful bravura than its older sister up the road, and draws a younger crowd, who pack out the open-air balcony at its restaurant and bar on the weekends. They come to see European classics with a modern edge, new writing with an international flavour and collaborations with leading companies. Recent winners have included hard-hitting race musical *The Scottsboro Boys*, which had a lauded run in the West End, and the theatre has also been attracting some starry talent, with Gillian Anderson's stunning Blanche du Bois of 2014 followed by Mark Strong winning one of three Olivier awards for *A View from the Bridge* in 2015.

Dance

London is the home of two long-established classical dance companies. The **Royal Ballet**, resident at the Royal Opera House, is a company of global stature, which managed to lure star Russian ballerina Natalia Osipova into its ranks. Recent premières have included Christopher Wheeldon's *The Winter's Tale*, which will be followed by Liam Scarlett's *Frankenstein*, while Wayne McGregor continues to choreograph extraordinary contemporary ballet. The Royal's (friendly) rival is **English National Ballet**, a touring company that performs most often at the Coliseum (*see p287*) and, for the regular *Swan Lake* 'in the round', at the **Royal Albert Hall** (*see p285*), but has recently expanded into venues more suitable to contemporary dance such as the **Barbican** (*see p283*) and **Sadler's Wells**.

The ENB's busy artistic director, Tamara Rojo – also a principal dancer with the company – has breathed real vigour into the ENB, but caused controversy in 2015 when bemoaning the lack of a work ethic among local dancers. On the contemporary side, choreographers Akram Khan, Hofesh Shechter and Lloyd Newson of DV8 Physical Theatre went further, suggesting that British ballet schools were failing to produce suitably rigorous dancers, creating a paucity of performers for their challenging work, a claim the schools naturally denied. London's dance fans await developments with interest.

MAJOR VENUES

The **Coliseum** (*see p287*) is home to the English National Ballet, but you'll also see performances there from the likes of the Peter Schaufuss Ballet and visiting Russian companies. The **Barbican** (*see p283*) attracts and nurtures experimental dance, especially in its perfectly intimate Pit Theatre, while London's other major multi-arts centre, the **Southbank Centre** (*see p287*) programmes everything from international contemporary dance and hip hop to South Asian dance at its cluster of venues.

★ Royal Opera House
For listings, see p288.
For the full ballet experience, nothing beats the Royal Opera House, home of the Royal Ballet. The current incarnation of the building is an appropriately grand space in which to see dreamy ballerinas including Marianela Nuñez and Lauren Cuthbertson. There's edgier fare in the Linbury Studio Theatre. Royal Ballet in Rehearsal sessions offer a rare – and thrillingly close-up – glimpse behind the scenes. The 90-minute sessions are held in the Clore Studio Upstairs, with a capacity of 175. This is ballet at its most stripped-down: no sets, no exquisite costumes and no grand stage. Instead, there's just the piano, the squeak of shoes on the scuffed grey floor, and the intense concentration of the dancers.

★ Sadler's Wells
Rosebery Avenue, Finsbury, EC1R 4TN (0844 412 4300, www.sadlerswells.com). Angel tube. **Box office** 10am-8pm Mon-Sat. **Tickets** £8-£60. **Map** p404 N3.
Built in 1998 on the site of a 17th-century theatre of the same name, this dazzling complex is home to impressive local and international performances of contemporary dance in all its guises. The Lilian Baylis Studio offers smaller-scale new works and works-in-progress; the Peacock Theatre (on Portugal Street in Holborn) operates as a satellite venue.

SMALLER VENUES

Greenwich Dance
Borough Hall, Royal Hill, Greenwich, SE10 8RE (8293 9741, www.greenwichdance.org.uk). Greenwich DLR/rail. **Box office** 9am-9pm Mon-Fri; 9am-3pm Sat. **Tickets** free-£15.
This art deco venue in Greenwich hosts classes and workshops and a regular tea dance, as well as unique cabaret nights, which deliver entertaining dance performances in short bursts. It has a partnership with Trinity Laban (*see below*).

★ The Place
17 Duke's Road, Bloomsbury, WC1H 9PY (7121 1100, www.theplace.org.uk). Euston tube/ Overground/rail. **Box office** *Non-performance days* 10am-6pm Mon-Sat. *Performance days* 10am-8pm performance days. **Tickets** £11-£14. **Map** p401 K3.
For genuinely emerging dance, look to the Place, which is home to the London Contemporary Dance School and the Richard Alston Dance Company. The theatre is behind the biennial Place Prize for choreography (next in 2016), which rewards the best in British contemporary dance, as well as regular seasons showcasing new work, among them Resolution! (Jan/Feb) and Spring Loaded (Apr/May).

Trinity Laban Conservatoire
Creekside, Deptford, SE8 3DZ (8305 9400, tickets 8463 9100, www.trinitylaban.ac.uk). Deptford DLR or Greenwich DLR/rail. **Open** 10am-5.30pm Mon-Fri. **Tickets** £4-£12.
Founded in Manchester by innovative and influential movement theoretician Rudolf Laban (1879-1958), the Laban Centre joined forces in 2005 with Trinity College of Music to create the first ever UK conservatoire for music and dance. The centre was designed by Herzog & de Meuron of Tate Modern fame and features an impressive curving, multicoloured glass frontage. The striking premises include a 300-seat auditorium and are home to Transitions Dance Company.
▶ *Also in Deptford, the Albany (Douglas Way, SE8 4AG, 8692 4446, www.thealbany.org.uk) specialises in hip hop theatre.*

Escapes & Excursions

Escapes & Excursions

You'll never run out of things to do in London. But everyone who lives here feels an irresistible urge to leave occasionally, so why would visitors be any different? And with good train services out of London, it's easy to reach some interesting destinations in under two hours. We also list some stellar day trips on the outskirts of the city, such as Hampton Court, Kew Gardens and the beautifully restored Eltham Palace, which can all be reached in less than an hour.

GETTING AROUND

All of the destinations included in this chapter are within easy reach of London. For the main attractions, we've included details of opening times and admission prices, but be aware that these can change without notice: it's best always to phone to check.

By Train

Britain's rail network is generally reliable. However, ticket prices on some services are high, and with different rail companies sharing some routes, it's easy to inadvertently pay too much or buy a ticket that limits your options. Factor in varying definitions of peak and off-peak travel and you'll usually be better off discussing your needs at a ticket office window rather than buying blind at a machine. If more than two of you are travelling, ask about family and group tickets, which offer excellent value.

The website www.nationalrail.co.uk has a good journey planner and gives live advice on engineering works and other delays, which are a regular occurence, particularly at weekends. You can buy tickets on the website, too, but there's generally no advantage, unless your journey takes you outside the south-eastern network (in which case, the further ahead you purchase, the lower the price). National Rail's phone number is 0845 748 4950.

If you need extra help, there are rail-travel centres in London's mainline stations, as well as at Heathrow and Gatwick airports. Staff can give you guidance on timetables and booking.

By Coach

Coaches operated by National Express (0871 781 8181, www.nationalexpress.com) run throughout the country. Services depart from Victoria Coach Station (164 Buckingham Palace Road, SW1W 9TP, 0871 781 8178, www.tfl.gov.uk), which is ten minutes' walk from Victoria rail and tube stations. Green Line Travel (0844 801 7261, www.greenline.co.uk) also operates coaches.

One-offs

ARUNDEL CASTLE

With its hilltop castle and cathedral, and the River Arun running beneath, Arundel looks more like a stage set for a medieval period drama than a real town. What's more, it's only 90 minutes from London by rail (trains leave from Victoria station).

Arundel Castle originated at the end of the 11th century and has been the family home of the Dukes of Norfolk and their ancestors for more than 850 years. Aside from the occasional reversion to the throne, it's one of the longest inhabited aristocratic houses in England. In 1643,

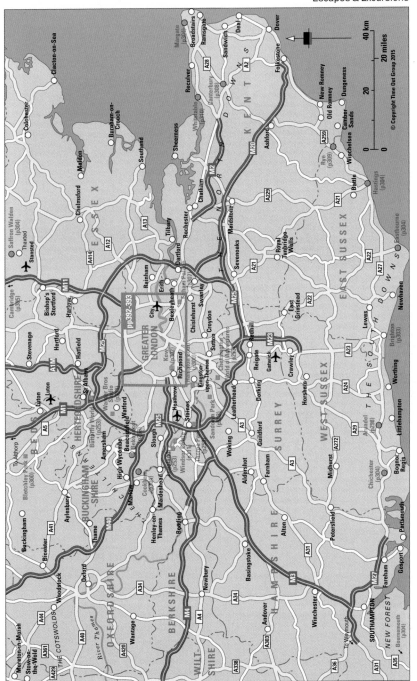

ESCAPES & EXCURSIONS

Arundel Castle.

during the Civil War, the castle was besieged, first by royalists then by General Waller (for Parliament) and the defences were partly demolished. Happily, many of the original features – such as the crenellated Norman keep, gatehouse and barbican, and the lower part of Bevis Tower – survived. The castle was almost completely rebuilt in the late 19th century.

The castle is worth exploring for its collection of paintings by Van Dyck, Gainsborough and Reynolds, among others, as well as its tapestries and furniture, and the gorgeous FitzAlan Chapel. Other treasures include a 14th-century two-handed sword, a jousting saddle (thought to be the only one in existence) and a silver icon of the Virgin and Child by Fabergé. A new formal garden was opened in 2008 as a tribute to Thomas Howard, 14th Earl of Arundel (1585-1646), known as 'the Collector'. An organic kitchen garden has been recreated, but the over-the-top decorations are based on what the Collector is thought to have enjoyed at his house in London. There's also a restaurant, café and gift shop. At weekends, outdoor events include medieval-style encampments with jousting and archery displays.

The castle is Arundel's main attraction, but the town also has many good eateries, wine bars, and independent shops, and the natural delights of the WWT Arundel Wetland Centre.

Arundel Castle

High Street, Arundel, West Sussex, BN18 9AB (01903 882173, www.arundelcastle.org). **Open** *Apr-Oct* 10am-5pm Tue-Sun (last admission 4pm); also Mon in Aug. Closed Nov-Mar. **Admission** £9-£18; £9-£15.50 reductions; £9 children; free under-5s; £41-£45 family.

BLETCHLEY PARK

The code-breaking centre – which famously broke the Nazis' Enigma cypher machine – remained shrouded in mystery until declassification after the Cold War. Bletchley's displays cover the story of its code-breakers and machines, and a new multimedia guide helps visitors to get the most from their visit; there's a special one for children too. There's also a computer museum (for which there's a separate charge), and the centre is surrounded by parkland. It's all easily accessible from London by rail (the journey north from Euston to Bletchley takes less than an hour, and the complex is close to Bletchley station).

Bletchley Park

The Mansion, Bletchley Park, Sherwood Drive, Bletchley, Milton Keynes, MK3 6EB (01908 640404, www.bletchleypark.org.uk). **Open** *Mar-Oct* 9.30am-5pm daily. *Nov-Feb* 9.30am-4pm daily. **Admission** £16.75; £10-£14.75 reductions; £38.50 family; free under-12s.

HAMPTON COURT PALACE

This spectacular palace, once owned by Henry VIII, is just a half-hour journey from central London – but will take you back 500 years through history. It was built in 1514 by Cardinal Wolsey, the high-flying Lord Chancellor, but Henry liked it so much he seized it for himself in 1528. For the next 200 years it was a focal point of English history: Elizabeth I was imprisoned in a tower by her jealous and fearful elder sister Mary I; Shakespeare gave his first performance to

James I in 1603; and, after the Civil War, Oliver Cromwell was so besotted by the building he ditched his puritanical principles and moved in to enjoy its luxuries.

Centuries later, the rosy walls of the palace still dazzle. Its vast size can be daunting, so it's a good idea to take advantage of the guided tours. If you do decide to go it alone, start with Henry VIII's State Apartments, which include the Great Hall, noted for its beautiful stained-glass windows and elaborate religious tapestries; in the Haunted Gallery, the ghost of Catherine Howard – Henry's fifth wife, executed for adultery in 1542 – can reputedly be heard shrieking. The King's Apartments, added in 1689 by Wren, are notable for a splendid mural of Alexander the Great, painted by Antonio Verrio. The Queen's Apartments and Georgian Rooms feature similarly elaborate paintings, chandeliers and tapestries, while the new Cumberland Art Gallery – in beautifully restored Georgian rooms – shows works from the Royal Collection by Holbein,

Rembrandt and Caravaggio. The Tudor Kitchens are great fun, with their giant cauldrons, fake pies and blood-spattered walls.

More extraordinary sights await outside, where the exquisitely landscaped gardens offer topiary, Thames views, a reconstruction of a 16th-century heraldic garden and the famous Hampton Court maze.

★ **Hampton Court Palace**
East Molesey, Surrey, KT8 9AU (0844 482 7777, www.hrp.org.uk). Hampton Court rail, or riverboat from Westminster or Richmond to Hampton Court Pier (Apr-Oct). **Open** *Palace Apr-Oct 10am-6pm daily. Nov-Mar 10am-4.30pm daily. Park dawn-dusk daily.* **Admission** *Palace, courtyard, cloister & maze Apr-Oct* £17.50; £8.75-£14.50 reductions; £43.80 family; free under-5s. *Nov-Mar* £16.50; £8.25-£14 reductions; £42.50 family; free under-5s. *Maze only* £4.50; £2.50 reductions. *Gardens only* £5.20; £4.80 reductions; free under-15s.

Hampton Court Palace.

ROYAL BOTANIC GARDENS (KEW GARDENS)

Kew's lush, landscaped beauty represents the pinnacle of our national gardening obsession. From the early 1700s until 1840, when the gardens were given to the nation, these were the grounds for two fine royal residences – the White House and Richmond Lodge. Early resident Queen Caroline, wife of George II, was very fond of exotic plants brought back by botanists voyaging to far-flung parts of the world. In 1759, the renowned 'Capability' Brown was employed by George III to improve on the work of his predecessors here, William Kent and Charles Bridgeman. Thus began the shape of the extraordinary garden that today attracts hundreds of thousands of visitors each year. Covering half a square mile, Kew feels surprisingly big – pick up a map at the ticket office and follow the handy signs. Head straight for the 19th-century greenhouses, filled to the roof with plants – some of which have been here as long as the enormous glass structures themselves. The Temperate House is closed until 2018 for much-needed restoration work, but the sultry Palm House remains open, with its tropical palms, bamboo, tamarind, fig and mango trees, as well as fragrant hibiscus and frangipani.

Also worth seeking out are the Princess of Wales Conservatory, divided into ten climate zones; the Marine Display, downstairs from the Palm House (it isn't always open, but when it is you can see the delightful seahorses); the lovely,

Royal Botanice Gardens (Kew Gardens).

quiet indoor pond of the Waterlily House (closed in winter); and the exquisite Victorian botanical drawings found in the fabulous Marianne North Gallery. The Xstrata Treetop Walkway has been a hugely popular addition to the gardens, giving a completely different woodland walk 60 feet up in the leaf canopy.

Though Kew's main appeal is the Gardens, the area rewards further exploration. Much of Kew has a rarified air, with leafy streets that lead you into a quaint world of teashops, tiny bookstores and gift shops, a sweet village green, ancient pubs and pleasant riverside paths.

▶ *Britain's smallest royal palace is also within the gardens: Kew Palace (www.hrp.org.uk/KewPalace, closed Oct-Mar, entry included in Gardens admission price) dates back to the 18th century.*

★ Royal Botanic Gardens (Kew Gardens)
Kew, Richmond, Surrey, TW9 3AB (8332 5655, www.kew.org). Kew Gardens tube/Overground, Kew Bridge rail or riverboat to Kew Pier. **Open** from 9.30am; check website for closing times. **Admission** £15; £14 reductions; free under-17s.

SANDOWN PARK

Sandown is attractively sited in a natural amphitheatre and is the winner of several 'Racecourse of the Year' awards. Racing takes place all year round, with April's Gold Cup the highlight of the jumping season and the Coral-Eclipse Stakes in July the main feature of the flat programme – both pushing horses to the limit on Sandown's infamous hill finish. There's also a run of summer evening meetings, most also featuring live music. Families are welcome; a free crèche is available for under-fives on Saturdays, and there's a dedicated picnic area during the summer.

Sandown Park
Sandown Park Racecourse, Portsmouth Road, Esher, Surrey, KT10 9AJ (01372 464348, www. sandown.co.uk). **Open** times vary according to racing schedule. **Admission** varies.

WARNER BROS STUDIO

Warner Bros Studios in Leavesden, near Watford on the outskirts of London, is where all eight Harry Potter blockbusters were created. For followers of the bespectacled child-wizard, the **Harry Potter Studio Tour** offers a rare opportunity to learn just how JK Rowling's magical world was brought to life in the highest-grossing film series of all time. The Leavesden Studios, a former aircraft hangar 20 miles north-west of London, are spread over 170,000 square feet – with a 20,000 square foot extension having been added in 2015 to accommodate the Hogwarts

> ### IN THE KNOW SHANKS' PONY
>
> South-east England is blessed with many fine long-distance paths. Sections of the Greensand Way, the North and South Downs Way, and the Thames Path – which runs from its Cotswolds source through London to the sea, can be walked in a day out from London. More information is available at www.nationaltrail.co.uk.
>
> For many more walks from London, all using public transport, buy *Time Out Country Walks*, volumes I and II, or see www.walkingclub.org.uk.

Express. The two- to three-hour walking tour takes in such iconic sets as Hagrid's hut and the Gryffindor common room, plus it offers the chance to check out the special effects, animatronics, props and costumes used in the films. Dumbledore's office is here – built for *Harry Potter and the Chamber of Secrets*, it is home to the Sorting Hat, the Sword of Gryffindor and Albus Dumbledore's desk – but for real wow-factor, head into the Great Hall. First seen in *Harry Potter and the Philosopher's Stone* and designed by BAFTA-winning production designer Stuart Craig, the hall is 120 feet long and 40 feet wide with a solid stone floor and the original tables and benches where Daniel Radcliffe, Emma Watson et al once sat. But the Hogwarts Express is a fine addition: visitors walk through clouds of smoke along the train's carriages to sit in the interior set, complete with 'windows' that show how scenes from the films, including a Dementor attack, were created. This was the setting for the very last scene to be shot, in which a grown-up Harry, Ron and Hermione wave their own children off to school. Hankies ready.

Warner Bros Studio Tour
Leavesden Studios, near Watford, WD25 7LR (08450 840 900, www.wbstudiotour.co.uk). **Tours** 10am-4.30pm Mon-Fri; 9am-7pm Sat, Sun. **Tickets** (must be booked in advance) £33; £25.50 reductions; £101 family; free under-5s.

Towns & Cities

BRIGHTON

With its bracing sea air and whiff of scandal, Brighton has been a favoured day trip for Londoners ever since the 19th century, when the pleasure-loving Prince Regent decamped to the southern coast to escape his father's watchful eye. Its Regency heyday left a rich legacy of stately

ART DAY TRIPS

Fabulous art galleries in easy reach of London.

Fry Art Gallery

Castle Street, Saffron Walden, Essex, CB10 1BD (01799 513779, www.fryartgallery.org). **Open** Easter Sunday-late Oct 2-5pm Tue, Thur, Fri; 11am- 5pm Sat; 2.15-5pm Sun. Closed Nov-Mar. **Admission** free.

All of the work displayed here is by artists who were part of a creative community that flourished in and around Great Bardfield before and after World War II, including 600 works by Edward Barden. It's a terrific collection, stuffed with prints, paintings, wallpapers and decorative designs.

Jerwood Gallery

Rock-a-Nore Road, Hastings, East Sussex, TN34 3DW (01424 728377, www.jerwood gallery.org). **Open** 11am-5pm Tue-Sun. **Admission** £8; £3.50-£5.50 reductions.

Set on the shingle beach close to the fishing boats, the Jerwood Gallery's 2,000 black exterior tiles blend in with the tarred boards of the nearby fishermen's net huts. As well as figurative and abstract works from the period between World War I and the 1960s, it holds contemporary pieces by artists such as Maggi Hambling and Prunella Clough.

Pallant House Gallery

9 North Pallant, Chichester, West Sussex, PO19 1TJ (01243 774557, www.pallant.org. uk). **Open** 10am-5pm Tue, Wed, Fri, Sat; 10am-8pm Thur; 11am-5pm Sun. **Admission** £8.50; free-£4 reductions.

This lovely gallery has an outstanding collection of 20th-century British art, featuring works by Henry Moore, Bridget Riley, Lucian Freud and Walter Sickert. Exciting contemporary-art shows and installations add to the appeal. There's also a restaurant.

Russell-Cotes Art Gallery & Museum

Russell-Cotes Road, East Cliff Promenade, Bournemouth, Dorset, BH1 3AA (01202 451858, www.russell-cotes.bournemouth.gov. uk). **Open** 10am-5pm Tue-Sun. **Admission** Apr-Sept £6; free-£4 reductions. Oct-Mar free.

The Russell-Cotes is housed in one of Bournemouth's few remaining Victorian villas – an eccentric-looking turret-topped affair. It's filled to the rafters with curios, artefacts and artworks – including an awful lot of female nudes. Being perched on a cliff, the café and gardens have great views.

Stanley Spencer Gallery

High Street, Cookham, Berkshire, SL6 9SJ (01628 471885, www.stanleyspencer.org.uk). **Open** Apr-Oct 10.30am-5.30pm daily. Nov-Mar 11am-4.30pm Thur-Sun. **Admission** £5; free-£4 reductions.

Sir Stanley Spencer lived in Cookham for much of his life, and made it the subject of many of his paintings and drawings, some 100 of which are gathered here. It's a rare delight to be able to explore the relationship between an artist and his surroundings. The gallery's website details an hour-long ramble around the village that passes many of the locations of Spencer's paintings.

Towner Gallery

Devonshire Park, College Road, Eastbourne, East Sussex, BN21 4JJ (01323 434660, www. townereastbourne.org.uk). **Open** 10am-5pm Tue-Sun. **Admission** free.

Eric Ravilious is the name usually associated with the Towner, and with good reason: the artist's work is a key element of the collection, with everything from woodcuts to the posters he designed for London Transport. However, it's home to more than 4,500 works of art, so you'll also see pieces by Vanessa Bell, Tacita Dean, Olafur Eliasson, Picasso and Wolfgang Tillmans.

Turner Contemporary

Rendezvous, Margate, Kent, CT9 1HG (01843 233000, www.turnercontemporary.org). **Open** 10am-6pm Tue-Sun. **Admission** free.

This dramatic silver structure opened in 2011 with new commissions by Daniel Buren, Russell Crotty, Ellen Harvey and Conrad Shawcross, and the programme has remained consistently interesting. Further pluses are the café and the sweeping views.

seafront terraces and squares to rival those of Bath, in contrast to the elaborate domes and minarets of the **Royal Pavilion** (0300 029 0900, www.brighton-hove-pavilion.org.uk), the Prince's ornate and outlandish country farmhouse-turned-mock-Mughal palace.

This is a city that shuns the mainstream and embraces counterculture, with an ebullient gay scene and a packed arts calendar, culminating in the three-week arts extravaganza of the **Brighton Festival** (01273 709709, www. brightonfestival.org). It's also home to a fiercely independent shopping scene, encompassing flea markets, art galleries, jewellery shops, delis and boutiques – perfect for a day of browsing and café-hopping. Further diversions are offered by **Brighton Pier** and all the traditional seaside resort trappings, not to mention seven miles of coastline – see them all from the **Brighton Wheel** (01273 722822, www.brightonwheel.com) or, when it reaches completion, the 530ft-tall **i360** observation tower (www.brightoni360.co.uk).

Brighton has a ridiculous number of dining possibilities for a town of its size. Easy-going all-day eateries include **Bill's** (the Depot, 100 North Road, 01273 692894, www.bills-website.co.uk), an organic deli and restaurant; **Terre à Terre** (71 East Street, 01273 729051, www.terreaterre. co.uk), an expensive but inventive vegetarian restaurant; and any number of coffee shops, cafés and pubs. Also try the **Basketmakers Arms** (12 Gloucester Road, 01273 689006, http://basket-makers-brighton.co.uk), with its comprehensive selection of cask ales and whiskies; real-ale

specialist the **Hand in Hand** (33 Upper St James Street, 01273 699595); and the wonderful **Lion & Lobster** (24 Sillwood Street, 01273 327299, www. thelionandlobster.co.uk).

CAMBRIDGE

Beautiful, intimidating Cambridge has the feel of an enclosed city. But pass through those imposing gates with their stern porters: within and behind the colleges are pretty green meadows and the idle River Cam, a place where time seems to have stopped back in the 18th century.

Each of the 31 Cambridge colleges is an independent entity, so entry times (and, for the more famous ones, prices) vary considerably: www.cam.ac.uk/colleges has the details. But Cambridge isn't only about the colleges. The **Fitzwilliam Museum** (01223 332900, www. fitzmuseum.cam.ac.uk) has a superb collection of paintings and sculpture (by Titian, Modigliani and Picasso), as well as ancient artefacts from Egypt, Greece and Rome, and it's just one of many museums in Cambridge. A short walk south, the 40 relaxing acres of the **Botanic Gardens** (01223 336265, www.botanic.cam.ac.uk) have 8,000 plants. The magnificently atmospheric **Kettle's Yard** (01223 748100, www.kettlesyard. co.uk) – Tate curator Jim Ede's home, preserved as a collection of early 20th-century artists, closed for restoration and expansion work in early 2015. Until it reopens, head to the cluster of museums around Downing Street, among which the fascinating **Museum of Archaeology &**

Brighton.

Cambridge.

ESCAPES & EXCURSIONS

Anthropology (01223 333516, http://maa.cam. ac.uk) was refurbished in 2012; nearby, the **University Museum of Zoology** (01223 336650, www.museum.zoo.cam.ac.uk) will reopen after major redevelopment in 2016.

Behind the main colleges, the beautiful meadows bordering the willow-shaded Cam are known as the **Backs**. Carpeted with crocuses in spring, the Backs are idyllic for summer strolling and punting. Punts can be hired, but they're more difficult to handle than you might imagine; **Scudamore's Boatyard** (01223 359750, www. scudamores.com) is the largest operator.

The **Cambridge Chop House** (1 King's Parade, 01223 359506, www.cambscuisine.com) is a great come-one, come-all bistro opposite King's College, where you can tuck into British comfort food and draught ales. Nearby, the busy subterranean **Rainbow Café** (9A King's Parade, 01223 321551, www.rainbowcafe.co.uk) serves

cheap, hearty vegetarian food. The legendary **Fitzbillies** (51-52 Trumpington Street, 01223 352500, www.fitzbillies.com), loved by generations of students, is still the place for tucking into a Chelsea bun or other teatime treat.

Cambridge has many creaky old inns in which to settle down and enjoy one of the city's decent local ales. The **Eagle** on Benet Street (01223 505020, www.eagle-cambridge.co.uk) is the most famous, but there are many others, including the **Pickerel Inn** (30 Magdalene Street, 01223 355068, www.taylor-walker.co.uk) and, down a back alley a little off the beaten track, the sweet little **Free Press** (7 Prospect Row, 01223 368337, www.freepresspub.com).

Tourist Information Centre *Peas Hill, Cambridge, CB2 3AD (0871 226 8006, www.visitcambridge. org).* **Open** *Apr-Oct* 10am-5pm Mon-Sat; 11am-3pm Sun. *Nov-Mar* 10am-5pm Mon-Sat.

THAT'S RICH

Visit a wonderfully restored – and reassuringly welcoming – stately home.

Fancy a game of billiards or a bit of dressing up? Just half an hour from central London, **Eltham Palace** is the place.

The building is a cut-and-shut job: a medieval hall with a fabulous 1930s mansion attached. Henry VIII lived here as a boy, but when millionaire couple Stephen and Virginia Courtauld were looking for a country house within easy reach of London, derelict Eltham Palace fitted the bill. The Great Hall that was once the heart of one of the country's most important royal palaces was being used as a barn.

The Courtaulds commissioned a state-of-the -art residence filled with mod cons: en-suite bathrooms (at a time when only posh hotels offered such luxury); underfloor heating; piped music; and a centralised vacuuming system that hooked up with every room – it occasionally backfired, smothering the maids with dust.

Today, it is in the custody of English Heritage, which completed major refurbishments in spring 2015. Now, you approach the building via the oldest medieval bridge in the country, crossing the moat just like the film stars, explorers, politicans and royalty whom the Courtaulds entertained in their fabulous party palace. In fact, everything about a visit is intended to make you feel like a guest rather than a punter. On entry, you'll be handed a cocktail-party invitation addressed to someone who

actually visited the house during its heyday, along with the excellent interactive guide that is now included with admission.

The huge, lavish reception rooms, along with Virginia and Stephen's separate bedrooms, bathrooms and sitting rooms, were all opened to the public in 1999, but the latest restoration has spruced up the gardens too, applying the same princples that influenced Stephen, a keen gardener, who had his prize-winning orchids evacuated to Kew at the start of World War II. There's a new children's playground and the restaurant has been moved from the servants' quarters to a more appealing location in the glasshouse. For the first time, you can slip into Virginia's walk-in wardrobe to drool over dreamy vintage clothes and accessories; you can even try on replicas of some outfits. Head to the basement where the impressive vacuum cleaner has its own spotlight.

In the games room, you're at liberty to play snooker billiards on the original table. This games room was where the servants slept during air raids; the family and guests adjourned to a nearby luxury bunker.

Eltham Palace & Gardens
Court Yard, SE9 5QE (8294 2548, www.english-heritage.org.uk). Eltham or Mottingham rail. **Open** 10am-5pm Mon-Thur, Sun. **Admission** £13; £11.80 reductions; £7.80 children; £33.80 family.

Canterbury.

CANTERBURY

The home of the Church of England since St Augustine became the first archbishop of Canterbury in 597, this ancient city is rich in atmosphere, with many soaring spires and enchanting medieval streets. The town's busy tourist trade and large university provide a counterweight to all this history. Everything you want to see, do or buy in Canterbury is within walking distance. And that includes the seaside – at least, it does if you fancy a long (seven-mile) walk or cycle along the Crab & Winkle Way, a disused railway line to pretty Whitstable (*see p310*).

The main sight is glorious **Canterbury Cathedral** (01227 762862, www.canterbury-cathedral.org); inside, you'll find superb stained glass, stone vaulting and a vast Norman crypt. St Augustine, the first Archbishop of Canterbury, founded the cathedral in 597. A plaque near the altar marks what is believed to be the spot where Archbishop Thomas Becket was murdered by knights of Henry II; the Trinity Chapel contains the site of the original shrine, plus the tombs of Henry IV and the Black Prince.

A pilgrimage to Becket's tomb was the focus of one of the earliest and finest long poems in English literature: Geoffrey Chaucer's *Canterbury Tales*, written in the 14th century. At the

Canterbury Tales Exhibition (St Margaret's Street, 01227 479227, www.canterburytales.org.uk), two minutes from the cathedral, visitors are given a device that they point at tableaux inspired by Chaucer's tales of a knight, a miller, a wife of Bath, and others, enabling them to hear the rollicking stories that Chaucer brought to vivid life.

Other places of interest are the **Beaney House of Art & Knowledge** (18 High Street, 01227 862162, www.thebeaney.co.uk), a monument to high Victorian values and a notable art museum and event space, and **Eastbridge Hospital** (25 High Street, 01227 471688, www.eastbridgehospital.org.uk) – founded to provide shelter for pilgrims – where visitors can admire the undercroft with its Gothic arches, the Chantry Chapel, the Pilgrims' Chapel and the refectory with an enchanting early-13th-century mural showing Christ in Majesty. There's also the **Roman Museum** (Butchery Lane, 01227 785575, www.canterbury.co.uk) and the ruins of **St Augustine's Abbey** (Longport, 01227 767345, www.english-heritage.org.uk).

Canterbury has plenty of eating and drinking options: the **Goods Shed** (Station Road West, 01227 459153, www.thegoodsshed.co.uk) occupies a former railway freight store. Only ingredients on sale in the farmers' market below are used in the restaurant.

Pub-wise, most of the better ones are owned by local brewery Shepherd Neame. The best for real ales is the **Unicorn** (61 St Dunstan's Street, 01227 463187, www.unicorninn.com), which also has a great pub garden for summer drinking. Built in 1370, the **Parrot** (1-9 Church Lane, St Radigands, 01227 454170, www.theparrotonline.com) is the oldest pub in Canterbury and serves a good choice of ales and cider in a charming setting. The refurbished **White Hart** (Worthgate Place, 01227 765091, www.whitehartcanterbury.co.uk) is also a good bet.

Tourist Information Centre *18 High Street, Canterbury, CT1 2RA (01227 862162, www.canterbury.co.uk)*. **Open** 9am-5pm Mon-Wed, Fri, Sat; 9am-7pm Thur; 10am-5pm Sun.

RYE

Almost too quaint to be true, Rye is an extraordinarily photogenic jumble of Norman, Tudor and Georgian architecture perched on one of the area's few hills. The well-preserved, attractive centre is a joy to walk around, with lots of shops, pubs and cafés, plus a fetching harbour area. Although much of the place is given over to genteel tourism, it remains a working town, with enough real stores and down-to-earth pubs – and a commercial fishing fleet – to prevent there being a theme park atmosphere. It's easy to get to by rail (the walk from the station to the heart of town takes about a minute).

The place has history galore – it became one of the Cinque Ports in the 13th century but declined in importance as access to the sea changed over the years; by the 18th century, smuggling played as big a role in the town's economy as maritime trade. Soak up the atmosphere and architecture by investigating cobbled streets such as West Street, Mermaid Street and also Church Square. From here there are wonderful views, especially if you make the climb to the top of 900-year-old St Mary's church.

Henry James lived in Rye for years, at **Lamb House** on West Street; later residents include novelists EF Benson and Rumer Godden. It's owned by the National Trust and has limited opening times, but these do include Saturday afternoons, from late March to late October (see www.nationaltrust.org.uk for details).

Finding somewhere to eat is easy – the streets are lined with decent options, from cheap and cheerful eateries such as **Anatolian Kebab** (16A Landgate, 01797 226868), **Kettle o' Fish** (25 Wish Street, 01797 223684) and **Simply Italian** (Strand, 01797 226024) to destination restaurants such as the **Fish Café** (17 Tower Street, 01797 222210), the **George** (98 High Street, 01797 222114, www.thegeorgeinrye.com) and the **Landgate Bistro** (5-6 Landgate, 01797 222829,

www.landgatebistro.co.uk) – and you're never far away from a tea shop. There's a good array of pubs too: have a drink in the **Mermaid Inn** (Mermaid Street, 01797 223065, www.mermaidinn.com) for its olde worlde charm and collection of signed photographs, or soak up the view in the beer garden at the **Ypres Castle Inn** (Gungarden, 01797 223248, www.yprescastleinn.co.uk) with a pint of Timothy Taylor.

East from Rye lies other-worldly **Romney Marsh**, flat as a pancake and laced with cycle paths. Bikes can be hired from **Rye Hire** (1 Cyprus Place, 01797 223033, www.ryehire.co.uk)

Rye.

ESCAPES & EXCURSIONS

Whitstable.

and are an ideal way to explore the lonely medieval churches that dot the level marsh, or to access the vast sandy beach of Camber Sands.

Tourist Information Centre *4-5 Lion Street, Rye, TN31 7LB (01797 229049, www.visit1066 country.com)*. **Open** *Apr-Sept* 10am-5pm daily. *Oct-Mar* 10am-4pm daily.

WHITSTABLE

The image of Whitstable as a weekend bolthole for London's middle classes is not undeserved, but this lovely old coastal town has enough character to withstand total gentrification – and it's still very much a working fishing town. To learn about the town's history, pop into **Whitstable Museum** (Oxford Street, 01227 276998, www.canterbury.co.uk). Exhibits include a display devoted to the town's most famous fan, Peter Cushing, who bought a seafront house here in 1959. It includes film stills, props and examples of the actor-turned-painter's art.

Whitstable has smartened itself up for visitors – for example, many of the old fishermen's huts on the seafront have been fashioned into holiday retreats – but it doesn't pander. Much of the town looks as it always has, from the Island Wall with its mid-19th-century cottages to the little alleys once used by fishermen to cut through the town to the sea (Squeeze Gut Alley is so narrow that many have to walk through it sideways). The main streets, running north from Oxford Street to High Street to Harbour Street, all lead towards the seafront and harbour. Here, you'll find a selection

of small shops, galleries and cafés. Look out for **Oxford Street Books** (no.20A, 01227 281727, www.oxfordstreetbooks.com), where every nook and cranny is stuffed with second-hand books, and the **Cheese Box** (59-61 Harbour Street, 01227 273711, www.thecheesebox.co.uk), a fantastic deli. North from Harbour Street to Tower Hill, **Whitstable Castle** sits on the border of Whitstable and the suburb of Tankerton. The recently restored castle and grounds is a good place to take in some sea air. If you climb to the top of the hill you'll come out opposite **Tower Hill Tea Gardens**, an idyllic and often quiet spot with sea views.

Running parallel to the shingle beach is Island Row, lined with pretty cottages; walk east to reach the harbour. Low tide reveals a natural spit of shingle on a clay bank, known as the Street. You can walk it for about half a mile, on the last of the town's land to the north, the rest having been eroded and swallowed by the sea. Keep an eye on the rising tide, though.

Whitstable has been praised for its oysters since Juvenal shucked a few here a couple of thousand years ago. These days, try them at the **Whitstable Oyster Festival** (www.whitstableoysterfestival.co.uk, end of July), or at the **Crab & Winkle** (South Quay, 01227 779377, www.crabandwinklerestaurant.co.uk), the **Pearson's Arms** (Sea Wall, 01227 773133, www.pearsonsarmsbyrichardphillips.co.uk), **English's of Whitstable** (48 Harbour Street, 01227 273373, www.thetapas.co.uk) or **Wheelers Oyster Bar** (8 High Street, 01227 273311, www.wheelersoysterbar.com) – or you

could push the boat out at the **Whitstable Oyster Fishery Company** (Royal Native Oyster Stores, Horsebridge, 01227 276856, www.whitstableoystercompany.com), a handsome building in a prime position on the beach. There are plenty of takeaway options too – try the fish market on South Quay (01227 771245; there are barbecues here in summer). For fish and chips, **VC Jones** is a favourite (25 Harbour Street, 01227 272703, www.vcjones.co.uk).

WINDSOR

The direct line from Waterloo station to Windsor & Eton Riverside (taking just under an hour) offers pleasing views of Windsor Castle as you roll into town. The castle (Her Majesty is in residence if the Royal Standard is flying) is immediately before you, as is the start of the 4,800-acre Great Park's Long Walk – a three-mile stretch of surfaced path that leads from the castle to the Copper Horse statue atop Snow Hill depicting George III. Windsor town centre offers high-class shopping at a less frenetic pace than London, while Eton College and the River Thames are further attractions.

The sights at **Windsor Castle** (7766 7304, www.royalcollection.org.uk) – the Queen's weekend pad and the world's biggest occupied castle – run from works by Rembrandt, Rubens, Gainsborough and Van Dyck, to Edward Lutyens' elaborate Queen Mary's Dolls' House, complete with flushing loos. Or you may prefer to leave the changing guards, castle tours and souvenir shops behind, and walk through the Great Park.

Depending on the timing of your walk, you might stop at the lovely **Two Brewers** (34 Park Street, SL4 1LB, 01753 855426, www.twobrewerswindsor.co.uk) first. Get back on track and the greatest joy of the Long Walk promenade soon becomes clear. You don't need a map. Simply relax and let your mind wander as you march ahead admiring gnarly old oak trees and – a little further along – the resident red deer.

Should you fancy straying from the path, there are ample, well-signposted diversions. One of the most fascinating is **Frogmore House and the Royal Mausoleum** (final resting place of Prince Albert and Queen Victoria; www.royalcollection.org.uk), set in the private Home Park. You'll have to plan ahead to visit it as the former royal residence is only open to the public for two weekends a year – typically August bank holiday weekend and another in either May or June. The landscaped gardens are vast and impressive, with tulip trees and giant redwoods among the many historic plantings.

Stay away from such detours and your walking efforts will be rewarded as you ascend Snow Hill for stunning views of the castle and out beyond (the arch of Wembley Stadium can be seen on a clear day).

For lunch, however, you'll need to take a left as you face the Copper Horse and walk towards Bishops Gate and the cosy **Fox & Hounds** (Bishops Gate, Englefield Green, Surrey, 01784 433098, www.thefoxandhoundsrestaurant.co.uk). Warming in winter and spot on for summer alfresco drinking, this atmospheric pub is a popular local choice.

In Context

History

The making of modern London.

Over the 2,000 years since London began life as a small trading station by a broad, marshy river, the city has faced plague and invasion, fire and war, religious turbulence and financial turmoil. There have been natural disasters and acts of terrorism, all borne by Londoners with a characteristic upbeat pessimism until the moment arrives when the frenzy of commerce can begin again. More than anything, this city's past is a tale of resilience.

In the City, Wren churches – built from the ruins of the Great Fire – have walls still blackened by the German incendiary bombs dropped during the Blitz, and shrapnel scars around Cleopatra's Needle beside the Thames remain from a World War I biplane raid. A fragment of glass, deeply embedded in a wall at the Old Bailey, tells of an IRA terrorist attack back in 1973, while 52 austere steel columns in Hyde Park commemorate those killed by suicide bombers in the summer of 2005.

Evidence of strife is everywhere in this city, and the true Londoner will cheerfully insist there's more and worse to come. Just don't bet against them handling their portion of strife with aplomb.

IN CONTEXT

LATIN LESSONS

The city's origins are hardly grand. Celtic tribes lived in scattered communities along the banks of the Thames before the Romans arrived in Britain – creating what archaeologists describe as a 'ritual landscape': a dispersed region of sacred monuments – but there's no evidence of a settlement that we might recognise as the seed of the future metropolis before the invasion of the Emperor Claudius in AD 43. During his conquest, the Romans forded the Thames at its shallowest point (probably near today's London Bridge) and, later, built a timber bridge there. A settlement developed on the north side of this crossing.

Over the next two centuries, the Romans built roads, towns and forts in the area. Progress was halted in AD 61 when Boudicca, the widow of an East Anglian chieftain, rebelled against the imperial forces who had seized her land, flogged her and raped her daughters. She led the Iceni in a revolt, destroying the Roman colony at Colchester before marching on London. The Romans were massacred and their settlement razed.

After order was restored, London was rebuilt; around AD 200, a two-mile-long, 18-foot-high wall was put up around it. Chunks of the wall survive today; the early names of the original gates – Ludgate, Bishopsgate, Newgate and Aldgate – are preserved on the map of the modern city, with the street known as London Wall tracing part of its original course. (For a guided walk around the remains of the Roman wall, *see p324* **Walk**.) But through to the fourth century, racked by invasions and internal strife, the Roman Empire was in decline. In 410, the troops were withdrawn, and London became a ghost town.

INTO THE DARK

During the fifth and sixth centuries, history gives way to legend. The Saxons crossed the North Sea; apparently avoiding the ruins of London, they built farmsteads and trading posts outside the city walls. Pope Gregory sent Augustine to convert the English to Christianity in 596; Mellitus, one of his missionaries, was appointed the first Bishop of London, founding a cathedral dedicated to St Paul inside the old city walls in 604.

From this period, the history of London is one of expansion. Writing in 731, monk and writer the Venerable Bede described 'Lundenwic' as 'the mart of many nations resorting to it by land and sea'. Only recently have archaeologists found traces of this Anglo-Saxon around Covent Garden and the Strand. Yet the city faced a new danger during the ninth century: the Vikings. The city was ransacked in 841 and again in 851, when Danish raiders returned with 350 ships. It was not until 886 that King Alfred of Wessex – Alfred the Great – regained the city, re-establishing London as a major trading centre, and refounding it within its old walls.

Throughout the tenth century the city prospered. Churches were built, parishes established and markets set up. However, the 11th century brought more harassment from the Vikings, and the English were forced to accept a Danish king, Cnut (Canute, 1016-35), during whose reign London replaced Winchester as the capital of England.

The country reverted to English control in 1042 under Edward the Confessor, who devoted himself to building England's grandest church two miles west of the City on an island in the river marshes at Thorney: 'the West Minster' (Westminster Abbey). Just a week after the consecration, he died. London now had two hubs: Westminster, centre of the royal court, government and law; and the City of London, centre of commerce. On Edward's death, foreigners took over. Duke William of Normandy was crowned king on Christmas Day 1066, having defeated Edward's brother-in-law Harold at the Battle of Hastings. The pragmatic Norman resolved to win over the City merchants by negotiation rather than force, and in 1067 granted the burgesses and the Bishop of London a charter – still available to researchers in the London Metropolitan Archives – that acknowledged their rights and independence in return for taxes. He also ordered strongholds to be built at the city wall 'against the fickleness of the vast and fierce population', including the White Tower (the tallest building in the Tower of London) and the now-lost Baynard's Castle.

PARLIAMENT AND RIGHTS

In 1295, the Model Parliament, held at Westminster Hall by Edward I and attended by barons, clergy and representatives of knights and burgesses, agreed the principles of English government. The first step towards establishing personal rights and political liberty, not to mention curbing the power of the king, had already been taken in 1215 with the signing of the Magna Carta by King John. Then, in the 14th century, subsequent assemblies gave rise to the House of Lords and the House of Commons. During the 12th and 13th centuries, the king and his court travelled the kingdom, but the Palace of Westminster was now the permanent seat of law and government; noblemen and bishops began to build palatial houses along the Strand from the City to Westminster, with gardens stretching down to the river.

Relations between the monarch and the City were never easy. Londoners guarded their privileges, and resisted attempts by kings to squeeze money out of them to finance wars and construction projects. Subsequent kings were forced to turn to Jewish and Lombard moneylenders, but the City merchants were intolerant of foreigners too.

The self-regulation privileges granted to the City merchants under Norman kings were extended by the monarchs who followed – in return for finance. In 1191, the City of London was recognised by Richard I as a self-governing community; six years later, it won control of the Thames. In 1215 King John confirmed the city's right 'to elect every year a mayor', a position of authority with power over the sheriff and the Bishop of London. A month later, the mayor joined the rebel barons in signing the Magna Carta.

Over the next two centuries, the power and influence of the trade and craft guilds (later known as the City Livery Companies) increased as dealings with Europe grew. The City's markets drew produce from miles around: livestock at Smithfield, fish at Billingsgate, poultry at Leadenhall. The street markets ('cheaps') around Westcheap (now Cheapside) and Eastcheap were crammed with a variety of goods. The population within the city walls grew from about 18,000 in 1100 to well over 50,000 in the 1340s.

WAKE UP AND SMELL THE ISSUE

Lack of hygiene became a serious problem. Water was provided in cisterns, but the supply, more or less direct from the Thames, was limited and polluted. The street of Houndsditch was so named because Londoners threw their dead animals into the furrow there; in the

Saxon invasion.

streets around Smithfield (the Shambles), butchers dumped entrails into the gutters. These conditions helped to foster the greatest catastrophe of the Middle Ages: the Black Death of 1348 and 1349, which killed about 30 per cent of England's population. The plague came to London from Europe – probably carried by rats on ships, although research in 2015 suggested gerbils may have been to blame – and the plague was to recur in London several times during the next three centuries.

Disease left the harvest short-handed, causing unrest among the peasants whose labour was in such demand. Then a poll tax of a shilling a head was imposed. It was all too much: the Peasants' Revolt began in 1381. Thousands marched on London, led by Jack Straw from Essex and Wat Tyler from Kent; the Archbishop of Canterbury was murdered and hundreds of prisoners were set free. After meeting the Essexmen near Mile End, the 14-year-old Richard II rode out to the rioters at Smithfield and spoke with Tyler. During their discussion, Tyler was fatally stabbed by the Lord Mayor; the revolt collapsed and the ringleaders were hanged. But no more poll taxes were imposed.

ROSES, WIVES AND ROYAL DOCKS

Its growth spurred by the discovery of America and the opening of ocean routes to Africa and the Orient, London became one of Europe's

IN CONTEXT

largest cities under the Tudors (1485-1603). The first Tudor monarch, Henry VII, had ended the Wars of the Roses by might, defeating Richard III at the Battle of Bosworth and, by policy, marrying Elizabeth of York, a daughter of his rivals. By the time his son took the throne, the Tudor dynasty was firmly established. But progress under Henry VIII was not without its hiccups. His first marriage, to Catherine of Aragon, failed to produce an heir, so in 1527 he determined the union should be annulled. When the Pope refused to co-operate, Henry defied the Catholic Church, demanding to be recognised as Supreme Head of the Church in England and ordering the execution of anyone who opposed the plan (including Sir Thomas More, his otherwise loyal chancellor). The subsequent dissolution of the monasteries transformed the face of the medieval city.

When not transforming the politico-religious landscape, Henry found time to develop a professional navy, founding the Royal Dockyards at Woolwich in 1512. He also established palaces at Hampton Court and Whitehall, and built a residence at St James's Palace. Much of the land he annexed for hunting became today's Royal Parks, among them Greenwich, Hyde and Regent's parks.

RENAISSANCE MEANS REBIRTH

Elizabeth I's reign (1558-1603) saw the founding of the Royal Exchange in 1566, which enabled London to emerge as Europe's commercial hub. Merchant venturers and the first joint-stock companies established new trading enterprises, as pioneering seafarers Francis Drake, Walter Raleigh and Richard Hawkins sailed to the New World. As trade grew, so did London: it was home to 200,000 people in 1600, many living in overcrowded conditions. The most complete picture of Tudor London is given in John Stow's *Survey of London* (1598), a fascinating first-hand account by a Londoner whose monument stands in the church of St Andrew Undershaft.

These were the glory days of English drama. The Rose (1587) and the Globe (1599, now recreated; *see p57*) theatres were erected at Bankside, providing homes for the works of popular playwrights William Shakespeare and Christopher Marlowe. Deemed 'a naughty place' by royal proclamation, 16th-century Bankside was a vibrant mix of entertainment and 'sport' (bear-baiting, cock-fighting), drinking and whoring – all within easy reach of the City, which had outlawed theatres in 1575.

In 1605, two years after the Tudor dynasty ended with Elizabeth's death, her Stuart successor, James I, escaped assassination on 5 November, when Guy Fawkes was found underneath the Palace of Westminster. Commemorated with fireworks each year as Bonfire Night, the Gunpowder Plot had been hatched in protest at the failure to improve conditions for the persecuted Catholics, but only resulted in an intensification of anti-papist sentiment. James I is more positively remembered for hiring Inigo Jones to design court masques (musical dramas) and London's first influential examples of the classical Renaissance architectural style: the Queen's House (1616; *see p218*), the Banqueting House (1619; *see p73*) and St Paul's Covent Garden (1631; *see p140*).

ROYALISTS AND ROUNDHEADS

Charles I succeeded his father in 1625, but gradually fell out of favour with the City of London and an increasingly independent-minded Parliament over taxation. The country slid into civil war (1642-49), the supporters of Parliament (the Roundheads, led by Puritan Oliver Cromwell) opposing the supporters of the King (the Royalists).

Both sides knew that control of the country's major city and port was vital for victory, and London's sympathies were with the Parliamentarians. In 1642, 24,000

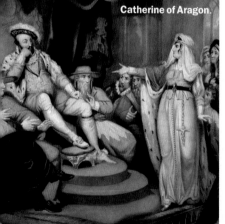

Catherine of Aragon.

Mass burial of victims of the **Plague**.

citizens assembled at Turnham Green to face Charles's army, but the King withdrew. The move proved fatal: Charles never threatened the capital again, and was eventually found guilty of treason. Taken to the Banqueting House in Whitehall on 30 January 1649, he declared himself a 'martyr of the people' and was beheaded. A commemorative wreath is still laid at the site of the execution on the last Sunday in January each year.

For the next decade, the country was ruled as a Commonwealth by Cromwell. But his son Richard's subsequent rule was brief: due to the Puritans closing theatres and banning Christmas (a Catholic superstition), the Restoration of the exiled Charles II in 1660 was greeted with great rejoicing. The Stuart king had Cromwell exhumed from Westminster Abbey, and his body was hung in chains at Tyburn (near modern-day Marble Arch). His severed head was displayed on a pole outside the abbey until 1685.

PLAGUE, FIRE AND REVOLUTION

The year 1665 saw the most serious outbreak of plague since the Black Death, killing nearly 100,000. Then, on 2 September 1666, a further disaster. The fire that spread from a carelessly tended oven in Thomas Farriner's baking shop on Pudding Lane raged for three days and consumed four-fifths of the City.

The Great Fire at least allowed planners the chance to rebuild London as a modern city. Many blueprints were considered, but Londoners were so impatient to get on with business that the City was reconstructed largely on its medieval street plan (albeit in brick and stone rather than wood). The prolific Sir Christopher Wren oversaw work on 51 of the 54 rebuilt churches. Among them was his masterpiece: the new St Paul's, completed in 1710 and effectively the world's first Protestant cathedral.

In the wake of the Great Fire, many well-to-do City dwellers moved to new residential developments west of the old quarters: the West End. In the City, the Royal Exchange was rebuilt, but merchants increasingly used the new coffee houses to exchange news. With the expansion of the joint-stock companies and the chance to invest capital, the City emerged as a centre not of manufacturing but of finance. Economic instability was common: the 1720 financial disaster known as the South Sea Bubble ruined Sir Isaac Newton.

Anti-Catholic feeling still ran high. The accession in 1685 of Catholic James II aroused such fears of a return to papistry that a Dutch Protestant, William of Orange, was invited to take the throne with his wife, Mary

DEATH AND URBAN PLANNING

Down in the ground where the dead men go.

The extraordinary growth of Victorian London brought with it many problems, a significant proportion of which were sanitary. When you suddenly stick a million extra people into streets that had barely changed since the Great Fire, things were bound to get stinky. This was a horse-drawn London before sewers, before dustmen, before toilets – and, crucially, before penicillin. In the squalor, diseases thrived, bringing further problems. What were they going to do with all the dead?

London bodies had traditionally been buried in churchyards, but these were overflowing – the earth was so stuffed with corpses, they literally popped out the ground. Londoners demanded new cemeteries, but at the same time refused to allow them to be built near where they lived. One inspired idea for a giant 94-step pyramid containing 215,296 catacombs atop Primrose Hill was rejected because of the £2.5m bill. A solution eventually came in the form of the 'Magnificent Seven', grand commercial cemeteries built between 1832 and 1841 in a cordon sanitaire outside central London at Kensal Green, West Norwood, Highgate (see p232), Abney Park (see p237), Nunhead,

Brompton (see p96) and Tower Hamlets. These weren't cheap, and were soon filled with magnificent monuments to the greats of Victorian society. The poor were left out, forcing public bodies to step in where the market had failed. Cheaper, smaller cemeteries were set up by the Board of Health and – with the exception of Brompton, which was bought by the state in 1852 – the 'Magnificent Seven' were largely abandoned to nature, a condition in which they remain, sepulchral monuments shrouded in ivy.

A bit like those cadavers re-emerging in Victorian churchyards, a strangely familiar row erupted in 2015. It centred on Camberwell Old Cemetery, which was built in Forest Hill after the heyday of the 'Magnificent Seven', and is distinguished by a fine Victorian lodge and the grave of FJ Horniman, founder of the Horniman Museum (see p238). This cemetery, having served its purpose, is now woodland, but Southwark Council want to restore parts to its original use. Locals are incensed and a campaign group called Save Southwark Woods (https://you.38degrees. org.uk/petitions/save-southwark-woods) has been set up to fight the plan.

Stuart (James's daughter). James fled to France in 1688 in what became known (by its beneficiaries) as the 'Glorious Revolution'. It was during William's reign that the Bank of England was founded, initially to finance the King's religious wars with France.

CREATION OF THE PRIME MINISTER

In 1714, the throne passed to George, the Hanover-born great-grandson of James I. The German-speaking king (he never learned English) became the first of four Georges in the Hanoverian line.

During George I's reign (1714-27), and for several years after, Sir Robert Walpole's Whig party monopolised Parliament. Their opponents, the Tories, supported the Stuarts and had opposed the exclusion of the Catholic James II. On the king's behalf, Walpole chaired a group of ministers (the forerunner of today's Cabinet), becoming, in effect, Britain's first prime minister. Walpole was presented with 10 Downing Street (built by Sir George Downing) as a residence; it remains the official prime ministerial home.

During the 18th century, London grew with astonishing speed. New squares and terraced streets spread across Soho, Bloomsbury, Mayfair and Marylebone, as wealthy landowners and speculative developers cashed in on the new demand for leasehold properties. South London also became more accessible with the opening of the first new bridges for centuries: Westminster Bridge (opened 1750) and Blackfriars Bridge (completed 1769) joined London Bridge, previously the only Thames crossing.

GIN-SOAKED POOR, NASTY RICH

In London's older districts, people were living in terrible squalor. Some of the most notorious slums were located around Fleet Street and St Giles's (north of Covent Garden), only a short distance from fashionable residences. To make matters worse, gin ('mother's ruin') was readily available at low prices; many poor Londoners drank excessive amounts in an attempt to escape the horrors of daily life. The well-off seemed complacent, amusing themselves at the popular Ranelagh and Vauxhall pleasure gardens or with trips to mock the patients at the Bedlam lunatic asylum. Public executions at Tyburn were popular events in the social calendar; it's said that

200,000 people gathered to see the execution (after he had escaped from prison four times) of the folk-hero thief Jack Sheppard in 1724.

The outrageous imbalance in the distribution of wealth encouraged crime, and there were daring daytime robberies in the West End. Reformers were few, though there were exceptions. Henry Fielding, author of the picaresque novel *Tom Jones*, was also an enlightened magistrate at Bow Street Court (now destined to become a hotel). In 1751, he and his blind half-brother John set up a volunteer force of 'thief-takers' to back up the ineffective efforts of the parish constables and watchmen who were, until then, the city's only law-keepers. This crime-busting group of proto-cops, known as the Bow Street Runners, were the earliest incarnation of today's Metropolitan Police (established in 1829).

Meanwhile, five major new hospitals were founded by private philanthropists. St Thomas's and St Bartholomew's were long-established monastic institutions for the care of the sick, but Westminster (1720), Guy's (1725), St George's (1734), London (1740) and the Middlesex (1745) went on to become world-famous teaching hospitals. Thomas Coram's Foundling Hospital (*see p151*) was another remarkable achievement.

INDUSTRY AND CAPITAL GROWTH

It wasn't just the indigenous population of London that was on the rise. Country folk, whose common land had been replaced by sheep enclosures, were faced with a choice between starvation wages or unemployment, and so drifted into the towns. Just outside the old city walls, the East End drew many poor immigrant labourers to build the docks towards the end of the 18th century. London's total population had grown to one million by 1801, the largest of any city in Europe. By 1837, when Queen Victoria came to the throne, five more bridges and the capital's first passenger railway (from Greenwich to London Bridge) gave hints of huge expansion.

As well as being the administrative and financial capital of the British Empire, London was its chief port and the world's largest manufacturing centre. On the one hand, it had splendid buildings, fine shops, theatres and museums; on the other, it was a city of poverty, pollution and disease. Residential areas were

IN CONTEXT

polarised into districts of fine terraces maintained by squads of servants, and overcrowded, insanitary slums.

The growth of the metropolis in the century before Victoria came to the throne had been spectacular, but during her reign (1837-1901), thousands more acres were covered with roads, houses and railway lines. If you visit a street within five miles of central London, its houses will be mostly Victorian. By the end of the 19th century, the city's population had swelled to more than six million, an incredible growth of five million in just 100 years.

'It was the opening of the first passenger railway that heralded the commuters of the future.'

IN CONTEXT

Despite the social problems of the Victorian era, memorably depicted in the writings of Charles Dickens, by the turn of the century steps were being taken to improve conditions for the majority of Londoners. The Metropolitan Board of Works installed an efficient sewerage system, street lighting and better roads. The worst slums were replaced by low-cost housing schemes funded by philanthropists such as the American George Peabody, whose Peabody Donation Fund continues to provide subsidised housing. The London County Council (created in 1888) also helped to house the poor.

The Victorian expansion would not have been possible without an efficient public-transport network with which to speed workers into and out of the city from the new suburbs. The horse-drawn bus appeared on London's streets in 1829, but it was the opening of the first passenger railway seven years later that heralded the commuters of the future. The first underground line, which ran between Paddington and Farringdon Road, opened in 1863 and proved an instant success, attracting 30,000 travellers on the first day. The world's first electric track in a deep tunnel – the 'tube' – opened in 1890 between the City and Stockwell, later becoming part of the Northern line.

THE CRYSTAL PALACE

If any single event symbolised this period of industry, science, discovery and invention, it was the Great Exhibition of 1851. Prince Albert, the Queen's Consort, helped to organise the triumphant showcase, for which the Crystal Palace, a vast building of iron and glass, was erected in Hyde Park. It looked like a giant greenhouse; hardly surprising as it was designed not by a professional architect but by the Duke of Devonshire's gardener, Joseph Paxton. Condemned by art critic John Ruskin as the model of dehumanisation in design, the Palace came to be presented as the prototype of modern architecture. During the five months it was open, the Exhibition drew six million visitors. The profits were used by the Prince Consort to establish a permanent centre for the study of the applied arts and sciences; the enterprise survives today in the South Kensington museums of natural history, science, and decorative and applied arts (see p87), and in three colleges (of art, music and science). After the Exhibition closed, the Crystal Palace was moved to Sydenham and was used as an exhibition centre until it burned down in 1936.

ZEPPELINS ATTACK FROM THE SKIES

London entered the 20th century as the capital of the largest empire in history. Its wealth and power were there for all to see in grandstanding monuments such as Tower Bridge (see p187) and the Midland Grand Hotel at St Pancras Station (see p158), both of which married the retro stylings of High Gothic with modern iron and steel technology. During the brief reign of Edward VII (1901-10), London regained some of the gaiety and glamour it had lacked in the later years of Victoria's reign. Parisian chic came to London with the opening of the Ritz; Regent Street's Café Royal hit the heights as a meeting place for artists and writers; gentlemen's clubs proliferated; and 'luxury catering for the little man' was provided at the new Lyons Corner Houses (the Coventry Street branch held 4,500 people).

Road transport, too, was revolutionised in this period. By 1911, horse-drawn buses were abandoned, replaced by motor cars, which put-putted around the city's streets, and the motor bus, introduced in 1904. Disruption came in the form of devastating air raids during World War I (1914-18; see p55 **For the Fallen**).

Around 650 people lost their lives in Zeppelin raids, but the greater impact was psychological – the mighty city and its populace had experienced helplessness.

CHANGE, CRISIS AND SHEER ENTERTAINMENT

Political change happened quickly after the war. At Buckingham Palace, the suffragettes had fiercely pressed the case for women's rights before hostilities began, and David Lloyd George's government averted revolution in 1918-19 by promising 'homes for heroes' (the returning soldiers). It didn't deliver, and in 1924 the Labour Party, led by Ramsay MacDonald, formed its first government.

A live-for-today attitude prevailed in the Roaring '20s among the young upper classes, who flitted from parties in Mayfair to dances at the Ritz. But this meant little to the mass of Londoners, who were suffering in the post-war slump. Civil disturbances, brought on by the high cost of living and rising unemployment, resulted in the nationwide General Strike of 1926, when the working classes downed tools en masse in support of striking miners. Prime Minister Baldwin encouraged volunteers to take over the public services, and the streets teemed with army-escorted food convoys, aristocrats running soup kitchens and students driving buses. After nine days of chaos, the strike was finally called off.

The economic situation only worsened in the early 1930s following the New York Stock Exchange crash of 1929. By 1931, more than three million Britons were jobless. During these years, the London County Council (LCC) began to have a greater impact on the city, clearing slums and building new houses, creating parks and taking control of public services. All the while, London's population increased, peaking at nearly 8.7 million in 1939 – it would be spring 2015 before the city's population exceeded that number. To accommodate the influx, the suburbs expanded, particularly to the north-west with the extension of the Metropolitan line to an area that became known as 'Metroland'. Gabled houses sprang up in their thousands.

At least Londoners were able to entertain themselves with film and radio. Not long after London's first radio broadcast was beamed from the roof of Marconi House in the Strand

Children made homeless by the **Blitz**.

in 1922, families were gathering around huge Bakelite wireless sets to hear the BBC (the British Broadcasting Company; from 1927, the British Broadcasting Corporation). TV broadcasts started on 26 August 1936, when the first telecast went out from Alexandra Palace, but few Londoners could afford televisions until the 1950s.

BLITZKRIEG

Abroad, events had taken on a frightening impetus. Neville Chamberlain's policy of appeasement towards Hitler's Germany collapsed when the Germans invaded Poland. Britain duly declared war on 3 September 1939. The government implemented precautionary measures against air raids, including the evacuation of 600,000 children and pregnant mothers, but the expected bombing raids didn't happen during the autumn and winter of 1939-40 (the so-called 'Phoney War'). Then, in September 1940, hundreds of German bombers dumped explosives on east London and the docks, destroying entire streets and killing or injuring more than 2,000 in what was merely an opening salvo. The Blitz had begun. Raids on London continued for 57 consecutive nights, then intermittently for a further six months. Londoners reacted with stoicism, famously

WALK THE ROMAN WALLS

A stroll around the City's ancient perimeter.

Start by walking north from Blackfriars. Turn left on Bride Lane, nip up the St Bride Foundation stairs and do a slow U-turn on to Dorset Rise and then into the main entrance of Wren's lovely **St Bride's** (see p174). Downstairs is a fascinating little museum, in which a pair of angled mirrors show tessellated Roman pavement. Upstairs again, the side door takes you on to Fleet Street. On the way to **St Paul's Cathedral** (see p176) stop off at another Wren church: St Martin within Ludgate. This was the site of ancient Ludgate, as a sign inside points out.

Turn left out of the church, head through Stationers' Hall courtyard and go left on Newgate Street. When you're on the Holborn Viaduct, look south. See that slope down to the right-hand side of Farringdon Street? In Roman times, it was the bank of a river – later the Fleet – that ran just outside the city, and you'd have been standing on the bridge legionaries marched over on their way to St Albans (Verulamium) along what was then Watling Street. Retrace your steps until you can turn left on to Foster Lane. North is

Noble Street where, among the modern towerblocks, you'll see your first substantial remains of Roman London – exposed by the Blitz in 1940. In the early 2nd century AD, this was the corner of a square Roman fort. Up the stairs at the end of the ruins, the elevated walkway leads you to the fine Roman exhibits in the **Museum of London** (see p180) – watch out for the graffiti about a lazy Roman bricklayer.

Leave the museum heading east on the Bastion Highwalk, but take the first staircase on your left down to the ground. In the park on your left are further Roman and medieval walls, while to the north a medieval bastion overlooks an artificial lake. Head back and turn left out of the park up the curving slope and back up on to the walkway. Keep east, turning left at 125 London Wall. Follow the sign downstairs to **St Giles Cripplegate** (see p179), which has another impressive run of wall on the far side of a quietly reflective moat. Stroll round the church but don't go back up the stairs: instead, turn right on to Wood Street and take a detour left on to St

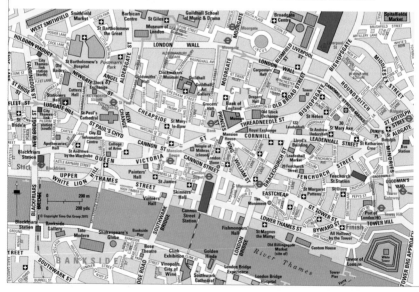

Alphage Gardens, where further ruins were laid out as a garden in 1872, according to a battered stone plaque.

Back on Wood Street, head south to the isolated tower of St Alban's (again by Wren) and go left on Love Lane, then right and into the courtyard of the **Guildhall** (see p182). The dark grey curve of tiles in the ground to your right indicates the 6,000-seater Roman amphitheatre, whose actual remains are in the **Guildhall Art Gallery** (see p183) opposite, along with a few artefacts. Keep on in the same direction, jinking left then hard right through Masons Avenue and left up Coleman Street. You're now on London Wall, which does indeed trace the line of the ancient perimeter. But only All Hallows-on-the-Wall, on your left, has any visible remains.

London Wall becomes Camomile Street, Bevis Marks and eventually Duke's Place. Turn left down Minories, where a superb Roman eagle sculpture was found in 2013 under what's now Motel One. Go right on to Crosswall then left, under the railway, along Coopers Row. Nose into the Grange City Hotel's car park for a lovely bit of Roman and medieval wall, its arched windows still visible. Then it's south, turning left after Tower Hill underground to be confronted by a massive chunk of masonry – and a rather fey statue of Emperor Trajan. Through the pedestrian tunnel are the footings of a medieval bastion.

Head right, rejoining the main road, as far as **All Hallows by the Tower** (see p186) for another old-fashioned but fascinating basement museum, with further artefacts, inscriptions and more Roman pavement, some of which you walk across to enter. Even better, there's a model of Roman London: you can see where the Fleet meets the Thames outside the western wall, and trace the journey you've just made, up from Blackfriars, past the square fort, along London Wall and down to the Thames again – 2,000 years in just a couple of hours.

For more details, buy the Museum of London's Londinium map guide or download their free app Streetmuseum: Londinium.

asserting 'business as usual'. After a final raid on 10 May 1941, the Nazis had left a third of the City and the East End in ruins.

From 1942 onwards, the tide began to turn, but Londoners had a new terror to face: the V1 or 'doodlebug'. Dozens of these deadly, explosive-packed, pilotless planes descended on the city in 1944, causing widespread destruction. Later in the year, the more powerful V2 rocket was launched. The last fell on 27 March 1945 in Orpington, Kent, around six weeks before Victory in Europe was declared on 8 May 1945.

'NEVER HAD IT SO GOOD'
World War II left Britain almost as shattered as Germany. Soon after VE Day, a general election was held and Winston Churchill was defeated by the Labour Party under Clement Attlee. The new government established the National Health Service in 1948, and began a massive nationalisation programme that included public transport, electricity, gas, postal and telephone services. For most people, however, life remained regimented and austere. In war-ravaged London, local authorities struggled with a critical shortage of housing. Prefabricated bungalows provided a temporary solution for some (60 years later, six prefabs on the Excalibur estate in Catford, south-east London, were given protection as buildings of historic interest), but the huge new high-rise housing estates proved unpopular with their residents.

There were bright spots. London hosted the Olympic Games in 1948; three years later came the Festival of Britain, resulting in the full redevelopment of the riverside site into the South Bank (now Southbank) Centre. As the 1950s progressed, prosperity returned, leading Prime Minister Harold Macmillan in 1957 to proclaim that 'most of our people have never had it so good'. However, Londoners were leaving. The population dropped by half a million in the late 1950s, causing a labour shortage that prompted huge recruitment drives in Britain's former colonies. London Transport and the National Health Service were both particularly active in encouraging West Indians to emigrate to Britain. Unfortunately, as the Notting Hill race riots of 1958 illustrated, the welcome these new immigrants received was rarely friendly. Still, there were several areas of tolerance:

IN CONTEXT

Soho, for instance, which became famous for its mix of cultures and the café and club life they brought with them.

THE SWINGING '60S

By the mid 1960s, London had started to swing. The innovative fashions of Mary Quant and others broke the stranglehold Paris had on couture: boutiques blossomed along the King's Road, while Biba set the pace in Kensington. Carnaby Street became a byword for hipness as the city basked in its new-found reputation as music and fashion capital of the world – made official, it seemed, when *Time* magazine devoted its front cover to 'swinging London' in 1966. The year of student unrest in Europe, 1968, saw the first issue of *Time Out* hit the streets in August; it was a fold-up sheet, sold for 5d. The decade ended with the Rolling Stones playing a free gig in Hyde Park that drew around 500,000 people.

Then the bubble burst. Many Londoners remember the 1970s as a decade of economic strife, the decade in which the IRA began its bombing campaign on mainland Britain. After the Conservatives won the general election in 1979, Margaret Thatcher instituted an economic policy that cut public services and widened the gap between rich and poor. Riots in Brixton (1981) and Tottenham (1985) were linked to unemployment and heavy-handed policing, keenly felt in London's black communities. The Greater London Council (GLC), led by Ken Livingstone, mounted vigorous opposition to the government with a series of populist measures, but it was abolished in 1986.

THINGS CAN ONLY GET BETTER?

In May 1997, the British electorate ousted the Tories and gave Tony Blair's Labour Party the first of three election victories. Blair left London with two significant legacies. First, the government commissioned the Millennium Dome, whose turn-of-the-century celebrations it hoped would be a 21st-century rival to the Great Exhibition of 1851. Instead, the Dome ate £1 billion and became a national joke. However, as Labour's fortunes declined, the Dome's saw an upturn. As the O2 Arena, it has hosted gigs by the likes of Prince, Lady Gaga and the reformed Led Zeppelin. Second, following a referendum, Labour instituted the Greater London Assembly (GLA) and London

mayoralty. Thus 2000 saw Ken Livingstone return to power as London's first directly elected mayor. He was re-elected in 2004, a thumbs-up for policies that included a traffic congestion charge. Summer 2005 brought elation, as London won the bid to host the 2012 Olympic Games, and devastation the very next day, as bombs on tube trains and a bus killed 52 people and injured 700.

Aided by support from the suburbs, which felt neglected by Livingstone, thatch-haired Tory Boris Johnson became mayor in 2008 with a healthy majority, and again in 2012 by a slimmer margin – again against Livingstone. His early policies, such as banning alcohol on London transport, scrapping the western extension of the Congestion Charge, as well as introducing a bike-rental scheme and developing an updated Routemaster bus, were popular. The latter were launched as self-financing through revenue and private sponsorship; both have instead been regularly topped up with money from Transport for London's already stretched public transport budget, even as public transport costs continued a relentless rise – until the year before before the 2015 General Election, in which Johnson was coincidentally standing as a Member of Parliament.

The riots and looting of August 2011, whose flashpoint was again in Tottenham, brought issues of youth unemployment, alienation and policing to the fore; how to build enough affordable housing for Londoners is another major problem. The 2012 Olympics and Paralympics were an unbridled success, yet the promised 'legacy' of improvements at a local level in some of London's poorest areas remains frustratingly elusive.

Johnson won't serve both as mayor and MP, so London will have a new mayor after the 5 May 2016 election. London's population continues to grow and house prices are stratospheric. The banking industry seems back to business as usual. The vast new Crossrail train link has burrowed its way right under the city. Whole new districts have grown up: the ambition of the King's Cross Central and the Olympic Park redevelopments may well be matched at Battersea Power Station and Vauxhall, though the social value of new developments is now routinely criticised. The city's future looks as turbulent – and fascinating – as its past has been.

IN CONTEXT

KEY EVENTS

43 The Romans invade; the settlement of Londinium is founded on the remains of an ancient ritual landscape.

61 Boudicca burns Londinium; the city is rebuilt and made provincial capital.

200 A city wall is built.

410 Roman troops evacuate Britain.

c600 Saxon London is built to the west.

604 Mellitus is consecrated bishop of London.

841 The Norse raid for the first time.

c871 The Danes occupy London.

886 Alfred the Great takes London.

1042 Edward the Confessor builds a palace and 'West Minster' upstream.

1066 William I is crowned in Westminster Abbey.

1078 The Tower of London is begun.

1123 St Bart's Hospital is founded.

1197 Henry Fitzalwin is the first mayor.

1215 The mayor signs Magna Carta.

1240 First Parliament at Westminster.

1290 Jews are expelled from London.

1348 The Black Death arrives.

1381 The Peasants' Revolt.

1397 Richard Whittington is Lord Mayor.

1476 William Caxton sets up the first printing press at Westminster.

1534 Henry VIII cuts England off from the Catholic Church.

1555 Martyrs burned at Smithfield.

1565 Sir Thomas Gresham proposes the Royal Exchange.

1572 First known map of London.

1599 The Globe Theatre opens.

1605 Guy Fawkes's plot to blow up James I fails.

1642 The start of the Civil War.

1649 Charles I is executed; Cromwell establishes the Commonwealth.

1665 Outbreak of the Great Plague.

1666 The Great Fire.

1675 Building starts on the new St Paul's Cathedral.

1694 The Bank of England is set up.

1766 The city wall is demolished.

1773 The Stock Exchange is founded.

1824 The National Gallery is founded.

1836 The first passenger railway opens; Charles Dickens publishes *The Pickwick Papers*, his first novel.

1851 The Great Exhibition takes place.

1858 The Great Stink: pollution in the Thames reaches hideous levels.

1863 The Metropolitan line opens as the world's first underground railway.

1866 London's last major cholera outbreak; the Sanitation Act is passed.

1868 The last public execution is held at Newgate prison (now the Old Bailey).

1884 Greenwich Mean Time is established as a global standard.

1888 Jack the Ripper prowls the East End; London County Council is created.

1890 The Housing Act enables the LCC to clear the slums; the first electric underground railway opens.

1897 Motorised buses are introduced.

1908 London hosts the Olympic Games for the first time.

1915 Zeppelins begin three years of bombing raids on London.

1940 The Blitz begins.

1948 London again hosts the Olympics.

1951 The Festival of Britain is held.

1952 The last 'pea-souper' smog.

1953 Queen Elizabeth II is crowned.

1981 Riots in Brixton.

1982 The last London docks close.

1986 The Greater London Council is abolished.

1992 One Canada Square tower opens on Canary Wharf.

2000 Ken Livingstone becomes London's first directly elected mayor; Tate Modern and the London Eye open.

2005 The city wins its bid to host the 2012 Games; suicide bombers kill 52 on public transport.

2008 Boris Johnson becomes mayor.

2010 Hung parliament leads to new Conservative–Lib Dem coalition.

2011 Riots and looting around the city.

2012 London becomes the second city to host the Olympic Games for a third time.

2015 The population of Greater London reaches 8.7m, the largest number in its history.

IN CONTEXT

Architecture

*A wonderful jumble of
world-class buildings.*

London's new architectural obsession is height. Girdled by the protected Green Belt, which by preventing spread keeps land values high, the city's only way is up. By one estimate, there are more than 260 buildings of 20 storeys or more currently in planning or under way, with Rafael Viñoly's 38-storey 'Walkie Talkie' and Richard Rogers's even taller 'Cheesegrater' only the most notable additions to a cluster of City skyscrapers – the Gherkin, Tower 42 and Heron Tower – looked down on from the far bank of the river by Renzo Piano's 1,016-foot Shard.

For all the annual lists of London's worst new buildings, the best modern architecture is swiftly appreciated: witness the Saw Swee Hock Student Centre, for instance. Other buildings become classics over time: the Brutalist National Theatre and Barbican are perfect examples of the changing nature of architectural taste.

None of this is new: in the 17th century, the authorities objected to Wren's magnificent St Paul's Cathedral because it looked too Roman Catholic for their Anglican sensibilities. In fact, London's defining characteristic is its aesthetically unhappy mix of buildings, a mess of historic bits and modern bobs that gives the city its a unique capacity to surprise and delight.

Monument

IN CONTEXT

ANCIENT STREETS, NEW CITY

Modern London sprang into being from the ashes left after the Great Fire of 1666, which destroyed four-fifths of the City of London, burning 13,200 houses and 89 churches. The devastation was explicitly commemorated by Sir Christopher Wren's 202-foot **Monument** (see p186), but many of the finest buildings in the City stand testament to his talent as the architect of the great remodelling, and to the work of his successors.

London had been a densely populated place built largely of wood, and fire control was primitive. It was only after the three-day inferno that the authorities insisted on a few basic regulations. Brick and stone became the construction materials of choice, and key streets were widened to act as firebreaks. Yet, despite grand, Classical proposals from several architects (Wren among them), London reshaped itself around its old street pattern, and some structures that survived the Fire still stand as reminders of earlier building styles. Chief of these are the City's fragments of Roman wall (Tower Hill tube station and the grounds of the Museum of London, see p180, have good examples) and the central Norman keep at the **Tower of London** (see p187), begun soon after William's 1066 conquest and extended over the next 300 years; the Navy saved the Tower from the flames by blowing up surrounding houses before the inferno could reach it.

Another longstanding building, **Westminster Abbey** (see p75) was begun in 1245 when the site lay far outside London's walls; it was completed in 1745 by Nicholas Hawksmoor's distinctive west towers. The abbey is the most French of England's Gothic churches, but the chapel – begun by Henry VII – is pure Tudor. Centuries later, the American writer Washington Irving gushed: 'Stone seems, by the winning labour of the chisel, to have been robbed of its weight and density, suspended aloft, as if by magic.'

A LATE FLOWERING

The European Renaissance came late to Britain, making its London debut with Inigo Jones's 1622 **Banqueting House** (see p73). The sumptuously decorated ceiling, added in 1635 by Rubens, celebrated the Stuart monarchy's Divine Right to rule, although 14 years later King Charles I provided a greater

spectacle as he was led from the room and beheaded on a stage outside. Tourists also have Jones to thank for **St Paul's Covent Garden** (see p140), and the precise little **Queen's House** (see p218) in Greenwich, but they're not his only legacies. He mastered the art of piazzas (notably at Covent Garden), porticoes and pilasters, changing British architecture forever. His work influenced the careers of succeeding generations of architects and introduced a habit of venerating the past that it would take 300 years to kick.

Nothing cheers a builder like a natural disaster, and one can only guess at the relish with which Wren and co began rebuilding after the Fire. They brandished Classicism like a new broom: the pointed arches of English Gothic were rounded off, Corinthian columns made an appearance and church spires became as complex, frothy and multi-layered as a wedding cake.

Wren blazed the trail with his daring plans for **St Paul's Cathedral** (see p176), spending an enormous (for the time) £500 on just the oak model of his proposal. But the scheme, incorporating a Catholic dome rather than a Protestant steeple, was too Roman for the establishment and the design was rejected. Wren quickly produced a redesign and gained planning permission by incorporating a spire, only to set about a series of mischievous U-turns to give us the building, domed and heavily suggestive of an ancient temple, that survives to this day.

Wren's work was continued by Nicholas Hawksmoor and James Gibbs, who benefited from a 1711 decree that 50 extra churches should be built using the money raised by a tax on coal. Gibbs became busy around Trafalgar Square with the steepled Roman temple of **St Martin-in-the-Fields** (see p69), as well as the Baroque **St Mary-le-Strand** and the tower of **St Clement Danes** (for both, see p146). His work was well received, but the more experimental Hawksmoor had a rougher ride. For one thing, not everyone admired his stylistic innovations; for another, even fewer approved of his financial planning, or lack of it: **St George's Bloomsbury** (see p154) cost three times its £10,000 budget and took 15 years to build. Nonetheless, Hawksmoor designed, in whole or in part, eight new places of worship. Like Wren, Hawksmoor loved the Classical temple, a style at odds with the Act's insistence on spires. **St George-in-the-East**, **St Anne**

Limehouse and **St Mary Woolnoth** (see p182) are all unorthodox resolutions of this contradiction, but the 'spire' of St George's Bloomsbury is the barmiest. Aping the Mausoleum of Halicarnassus, Hawksmoor created a peculiar stepped pyramid design, plopped a giant statue of George I in a toga on top and then added unicorns and lions. Hawksmoor's ruinous overspends were one reason why just a dozen of the proposed 50 churches were built.

After action, reaction: one of a large family of Scottish architects, Robert Adam found himself at the forefront of a movement that came to see Italian Baroque as a corruption of the real thing, with architectural exuberance dropped in favour of a simpler interpretation of ancient forms. The best surviving work of Robert and his brothers James, John and William can be found in London's great suburban houses, including **Kenwood House** (see p231), but the project for which they're most famous no longer stands: the cripplingly expensive Adelphi housing estate. Almost all of the complex was pulled down in the 1930s and replaced by an office block, apart from the **Royal Society of Arts** building, just off the Strand on John Adam Street.

IN CONTEXT

St George-in-the-East.

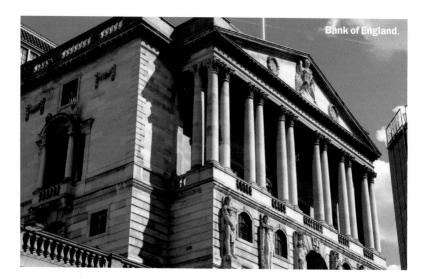
Bank of England.

SOANE AND NASH

Just as the first residents were moving into the Adelphi in the early 1770s, a young unknown called John Soane was embarking on a domestic commission in Ireland. It was never completed, but Soane eventually returned to London and went on to build the **Bank of England** (see p181) and **Dulwich Picture Gallery** (see p238). The Bank was demolished between the wars, leaving only the perimeter walls of Soane's masterpiece, but his gracious Stock Office has been reconstructed in the Bank's museum (see p182). A further glimpse of what the bankers might have enjoyed can be gleaned from his own house, the quirkily marvellous and recently extended **Sir John Soane's Museum** (see p166), an exquisite architectural experiment.

A near-contemporary of Soane's, John Nash was a less talented architect, but his contributions – among them the inner courtyard of **Buckingham Palace** (see p79), the **Theatre Royal Haymarket** and **Regent Street** (see p114) – have comparable influence in the look of contemporary London to those of Wren. Regent Street began as a proposal to link the West End to the planned park further north, as well as a device to separate the toffs of Mayfair from the riff-raff of Soho; in Nash's own words, a 'complete separation between the Streets occupied by the Nobility and Gentry, and the narrow Streets and meaner houses occupied by mechanics and the trading part of the community'.

By the 1830s, the Classical form of building had been established in England for some 200 years, but this didn't prevent a handful of upstarts from pressing for change. In 1834, the **Houses of Parliament** (see p73) burned down, leading to the construction of Sir Charles Barry's Gothic masterpiece. Barry sought out Augustus Welby Northmore Pugin. Working alongside Barry, if not always in agreement with him (of Barry's symmetrical layout, Pugin famously remarked, 'All Grecian, sir. Tudor details on a Classic body'), Pugin created a Victorian fantasy that would later be condemned as the Disneyfication of history.

GETTING GOTHIC

This was the beginning of the Gothic Revival, a move to replace what was considered to be foreign and pagan with something that was native and Christian. Architects would often decide that buildings weren't Gothic enough; as with the 15th-century Great Hall at the **Guildhall** (see p182), which gained its corner turrets and central spire only in 1862. The argument between Classicists and Goths erupted in 1857, when the government hired Sir George Gilbert Scott, a leading light of the Gothic movement, to design a new home for the Foreign Office. Scott's design incensed anti-Goth Lord Palmerston, then prime minister, whose diktats prevailed. But Scott exacted his revenge by building an office in which everyone hated working, and by going on to construct wonderful Gothic edifices all over town, among them the **Albert Memorial** (*see p87*) and what is now the **Renaissance St Pancras** hotel (*see p357*), which still forms the front of St Pancras train station (*see p158*).

St Pancras was completed in 1873, after the Midland Railway commissioned Scott to build a London terminus that would dwarf that of its rivals next door at King's Cross. Using the project as an opportunity to show his mastery of the Gothic form, Scott built an asymmetrical castle that obliterated views of the train shed behind, itself an engineering marvel completed earlier by William Barlow.

Other charming, imposing neo-Gothic buildings around the city include the **Royal Courts of Justice** (*see p175*), the **Natural History Museum** (*see p87*) and **Tower Bridge** (*see p187*). Under the influence of the Arts and Crafts movement, medievalism morphed into such mock Tudor buildings as the wonderful half-timbered **Liberty** department store (*see p116*).

Broadcasting House.

Albert Memorial.

IN CONTEXT

BEING MODERN

World War I and the coming of modernism led to a spirit of renewal and a starker aesthetic. **Freemasons' Hall** (*see p140*) and the BBC's **Broadcasting House** (*see p103*) are good examples of the pared-down style of the 1920s and '30s, but perhaps the finest example of between-the-wars modernism can be found at **London Zoo** (*see p197*). Built by Russian émigré Bertold Lubetkin and the Tecton group, the spiral ramps of the former Penguin Pool were a showcase for the possibilities of concrete. The material was also put to good use on the London Underground, enabling the quick, cheap building of cavernous spaces with sleek lines and curves: the collaboration between London Underground supremo Frank Pick and architect Charles Holden created design masterpieces such as **Southgate** and **Arnos Grove stations** at the north end of the Piccadilly line, and **Chiswick Park station** to the west on the District line, as well as the transport headquarters at **55 Broadway** – which featured sculptures by modern masters Jacob Epstein, Eric Gill and Henry Moore. Even local government offices were built with care and skill: see for yourself at the likes of **Hornsey Town Hall** (www.hthartscentre. co.uk), which reopened to the public in 2014. Further innovations were employed on the gorgeous **Daily Express** building

30 St Mary Axe ('the Gherkin').

Lloyds of London.

IN CONTEXT

(121-128 Fleet Street), built in 1931 using the pioneering 'curtain wall' construction, its radical black vitrolite and glass façade hung on an internal frame.

The bombs of World War II left large areas of London ruined, providing another opportunity for builders to cash in. Lamentably, the city was little improved by the rebuild; in many cases, it was left worse off. The destruction left the capital with a dire housing shortage, so architects were given a chance to demonstrate the grim efficiency with which they could house large numbers of families in tower blocks. There were post-war successes, however, including the **Royal Festival Hall** (see p50) on the South Bank. The sole survivor of the 1951 Festival of Britain, the RFH was built to celebrate the end of the war and the centenary of the Great Exhibition, held in 1851 and responsible for the foundation in South Kensington of the Natural History Museum, the Science Museum and the V&A. Next to the RFH, the **Hayward Gallery** (see p51) is an exemplar of the 1960s vogue for Brutalist architecture, a style more thoroughly explored at the **Barbican** (see p179).

HERE COME THE STARCHITECTS

The 1970s and '80s offered a pair of alternatives to concrete: postmodernism and high-tech. The former is represented by César Pelli's blandly monumental **One Canada Square** (see p242) in Docklands, an oversized obelisk that's perhaps the archetypal expression of late '80s architecture – and whose impact is hard to imagine now it stands in a copse of inferior office blocks. Richard Rogers's high-tech **Lloyd's of London** building (see p184) is much more widely admired. A clever combination of commercial and industrial aesthetics that adds up to one of the most significant British buildings since the war, it was mocked on completion in 1986; opposite, Rogers' disappointing 48-storey **122 Leadenhall** ('the Cheesegrater') is now complete, while nearby Bishopsgate has both the City's current tallest building – the 755-foot, 46-storey **Heron Tower** – and the footings of the building that may one day exceed it: a long-stalled project that was once to be the 945ft **Pinnacle**.

Apart from Rogers, the city's most visible contemporary architect has been Norman Foster, whose **City Hall** and **30 St Mary Axe** (universally known as 'the Gherkin', for obvious reasons; see p185) caught up with Big Ben and black taxis as movie shorthand for 'Welcome to London!' – only to be overtaken in 2012 by the giant glass spike of Renzo Piano's **Shard** (see p63), facing the City across the Thames. Foster's prolific practice set new standards with the exercise in complexity that is the £100-million Great Court at the **British Museum** (see p150). The Great Court is the largest covered square in Europe, but each of the 3,300 triangular glass panels that make up its roof is unique.

Much new architecture is to be found cunningly inserted into old buildings. Herzog & de Meuron's fabulous transformation of a Bankside power station into **Tate Modern** (see p57) is the most famous example – the firm aims to repeat its success with an ambitious new extension, a vast pyramid unfolding itself upwards like self-assembled origami (due to open in 2016).

LOOKING AT LONDON

Get the inside view on the city's architecture.

Both the **Architectural Association** (36 Bedford Square, WC1B 3ES, 7887 4000, www.aaschool.ac.uk, closed Sun) and **Royal Institute of British Architects** (66 Portland Place, W1B 1AD, 7580 5533, www.architecture.com, closed Sun) have terrific exhibitions on different aspects of architecture, but for a focused look at London's architectural future, get off the tube at Goodge Street and visit **New London Architecture** (26 Store Street, WC1E 7BT, 7636 4044, www.newlondonarchitecture. org, closed Sun). To celebrate its tenth anniversary, NLA is rebooting its centrepiece: a 39-foot-long scale model of the city, with all major developments with planning permission indicated. The new version will have a broad range of interactives and enhanced information. It promises to offer real insight into the city's recent and future architecture and plans. In addition, Open-City's **Open-House London** (see p37) festival is a key date in the architecture calendar each year. It does a terrific job of getting locals engaged with their city by giving public access to amazing buildings of all epochs.

IN CONTEXT

New London Architecture.

LOCAL COLOUR AND OPEN ARTS

Architecture hasn't all been about headline projects and eye-troubling commercial developments. Will Alsop's multicoloured **Peckham Library** (122 Peckham Hill Street) helped to redefine community architecture in 2000, and architects have continued to play a major role in redefining public libraries. David Adjaye subsequently designed the **Idea Stores** (www.ideastore.co.uk) in Poplar (1 Vesey Path, East India Dock Road) and Whitechapel (321 Whitechapel Road), with a crisp, softened industrial aesthetic that is a world away from the familiar Victorian versions of libraries, while at the end of 2011 Piers Gough's upside-down pyramid, **Canada Water Library** (21 Surrey Quays Road), provided a focus for a rather incoherent district in south-east London. The subtle Robbrecht en Daem expansion of **Whitechapel Gallery** (*see p205*) into the stylistically very different former library next door reversed this process, giving a new democratic openness to a pair of landmark Victorian buildings, while the **Saw Swee Hock Student Centre** (Houghton Street) by O'Donnell+Tuomey is at once a dramatically shaped building and an ingenious response to an extremely restricted plot surrounded by other buildings just off the Kingsway.

THE END – OR BEGINNING? – OF THE MEGABUILDS

In the north of London, the transformation of King's Cross is approaching its conclusion. Here, you'll find the reopened St Pancras International station; a refurbished **King's Cross station** with a spectacular new roof; the new-build office/concert venue **Kings Place** (*see p284*); and **Central Saint Martins** art college, in a redeveloped Victorian granary on a fine new square with restaurants, geometric, choreographed fountains and terracing down to the canal. This 67-acre brownfield redevelopment, King's Cross Central, will eventually also comprise 1,900 new homes, serviced by 20 new streets and another four squares, in a part of London that has its very own new postcode: N1C.

Even more impressive – and also with its own postcode, E20, cannily borrowed from the fictional London borough in long-running BBC TV soap opera *EastEnders* – is the

King's Cross Station.

Olympic Park (*see p241*). Having admirably fulfilled its function as the major venue for the 2012 Olympics and Paralympics, it is being made fit for public ('legacy' in the jargon) use – and the taxpayer has reason to expect rather a lot from a project for which the original £2.4-billion budget had to be increased to an eye-watering £9.3 billion. With only the Olympic Stadium now out of public hands (it should reopen as West Ham's football ground for the 2016/17 season), the results are impressive: from a superb park, with excellent playgrounds, to the beautiful wood-clad Velodrome, Zaha Hadid's stunning Aquatics Centre (finally without its disfiguring temporary seating stands) and the cordially loathed red spirals of the Anish Kapoor-designed **ArcelorMittal Orbit** – which may just be beginning to win a place in local affections.

While the Olympic 'legacy' plays out, focus has shifted to regeneration, gentrification and, above all, how affordable housing can be provided. The regeneration currently feels a lot like gentrification in new 'town centres' at Stratford, on the eastern flank of the Olympic Park, where the **Westfield Stratford City** mall has been doing serious business, and in Woolwich. Big business is behind the £30-million Siemens sustainability centre on the Royal Docks, linked across the Thames by Mayor Boris Johnson's first vanity project – the **Emirates Air Line cable car** (*see p243*) – to the **O2 Arena** (*see p273*), with its own cluster of new buildings, including a university campus. (The Mayor's second vanity project, the **Garden Bridge**, planned to link the Embankment to the South Bank in central London, also looks great but serves little infrastructural purpose.)

Planners have pointed to the eastern docks area of London, the 'Thames Gateway', as the city's future for many years – that possibility is underpinned by the progress of the colossally ambitious **Crossrail** project. Not due to complete until 2018, this railway has already wormed its way under key areas of the city, including Oxford Street, to connect the suburbs and beyond to east and west with the centre of London. It is an extraordinary feat of civil engineering.

Are we on the way to a better future city? The arguments on both sides are fierce. But one thing is clear: heading up, out and under, one way or another, we are well on our way to a bigger future London.

IN CONTEXT

Olympic Park.

Essential Information

Hotels

Even at the height of the recession, London's hoteliers seemed to think it was boomtime, and the pace of deluxe openings hasn't slowed. A top-class hotel has opened in Mayfair, the area's first new addition for ten years – and the Beaumont is a beauty. The lofty Shangri-La at the Shard overlooks all other London hotels, and the Mondrian at Sea Containers has stunning riverside views, but everything feels a little in the shadow of Marylebone's none-more-trendy Chiltern Firehouse. It's not all top-dollar here, mind you. The pioneering Hoxton has opened a sister hotel that's just as cool and affordable as the original, while citizenM is soon to expand its brand of bargain chic into Shoreditch. On the whole, though, room prices remain high across town. Significantly, the new Hospital Club rooms followed Soho House's lead: their bargain rooms are bluntly described as 'Small'. And in fact, for London, they're not even all that small.

OUR LISTINGS

In London, the average price of a double room for the night is not much shy of £130. So we've classified the hotels in this chapter – by average prices for a double – as follows: you can expect to pay more than £300 a night for hotels in the **Deluxe** category, £200-£300 for **Expensive** hotels, £100-£200 for **Moderate** properties and under £100 a night for hotels listed as **Budget**.

The classifications we use are just a guide. A hotel's rates can vary widely, both top to bottom and over the course of the year. As a rule, it's best to book as far ahead as possible, and always try hotels' own websites first: many offer special online deals throughout the year; pretty much every business hotel will offer steep reductions for a Sunday night stay.

If you do arrive in town without a bed booked, staff at **Visit London** (1 Lower Regent Street, 0870 156 6366, www.visitlondon.com) will be happy to help you out.

Be aware that a few hotels don't include VAT in the rates they quote. And watch out for added extras. If you're bringing a car (not recommended), always check with the hotel before you arrive: few central hotels offer parking, and those that do charge steeply for it.

THE SOUTH BANK & BANKSIDE
Deluxe

★ Mondrian at Sea Containers
20 Upper Ground, SE1 9PD (3747 1000, www.morganshotelgroup.com/mondrian/mondrian-london). Blackfriars tube.
Rooms 359. **Map** p404 7N.

Location's everything here: this Mondrian is right on the Thames, with the views on the bank side of the building among the best in London – low enough to feel part of the city, high enough to feel exclusive. The rooms are nicely furnished by Tom Dixon in a kind of post-modern deco style, minimalist without leaving you feeling the sharp edges. Public spaces are terrific and playfully ship-themed (not least the prow that encases the reception desks) and there are plenty of areas for meetings. There's a connoisseurs' bar (Dandelyan; *see p208*) and less accomplished restaurant on the ground floor, as well as a blingier bar in a glass cube on the roof (the Rumpus Room, closed Sun, Mon) and a cosy Curzon cinema.

★ Shangri-La at the Shard

31 St Thomas Street, SE1 9QU (7234 8000, www. shangri-la.com/london). London Bridge tube/rail. **Rooms** 202. **Map** p405 Q8.

The Shangri-La is unusual in many ways. The hotel proper starts on floor 35 with a spacious foyer and restaurant: the ground floor is just a pre-reception and security bag scanner before the uncannily smooth and swift lift. The building's pyramid shape means every room is different, with most floor space and hence the poshest suites on 36 and 37, not at the top. And the rooms are priced by view: the most expensive look north, offering 180° Thames vistas. Those views are amazing, as you'd expect: absorbing as dusk falls and the city lights come on, especially from the lobby and restaurant. The Skypool, fitness room and bar feel a bit remote, way up on floor 52. The decor is cosmopolitan Asian neutral, with some unimpressive bits of design offset by imaginative touches (binoculars for you to enjoy the view, torches to ease jetlagged room navigation in bedside drawers). And the multicultural staff was friendly, thoughtful and tuned in, cheerfully solving problems and seeming rather pleased to be here.

Moderate

Bermondsey Square Hotel

Bermondsey Square, Tower Bridge Road, SE1 3UN (08744 015 9834, www.bespokehotels.com). Borough tube or London Bridge tube/rail. **Rooms** 100. **Map** p405 Q10.

This is a deliberately kitsch new-build hotel on a redeveloped square. Loft suites are named after the heroines of psychedelic rock classics (Lucy, Lily, Jude, Ruby and Eleanor); some have private terraces or a hammock, or Japanese baths. Rooms have classic discs on the walls, and you can kick your heels from the suspended Bubble Chair at reception. But, although occupants of the Lucy suite get a multi-person jacuzzi (with a great terrace view), the real draw isn't the gimmicks – it's well-designed rooms, with free Wi-Fi, for competitive prices. The restaurant-bar has been through a few hit-and-miss incarnations, but the bar's lounge area remains a good spot to relax in and the staff are helpful.

▶ *Bermondsey is now full of design studios and funky shops; the Fashion & Textile Museum (see p62) is a short walk away.*

ESSENTIAL INFORMATION

Mondrian at Sea Containers.

★ citizenM London Bankside
20 Lavington Street, SE1 0NZ (020 3519 1680, www.citizenm.com). Southwark tube. **Rooms** 192. **Map** p404 O8.

This casually stylish new-build is a superbly well-designed – and well-located – addition to London's affordably chic hotels. The ground floor is a slick yet cosy café-bar and reception area: self-check-in, but with staff on hand to help and, where better rooms are available, offer upgrades. Guests are invited to use this area as their 'living room' and – thanks to the neat design – do so. The rooms themslves are tiny but well thought through: there are blackout blinds, free Wi-Fi, drench showers with removeable sideheads, storage under the bed and free movies. The rooms are also fun: those blinds are automatic, controlled – as are the movies, air-con and funky coloured lighting – from a touch-sensitive tablet.

Premier Inn London County Hall
County Hall, Belvedere Road, SE1 7PB (0871 527 8648, www.premierinn.com). Waterloo tube/rail. **Rooms** 314. **Map** p401 M8.

This Premier Inn's position right by the London Eye, the Thames, Westminster Bridge and Waterloo Station is a gift for out-of-towners on a bargain weekend break. Extra points are garnered for its friendly and efficient staff, making this newly refurbished branch of the Premier Inn chain the acceptable face of budget convenience. Check-in is quick and pleasant; rooms are spacious, clean and warm, with comfortable beds and decent bathrooms with very good showers. Breakfast, a buffet-style affair in a comfortable dining room, is extra but provides ballast for a day of sightseeing, shopping, or, indeed, meetings. Wi-Fi costs £3 a day, but guests get a 30-minute free session.

WESTMINSTER & ST JAMES'S
Deluxe

Corinthia
Whitehall Place, SW1A 2BD (7930 8181, www.corinthia.com). Embankment tube or Charing Cross tube/rail. **Rooms** 294. **Map** p401 L8.

Firmly in the grand-hotel tradition, the Corinthia actually spent years as government offices before its conversion to a hotel. The colossal Baccarat chandelier (with 1,000 clear crystal globes, plus one in red) in the expansive lobby complete with central dome; the dark wood and silk-covered walls in the high-spec rooms; the luxurious bathrooms with pool-like oval baths: everything is as you would expect for a hotel in this price range, and it's done well and with a light, modern touch that avoids self-importance or stuffiness. The Espa spa and subterranean pools (with jacuzzi, steam room, sauna and hot seats) form a complex over two floors. Espa products are in the bathrooms too. Afternoon tea is a stylish affair, served in the lobby. The Bassoon bar is an intimate, after-dark retreat, while the Northall restaurant serves British food in a dramatic circular space with floor-to-ceiling windows.

Ritz
150 Piccadilly, W1J 9BR (7493 8181, www.theritzlondon.com). Green Park tube. **Rooms** 136. **Map** p400 J8.

If you like the idea of a world where jeans and trainers are banned and jackets must be worn by gentlemen when dining (the requirement is waived for breakfast), the Ritz is the place for you. Founded by hotelier extraordinaire César Ritz, the hotel is deluxe *in excelsis*. The show-stopper is the ridiculously ornate, vaulted Long Gallery, an orgy of chandeliers, rococo mirrors and marble columns, but all the high-ceilinged, Louis XVI-style bedrooms have been painstakingly renovated to their former glory in restrained pastel colours. But amid the old-world luxury, there are plenty of mod cons, including free wireless and large TVs in most rooms. ▶ *Fancy being an interloper? Book (well in advance) for an elegant afternoon tea in the Palm Court.*

IN THE KNOW CHAINS

Chain hotels aren't covered in this chapter, unless they're new, especially well located (**Premier Inn London County Hall**; *see left*) or otherwise unusually praiseworthy. This is simply because the internal logic of chain hotels is that one should be as similar as possible to another, with reliability one major virtue – and price the other. You can find double rooms for around £100 at **Holiday Inn** and **Holiday Inn Express** (www.ihg.com/holidayinn), **Ibis** (www.ibis.com) and **Travelodge** (www.travelodge.co.uk), while the newcomer **Motel One Tower Hill** (24-26 Minories, EC3N 1BQ, 7481 6420, www.motel-one.com) combines good prices and a good location for both business and sightseeing.

The 'no-frills' approach is another way to go – very low rates, but nothing inessential is included. Airline-offshoot **EasyHotel** (www.easyhotel.com) was the first, but we prefer **Tune** (www.tunehotels.com), which now has five London hotels; the first is located not far from the South Bank, across the river from the Houses of Parliament. Rooms are usually around £115 a night. If you've got an awkward departure time from Gatwick or Heathrow, consider the neat 'pod' rooms at a **Yotel** (www.yotel.com); a four-hour stay will cost around £60. And open now at Gatwick is London's first **Bloc** hotel (www.blochotels.com) – a high-tech, no-frills enterprise priced around £65.

Number Sixteen. *See p346.*

Expensive

Eccleston Square Hotel

37 Eccleston Square, SW1V 1PB (3489 1000, 3503 0692, www.ecclestonsquarehotel.com). Pimlico tube or Victoria tube/rail. **Rooms** 39. **Map** p400 H11.

This Grade II-listed Georgian house has been transformed into a smart, urbane and rather masculine boutique hotel, in a palette of grey, black and white, with high-quality fittings such as Italian marble chevron flooring throughout the ground floor and black Murano glass chandeliers. Upstairs, the monochrome continues, with leather headboards, and silk wallpaper and curtains, all in shades of grey. It's in the rooms that the hotel's USP becomes apparent: it's all about the tech. Whether it's the underfloor heating in the bathroom, the lighting or the curtains, it's all operated by finger-tip control pads. The most snazzy is the one that turns the 'smart glass' of the white marble bathroom walls opaque for privacy. (Bath-lovers should note that tubs are eschewed in favour of rainfall showers.) The hotel doesn't take guests under 13.

Trafalgar

2 Spring Gardens, Trafalgar Square, SW1A 2TS (7870 2900, www.thetrafalgar.com). Charing Cross tube/rail. **Rooms** 129. **Map** p401 K7.

The Trafalgar is part of the Hilton chain of hotels, but you'd hardly notice. The mood is young and dynamic at the chain's first 'concept' hotel, for all that it's housed in the imposing edifice that was once the headquarters of Cunard (this was where the *Titanic* was conceived). To the right of the open

reception is the Rockwell Bar, which is boisterous at night, although thick walls should prevent sound leaking up to the rooms; breakfast downstairs is accompanied by gentler music, sometimes played live. It's the none-more-central location, however, that's the hotel's biggest draw – the handful of corner suites look directly into the square (prices reflect location). Anyone without their own view can always avail themselves of the little rooftop bar, which is also open to the public in summer.

Moderate

B+B Belgravia

64-66 Ebury Street, SW1W 9QD (7259 8570, www.bb-belgravia.com). Victoria tube/rail. **Rooms** 17. **Map** p400 H10.

How do you make a lounge full of white and black contemporary furnishings seem cosy and welcoming? Hard to achieve, but the owners have succeeded at B+B Belgravia, which takes the B&B experience to a new level. It's fresh and sophisticated without being hard-edged: there's nothing here that will make the fastidiously design-conscious wince (leather sofa, arty felt cushions, modern fireplace), but nor is it overly precious. A gleaming espresso machine provides 24/7 caffeine, and there's a large but somewhat dark garden sit in at the back.

Budget

Morgan House

120 Ebury Street, SW1W 9QQ (7730 2384). Pimlico tube or Victoria tube/rail. **Rooms** 11. **Map** p400 G10.

The Morgan has the understated charm of the old family home of a posh but unpretentious English friend: a pleasing mix of nice traditional wooden or iron beds, with pretty floral curtains and coverlets in subtle hues, the odd chandelier or big gilt mirror over original mantelpieces, and padded wicker chairs and sinks in every bedroom, along with free Wi-Fi. Though there's no guest lounge, guests can sit in the little patio garden in better weather and, for Belgravia, the prices are a steal.

SOUTH KENSINGTON & CHELSEA

Deluxe

The landmark **Lanesborough** hotel (7259 5599, www.lanesborough.com) at Hyde Park Corner was closed for renovations at the time of writing, but due to open shortly after we've gone to press.

Blakes

33 Roland Gardens, SW7 3PF (7370 6701, www.blakeshotels.com). Gloucester Road or South Kensington tube. **Rooms** 47. **Map** p397 D11.
As original as when Anouska Hempel opened it in 1983 – the scent of oranges and the twittering of a pair of lovebirds fill the dark, oriental lobby – Blakes and its maximalist decor have stood the test of time, a living casebook for interior design students. Each room is in a different style, with influences from Italy, India, Turkey and China. Exotic antiques picked up on the designer's travels – intricately carved beds, Chinese birdcages, ancient trunks – are set off by

sweeping drapery and piles of plump cushions. Downstairs, the Eastern-influenced restaurant caters for a celebrity clientele enticed by the hotel's discreet, residential location.

Gore

190 Queen's Gate, SW7 5EX (7584 6601, www.gorehotel.com). South Kensington tube. **Rooms** 50. **Map** p397 D9.
This fin-de-siècle period piece was founded by descendants of Captain Cook in two grand Victorian townhouses. The lobby and staircase are hung with old paintings, and the bedrooms all have fantastic 19th-century carved oak beds, sumptuous drapes and shelves of old books. The suites are spectacular: the Tudor Room has a huge stone-faced fireplace and a minstrels' gallery, while tragedy queens should plump for the Judy Garland room with her old bed (and replica ruby slippers). Bistrot 190 provides a casually elegant setting for great breakfasts, while the warm, wood-panelled 190 bar is a charming and sophisticated setting for cocktails.

Milestone Hotel & Apartments

1-2 Kensington Court, W8 5DL (7917 1000, www.milestonehotel.com). High Street Kensington tube. **Rooms** 56; 6 long-stay apartments. **Map** p394 C8.
Wealthy American visitors make annual pilgrimages here, their arrival greeted by the comforting, gravelly tones of their regular concierge, as English as roast beef, and the glass of sherry in the room. Yet amid the old-school luxury (butlers on 24-hour call) thrives inventive modernity (the resistance pool in the spa).

ESSENTIAL INFORMATION

San Domenico House . *See p346.*

Beaumont. *See p349.*

The rooms that overlook Kensington Gardens feature the inspired decor of South African owner Beatrice Tillman: the Safari suite contains tent-like draperies and leopard-print upholstery; while in the Regency Suite, an early 19th-century screen conceals a copper bath. Afternoon tea is served in the Park Lounge, a glorious melding of library and boudoir.

Expensive

Myhotel Chelsea

35 Ixworth Place, SW3 3QX (7225 7500, www.myhotels.com). South Kensington tube.
Rooms 45. **Map** p397 E11.

The Chelsea myhotel feels a world away from its sleekly modern Bloomsbury sister (*see p356*). The Sloane Square branch has an aesthetic that is softer and decidedly more English – with a floral sofa and plate of scones in the lobby, and white wicker headboards, velvet cushions and Bee Kind toiletries in the guestrooms. These feminine touches contrast nicely with the mini-chain's feng shui touches, Eastern-inspired treatment room and sleek aquarium. Breakfast and cold dishes are served in a bar-restaurant with a modernised farmhouse feel, while Pellicano serves Italian food. The central library, which is done out in conservatory style, is simply wonderful. Just pick up a book, sink into one of the ample comfy chairs and listen to the tinkling water feature.

Number Sixteen

16 Sumner Place, SW7 3EG (7589 5232, www. firmdalehotels.com). South Kensington tube.
Rooms 41. **Map** p397 D10.

This may be Kit Kemp's most affordable hotel but there's no slacking in the typical Firmdale hotel style stakes – witness the fresh flowers and origami-ed bird-book decorations in the comfortable drawing room. Bedrooms are generously sized, bright and very light, and carry the Kemp trademark mix of bold and traditional. The whole place has an appealing freshness about it, enhanced by a large, tree-filled back garden complete with a central water feature. By the time you finish breakfast in the pretty conservatory, you'll have forgotten you're in the middle of the city. *Photo p344.*
▶ *This is an excellent location for visiting South Kensington's museums early, when they're less busy.*

San Domenico House

29-31 Draycott Place, SW3 2SH (7581 5757, www.sandomenicohouse.com). Sloane Square tube.
Rooms 17. **Map** p397 F11.

Along a quiet terrace of late 19th-century red-stone buildings just off Sloane Square, San Domenico owes much of its tasteful, historic look to previous owner Sue Rogers, the interior designer who transformed this former private residence into a boutique hotel masterpiece. All the categories of guestroom, including the split-level gallery suites and a new junior suite, feature original furnishings or antiques. Royal portraits, Victorian mirrors and Empire-era travelling cases are complemented by fabrics of similar style and taste, offset by contemporary touches to bathrooms. The spacious bedrooms enjoy wide-angle views of London, some from little balconies, and have free Wi-Fi. Breakfasts are taken up to guests or laid out in the room downstairs, while main meals may be taken in the sumptuous coffee room by the lobby. *Photo p345.*

ROOM WITHOUT A VIEW

The suite where luxury seeks cosmic balance with austerity.

When the Grosvenor Estate got together with ace restaurateurs Chris Corbin and Jeremy King over transforming a Grade II-listed block of offices into the **Beaumont** (for listings, *see p349*) there was one unusual stipulation: the design had to include a piece of public art. So Corbin and King contacted the sculptor Anthony Gormley – who was interested, but didn't initially grasp how radical these new hoteliers were prepared to be for their debut hotel. Judging by what was eventually unveiled, the answer is pretty darn radical.

Gormley's ROOM isn't so much an acquired taste as an entirely new sensation. From the outside, the sculpture is striking enough: it's a man, as if made of giant pixels of grey metal for some kind of pre-*Tron* arcade game, sat on his haunches two storeys up one side of the hotel. But inside, it's a suite unlike any other in the world. The sitting room, hallway and guest bathroom are in the same immaculate art-deco style as the rest of the hotel – all heavy woods, metal accents and objets d'art. Then, in the main bathroom, things begin to shift. Conceived as a kind of ritual transition

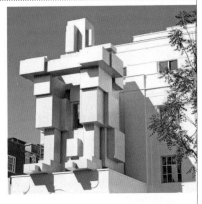

space, the bathroom in this suite eschews the contrasting black-and-white tiles that help smarten up the rest of the hotel. Instead, there's pure white marble. A further sense of ceremony is created by a black velvet curtain, drawn across the nine steps leading up to the suite's single bedroom. And in that room you'll find nothing but a bed.

The room is heavily clad in chunky, very dark, oak timbers – a match for the heavy pixels of the crouching man outside. Into the sombre space is pierced a single window, so high up the wall as to look out on nothing but sky. There's no TV, no phone, no distractions. It's suggested you turn your mobile off while you're here. It's just a dark, meditative womb-like space. Indeed, that single window is set through the belly of the sculpture.

Gormley wanted to conjure the sense of actually being inside his sculpture. He also felt the dark, enclosed space there could be soothing, comforting even – an escape from the rigours and rush of modern life, a way to step out of the hotel into something different.

Want to experience it for yourself? Rather than creating public art that could only be gawped at from Brown Hart Gardens, Corbin and King have decided the suite will let in members of the public twice a year. Not mobs of camera wielders, we're told, but nonetheless properly open – perhaps we should imagine some kind of Open-House (*see p37*) ballot system. The details were still being decided as we went to press, so visit the website for the latest.

ESSENTIAL INFORMATION

Moderate

Ampersand

10 Harrington Road, SW7 3ER (7589 5895, www.ampersandhotel.com). South Kensington tube. **Rooms** 111. **Map** p397 D10.

In a Victorian stucco property, Ampersand has a strong design ethos, with dove greys and duck-egg blues enlivened by splashes of purples, yellows and reds, bringing together a striking and distinctive look. A whimsical twist on the classic comes from the likes of tall purple padded headboards reaching nearly to the ceiling and dove drawings on the dove-grey walls in the ornithologically inspired deluxe rooms. In the corridors, botanical drawings and interesting representations of scientific instruments reference the museums nearby, while the colourful lounge area – where afternoon tea is served – has deep sofas and studded armchairs in scarlet velvets and kingfisher blues and a multicoloured teapot collection in a wall cabinet. Breakfast and dining is found downstairs in the white-tiled Mediterranean-oriented Apero restaurant.

Vicarage Hotel

10 Vicarage Gate, W8 4AG (7229 4030). High Street Kensington or Notting Hill Gate tube. **Rooms** 17. **Map** p394 B8.

Scores of devotees return regularly to this tall Victorian townhouse, which has a great location, tucked in a quiet leafy square just off High Street Ken, hard by Kensington Gardens. It's a comfortable, resolutely old-fashioned establishment – and that's

what the punters come for. The refurbished entrance hall is wonderfully grand, with red and gold striped wallpaper, a huge gilt mirror and chandelier. A sweeping staircase ascends from there to an assortment of good-sized rooms, furnished in pale florals and nice old pieces of furniture.

OXFORD STREET, MAYFAIR & MARYLEBONE

Deluxe

45 Park Lane

45 Park Lane, W1K 1PN (7493 4576, www. dorchestercollection.com). Hyde Park Corner tube. **Rooms** 45. **Map** p400 G8.

The sprightly offspring of the venerable Dorchester (*see p350*), which it faces across a twinkly-treed forecourt, 45 Park Lane has translated the famously high standards of its parent into a buzzier, boutiquier, even blingier form. Where the Dorchester offers liveried concierges, 45 Park Lane allocates guests a personal host sharply suited in grey; the Dorchester can arrange a limo… well, so can 45 – or it will lend you a folding bike. Wolfgang Puck brings informal glamour and high-end steaks to the Cut restaurant, and Bar 45 has the largest collection of American wines in the UK. Rooms are standard rectangles given character by well-chosen art, quality furnishings, great views (ask for an upper floor) and considered touches such as a yoga mat, designer glassware and in-safe electrical outlet. Technology is state of the art; enormous flatscreens

Chiltern Firehouse.

swing out from the walls; a TV is embedded in the bathroom mirror (so that you can watch from the giant marble bath); and touchscreens control room functions electronically.

★ Beaumont

Brown Hart Gardens, W1K 6TF (7499 1001, www.thebeaumont.com). Bond Street tube. **Rooms** 75. **Map** p398 G6.

Oddly, the Grade II-listed façade is the least impressive part of this hotel. The first new Mayfair hotel for a decade is set in the vast 1926 garage where Selfridge's shoppers used to get their jalopies tuned up, but it is in the painstakingly and totally rebuilt interiors – bland hire-car offices in 2011 – that this art deco fantasia sings. The bar's great (American Bar; *see p118*) and there's smooth service and a lovely private bar/drawing room off the foyer. The staff gets the marriage of glamorous formality and approachability just right, and the owners' personal travel bugbears have created some really thoughtful touches, from the sliding screens that isolate beds from bathrooms to the free soft drinks, movies and shoeshines. For the Antony Gormley-designed suite, *see p347* **Room Without a View**.

Brown's

Albemarle Street, W1S 4BP (7493 6020, www.roccofortecollection.com). Green Park tube. **Rooms** 117. **Map** p400 J7.

Brown's was opened in 1837 by James Brown, butler to Romantic poet, hedonist and freedom-fighter Lord Byron. The first British telephone call was

made from here in 1876, five years after Napoleon III and Empress Eugenie took refuge in one of the considerable suites after fleeing the Third Republic. Ethiopian Emperor Haile Selassie and Rudyard Kipling were also guests. The bedrooms are all large and extremely comfortable, furnished with original art, collections of books and, in the suites, fireplaces; its elegant, classic British hotel restaurant, Hix Mayfair, gives a nod to modernity with a series of contemporary British artworks, including pieces by the likes of Tracey Emin and Bridget Riley, but the public spaces of the hotel thrum with history. Non-residents can visit: try the afternoon tea in the English Tea Room or sip a cocktail in the classily masculine Donovan Bar.

Chiltern Firehouse

1 Chiltern Street, W1U 7PA (7073 7690, www.chilternfirehouse.com). Baker Street or Bond Street tube. **Rooms** 26. **Map** p398 G5.

This Grade II-listed red-brick former fire station was for years the secret location of London's most-anticipated new hotel. The key factor was André Balazs who, as the man behind the celeb-friendly Chateau Marmont in LA and New York's Mercer, has a gift for creating exclusive hotels with incredible buzz. The see-and-be-seen restaurant (*see p110*) opened first, under visionary chef Nuno Mendes, and was immediately block-booked; ditto the 26 refined suites, each a model of intelligent, comforting design, retro of course, but not stuck in the past. Service is relaxed but crisp – exemplified by the note alongside the phone in each room, replacing the usual book of instructions, simply instructing one to 'Dial 0 for anything'.

★ Claridge's

55 Brook Street, W1K 4HR (7629 8860, www.claridges.co.uk). Bond Street tube. **Rooms** 203. **Map** p398 H6.

Claridge's is sheer class and pure atmosphere and, with its signature art deco redesign, still simply dazzling. Photographs of past guests, including Churchill and sundry royals, grace the grand foyer, as does an absurdly over-the-top Dale Chihuly chandelier. Without departing too far from the traditional, Claridge's has managed to keep its main restaurant Fera actively fashionable (the excellent Simon Rogan is in charge), and A-listers can gather for champers in the discreet bar. The rooms divide evenly between deco and Victorian style, with period touches such as deco toilet flushes in swanky marble bathrooms. Bedside panels control the mod-con facilities at the touch of a button. If money's no object, opt for a David Linley suite, in duck-egg blue and white, or lilac and silver.

Connaught

Carlos Place, W1K 2AL (7499 7070, www.the-connaught.co.uk). Bond Street tube. **Rooms** 121. **Map** p400 H7.

ESSENTIAL INFORMATION

This isn't the only hotel in London to provide butlers, but there can't be many that offer 'a secured gun cabinet room' for the hunting season. This is traditional British hospitality for those who love 23-carat gold leaf trimmings and stern portraits in the halls, but all mod cons in their room, down to flatscreens in the en suite. Too lazy to polish your own shoes? The butlers are trained in shoe care by the expert cobblers at John Lobb. Both of the bars – gentleman's club cosy Coburg (*see p118*) and cruiseship deco Connaught – and the Hélène Darroze restaurant are very impressive. In the new wing, which doubled the number of guestrooms, there's a swanky spa and 60sq m swimming pool.

Dorchester
53 Park Lane, W1K 1QA (7629 8888, www. thedorchester.com). Hyde Park Corner tube. **Rooms** 250. **Map** p400 G7.
A Park Lane fixture since 1931, the Dorchester's interior may be thoroughly, opulently classical, but the hotel is cutting-edge in attitude, providing an unrivalled level of personal service. With the grandest lobby in town, amazing views of Hyde Park, state-of-the-art mod cons and a magnificent spa, it's small wonder the hotel continues to welcome movie stars (the lineage stretches from Elizabeth Taylor to Tom Cruise) and political leaders (Eisenhower planned the D-Day landings here). It's said to have the deepest baths in London. You're not likely to be eating out, either: the Dorchester employs 90 full-time chefs at the Grill Room, Alain Ducasse and the wonderfully atmospheric China Tang. There's even an angelic tearoom in the spa: the Spatisserie. A few years ago, the Dorchester opened an entirely new hotel, 45 Park Lane (*see p348*), in the former Playboy Club premises, almost opposite the entrance to its predecessor.

Expensive

Montagu Place
2 Montagu Place, W1H 2ER (7467 2777, www. montagu-place.co.uk). Baker Street tube. **Rooms** 16. **Map** p398 G5.
A small, fashionable townhouse hotel, Montagu Place fills a couple of Grade II-listed Georgian residences with sharply appointed rooms graded according to size. The big ones are entitled Swanky, and have super king-size beds and big bathrooms with walk-in showers – some have narrow front terraces. More modest in size, the Comfy category has double beds and, being at the back of the building, no street views. All rooms have a cool and trendy look, with cafetières and ground coffee instead of Nescafé sachets, as well as flatscreen TVs and free Wi-Fi. The decision to combine bar and reception desk (situated at the back of the house) means you can get a drink at any time and retire to the graciously modern lounge. Service is at once sharp and very obliging.

No.5 Maddox Street
5 Maddox Street, W1S 2QD (7647 0200, www. living-rooms.co.uk). Oxford Circus tube. **Rooms** 12. **Map** p398 J6.
This bolthole just off Regent Street is perfect for visiting film directors looking to be accommodated in a chic apartment at a reasonable long-term rate. Here, they can shut the discreet brown front door, climb the stairs and flop into a home from home with all contemporary conveniences. The East-meets-West decor is classic 1990s minimalist, but very bright and clean after a gentle refurbishment. Each apartment has a fully equipped kitchen, but room service will shop for you, as well as providing the usual hotel amenities. There's no bar, but breakfasts and snacks are served, and there's a Thai restaurant (Patara) on the ground floor.

Moderate

22 York Street
22 York Street, W1U 6PX (7224 2990, www.22yorkstreet.co.uk). Baker Street tube. **Rooms** 10. **Map** p398 G5.
Bohemian French chic – white furniture, palest pink lime-washed walls, mellow wooden floors, subtly faded textiles and arresting *objets d'époque* – makes this delightfully unpretentious bed and breakfast in the heart of Marylebone a sight to behold. It doesn't announce itself from the outside, so you feel as if you've been invited to stay in someone's arty home, especially when you're drinking good coffee at the gorgeous curved table that dominates the breakfast room-cum-kitchen. Guests are also given free rein with the hot beverages in a lounge full of knick-knacks upstairs, while a cluttered smaller room downstairs has an internet station (the Wi-Fi is free). All rooms are a decent size and have en suite baths, a rarity at this price and in this part of London.

Sumner
54 Upper Berkeley Street, W1H 7QR (7723 2244, www.thesumner.com). Marble Arch tube. **Rooms** 20. **Map** p395 F6.
The Sumner's cool, deluxe looks have earned it many fans, not least in the hospitality industry, where it has won a number of awards. You won't be at all surprised when you get here: from the soft dove and slatey greys of the lounge and halls you move up to glossily spacious accommodation with brilliant walk-in showers. The breakfast room feels soft and sunny, with a lovely, delicate buttercup motif and vibrant Arne Jacobsen chairs to cheer you on your way to the museums, but the stylishly moody front sitting room is also a cosy gem.

Budget

Pavilion
34-36 Sussex Gardens, W2 1UL (7262 0905, www.pavilionhoteluk.com). Edgware Road

ESSENTIAL INFORMATION

tube, or Marylebone or Paddington tube/rail.
Rooms 30. **Map** p395 E5.
A hotel that describes itself as 'fashion rock 'n' roll' is never going to be staid, but Danny and Noshi Karne's Pavilion is quite mind-bogglingly excessive. The rooms have attention-grabbing names – such as 'Enter the Dragon' (you've guessed, Chinese themed), 'Honky Tonk Afro' (a tribute to the 1970s) 'Flower Power' (blooming flowery) and 'Cosmic Girl' (way out there, man) – and they are frequently used for fashion shoots. The website has an impressive list of celebrities who have rocked up here over the years. Bizarre and voluptuous choice of decor notwithstanding, this crazy hotel actually offers excellent value and has the usual amenities, including free Wi-Fi. You might be disappointed if you want cool contemporary elegance and poncey toiletries – the Pavilion's much more fun than that.

SOHO & LEICESTER SQUARE

Deluxe

★ Ham Yard Hotel
1 Ham Yard, W1D 7DT (3642 2000, www. firmdalehotels.com). Piccadilly Circus tube.
Rooms 91. **Map** p401 K7.
We're fans of all the Firmdale hotels – and co-owner Kit Kemp's trademark splashy, clashy colours, winningly teamed with antique and distressed furniture – but Ham Yard has immediately leapt to the top of our list. It's partly just a matter of scale: Firmdale took over a whole yard in central London, and have built there a grandly proportioned hotel, a separate block of hotel apartments and a cluster of curated shops around a cental courtyard that's well-populated with diners and sippers on warm days. Guests won't feel lost in all this vastness, due to unusually friendly service, and Kemp's ability to combine conversation-starter decor (witness the deconstructed loom over reception) with intimate, arty detailing. There's a library and drawing room, a big ground-floor bar and restaurant with rear conservatory, exquisite basement bowling alley and, of course, fabulously appointed rooms: expect marble fittings and flatscreens in the bathroom, bespoke toiletries and tech that actually works – first time.

Haymarket Hotel
1 Suffolk Place, SW1Y 4HX (7470 4000, www. firmdale.com). Piccadilly Circus tube. **Rooms** 50.
Map p401 K7.
A terrific addition to Kit Kemp's Firmdale portfolio, this block-sized building was designed by John Nash, the architect of Regency London. The public spaces are a delight, with Kemp's trademark combination of contemporary arty surprises and plump, floral sofas. Wow-factors include the bling basement swimming pool and bar (shiny sofas, twinkly roof) and the central location. Rooms are generously sized (as are the bathrooms), individually

decorated and discreetly stuffed with facilities, and there's plenty of attention from the switched-on staff. The street-side bar and restaurant are top-notch and the breakfast is exquisite.

Soho Hotel
4 Richmond Mews, W1D 3DH (7559 3000, www.firmdale.com). Piccadilly Circus or Tottenham Court Road tube. **Rooms** 91.
Map p399 K6.
You'd hardly know you were in the heart of Soho once you're inside Firmdale's edgiest hotel: tucked away in a mews, the place is wonderfully quiet, with what was once a car park now feeling like a converted loft building. The big bedrooms exhibit a contemporary edge, with modern furniture, industrial-style windows and nicely planned mod cons (digital radios as well as flatscreen TVs), although they're also classically Kit Kemp with bold stripes, traditional florals, plump sofas, oversized bedheads and upholstered tailor's dummies. The quiet drawing room and other public spaces feature groovy colours, while Refuel, the loungey bar and restaurant, has an open kitchen and, yes, in a nod to its past, a car-themed mural.

Z Soho. See p352.

W London Leicester Square

10 Wardour Street, W1D 6QF (7758 1000, www. wlondon.co.uk). Leicester Square tube. **Rooms** 192. **Map** p401 K7.

The old Swiss Centre building on the edge of Leicester Square has been demolished and in its place is the UK's first W Hotel. The brand made its name with a series of hip hotels around the world that offer glamorous bars, upmarket food and functional but spacious rooms. The London W is no exception: Spice Market got its first UK restaurant here; Wyld is a large nightclub/bar space and the W lounge does classy cocktails. The rooms – across ten storeys – are well equipped, with their own munchie boxes. FIT (the hotel's state-of-the-art fitness facility), placed next to the pale and serene Away spa on the sixth floor, offers fine views over Soho. Also of note is the exterior: the entire hotel is veiled in translucent glass, which is lit in different colours through the day (although the presence of M&M World downstairs dials the wow-factor down a little). The private 3D cinema might dial it up again.

Expensive

★ Dean Street Townhouse & Dining Room

69-71 Dean Street, W1D 3SE (7434 1775, www. deanstreettownhouse.com). Leicester Square or Piccadilly Circus tube. **Rooms** 39. **Map** p399 K6.

This Grade II-listed, 1730s townhouse has been converted into another winning enterprise from the people behind Soho House members' club, Shoreditch Rooms (*see p361*) and High Road House. To one side of a buzzy ground-floor restaurant are four floors of bedrooms that run from full-size rooms with early Georgian panelling and reclaimed oak floors to half-panelled 'Tiny' rooms that are barely bigger than their double beds – but which can be had from the website for as little as £145. The atmosphere is that of a gentleman's club (there are cookies in a cute silver Treats container in each room), but modern room types also get to enjoy rainforest showers, 24-hour room service, Roberts DAB radios, free wireless internet and big flatscreen TVs. Even the calm little library room behind reception manages to be both low-key and luxurious.

★ Hazlitt's

6 Frith Street, W1D 3JA (7434 1771, www. hazlittshotel.com). Tottenham Court Road tube. **Rooms** 30. **Map** p399 K6.

Four Georgian townhouses make up this absolutely charming place, named after William Hazlitt, the spirited 18th-century essayist who died here in abject poverty. With flamboyance and staggering attention to detail, the rooms evoke the Georgian era, all heavy fabrics, fireplaces, free-standing tubs and exquisitely carved half-testers. Yet modern luxuries – air-conditioning, free Wi-Fi, TVs in antique cupboards and double-glazed windows – have

been subtly attended to as well. It gets creakier and more crooked the higher you go, culminating in enchanting garret single rooms with rooftop views. Of seven new bedrooms, the main suite is a real knock-out: split-level, with a huge eagle spouting water into the raised bedroom bath and a rooftop terrace with sliding roof, it's a joyous extravaganza. From the back alley outside, the extension has been made to look like 1700s shopfronts.

Budget

Z Soho

17 Moor Street, W1D 5AP (3551 3701, www. thezhotels.com). Leicester Square or Tottenham Court Road tube. **Rooms** 85. **Map** p399 K6.

For the money, the Z is a cast-iron bargain. First, the location is superb: it really means Soho, not a short bus-ride away – the breakfast room/bar exits on to Old Compton Street. Then there's the hotel itself, which is surprisingly chic – especially the unexpected interior courtyard, with open 'corridors' stacked above it, and room to sit and drink or smoke at the bottom – and very cheerfully run, down to free wine and nibbles of an evening. The rooms are quite handsome, and have everything you need, from a little desk to free Wi-Fi, but not much more. Including space: expect beds (perhaps a little short for anyone over 6ft tall) to take up most of the room, a feeble shower, and no wardrobes or phones. A great little hotel – in both senses – and, we're pleased to report, expanding rapidly. *Photo p351.*

Other locations 5 Lower Belgrave Street, Victoria, SW1W 0NR (3589 3990); 2 Orange Street, Piccadilly, WC2H 7DF (3551 3720); 136-144 City Road, Shoreditch, EC1V 2RL (3551 3702).

COVENT GARDEN & THE STRAND

Deluxe

★ Covent Garden Hotel

10 Monmouth Street, WC2H 9HB (7806 1000, www.firmdalehotels.com). Covent Garden or Leicester Square tube. **Rooms** 58. **Map** p399 L6.

The excellent location – in the heart of London's theatre district – and tucked-away screening room of this Firmdale hotel ensure that it continues to attract starry customers, with anyone needing a bit of privacy able to retreat upstairs to the lovely panelled private library and drawing room. In the guest-rooms, Kit Kemp's distinctive style mixes pinstriped wallpaper, pristine white quilts and floral upholstery with bold, contemporary elements; each room is unique, but each has the Kemp trademark upholstered mannequin and granite and oak bathroom. On the ground floor, the 1920s Paris-style Brasserie Max and the retro zinc bar retain their buzz – outdoor tables give a perfect viewpoint on Covent Garden boutique life in summer.

JOINING THE CLUB

The fine new rooms at the Hospital Club pick up where Soho House left off.

For a long time, private clubs offered their members overnight accommodation for those evenings when the journey home was too much after a trying night – or staying out seemed like it might be more fun. Since 2010, when it opened Dean Street Townhouse (see p352), **Soho House** have done rather well out of an extension of the concept: preferential rates for members on rooms that can be booked by non-members too. The concept's been such a success, Soho House plans further rooms in the former BBC Television Centre in Shepherd's Bush, in addition to three current London locations and outposts in Berlin, New York and Miami. It's no surprise the **Hospital Club** (for listings, see p355) decided to join the fun.

Opening 15 rooms in early 2015, there are many parallels in what's on offer. Rooms are named and priced honestly according to their size: from Tiny to Bigger at Dean Street; from Small to Large at Hospital Club. In each category here, however, there's another option: the Sleeper. They don't have a window, but you get more room for your money and the cossetting decor – with Russell Sage Studios stained glass and dignified woods, including a rather snazzy headboard-cum-canopy over each bed – makes these Sleeper rooms feel cosy rather than sequestered. The Hospital Club provides crowd-pleasing eating and drinking options, one bar with a handy little smoking terrace. There are high-quality toiletries and high-spec fittings in all rooms, curious artworks, plenty of upscale retro tech (digital radios, docking stations) and high-fashion sex toys to spice things up.

Opened in an 18th-century hospital building in 2004 by Paul Allen and Dave Stewart of 1980s electropopsters the Eurhythmics, the Hospital Club was designed as a place where creative people (rather than necessarily creatives) could exchange inspiration. It has frequent exhibitions in a ground-floor gallery, as well as hosting talks and seminars, and hosting events for London Fashion Week (see p37), when Endell Street can become a hive of paparazzi. And a stay here means – unless you choose to retire in seclusion – that you'll mingle with the creative crowd, perhaps at the regular film screenings or while grabbing a bit of Wi-Fi in a comfy break-out space, or perhaps swirling a martini on the terrace with the late-night crowd.

Hub London
Covent Garden.

ME by Meliá London

336-337 the Strand, WC2R 1HA (7393 3400, www.melondonuk.com). Covent Garden or Temple tube. **Rooms** 157. **Map** p401 M7.

London's first ME by Meliá – its predecessors are in Madrid, Barcelona, Cancún, Cabo San Lucas and Vienna – is a beauty. Designed by Foster + Partners, the finishes are expensive and carefully modelled on what was there before – respecting the lines of Marconi House next door, from where the fledgling BBC made its first radio broadcast, using a transmitter built by Guglielmo Marconi, in November 1922. But it now contains a genuinely breathtaking atrium, a pyramid nine floors tall, coolly minimal in style – and starting not at ground-floor level, but from the first floor. Here, guests can sit and calmly sip champagne as they're checked in by personal 'Aura managers'.

In the rooms, the tech and textile details are all taken care of, naturally, but idiosyncratic design touches include triangular windows you can't resist stepping into to peer up and down the Aldwych. The social spaces have different moods neatly covered: from a bling American steakhouse and a basement events space into which cars can be driven, via

a more relaxed Italian restaurant, and up to Radio, the rather elegant tenth-floor roof terrace bar, where the Thames-side seats with their exceptional views are hugely in demand.

One Aldwych

1 Aldwych, WC2B 4BZ (7300 1000, www. onealdwych.com). Covent Garden or Temple tube, or Charing Cross tube/rail. **Rooms** 105. **Map** p401 M7.

You only have to push through the front door and enter the breathtaking Lobby Bar to know that you're in for a treat. Despite the building's weighty history – the 1907 structure was once the offices of the *Morning Post* – One Aldwych is a thoroughly modern establishment, with Frette linen, bathroom mini-TVs and an environmentally friendly loo-flushing system. Flowers and fruit are replenished daily, and a card with the next day's weather forecast appears at turndown. One of two on-site restaurants, Axis, serves modish British food with an emphasis on foraged ingredients. The location is perfect for the West End theatres and has become popular with attendees of London Fashion Week, particularly since many of the events are now held in nearby Somerset House. The three round corner suites are very romantic; a cosy screening room, excellent spa and a downstairs swimming pool with an underwater sound system playing soothing music may dissuade you from ever stepping outside.

St Martins Lane Hotel

45 St Martin's Lane, WC2N 4HX (7300 5500, www.morganshotelgroup.com). Leicester Square tube or Charing Cross tube/rail. **Rooms** 204. **Map** p401 L7.

When it opened over a decade ago, the St Martins was the toast of the town. The flamboyant, theatrical lobby was constantly buzzing, and guests giggled like schoolgirls at Philippe Starck's playful decor. To get back that wow factor, the hotel is renovating its lobby, restaurant and bar as we go to press, but work has been completed on the guest rooms: now interactive light displays have taken the place of slightly chilly minimalism, but the stunning floor-to-ceiling windows remain. Special garden rooms have private terraces full of flowers.

Savoy

Strand, WC2R 0EU (7836 4343, www.fairmont. com/savoy-london). Covent Garden or Embankment tube, or Charing Cross tube/rail. **Rooms** 268. **Map** p401 L7.

The super-luxe, Grade II-listed Savoy reopened after more than £100m of renovations in 2010 – the numerous delays testimony to the difficulty of bringing a listed building, loved by generations of visitors for its discreet mix of Edwardian neoclassical and art deco, up to scratch as a modern luxury hotel. Built in 1889 to put up theatregoers from Richard D'Oyly Carte's Gilbert & Sullivan shows, the Savoy is the hotel from which Monet painted the Thames, where Vivien Leigh met Laurence Olivier, where Londoners learned to love the martini. The famous cul-de-sac at the front entrance now has a garden of new topiary and centrepiece Lalique crystal fountain, but the welcome begins before you arrive with a phone call to ascertain your particular requirements. There's a new tearoom with glass-roofed conservatory; the leather counter of the new Beaufort champagne bar is set on a stage that once hosted big bands for dinner dances; and the Savoy Grill is again under the control of Gordon Ramsay. Highlight of the fitness and beauty centre is a pool in its own atrium, with a jet-stream for those who choose to swim against the current. Traditionalists can relax, though: the American Bar remains unchanged.

Moderate

★ Hospital Club

24 Endell Street, WC2H 9HQ (7170 9100, www.thehospitalclub.com). Covent Garden tube. **Rooms** 15. **Map** p399 L6.
See p353 **Joining the Club.**

Budget

Hub London Covent Garden

110 St Martin's Lane, WC2N 4BA (0333 321 3104, www.premierinn.com/en/hotel/LONSTM/ london-covent-garden). Charing Cross tube/rail or Leicester Square tube. **Rooms** 163. **Map** p401 L7.

Gimmick? Genuine convenience? We're still undecided about the central feature of this new hotel 'concept' by budget chain Premier Inn: it's all run by an app, from booking and checking in to basic room controls (temperature, light, food orders, entertainment) – it even gives you a guide to the local area. The rooms owe plenty to the pod hotels that started appearing a few years ago and so they're small, but they're also well designed (luggage storage under the bed and so on) and they are keenly priced for such a central location.

▶ *For Premier's South Bank location see p343.*

Charlotte Street Hotel. See p356.

BLOOMSBURY, KING'S CROSS & FITZROVIA

Deluxe

Charlotte Street Hotel

15-17 Charlotte Street, W1T 1RJ (7806 2000, www.firmdale.com). Goodge Street or Tottenham Court Road tube. **Rooms** 52. **Map** p399 K5.

Now a fine exponent of Kit Kemp's much imitated fusion of flowery English and avant-garde, this gorgeous hotel was once a dental hospital. Public rooms have Bloomsbury Set paintings by the likes of Duncan Grant and Vanessa Bell, while bedrooms mix English understatement with bold flourishes. The huge, comfortable beds and trademark polished granite and oak bathrooms are suitably indulgent, and some rooms have unbelievably high ceilings. The Oscar restaurant and bar are classy and busy with a smart crowd of media and ad people. At 5pm on Sundays, the mini-cinema holds screenings. *Photo p355.*

Sanderson

50 Berners Street, W1T 3NG (7300 1400, www.morganshotelgroup.com). Oxford Circus tube. **Rooms** 150. **Map** p398 J5.

No designer flash in the pan, the Sanderson remains a statement hotel, a Schrager/Starck creation that takes clinical chic in the bedrooms to new heights. Colour is generally conspicuous by its absence: the design throughout is all flowing white net drapes, gleaming glass cabinets and retractable screens. The residents-only Purple Bar sports a button-backed purple leather ceiling and fabulous cocktails; in particular, try the Vesper. The 'billiard room' has a purple-topped pool table, surrounded by strange tribal adaptations of classic dining room furniture.

Expensive

Myhotel Bloomsbury (11-13 Bayley Street, WC1B 3HD, 3004 6000, www.myhotels.com) is a grown-up, urban brother to myhotel Chelsea (*see p346*), giving the trademark Asian touches a masculine, minimalist twist.

★ Great Northern Hotel

King's Cross St Pancras Station, Pancras Road, N1C 4TB (3388 0800, www.gnhlondon.com). King's Cross tube/rail. **Rooms** 91. **Map** p399 L3.

Designed by Lewis Cubitt, the city's first railway hotel (take that, St Pancras Renaissance) opened in 1854, part of the Victorian railway explosion. It has had plenty of rough times since then, not least the 12 years it was dark, but almost £40m of renovation has recreated the place as a classic. The furniture is by artisans and, in many cases, bespoke: witness the Couchette rooms, each with a double bed snugly fitted into the window to playfully echo sleeper carriages; the neatly upholstered bedside cabinets; or the ceiling lights raised and lowered by fabulously

Great Northern Hotel.

steampunk pulleys. You're not expected to suffer the privations of a Victorian traveller, though: free Wi-Fi, film and music libraries on the 40-inch TV, Egyptian cotton sheets and walk-in showers are all standard. There's no room service but each floor has a simply charming pantry, full of jars of vintage sweets, a stand of fresh cakes, tea and coffee, newspapers and books – even a USB printer. There's also Plum + Spilt Milk, a grand restaurant with a quiet bar, on the first floor, while the busy ground-floor GNH Bar has direct access to King's Cross station.

London Edition
10 Berners Street, W1T 3NP (7781 0000, www.editionhotels.com/london). Oxford Circus or Tottenham Court Road tube. **Rooms** 173. **Map** p398 J6.

The London Edition makes a big impact as you walk into its grand hall of a lobby, complete with double-height rococo ceilings, floor-to-ceiling windows and marble pillars. And there's more to the space: it's the setting for the lobby bar, with an eclectic mix of comfortable, snazzy seating: sofas with faux-fur throws and wing-backed chairs, a snooker table, plus a blackened steel bar, a real fire and a colossal silver egg-shaped object hanging where you might expect a chandelier. Off on one side is the equally opulent Berners Tavern (*see p161*), where Jason Atherton is executive chef. With banquette seating and many paintings, it has the vibe of a grand café and a brasserie-style menu to match. Hidden away at the back of the public area is the clubby, wood-panelled Punch Room bar, where the speciality is – you've guessed it – punch. Bedrooms are a contrast: akin to lodges or dachas, with matte oak floors, wood-panelled walls and more faux-fur throws tossed on luxurious beds. Larger rooms come with sofas, some have large furnished terraces, and all have rainforest showers, Le Labo toiletries (with the hotel's woody signature scent), iPod docks and free Wi-Fi.

St Pancras Renaissance
Euston Road, NW1 2AR (7841 3540, http://st pancras.com). King's Cross St Pancras tube/rail. **Rooms** 245. **Map** p399 L3.

A landmark hotel in every sense of the word, the St Pancras Renaissance is the born-again Midland Grand, the pioneering railway hotel designed into the station's imposing Gothic frontage. It opened in 1873 but fell into disuse in the 20th century (except for appearances as a Harry Potter backdrop and in the Spice Girls' 'Wannabe' video, among other screen roles). The Renaissance group (fittingly) has done a beautiful and painstaking job of restoring it to its breathtaking, Grade I-listed best while adding modern comforts. The 120 rooms and suites in the historic hotel (there's a new wing too) have high ceilings, original features and awesome views over the station concourse or forecourt. Facilities are high-spec – Bose stereo, Nespresso machines, REN toiletries, marble baths – and the furniture is modern

classic in style. Design is sensitive to the context, re-using motifs from the original decor in the carpets, for example. The subterranean spa includes saunas, a steam room and a Victorian tiled relaxation pool. Public areas, including both restaurants (for the Booking Office, *see p160*) and the gorgeous grand staircase, are similarly splendid. London loves it.

Moderate

Academy
21 Gower Street, WC1E 6HG (7631 4115, www.theacademyhotel.co.uk). Goodge Street tube. **Rooms** 49. **Map** p399 K5.

The Academy goes for the country intellectual look, in keeping with Bloomsbury's studious yet decadent history. It's made up of five Georgian townhouses, and provides in all its rooms a tranquil generosity of space that's echoed in the Georgian squares sitting serenely between the arterial traffic rush of Gower Street and Tottenham Court Road. There's a restrained country-house stylishness in summery florals and checks, and a breath of sophistication in the handsome, more plainly furnished suites. The library and conservatory open on to fragrant walled gardens, the ideal place for the drinks and breakfast that are served there during the summer.

Harlingford Hotel
61-63 Cartwright Gardens, WC1H 9EL (7387 1551, www.harlingfordhotel.com). Russell Square tube or Euston tube/rail. **Rooms** 40. **Map** p399 L4.

An affordable hotel with tons of charm in the heart of Bloomsbury, the perkily styled Harlingford has light, airy rooms with evident boutique aspirations, and free Wi-Fi. The decor is lifted from understated sleek to quirky with the help of vibrant splashes from coloured glass bathroom fittings and mosaic tiles – overall, the hotel has something of a Scandinavian feel. The crescent it's set in has a lovely and leafy private garden where you can lob a tennis ball about or just dream under the trees on a summer's night.

Morgan
24 Bloomsbury Street, WC1B 3QJ (7636 3735, www.morganhotel.co.uk). Tottenham Court Road tube. **Rooms** 21. **Map** p399 K5.

This brilliantly located, comfortable and reasonably priced hotel in Bloomsbury is done out in neutral shades. The rooms are well equipped and all are geared up for the electronic age with wireless, voicemail, flatscreen TVs with Freeview, and air-conditioning. A good, slap-up English breakfast is served in a pleasant room with wood panelling, London prints and blue and white china plates. The spacious flats are excellent value.

Rough Luxe
1 Birkenhead Street, WC1H 8BA (7837 5338, www.roughluxe.co.uk). King's Cross tube/rail. **Rooms** 9. **Map** p399 L3.

ESSENTIAL INFORMATION

In a bit of King's Cross that's choked with ratty B&Bs and cheap chains, this Grade II-listed property takes shabby chic to extremes with artfully distressed walls, torn wallpaper, signature works of art and old-fashioned TVs that barely work. It even retains the sign for the hotel that preceded Rough Luxe: 'Number One Hotel'. All rooms have free wireless internet, but otherwise have totally different characters: there's the one with the free-standing copper tub, the one with the rose motif, and so on. The set-up is flexible, too: rooms with shared bathrooms can be combined for group bookings, and the owners are more than happy to chat with guests over a bottle of wine in the back courtyard, where a great breakfast is served. A place to stay if you're looking for somewhere different from the norm.

Budget

Clink78

78 King's Cross Road, WC1X 9QG (7183 9400, www.dinkhostels.com). King's Cross St Pancras tube/rail. **Beds** 717. **Map** p399 M3.

Located in a listed ex-courthouse, the Clink set the bar high for party-style hosteldom when it opened a few years back. There was the setting: the hostel retains the superb original wood-panelled lobby and courtroom where the Clash once stood before the beak. Then there's the urban-chic ethos that permeates the whole enterprise, from the streamlined red reception counter to the Japanese-style 'pod' beds. A thorough redesign of the public areas and licensed café/bar downstairs (no alcohol is allowed to be brought into the hostel), with computer screens for internet access (£2/hr), has given things a new rock 'n' roll fillip, with street-art decor and more comfortable furniture to enhance the place's good-time vibe. Clink261, nearby, might be a better choice for older and calmer hostellers.

Other location Clink261, 261-265 Gray's Inn Road, Bloomsbury, WC1X 8QT (7183 9400).

Generator

37 Tavistock Place, WC1H 9SE (7388 7666, http:// generatorhostels.com). Russell Square tube. **Beds** 872. **Map** p399 L4.

With a handily central Bloomsbury location, the Generator is a good option for those on ultra-tight budgets. It has been part of a global refit of the chain, creating private rooms for £50 or so a night, and adding an in-house cinema and individual room lockers (to be fastened with your own padlock). There's free Wi-Fi throughout, of course, plus a lounge that hosts regular gigs and DJs. The laundry, luggage store and hotel-style reception all stay open 24hrs a day.

Jenkins Hotel

45 Cartwright Gardens, WC1H 9EH (7387 2067, www.jenkinshotel.co.uk). Russell Square tube or King's Cross St Pancras tube/rail. **Rooms** 19. **Map** p399 K3.

This well-to-do Georgian beauty has been a hotel since the 1920s, and was refurbished in 2013. It still has an atmospheric, antique air, although the rooms have mod cons enough – TVs, mini-fridges, tea and coffee, and free Wi-Fi. Its looks have earned it a role in *Agatha Christie's Poirot*, but it's not chintzy, just floral. The breakfast room is handsome, with snowy cotton tablecloths and Windsor chairs, and the buffet breakfast – which includes hot options – is free.

YHA London Central

104 Bolsover Street, W1W 5NU (0845 371 9154, www.yha.org.uk). Great Portland Street tube. **Beds** 302. **Map** p398 J5.

The Youth Hostel Association's newest hostel is one of its best – as well as being one of the best hostels in London. The friendly and well-informed receptionists are stationed at a counter to the left of the entrance, in a substantial café-bar area. The basement contains a well-equipped kitchen and washing areas; above it, five floors of clean, neatly designed rooms, many en suite. Residents have 24hr access and the location is quiet but an easy walk from most of central London.

Other locations throughout the city.

THE CITY

Deluxe

Andaz Liverpool Street

40 Liverpool Street, EC2M 7QN (7961 1234, www.london.liverpoolstreet.andaz.com). Liverpool Street tube/rail. **Rooms** 267. **Map** p405 R6.

A faded railway hotel until its £70m Conran overhaul in 2000, the red-brick Great Eastern became in 2007 the first of Hyatt's new Andaz portfolio. The new approach means out with gimmicky menus, closet-sized minibars and even the lobby reception desk, and in with down-to-earth, well-informed service and eco-friendliness. The bedrooms still wear style-magazine uniform – Eames chairs, Frette linens – but free services (local calls, wireless internet, healthy minibar) are an appreciated touch. Restaurant options include British nosh at the 1901 restaurant in a magnificent former ballroom with a stained-glass dome or Japanese at Miyako. The cinema – set in the basement Masonic Temple, a feature of the original hotel – appropriately favours horror movies.

Expensive

Malmaison

18-21 Charterhouse Square, EC1M 6AH (0871 943 0350, www.malmaison.com). Barbican tube. **Rooms** 97. **Map** p402 O5.

Malmaison is deliciously located, looking out on a lovely cobbled square on the edge of the Square Mile, near the bars, clubs and better restaurants of the East End. This being design-conscious Clerkenwell,

Generator.

it's no surprise that the decor throughout makes a cool statement (note the Veuve Clicquot ice buckets built into the love seats at reception). The rooms overlooking the square are the pick of the bunch, with the best of the views and morning sunshine that pours through large sash windows on to big, white firm beds. After a recent redesign, they now feature wallpapers and stripped wooden floors. There's smiley service downstairs in the lovely basement brasserie, and internet usage is free.

★ Rookery

12 Peter's Lane, Cowcross Street, EC1M 6DS (7336 0931, www.rookeryhotel.com). Farringdon tube/rail. **Rooms** 33. **Map** p402 O5.

Sister hotel to Hazlitt's (*see p352*), the Rookery has long been something of a celebrity hideaway deep in the heart of Clerkenwell. Its front door is satisfyingly hard to find; when Fabric (*see p267*) devotees are about the front rooms can be noisy, but the place is otherwise as creakily calm as a country manor house. Once inside, guests enjoy an atmospheric warren of rooms, each individually decorated in the style of a Georgian townhouse: huge clawfoot baths, elegant four-posters, antique desks, old paintings and brass shower fittings. Modernity isn't forgotten though: there's free Wi-Fi. There's an honesty bar in the bright and airy drawing room at the back, which opens on to a sweet little patio. The ground-floor suite has its own hallway, a cosy boudoir and a subterranean bathroom with a double-ended cast-iron bath. Topping it all is the huge split-level Rook's Nest suite, which has views of St Paul's Cathedral.

South Place Hotel

3 South Place, EC2M 2AF (3503 0000, www. southplacehotel.com). Moorgate or Liverpool Street tube/rail. **Rooms** 80. **Map** p403 Q5.

D&D runs some of the swankiest restaurants in London, so much was expected of its first hotel. South Place delivers. It manages the difficult balance of sufficient formality to keep expense-accounters satisfied that their needs are being attended to, with enough levity for you to want to spend the evening here. The muted top-floor Angler restaurant is a superbly oiled operation, there's a pretty interior courtyard garden bar, and the ground-floor 3 South Place bar-diner segues neatly from smooth breakfast operation to boisterous bar. The attention to detail impresses: from conversation-piece art (wire high-heels in one cabinet, a light feature of suspended aeroplanes, steampunk drawings) to touch controls in the rooms, or the Bond-themed pool room and library complete with vinyl and turntable.

Threadneedles

5 Threadneedle Street, EC2R 8AY (7657 8080, www.hotelthreadneedles.co.uk). Bank tube/DLR. **Rooms** 74. **Map** p405 Q6.

Threadneedles boldly slots some contemporary style into a fusty old dame of a building in the heart

ESSENTIAL INFORMATION

of the City; it was formerly the grand Victorian HQ of the Midland Bank, bang next to the Bank of England and the Royal Exchange. The etched glass-domed rotunda of the lobby soars on columns over an artful array of designer furniture and shelving that looks like the dreamchild of some powerful graphics software – it's a calm space, but a stunning one. The bedrooms are individual, coherent and soothing examples of City-boy chic, in muted beige and textured tones, with limestone bathrooms and odd views of local landmarks: St Paul's, Tower 42 and the Lloyd's building. Drinks are served under the stained-glass central dome, and the pillared restaurant (run by Marco Pierre White) is also an impressive space. It's all smoothly run.

★ Zetter

86-88 Clerkenwell Road, EC1M 5RJ (7324 4444, www.thezetter.com). Farringdon tube/rail. **Rooms** 59. **Map** p402 O4.

Zetter is a fun, laid-back, modern hotel with some interesting design notes. There's a refreshing lack of attitude and a forward-looking approach, with friendly staff and firm eco-credentials (such as free Brompton bikes for guests' use). The rooms, stacked up on five galleried storeys around an impressive atrium, look into an intimate and recently refreshed bar area. They are smoothly functional, but cosied up with choice home comforts such as hot-water bottles and old Penguin paperbacks, as well as having walk-in showers with REN smellies. The downstairs restaurant Bistrot Bruno Loubet has, for now, become a more experimental version of Loubet's excellent King's Cross restaurant Grain Store (*see p159*), while the fabulous Zetter Townhouse, in a historic building just across the square, has a fantastic cocktail bar (*see p173*) and far cuddlier rooms with a hip vintage feel.

Moderate

Apex London Wall

7-9 Copthall Avenue, EC2R 7NJ (0845 365 0000, www.apexhotels.co.uk). Moorgate tube/rail. **Rooms** 89. **Map** p405 Q6.

The mini-chain's second London hotel shares the virtues of the first. The service is obliging, the rooms are crisply designed with all mod cons, and there are comforting details: a rubber duck in the impressive bathrooms; free jelly beans; free local calls and internet; kettle and iron provided. The City of London branch has the better location for tourists, a short walk from the Tower of London, but this one is handier for business. From the suites, a terrace peers over commercial buildings, but the view from the restaurant – of the flamboyantly sculpted frieze on a business institute – is rather pleasing. Prices are decent for the City location, but book well ahead to get the best deals.

Other location Apex City of London, City, 1 Seething Lane (7702 2020).

Ace Hotel London Shoreditch.

Fox & Anchor

115 Charterhouse Street, EC1M 6AA (7250 1300, www.foxandanchor.com). Barbican tube or Farringdon tube/rail. **Rooms** 6. **Map** p402 O5.

Check in at the handsome attached boozer (*see p172*) and you'll be pointed to the separate front entrance for the hotel, with its lovely floor mosaic, leading to a handful of well-appointed, atmospheric and surprisingly luxurious rooms. All are different, but the high-spec facilities (big flatscreen TV, roll-top bath and drench shower) and quirky attention to detail (bottles of ale in the minibar, the 'Nursing hangover' privacy signs) are common throughout. Expect some clanking noise in the early mornings as the traders roll in, but proximity to the historic Smithfield meat market also means you get a feisty fry-up in the morning in the pub.

★ Hoxton Holborn

199-206 High Holborn, WC1V 7BD (7661 3000, https://thehoxton.com). Holborn tube. **Rooms** 174. **Map** p399 L5.
See p362 **Hoxton and On.**

ESSENTIAL INFORMATION

CAMDEN

If it's important for you to stay in Camden itself, the **Holiday Inn** (*see p343* **In the Know**) on Jamestown Road is right in the heart of things – some rooms overlook the Lock.

EAST END

Expensive

Ace Hotel London Shoreditch

100 Shoreditch High Street, Shoreditch, E1 6JQ (7613 9800, www.acehotel.com/london). Liverpool Street tube/rail or Shoreditch High Street Overground. **Rooms** 258. **Map** p403 R4.

Ace arrived in Shoreditch from the US a couple of years ago, taking over a dowdy Crowne Plaza hotel. The look of the spacious rooms is comfortable and a bit bohemian, with wall-to-wall daybeds/sofas, sturdy oak or metal storage units, round oak tables and luxury denim coverings. Furniture and accessories reflect the Ace appreciation of artisans. You might find an Ally Capellino leather change box (her shop is just down the road) or a lovely CF Martin & Co guitar in your room. The lobby vibe is egalitarian and informal: a long communal table holds computers and there are DJs every night. There's a cute juice bar, Lovage, a nook of a coffee shop, a bar tucked into a further nook, a flower shop even, and the fine wood-clad brasserie Hoi Polloi (*see p207*).

★ Boundary

2-4 Boundary Street, Shoreditch, E2 7DD (7729 1051, www.theboundary.co.uk). Liverpool Street tube/rail or Shoreditch High Street Overground. **Rooms** 17. **Map** p403 R4

Design mogul Sir Terence Conran's Boundary Project warehouse conversion was a labour of love. Its restaurants – which include Albion (*see p207*), a downstairs fine-dining establishment and a rooftop bar – are high quality but relaxed places, and all 17 bedrooms are beautifully designed. Each has a handmade bed, but all are otherwise individually furnished with classic furniture and original art. The five split-level suites range in style from the bright and sea-salt fresh Beach to a new take on Victoriana by Polly Dickens, while the remaining rooms (the slightly larger corner rooms have windows along both external walls) are themed by design style: Mies van der Rohe, Eames, Shaker. There's also a charming Heath Robinson room, decorated with the cartoonist's sketches of hilariously complex machines.

Town Hall Hotel

Patriot Square, Bethnal Green, E2 9NF (7871 0460, www.townhallhotel.com). Bethnal Green tube. **Rooms** 98.

A few years back, a grand, Grade II-listed, early 20th-century town hall was transformed into this classy modern aparthotel – despite its unpromising location between a council estate and a scruffy row of shops. The decor is minimal, retaining many features – walnut panelling and marble for the interior, Portland stone outside, stained glass, and fire hoses on old brass reels scattered about – that would be familiar to the local-government bureaucrats who used to toil here, but jazzed up with contemporary art and a patterned aluminium 'veil' that covers the new floor at the top of the building. The pale-toned, spacious apartments are well equipped for self-catering, but hotel luxuries such as free wireless internet and TV/DVD players are also in place. The De Montfort suite is the size of most houses, stretching over three floors, with a living room as big as a council chamber. The hotel's new restaurant, the Typing Room (*see p212*), and bar, the Peg & Patriot, are much praised. Under a conservatory roof, there's a narrow basement swimming pool with sparkly tiles.

Moderate

★ Hoxton Shoreditch

81 Great Eastern Street, Shoreditch, EC2A 3HU (7550 1000, www.thehoxton.com). Old Street tube/rail. **Rooms** 210. **Map** p403 Q4.

Famous for its low rates, the Hoxton deserves credit for many other things. First, there's the hip Shoreditch location – hip enough for Soho House to have taken over the downstairs bar-brasserie a few years ago. Then there are the great design values. Finally, the rooms are well thought out, if mostly rather small, with lots of nice touches – free fresh milk in the fridges, a cold snack for breakfast, free Wi-Fi. Nowadays, there are even some individually designed suites – at the same price as the other rooms, but first-come, first-served. The downside? Popularity. If you don't book well in advance and plan to visit during the week rather than at the weekend, you could pay as much as at one of the big chains. A major refurbishment has opened out the original bar and added another, as well as putting red leather booths in the lobby; a new coffee bar is on the way. And the Hoxton finally has a sibling: the Hoxton Holborn (*see p360*).

★ Shoreditch Rooms

Ebor Street, Shoreditch, E1 6AW (7739 5040, www.shoreditchhouse.com). Shoreditch High Street Overground. **Rooms** 26. **Map** p403 S4.

The most recent hotel opening from Soho House members' club – joining Dean Street Townhouse (*see p352*) and High Road House – might even be the best, perfectly catching the local atmosphere with its unfussy, slightly retro design. The rooms feel a bit like urban beach huts, with pastel-coloured tongue-and-groove, shutters and swing doors to the en suite showers. They feel fresh, bright and comfortable, even though they're furnished with little more than a bed, an old-fashioned phone and DAB radio, and

ESSENTIAL INFORMATION

HOXTON AND ON

The brilliant affordable-chic hotel does it again.

Back in 2006, Sinclair Beecham, who had previously built the Pret a Manger sandwich empire, came up with an outlandish notion: fashionable accommodation with airline pricing – your room costs more when there's more demand, but otherwise it could be had for a bargain price. The most extraordinary thing wasn't that the Hoxton (now **Hoxton Shoreditch**, *see p361*) was an immediate roaring success. It was that it made so little impact on the rest of the industry.

It wasn't until 2012 that a real competitor for the Hoxton emerged: **citizenM London Bankside** (*see p343*) shares the Hoxton's youthful energy and zippy design values and was, of course, an instant hit. Now, with citizenM due to found a colony in Shoreditch, near St Paul's Cathedral and close to the Tower of London, the Hoxton has roused itself to reclaim its crown as the hotelier the public loves to stay with – and where they can actually afford to pay for a room.

Apart from its self-contradictory name, the **Hoxton Holborn** (for listings, *see p360*) is every bit as good as its predecessor – in fact, it's a little better. The location is excellent for a holiday: sure, Shoreditch may be a few degrees cooler, but in Holborn you are an easy walk from the British Museum, say, and not much further from Covent Garden or Soho's restaurants. There's the same partnership on catering as in Shoreditch, with the near-ubiquitous Soho House running one of its endlessly popular junk-food palaces, Chicken Shop, in the basement; on the ground floor are the Daily Grind coffee bar, the Cheeky nail salon and extensive bar-restaurant Hubburd & Bell. The foyer area is handsome, and popular with the Wi-Fi coffee geeks at their open laptops.

As for the rooms, expect a masculine feel and stylish attention to detail similar to Hoxton Shoreditch – although the decor feels bolder, with a hashtag motif on the pillows and big round mirror on the walls. Perhaps most significantly, the Hoxton Holborn is a refit of a former post office building rather than a new-build like its predecessor. This means the rooms are different sizes, so the Holborn has adopted the Soho House model of cheeky names and different categories: Roomy down to the neat but not tight Shoebox, which you might get for less than £80 all in on a Sunday.

a big, solid dresser (minibar, hairdryer and treats within, flatscreen TV on top). Guests get access to the fine eating, drinking and fitness facilities (yes, there is a gym, but more importantly an excellent rooftop pool) in the members' club next door. Everything's put together with a light touch, from the 'Borrow Me' bookshelf by the lifts (jelly beans, umbrellas, boardgames) to the room grades: Tiny (from just £105), Small or Small+ (with little rooftop balconies from which to survey the grey horizon).

Budget

Qbic Hotel London City

42 Adler Street, Whitechapel, E1 1EE (no phone, www.qbichotels.com). Aldgate East or Whitechapel tube. **Rooms** 171. **Map** p405 S6.

The second line of the Dutch invasion of stylish budget hotels (citizenM, *see p343*, is the other) is cheaper and more focused on community and sustainability: in fact, the hotel was created by the incredibly rapid fit-out of a former office building using modular 'Cubi' bedrooms. The hotel also works with local cycling charity Bikeworks and with Food Cycle, which provides free soup every afternoon. The rooms are sold at four levels – starting at £59 a night for no view, and increasing in price if you want to see the Whitechapel Road, the inner courtyard or Altab Ali Park. Prices are pegged by keeping down the numbers of staff, which means self-check-in and no cash accepted – even vending machines are credit card only. Still, the essentials are covered: TVs in each room, free wireless internet throughout, free snack breakfast (or £7.50 for a continental) in the natty social space downstairs. The location is gritty but great: minutes from Brick Lane.

GREENWICH

Greenwich is one of London's finest visitor attractions, but has few exceptional places to stay. It has several predictable chain hotels and a range of old-fashioned B&Bs, but nothing to persuade you to choose this over other areas.

NOTTING HILL & HOLLAND PARK

Expensive

Portobello Hotel

22 Stanley Gardens, Notting Hill, W11 2NG (7727 2777, www.portobellohotel.com). Holland Park or Notting Hill Gate tube. **Rooms** 21.

The Portobello is a hotel with nearly half a century of celebrity status, having hosted the likes of Johnny Depp, Kate Moss and Alice Cooper, who used his tub to house a boa constrictor. It remains a pleasingly unpretentious place, with a more civilised demeanour than its legend might suggest. There is now a lift to help rockers who are feeling their age up the five

floors, but there's still a 24-hour guest-only bar downstairs for those who don't yet feel past it. The rooms are themed – the superb basement Japanese Water Garden, for example, has an elaborate spa bath, its own private grotto and a small private garden – but all are stylishly equipped with a large fan, tall house plants, free Wi-Fi and round-the-clock room service.

Moderate

★ La Suite West

41-51 Inverness Terrace, Bayswater, W2 3JN (7313 8484, www.lasuitewest.com). Bayswater or Queensway tube. **Rooms** 80. **Map** p394 C6.

A typical row of west London townhouses on the outside, La Suite has been transformed on the inside by designer Anouska Hempel, with sleek lines and a black and white palette – the antithesis of her maximalist Blakes (*see p345*). A discreet side entrance leads into a long, minimalist reception area with an open fire and a zen-like feel. An Asian influence persists in the rooms, with slatted sliding screens for windows, wardrobe and bathrooms helping to make good use of space (which is limited in the cheaper rooms). Thoughtfully designed white marble bathrooms, with rainforest shower and bath, give a feeling of luxury despite not being huge. The large terrace running along the front of the building, with trees planted for an arbour-like effect, is a big summer asset for drinks, lunch or dinner, and the Raw vegetarian restaurant is an unusual take on hotel dining. All in all, clever design, a friendly vibe and – importantly – keen pricing make for a great hotel for this price range. Highly recommended.

New Linden

59 Leinster Square, Bayswater, W2 4PS (7221 4321, www.newlinden.co.uk). Bayswater tube. **Rooms** 50. **Map** p394 B6.

Modern, modish and moderately priced – that's the Mayflower Group for you. This is its Bayswater baby. It looks very cool, however, and it is a fantastically comfortable place to stay. The lobby and lounge are slick and glamorous – there's a beautiful teak arch in the lounge and the rooms are low-key with some vibrant, twirly eastern influences. Some of the larger family rooms retain their elaborate period pillars and cornicing. The bathrooms are a symphony in marble; the walk-in showers have deluge heads. There's a pleasant little patio, upstairs at the back, for morning coffee and evening drinks.

Vancouver Studios

30 Prince's Square, Bayswater, W2 4NJ (7243 1270, www.vancouverstudios.co.uk). Bayswater or Queensway tube. **Rooms** 47. **Map** p394 B6.

Step into the hall or comfortably furnished sitting room of this imposing townhouse and it feels like the gracious home of a slightly dotty uncle, with decor in the public spaces comprising colonial swords and historic prints. The studio and apartment

ESSENTIAL INFORMATION

Shoreditch Rooms. See p361.

accommodation is more modern in tone. Each room has its own style – from cool contemporary lines to a softer, more homely feel – and all are well equipped with kitchen appliances so that guests can do a bit of self-catering, should they wish. There's free Wi-Fi too. Zeus the cat lords it over the building and may, if he deems you worthy of his attention, show you into the pretty garden with its fountain and heady scent of jasmine – a shady stunner.

Budget

Garden Court Hotel

30-31 Kensington Gardens Square, Bayswater, W2 4BG (7229 2553, www.gardencourthotel. co.uk). Bayswater or Queensway tube. **Rooms** 39. **Map** p394 B6.

Once people have discovered the Garden Court Hotel, they tend to keep coming back, says Edward Connolly, owner-manager of this long-established hotel, with quiet pride. There aren't many places this close to Hyde Park and Portobello Market that give such excellent value for money and impeccable service. The rooms in this grand Victorian terrace have a bright, modern look and plenty of space, and the lounge, with its wood floor, leather-covered furniture, sprightly floral wallpaper and elegant mantelpiece, is a lovely place to linger.

Stylotel

160-162 Sussex Gardens, Paddington, W2 1UD (7723 1026, www.stylotel.com). Edgware Road tube, or Marylebone or Paddington tube/rail. **Rooms** 48. **Map** p395 E6.

Partly due to the young manager's enthusiasm, it's hard not to like this place. It's a retro-futurist dream: metal floors and panelling, lots of royal blue (the hall walls, the padded headboards) and pod bathrooms. But the real deal at Stylotel is its bargain studio and apartment (respectively, £120-£150 and £150-£200, with breakfast included), around the corner above a pub. Designed – like the rest of the hotel – by the owner's son, they suggest he's calmed down with age. Here's real minimalist chic: sleek brushed steel or white glass wall panels; simply styled contemporary furniture upholstered in black or white.

FURTHER AFIELD

We've divided this chapter into sections that correspond with the Explore chapters earlier in the book. This final section gathers some disparate recommendations: a classic in the beautiful back of beyond; and a cluster of useful and affordable options – one in Hampstead, one in Docklands and a few around Earl's Court.

Expensive

★ Bingham

61-63 Petersham Road, Richmond, Surrey, TW10 6UT (8940 0902, www.thebingham.co.uk). Richmond tube/Overground/rail. **Rooms** 15.

Blessed with a wonderful riverside location, a visit to the Bingham is like a holiday out of town. Six of its individually styled and high-ceilinged rooms overlook the Thames; all of them are named after a poet or poem, in honour of the Bingham's artistic past (lesbian aunt-and-niece couple Katherine Harris Bradley and Edith Emma Cooper lived here in the 1890s, regularly hosting members of the Aesthetic Movement while they were in residence). Each room accommodates an ample bathtub and shower, art deco touches to the furnishings and irresistibly fluffy duck-and-goose-feather duvets. Run by the Trinder family for the last 25 years, the Bingham manages to feel both grand and boutique. It's a real away-from-home treat.

Moderate

Aloft

One Eastern Gateway, Royal Victoria Dock, Docklands, E16 1FR (3203 0700, www. aloftlondonexcel.com). Custom House or Prince Regent DLR. **Rooms** 252.

In the (Dock)land where chain mediocrity or bland corporate efficiency prevails, Aloft – a cheaper option from the swanky W chain (see p352) – is refreshing. Outside, the design is rather cool, a swoop of shiny surfaces with charming coloured lighting; inside, service is winningly offhand. Shove your credit card into the self-check-in and your key card is dispensed, giving you access to the upper floors by lift, where further funky lighting guides you to your room (nicely finished, masculine decor; remote keyboard to operate the telly; free Wi-Fi; decently appointed wet room). Your card also gets you into the pool and gym, while careless packers have a coin-op mobile phone charger in the lobby. Aloft is right at the exit from the ExCeL convention centre, so Friday night in the bar-diner is lively with post-convention hair being let down.

Garret

Troubadour, 263-267 Old Brompton Road, Earl's Court, SW5 9JA (7370 1434, www.troubadour. co.uk). West Brompton tube/Overground/rail. **Rooms** 2. **Map** p396 B11.
This idiosyncratic attic apartment is an absolute treat. High above the Troubadour, a 1960s counter-culture café that still hosts poetry and music events, it's unjustly named: yes, the rooms are in the attic and have charming pitched roofs, but there are acres of space for two – and even enough for a small family, if the kids sleep on the pull-out sofa in the lounge-kitchen. The huge, high main bed lies under a skylight and there's a writing desk, but any thought of poetic torment is banished by the well-executed Arts and Crafts decor and fully equipped kitchen area, right down to the cafetière and wines. A new room, the Eleanor, has recently been added.

Mayflower Hotel

26-28 Trebovir Road, Earl's Court, SW5 9NJ (7370 0991, www.themayflowerhotel.co.uk). Earl's Court tube. **Rooms** 56. **Map** p396 B11

After fighting on the front lines of the Earl's Court budget-hotel style revolution, the Mayflower's taken the struggle to other parts of London (New Linden; *see p363*). But this is where the lushly contemporary house style evolved, proving that affordability can be opulently chic. The recent complete refurbishment of the hotel, involving public areas and all the guestrooms, shows that it's not resting on its laurels. Hand-carved Asian artefacts complement the richly coloured fabrics. The facilities, too, are well up to scratch, featuring marble bathrooms, Egyptian cotton sheets, free Wi-Fi and CD players in the rooms.

Twenty Nevern Square

20 Nevern Square, Earl's Court, SW5 9PD (7565 9555, www.20nevernsquare.com). Earl's Court tube. **Rooms** 25. **Map** p396 A11.
Only the less-than-posh location of this immaculate boutique hotel keeps the rates reasonable. Tucked away in a private garden square, it feels far from its locale. The modern-colonial style was created by its well-travelled owner, who personally sourced many of the exotic and antique furnishings (as well as those in sister hotel the Mayflower; *see left*). In the sleek marble bathrooms, toiletries are tidied away in decorative caskets, but the beds are the real stars: from elaborately carved four-posters to Egyptian sleigh styles, all with luxurious mattresses. The vaguely Far Eastern feel extends into the lounge and the airy conservatory, with its dark wicker furniture.

Budget

Hampstead Village Guesthouse

2 Kemplay Road, Hampstead, NW3 1SY (7435 8679, www.hampsteadguesthouse.com). Hampstead tube. **Rooms** 11.

Qbic Hotel London City. *See p363.*

ESSENTIAL INFORMATION

Owner Annemarie van der Meer loves to point out all the quirky space-saving surprises as she shows you round her wonderful and idiosyncratic bed and breakfast: here's the folding sink, there's the bed that pops out of an antique wardrobe… The special atmosphere at this double-fronted Victorian house, set on a quiet Hampstead street, means that guests return year after year. Each room is uniquely decorated with eclectic furnishings and there's a self-contained studio with its own kitchen. All guests may make use of a range of home comforts, from hot-water bottles to mobile phones, as well as a laptop to borrow and free Wi-Fi. Breakfast (which costs extra) may be taken in the garden that surrounds this lovely property on all four sides.

APARTMENT RENTAL

Holiday Serviced Apartments (0808 123 4477, www.holidayapartments.co.uk) specialises in holiday lets. **London Holiday Accommodation** (7265 0882, www. londonholiday.co.uk) offers half a dozen decent-priced self-catering options next to Tower Bridge. For serviced apartments, try the South Bank or Earl's Court 'campuses' run by **Allstay Apartments** (3465 9100, www.allstay.co.uk). **Accommodation Outlet** (www.outlet4 property.com) is a lesbian and gay agency that has some excellent properties across London.

CAMPING & CARAVANNING

If putting yourself at the mercy of English weather in a far-flung suburban field doesn't put you off, the difficult transport links into central London might do the job instead. Still, you can't really beat the prices.

Crystal Palace Caravan Club *Crystal Palace Parade, Crystal Palace, SE19 1UF (8778 7155, www.caravanclub.co.uk). Crystal Palace Overground/rail or bus 3.* **Open** *Mar-Sept* 9am-6pm daily. *Oct-Jan* 9.30am-5.30pm daily.

STAYING WITH THE LOCALS

Several agencies can arrange for individuals and families to stay in Londoners' homes. The **B&B and Homestay Association** (www.bbha.org. uk) lists many of them. They include **At Home in London** (8748 2701, www.athomeinlondon. co.uk), **London Bed & Breakfast Agency** (7586 2768, www.londonbb.com) and **London Homestead Services** (7286 5115, www. lhslondon.co.uk). There is usually a minimum length of stay. Of course, all this seems a little old-fashioned now: **www.airbnb.co.uk** has made a rapid transition from in-the-know insider funkiness to the mainstream, with its offer of 'unique places to stay from local hosts'. It doesn't

offer a curated selection of properties, of course, and that notion of 'hosting' has rather gone since the early days, but you'll get a good range of places to choose from – and plenty of feedback from other clients to keep you from bad decisions.

UNIVERSITY RESIDENCES

During vacations, much of London's dedicated student accommodation is available to visitors. Central locations can make these a bargain.

International Students House *229 Great Portland Street, Marylebone, W1W 5PN (7631 8300, www.ish.org.uk). Great Portland Street tube.* **No credit cards.** **Map** p398 H4.
King's College Conference & Vacation Bureau *Strand Bridge House, 138-142 the Strand, Covent Garden, WC2R 1HH (7848 1700, www.kings venues.com). Temple tube.* **No credit cards.** **Map** p401 L7.
LSE *Sardinia House Houghton Street, WC2A 2AE (7955 7676, www.lsevacations.co.uk). Holborn or Temple tube.* **Map** p404 O8.
The LSE has vacation rentals across town, but Bankside House is the best located.

YOUTH HOSTELS

For Youth Hostel Assocation (YHA) venues, you can get extra reductions on the rates detailed below if you're a member of the IYHF (International Youth Hostel Federation): you'll pay £3 less a night. Joining costs only £20 (£10 for under-26s), and can be done on arrival or through www.yha.org.uk prior to departure. YHA hostel beds are arranged either in dormitories or in twin rooms. Our favourite hostels are reviewed (**YHA London Central**, *see p358*; **Clink78**, *see p358*), but those listed below are all handily located across town.

Earl's Court *38 Bolton Gardens, Earl's Court, SW5 0AQ (0845 371 9114, www.yha.org.uk). Earl's Court tube.* **Open** 24hrs daily. **Map** p396 B11.
Meininger Baden-Powell House *65-67 Queen's Gate, South Kensington, SW7 5JS (3318 1407, www.meininger-hostels.com). Gloucester Road or South Kensington tube.* **Map** p397 D10.
Oxford Street *14 Noel Street, Soho, W1F 8GJ (0845 371 9133, www.yha.org.uk). Oxford Circus tube.* **Open** 24hrs daily. **Map** p398 J6.
St Pancras *79-81 Euston Road, King's Cross, NW1 2QE (0845 371 9344, www.yha.org.uk). King's Cross St Pancras tube/rail.* **Open** 24hrs daily. **Map** p399 L3.
St Paul's *36 Carter Lane, the City, EC4V 5AB (0845 371 9012, www.yha.org.uk). St Paul's tube or Blackfriars rail.* **Open** 24hrs daily. **Map** p404 O6.

Getting Around

ARRIVING & LEAVING

By air

Gatwick Airport *0844 892 0322, www.gatwickairport.com. About 30 miles south of London, off the M23.* Of the three rail services that link Gatwick to London, the quickest is the **Gatwick Express** (0345 850 1530, www.gatwickexpress.com) to Victoria; it takes 30mins and runs 4.30am-12.30am daily. Tickets cost £19.90 single or £34.90 for an open return. Under-16s pay £9.95 for a single and £17.45 for returns; under-5s go free. Online prices are cheaper.

Southern (0345 127 2920, www. southernrailway.com) also runs a rail service between Gatwick and Victoria, with trains every 5-10mins (hourly 2-4am and every 15-30mins midnight-2am, 4-6am). It takes about 35mins, and costs £15.40 for a single, £15.50 for a day return (after 9.30am) and £29 for an open period return. Under-16s get half-price tickets; under-5s go free. Book online and save 10%.

Thameslink Great Northern (www.thameslinkrailway.com) costs £16.40 single and £19.30 day return (after 9.30am).

A **taxi** to the centre costs about £100 and takes a bit over an hour.

Heathrow Airport *0844 335 1801, www.heathrowairport.com. About 15 miles west of London, off the M4.* The **Heathrow Express** train (0845 600 1515, www.heathrow express.co.uk) runs to Paddington every 15mins (5.10am-11.25pm daily) and takes 15-20mins. Tickets cost £21.50 single and £35 return (more if you buy on board); under-15s travel at half-price; under-2s free. Many airlines have check-in desks at Paddington Station.

The journey by tube is longer but cheaper. The 50-60min **Piccadilly line** ride into central London costs £5.70 one way (£3 11-15s). Trains run every few minutes from about 6am to 12.30am daily (7am-11.30pm Sun). Fares using Oyster cards are cheaper (£5.10 and £0.75 11-15s).

The **Heathrow Connect** (0345 604 1515, www.heathrowconnect. com) rail service offers direct access to Hayes, Southall, Hanwell, West Ealing, Ealing Broadway and Paddington stations in west and north-west London. The trains run

every half-hour, from 4.42am to 11.05pm, terminating at Heathrow Central (Terminals 1, 2 and 3). From there to Terminal 4 get the free shuttle; between Central and Terminal 5, there's free use of the Heathrow Express. A single from Paddington is £10.10; an open return is £20.20.

National Express (0871 781 8178, www.nationalexpress.com) runs daily coach services to London Victoria (90mins, 4.20am-10.05pm daily), leaving Heathrow Central bus terminal every 20-30mins. It's £6 for a single (£3 under-16s) or £11 (£5.50 under-16s) for a return.

A **taxi** into town will cost £45-£85 and take 30-60mins.

London City Airport *7646 0088, www.londoncityairport.com. About 9 miles east of London.* The **Docklands Light Railway** (DLR) includes a stop for London City Airport and runs every 8-15mins. The journey to Bank station in the City takes around 20mins, and trains run 5.36am-12.16am Mon-Sat, 7.06am-11.16pm Sun. Tickets cost £4.80; £2.40 11-15s. A **taxi** costs around £40 to central London.

Luton Airport *01582 405100, www. london-luton.com. About 30 miles north of London, J10 off the M1.* It's a short shuttle bus ride from the airport to Luton Airport Parkway station. From here, the **Thameslink Great Northern** rail service (*see left*) calls at many stations; journey time is 35-45mins. Trains leave every 15mins or so and cost £13.50 one-way and £23.50 return. Trains between Luton and St Pancras run at least hourly all night.

By coach, the Luton to Victoria journey takes 60-90mins. **Green Line** (0844 801 7261, www.green line.co.uk) runs a 24hr service. A single is £10 and returns cost £15; under-15s £7 single, £10 return; under-5s free.

A **taxi** to London costs £100.

Stansted Airport *0844 335 1803, www.stanstedairport.com. About 35 miles north-east of London, J8 off the M11.* The **Stansted Express** train (0845 748 4950, www.stansted express. com) runs to and from Liverpool Street Station; the journey time is 40-45mins. Trains leave every

15mins, and tickets cost £19 single, £32 return; under-16s travel half-price, under-5s free.

Several companies run coaches to central London. The **National Express** service (0871 781 8178, www.nationalexpress.com) from Stansted to Victoria takes at least 80mins. Coaches run roughly every 15mins (24hrs daily), more at peak times. A single is £10.50 (£6 for under-16s), return is £20 (£9.50 for under-16s).

A **taxi** into the centre of London costs around £100.

By coach

Coaches run by **National Express** (0871 781 8178, www.national express.com), the biggest coach company in the UK, arrive at **Victoria Coach Station** (164 Buckingham Palace Road, SW1W 9TP, 0343 222 1234, www.tfl.gov.uk), a good 10min walk from Victoria tube station. This is where companies such as **Eurolines** (0871 781 8178, www.eurolines.co.uk) dock their European services.

By rail

Trains from mainland Europe run by Eurostar (0342 186 186, www. eurostar.com) arrive at **St Pancras International** (Pancras Road, Euston Road, N1C 4QP, 7843 7688, www.stpancras.com).

PUBLIC TRANSPORT

Information

Details on timetables and other travel information are provided by **Transport for London** (0343 222 1234, www.tfl.gov.uk). Complaints or comments on most forms of public transport can also be taken up with **London Travel Watch** (3176 2999, www.londontravelwatch.org.uk).

Information Centres
These offer help with the tube, buses and DLR; unless stated otherwise, you'll find them in the stations below. They are undergoing a minor expansion, due to finish in summer 2015: expect opening hours to be extended at Paddington, Gatwick and Euston. Call 0343 222 1234 for more information.

Euston *opposite Platform 10*
7.15am-7pm Mon-Thur; 7.15am-8pm Fri, Sat; 8.15am-7pm Sun.
Gatwick *North Terminal arrivals*
9.15am-5pm daily.
Heathrow Terminals 1, 2, 3
7.30am-7.30pm daily.
King's Cross *Western Ticket Hall* 7.15am-8pm Mon-Sat; 8.15am-7pm Sun.
Liverpool Street 7.15am-7pm Mon-Thur, Sat; 7.15am-8pm Fri; 8.15am-7pm Sun.
Paddington *opposite Platform 1* 8.15am-3pm daily.
Piccadilly Circus 8am-7pm Mon-Fri; 9.15am-7pm Sat; 9.15am-6pm Sun.
Victoria *opposite Platform 8* 7.15am-8pm Mon-Sat; 8.15am-7pm Sun.

Fares & tickets

Tube and DLR fares are based on a system of six zones, stretching 12 miles out from the centre of London. A flat cash fare of £4.80 per journey applies across zones 1-3 on the tube, and £6 for zones 1-6; customers save up to £2.50 per journey with a pre-pay Oyster card or by paying with a contactless debit or credit card. Anyone caught without a ticket, Oyster or contactless card is subject to an £80 on-the-spot fine (reduced to £40 if you pay within three weeks).

Using the system It is best to use either your contactless credit/debit card or to get an Oyster card (for both, *see right*). The latter can be obtained from www.tfl.gov.uk/tickets, by calling 0343 222 1234, at tube stations, Travel Information Centres, some rail stations and newsagents.

To enter and exit the tube using an Oyster (or contactless) card, simply touch it to the yellow reader, which will open the gates. Make sure you also touch the card to the reader when you exit the tube, or you'll be charged a higher fare when you next use your card to enter a station. On certain lines, you'll see a pink 'validator' – touch this reader in addition to the yellow entry/exit readers and on some routes it will reduce your fare.

Alternatively, paper single or day tickets can be bought from self-service ticket machines. TfL is in the process of closing all Underground ticket offices; carry a charged-up Oyster card to avoid being stranded. If you are using a paper ticket, enter by placing it in the slot with the black magnetic strip facing down, then pull it out of the top to open the gates. Exiting is done in much the same way; however, if you have a single journey ticket, it will be retained by the gate as you leave.

Oyster cards A pre-paid smart-card, Oyster is a far cheaper way of getting around on public transport than buying paper tickets. You can charge up standard Oyster cards at tube stations, Information Centres (*see p367*), some rail stations and newsagents. There is a £5 refundable deposit payable on each card; to collect your deposit, call 0343 222 1234. Young visitor cards are also available for children.

Visitor Oyster cards are available from Gatwick Express outlets, National Express coaches, Superbreak, www.visitbritainshop.com, Oxford Tube coach service and on Eurostar services. The only difference between Visitor Oysters and 'normal' Oysters is that they come pre-loaded with money.

A tube journey in zone 1 using Oyster pay-as-you-go costs £2.30 (85p 11-15s), compared to the cash fare of £4.80. A single tube ride within zones 2, 3, 4, 5 or 6 costs £2.80 (85p 11-15s); single journeys from zones 1 through to 6 using Oyster are £5.10 (6.30-9.30am, 4-7pm Mon-Fri) or £3.10 (all other times), or 85p for 11-15s. Up to four children under 11 can travel for free when travelling with an adult.

Oyster now has day capping of £6.40 if you're travelling between zones 1-2 off peak, £9.20 between zones 1-4 off peak, and £11.70 between zones 1-6 off peak – it thus works out cheaper than a Day Travelcard (*see below*).

Contactless payment At the end of 2014, TfL launched contactless payment. If you have a credit or debit card with the contactless symbol (»))), you can use it instead of getting an Oyster card – and you will pay the same fare. Just place it on the yellow or pink readers in exactly the same way as you would an Oyster. If you use public transport every day for a week during your stay, it's likely to be marginally cheaper even than Oyster: usage is capped at the level of a weekly – not daily – Travelcard.

Day Travelcards If you're only using the tube, DLR and buses, using Oyster to pay-as-you-go will always be capped at the same price as or slightly lower than an equivalent Day Travelcard. However, if you're also using certain National Rail services, Oyster may not be accepted: opt, instead, for a Day Travelcard, a standard ticket with a coded stripe that allows travel across all networks.

Anytime Day Travelcards can be used all day. They cost from £12

for zones 1-2 (£6 child), up to £17 for zones 1-6 (£8.50 child). Tickets are valid for journeys begun by 4.30am the next day. The cheaper **Off-Peak Day Travelcard** allows travel after 9.30am Mon-Fri and all day at weekends and public holidays. It costs £12 for zones 1-6.

Children Under-5s travel free on buses without the need to provide any proof of identity. Five-to 10-year-olds can also travel free, but need to obtain a 5-10 Zip Oyster photocard. For details, visit www.tfl.gov.uk/tickets or call 0343 222 1234.

An 11-15 Zip Oyster photocard is needed by 11- to 15-year-olds to pay as they go on the tube/DLR and to buy 7-day, monthly or longer period Travelcards.

Photocards Photocards are not required for 7-Day Travelcards or Bus Passes, adult-rate Travelcards or Bus Passes charged on an Oyster card. For details of how to obtain 5-10, 11-15 or 16+ Oyster photocards, see www.tfl.gov.uk/tickets or call 0343 222 1234. There is a non-refundable £10 administration fee for each ID card.

London Underground

Delays are fairly common, with lines or sections of lines frequently closed at weekends for engineering work. Trains are hot and crowded in rush hour (7.30-9.30am and 4.30-6.30pm Mon-Fri) – avoid the rush by travelling after 9.30am and you'll also pay less for your fare. The 12 colour-coded lines that together comprise the underground rail system (for a map, *see pp414-415*) – also known as 'the tube' – remain the quickest way to get around, carrying some 3.5 million passengers every weekday. Comments or complaints are dealt with by **TfL Customer Services** on 0343 222 1234 (8am-8pm daily).

Timetables Tube trains run daily from around 5.30am (except Sunday, when they start an hour or so later, and Christmas Day, when there's no service). You shouldn't have to wait more than 10mins for a train; during peak times, services should run every 2-3mins. Times of last trains vary; they're usually around 12.30am daily (11.30pm on Sun). The tubes currently run all night only on New Year's Eve, but a limited 24hr weekend service (the 'night tube') is promised from September 2015, with rapid expansion of that service mooted. Otherwise, you're limited to night buses (*see p369*).

ESSENTIAL INFORMATION

Fares The single fare for adults across the network is £4.80 for journeys within zones 1-3; £6 for zones 1-6; £7 for zones 1-7; £12 for zones 1-9. Using Oyster pay-as-you-go or a contactless card, journeys within zone 1 cost £2.30; zones 1-2 costs £2.30 or £2.90, depending on the time of day; zones 1-6 costs £3.10 or £5.10. The single fare for children aged 5-15 is 75p or 85p for any journey in zones 1-6 depending on the time of day. Under-5s travel free.

Overground

The Overground (0343 222 1234) was one of former mayor Ken Livingstone's more significant legacies to London. A patchwork of different rail services, tracing a complex orbital route roughly following the boundary of zones 2 and 3, was stitched together and opened in 2010 as the Overground, under the control of Transport for London and with coherent new branding (the orange-and-white line on the tube map; *see p414-415*). For those planning to visit areas of London with poor Underground coverage – notably (and perhaps not coincidentally) some of the buzzier bits of east and south London – the Overground is a valuable friend.

Fares Fares on the Overground are the same as for the tube.

National Rail services

Independently run commuter services co-ordinated by **National Rail** (0845 748 4950, www.national rail.co.uk) leave from the city's main rail stations. Visitors heading to south London, or to more remote destinations such as Hampton Court Palace, use these services.

Fares Travelcards are valid on these services within the right zones, but not all routes accept Oyster pay-as-you-go or contactless payments.

Docklands Light Railway

The mostly elevated DLR trains (0343 222 1234, www.tfl.gov.uk/dlr) run from Bank station (where they connect with the Central, Northern and Waterloo & City lines) or Tower Gateway, close to Tower Hill tube (Circle and District lines). At Westferry station, the line splits east and south via Island Gardens to Greenwich and Lewisham; a change at Poplar or Canning Town can take you north to Stratford. The easterly branch forks after Canning Town to

either Beckton or Woolwich Arsenal. Trains run 5.30am-12.40am daily, and there are lots of good views of Docklands to be enjoyed.

Fares Fares are the same as the tube.

Buses

Buses are now cash-free, so you must have a ticket, valid pass or, better, an Oyster card or contactless payment card (for both, *see p368*) before boarding any bus. You can buy a ticket from machines in tube and rail stations. Inspectors patrol buses at random; if you don't have a ticket, card or pass, you may be fined £80 (£40 if you pay within 21 days).

All buses are now low-floor vehicles that are accessible to wheelchair-users and passengers with buggies. The only exception is Heritage route 15, which is served by the historic and world-famous open-platform Routemaster buses.

Fares Using Oyster pay-as-you-go costs £1.50 a trip; your total daily payment, regardless of how many journeys you take, will be capped at £4.40. Under-16s travel for free (using an Under-11 or 11-15 Oyster photocard, as appropriate; *see p368*).

Night buses Many bus routes operate 24hrs a day, seven days a week. There are also some special night buses with an 'N' prefix, which run from about 11pm to 6am – they're used by a sometimes exhilarating combination of nightshift workers and partiers, in different proportions depending on the time of night. Most night services run every 15-30mins, but busier routes run every 10mins or so. Fares are the same as for daytime buses; Bus Passes and Travelcards can be used at no extra fare until 4.30am of the morning after they expire, with Oyster day-capping in effect until then too.

Green Line buses These serve the suburbs within 40 miles of London (0844 801 7261, www.greenline. co.uk); services run 24hrs a day.

Water transport

Most river services operate every 20-60mins between 10.30am and 5pm, and may run more often and later in summer. For commuters, **Thames Clippers** (www.thames clippers.com) runs a service between Embankment Pier and Royal Arsenal Woolwich Pier (limited period, otherwise to North Greenwich);

stops include Blackfriars, Bankside, London Bridge, Canary Wharf and Greenwich. A standard day roamer ticket (valid 9am-9pm) costs £17.35, £8.65 for a child, while a single from Embankment to Greenwich is £7.15, £3.60 under-16s, or £6.44 for Oyster cardholders.

Westminster Passenger Service Association (7930 2062, www.wpsa.co.uk) runs a daily service from Westminster Pier to Kew, Richmond and Hampton Court from April to October. At around £12 for a single, it's not cheap, but it is a lovely way to see the city, and there are discounts of 33%-50% for Travelcard holders.

Thames River Services (7930 4097, www.thamesriverservices. co.uk) operates from the same pier, with trips to Greenwich and Tower Pier, and the Thames Barrier from May to Oct. A trip to Greenwich costs £12.25. Travelcard holders get a third off.

TAXIS
Black cabs

The licensed London taxi, aka 'black cab' (although they now come in many colours), is a much-loved feature of London life. Drivers must pass a test called 'the Knowledge' to prove they know every street in central London, and the shortest route to it.

If a taxi's orange 'For Hire' sign is lit, it can be hailed. If a taxi stops, the cabbie must take you to your destination if it's within seven miles. Fares rise after 8pm on weekdays and at weekends.

You can book black cabs using the the very handy free **Hailo** app, or from **Radio Taxis** (7272 0272) and **Dial-a-Cab** (7253 5000); credit cards only, with a booking fee of £2 plus a 12.5% handling charge). Complaints about black cabs should be made to the **Public Carriage Office** (0845 602 7000, www.tfl.gov.uk/pco). Note the cab's badge number, which should be displayed in the rear of the cab and on its back bumper.

Minicabs

Minicabs (saloon cars) are generally cheaper than black cabs, but can be less reliable. The police and TfL regularly warn against the use of any but licensed firms (look for a disc in the front and rear windows), so be sure to avoid drivers who illegally tout for business in the street: if they're unlicensed they might well be uninsured and may be dangerous.

ESSENTIAL INFORMATION

ESSENTIAL INFORMATION

If you text **HOME** to 60835 ('60TFL'), Transport for London will reply with the numbers of the two nearest licensed minicab operators and the number for **Radio Taxis**, which provides licensed black taxis in London (it costs 35p plus standard call rate). You can also use the **Uber** app – controversial with black cab drivers, who regard the app as a kind of metering – to hail a minicab. Fully licensed minicab firms include **Addison Lee** (7487 9000) and **Ladycars** (8558 8510; women-only drivers). Whatever method you use to call your cab, ask the price when you book and confirm it with the driver before you get in.

DRIVING

London's roads are often clogged with traffic and roadworks, and parking (*see right*) is a nightmare: walking or using public transport is almost always the better option. If you hire a car, you can use any valid licence from outside the EU for up to a year after arrival. Speed limits in the city are generally 20 or 30mph.

Congestion charge

Drivers coming into central London between 7am and 6pm Monday to Friday have to pay £11.50, a fee known as the congestion charge. The congestion charge zone is bordered by Marylebone, Euston and King's Cross (N), Old Street roundabout (NE), Aldgate (E), Tower Bridge Road (SE), Elephant & Castle (S), Vauxhall, Victoria (SW), Park Lane and Edgware Road (W). You'll know when you're about to drive into the charging zone from the red 'C' signs on the road. Enter the postcode of your destination at www.tfl.gov.uk/modes/congestioncharging to discover if it's in the charging zone.

Passes can be bought from some newsagents, garages and NCP car parks; you can also pay online at www.tfl.gov.uk/modes/congestion charging, by phone on 0343 222 2222 or by SMS. You can pay any time during the day; payments are also accepted until midnight on the next charging day, although the fee is £14 if you pay then. You only pay once per day, no matter how many times you go in and out of the zone. Expect a fine of £65 if you fail to pay, rising to £130 if you delay payment.

Breakdown services

AA (Automobile Association) *0800 917 8612 information, 0845 788 7766 breakdown, www.theaa.com.*

ETA (Environmental Transport Association) *0333 000 1234, www.eta.co.uk.*
RAC (Royal Automobile Club) *01922 437 000 information, 0800 073 7283 breakdown, www.rac.co.uk.*

Parking

Central London is scattered with parking meters, but finding an unoccupied one is usually difficult. Meters cost upwards of £1 for 15mins, and in some areas they are limited to 2hrs; if you're going to spend a lot of time driving in particular areas, find out whether there's an app for that location that allows easy payment – sometimes even permitting remote top-up payments. Parking on a single or double yellow line, a red line or in residents' parking areas during the day is illegal, and you may be fined, clamped or towed.

However, in the evening (from 6pm or 7pm in much of central London) and at various times at weekends, parking on single yellow lines is legal and free. If you find a clear spot on a single yellow line during the evening, look for a sign giving the local regulations. Meters also become free at certain times during evenings and weekends. Parking on double yellow lines and red routes is always illegal. Use an app like **AppyParking** to help you find the nearest free car parking; otherwise, there are many **NCP** car parks (0345 050 7080, www.ncp.co.uk), open 24hrs a day.

Clamping & vehicle removal The immobilising of illegally parked vehicles with a clamp is common in London. You'll have to stump up a release fee (£125) and show a valid licence. The payment centre will de-clamp your car within four hours. If you don't remove your car at once, it may get clamped again, so wait by your vehicle.

If your car has disappeared, it's either been stolen or, if it was parked illegally, towed to a car pound by the local authorities. A release fee of £200 is levied for removal, plus upwards of £21 per day from the first midnight after removal. You'll also probably get a parking ticket, typically £130 (reduced by 50% if paid within 14 days). Call the **Trace Information Service** hotline (0845 206 8602).

CYCLING

There has been a lot of talk about improving provision for cyclists in London – especially since six cyclists

were killed in a single fortnight at the end of 2013 – and impressive sums of transport budget set aside for the purpose. Certain notorious junctions have been improved and work has begun on the 'superhighways' – segregated north–south and east–west cycling routes through the centre of town – but it will be a good while before their success can be judged. Nonetheless, no one needs to be scared of London's streets – some 180 million journeys are made each year by bike, almost all of them safely. Ride calmly, assertively and obeying the rules of the road, and *always* avoid getting caught on the inside of a left-turning bus or lorry. TfL's 'Cycle safety tips' are at www.tfl.gov.uk/modes/cycling. Serious cyclists can contact the **London Cycle Network** (www.londoncycle network.org.uk) and **London Cycling Campaign** (7234 9310, www.lcc.org.uk).

TfL also runs a handy **cycle hire scheme** (0843 222 1234, www.tfl.gov.uk) that has been deemed sufficiently successful to see expansions east and west of an initial zone of operations in central London, even though claims the scheme would be self-funding through sponsorship deals and hire fees remain wide of the mark. Nicknamed 'Boris Bikes' after Mayor Johnson, who introduced them, the cycles – distinguished by their red Santander sponsorship branding – are picked up from and returned to a string of 24hr bicycle stations. To hire a bike, go to a docking station, touch the 'Hire a cycle' icon and insert a credit or debit card. The machine will print out a five-digit access code, which you then tap into the docking point of a bike, releasing the cycle, and away you go. £2 buys 24-hour access to the bikes and the first 30 minutes are free.

WALKING

By far the best way to see London is on foot, but the city's street layout is complicated. We've included street maps of central London in the back of this book, as well as area maps in the appropriate chapters for the city's most important districts; the standard Geographers' *London A-Z* or Collins' *London Street Atlas* are useful supplements. There's route advice at www.tfl.gov.uk/modes/find-your-way, and look out for the yellow-topped 'Legible London' information posts as you stroll around (www.tfl.gov.uk/microsites/legible-london/). And no matter how well you know our city, going for a walk will reveal further secrets.

Resources A-Z

TRAVEL ADVICE

For up-to-date information on travel to a specific country – including the latest on safety and security, health issues, local laws and customs – contact your home country government's department of foreign affairs. Most have websites with useful advice for would-be travellers.

AUSTRALIA
www.smartraveller.gov.au

CANADA
www.voyage.gc.ca

NEW ZEALAND
www.safetravel.govt.nz

REPUBLIC OF IRELAND
foreignaffairs.gov.ie

UK
www.fco.gov.uk/travel

USA
www.state.gov/travel

ADDRESSES

London postcodes are less helpful than they could be for locating addresses. The first element starts with a compass point – N, E, SE, SW, W and NW, plus the smaller EC (East Central) and WC (West Central). However, the number that follows relates not to geography (unless it's a 1, which indicates central) but to alphabetical order. So N2 is way out in the boondocks (East Finchley), while W2 covers the very central Bayswater district.

AGE RESTRICTIONS

Buying/drinking alcohol 18.
Driving 17.
Sex 16.
Smoking 18.

CUSTOMS

Citizens entering the UK from outside the EU must adhere to duty-free import limits:

● 200 cigarettes or 100 cigarillos or 50 cigars or 250g of tobacco
● 4 litres still table wine plus either 1 litre spirits or strong liqueurs (above 22% abv) or 2 litres fortified wine (under 22% abv), sparkling wine or other liqueurs
● other goods to the value of no more than £390

The import of meat, poultry, fruit, plants, flowers and protected animals is restricted or forbidden; there are no restrictions on the import or export of currency if travelling from another EU country. If you are travelling from outside the EU, amounts over €10,000 must be declared on arrival.

People over the age of 17 arriving from an EU country are able to import unlimited goods for their own personal use, if bought tax-paid (so not duty-free). For more details, see www.gov.uk.

DISABLED

As a city that evolved long before the needs of disabled people were considered, London is difficult for wheelchair users, though access and facilities are slowly improving. The capital's bus fleet is now low-floor for easier wheelchair access; there are no steps for any of the city's trams; and all DLR stations have either lifts or ramp access. However, steps and escalators to the tube and overland trains mean they are often of only limited use to wheelchair users. A blue symbol on the tube map (see pp414-415) indicates stations with step-free access. The *Step-free Tube Guide* map is free; call 0843 222 1234 for more details. For London Overground, call 0343 222 1234.

Most major attractions and hotels offer good accessibility, though provisions for the hearing- and sight-disabled are patchier. Enquire about facilities in advance. *Access in London* is an invaluable reference book for disabled travellers. It's available for a £10 donation (sterling cheque, cash US dollars or via PayPal to accessinlondon@gmail.com) from **Access Project** (39 Bradley Gardens, W13 8HE, www. accessinlondon.org).

Artsline
www.artsline.org.uk.
Information on disabled access to arts and culture.
Can Be Done
Congress House, 14 Lyon Road, Harrow, Middx, HA1 2EN (8907 2400, www.canbedone.co.uk). Harrow on the Hill tube/rail. **Open** 9.30am-5pm Mon-Fri.
Disabled-adapted holidays and tours in London, around the UK and worldwide.
Disability Rights UK
Ground floor, CAN Mezzanine, 49-51 East Road, Islington, N1 6AH (0808 800 0082, 0084 textphone, www. disabilityrightsuk.org). Old Street tube/rail. **Open** 9am-8pm Mon-Fri; 10am-2pm Sat. **Map** p402 P3.
A national organisation for disabled voluntary groups, publishing books and offering advice, links to other organisations for help and courses.
Tourism for All
0845 124 9971, www.tourismforall. org.uk. **Open** Helpline 9am-5pm Mon-Fri.
Information for older people and people with disabilities in relation to accessible accommodation and other tourism services.
Wheelchair Travel & Access Mini Buses
Unit 44, Martlands Industrial Estate, Smarts Heath Lane, Woking, Surrey, GU22 0RQ (01483 233640, www. wheelchair-travel.co.uk).
Hires out converted vehicles (a driver is optional), plus cars with hand controls and wheelchair-adapted vehicles.

DRUGS

Illegal drug use remains higher in London than the UK as a whole, though it's becoming less visible on the streets and in clubs. Despite fierce debate, cannabis has been reclassified from Class C to Class B (where it rejoins amphetamine), but possession of a small amount might attract no more than a warning for a first offence. More serious Class B and A drugs (ecstasy, LSD, heroin, cocaine and the like) carry stiffer penalties, with a maximum of seven years in prison for possession plus a fine.

ESSENTIAL INFORMATION

ELECTRICITY

The UK uses the European standard 220-240V, 50-cycle AC voltage. British plugs have three pins, so travellers with two-pin European appliances should bring an adaptor.

Anyone using US appliances, which run off 110-120V, 60-cycle, will need to bring or buy a voltage converter.

EMBASSIES & CONSULATES

American Embassy
24 Grosvenor Square, Mayfair, W1A 2LQ (7499 9000, http://london.usembassy.gov). Bond Street or Marble Arch tube. **Open** 8.30am-5.30pm Mon-Fri. **Map** p400 G7.

Australian High Commission
Australia House, Strand, Holborn, WC2B 4LA (7379 4334, www. uk.embassy.gov.au). Holborn or Temple tube. **Open** 9am-5pm Mon-Fri. **Map** p401 M6.

Canadian High Commission
Canada House, Trafalgar Square, Westminster, SW1Y 5BJ (7004 6000, www.canada.org.uk). Charing Cross tube/rail. **Open** 8am-4.30pm Mon-Thur; 8am-1.30pm Fri. **Map** p400 H7.

Embassy of Ireland
17 Grosvenor Place, Belgravia, SW1X 7HR (7235 2171, 7373 4339 passports & visas, www.embassy ofireland.co.uk). Hyde Park Corner tube. **Open** 9.30am-4.30pm Mon-Fri. **Map** p400 G9.

New Zealand High Commission
New Zealand House, 80 Haymarket, St James's, SW1Y 4TQ (7930 8422, www.nzembassy.com). Piccadilly Circus tube. **Open** 9am-5pm Mon-Fri. **Map** p401 K7.

EMERGENCIES

In the event of a serious accident, fire or other incident, call 999 – free from any phone, including payphones – and ask for an ambulance, the fire service or police.

For hospital Accident & Emergency departments, *see right*; for helplines, *see p373*; for police stations, *see p375*.

GAY & LESBIAN

For information on gay and lesbian life in London, *see pp259-265*. The phonelines that we list below provide general help and information for gay and lesbian people; for HIV and AIDS services, *see p373*.

London Friend
7837 3337, http://londonfriend.org. uk. **Open** 7.30-9.30pm Mon-Wed.
London Lesbian & Gay Switchboard
0300 330 0630, www.llgs.org.uk. **Open** 10am-11pm daily.

HEALTH

British citizens or those working in the UK can go to any general practitioner (GP). People ordinarily resident in the UK, including overseas students, are also permitted to register with a National Health Service (NHS) doctor. If you fall outside these categories, you will have to pay to see a GP. Your hotel concierge should be able to recommend one.

A pharmacist may dispense medicines on receipt of a prescription from a GP. NHS prescriptions cost £8.05; under-16s, those on benefits and over-60s are exempt from charges. Contraception is free for all. If you're not eligible to see an NHS doctor, you'll be charged cost price for any medicines prescribed.

Free emergency medical treatment under the NHS is available to:

● EU nationals and those of Iceland, Norway and Liechtenstein; all may also be entitled to state-provided treatment for non-emergency conditions with an EHIC (European Health Insurance Card)
● nationals of New Zealand, Russia, most former USSR states and the former Yugoslavia
● residents (irrespective of their nationality) of Anguilla, Australia, Barbados, the British Virgin Islands, the Falkland Islands, the Isle of Man, Montserrat, Poland, Romania, St Helena and the Turks & Caicos Islands
● anyone who has been in the UK for the previous 12 months, or who has come to the UK to take up permanent residence
● students and trainees whose courses require more than 12 weeks in employment in the first year
● refugees and others who have sought refuge in the UK
● people with HIV/AIDS at a special STD treatment clinic

The NHS does not charge for the following services:

● treatment in A&E wards
● emergency ambulance transport to a hospital
● diagnosis and treatment of certain communicable diseases
● family-planning services
● compulsory psychiatric treatment

Accident & emergency

Listed below are most of the central London hospitals that have Accident & Emergency (A&E) departments which are open 24 hours daily.

Charing Cross Hospital
Fulham Palace Road, Hammersmith, W6 8RF (3311 1234, www.imperial. nhs.uk). Hammersmith tube.
Chelsea & Westminster Hospital
369 Fulham Road, Chelsea, SW10 9NH (3315 8000, www.chelwest.nhs. uk). South Kensington tube. **Map** p396 C12.
Royal Free Hospital
Pond Street, Hampstead, NW3 2QG (7794 0500, www.royalfree.nhs.uk). Belsize Park tube or Hampstead Heath Overground.
Royal London Hospital
Whitechapel Road, Whitechapel, E1 1BB (3416 5000, www.bartshealth. nhs.uk). Whitechapel tube/ Overground.
St Mary's Hospital
Praed Street, Paddington, W2 1NY (3312 6666, www.imperial.nhs.uk). Paddington tube/rail. **Map** p395 D5.
St Thomas' Hospital
Westminster Bridge Road, South Bank, SE1 7EH (7188 7188, www.guysandstthomas.nhs.uk). Westminster tube or Waterloo tube/rail. **Map** p401 L9.
University College Hospital
235 Euston Road, NW1 2BU (3456 7890, www.udh.nhs.uk). Euston Square or Warren Street tube. **Map** p398 J4.

Contraception & abortion

Family-planning advice, contraceptive supplies and abortions are free to British citizens on the NHS, and to EU residents and foreign nationals living in Britain. Phone 0845 122 8690 or visit www.fpa.org. uk for your local Family Planning Association. The 'morning after' pill (around £25), effective up to 72 hours after intercourse, is available over the counter at pharmacies.

British Pregnancy Advisory Service
03845 730 4030, www.bpas.org. **Open** *Helpline* 8am-8pm Mon-Fri; 8.30am-2.30pm Sat, Sun. Callers are referred to their nearest clinic for treatment.
Brook Advisory Centre
7284 6057, 0808 802 1234 helpline, www.brook.org.uk. **Open** *Helpline* 11am-3pm Mon-Fri.

Information on sexual health, contraception and abortion, plus free pregnancy tests for under-25s.

Marie Stopes House
Family Planning Clinic/Well Woman Centre, 108 Whitfield Street, Fitzrovia, W1T 5BE (0845 300 8090, www.mariestopes.org.uk). Warren Street tube. **Open** *Clinic* 8am-4pm Mon, Tue; 9am-4pm Wed; 11am-5pm Fri. *Helpline* 24hrs daily. **Map** p398 J4.
Contraceptive advice, emergency contraception, pregnancy testing, an abortion service, cervical and health screening or gynaecological services. Fees may apply.

Dentists

Dental care is free for resident students, under-18s and people on benefits. All others must pay. To find an NHS dentist, contact the local Health Authority or a Citizens' Advice Bureau (*see right*).

Dental Emergency Care Service
Guy's Hospital, floors 17-28, Tower Wing, Great Maze Pond, SE1 9RT (7188 8006). London Bridge tube/rail. **Open** 9am-5pm Mon-Fri. **Map** p404 Q8.
Queues start forming at 8am; arrive by 10am if you're to be seen at all.

Hospitals

For a list of hospitals with Accident & Emergency departments, *see p372*; for other hospitals, check www.yell.com.

Pharmacies

Also called 'chemists' in the UK. Branches of Boots (www.boots.com) and larger supermarkets have a pharmacy. Most keep shop hours (9am-6pm Mon-Sat) but the Boots store at 44-46 Regent Street, Mayfair, W1B 5RA (7734 6126), opens until midnight (6.30pm Sun).

STDs, HIV & AIDS

NHS Genito-Urinary Clinics (such as the Centre for Sexual Health) are affiliated with major hospitals. They provide free, confidential STD testing and treatment, as well as treating other problems such as thrush and cystitis. They also offer counselling about HIV and other STDs, and can conduct blood tests.
    The NHS website (www.nhs.uk) also has information, including clinic locations. For helplines, *see right*; for abortion and contraception, *see p372*.

Mortimer Market Centre for Sexual Health
Mortimer Market, Capper Street, off Tottenham Court Road, Fitzrovia, WC1E 6JB (3317 5100, www.cnwl. nhs.uk). Goodge Street or Warren Street tube. **Open** 9am-6pm Mon, Thur; 9am-7pm Tue; 1-6pm Wed; 9am-3pm Fri. **Map** p398 J4.

Terrence Higgins Trust
314-320 Gray's Inn Road, King's Cross, WC1X 8DP (0808 802 1221, www.tht.org.uk). King's Cross St Pancras tube/rail. **Open** *Helpline* 10am-10pm Mon-Fri; noon-6pm Sat, Sun. **Map** p399 M5.
Advice for those with HIV/AIDS, their relatives, lovers and friends.

HELPLINES

Helplines dealing with sexual health issues are listed under STDs, HIV & AIDS (*see above*).

Alcoholics Anonymous *0845 769 7555, www.alcoholics-anonymous. org.uk.* **Open** 10am-10pm daily.
Citizens' Advice Bureaux *www. citizensadvice.org.uk.*
The council-run Citizens' Advice Bureaux offer free legal, financial and personal advice. Check the phone book or see the website for the address of your nearest office.
Missing People *0116 000 freephone, www.missingpeople.org. uk.* **Open** 24hrs daily.
Information on anyone who is reported missing.
NHS Direct *111, www.nhsdirect. nhs.uk.* **Open** 24hrs daily.
A free, first-stop service for medical advice on all subjects.
Rape Crisis *0808 802 9999, www. rapecrisis.org.uk.* **Open** noon-2.30pm, 7-9.30pm daily.
Information and support.
Samaritans *0845 790 9090, www. samaritans.org.* **Open** 24hrs daily.
General helpline for those under emotional stress.
Victim Support *0808 168 9111, www.victimsupport.org.uk.* **Open** 9am-9pm Mon-Fri; 9am-7pm Sat, Sun. **Map** p398 H5.
Emotional and practical support for victims of crime.

ID

Passports and photographic driver's licences are acceptable forms of ID.

INTERNET

Most hotels have free high-speed internet (though some of the more expensive ones still charge a fee) and establishments all over town,

especially cafés, have wireless access, usually free. Even the Tube is wired: see www.tfl.gov.uk/wifi.

LEFT LUGGAGE

Airports

Gatwick Airport *01293 734 887.*
Heathrow Airport *8759 3344.*
London City Airport *7646 0000.*
Luton Airport *01582 809174.*
Stansted Airport *0844 824 3109.*

Rail & bus stations

London stations tend to have left-luggage desks rather than lockers. Call 0845 748 4950 for details.
Charing Cross *7930 5444.*
Open 7am-11pm daily.
Euston *7387 1499.*
Open 7am-11pm daily.
King's Cross *7837 4334.*
Open 7am-11pm daily.
Paddington *7262 0344.*
Open 7am-11pm daily.
Victoria *7963 0957.*
Open 7am-midnight daily.

LEGAL HELP

Those in difficulties can visit a Citizens' Advice Bureau (*see left*) or contact the Law Centres Federation (*see below*). Try the **Legal Services Commission** (0845 345 4345, www. legalservices.gov.uk) for information. If you're arrested, you should call your embassy (*see p372*).

Law Centres Federation
3637 1330, www.lawcentres.org.uk. **Open** 11am-5.30pm Mon-Fri.
Free legal help for people who can't afford a lawyer and live or work in the immediate area; this office connects you with the nearest centre.

LOST PROPERTY

Always inform the police if you lose anything, if only to validate insurance claims. Only dial 999 if violence has occurred; use 101 for non-emergencies. Report lost passports both to the police and to your embassy (*see p372*).

Airports

For items left on the plane, contact the relevant airline. Otherwise, phone the following:

Gatwick Airport *01293 503162.*
Heathrow Airport *0844 824 3115.*
London City Airport *7646 0000.*
Luton Airport *01582 395219.*
Stansted Airport *0844 824 3109.*

ESSENTIAL INFORMATION

Public transport

If you've lost property in a national railway station or on a train, call 0870 000 5151, and give the operator the relevant details.

Transport for London
Lost Property Office, 200 Baker Street, Marylebone, NW1 5RZ (0343 222 1234, www.tfl.gov.uk/lostproperty). Baker Street tube. **Open** 8.30am-4pm Mon-Fri. **Map** p398 G4.
Allow two to ten working days from the time of loss. If you lose something on a bus, call 0343 222 1234 and ask for the numbers of the depots at either end of the route. For tube losses, pick up a lost-property form from any station. There is a fee to cover costs.

Taxis

The Transport for London office (*see above*) deals with property found in registered black cabs. Allow two to ten days from the time of loss. For items lost in a minicab, contact the relevant company.

MEDIA

Magazines & newspapers

Time Out remains London's only quality listings magazine – and it's free. If you want to know what's going on and whether it's any good, this is the place to look. It's widely available in central London every Tuesday. The capital's main daily paper (also free) is the sensationalist *Evening Standard*, published Monday to Friday. In the mornings, in tube station dispensers and discarded in the carriages, you'll find *Metro*, a free *Standard* spin-off.

Radio

The stations below are broadcast on standard wavebands as well as digital, where they are joined by some interesting new channels (mostly from the BBC).

Absolute *105.8 FM.* Laddish rock.
BBC London *94.9 FM.* All things to do with the capital.
BBC Radio 1 *98.8 FM.* Youth-oriented pop, indie and dance.
BBC Radio 2 *89.1 FM.* Bland during the day; better after dark.
BBC Radio 3 *91.3 FM.* Classical music dominates, but there's also discussion, world music and arts.
BBC Radio 4 *93.5 FM,* 198 LW. The BBC's main speech station is led by

news agenda-setter Today (6-9am Mon-Fri, 7-9am Sat).
BBC Radio 5 Live *693, 909 AM.* Rolling news and sport. Avoid the morning phone-ins.
BBC World Service *648 AM.* Some repeats, some new shows, transmitted globally.
Capital FM *95.8 FM.* Pop and chat.
Classic FM *100.9 FM.* Easy-listening classical.
Heart FM *106.2 FM.* Capital for grown-ups.
Kiss *100 FM.* Dance music.
LBC *97.3 FM.* Phone-ins and talk.
Magic *105.4 FM.* Familiar pop.
Resonance *104.4 FM.* Arts radio – an inventively oddball mix.
Smooth *102.2 FM.* Aural wallpaper.
XFM *104.9 FM.* Alternative-ish rock.

Television

With a multiplicity of formats, there are plenty of pay-TV options. However, the relative quality of free TV keeps subscriptions from attaining US levels.
The five main free-to-air networks are as follows:

BBC One The Corporation's mass-market station. Relies too much on soaps, game shows and lifestyle TV, but has high-quality offerings too. Excellent news coverage. As with all the BBC stations: no commercials.
BBC Two A reasonably intelligent cultural cross-section, but now upstaged by BBC Four.
ITV Weekday mass-appeal shows, with ITV2 producing similar fare.
Channel 4 Successful US imports, more or less unwatchable home-grown entertainment, some great documentaries and quality news.
Channel Five From high culture to lowbrow filth. A strange, unholy mix.

Satellite, digital and cable channels include the following:

BBC Three Often awful home-grown comedy and dismal documentary – plans are to move it to online only at some point in 2015.
BBC Four Highbrow stuff, including fine documentaries and dramas.
BBC News Rolling news.
BBC Parliament Live debates.
CBBC, CBeebies Children's programmes – the latter for toddlers.
Discovery Channel Science and nature documentaries.
E4, More4, Film4 Channel 4's entertainment and movie channels.
5USA US comedy and drama, plus Australian soaps.
ITV2, ITV3, ITV4 US shows on 2, British reruns on 3 and 4.

Sky News Rolling news.
Sky One Sky's version of ITV.
Sky Sports Four channels.

MONEY

Britain's currency is the pound sterling (£). One pound equals 100 pence (p). Coins are copper (1p, 2p), silver (round: 5p, 10p; seven-sided: 20p, 50p), yellow-gold (£1) or silver in the centre with a yellow-gold edge (£2). Paper notes are blue (£5), orange (£10), purple (£20) or red (£50). You can exchange foreign currency at banks, bureaux de change and post offices; there's no commission charge at the last of these (for addresses of the most central, *see p375*). Many large stores also accept euros (€).

Western Union *0808 234 9168, www.westernunion.co.uk.*
The old standby. Chequepoint (*see p376*) also offers this service.

Banks & ATMs

ATMs can be found inside and outside banks, in some shops and in larger stations. Machines in many commercial premises levy a charge for each withdrawal, usually £1.85. If you're visiting from outside the UK, your card should work via one of the debit networks, but check charges in advance. ATMs also allow you to make withdrawals on your credit card if you know your PIN; you'll be charged interest plus, usually, a currency-exchange fee. Generally, getting cash with a card is the cheapest form of currency exchange but there are hidden charges, so do your research.
Credit cards, especially Visa and MasterCard, are accepted in most shops (except small corner shops) and restaurants (except caffs). However, American Express and Diners Club tend to be accepted only at more expensive outlets. You will usually have to have a PIN number to make a purchase.
No commission is charged for cashing sterling travellers' cheques if you go to one of the banks affiliated with the issuing company. You do have to pay to cash travellers' cheques in foreign currencies, and to change cash. You will always need to produce ID when you want to cash travellers' cheques.

Bureaux de change

You'll be charged for cashing travellers' cheques or buying and selling foreign currency at bureaux de change. Major stations have bureaux, and there are many in tourist areas and on major shopping streets. Most open 8am-10pm.

Chequepoint
550 Oxford Street, W1C 1LY (7724 6127, www.chequepoint.com). Marble Arch tube. **Open** 24hrs daily. **Map** p398 G6. **Other locations** throughout the city.

Covent Garden FX
30A Jubilee Market Hall, Covent Garden, WC2E 8BE (7240 9921, www.coventgardenfx.com). Covent Garden tube. **Open** 9.30am-6pm Mon-Fri; 10am-4pm Sat; 10am-2pm Sun. **Map** p401 L7.

Thomas Exchange
5 Market Place, W1W 0AE (7637 7336, www.thomasexchange.co.uk). Oxford Circus tube. **Open** 9am-6pm Mon-Fri; 10am-5pm Sat. **Map** p398 J6.

Lost/stolen credit cards

Report lost or stolen credit cards both to the police and to the 24-hour phone lines listed below.

American Express *01273 696 933, www.americanexpress.com.*
Diners Club *0845 862 2935, www. dinersclub.co.uk.*
MasterCard *0800 964 767, www. mastercard.com.*
Visa *0800 891 725, www.visa.co.uk.*

Tax

With the exception of food, books, newspapers and a few other items, purchases in the UK are subject to Value Added Tax (VAT), aka sales tax. The rate is currently set at 20%. VAT is included in all prices quoted by mainstream shops, although it may not be included in hotel rates.

Foreign visitors may be able to claim back the VAT paid on most goods that are taken out of the EC (European Community) as part of a scheme generally called 'Tax Free Shopping'. To be able to claim a refund, you must be a non-EC visitor to the UK, or a UK resident emigrating from the EC. When you buy the goods, the retailer will ask to see your passport, and will then ask you to fill in a simple refund form. You need to have one of these forms to make your claim; till receipts alone will not do. If you're leaving the UK direct for outside the EC, you must show your goods and refund form to UK customs at the airport/port from which you're leaving. If you're leaving the EC via another EC country, you must show your goods

and refund form to customs staff of that country.

After customs have certified your form, get your refund by posting the form to the retailer from which you bought the goods, posting the form to a commercial refund company or handing your form at a refund booth to get immediate payment. Customs are not responsible for making the refund: when you buy the goods, ask the retailer how the refund is paid.

OPENING HOURS

Government offices close on bank (public) holidays (*see p31*), but big shops often remain open, with only Christmas Day sacrosanct. Most attractions remain open on the other public holidays.

Banks 9am-4.30pm (some close at 3.30pm, some 5.30pm) Mon-Fri; some also Sat mornings.
Businesses 9am-5pm Mon-Fri.
Post offices 9am-5.30pm Mon-Fri; 9am-noon Sat.
Pubs & bars 11am-11pm Mon-Sat; noon-10.30pm Sun; many pubs and bars, particularly in central London, stay open later.
Shops 10am-6pm Mon-Sat, some to 8pm. Many also open on Sun, usually 11am-5pm or noon-6pm.

POLICE

For emergencies, call 999. The non-emergency number is 101.

London's police are used to helping visitors. If you've been robbed, assaulted or a victim of crime, go to your nearest police station. (We've listed a handful in central London; look under 'Police' in Directory Enquiries or call 118 118, 118 500 or 118 888 for more.)

If you have a complaint, ensure that you take the offending officer's identifying number (it should be displayed on his or her epaulette). The Independent Police Complaints Commission website, www.ipcc.gov. uk, has details of how to complain to the relevant police force.

Belgravia Police Station
202-206 Buckingham Palace Road, Pimlico, SW1W 9SX (111). Victoria tube/rail. **Map** p400 H10.
Charing Cross Police Station
Agar Street, Covent Garden, WC2N 4JP (111). Charing Cross tube/rail. **Map** p401 L7.
Chelsea Police Station
2 Lucan Place, Chelsea, SW3 3PB (111). South Kensington tube. **Map** p397 E10.

Holborn Police Station
10 Lambs Conduit Street, Bloomsbury, WC1N 3NR. Holborn tube. **Map** p399 M5.
Islington Police Station
2 Tolpuddle Street, Islington, N1 0YY (111). Angel tube. **Map** p402 N2.
West End Central Police Station
27 Savile Row, Mayfair, W1S 2EX (111). Oxford Circus tube. **Map** p400 J7.

POSTAL SERVICES

The UK has a reliable postal service. Customer Services are on 0845 774 0740. For business enquiries, call 0845 795 0950.

Post offices are usually open 9am-5.30pm during the week and 9am-noon on Saturdays, although some post offices shut for lunch and smaller offices may close for one or more afternoons each week. Some central post offices are listed below; for others, call the **Royal Mail** on 0845 611 2970 or check online at www.royalmail.com.

You can buy individual stamps at post offices, and books of four or 12 first- or second-class stamps at newsagents and supermarkets that display the appropriate red sign. A first-class stamp for a regular letter costs 63p; second-class stamps are 54p. It costs 88p to send a postcard abroad. For details of other rates, see www.royalmail.com.

Post offices

Post offices are usually open 9am-5.30pm Mon-Fri and 9am-noon Sat, with the exception of Lower Regent Street Post Office (11 Lower Regent Street, SW1Y 4LR, 0845 611 2970), which opens 8am-6.30pm Mon-Fri; 9am-5.30pm Sat; noon-4pm Sun. Listed below are the other main central London offices. For general enquiries, call 0845 611 2970 or consult www.postoffice.co.uk.

Albemarle Street *nos.43-44, Mayfair, W1S 4DS. Green Park tube.* **Map** p400 J7.
Baker Street *no.111, Marylebone, W1U 6SG. Baker Street tube.* **Map** p398 G5.
Great Portland Street *nos.54-56, Fitzrovia, W1W 7NE. Oxford Circus tube.* **Map** p398 H4.
High Holborn *no.181, Holborn, WC1V 7RL. Holborn tube.* **Map** p399 L6.

Poste restante

If you want to receive mail while you're away, you can have it sent to Lower Regent Street Post Office (*see p375*), where it will be kept for a month. Your name and 'Poste Restante' must be clearly marked on the letter. You'll need ID to collect it.

PUBLIC HOLIDAYS

On public holidays (bank holidays), many shops remain open, but public-transport services generally run to a Sunday timetable. On Christmas Day, almost everything, including public transport, closes down. For the dates for 2015 and 2016, *see p31*.

RELIGION

Times of services may vary, particularly at festivals and holy days; phone to check.

Anglican & Baptist

Bloomsbury Central Baptist Church
235 Shaftesbury Avenue, Covent Garden, WC2H 8EP (7240 0544, www.bloomsbury.org.uk). Tottenham Court Road tube. **Services & meetings** 11am, 5.45pm Sun. **Map** p399 Y1.

St Paul's Cathedral
For listings, see p177. **Services** 7.30am, 8am, 12.30pm, 5pm Mon-Sat; 8am, 10.15am, 11.30am, 3.15pm, 6pm Sun. **Map** p404 O6.

Westminster Abbey
For listings, see p76. **Services** 7.30am, 8am, 12.30pm, 5pm Mon-Sat; 8am, 10am, 11.15am, 3pm, 5.45pm Sun. **Map** p401 K9.

Buddhist

Buddhapadipa Thai Temple
14 Calonne Road, Wimbledon, SW19 5HJ (8946 1357, www.buddhapadipa. org). Wimbledon tube/rail then bus 93. **Open** *Temple* 9am-6pm Sat, Sun. *Meditation retreat* 7-9pm Tue, Thur; 4-6pm Sat, Sun.

London Buddhist Centre
51 Roman Road, Bethnal Green, E2 0HU (8981 1225, www.lbc.org.uk). Bethnal Green tube. **Open** 10am-5pm Mon-Sat.

Catholic

Brompton Oratory
For listings, see p94. **Services** 7am, 8am (Latin mass), 10am, 12.30pm, 6pm Mon-Fri; 7am, 8am, 10am, 6pm Sat; 8am, 9am (tridentine), 10am, 11am (sung Latin), 12.30pm, 4.30pm, 7pm Sun. **Map** p397 E10.

Westminster Cathedral
For listings, see p78. **Services** 7am, 8am, 10.30am, 12.30pm, 1.05pm, 5.30pm Mon-Fri; 8am, 9am, 10.30am,

12.30pm, 6pm Sat; 8am, 9am, 10.30am, noon, 5.30pm, 7pm Sun. **Map** p400 J10.

Islamic

East London Mosque
82-92 Whitechapel Road, Whitechapel, E1 1JQ (7650 3000, www.eastlondonmosque.org.uk). Aldgate East tube. **Services** times vary; check website for details. **Map** p405 S6.

Islamic Cultural Centre & London Central Mosque *146 Park Road, Marylebone, NW8 7RG (7724 3363, www.iccuk.org). Baker Street tube or bus 13, 113, 274.* **Services** times vary; check website for details.

Jewish

Liberal Jewish Synagogue
28 St John's Wood Road, St John's Wood, NW8 7HA (7286 5181, www.ljs.org). St John's Wood tube. **Services** 6.45pm Fri; 11am Sat.
West Central Liberal Synagogue
The Montagu Centre, 21 Maple Street, Fitzrovia, W1T 4BE (7636 7627, www.wds.org.uk). Warren Street tube. **Services** 3pm Sat. **Map** p398 J4.

Methodist & Quaker

Methodist Central Hall
Storey's Gate, Westminster, SW1H 9NH (7654 3809, www.methodist-central-hall.org.uk). St James's Park tube. **Services** 12.45pm Wed; 11am, 6.30pm Sun. **Map** p401 K9.
Religious Society of Friends (Quakers)
173-177 Euston Road, Bloomsbury, NW1 2BJ (7663 1000, www.quaker. org.uk). Euston tube/Overground/rail. **Meetings** 11am daily; 6.30-9pm Mon; 6.30pm Thur; 11am Sun. **Map** p399 K3.

SAFETY & SECURITY

Despite the riots during 2011, London is not a violent city. You're much more likely to get hurt in a car accident than as a result of criminal activity, but pickpockets do haunt busy shopping areas and transport nodes as they do in all cities.

Use common sense and follow some basic rules. Keep wallets and purses out of sight, and handbags securely closed. Never leave bags or coats unattended, beside, under or on the back of a chair – even if they aren't stolen, they're likely to trigger a bomb alert. Don't put bags on the floor near the door of a public toilet. Don't take short cuts through dark

alleys and car parks. Keep your passport, cash and credit cards in separate places. Don't carry a wallet in your back pocket. And always be aware of your surroundings.

SMOKING

July 2007 saw the introduction of a ban on smoking in all enclosed public spaces, including pubs, bars, clubs, restaurants, hotel foyers and shops, as well as on public transport. Smokers now face a penalty fee of £50 or a maximum fee of £200 if they are prosecuted for smoking in a smoke-free area. Many bars and clubs offer smoking gardens or terraces for smokers.

TELEPHONES

Dialling & codes

London's dialling code is 020; standard landlines have eight digits after that. You don't need to dial the 020 from within the area, so we have not given it in this book.

If you're calling from outside the UK, dial your international access code, then the UK code, 44, then the full London number, omitting the first 0 from the code. For example, to make a call to 020 7813 3000 from the US, dial 011 44 20 7813 3000. To dial abroad from the UK, first dial 00, then the relevant country code from the list below. For more international dialling codes, check the phone book or see www.kropla.com/dialcode.htm.

Australia 61
Canada 1
New Zealand 64
Republic of Ireland 353
South Africa 27
USA 1

Mobile phones

Mobile phones in the UK operate on the 900 MHz and 1800 MHz GSM frequencies common throughout most of Europe. If you're travelling to the UK from Europe, your phone should be compatible; if you're travelling from the US, it may not be. Either way, check your phone is set for international roaming, and that your service provider at home has a reciprocal arrangement with a UK provider.

The simplest option may be to buy a 'pay-as-you-go' phone (about £10-£200); there's no monthly fee – you top up talk time using a card. Check before buying whether it can make and receive international calls.

LOCAL CLIMATE

Average temperatures and monthly rainfall in London.

	High (°C/°F)	Low (°C/°F)	Rainfall (mm/in)
Jan	6 / 43	2 / 36	54 / 2.1
Feb	7 / 44	2 / 36	40 / 1.6
Mar	10 / 50	3 / 37	37 / 1.5
Apr	13 / 55	6 / 43	37 / 1.5
May	17 / 63	8 / 46	46 / 1.8
June	20 / 68	12 / 54	45 / 1.8
July	22 / 72	14 / 57	57 / 2.2
Aug	21 / 70	13 / 55	59 / 2.3
Sept	19 / 66	11 / 52	49 / 1.9
Oct	14 / 57	8 / 46	57 / 2.2
Nov	10 / 50	5 / 41	64 / 2.5
Dec	7 / 44	4 / 39	48 / 1.9

Operator services

Call 100 for the operator if you have difficulty in dialling; for an alarm call; to make a credit card call; for information about the cost of a call; and for help with international person-to-person calls. Dial 155 for the international operator if you need to reverse the charges (call collect) or if you can't dial direct; this service is very expensive.

Directory enquiries

This service is now provided by various six-digit 118 numbers. They're pretty pricey to call: dial (free) 0800 953 0720 for a rundown of options and prices. The best known is 118 118. Calls from a landline cost £4.45 per call, then £2.57 per minute thereafter; 118 888 charges 59p per call, then £1.99 per minute; 118 811 charges 50p per call; calls from a mobile may cost more. BT customers can call 118 707 and request two numbers for £1.20. Online, the www.ukphonebook.com offers ten free credits a day to UK residents; overseas users get the same credits if they keep a positive balance in their account.

Yellow Pages This 24-hour service lists phone numbers of businesses in the UK. Dial 118 247 (£1.50 connection charge plus 70p/min) and identify the type of business you require, and where in London. Online, try www.yell.com.

Public phones

Public payphones take coins or credit cards (sometimes both). The minimum cost is 60p (including a 40p connection charge); local and national calls are charged at 60p for 30mins then 10p for each subsequent

15mins. Some payphones, such as the counter-top ones found in pubs, require more. International calling cards, offering bargain minutes via a freephone number, are widely available in shops.

TIME

London operates on Greenwich Mean Time (GMT), five hours ahead of the US's Eastern Standard Time. In spring (27 March 2016) the UK puts its clocks forward by one hour to British Summer Time. In autumn (25 October 2015, 30 October 2016), the clocks go back to GMT.

TIPPING

In Britain, it's accepted that you tip in taxis, minicabs, restaurants (some waiting staff rely heavily on tips), hotels, hairdressers and some bars (not pubs). Around 10% is normal, but some restaurants add as much as 15%. Always check whether service has been included in your bill: some restaurants include an automatic service charge, but also give the opportunity for a gratuity when paying with a card.

TOILETS

Pubs and restaurants generally reserve the use of their toilets for customers. However, all mainline rail stations and a few tube stations – Piccadilly Circus, for one – have public toilets (you may be charged a small fee: have some coins handy for the entrance gate). Department stores usually have loos that you can use free of charge, and museums (most no longer charge an entry fee) generally have good facilities. At night, options are worse. The coin-operated toilet booths around the city may be your only option.

TOURIST INFORMATION

In addition to the tourist information centres listed below, there are travel information centres, selling tickets for travel and London attractions, at King's Cross, Euston, Liverpool Street and Victoria stations, and at Piccadilly Circus tube station (*see p368*).

City of London Information Centre *St Paul's Churchyard, City, EC4M 8BX (7332 3456, www. cityoflondon.gov.uk).* **Open** 9.30am-5.30pm Mon-Sat; 10am-4pm Sun. **Map** p404 O6.
Greenwich Tourist Information Centre *Discover Greenwich, Pepys House, 2 Cutty Sark Gardens, Greenwich, SE10 9LW (0870 608 2000, www. visitgreenwich.org.uk). Cutty Sark DLR.* **Open** 10am-5pm daily.
Holborn Information Kiosk *89-94 Kingsway, outside Holborn tube, Holborn, WC2B 6AA (no phone).* **Open** 8am-6pm Mon-Fri. **Map** p399 L5.
Twickenham Visitor Information Centre *44 York Street, Twickenham, Middx, TW1 3BZ (8891 1441, www. visitrichmond.co.uk). Twickenham rail.* **Open** 9am-5.15pm Mon-Thur; 9am-5pm Fri.

WEIGHTS & MEASURES

The UK is moving slowly and reluctantly towards full metrication. Distances are still measured in miles but all goods are officially sold in metric quantities, with no legal requirement for the imperial equivalent to be given. Nonetheless, imperial measurements are still more commonly used, so we use them in this guide.

Below are listed some useful conversions, first into the metric equivalents from the imperial measurements, then from the metric units back to imperial:

1 inch (in) = 2.54 centimetres (cm)
1 yard (yd) = 0.91 metres (m)
1 mile = 1.6 kilometres (km)
1 ounce (oz) = 28.35 grams (g)
1 pound (lb) = 0.45 kilograms (kg)
1 UK pint = 0.57 litres (l)
1 US pint = 0.8 UK pints or 0.46 litres

1 centimetre (cm) = 0.39 inches (in)
1 metre (m) = 1.094 yards (yd)
1 kilometre (km) = 0.62 miles
1 gram (g) = 0.035 ounces (oz)
1 kilogram (kg) = 2.2 pounds (lb)
1 litre (l) = 1.76 UK pints or 2.2 US pints

Further Reference

BOOKS

Fiction

Peter Ackroyd *Hawksmoor; The House of Doctor Dee; The Great Fire of London* Intricate fiction about the arcane city.

Martin Amis *London Fields* Darts and drinking way out east.

Ned Beauman *Glow* Bright young novelist takes on the rave scene in noughties south London.

Anthony Burgess *Dead Man in Deptford* Fictionalised biography of Marlowe.

Norman Collins *London Belongs to Me* Witty saga of '30s Kennington.

Sir Arthur Conan Doyle *The Complete Sherlock Holmes* Reassuring sleuthing shenanigans.

Joseph Conrad *The Secret Agent* Anarchism in seedy Soho.

Charles Dickens *Oliver Twist; David Copperfield; Bleak House* Three of the Victorian master's most London-centric novels.

Anthony Frewin *London Blues* Kubrick assistant explores the 1960s Soho porn-movie industry.

Jeremy Gavron *An Acre of Common Ground* Best of the noughties glut of Brick Lane fiction.

George the Poet *Search Party* Buzzy debut from the Harlesden-born, Cambridge-educated poet.

Graham Greene *The End of the Affair* A tale of adultery, Catholicism and the Blitz.

Patrick Hamilton *Twenty Thousand Streets Under the Sky* Dashed dreams at the bar of the Midnight Bell in Fitzrovia.

Neil Hanson *The Dreadful Judgement* Embers of the Great Fire.

Melissa Harrison *Clay* The dispossessed of south London encounter nature.

Alan Hollinghurst *The Swimming Pool Library; The Line of Beauty* Gay life around Russell Square; metropolitan debauchery.

BS Johnson *Christie Malry's Own Double Entry* A London clerk plots revenge on…everybody.

Doris Lessing *The Golden Notebook; The Good Terrorist* Nobel winner's best London books.

Colin MacInnes *City of Spades; Absolute Beginners* Coffee 'n' jazz, Soho 'n' Notting Hill.

Gautam Malkani *Londonstani* A violent tale of South Asian immigrants in Hounslow.

Michael Moorcock *Mother London* A roomful of psychiatric patients live a love letter to London.

Alan Moore *From Hell* Dark and epic graphic novel on the Ripper.

Nick Papadimitriou *Scarp* Hallucinatory explorations of the high ground north of London.

Derek Raymond *I Was Dora Suarez* The blackest London noir.

Nicholas Royle *The Matter of the Heart; The Director's Cut* Abandoned buildings and secrets.

Iain Sinclair *Downriver; White Chappell/Scarlet Tracings* Thames-based *Heart of Darkness*; the Ripper and book dealers.

Sarah Waters *The Night Watch* World War II on the Home Front.

Virginia Woolf *Mrs Dalloway* A kind of London *Ulysses*.

Non-fiction

Peter Ackroyd *London: The Biography; Thames: Sacred River* Loving and obscurantist histories of the city and its river.

Richard Anderson *Bespoke: Savile Row Ripped and Smoothed* Inside story of a Savile Row tailor.

Nicholas Barton *The Lost Rivers of London* A classic study.

David Bownes, Oliver Green & Sam Mullins *Underground* Illustrated celebration of 150 years of the Tube, which opened in 1863.

James Cheshire & Oliver Uberti *The Information Capital* Fabulous infographics about all aspects of London life.

Mark Daly *Unseen London* Fine behind-the-scenes pics of the city.

Paul Du Noyer *In the City* London in song.

Ed Glinert *A Literary Guide to London; The London Compendium* Essential London minutiae.

Sarah Hartley *Mrs P's Journey* Biography of the woman who created the *A–Z*.

Leo Hollis *The Stones of London* A superb take on the city's history – through 12 of its key buildings.

Simon Inglis *Played in London* Comprehensive and riveting account of London's sporting heritage.

Lee Jackson *Dirty Old London* Gripping tale of how the Victorians fought to clean up the Big Smoke – and what they were up against.

Edward Jones & Christopher Woodward *A Guide to the Architecture of London*

Paul L Knox *London: Architecture, Building and Social Change* How our buildings affect how we live.

Jenny Landreth *The Great Trees of London* Ancient trees in famous and unlikely city locations.

David Lawrence (ed) *Omnibus* Social history of the London bus.

Jenny Linford *London Cookbook* Unsung producers and chefs share their food secrets.

Jack London *The People of the Abyss* Poverty in the East End.

Anna Minton *Ground Control* Important questions about Canary Wharf-style developments – updated to cover the Olympic Park.

HV Morton *In Search of London* A tour of London from 1951.

George Orwell *Down and Out in Paris and London* Waitering, begging and starving.

Samuel Pepys *Diaries* Plagues, fires and bordellos.

Cathy Phillips (ed) *London through a Lens; Londoners through a Lens* Captivating photographs of the city from the Getty archive.

Roy Porter *London: A Social History* An all-encompassing work.

Sukhdev Sandhu *Night Haunts* London and Londoners after dark.

Iain Sinclair *Lights Out for the Territory; London Orbital* Time-warp visionary crosses and then circles London.

Craig Taylor *Londoners: The Days and Nights of London Now* A superb and revealing collection of interviews with modern Londoners.

Richard Trench & Ellis Hillman *London under London* Tunnels, lost rivers, disused tube stations and military bunkers.

Ben Weinreb & Christopher Hibbert (eds) *The London Encyclopaedia* Indispensable.

Jerry White *London in the 18th Century; London in the 19th Century; London in the 20th Century* How London became a global city.

FILMS

Alfie *dir Lewis Gilbert, 1966* What's it all about, Michael?

Blow-Up *dir Michelangelo Antonioni, 1966* Unintentionally hysterical film of Swinging London.

Death Line *dir Gary Sherman, 1972* Lost Victorian cannibal race is discovered in Russell Square tube.

Dirty Pretty Things *dir Stephen Frears, 2002* Body-organ smuggling.

Fires Were Started *dir Humphrey Jennings, 1943* War propaganda about the London Fire Brigade.

How We Used to Live *dir Paul Kelly, 2013* Rare post-war footage, with Saint Etienne soundtrack.

Hyena *dir Gerard Johnson, 2015* London-set crime flick.

The Krays *dir Peter Medak, 1990* The life and times of the most notorious of East End gangsters.

The Ladykillers *dir Alexander Mackendrick, 1951* Classic Ealing comedy.

Life is Sweet; Naked; Vera Drake; Happy-Go-Lucky; Mr Turner *dir Mike Leigh, 1990-2014* Metroland; urban misanthropy; sympathy for a post-war abortionist; day and night with a north London optimist; London's greatest artist.

Lock, Stock & Two Smoking Barrels; Snatch; RocknRolla *dir Guy Ritchie, 1998-2008* Former Mr Madonna's cheeky London faux-gangster flicks.

London; Robinson in Space *dir Patrick Keiller, 1994, 1997* Arthouse documentaries tracing London's lost stories.

London: The Modern Babylon *dir Julien Temple, 2012* Rousing montage portrait, driven by music, of London from the birth of cinema.

The Long Good Friday *dir John MacKenzie, 1989* Classic London gangster flick.

The National Gallery *dir Frederick Wiseman, 2015* Inquisitive documentary on the employees and paintings of the historic gallery.

Oliver! *dir Carol Reed, 1968* Fun musical Dickens adaptation.

Paddington *dir Paul King, 2014* The immigrant Peruvian bear gets his own movie.

Passport to Pimlico *dir Henry Cornelius, 1949* Ealing comedy classic.

Peeping Tom *dir Michael Powell, 1960* Creepy serial-killer flick.

Performance *dir Nicolas Roeg & Donald Cammell, 1970* Cult movie to end all cult movies.

Sex & Drugs & Rock & Roll *dir Mat Whitecross, 2009* Delirious biopic of splenetic rocker Ian Dury.

Skyfall *dir Sam Mendes, 2012* See the SIS building blown up and Bond nearly run over by the Tube.

28 Days Later *dir Danny Boyle, 2002* Post-apocalyptic London, with bravura opening sequence.

We Are the Lambeth Boys *dir Karel Reisz, 1959* 'Free cinema' classic doc on Teddy Boy culture.

Withnail & I *dir Bruce Robinson, 1987* Classic Camden lowlife comedy.

Wonderland *dir Michael Winterbottom, 1999* Love, loss and deprivation in Soho.

MUSIC

Billy Bragg *Must I Paint You a Picture? The Essential Billy Bragg* The bard of Barking's greatest hits.

Blur *Parklife* Key Britpop album.

Burial *Untrue* Pioneering dubstep album – still the benchmark.

Chas & Dave *Don't Give a Monkey's* Cockney singalong.

The Clash *London Calling* Era-defining punk classic.

Dizzee Rascal *Boy in Da Corner* Rough-cut sounds and inventive lyrics from a Bow council estate.

Hot Chip *The Warning* Wonky electro-pop.

Ian Dury *New Boots & Panties!!* Cheekily essential listening from the Essex pub maestro.

The Jam *This is the Modern World* Weller at his fiercest and finest.

Kate Tempest *Everybody Down* Young Brockley-born street poet's debut album.

The Kinks *Something Else* 'Waterloo Sunset' and all.

Linton Kwesi Johnson *Dread, Beat an' Blood; Forces of Victory; Bass Culture* Angry reggae from the man Brixton calls 'the Poet'.

Madness *Ultimate Madness* The Nutty Boys' wonderful best.

Melt Yourself Down *Melt Yourself Down* Wigged-out psych-jazz-funk supergroup.

MIA *Arular* Agit-pop raver's debut album – and still her best.

Public Service Broadcasting *Inform–Educate–Entertain* Documentary narration set to music – shouldn't work, but it does.

Saint Etienne *Tales from Turnpike House* Kitchen-sink opera by London-loving indie dance band.

Squeeze *Greatest Hits* Lovable south London geezer pop.

The Streets *Original Pirate Material* Pirate radio urban meets Madness on Mike Skinner's debut.

The xx *xx* Shiny, slinky melancholia from the 2010 Mercury Prize winners.

WEBSITES

www.bbc.co.uk/london News, travel, weather, sport.

www.britishpathe.com Archive newsreel footage, from spaghetti-eating contests to pre-war Soho.

http://catsmeatshop.blogspot. co.uk Expert on Victorian hygiene explains urine deflectors and the like.

www.classiccafes.co.uk Great archive of 1950s and '60s caffs.

http://diamondgeezer.blogspot. com One of London's key bloggers.

www.filmlondon.org.uk London's cinema organisation – with mapped location tours.

http://greatwen.com Engaged, fun and often thought-provoking blog by our 'London Today' author.

www.hidden-london.com Undiscovered gems – and a neat place names pronunciation guide.

www.london.gov.uk The official website for the Greater London Assembly, the city's government.

http://londonist.com News, culture and things to do.

http://londonreconnections. blogspot.com Heaven for transport geeks: everything from rolling stock plans to major infrastructure work.

www.londonremembers.com Definitive site for London memorials.

http://mappinglondon.co.uk Great-looking site with the best maps – and ways of mapping – the city.

http://mel-talesofthecity. blogspot.co.uk Nature in the city, lovingly, authoritatively described by *Clay* author Melissa Harrison.

www.nickelinthemachine.com Terrific blog on history, culture and music of 20th-century London.

http://spitalfieldslife.com Lovely London blog: focused, charming, informative and very human.

www.timeout.com Eating and drinking reviews, features and events listings – a vital resource.

www.tfl.gov.uk Information, journey planners and maps from Transport for London, the city's central travel organisation.

APPS

Appy Parking (free) Extremely helpful: shows you free parking spaces across London.

City Mapper (free) Simply the greatest London journey planner, smoothly integrating multimodal transport – tube, rail, bus and bike – with estimated times and much more.

Hailo (free) Calls a black cab, tells you how long it will be, and deducts the meter fare from your account.

London: A City Through Time (£10.49) Expensive for an app – but you get the superb *London Encyclopaedia*, plus interactives.

StreetMuseum (free) Brilliant Museum of London app – archive shots geolocated to where you're standing, with informative captions.

StreetMuseum Londinium (free) StreetMuseum, but for Romans.

Time Out London Magazine (free) Our indispensable guide to the week's happenings in the capital.

Toiluxe – central London (69p) Where's the nearest public loo?

Uber (free) Hails a minicab, with fare quotes – the cab is paid for through the app (prices rise, airline-style, with demand), so no cash is needed.

ESSENTIAL INFORMATION

Index

INDEX

LONDON.
IN HIGH DEFINITION.

THE VIEW
FROM THE SHARD

AT THE TOP OF WESTERN EUROPE'S TALLEST BUILDING
THE VIEW FROM THE SHARD IS THE HIGHEST VIEWING PLATFORM IN LONDON,
WITH STUNNING PANORAMIC VIEWS STRETCHING UP TO 40 MILES.

THEVIEWFROMTHESHARD.COM

INDEX

INDEX

Made with

INDEX

Advertisers' Index

Please refer to the relevant pages for contact details.

Maps

THAMES PATH
Hungerford Bridge

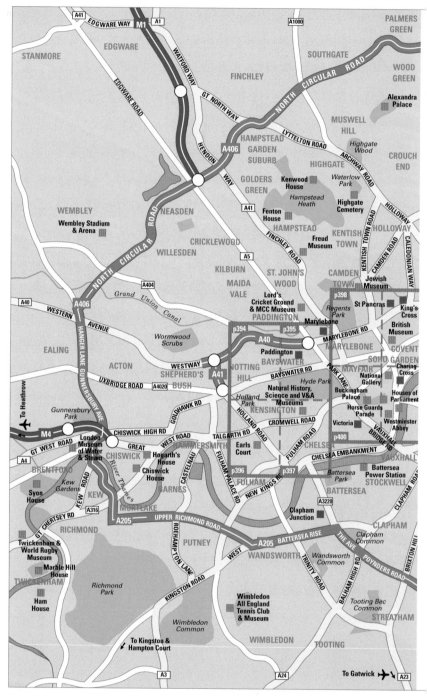

MAPS

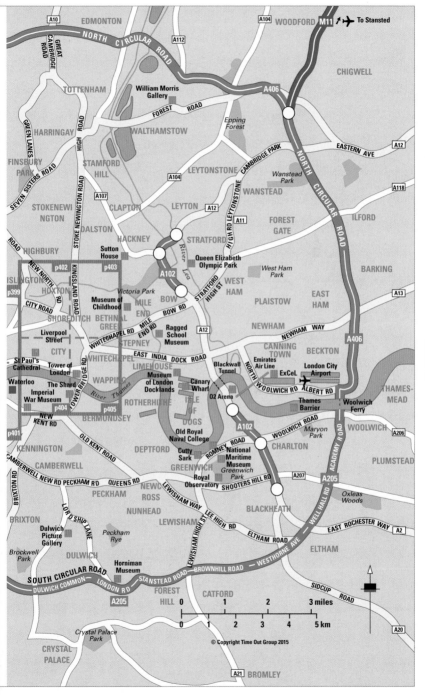

To Stansted

MAPS

© Copyright Time Out Group 2015

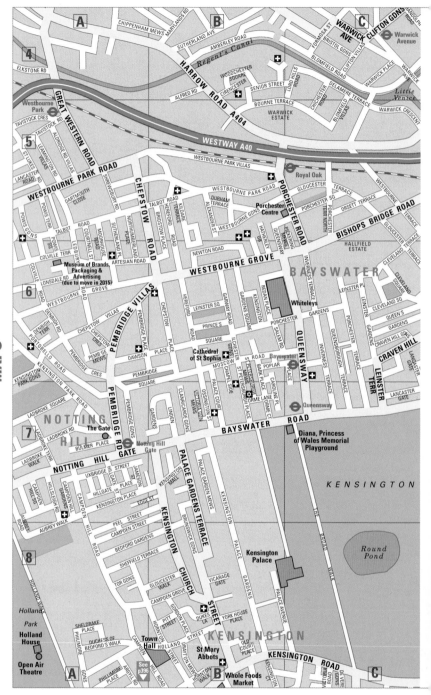

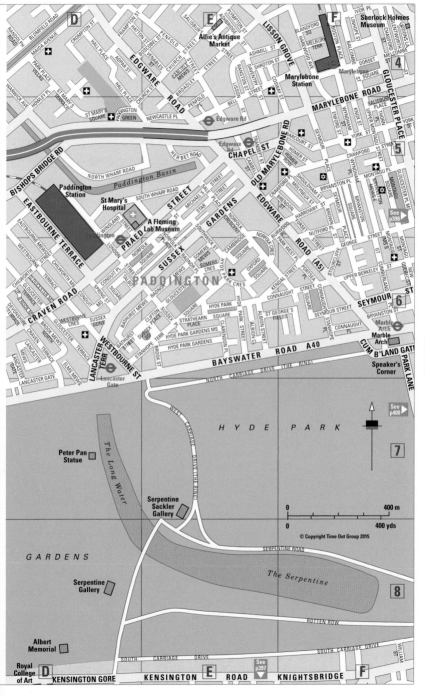

MAPS

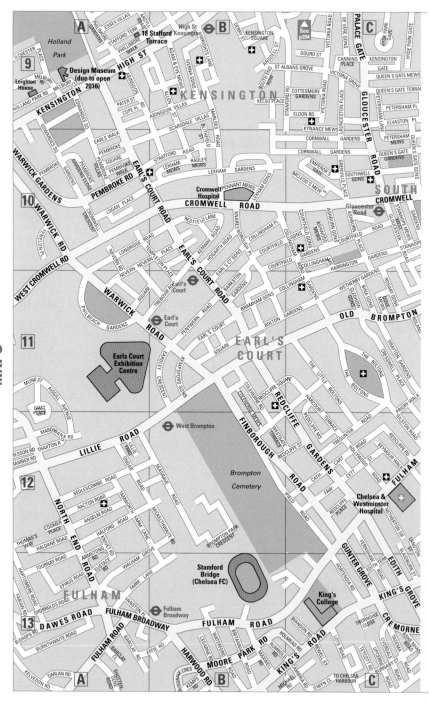

MAPS

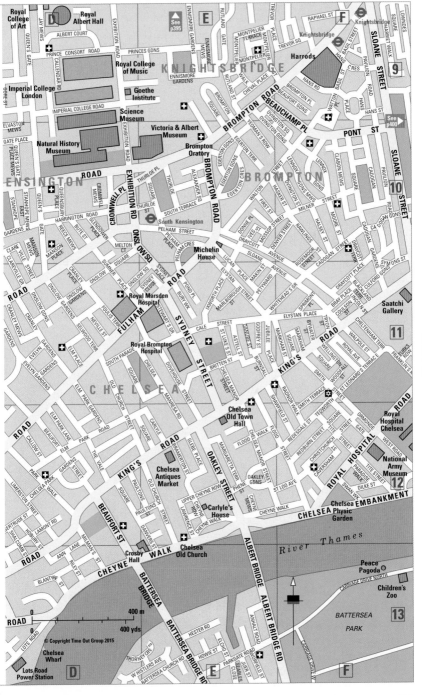

MAPS

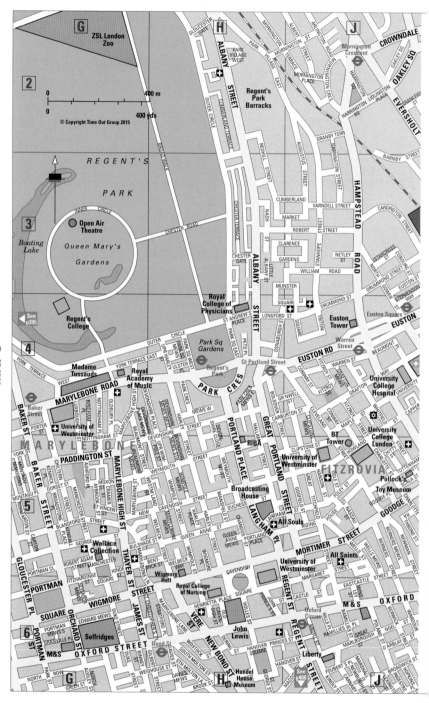

MAPS

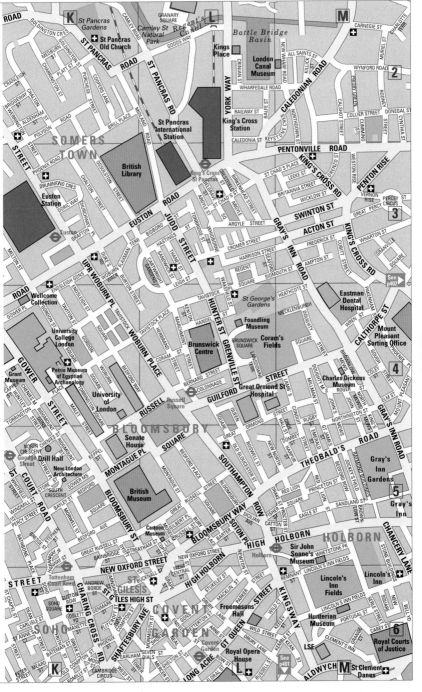

MAPS

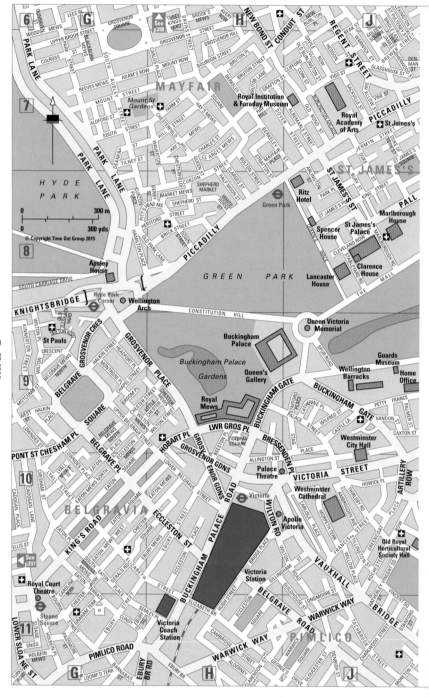

MAPS

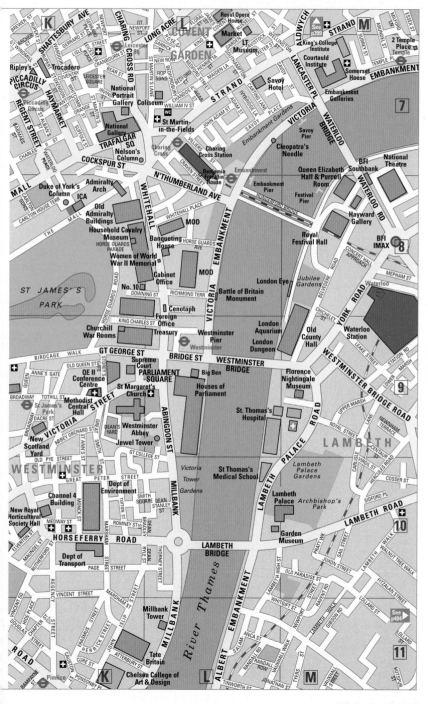

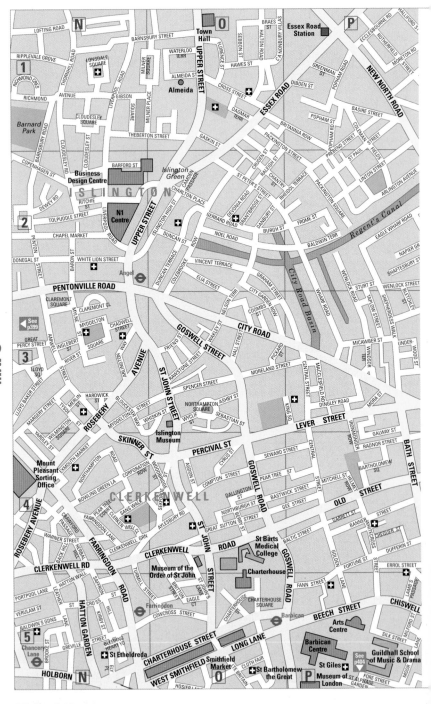

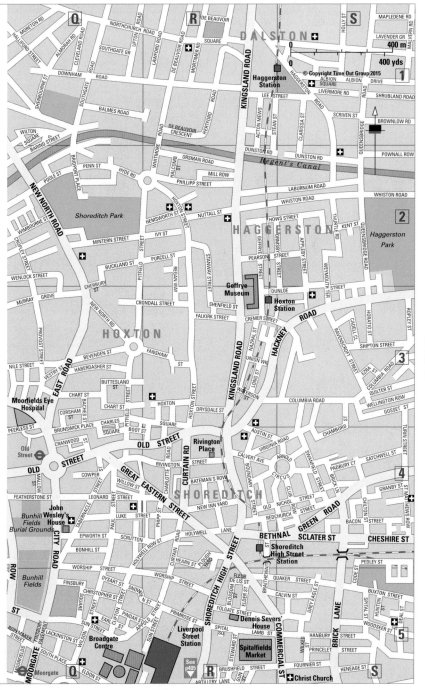

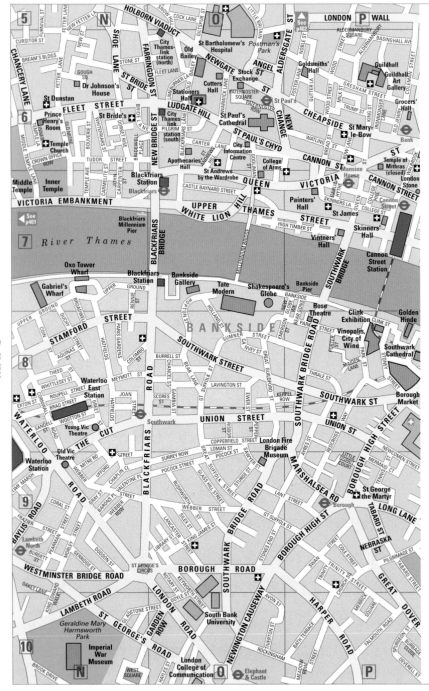

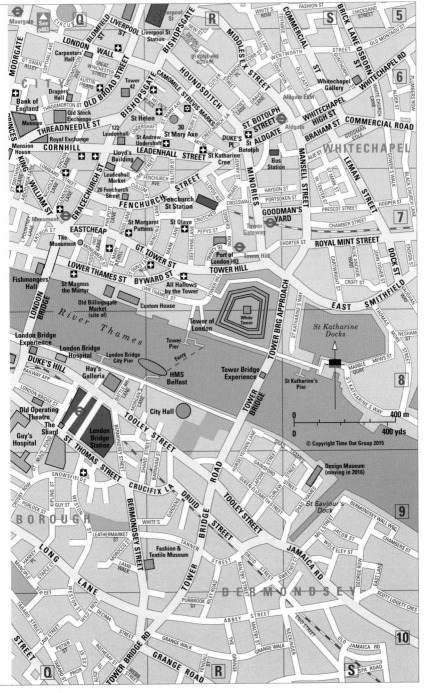

Street Index

STREET INDEX

STREET INDEX

STREET INDEX

STREET INDEX

STREET INDEX

MAPS

Bakerloo	Metropolitan	○ Interchange stations
Central	Northern	Ⓐ Step-free access from street to train
Circle	Piccadilly	Ⓐ Step-free access from street to platform
District	Victoria	≷ National Rail
District open weekends, public holidays and some Olympia events	Waterloo & City	⛴ Riverboat services
Hammersmith & City	DLR	▭▭ Tramlink
	London Overground	✈ Airport
Jubilee	Emirates Air Line	Ⓔ Emirates Air Line

MAYOR OF LONDON

⊕ tfl.gov.uk

ℹ 24 hour travel information
0343 222 1234*

*Service and network charges may apply. See tfl.gov.uk/terms for details.

© Transport for London   Reg. user No. 15/2834/P   **Improvement works may affect**